EDUCATION and CULTURAL PROCESS

Toward an Anthropology of Education

EDUCATION and CULTURAL PROCESS

Toward an Anthropology of Education

Edited by **George Dearborn Spindler**
Stanford University

HOLT, RINEHART AND WINSTON, INC.
New York Chicago San Francisco Atlanta
Dallas Montreal Toronto London Sydney

ACKNOWLEDGMENTS

It is customary to acknowledge at least the direct help that one has received in the preparation of a book. But it is impossible to mention everyone who helped in the making of this volume—the list would go on and on.

I am particularly grateful to the contributing authors for the patience they demonstrated over the several years it took to prepare this book. By the same token, I am grateful to David Boynton, Social Science Publisher at Holt, Rinehart and Winston, for not harassing me about its completion, as well as for active support. Special thanks are due to Julia Kringel for a great deal of help in the preparation of the manuscript. I am deeply grateful to the many students and colleagues who shared their thoughts and writings with me. Some of these writings are represented in this book. As always, I am in debt to Louise Spindler for her invaluable counsel and personal support.

Lastly, I wish to thank the Executive Heads of the Department of Anthropology and the Deans of the School of Education who have made a joint appointment in anthropology and education workable over the twenty-three years I have been associated with Stanford University.

Library of Congress Cataloging in Publication Data

Spindler, George Dearborn.
Education and cultural process.

Includes bibliographical references.
1. Educational anthropology—Addresses, essays, lectures. I. Title.
LB45.S64 301.5′6 74-1347
ISBN: 0-03-085180-7

Printed in the United States of America
4567 090 987654321

I claim the privilege, as editor, of dedicating this book to
The Women in My Life
Winifred
Corabelle
Louise
Sue
Vicki
Rebecca
To my father, Frank Nicholas Spindler, who taught psychology, ethics and philosophy, and uncommon sense at Central State Teachers College for many years, and to students everywhere.

PREFACE

Anthropology is comprised of several major areas—biological, archeological, linguistic, and cultural—and many divisions of these. Some workers distinguish a social from a cultural anthropology, but for most American anthropologists the latter term covers both the social and cultural dimensions. In this book we are concerned with some of the significant ways in which the concepts, methods, and information subsumed by cultural anthropology can be applied to the analysis of educational process.

Our focus is on cultural transmission, but even this focus is very broad. The ways in which we draw from this breadth will become clear as the stratagems of this book proceed. There are other ways to draw from it, and the exploitation of the resources of anthropology that are relevant to education has only begun.

This diversity of interests, skills, and knowledge is one of the primary assets of anthropology and makes anthropological analyses different from those of psychology and sociology. Certainly no anthropologist controls the essential knowledge in all these major fields and topical areas. But most cultural anthropologists are *aware* of these fields and areas and of some of the significant ideas and findings in them. This awareness makes a difference in the way anthropologists study phenomena and what they make of their study. There is an eclecticism, an eagerness for new approaches, a willingness to borrow from other disciplines, and a manner of seeing relationships that are more often left unrelated and unseen, that seem less characteristic of other disciplines.

The transcultural perspective is also a special feature of anthropology. Every anthropologist reads about other ways of life both casually and professionally, often in great detail and breadth, and puts the information into a more or less systematic frame of reference, so the data are not mere curiosa. One's fieldwork is nearly always in a cultural context other than one's own, and usually in a language one has had to learn. The transcultural experience makes one view behavior differently—it may even make one a different kind of person. The transcultural context is one of the factors that makes the treatment of the topics covered here anthropological, for the topics themselves are not the exclusive domain of anthropology. The transcultural perspective is not always made explicit in data presentation and analysis. It is present, however, even when—perhaps particularly when—the anthropologist studies his own culture. The alert reader will detect it in nearly every chapter of this book.

This volume began as a revision of *Education and Culture: Anthropological Approaches,* which was in turn a revision of *Education and Anthropology.*[1] It has evolved into an almost entirely different book. Only two chapters are republished from the previous book—Dorothy Eggan's "Instruction and Affect in Hopi Cultural Continuity" and C. W. M. Hart's "Contrasts between Prepubertal and Postpubertal Education." We considered them indispensible to the arguments presented in the section on education and cultural process in traditional and modernizing societies. The article by Bernard Siegel, "Cultural Approaches to Models for Analysis of Educational Process in American Communities," appeared in a preliminary form in *Education and Culture.* It was especially revised for this new volume. Of the twenty-six chapters in the present book nineteen are published here for the first time. It is, then, a new book representing significant contemporary concerns of those anthropologists now producing an anthropology of education.

Education and Cultural Process does not sample everything in contemporary educational anthropology. The field is expanding rapidly and going in many different directions. The Previews to each section suggest further readings to expand one's grasp of this dynamic field. There are not only many specific areas of contemporary educational anthropology that can be represented in any single volume only tangentially, if at all, but there are also many people whose work cannot be represented. I have chosen as a strategy to favor papers written specifically for this volume or written for professional meetings but not published. This has automatically eliminated works from some of the most significant contributors to an educational anthropology, such as Margaret Mead, Solon Kimball, Jacquetta Burnett, Nancy Modiano, Ethel Alpenfels, Francis Ianni, Jules Henry, Rosalie and Murray Wax, Henry Burger, Fred Gearing, Theodore Brameld—the list could go on. Their influence, of course, is represented pervasively throughout the book. I have also favored papers by people with whom I have worked closely, such as John Singleton, Bernard Siegel, R. P. McDermott, John Hostetler, Harry Wolcott, Peter Sindell, Bruce Grindal, Richard Warren, A. Richard King, and Diane and Norman Reynolds. Many of these people were graduate students at Stanford. Naturally I am biased favorably toward their work.

Each of the five parts of this volume is organized around certain themes. These themes are discussed in the Previews to each section. In Part I our purpose is to set the stage. All of the papers are concerned with ways in which anthropological concepts have or can be applied to the analysis of education. In Part II there are several themes: the ways in which culture is transmitted so as to advantage some students and disadvantage others, the ways in which rituals mark certain significant stages of cultural transmission, an alternative solution to the problems of relationship between minority groups and the

[1] George D. Spindler, *Education and Anthropology* (Stanford, Calif.: Stanford University Press, 1955); and George D. Spindler, *Education and Culture: Anthropological Approaches* (New York: Holt, Rinehart and Winston, Inc., 1963).

dominant society, and the complex interaction between educational institutions and processes and the societies and cultural systems they serve in modern societies. In Part III there are two basic themes: education and cultural transmission in whole traditional cultural systems and the effects of modernization upon education and cultural transmission in formerly nonliterate traditional societies. In Part IV we discuss strategies of field research in schools and classrooms. The major theme, selected from a number of possible alternatives, focuses upon the keystone of anthropological fieldwork—participant observation, its advantages and pitfalls. Part V, "The Teaching of Anthropology," emphasizes the necessity for as direct an exposure as possible to the data of cultural life through the use of audiovisual materials and case studies. We end with a review of the ways in which existing textbooks used in social studies curricula in the public schools may teach prejudice against minority groups and damage the self-esteem of those groups.

This book is intended as a text in the anthropology of education, for courses and seminars that utilize anthropological materials and perspectives in the analysis of educative processes. These courses and seminars are offered to both the upper-division undergraduate and the first- or second-year graduate student. Some are given in schools of education, others in departments of anthropology. Many are listed in both, as they are at Stanford. This book may also be used as a text or collateral reading in the cultural foundations of education, the sociology of education, in teacher-training and curricular courses, and in other foundational areas, such as philosophy, history, and psychology, as well as in applied anthropology and cultural dynamics courses that are in part concerned with education. It must therefore serve a wide range of interests and expertise in both anthropology and education. It is designed with this diverse audience in mind. Anthropology lends itself comfortably to this use.

Stanford, California
February 1974

G. D. S.

CONTENTS

EDUCATION and CULTURAL PROCESS

Toward an Anthropology of Education

PART I

Engagements between Anthropology and Education

PREVIEW

This section of *Education and Cultural Process* is concerned with engagements between education and anthropology. This phrase refers to various points of contact and confrontation between these two cultural systems. The engagements between education and anthropology have a fairly long history, which begins officially with Edgar Hewett's prescient papers in the *American Anthropologist* (Hewett 1904, 1905). It has continued fitfully up to the present. The past five years in particular have seen a remarkable acceleration of activity in this arena with the establishment in 1970 of the Council on Anthropology and Education, now a part of the American Anthropological Association; the publication of a newsletter, the *CAE,* now about to assume the status of a journal; the conducting of programs in education and anthropology at nearly all recent meetings of the American Anthropological Association, its associates, and its regional branches. Publication has likewise accelerated, as evidenced in review papers by Harry Wolcott (1967), Peter Sindell (1970), and Nancy Modiano (1970). Articles on various aspects of the educational process have been published in core anthropological journals such as *Human Organization* and the *American Anthropologist.* Useful collections of papers both reprinted and contributed have recently appeared, among them *Cultural Relevance and Educational Issues,* edited by Francis Ianni and Edward Storey (1973), and *Anthropological Perspectives on Education,* edited by Murray Wax, Stanley Diamond, and Fred Gearing (1971).

Rather than include a review article that would become more dated each year this book lives on, I have opted as editor for chapters that deal with established contributions or that set up models for future possibilities in the interaction of anthropology and education. Robert Nash's chapter is of the first type. Those by Singleton and Siegel are of the second. They serve well the purpose of the first section—to lay out some of the most significant points of past and future engagements between anthropology and education.

Professor Nash, a philosopher of education, reviews works of nine anthropologists who are veterans of these engagements and whose interests in education have constituted a significant part of their professional lives. The works he reviews here were all written prior to 1970. As a matter of fact, only three of the contributors—Margaret Mead, Ashley Montagu, and this editor—are still living. The analysis by Professor Nash of these works provides a sample of the background against which an emerging anthropology of education must be cast, as it is these works which have influenced the present shape of the engagement. In the second half of his chapter Professor Nash develops a case for the hermeneutical scientist, a mediator who tries to avoid the schism between fact and value and who applies the findings of the methodological scientist to the existential dilemmas which have vexed humans for centuries. It is not an accident that he develops this case by drawing largely from the work of educators rather than anthropologists, but he shows how some anthropologists fall within this category as well. He provides some suggestions as to how a working relationship between education and anthropology may be developed, given certain characteristic approaches in each field and a willingness on the part of anthropologists to examine their own value positions and make them explicit.

John Singleton in his chapter on the implications of education as cultural transmission provides us with further understanding of real and possible education-anthropology engagements. His argument that education can be productively conceptualized as cultural transmission leads into Parts II and III where this is a basic stance. He shows how some of our current problems were recognized by Edgar J. Hewett in 1904 and advocates certain research strategies and conceptual approaches to a range of problems defined in modern terms. Readers will find a sample of these efforts, as well as others, in this volume.

Bernard Siegel approaches engagements between education and anthropology from a distinctive but related viewpoint. He too conceives of education as cultural transmission. Within this broad framework he develops three models as a way of thinking about the kind of effects the educational system has upon the young. He hopes that the models he suggests will have some constructive value in formulating research projects. His guiding hypothesis is that what is taught in schools is screened, interpreted, and reinterpreted at several levels as a consequence of the carrying networks of role relationships. The first of his models is based upon the acculturation process, the second utilizes the channels theory proposed by Kurt Lewin in a study of food habits, and the third draws from information theory, which, in turn, is a part of general systems theory. In his conclusions Professor Siegel takes a hermeneutical stance as described by Donald Nash in the first chapter in this section when he calls for viable alternatives to narrow conceptions of educational functions as exemplified by such cherished norms as compulsory attendance and isolation from the larger world.

The reader will find that most of the ideas touched upon in this first section are expanded in subsequent chapters or serve as starting points for innovative analyses.

References

Ianni, Francis A. J., and Edward Storey, eds., 1973, *Cultural Relevance and Educational Issues: Readings in Anthropology and Education.* Boston: Little, Brown and Company.

Modiano, Nancy, 1970, "Educational Anthropology: An Overview." Paper presented at the Annual Meetings of the American Educational Research Association.

Sindell, Peter S., 1970, "Anthropological Approaches to the Study of Education," *Review of Educational Research,* 39(5): 593–605.

Wax, Murray L., Stanley Diamond, and Fred O. Gearing, eds., 1971, *Anthropological Perspectives on Education.* New York: Basic Books, Inc.

Wolcott, Harry F., 1967, "Anthropology and Education," *Review of Educational Research* 3:82–95.

Hewett, Edgar L., 1904, "Anthropology and Education," *American Anthropologist* 6:574–575.

——, 1905, "Ethnic Factors in Education," *American Anthropologist* 7:1–16.

ROBERT J. NASH/*University of Vermont*

1 *The Convergence of Anthropology and Education*

There are many American anthropologists who have expressed a concern for education. I have selected nine for discussion in this chapter. Although their interests have been sporadic, and, at times, nonsystematic, each has recognized the similarity of interests which converge at the core of both disciplines. All nine provide a representative cross-section of anthropological writings investigating the theory and practice of education in the United States up to the seventies. And all nine are veterans rather than newcomers to the scene. In the next part of this chapter, I will discuss selected educational contributions to anthropology and education.

Contributions to Anthropology and Education

Franz Boas, the father of American anthropology, wrote a great deal about education, and his writings can be categorized in two ways: by the objective, empirical research which he undertook in the educational milieu and by the speculative, normative visions which he often articulated for schools in the United States. One part of his research was rigorously scientific. Another part was rich in philosophic generalization—an expression of his humanism. Rarely did he relate the two with any degree of explicitness.

As an empirical scientist preoccupied with "hard" data, Boas was primarily interested in studies of race and physical growth and development. In his educational studies of children, he abandons the conventional anatomic approach to the study of physical types and substitutes instead the application of biometric techniques to his analysis of data. His anthropometric studies of schoolchildren in America substantiate his thesis that the human organism is not entirely determined by hereditary causes (Boas 1941:339). For Boas, the anthropologist's most significant contribution to educational theory is in the collection and interpretation of hard, empirical evidence so that educators can understand that the rate of a child's development is not solely or sufficiently determined by heredity. Environmental causes are primary in the formation of the individual personality, and formal education must include an adaptive dimension if it is to be successful—that is, the child must be taught how to survive in his struggle for existence in hostile environments.

The teacher's judgment must always be based on the observation of individual behavior with careful, painstaking regard to the cultural background which determines the motivation of action (Boas 1940:144).

The second part of Boas's research includes fifteen separate essays on education, written during the years 1938 to 1943, on subjects ranging from intellectual freedom in Nazi Germany to his statements on education as the very foundation of a healthy democracy. During these years, Boas spoke out on social issues and he often conceived of "comparative anthropology" as an educational aid which could be used in the solution of social problems in the United States. In the liberal tradition of the forties, Boas opted with passion and eloquence for a world federation of nations, the diminution of tradition, the correspondingly greater wisdom of the urban masses as against the so-called "classes," and the modernization and humanization of harsh, unrealistic sexual conventions. In his educational speculations, he spoke out for intellectual freedom and for student and faculty control of universities and colleges; and in the early forties he railed against those teachers who brought into their classrooms wild generalizations about human nature which bordered on racism and which resulted in "unthinking conservatism," "willing subordination to tradition," and "racial bigotry" (Boas 1945:177, 197).

Ruth Benedict, Boas's graduate student at Columbia, studied education in the American culture in its three traditional roles: the transmissive, the transitional, and the transformative. Benedict maintained that in the United States education has been transmissive in the sense that it has imparted such enduring democratic qualities as initiative, independence, and a sense of justice, autonomy, and freedom. During the war years, Benedict asserted that the adjustment of the pupil's emotions, will power, and motivation to the values of American democracy must be the primary task of the educator. Based upon her studies in nonliterate cultures, she came to believe that "education must fit the cooperative arrangements of a child's culture; there must be a specific consonance between child training and the kind of character structure which can operate to advantage in the culture." The transmissive function of education was especially important during the war years, Benedict contended, because education had the power to "make or break" the established social order, and young people must develop a clear idea of their responsibilities and expectations in a democratic society (Benedict 1943:724–725).

Education is transitional in the sense that it should prepare the child to move, with autonomy and self-understanding, into the adult years. However, much of Benedict's educational research was based upon her observation that the continuities and discontinuities in cultural conditioning in the United States were resulting in some turbulent crises in American formal education, and also in the informal processes of early child rearing. Education had a responsibility to help the child bridge the chasm between child and adult roles by helping young people become adults. However, what was happening was that both formal and informal education in the United States was reinforcing the rampant discontinuities and conflicts in the culture by conditioning young people to be irresponsible, submissive, and feel guilty about sex (Benedict 1936:164). According to Benedict, this kind of education had exacted an overwhelming cost to the American psyche.

Education is transformative in that it can begin to resolve many of the discontinuities in the culture, by surveying "the major wastages in our culture" and by looking to other cultures for ways they have utilized to meet similar situations" (Benedict 1940–1944:127). Benedict suggested that educators can more sharply understand human behavior by studying how patterned pressures and expectations are built into the individual in babyhood and in childhood, and then continued or controverted in adulthood. She also advocated that educators engage in a continual, exhaustive examination of the educational techniques of other cultures, both nonliterate and literate, in order to understand how harmony, integration, and continuity are achieved as children become adults. And, finally, education is transformative in the sense that it can improve the lot of humankind through the scientific study of race. She wrote extensively about educators' responsibility to eliminate racial conflict by saturating their curricula with the conclusions of scientists that the superiority of race is a myth (Benedict 1942:17, 19, 20).

Benedict's contribution to the convergence of anthropological and educational theory was in pointing out to the educator of her day that cultural transmission is often complicated by the rapidity of social and cultural change, and by discontinuities, which result in the intensive psychological upsets of individual members of the culture. Consequently, cultural crises occur when the tradition to be transmitted no longer conforms to the more secular interests and practices of everyday life, when the younger generation loses cultural contact with the older, and when one section or class of the community ceases to function in conformity with the interests and ideals of the whole community.

Margaret Mead, another student of Boas, has written extensively about education, and her writings can be summarized in two stages. Her *early* research in the twenties, thirties, and forties was a response to those progressive educators whom she felt were distorting the ideals of John Dewey. Much of her early work revealed her belief that those educators in the United States who were emphasizing child-centeredness, life-adjustment, and untrammeled freedom in their learning theories, were paralyzing initiative, generating deep-seated psychological conflict, and failing to provide the smooth transition from childhood to adulthood which any complex culture requires if it is to remain stable. Based upon her early South Sea studies, Mead concluded that while human nature is malleable, the malleability is limited. Educators must provide models, as parents do in Samoa and New Guinea, so that children can become typical, nonneurotic members of their society (Mead 1931:107–108).

Mead decided that when educators encourage students to discard their "cultural anchors" and when they advocate the abandonment of fixed social patterns and sanctions (as progressive educators were doing), student identity crises are inevitable. She advocated, instead, that teachers must inculcate in their students a cultural character which is congruent with the best ideals of the United States. Children need the stability of the cultural heritage, especially when their society is marked by rapid change (Mead 1951:34).

Mead's later educational research includes both a critical analysis of education in this country and a normative program for cultural amelioration. She has written that racism is scientifically untenable. She has also come to express a faith in the innovative tendencies of education which earlier in her career she was unwilling to consider. She has asked for a new conception of learning called "lateral" which enables individuals to become aware of and to rectify obsolescences in the more traditional or "vertical" cultural heritage (Mead 1959a:1; 1959b:14). Her work in adult education illustrates her understanding that enculturation is a lifelong process whereby creativity is possible at all points on the learning continuum. She has claimed that education should prepare adults to participate freely and creatively in the "business of living in a dynamic culture" so that they might develop a life-style which allows them "to effect change in established institutions" (Mead 1961:38; 1966:52–62).

Mead's latest contribution to educational theory has been to reveal those practices in American education which have generated deep-seated psychological conflict. She has examined the extent to which our educational system has fit the different temperamental types—genetic and constitutional—to the culture's basic configurations, and the correlative extent to which the educational system has reflected the dislocations in the culture. In a recent statement, Mead has distinguished three types of enculturation. The *postfigurative* is one where children learn primarily from their forbears. Primitive societies, and microcosmic religious and ideological enclaves are postfigurative, deriving authority from tradition. Education is transmitted unilaterally from elders to other members of the society. The *cofigurative* is one where both children and adults learn from peers. Even though elders still set the style and define the limits of the educational experience, a cofigurative education is clearly marked by a predominant clique or group-behavior influence. Adults are virtually nonexistent as behavior models. The *prefigurative* is one where adults learn from their children. In complex, postindustrial societies in flux, it is not the elders but the very young who become the symbol of future life. Thus, the young, free to act on their own initiative, are able to lead their elders into the direction of an unknown future (Mead 1970).

Mead and Benedict have advocated the comparative study of educational systems. Both have grounded their culture-and-personality studies in the belief that if the type of upbringing a child receives determines, in large part, his adult behavior, then only a dynamic conception of child rearing, geared to the realities of social change, will produce the kind of dynamic adults needed to guide the world through its most frenzied moments.

Melville J. Herskovits has remarked at length on the transmissive dimension of enculturation, a word which he borrowed from a colleague (E. A. Haggard) and which he has clarified conceptually more extensively than any single anthropologist. For Herskovits, enculturation included all "the aspects of the learning experience which mark off man from other creatures. . . ." Enculturation is the process of conscious and unconscious, formal and informal, cultural conditioning, exercised always within the boundaries sanctioned by a given body of custom (Herskovits 1948:39, 51). For Herskovits, the enculturation process is the basis for much of his research on education in other cultures. Enculturation is the key to several anthropological and educational enigmas: it unlocks the mystery of the relation of the individual to his culture, resolves the question of cultural conservatism and cultural change, and validates the philosophical function of cultural relativism. In Herskovits's own words: "The enculturation of the individual in the early years of his life is the prime mechanism making for cultural stability, while the process, as it is operative on more mature folk, is highly important in inducing change" (1948:40).

The existence of the enculturation process in every known culture demands a relativistic point of view. Cultures and human beings are what they are because of enculturative factors which perpetuate, recondition, and occasionally renew the way of life of a people. And as a corollary of enculturation, people tend to feel that their judgments and perceptions are to be preferred to all others. Herskovits infers from the ethnocentrism inherent in most enculturative experiences that evaluation of cultures is at best relative, and that attitudes, beliefs, perceptions, and standards of behavior are also relative. The infinite expression of these "is simply based on the circumstance of enculturative conditioning" (1948:70, 627, 677, 642–655).

Herskovits' empirical studies in education deal preponderantly with blacks in the New World, based upon his research into black life in other parts of the world. He has helped to destroy the myth of racial inferiority. Back in the late twenties and early thirties, Herskovits examined the diverse ways in which blacks had accommodated themselves to the different cultural backgrounds into which they had been brought as slaves, and the force of the enculturation process in the United States in either reinforcing and/or extinguishing the earlier ancestral enculturation of blacks in the Old World. His research on intelligence tests proved in 1927 that the basic hypothesis of white superiority in general social efficiency and innate intelligence was unwarranted because intelligence tests tend to measure standardized individual reactions to environments and natural background and not innate behavior (Herskovits 1927:3). His research on Dahomey education in Africa provided him with the understanding that education in the Old World was directed toward the maintenance of cultural stability. However, in the New World, first-, second-, or third-generation blacks had to make profound cultural changes. Herskovits concluded that in the case of most New World blacks, early African enculturation had been a prohibitive, almost insurmountable obstacle to Euro-American assimilation (Herskovits 1954:3–7).

Herskovits' single greatest contribution to the convergence of educational and anthropological theory is the degree to which he has pointed out that ethnocentrism is implicit in curricula, in the attitudes of teachers toward members of minority groups, and in the widespread but mistaken assumption that other cultures are somehow inferior to our own because of our technological superiority. Herskovits held that one of the anthropologist's primary tasks was to convince educators that truth is dynamic, "that it develops forms in one generation and for one people which it does not have at other times or in other places" (Herskovits 1947:217). Shibboleths of racial, ethnic, or cultural supremacy are both unscientific and illogical; they are predicated on an ethnocentrism which is ignorant of the infinity of enculturative possibilities in other cultural and subcultural units.

Robert Redfield's educational research is far-ranging. He often alleged that an understanding of education in complex societies can be gained through a consideration of education in primitive or folk societies. As a result of his several field studies in Guatemala, Yucatan, and in a Mexican village, Tepoztlan, Redfield discovered that there were universal elements of education which have evolved from the simplest cultures and which are expressed today in complex urban cultures. He found that in all cultures, whether folk or urban or mixed, education has an exploratory, a conversational, and a creative dimension (Redfield 1962:273; 1963:30–73). He contended that because all cultures are somewhat integrated, then teaching itself should be perceived as a more or less integrated element in the culture of any community: "Teaching is effective in so far as it tends toward the development in the young person of a coherent body of attitudes and values adequate to the life-needs in his particular community" (1963:97). The single greatest lesson which modern society can learn from education in folk society is its consistency and its high regard for the heritage of the culture.

Redfield's major contribution to educational theory in the United States is his response to a question which he often asked: "What should education in the United States do in order to enrich the human potential of every single individual and to allow each person to achieve the good life?" (1963:71). In his longest essay on education, he asked educators to advance the value of individual worth; this could find expression in the exploration of the enduring values found in the great literary works, in the intellectual and moral conversation which rational students can have with their teachers. It could also be expressed in the creative spirit of a thinker like Alfred North Whitehead, who encouraged students to recreate themselves by rearranging their value priorities, based upon the most universal and long-lasting values found in the great literature of the world (1963:22–23).

Clyde Kluckhohn has written that "the matter of values is the prime intellectual issue of the present day" (Kluckhohn 1962:286). In many of his educational writings he held that the cohesiveness and strength of the American people depend upon the clarity and the force with which schools are willing to undertake the task of making explicit for Americans and the rest of the world the value assumptions which underlie their own behavior (1962:286). Kluckhohn advocated an exhaustive examination of postulated universal values with the possibility of constructing blueprints outlining a future world community dedicated "to the self-integrating multiplicity of the culture-patterns that are indigenous to disparate areas of the earth's surface" (1962:300). While he did not give concerted attention to the analysis of the educational process in his fieldwork, he did attempt to help educators in this country to deal with hypotheses such as universal human values in the classroom. One form which this might take would be to study the value systems and institutions of other cultures with the explicit intention of gradual modification of our own self-defeating norms. This means, according to Kluckhohn, that educators, like many anthropologists, "must concentrate on the universally human techniques of living which all cultures have contrived within the context of broad, panhuman values" (Brameld 1957:xii).

Kluckhohn proposed that educators must confront each human being in the classroom as an integrated personality. Educators must be able to admit to youngsters that cultural discrepancies do exist and that values can be critically examined in the schools, as well as in the home or church. Educators must construct curricula rooted in the "potentialities" of the human personality and the limitless possibilities for personality growth. While Kluckhohn rarely stated with explicitness that education's most pressing goal should be the search for fresh, integrating principles appropriate to a world culture, he has suggested that educators, as well as scholars from other disciplines, might help to investigate the nature and causes of human conflict and devise means for its reduction (Kluckhohn 1963:244).

Kluckhohn's major contribution to educational theory was his movement away from the position of value relativism, and away from a conception of personality which is behavioristic, to a recognition that there may be universal values worth examining in the classroom. He suggested the far-reaching possibilities of personal autonomy and encouraged a pattern of education which allows for the free growth of the personality so necessary in a mobile and changing culture.

Ashley Montagu has reasoned that because a person is such a plastic, educable organism, then educators must stop "instructing" (merely imparting the three R's); they must become aware that man's only hope for survival rests in his learning to become more human. That is, human beings must learn to give in to their natural tendency to become cooperative and loving. According to Montagu, educators must be responsible for sensitizing students all over the world to the "indisputable socio-biological fact" of interhuman cooperation. Therefore, all of education should be based on the necessity for loving human relations (Montagu 1958:79, 31–33).

Montagu believes that anthropology and education converge at a point where the scientific evidence for a theory of human nature is unquestionable. As a result of his research in the fields of social biology and cultural and physical anthropology, he asserts that the scientific evidence attesting to the innate tendency of all organisms toward "life, love, and mutual aid" should convince educators that learned aggressive responses can be replaced by learned cooperative ones. Educators should become students of human nature by turning to the research of natural and social scientists and then by teaching the value of interdependent human relations in the classroom. Education for human relations can achieve two goals: it will eliminate racism in social life, and it will reveal to students that competition, aggression, and conflict are the negative by-products of an inhuman, capitalistic social structure. If students are allowed to see that racism is the indispensable correlate of the dysfunctional ideals of a rugged American individualism, laissez-faire capitalism, and Social Darwinism (because minority groups pose a threat to the security of people whose personalities are structured in terms of those disoperative ideals), then the possibility of a more humanistic way of life can become a reality. According to Montagu, an education directed to better human relations will enable man to humanize his technology, reconstruct his divisive, predatory society, and achieve a peaceful and loving world order.

Jules Henry's contribution to educational theory was based upon firsthand educational observations in several cultures, including direct fieldwork in U.S. classrooms. He has shown that education in this country cannot be understood apart from the study of culture as an integrated whole. By concentrating on communications and psychological theory, he pointed out the implicit and explicit teaching of values which comprise the American natural character. And because the school is part of a self-reinforcing, interlocking cultural system, and because its primary function is to "drill children in cultural orientations" (Henry 1965:45, 127, 283). Henry maintains that the American public school reflects the division within the total culture between "hedonistic mindlessness" and "austere intelligence." He has depicted at length the subtle and obvious ways that teachers transmit values to their students. Because education is a "polyphasic" (learning more than one thing at a time) endeavor, teachers convey values to their students, not only through the subject matter but through signals, signs, and cues (Henry 1965:108, 206).

Henry utilized the techniques of the anthropologist-observer in the classroom to illustrate the degree to which the school is a reflector of all the drives, the conflicts, and the discontinuities inherent in the culture as a whole. What is being transmitted in the schools, according to Henry, is a "culture of death" which portrays the irrevocable effects upon the personality of the American economic scheme and its concomitant value structure. In the classroom, teachers consciously and unconsciously foster the spirit of competitiveness, fear, and docility, all of which reinforce the key cultural drive of "technological driveness," calculated to make Americans mindless, acquisitive consumers. What results is a human personality which is competitive and aggressive, in spite of its craving for love and security. Henry has shown educators the extent to which the American natural character is split with conflict. He has also underscored the degree to which the schools have produced individuals who fit the acquisitive requirements of the culture, but in so doing, have made love among people a virtual impossibility. His latest work, published posthumously, extended his educational interests into American family life where he studied families with psychotic children. The primary goals of these extensive daily observations were to furnish new insights into psychotic breakdown and to ascertain the relationships between family life and people's behavior in several other cultural institutions, including the educational system (Henry 1972).

George Spindler has been one of the pioneers in systematically stimulating cross-fertilization between anthropological and educational theory (Spindler 1955, 1963). Much of his educational research has been based upon a theoretical position which he describes as "configurative" and "functionalistic." That is, he has shown how the school is an interrelated, functionally interdependent, self-reinforcing system, with both teachers and students profoundly influenced by life experiences outside the classroom. Spindler has demonstrated how the educational process is a basic reflector of the value conflicts which rage within the cultural milieu surrounding the school, and has clarified the teacher's role as a transmitter of the culture. He has examined such problems as how the conflicting values of the teacher often influence his perception of student behavior, how the transmission of manifest and latent values in the classroom has often resulted in the defeat of such worthwhile teacher goals as democratic choice and equality of student opportunity (Spindler 1959), and how the role of the school administrator is a direct projection of core American cultural values. Because these values (achievement, individualism, leadership) are at best tenuous and controversial, the administrator's position in the community is often an uncertain one. Consequently, his professional function becomes a "balancing" or mediating one (Spindler 1963). Spindler has also engaged in an examination of educational processes among the Menomini Indians (in Spindler 1963), and he and his wife, Louise Spindler, have edited a series of paperbacks on education in other cultures (G. and L. Spindler 1965).

By advocating an "anthropology of education" Spindler has emphasized the teachers' need to become aware of the functional interdependence of cultural institutions, of the conflicting values inherent in the American culture, and the overall influence of culture as a patterned system influencing human behavior. Thus, the professional anthropologist must work closely with teachers in the role of a "culture therapist," with the ultimate goal of increasing the teacher's awareness of his own value orientation, the relationship of his values to the larger cultural context, and the ways that the teacher's value conflicts are transmitted to students (Spindler 1959).

In general, these nine anthropologists who have written about education perceive their role as descriptive, diagnostic, and reportorial in scope. Most have described the educational process in the United States, and they have used their observations of education in other cultures to diagnose what they consider to be dislocations in the American education environment. All have approached the study of American educational processes by comparative references to nonliterate and literate cultures throughout the world. Generally, all have dealt with the following problem areas in education: personality development, learning theory, the transmission of values, the transmission of the cultural heritage, communication among students, parents, teachers, and administrators, social structure and function, role behavior, ethnocentrism, universal and relative values, pattern, configuration, and race.

Educational Contributions to Anthropology and Education

Henry Winthrop, a social scientist and a philospher, characterizes two possible kinds of interdisciplinary research: methodological and hermeneutical. Because most educational theorists writing about anthropology tend to perceive their function as one of *applying* the insights of anthropologists to their own field, they can be identified by one of the two Winthrop categories.

According to Winthrop, the *methodological* interdisciplinarian is interested in other disciplines because they pose new problems, provide an opportunity for new methods of analysis, and suggest fresh analogies and models. These modes of analysis represent an empirical departure from the purely theoretical and speculative interests of the hermeneutical interdisciplinarian. They show immediate practical value, they can be undertaken with scientific objectivity and value neutrality, and they avoid the synoptic concerns of metaphysical system builders. The methodological researcher is a dispassionate reporter of empirical findings who scrupulously avoids explicit normative considerations.

Conversely, the *hermeneutical* scientist is a mediator. He tries to avoid the schism between fact and value (between what is and what ought to be) by creating a working partnership between facts and theory on the one hand, and questions of personal, cultural and social value on the other. The hermeneutical scientist is an interpreter of the human situation: he attempts to apply the findings of the methodological scientist to the resolution of those existential dilemmas which continue to baffle modern man. He is eager to explore the social, spiritual, and intellectual implications of scientific research, and often, is willing to suggest bold resolutions to the various personal and social crises which occur in the postindustrial state with disturbing frequency (Winthrop 1968:1–15). Many of the educational contributions to the partnership between anthropology and education have been marked by a hermeneutical tendency, greater in some writers than in others. What follows is a brief examination of some representative educational contributions to the convergence of educational and anthropological theory.

Two textbooks, by educators, illustrate the hermeneutical technique described by Winthrop. One book, by Thomas M. Weiss and Kenneth H. Hoover, was written to give students an opportunity to understand the "serious conflicts in their own cultures" (Weiss and Hoover 1960:130). In the section on culture, Hoover tries to define those problems the educator faces in reeducating students who are culturally impoverished and the extent to which inconsistent cultural norms often affect the mental health of students. Hoover believes that an understanding of an individual's behavior as culturally determined will help teachers to question their own beliefs and habits which are cultural in nature and which lead to conflict and inconsistency in everyday life. Using Kingsley Davis's six potential conflict areas (conflicting norms; competing authorities; ill-defined steps in parental authority; small, single-unit families; open competition for social status; and sex tensions) as potential stress areas for adolescents in this country, Hoover looks to cultures such as the Samoan and Burmese to see how they resolve these universal adolescent conflicts. He concludes his analysis of the anthropological literature with five generalizations which he believes will offer many insights to educators. 1. Culture determines how individuals think, but, nevertheless, human behavior is infinitely flexible. 2. The inconsistencies between what boys and girls ought to do and the frustration and conflict which arise often lead to open rebellion. 3. Some cultures produce very few conflict situations. 4. Language differences between various cultural groups create needless misunderstandings. 5. The school is an agent of cultural transmission and any revision of education should reflect the needs of a changing culture.

Hoover, like other educational authors and editors of textbooks in the hermeneutical tradition, advocates a partnership with anthropology mainly because of its practical and applicational value for educators (Lindquist 1970). He believes that an understanding of basic anthropological principles can help teachers scrutinize more realistically the traditional beliefs of their students and themselves in order to minimize further educational crises.

Another textbook, edited by three educators, has as its immediate objective in presenting pieces by Clyde Kluckhohn, Leslie A. White, John and Mavis Biesanz, Dorothy Lee, Ralph Linton, Margaret Mead, Robert Redfield, and others the cultivation of an "awareness of the factors in society and in culture that influence learning and the acquisition of skills important to survival and self-fulfillment" (Chilcott, Greenberg, and Wilson 1968:28).

The editors have selected articles by leading anthropologists which they believe will increase the educator's awareness of cultural alternatives available to him and will enable him to choose wisely among those alternatives. For example, in the section on "the science of culture in education," the articles convey the increasing complexity of education in industrial societies. As a result of the United States' increase in cultural content, children are often presented with conflicting views of the adult world. They experience adult life mainly through the media, and the value distortions which they receive leave them unprepared for a responsible, self-actualizing adult life. The editors conclude that because the early years of a child's enculturation are so influential in his life, individual stress is inevitable when the child is expected to adjust to new cultural norms effected by technological upheavals in the American value system. They believe that anthropology is of value to teachers mainly as it prepares them to be "culturally literate"—that is, teachers should be given courses in "the science of culture" so that they may be able to analyze their way of life in order to determine the culturally defined limits within which they must transmit the heritage to children.

Solon T. Kimball and James E. McClellan, Jr., the one an anthropologist and the other a philosopher of education, have collaborated to write a provocative analysis of American life. Their elaborate examination of the functions of education in a rapidly changing technological society makes a brief summary difficult. The authors, in the hermeneutical tradition, undertake a structural and systemic analysis of American society in order to identify problems and then to suggest remedies which might restore a sense of commitment to individual self-realization—this in the face of the overwhelming demands made on human beings by a "complex, impersonal, public, corporate world" (Kimball and McClellan 1966:17). The authors begin their analysis in agrarian America just after the Civil War and trace the transition of the United States from an agrarian to an industrial economy. They examine the family structure, the school, the community, and the corporate system as the primary groups in which the individual learns and expresses his sense of self. The fundamental objective of their study is to get both teachers and students to commit themselves, first to an awareness that public and private worlds are refractory and necessary parts of the given social system, and, second, that the school can help the student create meaning and purpose in his life only if it understands that wholly new forms of human association and new symbolic relationships between the person and his external world have evolved since the time of John Dewey.

Kimball and McClellan typify the technique of the hermeneutical scientist. They utilize the analytic methods of the cultural anthropologist and the educational philosopher in order to study and to explain the influence of the corporate system on the private life of the individual. They maintain that the value of such a study resides in the intellectual contribution it can make to the individual's understanding of his world. They predict that because the individual is equipped with such a critical understanding of the tension between his public and private worlds, he may be able to tolerate the tension more easily and construct a meaningful life with the tools and symbols provided him from both worlds.

Theodore Brameld, an educational philosopher, has examined the order, process, and goals of culture in the hermeneutical spirit of achieving a more humanistic and democratic world community. Brameld contends that the presence of anthropology in teacher-training curricula is vital if educators are to comprehend the temporal-spatial pattern and structure of their culture, the nature of change which is inherent in all dimensions of cultural life, and the value system which motivates individuals to opt for one way of life over another. In one of the earliest systematic statements developing the convergence of educational and anthropological theory, Brameld marshals an impressive collection of evidence provided by cultural anthropologists and other social scientists in order to show the relevance of culture theory to education (Brameld 1957).

In his study, Brameld is both methodological and hermeneutical—methodological in his structured and systematic analysis and elucidation of all areas of cultural anthropology and hermeneutical in the sense that his analysis culminates in the prescription that educators, acting on the empirical findings of the social sciences, ought to begin to construct a better way of life for themselves and their fellows. During the sixties, Brameld taught two courses at Boston University dealing explicitly with the culture concept. The first course, "Cultural Foundations of Education," exposed students to the science of culture, to the writings of several great figures in the field, and to many central anthropological concepts used by the nine anthropologists discussed in the first section of this chapter. The companion course, "Educational Anthropology," had a dual purpose: it was methodological because students were given the opportunity to apply the conceptual tools (developed in the first course) to actual field experience (Brameld 1967); it was hermeneutical because students were constantly encouraged to construct a scientifically defensible theory of human behavior. The ultimate objective of the course was to help others identify and improve the self-defeating aspects of their personal and social living. To use Brameld's term, the educator, acting as an "anthropotherapist," strives to help people help themselves by making scientifically plausible value judgments, based upon intensive and extensive analysis of cultural conflicts, with the ultimate goal of resolving troublesome and destructive cultural practices (Brameld 1965). The second course, "Educational Anthropology," was a normative, applied extension of the scientific theories derived from the first. It is Brameld's contention that education and anthropology converge at the point which makes the greatest difference to human beings. This point of contact exists where the quality of individual and communal living can be improved and enriched through the efforts of educators acting in the best interests of their students, and always on the basis of a scientific and humanistic consensus of what is good for man.

In general, educators who have written about the convergence of anthropological and educational theory are interested in the applicative and practical benefits of such a union. They often stress the need for a cultural awareness on the part of educators. They engage in diagnostic practices utilizing the research of anthropologists to identify and clarify trouble spots in the educational environment. They are hermeneutical in the sense that most are genuinely concerned about the normative implications for educational theory and practice as a result of the anthropologist's interest in their field. And most educators look with expectancy to anthropology for a theory of human behavior which is both explanatory and predictive and which is able to illuminate the many stress areas in contemporary education.

A Critical Summary

In the past, educators have turned to the social sciences in a fit of frenzied and slavish desperation. Most of the original research in learning theory, cognitive development, I.Q. studies, the sociocultural pressure on students, urban education, and educational economics has come not from scholars trained in the pedagogy and theory of education, but from social scientists representing such disciplines as psychology, sociology, and economics. Likewise, much of the work in education—and anthropology—is still marked by an uncritical acceptance by harried, crisis-oriented educators of the basic findings of cultural anthropologists. Educators often overlook the fact that cultural anthropology is in the process of correcting many of its own earlier excesses by revising its conceptual foundations, terminology, and methodology. In retrospect, there appear to be four interrelated problem areas which emerge from this cursory examination of educational and anthropological theory. Obviously, anthropologists have contributed a great deal to educational thought and practice. But if there is ever to be a more tenable union between the two disciplines, then educators and anthropologists must become sensitive to the following theoretical tensions which exist between the two disciplines (Kurtz and Handy 1964).

How Scientific Is Education?

Some critics regard education mainly as an applied field or as a policy science. Educators themselves have expended a great amount of energy in applying the results of the other behavioral sciences to their own interests in motivation, learning, and socialization. In the past there has been a general reluctance on the part of educators to experiment and to develop fresh techniques and methods (although this is being done more now in the technological and behavioral modification areas). Educators have tended to wait for social scientists to identify research areas in education, and then to contribute to the research in education with empirical studies of their own. Educational theorists have usually been defensive about the scientific validity of their own subject; or else they have made preposterous scientific claims in their research which have been completely unwarranted. Generally, educational theorists have rushed to the more prestigious sciences for empirical evidence to decide controversial questions and to measure specific educational outcomes.

In the future, educational theorists must also contribute with originality to anthropological work on such topics as socialization and learning theory. If interdisciplinary study is to be reciprocal, educators must begin to determine the reasonable and desirable extent to which they can formulate warranted, descriptive assertions about human behavior in and out of the classroom. They must decide the degree to which it is possible to determine whether behavior B in educational situations will recur if antecedent conditions A occur. While educators should continue to develop highly generalized, testable hypotheses of their own in such areas as cognitive performance, effective learning environments, and predictable short- and long-range intellectual outcomes, they must be careful *not* to succumb to the danger of trivialization in their research. Currently there is too much concern with measuring minute learning outcomes, tabulating irrelevant behavior changes, and undertaking cost-benefits research in education. In their understandable desire to contribute equally to social science research, educators are concentrating on the most easily measurable topics (usually the most banal), and neglecting the more pressing sociopolitical implications of educational policy-making.

Educators must also strive for terminological clarity if their discipline is to become respectable. Perhaps the single greatest contribution which anthropology can make to education is to help in clarifying such traditional terminological confusions as "teaching," "learning," "individual needs," "curriculum," "motivation," and "relevant education." Of course, this suggestion presupposes the awareness by anthropologists of the verbal imprecisions in their own field. In other words, to the extent that educators become less grandiose in their theorizings, more experimental in their inquiries, and more willing to engage in an analysis of controversial sociopolitical policies and proposals affecting education (even at the cost of surrendering the much-vaunted neutralism of objective research), then they can become more sensitive to the problems of the other social sciences, including anthropology, and the danger of importing those problems into the field of education.

How Can the Anthropologist Be of Maximum Help to the Educator?

Anthropologists have used a variety of heuristic models in their research, including the causal, functional, historical, logical, aesthetic, symbolic, and configurational. Some anthropologists reviewed in this study visualize their primary interdisciplinary role as accumulating empirical evidence concerning the observable processes of culture change, based upon one or more of the above models, and then describing (recording) the varied effects of culture change on education in the United States. Others have devised more abstract schemes to explain human behavior, and then have attempted to fit the data to the a priori scheme, in order to speculate about the role of education in resolving cultural crises. And at least one other anthropologist has stressed the need for more precise quantitative observation in education.

Educators and anthropologists must agree on the emphasis to be given to theory, methodology (deductive, inductive, hypothetico-deductive, participant-observer, observant-participant, recorder, diagnostician, prognostician), data accumulation, speculation, and the development and testing of scientific models. Much of the educational research undertaken by anthropologists has hitherto concentrated on problems in culture-and-personality, cognitive studies, communications, race, cultural transmission, and value orientation. In the future, educators will have to determine the priority of problems and methodologies to be explored and used in educational research. Perhaps structural functional studies, linguistics, symbolic interaction, physical anthropology, and acculturation can be of help to educators. There is no reason why educators trained in the science of culture cannot contribute to anthropological research more actively by identifying problem areas in education and by investigating the potential of the many techniques and models employed by anthropologists.

Thus far, the independent anthropological research of the educator, while promising, has largely been disappointing. Some educators are content to edit books of previously published anthropological selections. These readings usually lack an overall theoretical focus, purpose, coordination, or any type of discernible practical benefit. Also, because the same anthropologists are included in many volumes, there is rarely a variety of investigative models or procedures presented. McClellan and Kimball's work, referred to earlier, is insightful. However, their conclusions are marred by a reluctance to venture beyond a historical, hypothetico-deductive treatment of American society. Consequently, their study of education in the "new America" too often results in an uncritical defense of the corporate status quo. On the other hand, Brameld's work is the most genuinely hermeneutical. His research is original, important, and visionary. However, his tendency to manipulate anthropological constructs and methodologies in order to advance his "blueprint" for a world order runs the risk of exploiting interdisciplinary research for the promulgation of an ideology.

The time has come for anthropologists to encourage educators to initiate research on their own. In the beginning, some of that research will be crude, possibly even trivial. But, with the active help of anthropologists, educators can move from a parasitic, overly cautious reliance on the traditional rigors of the science to bolder, more visionary studies. This will happen only when anthropologists and educators engage in the continuing construction and testing of scientific models and strategies.

What Is the Place of Values in the Partnership between Anthropologists and Educators?

Some anthropologists discussed in this chapter believe that their strictly anthropological research should be value-free. They believe that it should be objective and make no overt prescriptions or recommendations. Only a few anthropologists have dealt explicitly with the personal, existential, or sociopolitical implications of their research. Educators tend to be more hermeneutical in their work, eager to apply the methodological findings of anthropologists to their own crisis areas. Actually, all anthropologists, especially those who have contributed to educational theory, hold many value preferences—on the "meta" level. Their writings abound with meta-scientific beliefs that education is primarily a transmissive process; that the school, at best, can only mirror the dislocations and turbulence in the larger culture; that culture exercises an irrevocable domination over man the creature; and that values are relative and contextual. Each anthropologist in this brief study has a "meta-image" of what the good life ought to be and what role the school should assume in achieving that good life.

Confusion occurs when educators, eager to apply the insights of anthropologists to their own field, force the application and then find it almost impossible to reconcile the hidden value assumptions of the anthropologist with their own. Also, many anthropologists appear unwilling to relate their basic anthropological work to their speculations about what education "ought" to achieve. For example, Redfield has not related with any specificity his educational prescriptions for a classical, "Great Books" education to such basic constructs as "folk society" or "world view." Montagu rarely makes explicit reference to his own research in physical anthropology when he speculates about an education for human relations. And Henry concentrates primarily on communications and psychological theory in his examination of the classroom milieu. Often much of the work undertaken by anthropologists in education is characterized by an eclectic, dilettantish tendency. At this time it is necessary for the anthropologist to become aware of his covert metaphysical assumptions and value biases, make these assumptions explicit, and then relate his educational research to these value assumptions—all the while making greater efforts to portray education in its strictly anthropological dimensions.

Educators too must make explicit their own underlying value assumptions, which are often confusingly understood and which result in the presentation of hazy value judgments and metaphysical preferences as if they were warranted assertions. Questions of value, decision-making, and policy preference must have both a normative and an empirically testable content. Too often the work of educators in advancing the findings of anthropologists and other social scientists is based upon a hasty, *ad hoc* application of empirical research to poorly understood social issues. Too few educators have a coherent, articulable understanding of their own basic philosophical positions. Even fewer have definable educational goals which give direction to the partnership between education and anthropology. Perhaps a distinction must be made between strictly descriptive sciences and the policy sciences. Such a distinction would ascribe to educators the responsibility of prescribing changes in their own areas. This distinction also implies that a "pure" descriptive science is attainable—a belief which has been the subject of controversy for a long time.

On What Level Can Anthropological and Educational Research Function Most Effectively?

Is the rapprochement between the two disciplines to result in a macro or a micro science? Is specialized research which is limited to specific individuals, educational procedures, or locales generalizable? Does the discovery of a similarity between a specific A and a general B imply that warranted assertions about A necessarily apply to B, or are all universalized assertions merely unscientific extrapolations of localized research? Should educational anthropologists concentrate only upon limited, middle-range hypotheses and problems, which can be analyzed and tested and which can then be cautiously advanced as applicable in similar situations? Anthropologists and educational theorists must decide upon the boundaries of their emerging discipline in order to avoid emphases in their work which border either on the nugatory or the overgeneralized extremes of the research continuum.

The micro-macro question, once resolved, can define for educational anthropologists those levels on which they can best examine such crucial contemporary issues as why education in big cities seems to be failing so tragically. Their diagnoses of the alleged failure of city schools will depend upon which area they choose to study, upon which level they wish to concentrate, and which causal phenomena can be advanced as similar in all urban situations. Educational anthropologists might focus on *individuals* who live in the core city, or *family* relationships, or *school* experiences, or welfare, housing, transportation, or work experiences. They might attempt to isolate and analyze the causal variables which result in racial conflict in the schools, like demographic changes, poverty, job scarcity or stagnation, factional politics, or the fragmentation or lack of concern on the part of city bureaucracies. The implications of such studies for teacher, counselor, and administrator training, curriculum construction and revision, and the functionality of gigantic educational bureaucracies (as opposed to smaller, community control of schools) are enormous. Before this is attainable, however, educators and anthropologists must agree upon the level where it is best (most analyzable and testable) to begin their research and which conclusions are generalizable to other situations.

Conclusion

The convergence of educational and anthropological theory will be most productive for students, teachers, theorists, and practitioners when there is a recognition that there are common problems in each discipline and that continuous and cooperative research into those common problems might result in a comprehensive view of human behavior. In this sense, the educational anthropologist becomes the embodiment of John Dewey's scientific prototype. He is the theorist who is scientific in method, who bases his recommendations and policies upon bold inquiries into the conditions and consequences of action, and who extracts from his interdisciplinary ventures the importance of value in a world of fact by creating and acting upon a scientific, humanistic program for personal, social, and cultural renewal.

Furthermore, the partnership between education and anthropology can be a dramatic way to satisfy the needs of young people to understand themselves, their institutions, and their human transactions. In a world shaken by personal and societal crises, students in the fields of education and anthropology ought to be given an opportunity to perceive human life in all of its complexity and diversity and in all of its commonality.

An anthropological examination of education should be both methodological (descriptive and scientific) and hermeneutical (normative and speculative). Students study such methodological concepts as acculturation, assimilation, innovation, and crisis. Through an understanding of such central concepts, the student will be better able to evaluate the merits of such educational experiments as community control, open education, accountability, and educational decentralization. In light of the reality of cultural dynamics, the methodologist can more keenly assess the effectiveness of such change concepts in education as operations research, linear programming, systems engineering, organization theory, game theory, group dynamics, and preferential behavior techniques.

An anthropological examination of education should also be hermeneutical. It must look beyond an excessive preoccupation with scientific description and methodology. Perhaps the most glaring weakness thus far in anthropological contributions to educational theory and practice has been the failure of anthropologists to make their value positions explicit. Very often there research has been nothing more than a thinly disguised acceptance of the social and cultural status quo. This is especially true when anthropological research has had as its primary (but usually unstated) objective the dispassionate description of educational processes in literate and nonliterate cultures, without the concomitant criticism of the larger social system which sustains and reinforces both beneficial and harmful educational practices.

Finally, an anthropological perspective on education is one which is rooted in the methodological and hermeneutical convergence of both disciplines. It is at this point that John Dewey's scientific prototype is most at home. He is acting upon the evidence generated by his scientific inquiries to create a world which is more defensibly humanistic and self-actualizing for human beings everywhere.

References*

Benedict, Ruth, 1936, "Continuities and Discontinuities in Cultural Conditioning," *Psychiatry* 1:161–167.

———, 1940–1944, "Educative Processes—A Comparative Note," *National Education Association Department of Supervisors and Directors of Instruction* 13:122–127.

———, 1942 "American Melting Pot, 1942 Model," *National Education Association Department of Supervisors and Directors of Instruction* 14:14–24.

———, 1943, "Transmitting Our Democratic Heritage in the School," *American Journal of Sociology* 48:722–727.

Boas, Franz, 1940, "Evidence on the Nature of Intelligence," *Harvard Educational Review* 10:144–149.

———, 1941, "The Relation Between Physical and Mental Development," *Science* 93:339–342.

———, 1945, *Race and Democratic Society.* New York: J. J. Augustin.

Brameld, Theodore, 1957, *Cultural Foundations of Education.* New York: Harper & Row.

———,1965, "Anthropotherapy—Toward Theory and Practice," *Human Organization* 24:288–297.

———, 1967, "Learning Through Involvement—Puerto Rico as a Laboratory in Educational Anthropology," *Journal of Education* 150:3–56.

Chilcott, John, Norman Greenberg, and Herbert Wilson, 1968, *Readings in the Socio-Cultural Foundations of Education.* Belmont, Calif.: Wadsworth Publishing Company.

Davis, Kingsley, 1940, "The Sociology of Parent-Youth Conflict," *American Sociological Review* 5:523–535.

Gruber, Frederick C., 1961, *Anthropology and Education.* Philadelphia: University of Pennsylvania Press.

Henry, Jules, 1965, *Culture Against Man.* New York: Vintage Books.

——, 1972, *Pathways to Madness.* New York: Random House.

Herskovits, Melville J., 1927, *The Negro and the Intelligence Tests.* Connecticut: Patriot Publishing Company.

———, 1947, "Social Science Units of the Northwestern Liberal Arts Program," *Journal of General Education* 1:216–223.

———, 1948, *Man and His Works.* New York: Alfred A. Knopf, Inc.

———, 1954, "Education in Changing Africa," *Institute of International Education Bulletin* 29:3–7.

*Throughout this book, Case Studies in Cultural Anthropology will be designated by CSCA following a book title; Case Studies in Education and Culture will be designated by CSEC following a book title; and Studies in Anthropological Method by SAM. All three series are published by Holt, Rinehart and Winston, Inc., New York.

Kimball, Solon T., and James E. McClellan, Jr., 1966, *Education and the New America.* New York: Vintage Books.

Kluckhohn, Clyde, 1957, "Cultures, Values, and Education," *Bulletin of the Research Institute of Comparative Education and Culture* 1:44–61.

———, 1962, *Culture and Behavior.* New York: The Free Press.

———, 1963, *Mirror for Man.* New York: Premier Books.

Kneller, George, 1965, *Educational Anthropology: An Introduction.* New York: John Wiley & Sons, Inc.

Kurtz, Paul, and Rollo Handy, 1964, *A Current Appraisal of the Behavioral Sciences.* Mass.: Behavioral Research Council.

Landes, Ruth, 1965, *Culture in American Education.* New York: John Wiley & Sons, Inc.

Lindquist, Harry M., 1970, *Education: Readings in the Process of Cultural Transmission.* Boston: Houghton Mifflin Company.

Mead, Margaret, 1931, "The Meaning of Freedom in Education," *Progressive Education* 8:107–111.

———, 1951, *The School in American Culture.* Cambridge, Mass.: Harvard University Press.

———, 1959a, "Why Is Education Obsolete?" *Education Digest* 24:1–5.

———, 1959b, "New Kind of Discipline," *Education Digest* 25:13–15.

———, 1961, "Continuing Our Present System Isn't Enough," *Notes and Essays on Education for Adults.* CSIEA. 34:34–38.

———, 1966, "The University and Institutional Change," *Notes and Essays on Education for Adults.* CSIEA. 2:52–62.

———. 1970, *Culture and Commitment. A Study of the Generation Gap.* New York: Doubleday & Company.

Montagu, Ashley, 1958, *Education and Human Relations.* New York: Grove Press.

Redfield, Robert, 1962, *Human Nature and the Study of Society: The Papers of Robert Redfield.* Chicago: University of Chicago Press.

———, 1963, *The Social Uses of Social Science.* Chicago: University of Chicago Press.

Spindler, George, ed., 1955, *Education and Anthropology.* Los Angeles: University of California Press.

———, 1959, *The Transmission of American Culture.* Cambridge, Mass.: Harvard University Press, for the Graduate School of Education.

———, ed., 1963, *Education and Culture: Anthropological Approaches.* New York: Holt, Rinehart and Winston, Inc.

Spindler, George and Louise, 1965–(continuing series), *Case Studies in Education and Culture.* New York: Holt, Rinehart and Winston, Inc.

Weiss, Thomas M., and Kenneth H. Hoover, 1960, *Scientific Foundations of Education.* Des Moines, Iowa: William C. Brown Company.

Winthrop, Henry, 1968, *Ventures in Social Interpretation.* New York: Appleton-Century-Crofts.

JOHN SINGLETON/*University of Pittsburgh*

2 *Implications of Education as Cultural Transmission**

The fact that anthropology can make only limited claims of a special contribution to educational research can be seen as an extension of past efforts by psychology and sociology—the two disciplines that have dominated this field of inquiry—which attempted to deal with the totality of human experience. The following is an attempt to contrast anthropological suggestions for educational research with what I believe have been the constraints imposed by psychological and sociological approaches to the study of education. In this way I would like to extend the questions that are asked about education and the methods by which answers will be sought.

In many ways our academic disciplines as social collectivities are like the primitive tribes with which anthropologists have traditionally dealt. They are composed of people who identify themselves and are identified by others as belonging to a particular tribe. Each disciplinary "tribe" has a certain territory, a language, a set of rules for guiding behavior, a mythology, a pattern for cultural transmission, a process of initiation, a social order, a series of rituals, and a system of social stratification.

In academia—or more specifically the modern university—disciplinary loyalties are strong and meaningful to many individuals and the physical and social structure of the university is usually built around these "tribal" groupings.

While anthropologists have not studied academic disciplines in these terms, I would like to use the tribal model in order to avoid questions of the logical division of our social science "turf." It is not then necessary to argue the uniqueness of our contributions to research on education—it is only necessary to describe what has been and what might yet be done under the banner of anthropology.

Lest the idea of applying anthropology to educational research be seen as something new, I would like to mention that a paper similar to mine was read in Philadelphia at the 1904 meeting of the American Association for the Advancement of Science. It was entitled "Ethnic Factors in Education" and was seen by its author, Edgar L. Hewett, as presenting a way of bringing together

*This article was first presented to the AAAS's Symposium on the Social Science Discipline: Contribution to Basic Research in Education, Philadelphia, December 29, 1971, under the title "Contribution of Anthropology to Basic Research in Education."

the fields of anthropological and educational research (Hewett 1905). In a note published earlier in the *American Anthropologist* (Hewett 1904), which also published his AAAS paper, Hewett had specifically suggested a joint meeting of the newly formed National Society for the Study of Education and the American Anthropological Association, under AAAS auspices, in order to "contribute to the progress of both." He believed that anthropology "needs closer definition by the masters, and its literature must be brought to a state that will place it in closer relations with education, through the schools of pedagogy, normal schools, and teachers' institutes."

Hewett's two concerns continue to attract anthropologists to the study of education. The first was the involvement of anthropologists in the construction of curriculum units for presentation in elementary and secondary schools, an involvement which seems to lead anthropologists to ask significant questions about the school as a social institution.

Hewett's major theme was that of ethnic differences in a system of common schooling. He was worried about the educational aims of Americanization among American Indians and Filipinos and wanted to bring anthropological attention to educational programs for these subject peoples. He must have been corrupted by some educational background, since he proposed an administrative solution—joining the then Federal Bureaus of Education and American Ethnology.

The reassertion of ethnic identity in the United States has again made us aware of the interaction of ethnic identity with school experience. It was, in part, the interest of anthropologists in contributing to school-based ethnic studies programs that lead to the formation in 1968 of the Council on Anthropology and Education within the American Anthropological Association.

Anthropologists, however, waited more than half a century before seriously taking up Hewett's proposal to explore their joint interests with educational researchers. Interest in these studies has increased considerably after the 1954 conference of anthropologists and educators, which was organized by George and Louise Spindler at Stanford (Spindler 1955).

Let me then describe some of the contributions which anthropology can make to the study of education. In this presentation I will focus on two areas. The first are the implications for stating problems in educational research when education is defined as cultural transmission. The second will suggest alternative strategies for educational research based upon the work of some anthropologists who have conducted significant studies in education.

Implications of Defining Education as Cultural Transmission

From an anthropological point of view, education is cultural transmission. Culture itself is often defined in essentially educational terms as "the shared products of human learning." More precisely, and from a psychological orientation, culture can be seen as "standards for deciding what is, standards for deciding what can be, standards for deciding how one feels about it, standards for deciding what to do about it, and standards for deciding how to go about doing it" (Goodenough 1963:258–259). Thus culture encompasses patterns of meaning, reality, values, actions, and decision-making that are shared by and within social collectivities. A culture is not, in this view, a group of people nor even a complete system of human behavior. It is a conceptual abstraction that helps us analyze individual human behavior as that behavior is shared among groups.

To look at education as cultural transmission implies, therefore, a set of basic assumptions about our unit of interest. It is no longer the individual, but a human group which shares a common cultural system. Information comes from individuals, based upon their social perceptions and interactions. Hence, our analysis should suggest the social structures and functions of the accepted patterns for transmitting culture.

Because anthropologists are so often connected with the study of social tradition, I must add that cultural transmission includes both the transmission of tradition from one generation to the next *and* the transmission of new knowledge or cultural patterns from anybody who "knows" to anyone who does not. We can, then, distinguish between enculturation as the process of generational continuity and acculturation as the process of individual and group change, caused by contact with various cultural systems. We ought also to acknowledge the dynamics of cultural systems in transmission. Robert Redfield spoke of education as "the process of cultural transmission and renewal" (Redfield 1963:13).

Applying the concept of education as cultural transmission in our educational research, suggests that we will be equally interested in all parties involved in educational systems and transactions, as well as in the social context within which learning is presumed to take place. This will include the intentions of a teacher, his manipulation of a learner, and the changes in the learner's behavior. Furthermore, we will want to know the meanings which the participants attach to their participation in the educational act, with whom and to what extent these meanings are shared, and the degree to which idiosyncratic behavior is reflective of shared understandings. Education as cultural transmission is viewed as a social process occurring within social institutions. Anthropological studies in isolated social systems provides a useful background for understanding the mechanisms and meanings of cultural transmission, but we cannot apply the original model of culture directly to modern mass social systems.

Few contemporary social systems exist in the kind of cultural isolation which was once assumed in ethnographic studies of American Indians, Africans, and Pacific Islanders. The understanding of the interrelatedness of contemporary social systems has been reflected only recently in anthropological studies, and it is therefore important that the original concepts and methods of anthropological study are being adapted to studies of the many interrelated sociocultural systems of modern mass societies. Such systems do not command the exclusive loyalties of all participants, but share their affiliation in both competitive and complementary relationships with other sociocultural systems. For example, national, ethnic, professional, religious, generational, and even sexual identities reflect sociocultural systems to which we belong.

As Charles Valentine has suggested (1968:1), use of the culture concept itself in anthropology implies three major assumptions:

1. Culture is universal. All people have cultures and therefore share a common humanity.
2. Culture is organized. There is a coherence and structure among the patterns of human behavior and meaning.
3. Culture is the product of human creativity. It is the collective product of human experience and shared interpretations of that experience as communicated within specific groups.

But the concept of culture also involves three seeming paradoxes related to these assumptions of universality, structured organization of cultural systems, and human cultural creativity. They indicate the difficulties which some researchers have had in using the culture concept.

1. Culture is universal in human experience, yet each local or regional manifestation of it is unique.
2. Culture is stable, yet it is also dynamic and manifests continuous and constant change.
3. Culture fills and largely determines the course of our lives, yet rarely intrudes into conscious thought (Herskovits 9148:18).

Even among anthropologists, it has not always been acceptable to use culture as a basic concept for defining the discipline's territory in the analysis of human behavior. For our purposes here, I believe that this concept of culture underlies a major contribution of anthropology for research on education. The implications of a cultural concept of education for the social institutions, processes, and organizations more commonly and narrowly labeled as educational by professional researchers in education will be suggested below. Anthropologists interested in education and culture would not limit themselves to the cognitive and affective domains of childhood experience—usually in modern school settings—either with explicit educational purposes or with behavioral objectives. What is appropriately labeled "basic" research in education the anthropologists may see as the "applied" aspect of his discipline. He would for his own purposes look for patterns of cultural transmission wherever they occur—as Gladwin did recently in a study of traditional navigational skills on the small Pacific island of Puluwat (Gladwin 1970).

The following implications to be suggested for educational research are neither logically free of overlap nor obviously inclusive of all the suggestions that might be made. I offer them as suggestive of the usefulness of an anthropological approach to the conceptualization of research problems in education.

There is what might be labeled the anthropologist's "declaration of intellectual equality," which comes from the concept of culture and from the objective stance of cultural relativism associated with anthropological research (Herskovits 1948:61–78).

One of the more recent groups of anthropologists to consider the scope of anthropology included first in its list of larger intellectual contributions of the discipline "the conviction as to the essential intellectual equality of all large groups of mankind irrespective of their biological characteristics" (Smith and Fischer, 1970:17). The universalistic implication of culture means that all people participate in one or more cultural systems. Those who would speak of "cultural deprivation" among well-enculturated residents of our central city neighborhoods are not speaking the anthropologist's language and use him in their footnotes only to their own peril. Some of our urban ethnic groups can rather be seen as subjects of a narrow cultural imperialism as they participate in urban institutions such as schools, courts, and social welfare agencies, but they are by no means lacking in culture (Liebow 1967, Valentine 1968). As Smith and Fischer stated: "By documenting the enormous range of cultural behavior in societies in all parts of the world; by studying societies under culture change, both internally generated and externally fostered; and by examining the process of cultural transmission from generation to generation, anthropologists have demonstrated beyond question that the precise structure of an individual's behavior is overwhelmingly the result of learning and is preponderantly determined by the cultural patterns of his group" (1970:17).

One of the important contributions, which anthropology is making to basic research in education is the questioning of the interpretation of findings of group differences in such matters as I.Q. test results (Jensen 1969). If tests of intelligence show group differences, then "intelligence" is referring to a specific cultural pattern and the tests, which are ultimately the only operational definition of intelligence, are inherently discriminatory in their measure of group response. The recent works of Rosalie Cohen (1969), the Baratzes (1969), and Valentine (1971) suggest some of the mechanisms by which black Americans are subordinated systematically within both traditional and new "compensatory" education programs. The anthropological research question is, then, "In what way is the larger social system organized to perpetuate the social hierarchy?" It was a sociologist, Rosalie Cohen, who went back to the I.Q. test items to examine what they could reveal of the cognitive system which they rewarded *and* the cognitive system which they discriminated against.

Not only are anthropologists and their intellectual sympathizers establishing the fact of systematic, or cultural, variation between blacks and mainstream American society, they are also infecting, via acculturation, a number of psychologists in educational research. The emphases on the cultural context of learning and the cognitive implications of cultural difference have suggested new research strategies involving cross-cultural comparison (Cole et al. 1971).

Second in my list of implications for educational research is the view that what takes place in schools is only one sector of the broad educational factors to which an individual is exposed and by which his development is influenced. The limited educational effects of formal schooling must be contrasted with the educational impact of the family, the peer group, ethnic associations, the mass media, and more formalized institutions such as those associated with medicine, law, government, social welfare, business, and religion (Silberman, 1970). Anthropologists have contributed most specifically to the understanding of early enculturation—the family's influence in child rearing—but the concept of culture suggests the importance of other social institutions, too. This general view of education has been most effectively applied to the studies of isolated tribes. It is time to take an equally broad approach to the understanding of modern man in his complex web of relationships with multiple sociocultural systems.

Accordingly, schools will be studied for the narrow range of their influence in the education of the individual, and other institutions will receive equal scrutiny of their educational functions. One of the most provocative studies of educational process in Japan, for instance, has come from a young anthropologist who chose to be a participant-observer in a training program for new employees of a Japanese bank (Rohlen 1971).

While schools are most often viewed as social instruments for educational purposes, it is probably more accurate to describe them as social institutions having a life and even culture of their own (Burnett 1970). This was suggested by Willard Waller, a seemingly renegade sociologist in the 1930s. His *Sociology of Teaching* (1932) still contains the most provocative outline for a study of schools in cultural perspective. The school itself as a miniature society, and the school as an integral social element of the community, are analyzed in a manner that should have had far more imitators. A research project entitled "Culture of the Schools" has, in fact, led to the most recent published collection of anthropological studies in education (Wax et al. 1971).

Schools need to be studied as instruments of a variety of specific functions rather than as what our educational ideology would claim for them. One of the most pervasive functions of schooling in many communities is to serve as a boundary-maintaining rather than a boundary-breaking structure between social classes and ethnic groups (Y. Cohen 1970, Hollingshead 1949). Recent critics of the schools have perceptively commented on baby-sitting, elite status justification, and political control functions of modern schools. The extent to which the schools serve these and social functions other than education ought to be studied as we attempt to understand the social institutions of education.

On the basis of experiences with ritual-behavior complexes in isolated societies based on different belief systems, we might suggest that much of what passes as formal education in modern schools can be better understood as ritualized reaffirmation of cultural patterns transmitted earlier in less explicit ways. Thus, the Japanese have credited pre-World War II programs of moral education for the tenacity and dedication shown by the Japanese people in their collective endeavors, including the war against the United States. It is highly dubious to me that one classroom hour per week of highly formalized instruction could have led to the social solidarity of the Japanese people. Rather, it would seem that attention to instruction in morality was primarily a ritualistic reaffirmation of a set of values inculcated in the institutions of family, neighborhood, mass media, and other institutions of Japanese society which had earlier and more intensive interaction with each child. Waller (1932), Fuchs (1969), and Burnett (1969) have given similar interpretations to their observations of American school patterns. As Bud Khlief (1971) and Ivan Illich (1970) have suggested, schools might be viewed as the new sacred institutions of our society, supplanting the churches which have turned to more secular functions.

Schools must be seen as the arena for cross-cultural conflict and other transactions between representatives of different cultural systems. The meaning of education within schools is inevitably influenced by cultural identities and experiences which teachers, students, parents, administrators, and bus drivers bring to their interactions with each other. Perhaps the most significant research yet conducted by anthropologists in education has been that directed to understanding education in settings where minority ethnic groups confront schools directed by agencies remote from their influence and experience. The Waxes' pioneering study of schools on the Pine Ridge Reservation (1964), together with American Indian studies by King (1967), Wolcott (1967), and Wintrob and Sindell (1968), have demonstrated the devastating manner in which such schooling may systematically subvert its own formal objectives. Margaret Mead has likewise pointed to the cultural dimensions of the generation gap in our contemporary society (1970) and Spindler has examined rural-urban cultural differences influencing the educational experiences of rural German students (1970).[1]

It is in the influence of ethnic identity upon students' school experiences that anthropologists are following the lead of Hewett and his 1904 AAAS paper. Indeed, the major differences in his analysis and our contemporary one is in the nature of the anthropological discipline. The schools still face the same problems. The U.S. government, for example, is still administering

[1] *Editor's note:* This preliminary report is greatly expanded in the chapter in this volume on Schooling in Schönhausen.

programs of education for American Indians and Pacific Islanders, and Micronesians and Samoans now are substituted for Filipinos in America's colonial system.

In summary, educators and schools must become the objects of studies—educational patterns cannot be understood through the students alone. Our formal attempts at education assume that there must be a teacher, live or canned, and it is this focus on teaching that differentiates our modern practices of education from those of our more isolated or "primitive" contemporaries. The school, as a social institution of education, cannot be understood if students are viewed as its only output and education as its only function.

Anthropological Strategies for Educational Research

Aside from the conceptualization of education as cultural transmission, there are a number of attributes of anthropological research methods offering alternative strategies for educational research. Anthropological research begins with systematic objective observation of human (and now animal) behavior in its natural settings. The recording and presentation of information derived from such direct observation is called ethnography. Only after a researcher has participated in this enterprise is he trusted by the anthropological "tribe" to proceed with the systematic analysis and comparison of his own and other ethnographic data. This cross-cultural comparative analysis is labeled ethnology. Unlike other social science disciplines, a great deal of effort and respect is given to the presentation of the basic ethnographic data. The hallmark of such presentations is the objective nonevaluative descriptions of behavioral systems—even when they rouse strong value responses in the anthropologist's own society or personality. Unlike the journalist and the novelist, the anthropologist seeks to present his data first in terms that will confront the reader directly rather than mediating it through his own native value systems.

The presentation of basic data is, of course, mediated by the anthropologist in terms of several disciplinary imperatives, including those described above under the concept of culture. Here cultural behavior is seen as universal, organized, systematic, and the creative product of people. Human behavior is more generally seen as having some universally shared characteristics influenced by a common biological heritage, some characteristics shared by the human groups an individual has associated with—culture-specific behavior—and some idiosyncratic behaviors that reflect personal creativity and adaptation to one's social and physical environment. The latter constitute potential contributions to cultural change.

Patterns of social organization and communication have an important part in the anthropologist's study of culture-specific behavior. He is variously interested in behaviors demonstrating these patterns as they would appear first to a Martian, who would have no basis for understanding such behavior, second to a human observer from another cultural setting—the anthropologist himself, and third to the people who are themselves full participants in the group under observation. This emphasis on the meaning of behavior to the participants stands in specific contrast to those experimental psychologists who treat the individual subject as a black box. The anthropologist insists on working with specifically named individuals and their web of social relationships. He does not discuss "subjects" deliberately stripped of their unique individual characteristics through controlled selection procedures. His subjects become anonymous only in his reports, and even then they usually are recognizable by their friends.

Two general characteristics of anthropological research can be labeled experimental and holistic. These are to be distinguished from the more common experimental and analytic characteristics of much contemporary social science.

The aexperimental nature of anthropological research, much like astronomy and geology in the physical sciences, means that naturalistic description is the first objective. While the astronomer has little choice, the anthropologist deliberately chooses not to approach his subject experimentally. "What happens in the real world?" is the basic question of the anthropologist who does not define behavioral variables before beginning observations. Controls on the observation are designed to promote reliability and objectivity and to minimize the interference of the investigator with the behavior he is observing—there is no observer-controlled "experimental treatment." The outlines for defining observational data will look like laundry lists derived from multiple observations in many other societies (Henry 1960).

The holistic nature of anthropological research stands in contrast to what might be called the analytic perspectives of psychology and sociology (Weiss 1966). Any naturally significant human group is seen as a system of interrelated elements which constitute the underlying structure of the phenomena to be observed rather than as a tangle of related variables which can be sifted out and associated in lawlike regularities for all human situations. Variables can be defined only after observation and usually form a statement of system characteristics or taxonomy. The aim often is to contribute to a typology of systems instead of a set of general laws of behavior. Variety and diversity in human life are the basic interest of the anthropologist.

Participant observation is the anthropologist's major method of ethnographic research. Unlike many observational studies in education, there are important elements that distinguish the anthropologist's technique. It is first important that the anthropologist come as a stranger to the group he studies. He is not an expert but a naive, unsophisticated outsider. Like a child, he must first learn the language and the social graces that will enable him to maintain communication with the individuals he is observing.

There is, of course, a dynamic tension between the participant and observer roles because the objectivity of the observer is as necessary for understanding a cultural system as is the experience of learning to share the unexamined and implicit assumptions upon which every cultural system is based. The following are features which distinguish the anthropologist's participant observation from other observational studies (Bruyn 1963):

1. The researcher is a stranger within the system which he is studying.
2. The researcher must learn the language of the system he is investigating.
3. The minimum time required for basic ethnographic description and analysis of a system is about one year.
4. The participant-observer must develop a social role within the system that allows him to become a natural part of the environment consistent with his research design.

Applying these research perspectives to what I like to call educational ethnography, a number of researchers are making significant contributions to our understanding of educational systems and processes. In anthropological style, I will finish this report by developing a short typology of their research efforts.

The study of individual actors in formal school settings is the first type. Case studies of individuals are used to understand the roles and actions of people in formally defined social positions. Carrying the disciplinary imperatives to their logical extreme, Wolcott, for instance, spent two years in the study of educational administration by following a willing, and obviously a typical, school principal in all of his professional and many of his private activities (Wolcott 1968). He began and finished his study as the naive participant-observer—in fact, his last request to teachers in the school of his administrator subject was to ask them to tell him what they thought he still did not know about their school. One teacher neatly summed up the inevitable limitations of participant observation when she replied that there were no Kotex dispensers in the faculty women's rest room.

Wolcott's ethnography of the school principal is now published (Wolcott 1973) and provides us with a better understanding of the expectations and behaviors which compose the job of a school administrator and of the complex social institution of the school in American society.

Another type of study is that of social systems at the classroom level focusing on the social transactions that occur within the school. Smith has described this as the "microethnography of the classroom" (Smith and Geoffrey 1968). Coming from a background of psychological research in education, he spent a year in an urban classroom taught by one of his graduate students. Together they split the participant-observer's role so that Smith could concentrate on the observation while his student was the participant-teacher.

Next are a number of studies where the ethnographer has taken a classroom teaching job and reported from this perspective upon the classroom, school, and community as an educational system. King (1968), for instance, using both classroom and community observations, reported on a Canadian Indian boarding school. Though originally entering the school as a way of supporting his studies in anthropology, Rosenfeld (1971) later used his experience to report on the social systems of a Harlem school. In both cases, the ethnographers were outsiders to their students and they paid special attention to the meaning of the school experience for their students.

In some cases observers outside the usual school roles have reported on school and community relationships in particular settings. The Waxes (1964) carried more obvious identification as researchers in their study of Pine Ridge Indian Reservation schools. In my study of a Japanese middle school (Singleton 1967) the participant-observer role in a school was acceptably defined as researcher, since all Japanese teachers were expected to develop their own research projects as part of their professional responsibility. In both Japan and Pine Ridge, it was necessary to develop close rapport between school personnel and the community—an easier task in Japan where school and community interests were more closely allied.

A few anthropologists have studied wider school systems, somewhat in the perspective of Willard Waller. Yehudi Cohen (1970) has been interested in delineating the role of schools in what he chooses to call "civilizational states." This requires a kind of national analysis that looks at structure and function of school institutions more broadly.

Studies of educational problems that relate specifically to anthropological interests in language, cultural and ethnic identity, or social stratification have been made. In this case, the educators' definition of a problem has been similar or complementary to basic anthropological interests. Language learning and the teaching of reading and writing have attracted the interests of anthropological linguists. Studies of foreign student experience in the United States, such as that reported by Bennett, Passin, and McKnight (1958) for Japanese students and those dealing with contemporary ethnic identity and schooling for American minority groups (Valentine 1971), have taken up the anthropologists' concern for the meaning of ethnic identity in contemporary national school systems.

Finally, what is called by Cole et al. (1971) "experimental anthropology," involves a real interest by and encouragement of psychologists to work jointly in the cross-cultural comparative experimentation. These joint efforts would make the psychologists' findings more relevant to the anthropologists' interests—and, hopefully, more universal.

References

Baratz, Joan C., and Stephen Baratz, 1970, "Early Childhood Intervention: The Social Science Base of Institutional Racism," *Harvard Educational Review* 40:29–50.

Bennett, John, Herbet Passin, and Robert McKnight, 1958, *In Search of Identity*. Minneapolis: University of Minnesota Press.

Bruyn, Severya, 1963, "The Methodology of Participant Observation," *Human Organization.*

Burnett, Jacquetta H., 1969, "Ceremony, Rites, and Economy in the Student System of an American High School," *Human Organization* 28:1–10.

———, 1970, "Culture of the School: A Construct for Research and Explanation in Education," *CAE Newsletter* (May), pp. 4–13.

Cohen, Rosalie, 1969, "Conceptual Styles, Culture Conflict, and Non-verbal Tests of Intelligence," *American Anthropologist* 71:828–856.

Cohen, Yehudi, 1970, "Schools and Civilizational States." In Joseph Fischer, ed., *The Social Sciences and the Comparative Study of Educational Systems.* Scranton, Pa.: International Textbook Company.

Cole, Michael, et al., 1971, *The Cultural Context of Learning and Thinking.* New York: Basic Books, Inc.

Fuchs, Estelle, 1969, *Teachers Talk.* New York: Doubleday & Company.

Gladwin, Thomas, 1970, *East is a Big Bird.* Cambridge: Harvard University Press.

Goodenough, Ward, 1963, *Cooperation in Change.* New York: Russell Sage Foundation.

Henry, Jules, 1960, "Cross-Cultural Outline for the Study of Education," *Current Anthropology* 1:267–305.

Herskovits, Melville J., 1948, *Man and His Works.* New York: Alfred A. Knopf.

Hewett, Edgar L., 1904, "Anthropology and Education," *American Anthropologist* 6:574–575.

———, 1905, "Ethnic Factors in Education," *American Anthropologist* 7:1–16.

Hollingshead, August B., 1949, *Elmtown's Youth.* New York: Science Editions.

Illich, Ivan, 1970, *Deschooling Society.* New York: Harper & Row.

Jensen, Arthur R., 1969, "How Much Can We Boost IQ and Scholastic Achievement?" *Harvard Educational Review,* vol. 39 (Winter).

Khlief, Bud B., 1971, "The School as a Small Society." In Murry L. Wax, Stanley Diamond, and Fred Gearing, eds., *Anthropological Perspectives on Education.* New York: Basic Books, Inc.

King, A. Richard, 1968, *The School at Mopass,* CSEC. New York: Holt, Rinehart and Winston, Inc.

Liebow, Elliot, 1967, *Tally's Corner.* Boston: Little, Brown & Company.

Mead, Margaret, 1970, *Culture and Commitment.* New York: Natural History Press/ Doubleday & Company.

Redfield, Margaret P., ed., 1963, *The Social Uses of Social Science: The Papers of Robert Redfield,* vol. 2. Chicago: University of Chicago Press.

Rohlen, Thomas C., 1971, "*Seishin Kyoikū* in a Japanese Bank," *CAE Newsletter* (February), pp. 3–8.

Rosenfeld, Gerry, 1971, *"Shut Those Thick Lips."* CSEC. New York: Holt, Rinehart and Winston, Inc.

Silberman, Charles, 1970, *Crisis in the Classroom.* New York: Random House.

Singleton, John, 1967, *Nichu: A Japanese School.* CSEC. New York: Holt, Rinehart and Winston, Inc.

Smith, Allan H., and John L. Fischer, eds., 1970, *Anthropology.* Englewood Cliffs, N.J.: Prentice-Hall, Inc.

Smith, Louis, and William Geoffrey, 1968, *The Complexities of an Urban Classroom.* New York: Holt, Rinehart and Winston, Inc.

Spindler, George, ed., 1955, *Education and Anthropology.* Stanford, Calif.: Stanford University Press.

Spindler, George, 1970, "Studying Schooling in Schönhausen," *CAE Newsletter* (October), pp. 3–10.

Valentine, Charles A., 1968, *Culture and Poverty.* Chicago: University of Chicago Press.

———, 1971, "Deficit, Difference, and Bi-Cultural Models of Afro-American Behavior," *Harvard Education Review* 41:136–157.

Waller, Willard W., 1932, *The Sociology of Teaching.* New York: John Wiley & Sons, Inc.

Wax, Murray L., 1971, Stanley Diamond, and Fred Gearing, eds., *Anthropological Perspectives on Education.* New York: Basic Books, Inc.

Wax, Murray, and Rosalie Wax, 1964, *Formal Education in an American Indian Community,* Supplement to *Social Problems* (Spring), Vol. 11, no. 4.

Weiss, Robert, 1966, "Alternative Approaches in the Study of Complex Situations," *Human Organization* 25:198–206.

Wintrob, Ronald M., and Peter S. Sindell, 1968, *Education and Identity Conflict Among Cree Indian Youth,* Annex 3 of the Final Report, McGill Cree Project. Ottawa: Rural Development Branch, Department of Regional Economic Expansion.

Wolcott, Harry, 1967, "An Ethnographic Approach to the Study of School Administration." Paper presented at the American Anthropological Association Meeting, 1968.

———, 1967, *A Kwakiutl Village and School.* CSEC. New York: Holt, Rinehart and Winston, Inc.

———, 1973, *The Man in the Principal's Office.* CSEC. New York: Holt, Rinehart and Winston, Inc.

BERNARD J. SIEGEL/*Stanford University*

3 *Conceptual Approaches to Models for the Analysis of the Educative Process in American Communities**

In this chapter I propose to raise certain questions about cultural transmission in the American school and community within appropriate frames of reference. The primary objective will be to analyze the forces that shape the career of things explicitly thought to be taught, between their entry into teacher-training institutions and their exposure to children in the classroom. From kindergarten through secondary grades certain curricula are offered in any given year in accordance with a set of ideas about what a young person at that stage of formal education ought to know. Somewhere along the line, some participants in the educative process concern themselves with the question *why* the young must have this information. Others are concerned with how best to present these subjects so as to elicit interest, discover domains of talent, devise alternate curricula for different kinds of learners, and so forth.

Ideally, this is a continual process, ever renewing in the light of public and professional beliefs, knowledge, prejudices, and priorities (reflected in, e.g., budgets for education). Only a few in the adult American community attack the value of compulsory formal education through a substantial part of the adolescent years. Education for what and in relation to whom comes under periodic scrutiny, and at times of social crisis different constituencies may propose, advocate, and demand quite different solutions to these important questions.

Obviously, this is a complex array of problems involving many variables. It is not surprising, therefore, that research and analysis attending to many facets of these concerns—by social scientists as well as by professional educators—bulk large. As part of our strategy for understanding the educational process as it takes place in the school and to put in order some of the many propositions that have been made or that one might investigate, I have found

---

* Reprinted with substantial revisions from *Education and Anthropology,* George D. Spindler, ed., with the permission of the publishers, Stanford University Press; copyright 1955 by the Board of Trustees of the Leland Stanford Jr. University.

it useful to construct a few models. Social scientists with different persuasions might suggest others more congenial to their theoretical orientations.

The notion of a model has the advantage, perhaps, of denoting structural properties of the phenomenon under consideration. The model should specify the elements of which it is composed and the relations that are thought to obtain among them. A theoretical model of this kind tends to create a familiar image that accounts for known or hypothetical situations and also for novel or unfamiliar ones that have similar properties. In this context it suggests a convenient way, or ways, of thinking about the kinds of effects that the educational system has upon the training of the young.

The following remarks are largely exploratory. They are not the results of specific researches carried on by the writer, nor do they constitute a critical appraisal of researches by others. Rather, they reflect the reactions of one social anthropologist to the challenging subject matter of this book.

Some Assumptions and Concepts

For purposes of argument I shall have to make explicit certain assumptions about the nature of the educational community and clarify whatever concepts may be used in the process. To begin with, by the "educational community" I refer to the "formal" school system—sites and interacting members, stated goals, and the role relations in terms of which the goals are translated into action. These, at least, are the primary elements of the system. It is recognized that in the dynamics of activating this system intrusive or intervening factors modify the intent of the formal blueprint in several respects. Principals and teachers may perceive and use their roles in different ways, in relation partly to personality factors and partly to situational conditions. Concerning the latter, the organization might have grown in size, so that patterns of communication, once successful, now break down at several points. Similarly, varying rates in the turnover in personnel can affect the degree of sharing of common goals and values of the institution. Compensatory adjustments for these and other disturbances within the educational community give rise to forms of communication and sets of relations that distort the formal system. These forces are obviously important, but I believe that their full significance can best be understood by a prior analysis of the organizational design originally intended for the school. It is also suggested that the formal system will yield useful insights into the processes of transmission and the alteration of cultural items once they are introduced into the school.

Articulating with the focal educational community are at least two additional and important segments of that community: the centers of higher learning and class and ethnic family units from which the students are drawn. A third segment, the membership of which is recruited from the above categories, is the school board. Presumably board decisions reflect prevailing community attitudes and sentiments, inasmuch as the positions are elective ones. But since the board has direct face-to-face relationships with school executives and operates more in a leadership capacity, it can be considered as an independent force.

The school, looked at from our point of view, is no isolated organization; its operational structure is continually affected by outside environmental forces. It does not set its own goals, nor can it seek to implement them completely independently of other community agencies. The relationship between the educational community and the community as a whole, however, is reciprocal and interacting. The former is not to be visualized as responding unilaterally and automatically to outside forces which impinge upon it. It obviously must make most of its day-by-day decisions and operate "as if it were" an independent organization. Moreover, its explicit goals (to educate the young for certain purposes and in certain ways) are better and more fully understood by the interacting participants than by outside members of the community as a whole. The educational community has its own culture—albeit a dependent and not an autonomous one—including norms for behavior of participants and values underlying and supporting these norms. What happens in the operation of the school system may also be expected to work back to affect the values, sentiments, and operations of the tangential segments with which it interacts, i.e., families and teacher-training centers.

As an organization that is also a local group, the school has a physical design and a geography. It has boundaries within which members must learn symbolic meanings relating to time and space. Individuals either have or do not have the option of entering and using certain places at given times (teachers' lounges, classrooms, assemblies, libraries, and so forth). They can come and go as they please, or they must move from one place to another in prescribed and specified ways.

The allocations of space and time—what we might designate the "settlement pattern" of the school—reflect beliefs and values and embrace a wide range of phenomena. They should describe how people are distributed, when they congregate and when they separate, in what numbers and densities, how controlled or how open communication is in these different settings, what kinds of discourse are permitted or demanded on different occasions and places, and the like (Goffman, 1962).[1] In a very imaginative analysis Friedenberg (1965:Chaps. 2 and 6) compares the young in the schools to colonies of peoples subordinated to a fundamentally authoritarian pattern of control, distrust, and punishment. He points out how so much of the colonial energies and activities deliberately conspire to the negation of such values as privacy, dignity, and creative nonconformism and to the reinforcement of those fac-

[1] For an interesting and relevant psychological analysis of the ecological basis of behavior see Festinger, Schachter, and Back 1950.

tors that inhibit any but the most ritualized communication among students from different class backgrounds. This it accomplishes in large measure, he asserts, by the almost complete usurpation of time and by very rigid teacher-administrator definitions of appropriate uses of space. The classroom, for example, should not be devoted only to the teaching of, for example, history but also to the special management of discussion, in the name of egalitarianism.

The settlement pattern pertains to the school in relation to the larger community as well as to its own ecology. Cases in point are the distances from user families and neighborhoods, conveyance, facilitation of or impedance to interaction between school and home, and the customary ways of scheduling and managing such interaction.

Like any other organization, the educational community exhibits certain regularities in the behavior of its members in carrying on the functions of the group. By charting these regularities we can construct a "structure of alignments," which will also indicate the varying "characteristics" of the different roles within the structure. Individuals who perform certain roles, for example, are in a position formally to make decisions and to display authority that affects some or all individuals who play other roles. Conversely, the roles of some will have built into them few or no rights of leadership and decision-making affecting others. The personnel are thus formally organized on a hierarchical (administrator-teacher) and a coordinate (teacher-grade) basis.

The school system, conceived as an educational community, has many structural and cultural features in common with other professional communities, for example, the hospital as a therapeutic community (Jones et al. 1953; Rapaport 1960). It differs from the hospital in the relatively low rank accorded to education as an end-value (in the sense of exciting the young about expanding the frontiers of knowledge). To a considerable extent education as a value is considered and treated as instrumental to the pursuit of other values (power, wealth, social position). Hence there is much possible ambiguity in the interpretation of its goals and methods within the greater locality. It has different kinds of attractions, interpretations, or repulsions for different segments of the community at large, as well as within the various levels of the educational community itself.

If one accepts these assumed formal characteristics of the school system and its tangential relationships as a point of departure, there are then several possible ways of collecting, organizing, and interpreting data about its operation. We are, of course, particularly interested in how its functioning affects what is taught (the messages that flow through it) and how what is taught is communicated and assimilated. My guiding hypothesis is that the flow of what is taught is screened, interpreted, and reinterpreted at several levels as a consequence of the carrying networks of role relationships.

In the remainder of this chapter I shall discuss three relevant models that are geared to phenomena of cultural transmission. One is the familiar process of acculturation. A second is the so-called channels theory proposed by Kurt Lewin (1951) in a study of food habits. And a third is based upon information theory that, in turn, is part of general systems theory. In several respects the last will be seen to cut across the first two approaches, but it addresses itself in special ways to questions raised about the effectiveness of educational processes in schools. I have tried to reduce as much as possible the special language in terms of which information theory is generally discussed. (It has been incorporated into a good deal of vulgar social science jargon, and there are few pretenders who do not bandy about words like "feedback," "inputs," "outputs," "networks"—even, heaven help us, "mutual causal deviation counteracting or amplifying relationships".) Its elaborate conceptual apparatus, and the fact that most of the mathematics required to adapt the theory to problems of the social scientist have yet to be developed, makes the task of adapting a difficult one. I have introduced it in the hope that some readers might want to pursue this mode of analysis for the educational system along lines suggested elsewhere (Easton 1965).

The Acculturation Model

Acculturation commonly refers to the process of culture change initiated by the continual interaction of individuals from two or more discrete groups and their cultures. It is also used in the sense of levels—more or less acculturated persons and groups, or groups that have made a special kind of adaptation in this process. The phenomenon in any event involves both process and product (Spindler 1955; Tremblay 1962; Siegel 1969). Initially it was derived from the observation of colonial situations—the relations between controlling and subject groups—and later assumed far broader applicability. The comparison with the school in which education is compulsory and the students captive members is an apt one.

The educational community is not autonomous, for it depends upon other collectivities for the recruitment of its personnel and, in part, for the carrying on of its policies. On the other hand, its teachers and administrative officers largely originate in distant localities, and its day-to-day operations are so extensively independent that we may be justified in speaking of it as quasi-autonomous.[2] It is in this sense that industrial concerns, hospitals, and similar social units have been treated as societies for the purposes of sociocultural analysis. We can therefore think of the school system as an organization

[2] In the same way, social theorists who think in terms of systems (social system, political system, and so on) do not worry about how discreet the unit of analysis is or how much relationship among the parts defines a system (Easton 1965:Chap. 2).

standing in apposition to other collectivities to which it must adapt, and which in turn it seeks to influence. Figure 3.1 summarizes these multiple relationships. It represents both the conscious structure of relationships and other

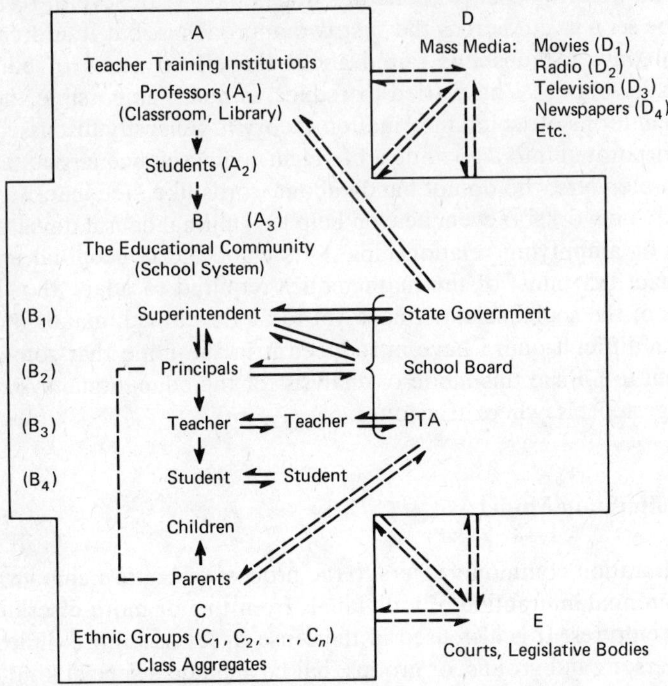

Figure 3.1. Acculturative factors affecting the transmission of cultural materials in the school system. A–E: major collectivities in interaction; → : main direction of influence and cultural dissemination; -→: intercultural relationships.

nonconscious structures generated by the way in which the former works—cliques, patterns, and norms of behavior developed by students and teachers in their attempts to cope with tensions fostered by the school environment. The nonconscious alignments and associated values perform important functions for shared needs of individuals arising from the deficiencies (from the clients' point of view) of the formal organization. As a matter of strategy, we might learn more about these needs and how urgently they are felt by prior consideration of formally available channels of cultural transmission.

Each of the collectivities and alignments, or smaller interactive units within them, represented by capital letters and their subscripts (A, A_1; B, B_1; and so on) may be conceived as exhibiting separate subcultures. The school as a whole is an organization that generates one culture, teacher-student relations another, teacher-teacher relations, a third, and so forth. We are primarily concerned with the way in which *what is meant to be imparted* to the student—the educational products[3]—actually reaches him from its point of origin. The educational products will be limited in our discussion to the formal contents (textbooks, classroom presentations and materials, teachers' manuals, reading assignments, and so on), prepared in part by teachers—for the most part by teachers of teachers.

Presumably a philosophy of education is implicit in these products, for example, in the selection of textbooks, in attempts at censoring reading materials, and in preparing curricula. The school edits and constrains what will be made available to the learner, and it must also respond to numerous and often conflicting demands placed upon it by varied public constituencies (Tyler 1960), a fact that many criticisms leveled against the public school fail to take into account.

It is also understood that many attitudes and biases—on sex and morality, punctiliousness, and cleanliness—are consciously or unconsciously betrayed in the classroom and that their impact is important to assess in relation to what orientations the young bring from other environments. In order to establish some control over the content of what is intended to be learned, I have arbitrarily restricted the problem to the transmission of formal materials, or explicit culture.

The way in which content is transmitted from level A to level B, is conditioned theoretically by several factors, such as (1) the degree of consistency of the values in each of the subcultures, (2) the extent of agreement of the members of the collectivities on these values, (3) the kinds of operational relations established between participants in the several subcultures (these have also been referred to as "intercultural role relations") (S.S.R.C. Seminar 1954), and (4) the perception of one's own roles and of content intended for transmission. Although no formal content originates in C, the latter is obviously significant as a third force in affecting what reaches the end products (children) and how it is perceived by them. The picture is structurally not unlike political third-force movements, in which one national unit stands between two other cultural units and must react continuously to the pushes and pulls exerted upon it from both directions.

Teaching members of the academic community tend to share a distinctive set of values which set them apart from other segments of the population.

[3] The term "educational products" is not meant to imply unchanging objects or contents that ultimately pass to the child intact. As will become abundantly clear from the text, these products may change their form and meaning for participants in each of the cultures involved; they may also have different adjustive functions for individuals at different levels and hence be *used* by them in different ways for varying ends. What is accented in A may be slighted in B and in C, or vice versa. They may be identified as specific objects, utterances, and the like, but for the above reasons they become different things to various categories of individuals who have anything to do with them. Thus a pupil may learn to engage in other activities he finds more rewarding, however counterproductive they may be from the teacher's point of view.

They look upon education not only as providing tools for the pursuance of other values but also as contributing to long-range satisfactions for the individual, or as an end in itself. They are concerned also with innovating both upon the content of what is transmitted and upon the ways in which this can be done. The process is a continuous one, in that the implications of traditional practice and of innovations are constantly subject to assessment and reevaluation. Hence the understanding which teachers of teachers will have, let us say, of Dewey's pragmatism in relation to education, is based upon a broad intellectual grasp and upon viewing its operation in a wide variety of contexts. The same might be said of their grasp of learning theories, of cultural processes, of child growth phases, and so on. If we can assume a rather extensive agreement upon ideology and objectives, at least among the professional educators of any given institution, we should still need to assess the degree of agreement between any two such training institutions. Failing that, we must confine our investigation to the members and teacher products of specific training centers.

In different geographical regions potential grade school personnel probably come from relatively homogeneous sociocultural backgrounds, although this presumption requires verification (Warner 1944).[4] If this is the case, we might hypothesize (1) a rather high degree of consistency in their understandings of values built into the school system, and (2) broad similarities in the way they perceive their own roles and in the way they internalize their training experience. Should their own backgrounds prove to vary more, as they do in the population as a whole, we should expect the contrary to be the case.

In their role as students in the academic setting, school personnel (actual or potential) are brought into contact with only a part of the cultural reservoir of A, and for a limited period of time (or intermittently for limited periods of time—summer courses and workshops). For this reason, and because they enter with a different set of attitudes and orientation to these ideas, they are apt to evaluate them from a limited (from the point of view of A) perspective. This is the nature of intercultural relations, namely, that they involve the operation of processes of perceptual selectivity.

As a consequence of this selectivity—the adjustment of new learning to previously assimilated patterns of thinking, doing, and believing—we can expect alterations in the educational product by the time they reach the educational community (B). At the latter point, moreover, a similar process occurs whereby students, the ultimate objects of our inquiry, make further choices about what they learn, for what purposes, and with what commitments.

It is common knowledge that grade-school children come from as wide a variety of family backgrounds as there are ethnic and class cultures, although

---

[4] This is so despite large differences in the qualities and excellence of individual teachers.

this fact is often slighted in discussions about problems of mass education. One well-known study, at least, has indicated certain implications of primary and secondary school education in America for reinforcing the tendency to freeze the inferior occupational roles of ethnic and racial groups. Thus several technical high schools in California steered members of different minority groups—for example, blacks and chicanos—into specific curricula and occupational-training classes which lead to lower-class levels of opportunity. Despite widespread opposition from parents, the vice-principal of one large school virtually segregated Mexican-American girls into domestic science courses which emphasize training in cooking, serving, and housework (Warner 1944; see also Ginsberg 1960, Vol. 3).

A more recent book describes in some depth a teacher-training experiment in southern California that paired cultural anthropology and education (Landes 1965). Among its several virtues, this study provides us with a wealth of interview material that portrays the profound barriers to intercultural communication that continue to exist between teacher, administrator, and student in multiethnic schools. As one dean exclaimed, with sudden insight: "We also have cultures, just like the minorities!" Slight as this distance may seem, he had really traveled far.

In this case there were obvious conflicts of self-conception of others between B and C. The actions of B members cannot be construed as direct applications of marginal participation in A, but rather as special interpretations of what they perceived and selected from it. One might equally wish to know something of the home stresses and motivations which prompt students to elect attending technical high schools in preference to general schools. Several other differences in value orientation and ratings between school and family cultures undoubtedly influence what content is presented in what ways, on the one hand, and how it becomes an object of interest by students, on the other. Among them are conceptions of time—of organizing and economizing time—and of "progressive" self-cultivation, of ranking talents, and so forth.

Informal peer groups and relatively unstructured relations with age mates among students (B_4) introduce yet another force—other patterns of values, interests, beliefs, and attitudes affecting the perceptual screening and selective learning of the child. Since children through high school find no entree to other productive social activities and are forcibly confined to the school, we should not be surprised to find that, among the several possible functions that peer relations perform elsewhere, here they assume certain characteristics because of the consuming amount of time that the young spend in each other's company. They are a collective response to demands and constraints thrust upon them, regardless of differences in preparation, background, and expectations about the future. To a large extent they are evidence, therefore, of certain lacks, unsatisfied desires, or frustrations within both home and school.

Like the defensive norms of behavior that work groups develop in factories (Sayles 1958), students—except for the scholastically oriented subgroups in large schools—appear rather universally to develop work-restricting norms aimed at "holding down effort to a level that can be maintained by all" (Coleman 1965:76). Coleman also suggests that one of the principal causes for the high status of athletics in secondary schools is that athletic contests provide about the only *collective* goals that students share. This was as true in middle-class schools with a high proportion of graduates going to college as it was in working-class schools (Coleman 1961:chap. 2). Otherwise, the particular emphasis placed upon interpersonal competition for grades in the classroom involves for the many a sustained high level of tension. Were educational standards more centrally governed with a minimum of local control, as they have been in Europe and Japan, we have reason to believe that the different institutional demands and rewards would lead to different group response (Coleman 1965:78, note 4).

In any event, it would be desirable to investigate the areas wherein barriers are erected against acceptance of content transmitted within the school, and the effectiveness of leadership within these associations as well as upon the behavior of nonparticipant children.

The cultural (value-interest) forces at work in the contact relations of B and C are several. First, parents and teachers have separate and direct influence upon the children. Second, parent-teacher relations are both formal (P.T.A.) and personal. The intended function of these meetings is to explicate the congruence and conflict of values between the home and school as they are evidenced in the child's patterns of adjustment, such as living up to ideals of conformity in the classroom. How these relations and interpretations are further communicated to the child—and with what effect on his learning tendencies—is an interesting subject for further investigation. Do the mother and teacher, for example, make the same criticisms and appreciate the same strengths in the child, so that their subsequent interaction with him leads to formation of different attitudes and learning readiness? Or are there conflicting reactions and judgments such that the child is reinforced in basic behavioral tendencies in the home, although these tendencies may already be prejudicial to assimilating educational content in the ways intended by the school?

The agreement or clash of explicit purposes between the school personnel and other public agencies, for example, the school board, is similarly important to assess, as are consequences of classroom experiences, such as reinforcement of generational conflict between children and parents. It becomes abundantly clear that an answer to the question, "How well does the school accomplish its objectives?" depends not only upon how well teachers and administrators know these objectives and techniques for achieving them; it depends also upon the dynamic interplay of value systems, interests, and diverse self-concepts in contact among the several collectivities involved in the formal transmission process (Conant 1959; Tyler 1960).

Members of the educational community are also targets of other forms of communication, of which we shall consider in particular the mass media. Ours is, among other things, a mass culture served and in no small measure shaped by mass media (Daedalus 1960), and it behooves us to know just what this means for the redefinition of educational goals and their implementation in the school. As Brodbeck (1955) has stated, "the really formidable questions about the mass media, and indeed about any socializing agency, begin when one attempts to discover and state the exact conditions under which the message succeeds or fails to take hold, quite independently of its usefulness."

In themselves, mass media are things and not organizations. However, they originate in organizations (broadcasting stations, production studios, publishing houses) that edit extensively, and, by making available additional images of reality, exert still other lines of influence upon the young, teachers, and administrators alike (Charters 1933; Klapper 1960; Schramm, Lyle, and Parker 1961). The information so communicated complicates our understanding and prediction of what happens during the course of transmission in the classroom, as do communications from any other source. However, if we were able to predict the effects of prior information upon subsequent choices of behavior by students, for example, we should then more fully and reliably be able to predict his response to things formally taught.[5] Exposure to any subject matter or to a belief outside the school provides part of the context within which new teaching and learning steps take place. If contemplative reading is encouraged in the home through exposure to magazines, books, and specially selected TV and radio programs, we should expect a higher level of interest in the mastery of these domains.

It is very difficult to assess the impact of continual instant communication through mass media upon the disciplined process of education stressed in classroom learning. Its importance cannot be overemphasized, however, since it pertains to much of the concern for relevance that the young so increasingly insist upon and many of the teachers respond to.

Neverthless the severe editing and summarizing of events through these channels create reactive dispositions, not only to the learning situation but also to reformation of the curriculm—to what is thought to be appropriate

---

[5] Compare this assertion with the following statement of an educator concerned with curriculum: "A curriculum is a sequence of content units arranged in such a way that the learning of each unit may be accomplished as a single act, *provided the capabilities described by specified prior units (in the sequence) have already been mastered by the learner* (Gagné 1967:23. Italics the author's). In fact, we must assume that prior capabilities are very broadly conditioned by forces at work outside the classroom. The element of uncertainty thus introduced, I submit, will more readily yield to resolution and understanding if one explicitly takes it into account than if the curriculum is considered in a more narrow context.

to learn about—and even its mode of presentation (advocacy of and constraints upon innovative teaching methods in the public schools). From the point of view of the educator and the educational policy-maker, random and uncontrolled amounts of information received outside the school renders very difficult predicting the outcomes of enculturation within it (Tyler 1960: 89).

The Channels Model

In 1942 Kurt Lewin directed a project designed to study food habits of a Midwestern town (Lewin 1951). The general question which he asked was, "How does food get on the table and why?" The answer to this question was conceived in terms of broad and narrow social channels through which food items passed from the points of origin to the table at which they were consumed. The characteristics of the channels and kinds of linkage from one to another were conceptually refined in the process of analysis to account for the adventures of food products, particularly at critical points along the traveled routes. For this purpose, culture was treated as a repetitive process rather than the product of some past history and was conceptualized as being in a state of dynamic equilibrium. "A culture," states Lewin, " . . . is not a static affair but a live process, like a river which moves but still keeps a recognizable form" (Lewin 1951:172–173).

It is unnecessary to concern ourselves with the details of this specific study, but the frame of reference utilized may have some possible utility for a consideration of cultural transmission in American school systems. As we shall see, the channels model is related to that of acculturation, and simply constitutes a slightly different—and to some, perhaps a more congenial—way of organizing and looking at the same phenomena. Instead of asking how food gets on the table, however, let us substitute the phrase, "How do educational products get into the child and why?" The student becomes the focal point of inquiry, and we then attempt to trace the channels through which understandings are molded and pushed in his direction, as he proceeds on his way to becoming a formally finished product. We are, in effect, dealing with the *learning habits and attitude-value formation* of the child, for they represent sets of behavioral tendencies that are created by a variety of converging forces (see Fig. 3.2). Had space permitted, we might have added other channels representing the total range of ecological forces related to the educational system, as for the acculturation chart.

The incorporation of new learning by a child is in large measure a product of past habit, what reaches him, the role relations (contexts) in which the flow of materials occurs, and the values and ways of perceiving that underlie these relations. The effectiveness of one or another channel for the child will depend partly on cultural values. Thus, in families where a high value is placed upon formal learning, greater application and better performance may be expected than in those where education as a value ranks low. In other words, children from families of the former type will make greater use of channel 1 than will children from those of the latter type. They may take maximum advantage of what is formally presented in the classroom and may even seek to go beyond it. From the anthropological point of view we might say that the meaning and functions of learning in channels 1 and 2 are very similar, hence mutually reinforcing.

Many things can happen to the content of what is transmitted in any channel as it passes from one section to another on its way to the child. The "gates" are opened by one or more "gatekeepers." In the academic community the form and meaning of transmitted material enter channel 1 through the teachers of teachers. They control what enters but not completely what happens to the materials, since student trainees may be expected to interpret cultural items in terms of the values they bring into the learning situation. For example, if the ideology of educational training centers emphasizes the values of individual differences in rates of learning, the trainee, on the other hand, may value the disciplinary aspects of the process; or else he may look upon the ideology in special truncated ways. Merely "putting the products" in the classroom or in the library will not guarantee that the trainee will retain either their meaning or their intended functions in this section of the channel.

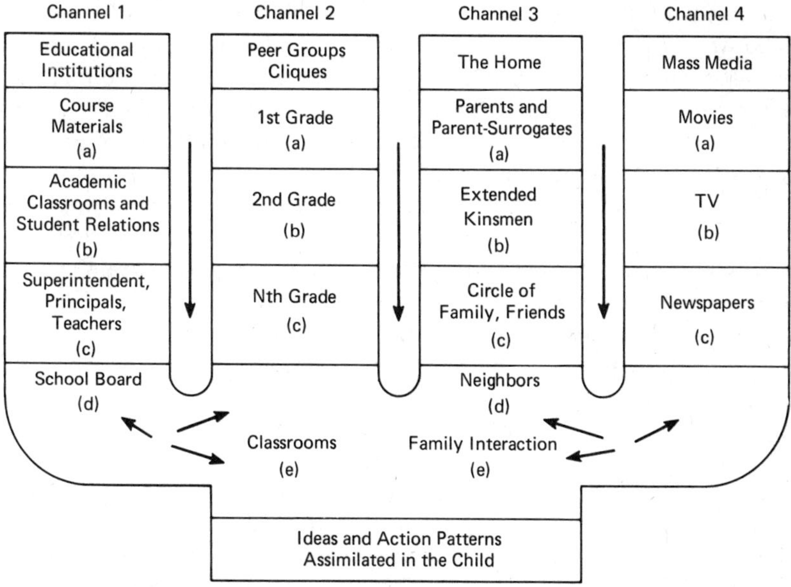

Figure 3.2. Channels through which explicit culture reaches the child. Solid lines within each channel mark off sections through which cultural content must pass. Arrows indicate the directions of stimuli and sociocultural forces. Small letters indicate sections within the channel.

The teachers and administrators are the principal gatekeepers of what enters into section B—the school system itself. The "keys" which they use to open the gates are their professional skills and motivations, consisting in part of the *needs fulfilled* by their professional roles (commitment to education as a job situation) and in part by the values which they bring from other collectivities.

Meanwhile, similar processes are at work in channels 2, 3, 4, and so forth. The peer-group channel is perhaps the most constant and consistent in the kinds of attitudes and action patterns that it instills. Participation itself in such relationships, as I have suggested earlier, is a response to tensions, needs, or frustrations felt within the school system. Leaders are the gatekeepers (the "leading set," originators and directors of clubs) and control entry of values and understandings that attract other members. The effectiveness of a teacher with respect to student learning in the teacher's terms will vary with the meaning that peer-group activity has for the child. The fact that the latter for the most part is counterproductive from this point of view is simply an artifact of school structures. They are not intrinsic to age-grades in themselves. Should we vary the content of any of the channels—change the motivations of teachers, amplify family perspectives about viable alternatives for their children, make the schools less like prisons for the young, provide more reasons for living in the larger environment—then we should expect peer activities to assume different characteristics in the educational process.

In channel 3 there is similarly relatively high consistency of understandings between the sections through which cultural objects and patterns flow toward the child. Except for purposes of expediency it would be more accurate also to depict the sections as coordinate rather than linear, since the hierarchy of values, system of beliefs, and behavior patterns of parents or parent surrogates are usually reinforced by kinsmen, family, friends, and other models insofar as the latter have meaningful relations with the children. It is unnecessary for our purposes to review known processes of personality development, socialization, and learning which take place within the home and other reference groups outside the school. An awareness of how they dispose the child to respond to stimuli at the point of contact with the educational community is obviously critical, however, as the problem is viewed in this paper.

In the schools themselves the several social channels converge, thus creating a broad stream of *interacting* (not verging) forces. Congruence or conflict of values now can be studied in the interaction of community representatives (board members, school administrators, teachers, and parents). To continue with our analogy, there are several gatekeepers who control the widened and deepened channel; the flow of *educational* products must compete with that of others. Explicit culture transmitted in the schools has a different weighting from understandings and orientations acquired outside them. At the final gate of this process, therefore, students will further select what they perceive as needed, desirable, anxiety-reducing, and rewarding in other ways. For example, the classroom situation need not exhibit basic agreement with family patterns in order for maximum transmission to occur. It may accomplish the same end for some children because it is an outlet for rebellion against home constrictions and pressures. It would be desirable to ascertain in which kinds of family cultures the one case prevails and in which kinds the other, if indeed any regularity exists in the matter.

In brief, forms of understanding, their content, and order of presentation are blocked, truncated, or expanded according to changing interpretations at each gate of the channel sections. Most gates require keys, and the keys are crucial in this process. They consist of cultural perceptions (terms in which people think about education), values (motivations to acquire, subvert, or to underplay cultural items), and personality dispositions to behavior.

An Information and Systems Theory Model

The argument of information theory, as Miller summarizes it, runs as follows:

> A well-organized system [think of this as the school system] is predictable—you know almost what it is going to do before it happens. When a well-organized system does something, you learn little that you didn't already know—you acquire little information. A perfectly organized system is completely predictable and its behavior provides no information at all. The more disorganized and unpredictable a system is, the more information you can get by watching it. Information, organization, and predictability room together in this theoretical house (1963:3).

In other words, if the school system were perfectly organized, every interaction between constituent elements would have completely predictable outcomes. All the actions originating with a teacher and responses from and among students would lead to planned and expected results. The process would then correspond to that shown in Figure 3.3. The school is less than perfectly organized in this sense, but one might indeed inquire whether that is not its goal. One can test this proposition by examining the controls exerted

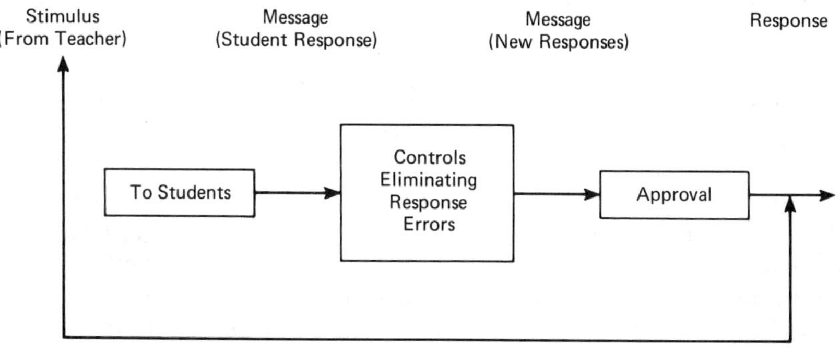

Figure 3.3.

by teachers over the things students say or do—the messages they give—by gesture, by tone of voice, and by other cues that they are not completely acceptable. When this occurs the teacher is saying, in effect, that the new information is in error; other students may quickly learn to correct for the variety of new fact or opinion introduced and rephrase responses until the "correct" one emerges.

In a small, relatively isolated society what is taught in one domain is reinforced in various ways in all others. Hence little attention might have to be paid to regulation of a given kind of formal education (let us say, puberty rites that mark beginning of the transition to adulthood), because that conduct is restated on all manner of other occasions—religious drama, toolmaking, storytelling—using the same precepts and emphasizing the same doctrine. Control mechanisms circulate throughout the entire society, conceived as a single system, much as I have described for one kind of classroom system in a much more idelogically complex environment. All kinds of information available to members sustains the social order in a given way.

If precepts of value and worthwhileness have come to be diverse and conflicting, as is true in our society, then any given value or norm is weakened, and conduct once penalized may be disregarded. The school may try to keep the system closed in various ways: by ignoring deviant values, by comparing them invidiously with those it tries to instill, by isolating, shaming, or otherwise reducing the influence of those who display unorthodox conduct, or by enlisting the power of other organizations in the social environment to the support of its value orientations. School systems that attempt to impose this kind of circularity of controls are subject to special strains, and these strains make the school vulnerable to conflicting values and experience (stresses), and demand redefinitions both of goals and procedures (Beals and Siegel 1966). As an anthropologist, I confess to view this state as desirable. Given the proliferation of alternatives and extensive interaction of its diverse kinds of people through modern communication techniques, contemporary society must remain increasingly open in order to adapt effectively to continuous environmental change.

Let us examine some of these matters further by reference to a different schematic presentation, based upon the same kind of reasoning (Figs. 3.4 and 3.5).

In Figure 3.4, T represents the degree of correspondence between student responses and information to which the student is formally exposed—by a teacher, a teaching machine, books, and other materials—for example, as measured by test scores. The remaining area in X represents information fed in to the student but not reflected in the latter's behavior in any measured way; it is lost, not understood, or rejected. The remaining area in Y represents information that is added in transmission, and is put out without being put in. A new interpretation may have been given to some items. Extraneous content may be fed in by the student from other sources to becloud otherwise predictable responses.

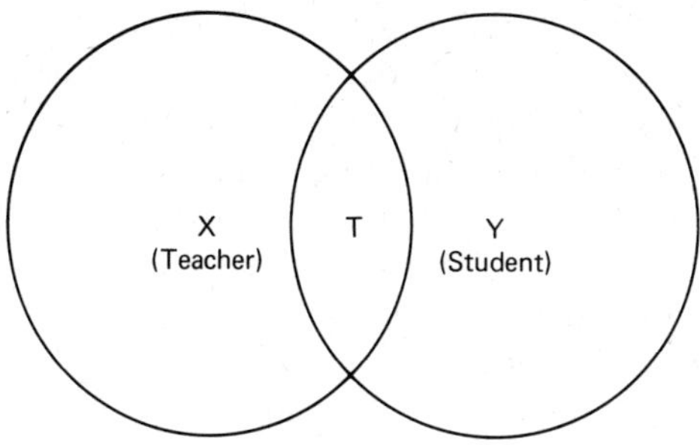

Figure 3.4. Quantities of information involved when messages are transmitted from one source (X) to the other (Y). T is the area of information common to X and Y.

In any event this way of conceptualizing the process raises questions relevant to those elicited earlier concerning the roles of teachers, what is taught, and about the products we hope to shape. If students are correct in saying that teachers want certain answers to given questions, or if discussion of issues raised in a classroom always proceeds until consensus is reached, we may assume that teachers seek to make T coextensive with X and Y. In these cases they consider communications good when they can account for all elements put into it.

This is the model of a perfectly traditional society, and it demands, as we have seen, special kinds of regulation and control. It may also be the desired model of technical learning. To put a man on the moon requires that all procedures have as perfectly predictable outcomes as possible; but, given that, it is a relatively simple matter. It also forms or selects a certain kind of person

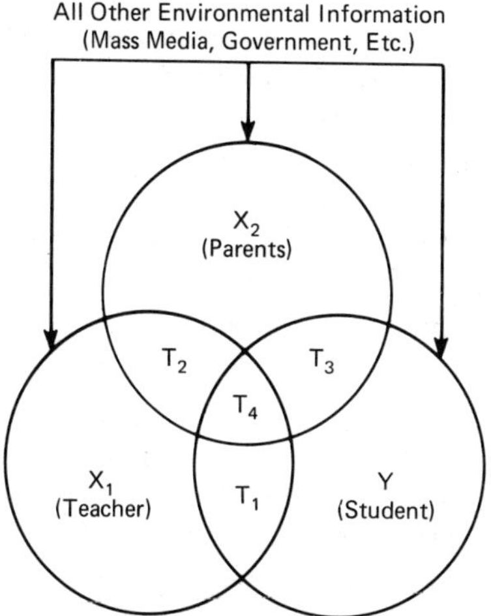

Figure 3.5. Quantities of information involved when messages are transmitted from two sources (X_1 and X_2) to a receiver (Y). T_1 is the area of information common to X_1 and X_2; T_3 is the area of information common to X_2 and Y; T_4 is the area of information common to X_1, Y, and X_2.

to participate successfully in this enterprise. Many well-educated individuals would admire his courage but otherwise not consider him very interesting. This kind of learning takes place in a highly circumscribed environment and is adapted to the solution of particular well-defined technological problems.

Most social problems do not yield themselves to such simple solutions, and indeed the application of corrective mechanisms to achieve agreed-upon outcomes or goals may exclude more desirable outcomes. Aside from what a skilled observer may have to say about these matters, potentially desirable outcomes are multiplied by the varied sources of information available in any complex society (Figure 3.5 and any ramification of same that embraces other sources, such as siblings, friends, independent reading). The goal of the teaching process may be to encourage a substantial area in Y to support spontaneity and creativity as a means of retaining openness in the solution of social problems and adaptation to change in the face of new experience. Assuming a learning procedure based upon the possibility of continually changing goals (a condition very nearly demanded in the modern world by the ever-expanding interaction of human groups) requires flexibility in the operating procedures, or rules, by which individuals choose among alternative behaviors. In human societies and cultures these rules consist of norms and values that guide the translation of preferences into action. Vickers points out that the total volume of behavior within the system (read for our purposes "the school system") becomes so large and contains so many inconsistencies that there is no longer only the right answer. "Conflict is endemic and universal; and its resolution involves valuation" (Vickers 1959: 219–234). The implication of this conclusion is that both the teacher and student, in approaching many subject matters, must learn to cope with ambiguity and with the expectation of being confronted with new needs that the resolution of current needs creates.[6] If a teacher is successful in completely regulating the behavior of the student by correcting his "errors," then he has succeeded in shaping the latter's operating rules to conform to his own. In the teaching of mathematics and spoken language this may be valuable; however, in teaching history, government, or literature it is open to serious doubt.

Explicit recognition that students in the classroom are also part of other systems, and that all of this experience is relevant to the purposes of education and learning, is tantamount to emphasizing the importance of deviancy in a creative society (Nett 1953:38–45). The same, of course, holds for teachers and administrators. The circularity of value systems is broken "only when rulers, judges, legislators, or for that matter, teachers and moralists apply or preach a doctrine in which they themselves do not believe" (Nadel 1953:73). This is what is implied by the horrendous phrase "deviation-amplifying mutual

---

[6] By this reasoning administrators ought rigorously to exclude authoritarian personality types from consideration as teacher candidates, by virtue of their intolerance of ambiguity. See Adorno et al. 1950.

causal processes" in information theory and is involved, among other things, in cultural evolution (Maruyama 1963:164–179).

This view of any operating community, such as the school, does not entail anarchy or uncontrolled change as a necessary consequence. Consistency and coherence of behavior can occur by bringing individuals in line with some preconceived goal, by continuing accommodation of any member—teacher, student-child, parent, superintendent, board member—with others with whom he is required to interact. "Shared agreements, underlying orderliness, are not binding and shared indefinitely but involve a temporal dimension implying eventual review, and consequent renewal or rejection" (Buckley 1968). In an enlightening study of a hospital this process has been spoken of as "negotiated order" (Strauss et al. 1963).

Curriculum and cultural products introduced within the school system itself should in large measure be perceived as elements in relation to other products introduced from other systems in the total environment. The stability that the school reveals at any point in time is simply the distillate of continuous sociocultural struggle that occurs in the interaction of teacher, student, principal, parents, and other sources of information at any given time. Tension and conflict are inherent in this process, so that any theory that allows consensus to define stability is inadequate. Students who are subject to authorities who attempt to constrain or exclude channels of information outside the classroom retain a high level of unreduced tension. In short, they find the school experience both dull and irrelevant and seek to relieve tensions in a variety of ways. The effects in some cases can be self-destructive; in other cases they lead to social movements and attempts at more meaningful cultural affirmations. The task seems to be that of lessening these constraints, thereby making creative use of student inputs, by assisting the student to relate that information to other relevant experience *in a disciplined way.*

Some time ago Edward Sapir put this conception of society and culture very elegantly:

> While we often speak of society as though it were a static structure defined by tradition, it is, in the more intimate sense, nothing of the kind, but a highly intricate network of partial or complete understandings between the members of organizational units of every degree of size and complexity. . . . It is only apparently a static sum of social institutions; actually it is being reanimated or creatively reaffirmed from day to day by particular acts of a communicative nature which obtain among individuals participating in it (1931:78).

Summary and Conclusions

The foregoing discussion has centered upon the problem of how we can estimate what part of the educational product—concrete understandings, norms of behavior, and attitudes toward new learning—is actually transmitted to the child in the school system, and with what effectiveness. The sociocultural factors that must be taken into consideration may be conceived a little differently, depending upon the particular frame of reference used for making and organizing observations about the process. In one case, attention is focused upon the cultures of several communities in interaction: the characteristics of the cultures and the nature of role relations established at points of contact. Backgrounds and contact conditions between the several collectivities constitute the ground and figure, respectively, of the transmission of shared understandings. In another case, the point of departure is the forces which permit cultural items to move in given forms and with intended meanings and functions through a variety of social agents until they reach the child. And in the third, our emphasis has shifted to a more particular concern with information flow in the educational process.

In any event we are concerned essentially with the screening effect of values and learning habits, derived from multiple backgrounds, upon successive reinterpretations and/or reinforcements of behavior patterns. What minimal forms of concrete knowledge, ideology, and behavior norms do academic formulators try to impart to teachers and administrators in training? What functions or consequences for child development do they intend such elements to have as presented, in the light of their own theoretical understandings? To what extent are the intended functions understood and shared in like ways by trainees, and to what extent are they accepted in cult fashion or rejected entirely? The notion of "permissiveness" has certain meanings when interpreted intellectually and critically in terms of psychoanalytic theory (or in terms of some other developmental framework); it may be taken over and subsequently imparted quite differently by teachers with deeply ingrained constricted values. Or, again, teachers of teachers may seek in the same way to transmit concepts of personality adjustment based upon certain social psychological theories, only to have them interpreted and conveyed to the child as conformity toward the middle level.

We may expect the same processes to operate in the relations of the school with other systems in the environment. How do values placed upon specific formal materials and upon education itself coincide or conflict? What rank order does the overall activity have in each group? And, finally, what use does the child make of his school experience in integrating it with extraschool experiences—previously or currently instilled goal orientations, self-conceptions, and role relations? These are illustrative of the central questions which emerge from the above analysis. Answers will be possible only in the course of systematic, long-range research programs, in which comparative case studies of each phase of the process become available.

Each of the three strategies considered in this paper brought our attention to the careers of curricula in the schools, for they represent most explicitly what the schools want to accomplish. But this is clearly not the end.

"A curriculum," we are informed (Stake 1967), "is an educational program. . . . Educational programs are characterized by their purposes, their content, their environment, their methods, and the changes they bring about. Usually there are messages to be conveyed, relationships to be demonstrated, concepts to be symbolized, understandings and skills to be acquired." The educationist literature on evaluation of these various dimensions of the curriculum is very large indeed. It tries to tell what happens in the course of instruction.

A hard search of this literature would yield precious little concern, however, with the larger goals of the socially and culturally diverse captive clientele for whom the curricula are presumably designed. Yet, to know something about the interaction of the social and cultural environments and the flow of communications among them in contrasting educational communities is an important step in new approaches to this more fundamental problem. If, as Friedenberg asserts, the school is genuinely interested in dealing more effectively with "culturally deprived" youngsters, it simultaneously despises their values and seeks to transform them into less mutilated versions of normal middle-class youth (Friedenberg 1965:194ff.). Apparently this is as true today as it was a generation ago. Even the more imaginative proposals for enlisting their more active participation in the educational process (Riessman 1962; Passow 1963) appear to be patronizing while sympathetic and tend to segregate the young by pandering to their values rather than making constructive use of them. The children of the rich, for other reasons, may fare even worse.

Is this really what we continue to want? If not, we might take a much harder look at some of our more cherished assumptions—compulsory attendance, isolation from the larger world, clinging to a specialized conception of educational functions—and seek to come up with more viable alternatives. A cogent argument can be made for voluntary education with a broad set of perspectives, geared to American society conceived as a community of publics rather than a monolithic mass. The school, of one kind or another, might then appeal to youth as a place they ought to be rather than as a place they have to be.

Natural history studies of educational communities generally embrace values in a neutral sense: they exist and should be described in terms of what they are and what they do. Review of the models discussed in this paper suggests that students of education have a responsibility to break through their own value orientations, to take different positions, seek their implementation, and study their consequences under controlled conditions. This is not an easy task, for we are not only observers of the social scene but participants in it. Nonetheless, it is a necessary one.

Whatever conclusions may be reached about goals, we shall be well advised to utilize relevant theoretical insights for investigating empirically what happens in the course of the enculturative process in a complex society such as our own. It is in this spirit that I have ventured to set out a few such models based upon promising available approaches.

References

Adorno, T. W., et al., 1950, *The Authoritarian Personality.* New York: Harper & Row.

Beals, Alan, and B. J. Siegel, 1966, *Divisiveness: An Anthropological Approach to the Study of Conflict.* Stanford, Calif.: Stanford University Press.

Brodbeck, A. J., 1955, "The Mass-Media as a Socializing Agency" (mimeo). Paper read to the American Psychological Association Symposium on Children and the Mass-Media, San Francisco.

Buckley, Walter, 1968, "Society as a Complete Adaptive System." In Walter Buckley ed., *Modern Systems Research for the Behavioral Scientist.* Chicago: Aldine Publishing Company, p. 504.

Coleman, James S., 1961, *The Adolescent Society.* New York: The Free Press, Chapter 2.

——1965, *Adolescents and the Schools.* New York: Basic Books, Inc.

Conant, James B., 1959, *The Child, the Parent and the State.* Cambridge, Mass.: Harvard University Press.

Daedalus, 1960, Proceedings, Journal of the American Academy of Arts and Sciences 89, no. 2 (Spring). Special number of "Mass Culture and Mass Media."

Easton, David, 1965, *A Systems Analysis of Political Life.* New York: John Wiley & Sons, Inc.

Festinger, Leon, S. S. Schachter, and Kurt Back, 1950, *Social Pressures in Informal Groups.* Stanford, Calif.: Stanford University Press, pp. 33–46.

Friedenberg, Edgar Z., 1965, *Coming of Age in America.* New York: Random House.

Gagné, Robert M., 1967, *Learning and Individual Differences.* Columbus, O.: Charles E. Merrill Books.

Ginsberg, Eli (ed.), 1960, *The Nation's Children.* New York: Columbia University Press, vol. 3.

Goffman, Erving, 1962, *Encounters: Two Studies in the Study of Interaction.* Chicago: Aldine Publishing Company.

Jones, Maxwell, et al., 1953, *The Therapeutic Community: A New Treatment Method in Psychiatry.* New York: Basic Books, Inc.

Klapper, J., 1960, *The Effects of Mass Communication.* New York: The Free Press.

Landes, Ruth, 1965, *Culture in American Education.* New York: John Wiley & Sons, Inc.

Lewin, Kurt, 1951, "Psychological Ecology." In Dorwin Cartwright, ed., *Field Theory in the Social Sciences.* New York: Harper & Row, pp. 170–187.

Maruyama, Magoroh, 1963, "The Second Cybernetics: Deviation-Amplifying Mutual Causal Processes," *American Scientist* 51:164–179.

Miller, George A., 1963, "What Is Information Measurement," *American Psychologist* 8:3–11.

Nadel, S. F., 1953, "Social Control and Self-Regulation," *Social Forces* 31:265–73.

Nett, Roger, 1953, "Conformity-Deviation and the Social Control Concept," *Ethics* 64:38–45.

Our Movie Made Children. Based upon the Payne Fund Motion Picture Appreciation Study (1929–33). New York: The Macmillan Company, 1933.

Passow, A. H., 1963, *Education in Depressed Areas.* New York: Bureau of Publications, Teachers College, Columbia University.

Rapaport, Robert N., 1960, *Community as Doctor: New Perspectives on a Therapeutic Community.* London: Tavistock Publications.

Riessman, Frank, 1962, *The Culturally Deprived Child.* New York: Harper & Row.

Sapir, Edward, 1931, "Communication," *Encyclopedia of the Social Sciences.* New York: Macmillan, vol. 4, p. 78.

Sayles, Leonard R., 1958, *Behavior of Industrial Work Groups: Prediction and Control.* New York: John Wiley & Sons, Inc.

Schramm, Wilbur, J. Lyle, and E. B. Parker, 1961, *Television in the Lives of our Children.* Stanford, Calif.: Stanford University Press.

Siegel, Bernard J., 1970, "Defensive Structuring and Environmental Stress," *American Journal of Sociology* 76(1):11–32.

Social Science Research Council Summer Seminar on Acculturation, 1954, "Acculturation: An Exploratory Formulation," *American Anthropologist* 56:973–1002.

Spindler, G. D., 1955, *Sociocultural and Psychological Processes in Menomini Acculturation.* Berkeley: University of California Press.

Stake, Robert E., 1967, "Toward a Technology for the Evaluation of Educational Programs." In R. Tyler, R. Gagné, and M. Scriven, *Perspectives of Curriculum Evaluation.* AERA Monograph Series on Curriculum Evaluation, vol. 1. Chicago: Rand McNally & Company.

Strauss, Anselm L. et al., 1963, "The Hospital and Its Negotiated Order," in Eliot Friedson, ed., *The Hospital in Modern Society.* New York: The Free Press, pp. 147–69.

Tremblay, Marc-Adelard, 1962, "Le Transfert Cultural: Fondement et Extension dans le Processus d'Acculturation," *Anthropologica,* IV, no. 2, pp. 293–319.

Tyler, Ralph, 1960, "Educational Objectives of American Democracy." In E. Ginzberg, ed., *The Nation's Children.* New York: Columbia University Press, vol. 2, pp. 70–92.

Vickers, George, 1959, "Is Adaptability Enough?" *Behavioral Science* 4:219–234.

Warner, W. L., R. J. Havighurst, and M. B. Loeb, 1944, *Who Shall Be Educated? The Challenge of Unequal Opportunities.* New York: Harper & Row.

PART II

Education and Cultural Process in Complex Modern Societies

PREVIEW

The purpose of Part I was to show how education and anthropology engage as cultural systems. In Part II we are concerned with the products of this engagement in analyses of educational processes in complex modern societies. This area is deliberately defined broadly. It is potentially concerned with any educational process treated anthropologically in any modern cultural system with a literate tradition. This includes, of course, both Western and non-Western societies as well as minoritics within these societies and the relationships of these minorities with the cultural mainstream. Most of the chapters in this part are about educational processes in the cultural system of the United States. The cross-cultural stance, which is at the heart of an anthropological approach to the analysis of educative process, is presented in Rohlen's chapter on the "spiritual training" in a Japanese bank and mine on an elementary school in a German village. This stance is carried farther in Part III.

Minority groups and their relationships with the mainstream culture via the school are a major focus of Part II. My chapter on minority groups in North America and McDermott's on "Achieving School Failure" are concerned with this theme. In both, the interaction of the teacher and students as cultural representatives in the social context of the classroom, engaged in both verbal and nonverbal communication, is stressed. John Hostetler's chapter on education among the Old Order Amish and the Hutterian Brethren is also about minority groups and their relationship with the mainstream culture. The Hutterites and Amish, however, are different from non-Anglo minorities in North America. They are not racially distinguishable from the dominant population, but their communities are defensively structured in relationship to that population and its culture. The Hutterite and Amish communities strive to keep the cultural input from the outside world under strict control so that the validity of their chosen and defended way of life is not damaged. Though there may be elements of this same orientation among other minority groups influenced by nationalistic movements or ideology, the major thrust of the Chicano, black, and American Indian minorities in

U.S. society has been toward a realization of the egalitarian philosophy that would permit them free access to the opportunities presumably afforded by a good education in our society. The Amish and Hutterites on the one hand, and the Chicanos and blacks on the other, make a comparison that places certain dilemmas of education in our society in sharp focus. The Hutterites and the Amish maintain an orderly, productive way of life by *excluding* educational (and cultural) input. However, in North American society education is considered to be one of the pillars of democracy, a means of personal fulfillment and a contribution to social and economic goals considered desirable for the national society as a whole. State and community education officials in the areas around the Hutterite colonies and Amish settlements have consistently attempted to force public education upon these people. For most other minorities the problem has been that of achieving free access to good education and its fruits, both of which were denied them through both explicit and implicit means. Some of these means are made clear in McDermott's and my chapters. Generally speaking, blacks, Chicanos, and American Indians accept the premise that education, opportunity, and achievement are closely interrelated. We are faced with the spectacle of a national society forcing education upon one minority group and effectively denying it to others while claiming pluralistic egalitarianism. This dilemma should be kept in mind when reading the first four chapters of this part.

Members of American minority groups, formerly nonliterate peoples, and peasants in other lands have complained that anthropologists are interested mainly in societies that have had essentially colonial relationships with the dominant society, of which the anthropologist is usually a representative. The remaining chapters in this section were selected as representative of a focus on social classes, ethnicity, and social participation that contradicts this characterization. My chapter on Beth Anne is a case study of culturally defined adjustment and teacher perceptions. Beth Anne is a child from an upper-middle-class Anglo setting. With this analysis I attempt to show how the process of cultural transmission in North American schools may be, under certain conditions, as damaging to the nonminority child as it is so often to the minority child. The same psychocultural processes are working, though the situations in which they are applied appear on the surface to be the reverse of each other.

The chapter by Schwartz and Merten, "Social Identity and Expressive Symbols: the Meaning of an Initiation Ritual," examines the relationship between expressive symbols and identity transformation implicit in adolescent education rituals in a high school in an upper-middle-class residential area of a large midwestern city. Their analysis shows how anthropological approaches may be made to the analysis of sociocultural phenomena in nonexotic settings. Essentially the same kinds of rituals appear to be operating as initiation rites in this urban community as those that have been reported by anthropologists in distant places and under the most exotic conditions imaginable. The role of ritual in modern life, and particularly in education, has been underemphasized, though articles such as that by Jacquetta Burnett (1969), as well as Hart's article reprinted in this volume, have made important contributions to the correction of this deficiency.

In "The Elementary School Principal: Notes from a Field Study" Harry Wolcott develops two major themes relevant to our discussion. The first is essentially methodological, and describes how he carried out an ethnographic study of an elementary school principal. The second is an ethnography of how principals are selected in one school system at a specific time. Wolcott shows how principals tend to perpetuate themselves by a selective process—something he calls "variety-reducing behavior." A conservative orientation is reinforced, and this influences the school—as a culture-transmitting agency—as a whole. Again, the focus is not upon ethnically differentiated minority groups or upon "primitive" or nonliterate peoples but rather upon selected phenomena in a middle-class North American setting.

In "Education, Schools, and Cultural Mapping" Marion Dobbert characterizes colleges and universities as initiation rituals in preparation for the priesthood—a priesthood whose essential function is the maintenance of the status quo in American society. The notion that education serves mainly to recruit new members and maintain the existing structure of society has been advanced several times in this volume. Heretofore, however, it has not been applied to higher education in our own society. This application makes most of us who are participants in the system of higher education acutely uncomfortable. We protest that in a democratic society education, and particularly higher education, serves as an instrument for self-improvement and for the improvement of our social, political, and economic structure. We are not surprised that in Socialist countries all educational institutions serve to recruit and maintain and that criticism of existing institutions must be constrained by ideological assumptions that make basic challenges to the Socialist status quo impossible. We resist the notion that we may be participants in the same relationship. Yet, we have known for some time that higher education is not working as it should in our society. Many, perhaps most, students are in some degree alienated, and not because they are intellectually dead or academically incompetent. Many young people have recently opted out of a college education. Could it be that they intuitively recognize the relationship Dobbert has described? Her paper should stimulate some interesting discussions. Is her analysis essentially correct? If so, how should matters be changed? Or is the relationship as she described it acceptable?

In the first chapter in this part, on education in a complex society other than North America, Thomas Rohlen describes *seishin kyōiku* (usually translated as "spiritual training") in a Japanese bank. His analysis moves us away from the school as the context of education and calls our attention to the fact that even under less dramatic circumstances than the one he describes, education is, indeed, not confined to the school, nor to children. His analysis also challenges certain assumptions that have guided educators at all levels in the United States. Like Christie Kiefer, who has written about the "examination hell" for Japanese school children as a kind of initiation ritual (Kiefer 1970), Rohlen deals with a process which may be termed conversion through suffering, which in turn may be regarded as a special form of dissonance resolution. This kind of education is fundamentally different from the verbal instruction, imparting of information, and explicit symbolic manipulation characterizing most schooling in the United States, or for that matter, most schooling in Western societies. The reader who is alert to the implications of Schwartz's and Merten's chapter will understand that it is a form of education that is not unknown to us; as he reads into Part III of this volume he will see that it is a significant type that is very widespread and of probable great time depth in human evolution.

My chapter on "Schooling in Schönhausen: A Study of Cultural Transmission and Instrumentatal Adaptation in an Urbanizing German Village," is likewise a study of a segment of a modern complex society. In this chapter I pursue two major goals. One is to describe the process of cultural transmission in a small elementary school. The second is to describe with some accuracy and objectivity the results of this cultural transmission as it has influenced the perception and thinking of the children in school. In order to achieve these aims I used traditional anthropological methods in that I became a participant observer in the school insofar as my age and status permitted. I also developed further a research procedure that Louise Spindler and I have applied elsewhere and which we term the Instrumental Activities Inventory, and further refined a theoretical model for it. Explicit theoretical models have been notably scarce in the anthropology of education, a condition to which Fred Gearing's recent paper (1973) is a glittering exception. The results of the application of the model and research technique show that the transmission of culture in the Schönhausen elementary school was effective at one level of cognitive organization, but that children were quite capable of exercising choices not dictated by the culture that was transmitted in the school. They also organized these choices in ways different from those that the culture transmitted by the school would allow one to predict. The underlying theme of the chapter is the role of the school in the transformation from a rural folk culture to an urbanized, industrialized environment. Though the setting is southern Germany there is much reported in the chapter that is directly comparable to various aspects of the situation in U.S. society or any other complex, urbanizing society.

Readers will find a paper by Joshua Fishman and Erika Lueders (1971) in the very useful volume *The Functions of Language in the Classroom,* a stimulating companion to my analysis of education in the Schönhausen elementary school. Fishman and Lueders use the teaching of high German to Schwäbisch- (a regional dialect) speaking children in the area in which

Schönhausen is located as the basis for an insightful discussion of verbal repertoire and functional differentiation, speech community, and other concepts applicable to situations where standardized forms of language are taught to native speakers with regional or class dialects.

References

Burnett, Jacquetta, 1969, "Ceremony, Rites, and Economy in the Student System of an American High School," *Human Organization* 28 (1): 1–10.

Fishman, Joshua, and Erika Lueders, 1971, "What Has the Sociology of Language to Say to the Teacher? (On Teaching the Standard Variety to Speakers of Dialectal or Sociolectal Varieties)." In Courtney Cazden, Vera John, and Dell Hymes, eds., *The Function of Language in the Classroom,* New York: Teachers College Press.

Gearing, Fred, 1973, "Where We Are and Where We Might Go: Steps toward a General Theory of Cultural Transmission," *Council on Education and Anthropology Newsletter* IV(1): 1–10.

GEORGE D. SPINDLER/*Stanford University*

4 *Why Have Minority Groups in North America Been Disadvantaged by Their Schools?**

In Harlem School?

A description of a first-grade class in a black ghetto in New York City follows. It is not a school in the poorest of the districts. It was considered "typical" for the grade.

> The teacher trainee (student teacher) is attempting to teach "rhyming." It is early afternoon. Even before she can get the first "match" (for example, "book" and "look") a whole series of events is drawn out.
>
> One child plays with the head of a doll, which has broken off from the doll, alternately hitting it and kissing it.
>
> The student teacher tells a boy who has left his seat that he is staying in after school. He begins to cry. Another child teases that his mother will be worried about him if he stays in after school. The boy cries even harder and screams at the teacher: "You can't keep me in until 15 o'clock."
>
> A girl tries to answer a question put to the class but raises her hand with her shoe in it. She is told to put her hand down and to put her shoe on.
>
> Another child keeps switching his pencil from one nostril to another, trying to see if it will remain in his nose if he lets go of it; he is apparently wholly unconcerned with the session in progress.
>
> One child is lying down across his desk, pretending to sleep while seeing if the teacher sees him. Just next to him another child leads an imaginary band. Still a different child, on his side, stands quietly beside his seat, apparently tired of sitting.
>
> While this is all going on the regular teacher of the class is out of the room. When she does return, she makes no effort to assist, or criticize, the student teacher. The student teacher later informed me that the regular teacher was not "just being polite." She rarely directed the student teacher, but simply let her "take over" the class on occasion. The student teacher also remarked that things were no different in the class when the regular teacher held forth.

---

*From *Culture in Process,* second edition, by Alan R. Beals, George D. Spindler, and Louise S. Spindler. Copyright © 1967, 1973, by Holt, Rinehart and Winston, Inc. Reprinted by permission of Holt, Rinehart and Winston, Inc.

> Fifteen minutes had gone by, but little "rhyming" had been accomplished. A boy begins to shadow box in the back; another talks to himself in acting out a scene he envisions.
>
> Still another child shakes his fist at the student teacher, mimicking her words: "cat-fat, hop-stop."
>
> Two children turn to each other and exchange "burns" on one another's forearms, while another child arranges and rearranges his desk materials and notebook, seemingly dissatisfied with each succeeding arrangement.
>
> A girl in the back has an empty bag of potato chips but is trying to use her fingers as a "blotter" to get at the remnants. She pretends to be paying attention to the lesson.
>
> Another child asks to go to the bathroom, but is denied.
>
> After a half-hour I left (Rosenfeld 1971:105).

As Gerry Rosenfeld, who taught in a Harlem school and did an anthropological field study there, pointed out, the schooling of these children is already patterned for them at the age of six or seven. "Not much is expected from them," they are from poor families, they are black, and they are "disadvantaged." By high school many of them will be dropouts, or "pushouts," as Rosenfeld terms them. As they get older they become less docile than the children described above, and some teachers in ghetto schools have reason to fear for their own safety. The teachers of this classroom did not have reason to fear their pupils, but they were ignorant about them. Their preparatory work in college or in teacher training had not prepared them for a classroom of children from a poor ghetto area in the city. The student teacher knew nothing about the neighborhood from which the children in her class came. She knew only that she "did not want to work with 'these' children when she became a regular teacher" (Rosenfeld, 1970:105).

As a teacher and observer at Harlem School, Rosenfeld found the teachers held an array of myths about poor children that they used to account for their underachievement and miseducation. At the benign liberal level there are beliefs about the nature of poverty and cultural disadvantage. These conditions become accepted as irrevocable givens. The child comes from such a background, therefore, there is nothing I, as a teacher, can do but try to get minimal results from this misshapen material. Among teachers who are explicitly bigoted in their views of the poor and black, the explanations for failure may be less benign. According to Rosenfeld, and his observations are supported by others, an underlying ethos pervades the slum school which prescribes and accepts failure for the child.

> Assistant principals function not as experts on curriculum and instruction but as stock boys and disciplinarians. Boxes are constantly being unpacked and children are being reprimanded and punished. The principal seems more concerned with maintaining a stable staff, irrespective of its quality at times, than with effecting school-community ties and fashioning relevant learning programs. Education appears as a process where children are merely the by-products, not the core of concern. Guidance counselors and reading specialists are preoccupied with norms

> and averages, not with the enhancement of learning for all the children. Theirs is a remedial task, and where one would not exist, they create it. School directives and bulletins are concerned with bathroom regulations and procedures along stairways, the worth of the children being assessed in terms of their ability to conform to these peripheral demands (Rosenfeld 1970:110).

The new teacher, however idealistic he or she may be at first, will be affected by the environment, and becomes a part of the social structure of the school. A socialization process occurs so that personal commitment and philosophy become ordered around the system. The clique structure among staff personnel also forces the newcomer to choose models and cultivate relationships. Communication must occur. There must be others with whom one can commiserate.

Teachers who keep their idealism, tempered as it is after a time by reality, turn more and more inward toward their own classroom. There one sees the results of the years of educational disenchantment. In the middle grades and beyond, the children are already two or more years behind standard achievement norms. The teacher realizes that for the children the school is an oppressive and meaningless place. He comes to understand also that children have developed counterstrategies for what they have perceived as their teachers' indifference, confusion, despair, and in some cases, outright aggression. But if the teacher persists in the effort to understand his or her pupils, eventually they become individuals. Most are alert and active. They are potentially high learners and achievers. Some are subdued and permanently detached. Some are irrevocably hostile towards schools, teachers, and white people. Others have surface hostilities but are willing to give trust and confidence when it is justified. Some are fast learners with strong curiosity and an eagerness to learn about the world. Others are apathetic or simply dull. Once the children become individuals, with sharp differences, they can no longer be treated as objects or as a collectivity.

The next step for the teacher who is going to become effective as a cultural transmitter and agent of socialization, as all teachers are, is to learn something of the neighborhood and of the homes from which the children come. But this is a step that is rarely taken. Rosenfeld describes the situation at Harlem School.

> Though Harlem School belonged to the neighborhood, it was not psychologically a part of it. On the contrary, teachers felt unwanted, estranged. Perhaps this was why few ventured off the "beaten paths" to the "hinterland" beyond the school, into the side streets and the homes where the children played out their lives. Some teachers at Harlem School had never been to a single child's household, despite the fact that they had been employed at the school for many years. Nothing was known of community self-descriptions, the activity and social calendar in the neighborhood, the focal points for assembly and dispersal, or the feelings of residents toward the "outside world." Teachers could not imagine that they could foster a genuine coming-together of neighborhood persons and

> themselves. They hid behind their "professionalism." They failed to realize that the apathy and disparagement they associated with parents were attributed by the latter to them. It is not to be underestimated how "foreign" teachers feel themselves to be at Harlem School, how disliked by the children. Why then do they remain on the job? Part of the answer is in the fact that the rewards of one's work are not always sought on the job itself, but in the private world. Teachers have little stake in the communities in which they work; that is why it may be necessary to link more closely teachers' jobs and children's achievement. It is my guess that all children (except those with proven defects) would achieve if teachers' jobs depended on this (Rosenfeld 1970:103).

It is clear that there are some parallels between the relationship of the school and teachers to the pupils and community in minority populations in the United States and the like relationship that has developed in many of the modernizing nations. Although there are profound differences in the two situations, the similarity is that the educational institutions in both cases are intrusive. These institutions stem from a conceptual and cultural context that is different from that of the people whose children are in the schools. This tends to be true whether "natives" or aliens are utilized as teachers and administrators for the schools. In the modernizing populations, as among the Sisala, the teacher, even though Sisala himself, is alien by virtue of his having been educated, removed from his community, socialized to norms, values, competencies, and purposes that are not a part of his community's culture (Grindal 1972). He is a member of a different class, for which there is as yet no clear place in the Sisala cultural system. He feels isolated from the community, and this isolation is reinforced by the character of the school in which he teaches. In Harlem School, or its prototypes, the teacher tends to be an alien whether he is white or black. Even among black teachers only some can maintain or acquire an identification with the people and community in which the school exists. The same processes of socialization and alienation that have taken place for the Sisala teacher have taken place for the black teacher in the United States. This is particularly true for the black teacher who comes from a middle-class background to begin with, then goes on to the university for advanced training. This teacher may be as far removed from the black community in a slum school as any white teacher. Of course not all black communities are in slums, but the slum school is the one we have been talking about.

At Rosepoint?

The interactions we are describing between school and culture occur elsewhere than in the urban slum. Martha Ward describes a community in what she calls Rosepoint, near New Orleans (1971). Rosepoint is a very small rural community, a former plantation occupied now by some of the people who worked on it, plus others. Rosepoint has its own culture—that of the black South together with a heavy French influence characteristic of the area as a whole, and the unique ecological characteristics of a community built along a levee of the Mississippi River. Martha Ward was particularly concerned with language learning and linguistic features. She found that there were many substantial differences in speech and learning to speak between Rosepoint adults and children and white people. These differences contribute to the separation between community and school, which is the focus of our attention, since the school is taught mostly by whites, although they are by no means the sole cause of this separation.

Rosepoint parents believe that most of the teachers in the schools their children attend—black or white—are authoritarian and punitive. They also see that their children attending white schools for the first time are subjected to discriminatory practices, sometimes subtle, sometimes very obvious. There is little communication between the home and the school, whether primary or high school. Parents have little notion how the school is run, what their children are taught, or how to cooperate with the school or teachers. And the schools show no understanding of the social problems or cultural characteristics of Rosepoint. The conflicts are profound. The irrelevancy of the school for most Rosepoint children is measured by a high dropout rate and low rates of literacy. From about eleven years of age on, states Martha Ward, staying in school is a touch-and-go proposition, especially for males. She describes certain characteristics of the school environment and expectations that are at odds with those of thc Rosepoint children.

> The school creates for the Rosepoint child an environment not as much unpleasant as unnatural. For years he has been determining his own schedule for eating, sleeping, and playing. The content of his play is unsupervised and depends on the child's imagination. His yard does not contain sand boxes, swings, clay, paints, nor personnel obliged to supervise his play. At school, however, play is supervised, scheduled, and centers around objects deemed suitable for young minds. There are firm schedules for playing, napping, eating, and "learning and studying" (with the implication that learning will occur only during the time allotted for it). The authority buttressing even minimal schedules is impersonal and inflexible with an origin not in face-to-face social relationships but in an invisible bureaucracy.
>
> Moreover, the Rosepoint home relies on verbal communication rather than on the written word as a medium. Adults do not read to children nor encourage writing. Extraverbal communication such as body movements or verbal communication such as storytelling or gossip are preferred to the printed page. The lack of money to purchase books, magazines, and newpapers partly explains this. . . . [sentence omitted] . . . for children of a culture rich in in-group lore and oral traditions the written word is a pallid substitute.
>
> Another conflict arising out of the home-school discrepancy is language—specifically, "bad" language. Remember, the Rosepoint child is rewarded for linguistic creativity . . . [three sentences omitted]

> In the classroom such language has an entirely different interpretation on it. Some educators discretely refer to it as "the M-F problem."[1] [sentence omitted] A nine-year-old girl was given a two-week suspension from classes for saying a four-letter word. This was her first recorded transgression of the language barrier. The second offense may be punished by expulsion . . . [two sentences omitted to end of paragraph] (Ward 1971:91–92).

The problems of Rosepoint and the schools that are intended to serve it are probably less overtly intense than those of Harlem School, its staff, and the community, but they are closely related to each other, and in turn to the problems of education among the Sisala, the Kanuri, and in Malitbog. The school in all of these situations is intrusive and the teachers are aliens. Resentment, conflict, and failures are present in communication from all sides.

We should be very careful here to realize that what we have been describing is not a problem of black minority populations alone. To some extent the disarticulation described between the school and community will be characteristic in any situation where the teachers and school stem from a different culture or subculture than that of the pupils and their parents. There is disarticulation between any formal school and the community, even where the school and community are not culturally divergent. Conflicts ensue when the school and teachers are charged with responsibility for assimilating or acculturating their pupils to a set of norms for behavior and thought that are different from those learned at home and in the community.

Education for minorities in North America is complicated by a variety of hazards. Harlem School operates in a depressing slum environment. No one wants to go there and the people there would like to get out. The conflicts and disarticulation germane to the school-community situation we have described are made more acute and destructive because of this. Rosepoint and its schools have their special circumstances also. The Rosepoint population has inherited the culture and outlook of a former plantation slave population. They are close to the bottom of the social structure. The teachers, particularly if they are white, have inherited attitudes toward black people from the South's past. Let us look for a moment at a quite different place and people, the Indians of the Yukon Territory of Canada and the Mopass Residential School.

In the Mopass Residential School

The children who come to this school represent several different tribes from quite a wide area of northwestern Canada. Many of these tribal societies adapted quickly to the fur trade economy that developed soon after the first white men arrived and many became heavily acculturated to the other aspects

[1] Refers to the use of obscenities in the school, including "Motherfucker."

of European culture. One could not say that on the whole the Native Americans of this area resisted the alien culture. In fact, they welcomed many of its technological and material advantages. As the northern territories have been opened for rapid development during the past decade, however, the Native Americans already there have found it increasingly difficult to find a useful and rewarding place in this expanding economy. The reasons for this are altogether the fault of neither the white Canadians nor the Indians, but certainly prejudice has played a role. One of the serious problems of the Indians, however, has been that, on the whole, they have had neither the skills that could be used in the expanding economy nor the basic education upon which to build these skills. The task of the school would seem to be that of preparing young Native Americans[2] to take a productive and rewarding role in the economy and society now emerging in the Northwest Territories. This is what it is like at Mopass Residential School, according to Richard King, who taught there for a year and did anthropological observations during that period.

> For the children, the residential school constitutes a social enclave almost totally insulated from the community within which it functions; yet Mopass School reflects in a microcosmic, but dismayingly faithful, manner the social processes of the larger society. Two distinct domains of social interaction exist independently: Whiteman society and Indian society. Where these domains overlap, they do so with common purposes shared at the highest level of abstraction—but with minimal congruence of purposes, values, and perceptions, at the operating levels of interaction. The Whiteman maintains his social order according to his own perceptions of reality. The Indian bears the burden of adaptation to a social order that he may perceive more realistically—and surely he perceives it with a different ordering of reality—than does the Whiteman. From his perceptions the Indian finds it impossible to accept the social order and, at the same time, impossible to reject it completely. He therefore creates an artificial self to cope with the unique interactive situations.
>
> In the residential school, the Whiteman staff and teachers are the end men of huge bureaucratic organizations (church and national government) that are so organized as to provide no reflection of the local communities. These employees derive their social, economic, and psychological identity from the organizations of which they are members. . . . [four sentences omitted]
>
> . . . The children of the school are little more than components to be manipulated in the course of the day's work. . . . No job at school is defined in terms of *outcomes,* expected, or observable, in children (King 1970:89–90).

King goes on to describe the factionalism among the adult faculty and staff in the school. He suggests that many of the people who take teaching jobs in the residential school are deviant or marginal personalities, and that the isolation of the school, and its nature as a closed system, tend to create a

[2] The term *Native Americans* is preferred by many American Indians. We use Indian and Native American interchangeably in recognition of this preference.

tense interpersonal situation. The children have to adjust to this as well as to the alien character of the institution itself.

> The school children become uniquely adept at personality analysis, since their major task is to cope with the demands of shifting adult personalities. But this analysis is limited to their needs as the children perceive them in specific situations (King 1967:88).

An artificial self is developed by the Indian child to cope with the total situation in which he finds himself. King says that the children sustain themselves with the conviction that their "real self" is not this person in the school at all. Through this, and other processes, the barriers between Whiteman and Indian are firmly developed

> not so much by a conscious rejection on the part of the Whiteman as by a conscious rejection on the part of the Indian child. The sterile shallowness of the adult model presented by the school Whitemen serves only to enhance—and probably to romanticise—memories of attachments in the child's primary family group, and to affirm a conviction prevalent among the present adult Indian generation that Indians must strive to maintain an identity separate from Whitemen (King 1967:88).

There is much more we could say about the social and learning environment that this school provided[3] the Indian children who attended it. King's case study should be read in order to understand it more thoroughly, for it is a startling example of miseducation—and with the best of intentions on the part of the sponsoring organizations and the teaching and administrative personnel of the school itself. All the features of disarticulation, isolation and nonrelatedness we have ascribed to the other schools discussed are present, but in a special and distorted form because the school is a closed residential institution even more removed from the community that it is intended to serve than the other schools. It is also a church school, run by the Episcopalian church for the Canadian government. Its curriculum is even less relevant to the Native American children who attend it than the curriculum of the Sisala school was to the Sisala children, for it is the same curriculum that is used in other Canadian schools at the same grade level. It appears that the Mopass Residential School intends to recruit children into the white culture and a religious faith (since religious observances and education are a regular part of the school life). It fails in these purposes and, in fact, creates new barriers to this recruitment and reinforces old ones. More serious by far is the fact that it does not prepare the children who attend it to cope with the new economy and society emerging in the north. The children leave the

---

[3] The school was closed in 1969. The "ethnographic present" is used in this description since it was in operation so recently and to be consistent with the other analyses.

school without necessary basic skills, alienated from what they see as white culture, alienated from themselves, and nonrelated to their own communities. This kind of schooling creates marginal people.[4]

Is There a Way Out of the Dilemma?

In the discussion so far we have dealt only with minority peoples who have had to operate in what some would describe as an essentially colonial situation. That is, they may have the theoretical rights of self-determination and self-regulation, but, in fact, do not and could not exercise these rights. There are now strong movements underway towards self-determination. Some are very militant, separatistic, and nationalistic. Others are more accommodative. But all share in striving for self-determination, and regulation of the schools is an important aspect of this determination. These people recognize, perhaps in different terms, what we have said—that education is a process of recruitment and maintenance for the cultural system. For minority people the schools have been experienced as damaging attempts to recruit their children into an alien culture. Their self-images and identities were ignored, or actively attacked.

There are some minority communities that have successfully resolved the problem. They have done so by creating and maintaining a closed cultural system that maintains a more or less defensive relationship toward the rest of the society. The Old Order Amish and the Hutterites are good examples of this solution. Both are nonaggressive pacifistic peoples, communal in orientation, and socioreligious in ideology and charter.

Amish communities are distributed principally throughout Pennsylvania, Ohio, and Indiana but are also found in several other states. The total Old Order Amish population is estimated at about 60,000. They are agrarian, use horsepower for agricultural work and transportation, and wear rather somber but distinctive dress. They strive to cultivate humility and simple living. Their basic values include the following: separation from the world; voluntary acceptance of high social obligations symbolized by adult baptism; the maintenance of a disciplined church-community; excommunication and shunning as a means of dealing with erring members and of keeping the church pure; and a life of harmony with the soil and nature—it is believed that nature is a garden and man was able to be a caretaker, not an exploiter. The goals of education are to instill the above values in every Amish child and maintain,

[4] Mopass Residential School is neither better nor worse than other residential schools for Native Americans because it is Episcopalian, and certainly not because it is Canadian. Most of the same conditions exist in residential schools in both the United States and Canada, in Protestant, Catholic, and non-denominational schools.

therefore, the Amish way of life. John Hostetler and Gertrude Huntington describe the concept of a true education from the Amish point of view.

> True education, according to the Amish, is "the cultivation of humility, simple living, and resignation to the will of God." For generations the group has centered its instruction in reading, writing, arithmetic, and the moral teachings of the Bible. They stress training for life participation (here and for eternity) and warn of the perils of "pagan" philosophy and the intellectual enterprises of "fallen man," as did their forefathers. Historically, the Anabaptist avoided all training associated with self-exaltation, pride of position, enjoyment of power, and the arts of war and violence. Memorization, recitation, and personal relationships between teacher and pupil were part of a system of education that was supremely social and communal (1971:9).

Realizing that state consolidation of schools constituted a severe threat to the continuity of their way of life and basic values, the Amish built the first specifically Amish School in 1925. By 1970 there were over three hundred such schools with an estimated enrollment of ten thousand pupils. When the population of the United States was predominantly rural and the major occupation was farming, the Amish people had no serious objections to public schooling. In the rural school of fifty years ago in most of the United States a curriculum much like that of the present Amish school was followed, the teacher was a part of the community, and the school was governed locally. Consolidation of schools in order to achieve higher educational standards shifted control away from the local area and the educational innovations that followed were unacceptable to the Amish. The Amish insist that their children attend schools near their homes so that they can participate in the life of the community and learn to become farmers. They also want qualified teachers committed to Amish values. Teachers who are merely qualified by state standards may be quite incapable of teaching the Amish way of life or providing an example of this way of life by the way they themselves live. The Amish also want to have their children educated in the basic skills of reading, writing, and arithmetic but training beyond that, they feel, should be related directly to the Amish religion and way of life. They do not agree with what they perceive to be the goals of the public schools, ". . . to impart worldly knowledge, to insure earthly success, and to make good citizens for the state." Ideally, from the Amish point of view, formal schooling should stop at about age fourteen, though learning continues throughout life. They feel that further schooling is not only unnecessary but detrimental to the successful performance of adult Amish work roles. The Amish pay for and manage their own schools in order to attain these goals (Hostetler and Huntington 1971:35–38).

Naturally there have been serious conflicts with state authorities about the schools. Forcible removal of the children from Amish communities has been attempted in some cases, and harassment in legal and interpersonal forms has characterized the relationship of state authority to the Amish in respect to the problem of education. The Amish have doggedly but nonviolently resisted all attempts to make them give up their own schools, for they realize that these schools are essential to the continuance of their cultural system. They have made accommodations where they could, as for instance in providing "vocational" schooling beyond elementary school to meet state educational age requirements concerning duration of schooling.

The Amish story is one that anyone interested in the processes and consequences of separatism should know about. Hostetler and Huntington's study is a good up-to-date overview that presents the case for the community-relevant school clearly and objectively and with a sympathetic understanding of the Amish point of view and lifeway.

The Hutterite culture is similar in many ways to that of the Old Order Amish, as seen from the outside, although the Hutterites are more communal in their economic organization and they used advanced agricultural machinery as well as trucks and occasionally cars. Hutterites are Anabaptists, like the Amish and the Mennonites, originating during the Protestant Reformation in the sixteenth century in the Austrian Tyrol and Moravia. They arrived in South Dakota in 1874 and have prospered since. There are about 18,000 Hutterites living on more than 170 colonies in the western United States and Canada. They are noted for their successful large-scale farming, large families, and effective training of the young.

Hutterites are protected from the outside world by an organized belief system which offers a solution to their every need, although they, like the Amish, have been subjected to persecution and harassment from the outside. The community minimizes aggression and dissension of any kind. Colony members strive to lose their self-identity by surrendering themselves to the communal will and attempt to live each day in preparation for death, and, hopefully, heaven. The principle of order is the key concept underlying Hutterite life. Order is synonymous with eternity and godliness; even the orientation of colony buildings conforms to directions measured with the precision of a compass. There is a proper order for every activity, and time is neatly divided into the sacred and the secular. In the divine hierarchy of the community each individual member has a place—male over female, husband over wife, older over younger, and parent over child. The outsider asks, "Why does this order work? How can it be maintained?" The implicit Hutterite answer is that "Hutterite society is a school, and the school is a society." The Hutterites, like the Old Amish, do not value education as a means toward self-improvement but as a means of "planting" in children "the knowledge and fear of God" (Hostetler and Huntington 1967).

We will not go into detail concerning Hutterite schools. Although they differ somewhat from the Amish schools in curriculum and style, particularly in being more strict and "authoritarian," the basic principles are the same. The Hutterites also understand that they must retain control of their schools and teachers if they are to retain their separatistic and particularly their communal and socioreligious way of life. They do this by retaining a "German school" that is in effect superimposed upon the "English school" required by the state or provincial law. The two schools have rather different curricula and teachers and of the two the former is clearly the one that carries the burden of cultural transmission that recruits youngsters into the Hutterite cultural system and helps maintain that system most directly.

The Hutterites serve as another example of how to solve the problem faced by the Sisala, the people of Malitbog, the Kanuri, the children of Harlem School and their parents, the people of Rosepoint, and the children in the Mopass Residential School.

The problem all of these people face is how to relate a culture-transmitting institution that is attempting to recruit their children to a cultural system different from that of the community, class, area, or minority from which the children come. The school and teacher are alien in all of these cases, and they are charged, by governments or the dominant population, with the responsibility of changing the way of life by changing the children. Understandably the consequences are at least disruptive, and at worst tragic.

The Hutterities and Amish have done exactly what is logical according to the anthropologist viewing the relationship between education and culture. Realizing the threat to the continuity of their way of life from the outside world, particularly from schooling and transmission of concepts and views alien to their fundamental principles, they have taken control of their schools to whatever extent they can, given the exigencies of survival in contemporary North America. The schools are so ordered as to recruit and help maintain the traditional cultural system. They are successful. The way of life, beleaguered though it is in both cases, survives, in fact, flourishes.

It is important to understand, however, that, from another point of view, the cost of this success is too great. The result of success is a closed cultural system in a defensive relationship to the rest of society. That there are restrictions on personal behavior, sharp limits on self-expression, and confinement in the very thought processes and world view in both cases, is undeniable. The values of spontaneity, individual creativity, discovery and invention, pursuit of knowledge, and innovation, that are important to men elsewhere, are not values in these or any other closed cultural systems. There is also a kind of self-created disadvantage imposed by the Hutterites and Amish upon themselves. Since they lack higher education, in fact are opposed to it, and control as vigorously as possible the context of primary education, they cannot participate fully in the give and take of our dynamic society. True, they do not want to, but it is a hard choice, and one that could be very disadvantageous to any minority group. Somehow the modernizing peoples of the world emerging from a tribal and then colonial past, and the minority peoples in vast societies like the United States and Canada, must balance the consequences of a closed system and the educational institutions to support it, and an open system and the educational institutions to support it. It is clear, however, that it is necessary for all peoples to exercise and develop the rights of self-determination and self-regulation in education, as well as in other areas of life. It may be that this can be done without creating closed, defensive, and confining cultural systems. It may help for us all to realize that we actually have little control over what happens in our schools, no matter who we are. The educational bureaucracy in a complex urban system functions in some ways like an alien cultural system in relation to the local community, the children in school, and their parents, whether these parents and children are members of minority or majority groups. We all have this problem in common. In this age of cultural pluralism in the United States it is difficult to discern what else we all have in common. Perhaps it is possible to agree that there are some competencies all children should acquire, such as functional literacy, concepts of mathematical processes, and so forth, that are necessary if they are not to be severely handicapped in later life in a complex society. But in the area of specific values, ideologies, and world views we cannot repeat the mistakes of the past, when we assumed that the melting pot would melt all ethnic differences down to the same blendable elements. The cultures of the American Indians, Afro-Americans, Mexican Americans, and Asian-Americans did not disappear as our ideology said they would. The challenge is to recognize and accept the differences without creating disadvantageous separatism or segregation, whether self-imposed or imposed from the dominant group. There are many paradoxes in the relationships we are discussing, and they are not easily resolved.

References

Grindal, Bruce T., 1972, *Growing Up in Two Worlds: Education and Transition among the Sisala of Northern Ghana.* CSEC. New York: Holt, Rinehart and Winston, Inc.

Hostetler, John A., and Gertrude E. Huntington, 1967, *The Hutterites in North America.* CSCA. New York: Holt, Rinehart and Winston, Inc.

Hostetler, John A., and Gertrude E. Huntington, 1971, *Children in Amish Society: Socialization and Community Education.* CSEC. New York: Holt, Rinehart and Winston, Inc.

King, A. Richard, 1967, *The School at Mopass: A Problem of Identity.* CSEC. New York: Holt, Rinehart and Winston, Inc.

Rosenfeld, Gerry, 1971, *"Shut Those Thick Lips!" A Study of Slum School Failure.* CSEC. New York: Holt, Rinehart and Winston, Inc.

Ward, Martha C., 1971, *Them Children: A Study in Language Learning.* CSEC. New York: Holt, Rinehart and Winston, Inc.

R. P. McDERMOTT/*Stanford University*

5 *Achieving School Failure: An Anthropological Approach to Illiteracy and Social Stratification*

Abstract

The mixture of intelligent, socially competent children from a low status minority or pariah community and hard working, well-intentioned teachers from a host or dominant community can bring about the same disastrous school records achieved by either neurologically disabled children or socially disabled, prejudiced teachers. Students and teachers in a pariah-host population mix usually produce communicative breakdowns by simply performing routine and practical everyday activities in ways their subcultures define as normal and appropriate. Because behavioral competence is differently defined by different social groups, many children and teachers fail in their attempts to establish rational, trusting and rewarding relationships across ethnic, racial or class boundaries in the classroom. As a result of this miscommunication, school learning is shunned by many minority children, and school failure becomes a peer group goal. The high rate of reading disabilities among minority children can be explained in terms of such miscommunication. The difficulty is usually neither "dumb kids" nor "racist teachers," but cultural conflict.

Introduction

This chapter is divided into four sections. The first defines a problem and asks a question. The problem is that children from minority communities appear to regenerate their parents' pariah status by learning how to act in

---

Comments on an earlier draft of this chapter were generously offered by Eric Arrow, Jacob Bilmes, Nancie Gonzalez, Robert McDermott, Harry Singer, and Stanley Wanat. I am most heavily indebted to Henry Beck, Harumi Befu, Charles Frake, Karl Pribram, and George Spindler for constant stimulation, encouragement and constructive criticism during the past two years. Even with their excellent counsel, however, the paper may harbor errors for which I am alone responsible.

ways condemned by the larger host community. The question asks where this learning comes from and whether or not it represents a rational adaptation to socialization attempts by host schools.

The second section examines the production of pariah-host social organizations in terms of what both pariah and host members must know about the daily business of treating each other as pariahs and hosts. Early experiences in the politics of everyday life determine the categories children develop for use in deciding how to act in similar situations at future times. In other words, the politics of everyday life socialize the identities, statuses and abilities of children and, as such, are the source of the persistence of social organizations, including pariah groups, across generations.

The third section discusses an example. Specifically, the social organization of learning to read in a host teacher and pariah student classroom is examined in terms of the politics of everyday life. For black American children in white-administered schools, it is argued that competence in reading and competence in classroom politics are inversely proportional. Inability to read is positively condemned by the host population and assures oppression and the assignment of pariah status by the host community. Nevertheless, not learning to read is accompanied by all the social skills essential to a peer-defined political success within the classroom. In peer group terms, it represents more of an achievement than a disability. Accordingly, the hypothesis examined is that a significant number of what are usually described as reading disabilities represent situationally induced inattention patterns which make sense in terms of the politics of the interethnic classroom. Pariah children learn not to read as one way of acquiring high status and strong identity in a host classroom.

The fourth section describes a starting point for culturally induced learning disabilities in terms of cultural or communicative code differences and conflicts. Specifically, it is hypothesized that minor differences in communicative codes can lead to disasters in everyday life. On the basis of communicative code conflicts, teachers classify their students into ability groups. Although in no way related in the first grade to potential reading or social leadership skills, the teacher's classificatory schema has great influence as a self-fulfilling prophecy. Many pariah children adapt to the senseless and degrading relational messages given them by unknowing teachers with different communicative codes by shutting down their attention skills in response to teacher tasks such as reading. Communicative code conflicts between black children and white teachers are discussed in detail, and the high rate of black school failure is tentatively explained.

The Ontogeny of Pariah Minorities

Most modern nations harbor one or more *pariah groups* "actively rejected by the host population because of behavior or characteristics positively condemned" by host group standards (Barth 1969:31). Host standards can be violated by an absurd collection of traits ranging from skin color and occupational specialties to culinary and sexual preferences. What is interesting is the persistence of both host group standards and pariah groups across generations. Even in the face of efforts by modern states to subdue the arbitrary and oppressive standards of host groups and to accommodate minority behavior patterns by programs of rationalization and equalization, pariah groups endure. For example, America has blacks, Native Americans, and Hispanic people; Japan has the Koreans (Mitchell 1967) and the racially indistinct Burakamin (DeVos and Wagatsuma 1966); Norway, the Lapps (Eidheim 1969); Northern Ireland, the Catholics; India, the outcasts; and Israel, the Oriental Jews. In all these groups, each generation of children will renew their parents' life styles, apparently oblivious to the condemnation and oppression that pariah status vis-à-vis the host group will bring down upon their heads.

How does this happen? How is pariah status acquired by each new generation? Despite years of special education, minority American children continue to speak low esteem dialects, fail in school, and attain occupational specialties which run afoul of public morality and legality. Apparently, the acquisition of pariah behavior patterns is a very complex process rooted in everyday life and is not going to be altered by formal training in a classroom for a few hours a week. Indeed, most pariah behavior patterns need not be altered. Black language, for example, bears a pariah label, but it is a perfectly efficient mode of communication with special social functions within the black community (Labov 1969). To treat it as an inferior or deprived language is wrong. To meddle with its use by way of a language arts program in order to homogenize it with the host language is not only wrong, but also naive. It indicates that we understand very little about how people acquire models of and guides to behavior in their own society and how these models are used to generate social structures complete with stratification. This chapter will attempt a better understanding of the acquisition of social structure (Cicourel 1970a)—how children acquire what has to be known in order to act in a culturally or subculturally appropriate way in specific social situations (Frake 1962, 1973).

Two positions are usually taken on the acquisition of pariah social status. To the distant observer and the pariah group member, it seems an obvious case of host populations working to defeat the efforts of each and every pariah child to break the degradation that bonds him without reason from his first day out of the womb. The child is simply tagged as he enters the world in such a way that the tag is available for all to see. Negative differential behavior is then applied to all the tagged regardless of acquired skills. Racial markers can, of course, do this job most efficiently: witness black America. Similar systems have been attempted without racial markers. Tattooing is one possibility. The Japanese of the Tokugawa era attempted another by having all members of the pariah Burakumin wear leather squares on the outside of all their garments (Cornell 1970). The point is that pariah children are made visible to all, defined as deviant because of their visibility, and treated badly as a result.

There is good reason for viewing the ascriptive system just described as too simple a representation of the acquisition of a particular status in a social structure. First, such clear-cut boundaries between host and pariah groups are seldom defined. Racial boundaries are not available in most societies in which there are pariah group problems. In fact, most observers must live in an area for a long time before they can start distinguishing between groups. The codes are subtle. Religion, language, dress and the minutiae of nonverbal communication very often function as markers for ascription. Even where biological boundaries can be drawn, as may be the case for outcastes in India, it takes either a native's eye or an anthropometrist's calipers to do the job (Beteille 1972). In such cases, identification involves much social work on the part of the interactants. The host population must be keyed to spotting certain cues, and the pariah population must in some way send off the cues which will allow them to be identified and abused.

A second problem with viewing status ascription as a simple tagging process is that in most contemporary societies such overt ascription is frowned upon by both legal constitutions and popular ideologies. Formal organizations which operate according to ascriptive criteria are officially prohibited. Japan and America stand out as two countries which have done a great deal to minimize overt ascription with universal schooling and uniform testing procedures for the placement of personnel in both the public and private sectors of their economies (Azumi 1969; Parsons 1959). Yet pariah boundaries remain firm, even within the school systems themselves (Shimahara 1971; Cicourel and Kitsuse 1963). Again it appears that something more than ascription is going on. How else could it be that, even after the demise of formal institutional powers to identify and operate against pariah people, pariah groups survive? The host population does not simply slot a child on the basis of its parentage and then keep a careful eye out for the child so that he never advances a slot. Rather, it seems as if the child must learn how to do it himself; he must learn a way of acting normally which the host population will be able to condemn according to the criteria the hosts have learned for evaluating, albeit arbitrarily, their own normal behavior. Pariah status appears almost as achieved as ascribed.

An alternative to the distant observer's view of the acquisition of pariah social status is the view of a host population native who usually sees in pariahs an obvious case of inferior persons begetting inferior persons. The argument is that pariah children acquire their low status because they are inferior. Unfortunately, each new pariah generation often reaffirms the soundness of the host's classificatory schema by apparently learning the codes of behavior essential to the schema's maintenance. Although there is no evidence that host classifications are accurate assessments of the natural order of people and their abilities, the host perception of pariah group behavior may not always be totally blinded by prejudice. Hosts may merely see what is there for them to see given the standards of evaluation that they use uniformly on all people regardless of race or ethnic identity. The question is, how is it that what is there for them to see is in fact there?

Consider an extreme example. The Burakumin minority in Japan has suffered a long history of political suppression due to its participation in condemned occupational specialties (Ninomiya 1933). Since the formal breakdown of the caste system during the Mejii Restoration a century ago, many Burakumin have attempted unsuccessfully to pass into the mainstream of Japanese life. At present, they are physically, linguistically, religiously, and, for the most part, occupationally indistinct from other Japanese. They can be discovered only on the basis of either their present or past residence in known Burakumin ghettos. Accordingly, most Japanese teachers are unaware of a child's Burakumin status in the early grades (Shimahara 1971). Yet, by puberty, a Burakumin identity will be visible and of increasing importance, as there is an increasing differential in the performances of Burakumin as opposed to non-Burakumin pupils. They lag behind on I.Q. and achievement tests and daily attendance, and they are the first to engage in delinquent activities (DeVos and Wagatsuma 1966; Brameld 1968). How does host group prejudice work against an invisible group? Obviously, it does not. It may be that unconscious host group standards work against Burakumin children in some subtle ways, however, for the children are eventually made visible, sorted out and condemned. But this is not obvious to a liberal and enlightened Japanese teacher, who, through no apparent fault of his own, winds up doing exactly the same job that a prejudiced teacher might do: he winds up failing many more Burakumin than non-Burakumin. The host-group stand appears strong. The teacher has only reacted to what was available for him to see, namely, obviously inferior performances by many Burakumin children. Again, pariah status seems almost as achieved as ascribed.

This Burakumin example sheds great light on this ascription versus inherent acquisition issue. The Burakumin child experiences teachers as prejudiced beings who inflict failing biographies on Burakumin children. The children are perhaps correct given the subtleties of interclass or interethnic communication. They are incorrect in viewing their school records as products of a blind ascription, for their invisibility protects them from such a fate. Host teachers have equally confusing experiences with school failure. They are correct in not assuming complete blame for the high rate of Burakumin school failure. Nevertheless, they are incorrect in viewing school failure as the result of an inherent acquisition, the unfolding of an inferior genetic stock or, at best, the unfolding of an inferior socialization process that leaves the child deprived. First, the Burakumin do not represent a gene pool (Taira 1971). Second, the social disadvantage perspective is almost as simplistic as the ascription stand, for it has never been able to account for how children with failing school records do so well in complex settings outside of school. Learning to talk and learning to behave sensibly in everyday life are far more complex than the tasks learned in school, and most so-called disadvantaged children excel at both, at least to the extent that such children have been carefully studied. Disadvantage is indeed a too simple, and often biased, account of minority school failure. Burakumin children do not come to school disadvantaged; they leave school disadvantaged. The question is, without some ascriptive mechanism working against them, how does this school failure and consequent disadvantage come about? In other words, if neither ascription nor inherent acquisition can completely account for pariah school failure, then how can the acquisition of pariah status be conceived?

A third position is possible. From their respective vantage points, both the pariah and the host groups are correct. To the pariah group, host behavior is indeed oppressive. To the host group, pariah behavior is indeed inadequate. If we understand how the two groups find this out about each other, we will have located the central problem. What is it that pariah people do that has host people react in oppressive ways, even if they do not want to be oppressive? And what is it that host people do that has pariah people react in antithesis to host expectations, even as they struggle to behave adequately according to host standards? If such misunderstandings take place very often in the early grades, the results can be disastrous. Once a host teacher treats a child as inadequate, the child will find the teacher oppressive. Often, once a child finds a teacher oppressive, the child will start behaving inadequately. After such a point, relations between the child and the teacher regress—the objectionable behavior of each will feed back negatively into the objectionable behavior of the other.

It is in this context that a third position makes sense: a child must achieve his pariah status. It is neither ascribed to the child nor naturally acquired by him in the sense that puberty is acquired. First, some form of miscommunication between a child and his teacher must take place. If this is not repaired quickly, a mutually destructive or regressive one-to-one relationship (Scheflen 1960) will be established between the teacher and the child. When teacher-student communication is complicated by interethnic code differences, regressive relations occur with enough frequency to result in the children forming alternatives to the teacher's organization of the classroom. Within the confines of these new social organizations, the children work at becoming visible. As a result, they leave themselves open to even further condemnation. The teacher's role as the administrator in charge of failure becomes dominant. And the children's revolt grows. School work gets caught in this battle, and a high rate of school failure results. A great deal of social work must be performed by both teachers and students in order for so many failures to occur. Whether the records list all passing or all failing grades, student records represent achievements in the sense that many difficult battles in the politics of everyday life had to be fought in their making. Teachers do not simply ascribe minority children to failure. Nor do minority children simply drag failure along, either genetically or socially, from the previous generation. Rather, it must be worked out in every classroom, every day, by every teacher and every child in their own peculiar ways.

Viewing school failure as an achievement implies that school failure can be understood as a rational adaptation by children to human relations in host schools. The rest of this chapter will be aimed at showing just that. The next section will consider, theoretically, how human relations are worked out face-to-face in the classroom. These relations have fantastic implications for the social organization of the classroom—who gets to interact with whom, when, and about what and who gets to learn from whom, when, and about what. In short, face-to-face relations help to organize status and abilities in the classroom. In the last two sections, the interference of interethnic human relations on learning to read is examined for black Americans.

The Social Organization of Status and the Politics of Everyday Life

It is considered a social fact (although actually it is either a native or a professional sociological model, but it is always treated as a fact) that there are different groups in the social organizations of modern states, and some of these are defined as pariah groups. It is this social fact that most social scientists want to explain. Beneath this fact, however, there are many other facts made of the little stuff of everyday life that helps produce larger social facts or patterns available for observation. A social organization is not a thing in itself as Durkheim would have us believe. Rather, it is an accomplishment, the product of great work in the everyday life of innumerable social actors. The term "social organization" is a shorthand term for the organization of social actions performed by social actors (Garfinkel 1956:181; cf. also, Miller, Galanter, and Pribram, 1960:98). The term social organization glosses all the hard work of social actors attempting to deal with each other. It hides all the achievements of everyday life. Social organizations are daily accomplishments, daily products of actors working out rational ways of dealing with each other.

If a social organization shows a division into pariah and host groups, then this is a division produced in everyday life; in their daily dealings, pariah and host people must classify each other into different groups and then treat each other in accordance with the dictates of their classification. Such a division cannot be taken by itself as a topic of our inquiry, for it is a mere gloss of the social acts that make it look like a fact. We must go deeper and ask how this fact is available for seeing and naming by either host or pariah members or the ethnographer. Let us examine, then, not the fact of such pariah-host relationships, the resource, but the fact of that fact, the topic; let us ask how it is that the persons involved in such relationships manage to organize and produce such relationships and to take them as the substance of everyday life (Beck 1972); let us "examine not the factual properties of status hierarchies, but the *fact* of the factual properties of status hierarchies" (Zimmerman and Pollner 1970:83). How is it then that host and pariah people, and the sociologists who study them, come to see their existence as related groups as facts?

The question we started with was how do the children of each generation acquire pariah status. This question has shifted somewhat in our discussion, and we must now ask how children learn to uniformly produce pariah-host statuses in their interactions with each other and their teachers. The designated statuses are not simple, cut and dried slots into which members of different groups are easily placed. *Statuses* do not specify everything that occurs in an interaction; rather they are the labels "used by the observer and actor as practical language games for simplifying the task of summarizing a visual field and complex stimuli that are difficult to describe in some precise, detailed way" (Cicourel 1970b:21). Status labels never reduce the complex stimulus fields so much that social life becomes easy. There is always interaction work to be done; social life is always in process.

One's place in a society is not easily acquired. Even if it is the lowest place on the stratification ladder, it is not simply worn as a piece of clothing. A selective way of seeing oneself in the position and of seeing others in relation to oneself must be developed. As Becker has written, an actor acquires a "symbolic mansion" established and maintained in interaction with other human beings; the symbols develop early in ontogeny and prescribe for the actor what situations he should attend, "what he should do in a particular social situation, and how he should feel about himself as he does it" (Becker 1962:84). Statuses, therefore, must be learned. Depending on how they are learned, a child develops specific identities and abilities for use in specific situations. First they are learned in the home in everyday interaction with family members. Many of these first statuses, identities, and abilities undergo considerable alterations in school on the basis of everyday interaction with class members and especially the teacher. School-specific social and intellectual skills must therefore be understood in terms of the politics of everyday life in the classroom. If the skills developed at home are relevant to what happens in the classroom, or if new skills must be developed, they will be visible, and they will make sense in terms of the politics of the classroom.

The *politics of everyday life* are built on messages of relationship passed between two or more social actors. According to Bateson's classic distinction, communication involves not only the transfer of information, but also the imposition of a relationship (Bateson 1972). A communicative act not only has a content which it reports, it also has command aspects which stipulate the relationship between the communicants. An army sergeant sends out messages of relationship with his uniform and an annoyed wife with her hands on her hips. These relational messages form the context for the transfer of information by classifying its intent (Watzlawick, Beaven, and Jackson 1967: 54). Such a context is read by the interpreter of a communicative act before the content of a message is attended. Thus, with open arms one sets a context which can be interpreted as specifying a love relationship, and everything said after that point will be measured for its value in this context; open arms with a gun in each hand asserts a different context and the information transferred, assuming one does not flee in fear of being shot, is understood differently. In both contexts the host may inform his guest that he has been anxiously awaiting his arrival, but the information transferred would be quite different depending upon the message of relationship sent off before any words were spoken.

Children are extremely well equipped by school age for entrance into the politics of everyday life. Messages of relationship are handled competently by neonates (Caudill and Weinstein 1969) and constitute the only form of communication allowed the child in its early years (Blurton-Jones 1972). Love, hate, support, antagonism, trust and deference are some of the relational messages transferred in daily life. Indeed, apparently few concerted practical activities are possible without the communication of such messages; even a slight eruption in their flow can cause a social breakdown (Garfinkel 1963). Children are especially expert in handling these messages as they have not yet developed competence in the verbal arts of saying what is not meant and interpreting what is not intended. Relational messages are more rooted in nonverbal channels which allow for more leakage and clues to deception than verbal channels (Ekman and Friesan 1969), and children decipher these without hindrance from message content.

At school age, the point at which children start acquiring their institutional biographies, relational messages continue in their dominance over information transfer. This is a decisive and delicate time in a child's life. School success, an essential ingredient in any child's avoidance of pariah status, is dependent upon high levels of information transfer. In these early stages of school, depending upon how the politics of everyday life are handled, the child defines his relations with his classmates and his teachers. These relations, remember, define the context of whatever information is to be transferred by a communicant. If the wrong messages of relationship are communicated, reading, writing, and arithmetic may take on very different meanings than they do for the child who is more successful in getting good feelings from the politics of the classroom. The wrong messages of relationship can result in learning disabilities. More will be said on this issue later. At present it is only essential to realize that children deal seriously in relationships, are profoundly affected by their abilities to do relational work, and acquire a social status and attendant skills on the basis of their successes and failures.

Let us try to describe the setting in which relational work is performed. Its general properties are really well known. Goffman (1963) has described the "primal sociological event" as one in which a person with an obvious stigma, no nose, for example, encounters a person without a stigma; in such a case, a tremendous amount of work must go into unspoken arrangements about how the two are to look at each other, at the nose, around the nose, or at the ground. Looking in this situation carries powerful relational messages. One has the power to induce confusion, embarrassment, anger, fright, trust, or love. The eyes will tell the stigmatized whether he has met a person with a similar stigma, with an acquaintance and understanding of the stigma, or with a fear or hate of the stigma. Goffman's point is that we all suffer from stigma of sorts. Every interaction is marked by some hiding and some probing. How much must be hidden, how much probing can go on, or indeed, whether hiding and probing are necessary at all, is dependent upon the messages of relationship exchanged. A policeman's uniform usually invokes hiding on ego's part and allows for probing on the policeman's part. Sexually suggestive clothing does the opposite. In the first case, ego shuts down, and in the second, an opening up is usually called forth. Situations in which these same cues invoke the opposite reactions can be imagined. The effort is to make as much sense as possible of the person's actions, to infer his intentions, and to then react sensibly given the intentions of both interactants (Schutz 1953).

The cues available in any situation are endless. People can send messages with their ecological setting, e.g., whether they are in a bar or a church (Barker 1968; J. McDermott 1969; Sommer 1969); with their posture (Scheflen 1964); with their spacing vis-à-vis their interpreter (Hall 1966); with their odor (Largey and Watson 1972); with their gaze (Kendon 1967); with their tone of voice (Crystal 1972; Laver 1968); with their sequencing of body and voice rhythms (Condon and Ogston 1966, 1971; Byers 1971; Kendon 1970, 1973); and so on. Everything available to the senses of the actors constitutes a possible contribution to the sense and rationality of an interaction.

More than the success of the interaction rides on how sensibly it can be made. Something important happens to the way in which the stigmatized person is going to interpret his next interaction; if one is treated to understanding and sympathy on one occasion, the next occasion will be attended and scanned for messages in a very different way than if the original interaction resulted in a fight. The selective perception skills that are carried from one situation to another of similar type, following Cicourel (1970b), are called status. In addition to his status, the stigmatized individual's feelings can undergo alteration. In talking about formative experiences during puberty, Erikson has noted that "it is of great relevance to the young individual's identity formation that he be responded to and be given function and status as a person whose gradual transformation makes sense to those who begin to make sense to him" (1968:156). Both status and identity are developed in daily interactions. A great deal is at stake in each and every one of them, for status and identity breakdowns are also developed in daily interactions.

An example of the social organization of status and identity in a classroom may be helpful here. Teachers often break their classes into ability groups in order to simplify their administration of the classroom. Not only the level of work engaged in, but also the people interacted with and the kind of feedback received from the teachers all depend upon the group to which the child is assigned. In this way, the teacher organizes the statuses and identities of the children in the class. What is most interesting is that the children seldom reject their assignment—even if they are assigned the lowest status in the classroom achievement hierarchy, they most often accept it as if it makes sense. If the child does not take his assignment, he may buckle down and work harder to catch the rest of the class. But revolt is seldom attempted. The reason is that the teacher generally assigns children to groups according to the same criteria that the children themselves use in their dealings with each other, and the same criteria that the children's parents and the rest of their community use in their dealings with the children. In short, the teacher handles the children in a way the children are used to being handled. Politically, the teacher, the children and the child's community are in harmony. Even if being placed in a low ability group is not good for the child's ego, the results of grouping, if it makes sense, will not be disastrous. The politics of everyday life in the classroom will be identical to the politics of everyday life outside the classroom, and the children's world will be in order.

The social organization of status and identity sometimes does not go so smoothly. Consider the case of an intense, bright child who arrives in school unable to keep up in reading because of some developmental lag specific to processing printed information. When this child is assigned to the lowest ability group, it makes no sense to him. He is treated as a gifted learner and a sociometric star outside the classroom; anything less than equivalent treatment in the classroom will be inadequate to the child's way of evaluating his place in the world. Of course, he revolts and "a negative motivational cycle" begins to take shape (Singer and Beardsley 1970). Later, the possibilities of a host group teacher successfully grouping minority children into the same ability groups that the minority community might itself perceive will be considered. From the high rate of revolt and "negative motivational cycles" in minority classrooms, the possibilities seem slim. The point here is that the politics of everyday life socially organize a classroom. Ability groupings help a teacher to isolate into accessible units children who are to receive fairly similar messages of relationship from the teacher. If the wrong children are assigned to the low ability groups, they will reject the messages of relationship forwarded from the teacher. They will demand a political reorganization of the classroom, one that is more commensurate with their statuses and identities outside the classroom. In the early weeks of a school year, the politics of the classroom feed the teacher's perception, and the classroom is organized accordingly. Then the children reorganize the class according to their own perceptions. If the teacher is insensitive to their demands, the remainder of the year can be occupied in small battles over each child's status and identity within the classroom. Whether or not anything is ever accomplished in the classroom depends upon how quickly these battles can be resolved. Thus, the development of abilities and disabilities also depends upon the politics of daily classroom life.

The specific division of abilities and disabilities among any pariah and host groups should be understood in terms of the politics of everyday life. It is in the very small political arenas constituted by dyads and only slightly larger groups that social organizations are produced. If we want to understand a large scale organizational division within a social organization, we must start asking how this division is produced. Pariah and host group members acquire different skills and produce the different behavior that makes for the organizational division between pariah and host groups. The division looks so real that we professional social scientists study it, and lay social scientists, or natives, perceive and use it as a model for their dealings with each other. In fact, the division is dependent for its existence on the daily differential use of abilities and disabilities by host and pariah group members. The employment of these abilities and disabilities depends upon man's delightful capacity to attend to, think about, and manipulate only certain selected aspects of his environment. Just what parts of an environment are attended and mastered depends upon the social meaning of the environment as recorded in the experiences of the developing child. For example, reading materials can or cannot be attended depending upon whether looking in a book is an acceptable activity in a particular social milieu and whether books contain information helpful to operating in a particular social environment. The social organization of reading materials will now be considered in more detail.

A Biobehavioral Ethnography of Reading Disabilities

Black children in America have a high rate of learning disabilities. Rates of functional black illiteracy are estimated around 50 percent (Thompson 1966) as compared to 10 percent for white Americans and only 1 percent for Japan (Makita 1968). The high rates of these disabilities do not point to a high rate of genetic inferiority, neurological damage, language deprivation, or any of the other intrapsychic causes suggested in social and behavioral science literature. Rather, the high rates of learning disorders point to learned patterns of selective inattention developed in the politics of everyday life in the classroom. Status and identity work is a dismal failure in early elementary school for many black children with white teachers and, as a result, they turn off, in the sense that they physiologically shut down. As a yoga or Zen master (Kasamatsu and Hirai 1966) may do for an entire environment, black children disattend reading materials and join their peers in the student subculture within the class. Reading disabilities and school failure result.

School failure is an important place to start an inquiry into the acquisition of pariah status, and social science literature on pariah group persistence across generations has often centered on school failure and its causes. Most of the work has centered on the children, independent of the schools they attend, as if there was something naturally wrong with their brains. To paraphrase crudely, the cause of pariah groups is that pariah children do not seem to think too well. This deprivation theme should be fairly offensive to social science; after all, has not a century of anthropology shown that to understand people is to discern difference and not deprivation? Yet the anthropological argument is difficult. Pariah children fail, and fail miserably. How can we claim that they are neither damaged nor deprived? One answer is that we have been measuring achievements with a biased set of standards. Achievements are realized only in particular situations. Rather than attempting to measure the development of absolute capacities that a child uses for all situations through time, perhaps we should center on the situations in which and for which particular skills are acquired. In other words, if we examine the classroom as a set of situations or an "occasion corpus" (Zimmerman and Pollner 1970), a child's failing performance on classroom tests might appear to be something of a situational achievement. Deprivation hypotheses are considerably weakened, if, instead of just looking at the skills stored in children's bodies, we look also at the social contexts in which the skills are turned into achievements.

Medicine, education, and psychology have all produced deprivation hypotheses for social scientists to adopt. Of late, pariah children have been described as genetically inferior (Jensen 1969). Another claim has it that an unspecified number suffer brain damage due to the poverty and ignorance that burdened their mothers in pregnancy and birth (Birch and Gussow 1970). Social science itself has had a hand in claiming that pariah children suffer perceptual handicaps (C. Deutsch 1968; Jensen 1966) and conceptual and linguistic handicaps (M. Deutsch 1963; Bernstein 1964; Entwisle 1971) due to low social class and its associated life-style. All these disciplines assume to discover facts out of context, raw facts about the world and the behavior of its inhabitants. Of course there are no such things. All behavior is context-bound. More important, all behavior is indexical or dependent upon our interpretation of the context in which the behavior is situated (Bar-Hillel 1954; Beck 1972; Cicourel, in press). Yet all assume that facts are available for all to see, and that these facts are invariable. In the case of learning disabilities, each discipline has assumed that whatever is located in the heads of the children studied is invariable. Whether a discipline uses a perceptual, cognitive, or language test, a projective technique or a sociometric status score, each has assumed that it describes the skills the individual has acquired for all occasions and tasks. This is, of course, incorrect. Each of these disciplines assumes too much.

My proposal is that each of these disciplines is describing the same social processes and merely indexing them differently. Scores on perceptual, intelligence, attitude, language competence, and even neurological tests are all remnants of the normal and practical work of persons in a particular situation. Ways of perceiving, thinking, feeling, talking, and the activities of the neural wetware processing our perceiving, thinking, feeling, and talking are all dependent upon the situations in which the person is placed. Testing offers a particular situation which may record little more than the way the subject defines the testing situation in response to the way in which the subject understands the tester's definition of the situation. In short, test scores always have discernible roots in the social world in which they take place (Cicourel, in press). We cannot expect tests to necessarily reveal very much about intrapsychic events and the capabilities of any subject. But tests can, if they are properly read, tell a great deal about interpsychic, social procedures in which a subject is engaged. For example, Cazden (1970) has described black children who do badly on language complexity tests in formal situations, and very well in informal situations; the opposite holds true for white children. What we can learn from such tests has nothing to do with a child's capacity to talk; but there is a great deal of information about social organization stored in this little test. Social organizations are made by people knowing approximately what to do in particular situations; a social organization is a cognitive phenomenon. When we look to tests for information about social organization, about the thinking underlying the social acts to be performed during the test, then they are very revealing.

Reading tests can significantly reveal the dynamics of social organization. Pariah children do very badly at them, almost certainly for social reasons. Reading is an act which apparently aligns the black child with the "wrong" forces in the social universe. In the classroom social organization produced by the politics of everyday life, reading takes its place as part of the teacher's "ecology of games" (Long 1958). To read is to accept these games and all the statuses and identities that accompany them. Not to read is to accept peer group games and their accompanying statuses and identities. In other words, given a particular social organization, reading failure is a social achievement. Conventional testing procedures could never reveal this trend. The battle grounds on which it is determined whether a child learns to read or not are drawn by the statuses and identities made available by the teacher and the peer group, in short, by social relations. If the teacher and the children can play the same games, then reading and all other school materials will be easily absorbed.

The success of educational settings directed by ethnic (Alitto 1969; Hostetler and Huntington 1971) and dialect (Fishman and Leuders-Salmon 1972) minorities for themselves illustrates this point nicely. If the children and the teacher generate their behavior from a shared set of interpretive procedures, efficient classroom learning can almost be assumed. This record contrasts, however, with educational settings designed and administered by outsiders to a community. Such settings often result in school failure. Centuries of failure in the white education of American Indians and blacks and Japanese failures in the education of Korean and Truk natives (Fischer 1961) illustrate this contrasting situation. If the classroom is divided into two separate worlds with teachers and students occupying different ecologies of games, school failure appears to be inevitable. The identities and statuses offered by a school system without roots in the community are apparently not worth seeking or are worth avoiding. For many children in such a situation, a social reorganization of the classroom becomes the main alternative to following the teacher's dictates.

An essential question at this point is how the politics of everyday life get inside a child's body and dictate what shall be perceived. This question can now easily be handled by recent advances in neuropsychology. Not all biology is reductionist, and there is good reason to attempt a view of social life by an examination of the biological foundations of behavior. Geertz alerted us to this possibility in his account of the dynamic, feedback relationship between biology and culture.

> As our central nervous system—and most particularly its crowning curse and glory, the neocortex—grew up in great part in interaction with culture, it is incapable of directing our behavior or organizing our experience without the guidance provided by systems of significant symbols . . . Such symbols are thus not mere expressions, instrumentalities, or correlates of our biological, psychological, and social existence; they are prerequisities of it. Without men, no culture, certainly; but equally, and more significantly, without culture, no men (1965:61).

Attention is the mechanism by which our bodies help us divide the world into significant and insignificant. As Wallace has suggested, man has created a rich and elaborate world for himself "by a process of selective attention to his total environment" (1965:277). Apparently, man suffers tremendous limitations in his ability to process all the information available to him at any one instant. Selection is a ubiquitous and unending process throughout our central nervous systems. Significance is stored not only in the social world, in the symbols out there, but in our equipment for decoding and interpreting the world. As Pribram has indicated, "societies are made up of persons whose brains shape the interactive matrix" (1969:37). What is organized in social organizations are individuals interpreting the world, human brains attending to some aspects of the social world and not to others.

A brief account of the psychophysiological concept of attention will hopefully suggest the importance of attention patterns for social scientists and detail for us how patterns of inattention can result in reading disabilities. The central nervous system has been increasingly conceived as a set of models depicting the world outside the body, in terms of which an organism attends, perceives, thinks, and acts (Sokolov 1969; Pribram 1971; MacKay 1972). Stimuli enter the body and if they are uninformative no attention will be paid to them. If the match is improper, the central nervous system will orient in search of new information which will either restore or redefine the model. In such a case, the organism is said to be "looking to see," and different parts of the brain will be activated in processing the new stimuli until harmony is again established (Pribram 1970). First a decision is made to look for a stimulus and only then is a second decision made as to whether or not the proper stimuli occur (Dewey 1896; N. Mackworth and Bagshaw 1970).

The human system is best discussed in terms of the feedback relations between pertinence, attention, and memory storage. Physiologists are not easily given to talking about pertinence centers in the brain, but they do talk about the efferent control of afferent stimuli on the basis of what central mechanisms deem to be the most pertinent information at any particular time. Central control of the models is called up from memory with plans. Furthermore, there is central control right down at the receptor sites as to what sort of information makes it to the brain for consideration and possible action (Pribram 1970, 1971; Rothblatt and Pribram 1972). The central nervous system is thus intimately involved in the organizational work that goes into the construction of significance in the world. The same symbols that are processed by our bodies are those processed in our social systems. Our bodies are the nodes in the communicative network that is society, and the work of these various nodes produces what has come to be seen as social organization. Statements of this proposition are unfortunately rare, but the trend is apparently changing (Bateson 1972; Beck 1971a,b). Nevertheless, we still have only a few anecdotes interrelating the organization of social events and the organization of neurological events. Pribram has given one delightful example:

> For many years there was an elevated railway line (the "el") on Third Avenue in New York that made a fearful racket: when it was torn down, people who had been living in apartments along the line awakened periodically out of a sound sleep to call the police about some strange occurrence they could not properly define. The calls were made at the times the trains had formerly rumbled past. The strange occurrences were, of course, the deafening silence that had replaced the expected noise (1971:50).

A model of the world for a particular time and place existed in the central nervous systems of many people up and down the Third Avenue El. When the environment did not supply the essential information, the people began orienting and paying attention. In this case, our ecology worked its way into our bodies and told us when to listen, namely at the time when the El had previously roared by; our social system then worked its way into our bodies and told us what to hear when we listened, perhaps a thief or another strange occurrence requiring police assistance. Society and ecology are merely two aspects of the environment with which we communicate. They send us messages about the adequacy of the internalized models of the time and space criteria in terms of which we perceive, think and act. We all live in a world of information which we decode according to the dictates of context. Much of this context is encoded in our memory and evidenced in our attention patterns.

There are many Third Avenue El trains in our lives. In every classroom in America, there is an organization of ecological and social happenings mediated by various neurologies with memory and attention biases wired into the wetware. To study one is to study the other, to study the brain is to study social organization, and vice versa. In this biobehavioral inquiry into reading disabilities, however, both systems are obviously involved. The epidemiological contours of reading disabilities run along ethnic and cultural lines and suggest that they are indeed socially organized. Yet unlike most behavior that we see as socially organized, reading skills or their diminution due to brain insult or socially induced inattention, obviously, rather than implicitly, involve neurological organization. Indeed, the picture we are developing of reading as a "psycholinguistic guessing game" (Goodman 1970; Wanat 1971) fits exactly the picture we have of the structure of the brain's activity in all behavior. In an excellent paper, J. Mackworth has laid the two side by side: reading involves

> a selective process that involves partial use of available language cues selected from the perceptual input on the basis of the reader's expectation, an interaction between thoughts and language. . .; the neuronal model anticipates the future probability and meaning of the next stimulus. A neuronal mechanism checks the meaning and nature of an incoming stimulus against the predictions of the neural model. Thus construction of a neural model is an active process, involving a two-way exchange of messages from environment and brain (1972:704, 708).

Both the environment and the brain are socially constructed. When a child is unable to read, part of the environment is not being processed by the brain. Because the epidemiology of reading disabilities follows a social organization, it is possible to claim that the organization of the proper neurological models for reading also follows a social organization. A brief look at the social organization of classrooms for black children in America will indicate how their brains appear disabled for reading. *In the politics of everyday life, black children in America learn how not to read; they learn how not to attend to printed information and as a result show high rates of reading disabilities.* The implications of this high rate of illiteracy for the acquisition of pariah status is obvious.

Almost a half a century ago, attention was a major focus of classroom research. Primarily this old research attempted to document whether or not children were paying attention to their teachers by noting their gaze direction during lessons. This is not a very efficient method of studying attention, for receptor orientation gives little information about just what a child is attending to during a boring lecture. The literature is significant, however, in documenting contrasting receptor attention patterns between middle American host schools then and minority classrooms now. In their check of gaze direction, it was shown that more than 90 percent of the host children had their eyes fixed on their teachers or their work at any given time (Jackson 1968). This contrasts considerably with estimates obtained from the contemporary classrooms that share in the early century pedagogical style of the teacher directing all attention in the classroom. M. Deutsch (1963) has found that teachers in Harlem elementary schools spent more than half their day calling children to attention. Attention patterns indeed appear to define the "scene of the battle" in pariah group education (Roberts 1970). School does not seem to work for many teachers and pariah children, and formal roles and statuses are not identically defined by teachers and students. The call for attention appears far more often and seems to have far less effect than it did in the twenties when these earlier studies were carried out.

There is much social organization in these attention and inattention patterns. In primate studies, attention patterns have recently been used to delineate the social organization of dominance hierarchies (Chance 1967). The more one baboon visually attends to another baboon, the more responsible it is to the leader's every movement. Similar, in the classroom where teachers and students produce leadership patterns for each other, attention is an issue. To attend to a teacher is to give the teacher a leadership role in the classroom; to attend to the peer group is to subvert the teacher's role. In the older studies, the primary fact is that all the children paid homage to the teacher's leadership role by attending, physically at least, to the teacher's activities. In schools populated by pariah children, this leadership role is much more subject to negotiation: some teachers can pull it off and some cannot; some children give their attention and others do not. It is in the context of this battle for attention that we must consider the nature of pariah reading disabilities. In many pariah classrooms, the politics of everyday life has been escalated into war games; there are teacher games and peer group games, and every student must make his choice. One takes sides by attending or not attending. Those who attend learn to read; those who do not attend do not learn how to read.

Attention patterns increasingly shift from teacher games to peer group games as a pariah child moves through elementary school. In addition to the often reported facts that pariah children learn less and misbehave more often as they get older, data on shifts in the perceptual, language structure and function, and attitude patterns of children in school are now available. The next few years promise to bring us far more information, not only on American blacks, the focus of all the work to be briefly discussed here, but on other pariah groups as well.

Perception

Much of the transmission of social know-how that occurs in the early years of school amounts to perceptual learning. Apparently different cultures learn how to perceive differently. This is especially the case for materials represented in two dimensions which apparently allow for more variability than the three-dimensional world of movement and action (Segall, Campbell. and Herskovits 1966; Forge 1970). Learning how to read involves a great deal of perceptual learning. Many children reverse their letters when first learning how to write, for there really is not much difference betwee p, d, g and b; o and e; u, n, m, v and w. Normals master these subtle differences, and disabled children continue to have difficulty distinguishing these forms after the first grade. Careful attention must be paid to differences in rotation, line-to-line curve, dimension and line-breaking transformations in order to make the proper distinctions between the letters which signal differences in word form and meaning. We develop these skills and store them deep in our nervous system. The more we read, the less work it takes to distinguish the different forms. The eye apparently learns just what to look for and orients only when a drastically misshapen form appears; the difficulties of proofreading illustrate just how well a good reader is programmed to read for meaning and to notice typographic irregularities only when they are given special attention.

Some black children do not permanently develop the essential skills for letter differentiation. In a test designed to analyze a child's competence at handling the perceptual transformations essential to letter discrimination, Gibson (1965) has shown that most children have trouble with rotation and line-to-curve transformations at age five. By age seven most children have mastered these transformations. This is the case for both black and white children. However, black children I tested at twelve years of age showed a mixed range in these skills; those who could read performed well, and those who could not read performed very poorly, scoring below younger black children on the same test. These children had apparently learned how not to see, or, more specifically, learned how not to look in order that they might not see. Reading apparently became a call for inattention, and they submerged the skills essential for a successful attending to reading materials.

Language Structure and Function

This shift in the perceptual properties of many black children is accompanied by subtle but highly significant changes in language structure and function. The brilliant work of Labov and his associates in Harlem has revealed that our language is indeed socially organized. The way in which our vocal chords allow for a passage of air to reverberate into the ears of other social actors depends greatly on just who the interactants are and how they are related. Depending upon who is doing the talking and who is doing the listening, not only will different points of information be passed, but the way of saying it may be remarkably different. Pariah children often learn to use one speech code or register for dealings with pariah people and another for host people; the differences in the code may be subtle lexemic markers as in Japan (Donoghue 1971), subtle phonemic shifts as between social classes and ethnic groups in New York City's Lower East Side (Labov 1964a), gross dialect shifts as between whites and blacks in America, or major language shifts as between French and English speakers in Canada or the Lapps and Norwegians in Norway (Eidheim 1969).

American blacks acquire a nonstandard or dialect English which is most often mutually intelligible with white English. When there is an intelligibility breakdown, the result can be disastrous. Gumperz gives the following example from a postbellum southern teacher's diary:

> I asked a group of boys one day the color of the sky. Nobody could tell me. Presently the father of one of them came by, and I told him of their ignorance, repeating my question with the same result as before. He grinned: "Tom, how sky stan'?" "Blue," promptly shouted Tom (1970:4).

This gross level of language interference was, of course, attributed by the teacher to the child's stupidity, and the teacher probably unconsciously related to the child the subordinate status that accompanies being "stupid" in a classroom.

For the most part, however, black and white verbal codes are mutually intelligible in content. Switching does not cause a problem at the structural level; rather the codes function to differentiate the games being played and the meaning attached to the behavior of various other actors in the game. Messages of relationship are differently stored in the codes. Indeed, using one and not the other is itself a powerful relational message. Switching codes causes a problem, then, for an actor's definition of situation. If an actor defines himself in terms of the ecology of games played by the peer group, then taking on the code which demands participation in the ecology of teacher and book games demands an existential leap and is neither easily nor healthily performed.

The differentiation of codes according to grammar alone deals only with what is systemically possible. Learning should not be blocked. Children merely learn new codes. The differentiation of codes on the basis of appropriateness is apparently a much more difficult chasm to bridge. When the social organization of communicative behavior is divided by two definitions of what is culturally appropriate, the one definition belonging to the teacher and the other to the pupils, communication across codes is much more limited than if codes are merely structurally at odds. It is not difficult to learn that "What color is the sky?" and "How sky stan'?" are equivalent, but, when your teacher deems you ignorant for using the one and your peer group shuns you for using the other, then the job of switching codes is difficult indeed.

The ecology of peer group games is well defined by the growth of a highly elaborate linguistic code restricted to peer group members. Labov has performed a masterful task in isolating these games in his delineation of the stages of acquisition of nonstandard English:

1. Up to age 5: basic grammatical rules and lexicon are taken from parents.
2. Age 5 to 12 the reading years: peer group vernacular is established.
3. Adolescence: "The social significance of the dialect characteristics of his friends become gradually apparent."
4. High school age: "The child begins to learn how to modify his speech in the direction of the prestige standard in formal situations or even to some extent in casual speech" (Labov 1964b:91).

The second and third stages are, of course, most important for a consideration of the implications of the school and the peer group registers for learning. The implications are not so obvious; what difference does it make if children use one register for interacting with teachers and reading materials and another for interacting with each other? The importance of these two registers lies in the fact that during the school years the two become mutually exclusive. As children participate more in their peer groups, the less importance is attached to school games. The more children participate in the ecology of games defined by their peers, the more deviant their linguistic registers; it is these linguistic features which help to mark off the peer group from the ecology of the schools.

Labov has documented these trends beautifully. Participation in peer groups, especially those with formal organizations such as street gangs, are accompanied by major phonological and grammatical shifts. One of the many charts presented in his Harlem study is reproduced here (Labov et al. 1968:182):

Percent of Standard Verb Agreement for Club Members, Lames and Whites

Present Tense Forms of Verb	*Club Members*	*Lames*	*Whites*
has (3rd sg.)	19	60	100
doesn't (3rd sg.)	03	36	32
were (2nd sg. + pl.)	14	83	100
does (3rd sg.)	00	13	100
says (3rd sg.)	04	00	100
(No. of subjects	31	10	8)

This illustrates the implications that peer group status has for the speech register employed by black adolescents. Lames do not participate in formally organized peer groups although they are in contact with the gangs and are part of the black speech community. In school, Lames are still open to interpreting favorably some cues from the teacher's ecology. The Inwood whites are of a low social class, but they do not show the extreme alienation patterns which characterize black children in school. Club members show the most extreme deviance from the standard English linguistic code, Inwood whites the least, and Lames fall in between. The same rank ordering can be made for the three groups' participation in school. This is not to say that linguistic difference causes alienation from school; rather it is a standard for nonacceptance of the ecology of games played in white schools. The rise in status of a black child in his peer group, the adoption of the peer group's linguistic register, and alienation from school all develop together.

In terms of this inquiry into reading disabilities, participation in peer group formal organizations and the employment of their linguistic registers are of great importance, for they correlate very well with reading scores. Labov and Robins (1969:57, 167) have shown perfectly the relation between the acquisition of reading skills and the participation in the peer group ecology of games. Not one out of 43 gang members was able to achieve a reading score on grade level and most are more than two years behind the national average. Participation in the peer group ecology of games appears indeed to be exclusive of a participation in the school ecology of games of which reading is a part. Printed materials appear to send few meaningful cues to those interested in improving their status among their peers.

Attitudes

Labov's findings are not limited to classrooms which harbor members of formally organized gangs in Harlem. In two classrooms in suburban New York City, the exact same trends were found. The children were not unaware of the trends, and their significance was readily apparent in the children's attitudes towards each other. This should not surprise us at all. In my high school, I remember that most of us could define others and make very accurate estimates of their grade point averages on the basis of clothes worn, speech patterns, and some postural cues. Our expertise was perhaps not as loaded as that of black children, for their expertise not only defines others but also determines who is to be popular or not. A series of sociometric tests administered in an all black, bottom track, sixth grade were consistent in placing nonreaders at the center of all peer group activities. Similar tests in an all black, nontracked, fifth grade also showed nonreaders at the center of most activities. Reading skills do not recommend an actor for leadership. Indeed, the acquisition of such skills can exclude an actor from the peer group ecology of games.

Ethnographic Summary

Many topics have been briefly touched in this short description of the black classroom, but its thrust can be summarized. Learning disabilities occur at very high rates in the American black population. The distribution of these disabilities overlaps with the distribution of social behavior that leads to the acquisition of nonmarketable and pariah biographies, behavior such as participation in street gangs and classroom subcultures specializing in disruption and failure. This nascent pariah population shows subtle shifts in its perceptual, linguistic, and attitude patterns. What the children are doing is learning to behave in new, culturally appropriate ways in educational settings, new ways which will determine their acquisition of pariah status vis-a-vis the host population. These new ways of behaving involve the development of new cues to be sent out in interaction with other humans, such as new phonemes and morphemes, and the development of new perceptual and evaluative skills, such as the abilities to hear new phonemes and perceive group leaders without confusion. What is being learned are new attention patterns, new ways of seeing, hearing, and construing the meaning of particular items of behavior shared with others in the subculture. When some items are attended, others are disattended, some of them actively so. Learning to behave in a culturally appropriate way in black classrooms in white school systems apparently involves learning to attend to cues produced in the peer group and learning to disattend teacher and school produced cues, such as shouts for attention or the introduction of tasks such as reading. These attention patterns are deeply programmed in the central nervous system. When the child attempts to attend to cues outside his learned competence, he fails. In this way, many black children fail in reading, and they appear neurologically impaired. Obviously, they are usually not impaired at all; they have merely learned to attend to different stimuli in a school situation. Ironically and tragically, for their successful and rational adaptation to the school situation, they are categorized as impaired and treated as inferiors. Thus they acquire pariah status.

Biculturation and the Acquisition of Pariah Status

Now that we have some notion of how a black classroom is organized in American schools and what black children must know in order to act in a subculturally appropriate way in the classroom, we must ask how this know-how is produced. Why is it that the social world of many black children is organized without a place for printed materials? Some observers might point to genes or to various kinds of deprivation leading to cognitive or motivational breakdowns. Others, especially radical educators (Holt 1969; Kohl 1967), black leaders, and P.T.A. groups, point to "underachieving schools" and the failure of teachers to do the job. Implicit in much of this rhetoric is the claim that racism is the primary factor in the failure of whites to educate black children; white teachers expect black children to fail and subtly induce their expectations into the children who indeed do fail.

These are the two alternatives offered by the literature: the children fail because there is something wrong with their heads; or the children fail because the schools are disasters and the teachers are racists. The first argument is far too simple. Gene pools (Montagu 1964) and cognitive and motivational systems are not easily located, and no one has shown why any of these systems fail in school and not in other settings in the social world. The second literature is a little more difficult to dismiss. Obviously, it is not only the schools that fail, for they serve different groups the same product with differential success. When racism is appended to the charge of school underachievement, the argument is intuitively more forceful. However, we have little idea just what racism means of late or, more importantly, how it works especially for the mostly well-meaning, hard-working, and ideologically nonracist teachers that staff our urban schools.

The proposal of this chapter is that reading disabilities are products of the way in which the people in the classroom use their categories for interaction to produce statuses and identities, or ways of attending stimuli, in the classroom setting. Although racist categories work their way into the production of the social organization of black-white relations, a teacher does not have to be a racist for the politics of everyday life to produce a classroom rigidly divided between teacher and peer group games. Any formal differences in the communicative styles of the teacher and the children can introduce havoc to their relations and the messages of relationship they consequently send to each other.

Consider the following important example. Two black Americans attending a Chicago college were introduced to each other. A film, shot at the rate of 24 frames per second, was made of their shaking hands. There was a definite rhythm to their handshake; for three frames their hands went up and for three frames down, and so on. Two Polish Americans at the same college produced a different but also fairly rhythmic interaction. One Pole and one black from each dyad produced a disastrous interaction (Leonard 1972): five up, one down, one up, two down, etc. There was no rhythm to their interaction. There they were, joined together at the hands, but with apparently little idea about what to do with each other. An analysis of the conversational false starts indicates that they also had little idea of what to say to each other. Rational and stigma-free interactions are difficult to make out of such material. Apparently, our communicative codes go into our bodies and establish rhythms and expectations about the rhythms of others. Interacting with a person with a slightly different code or rhythm can be a fatiguing and upsetting experience. On a one-to-one basis, these difficulties can be worked out or negotiated until the two interactants have managed consistent or rational ways of dealing with each other. In a classroom in which a teacher often stands one-to-thirty against a code of difference, negotiations are often not possible and at best limited (Byers, personal communications).

Communicative code differences in a classroom setting can have tremendous effects. A teacher out of phase with his students will undoubtedly fail in the politics of everyday life. Rational interaction with the group will hardly be possible. As a result, the teacher will fall back on his formal authority as a teacher, his so-called "role," to instruct the children in their classroom behavior. The children often reject this authority role and develop an idiosyncratic code, such as the nonstandard peer group code Labov has described. The children's actions make much sense. When rational interaction with a teacher is not possible, that is, when his position of authority makes no sense in terms of his relations with the children, they produce an alternative system and disown the teacher's authority. Reading skills get caught in this battle over which cues are to be attended—peer group cues or teacher cues.

This paper has suggested how a child learns to produce a pariah status in his work in everyday life. It has offered an example of this work in detailing how a large number of black children acquire statuses, identities, and behavioral patterns which produce a pariah biography. The statuses, identities, and behavioral patterns developed by black children in white school systems produce learning disabilities and enable the host population to exclude the black child from participation in the more lucrative institutions of American society. How are these statuses, identities and behavioral patterns produced? Three tasks remain if this question is to be answered.

Communicative Code Differences and the Inhibition of School Learning

First, examples of how minor differences in communicative codes can induce a selective inattention to school material must be given. One of the first reports of such interference was offered by Spindler (1959) in his work on the self-fulfilling prophecies of teachers unconsciously dominating classroom social organization. He showed how middle-class teachers attended to middle-class children and labeled them as the most talented and ambitious of the children in their classes. School success followed along identical lines, but more subtle evaluations of talent divided the populations along different lines. In this case, lower class children gave up trying and acquired failing "institutional biographies" (Goffman, 1963) because of an inability to give evidence of their intelligence in terms of the limited code that the teachers used to evaluate children.

A more specific example has been recently offered for a Boston elementary school with white teachers and black children. The effects of little things were in no way little in this school. Rist offers the following account of the classroom after it had been divided into three "ability groups," the fast, slow and nonlearners at Tables 1, 2, and 3, respectively:

> The organization of the kindergarten classroom according to the expectation of success or failure after the eighth day of school became the basis for the differential treatment of the children for the remainder of the school year. From the day that the class was assigned permanent seats, the activities in the classroom were perceivably different from previously. The fundamental division of the class into those expected to learn and those expected not to permeated the teacher's orientation to the class (1970: 423).

Assignment to each of the tables was based on the teacher's subjective evaluations which, after dissection by Rist, were shown to be rooted in the teacher's evaluation of the children's physical appearance and interactional and verbal behavior. At Table 1 are centered children with newer and cleaner clothes and more of them on cold days, slightly lighter skin, and processed hair. Children with reciprocal traits were positioned at lower tables. Class leaders or direction givers also clustered at Table 1. The children at the low tables spoke less in class, in heavy dialect when they did, and almost never to the teacher. What is most unfortunate is that by the third grade the children at the lower tables were still at the lower tables. Once the child is tracked, it is almost impossible for him to break loose. The lower his table, the less he gets in instructional time. In addition, teacher expectations follow him from year to year. Apparently, the acquisition of a school biography is completed within the first week of school, and all on the basis of a teacher's ethnocentric evaluation of a child's mannerisms.

A similar analysis can probably be carried out for every year of schooling that a child undergoes. Each year, more are sorted out until the "select few" reach college. The word "select" should not be taken in its elitist sense. By the time they enter college, some people may be more select because their enculturation to school equips them to do college work. We should not make the mistake, however, of thinking that the select few were selected for any reason other than that they were most like their teachers. Given Labov's speech data, we can see that the children at Table 3 are not the interactional and verbal dullards that the teacher supposed them to be. By the sixth grade, assuming Labov's data are predictive, the children at Table 3 will talk the most and be the best dressers and the most popular individuals in every class. Their native equipment for leading and learning is in perfect shape, although by the sixth grade it is understandably directed away from school. Why these children are not selected in their early years by teachers has to do with how well prepared both they and their teachers are for working out the conflicting points in their communicative code. The children are often more adaptable than their teachers. They are able and willing to develop new codes; indeed, they do so every day in the playgrounds. However, if the new code is used to degrade the children, as is the case for the children in "lower" ability groups, they will take flight and cut themselves off from whatever rewards the new code has to offer them. If a modus vivendi is not reached in the early grades, the children at the lower tables will create their own subculture defined partly in opposition to the classroom culture attempted by the teacher.

Pariah children invariably share some minor traits which help them to identify each other and to distinguish themselves from the host population. A particular phoneme, lexeme, or body movement can do the job. Invariably, these traits are at most minuscule factors in cognitive development. Even a dialect barrier great enough to produce mutual unintelligibility is not enough to stop German children from speaking and reading High German (Fishman and Leuders-Salmon 1972). Dialect differences between black children and white school officials and books, often claimed as a source of reading failure (Baratz and Shuy 1969), apparently present little formal interference to the reading process (Melmud 1971). It depends on what is done with the differences. In host-pariah teacher-student relations, the differences are used to do a great deal, and are allowed to intervene in interactions to the extent that they cut off the possibility of sense being made between the pair. The child gets stuck in a low ability group for reasons he cannot understand and the teacher finds the child's behavior equally incomprehensible. In such a case the teacher grasps onto a formal definition of the teacher's role in order to make sense of the situation: the teacher develops status or interaction skills in accordance with the definition of the teacher as a person to be listened to and learned from under any circumstances. Faced with this senseless rigidity of the teacher's role, the child develops his status and identity in the alternative source offered by his peer group. Recall the disabled child assigned low status in the classroom despite a high degree of acceptance outside the classroom. The child shut down his learning skills and turned to abnormal behavior (Singer and Beardsley 1970). The same senseless assignment to ability groups is often made in the interethnic classroom. The host teacher has different standards of evaluation than the minority child. Accordingly, the wrong children are often assigned to the low ability groups. Their assignment does not make sense to them, and they understandably shut down their learning skills and revolt. The difference between what happens to the disabled child who perceives a senseless status assignment and a minority child in an identical situation is that the minority child is never alone. The teacher invariably makes mistakes on a number of the children, and the ensuing revolt can develop earlier and more powerfully when a large number of children is involved.

The children in an interethnic classroom have three choices. They can take school as a source of identity; thus, the children at Table 1. They can take the peer group as a source of identity and fight the system; thus, the children at Tables 2 and 3 transformed by late elementary school into the gangs Labov has described. The third and perhaps the worst choice is represented by the children at the lower tables who accept the teacher's definitions and passively fail through school into pariah status. They also fail in their identity work. For the children to dispute the messages of relationship offered by a teacher to the lower ability groups causes havoc in the classroom but solid ego development in the children's own community. For the children to passively accept subordinate status creates classroom calm, but a weak ego. Either way, learning is blocked; in the first case by active selective inattention and misbehavior, in the second case with motivational lag and selective inattention. Neither group learns to read.

Black-White Communicative Code Differences

A second task is to describe possible points of conflict in black and white communicative skills and the difficulties of biculturation or the acquisition of competence in both codes. Work on this topic is just beginning, but already there are indications that the use of time and space in black culture is distinct from the use of time and space in white culture. Regardless of what these codes are an adaptation to, the point is that blacks and whites slice up the world in slightly different ways. When the black child enters a host school, he is asked to alter his codes drastically for spacing his body vis-a-vis (Aiello and Jones 1971; Hall 1971; Scheflen 1971; Johnson 1971) and his timing in conversation (Lewis, 1970; Gumperz and Herasimchuk, 1972; Leonard, 1972). This is very important, for it is in terms of these time and space coordinates that people send each other messages of relationship. If these code differences are not worked out, the teacher and students will tie into or punctuate (Bateson 1972; Watzlawick et al. 1967) each other in all the wrong ways.

Punctuation breakdowns are the stuff of the self-fulfilling prophecies described above. The child moves or speaks in the wrong way at the wrong time according to the teacher's code, and he will be branded hyperactive, out of control, or stupid. The teacher will appear equally disoriented according to the child's code and may well be branded cold and unfair. Slight differences in time and space use do not have to result in such a disaster, but they often do.

In an exciting article, Byers and Byers (1972) have described how black-white code differences can lead to pupil-teacher breakdown. The teacher in question is considered unbiased and talented. Byers and Byers filmed her interaction with four four-year-old girls, two black and two white. In the sequence analyzed, she looks at the black and white children almost an identical number of times. However, the black children look at the teacher more than three times as often as the white children. One might postulate that the children are anxious about their performance, or perhaps they are hyperactive, etc. The Byerses have a much more interesting conclusion to offer, after they add the most important information that the white children established eye contact with the teacher almost twice as often as the black children who are straining three times as hard to catch the teacher's eyes. This is very crucial, for it is during eye contact that the teacher can send the children messages of reassurance and affection, messages such as, "I love you," "You are doing well," "How smart!", or at least, "You are making sense to me." Why do these black and white eyes punctuate each other in all the wrong ways?

Consider what social work is performed by a glance of the eyes. The eyes are engaged in gathering information about the content and report of any interaction that a body is engaged in. Constant surveillance makes people uncomfortable, perhaps because it is a statement of distrust, a sign of one's unwillingness to suspend belief that nothing threatening is about to occur. So the eyes are used in brief spurts only, in passing glances. What is most interesting is that these glances are very well timed to occur at moments of maximum information transfer. Eye glances are paced by conversational rhythms, intonation patterns, and body movements and are sequenced rather neatly to other rhythms between two people. The white girls in the interaction that Byers and Byers have described appear to know just when to look at the white teacher in order to gain access to her eyes and whatever relational messages she is to dispense. The black girls do not appear to have the same information. They appear to be working off a slightly different interaction rhythm. Of course, this is just as Leonard's (1972) analysis of the black-white handshake and Gumperz's and Herasimchuk's (1972) analysis of black-white intonation rhythms predicted. Interaction is indeed an action between people, and if not perfectly timed the interaction will fail. In the case of this teacher and these children, the white-white interaction is successful, and the white-black interaction fails. For all their interactional work, the two black girls receive little relational support, and it is not difficult to predict that they will someday direct their interactional work towards each other. In time, achievement will be located in the peer group, and not in the teacher.

More blatant examples of teacher-student battles over time and space use exist in every American classroom in which teachers generally monopolize 85 percent of class space and 100 percent of class time (Sommer 1969). From the first to the last grade, the teacher attempts to dictate when and where a child should speak or move. In ghetto schools, this often leads to constant and open warfare. Teachers spend an inordinate amount of a child's six years in elementary school fighting with the class about just who is going to say and do what at a particular moment; manuals guiding a new teacher in instructional methods in such a school detail at length exactly how a teacher must rigidly structure time and space (Trubowitz 1968; Board of Education 1966). The children fight this particular structure to the extent that it stifles them; if their function and status in the structure do not make sense to them, that is, if the politics of classroom life do not make sense, they reject the structure and all that comes with it, including literacy.

A large percentage of American blacks are especially adept at making the code shifts essential to smooth interactions with whites. This is no easy task, for enculturation into two cultures, or biculturation (Valentine 1971), can have its drawbacks for ego development. The bicultural child must acquire two sometimes mutually exclusive ways of knowing how to act appropriately, one way for when whites are present and another for when the interaction matrix is all black. Where code shifting is most difficult is apparently in the bureaucratic setting in which the white code, in addition to being the only acceptable medium of information exchange, is also the medium for the expression of host group power and host group access to the essential and even luxurious utilities of the ecosystem that is contemporary America. The police station, the welfare office, the job interview and the classroom are all situations which demand complete subservience to host group codes. In each of these situations, people are being processed rather than negotiated with in an attempt to establish rationality. The rationale is already set. The bureaucrat has it down and the pariah does not. The bureaucrat already has the role defined, and the pariah must fit in if he is to be processed successfully. Even when the bureaucrat attempts to negotiate a rational interaction—to approach his public as he would normal people in everyday life, he is unable to do so because of the sheer numbers of people that must be processed. The teacher, for example, must deal with 30 children at a time, and the give and take that characterizes everyday life become impossible. Consequently, the teacher's code becomes the classroom code, and children are evaluated in its terms.

In the classroom, the teacher has the power; the teacher has the tools to supply the institutional biography that the child needs to escape his pariah origins. Teachers are quick to point this out to children and daily tell them that there is no success without school. If the child attempts biculturation, he adapts to the teacher's code, accepts the teacher's messages of power and dominance, and works hard at school. Many black children do not go this route. They reject the teacher's code and transform their minor differences in time and space use into large differences defining the classroom as the scene of the battle between the races. Code differences do not have to develop in this fashion, but they most often do. It is a measure of the teacher's adaptability in the early grades. The more sensible student-teacher relations can be made in the early grades, the less difference code differences will make. If the teacher fights the children with his formal authority from the early grades on, the children will equate the teacher's code with senseless suppression; it will become a difference that makes a difference. The children will reject the new code and seek the more rewarding alternatives offered by the peer group.

Host group teachers do not produce code differences. Both the teacher and his students partake in long ethnic traditions in their first years of life, and they then bring these traditions to school. The question is, how are ethnic differences made to make a difference? In the earlier grades, teachers make the difference as they are apparently not as adaptable as their students. In later years, as peer group lines solidify and code differences become the focus of most classroom social and political work, the children enforce the distinction between the teacher's code and their own code. In making their code make a difference, they are learning how to produce pariah status vis-a-vis the host group; they are learning to appear like "one-of-those"; they are producing a pariah biography which will haunt them until the next generation again plays the politics of everyday life in the classroom.

Identity and Mobility

The third task cannot be properly dealt with until we have detailed accounts of the politics of everyday life for many pariah groups both here in America and in other cultures. The third task is to explain why blacks do not fare as well as other minorities in classroom politics. All ethnic groups, Jews, Japanese, or Italians, for instance, bring some differences to the classroom. Shouldn't they all lead to communicative breakdowns, degrading relational messages between students and teachers, and, finally, learning disabilities? Yes, and indeed they do. Some groups have worked out ingenious strategies for by-passing host group discriminatory powers. American Catholics, for example, appear to have always understood the complexities of moving through host schools. Accordingly, they have always maintained their own school systems which have functioned not only as socializing agents, but also as protection against the sorting efforts of host group members. Whether or not their diplomas were equivalent in quality to host diplomas, Irish, Italian, and other Catholic Americans have always equipped their children with the institutional biographies required for at least minimally upward mobility.

The strategies of each group for identity work in the face of unacceptable messages of relationship in the classroom are probably deeply rooted in its history. The reasons for its having to develop such strategies exist in the politics of the classroom. If group identity work is necessitated by a breakdown in teacher-student relations, strategies as to what will be attended to and what will be acted upon will be worked out among the students. Learning abilities and disabilities are developed in such a context. School learning is almost always set back; the question is whether the group opts for learning how not to learn, the case described in this paper, whether the group merely opts to learn only about its own materials, as is the case for Hasidic Jews and the Pennsylvania Dutch, or whether the group overcomes the degrading messages and does scholastically better than host children even according to host group standards. The last case is most intriguing because of the records achieved by American Jews and American Japanese. Both groups have soared over mobility barriers and appear to have well escaped pariah status because of their mastery of the American school system. Of course, both groups reached the American shores with tremendous entrepreneurial skills and established traditions of literacy. Nevertheless, the essential question remains unanswered; namely, what did the Jews and the Japanese know that other pariah groups did not know? Alternatively, it can be asked what the host group knew about Jews and Japanese that it apparently does not know about other minorities (Spindler, personal communication). The point is that ethnic identity work defines what is to be learned and how it is to be learned, what is to be read and the strategies used for the reading act. What is different about the ethnic identity work of one group rather than another? Such a question will keep the next generation of scholars busy. If we achieve an answer, we will know a great deal.

Summary

Pariah groups are continually regenerated by host and pariah children learning how to assign *meanings* to particular social acts and how to *act appropriately* on the basis of the meanings assigned. These meanings are programmed into the *central nervous system* as patterns of *selective attention* to the stimuli particular to some acts and not to others. Patterns of selective attention, glossed in everyday language as *abilities, statuses* and *identitites.* shape a child's *institutional biography* and define whether the child, his abilities, statuses and identities, are to be assigned to a pariah or a host group in any situation.

The conclusion of this chapter is that the patterns of selective attention and inattention demonstrated by pariah children in school represent rational adaptations to the politics of everyday life in the classrooms. School failure and delinqency often represent highly motivated and intelligent attempts to develop the abilities, statuses, and identities that will best equip the child to maximize his utilities in the politics of everyday life. If the teacher is going to send degrading messages of relationship regardless of how the game is played, the child's best strategy is to stop playing the game.

The ability to read is taken up in some detail since it is one program which defines the boundary between pariah and host groups. Specifically, it is suggested that the politics of everyday life induce patterns of inattention for the reading task in particular groups. Host teachers and pariah children find each other occasionally unintelligible because of vocal and body language code differences and stereotypes. These differences are escalated into cues for intergroup conflict when degrading messages of relationship are appended by the teacher to the child's use of his own code for interpreting and generating behavior. The child is engaged in identity and status work and often rejects these messages as meaningless. The child then develops patterns of inattention to the teacher, the teacher's tasks such as behaving "properly" and reading, and, eventually, most stimuli generated by the host group. The high rate of black American illiteracy and pariah group membership is explained in this way.

References

Aiello, J., and S. Jones, 1971, "Field Study of the Proxemic Behavior of Young Children in Three Subcultural Groups," *Journal of Personality and Social Psychology* 19(7):351–356.

Allitto, S., 1969, "The Language Issue in Communist Chinese Education." In C. Hu, ed., *Aspects of Chinese Education.* New York: Teachers College Press.

Azumi, K., 1969, *Higher Education and Business Recruitment in Japan.* New York: Teachers College Press.

Baratz, J., and Shuy, R., eds., 1969, *Teaching Black Children To Read.* Washington, D.C. Center for Applied Linguistics.

Bar-Hillel, Y., 1954, "Indexical Expressions," *Mind* (n.s.) 63:359–379.

Barker, R., 1968, *Ecological Psychology.* Stanford, Calif.: Stanford University Press.

Barth, F., 1969, "Introduction." In F. Barth, ed., *Ethnic Groups and Boundaries.* Boston: Little, Brown and Company.

Bateson, G., 1972, *Steps to an Ecology of Mind.* New York: Ballantine Books.

Beck, H., 1971a, "The Rationality of Redundancy," *Comparative Political Studies* 3(4):469–478.

———, 1971b, "Minimal Requirements for a Biobehavioral Paradigm," *Behavioral Science* 16:442–456.

———, 1972, "Everyman Meets the Epistemologist." Paper presented at the 1972 Annual Meeting of the American Political Science Association.

Becker, E., 1962, *The Birth and Death of Meaning.* New York: The Free Press.

Bernstein, B., 1964, "Elaborated and Restricted Codes," *American Anthropologist* 66(6, part 2):55–69.

Beteille, A., 1972, "Race, Class and Ethnic Identity," *International Social Science Journal* 23(4):519–539.

Birch, H., and J. Gussow, 1970, *Disadvantaged Children: Health, Nutrition and School Failure.* New York: Harcourt Brace Jovanovich.

Blurton-Jones, N., 1972, "Nonverbal Communication in Children." In R. Hinde, ed., *Nonverbal Communication.* London: Cambridge University Press.

Board of Education, New York City, 1966, *Getting Started in the Elementary School.*

Brameld, T., 1968, *Japan: Culture, Education and Change in Two Communities.* New York: Holt, Rinehart and Winston, Inc.

Byers, P. 1971, "Sentics, Rhythms, and a New View of Man." Paper presented to the 138th Annual Meeting of the American Association for the Advancement of Science, Philadelphia, December 30, 1971.

———, and H. Byers, 1972, "Nonverbal Communication and the Education of Children." In C. Cazden, et al., eds., *Functions of Language in the Classroom,* New York: Teachers College Press.

Caudill, W., and H. Weinstein, 1969, "Maternal Care and Infant Behavior in Japan and America," *Psychiatry* 32:12–43.

Cazden, C., 1970, "The Situation: A Neglected Source of Social Class Differences in Language Use," *Journal of Social Issues* 26(2):35–60.

Chance, M., 1967, "Attention Structure as the Basis of Primate Rank Orders," *Man* (n.s.) 2(4):503–518.

Cicourel, A., 1970a, "The Acquisition of Social Structure." In J. Douglas, ed., *Understanding Everyday Life.* Chicago: Aldine.

———, 1970b, "Basic and Normative Rules in the Negotiation of Status and Role, *Recent Sociology* 2:4–45.

———, in press, "Ethnomethodology." In T. Sebeok, ed., *Current Trends in Linguistics,* vol. 12. The Hague: Mouton.

———, and J. Kitsuse, 1963, *Educational Decision Makers.* New York: Bobbs-Merrill.

Condon, W., and W. Ogston, 1966, "Sound Film Analysis of Normal and Pathological Behavior Patterns," *Journal of Nervous and Mental Disease* 143(4):338–347.

———, 1971, "Speech and Body Motion Synchrony of the Speaker-Hearer." In D. Horton and J. Jenkins, eds., *The Perception of Language.* Chicago: Charles Merrill.

Cornell, J., 1970, "'Caste' in Japanese Social Structure," *Monumenta Nipponica* 15(1–2):107–135.

Crystal, D., 1972, "Prosodic and Paralinguistic Correlates of Social Categories." In E. Ardener, ed., *Social Anthropology and Language.* London: Tavistock.

Deutsch, C., 1968, "Environment and Perception." In M. Deutsch, et al., eds., *Social Class, Race and Psychological Development.* New York: Holt, Rinehart and Winston, Inc.

Deutsch, M., 1963, "The Disadvantaged Child and the Learning Process." In A. Passow, ed., *Education in Depressed Areas.* New York: Teachers College Press.

DeVos, G., and H. Wagatsuma, eds., 1966, *Japan's Invisible Race.* Berkeley: University of California Press.

Dewey, J., 1896, "The Reflex Arc in Psychology," *Psychological Review* 3(4):357–370.

Donoghue, J., 1971, "An Eta Community in Japan: The Social Persistence of an Outcaste Group." In G. Yamamato and T. Ishida, eds., *Modern Japanese Society.* Berkeley: McCuthchan.

Eidheim, H., 1969, "When Ethnic Identity Is a Social Stigma." In F. Barth, ed., *Ethnic Groups and Boundaries.* Boston: Little, Brown and Company.

Ekman, P., and W. Friesen, 1969, "Nonverbal Leakage and Clues to Deception," *Psychiatry* 32(1):88–106.

Entwistle, D., 1971, "Implications of Language Socialization for Reading Models and for Learning to Read," *Reading Research Quarterly* 7(1):111–167.

Erikson, E., 1968, *Identity: Youth and Crisis.* New York: Norton.

Fischer, J., 1961, "The Japanese Schools for the Natives of Truk." In G. Spindler, ed., *Education and Culture.* 1963. New York: Holt, Rinehart and Winston, Inc.

Fishman, J., and E. Leuders-Salmon, 1972, "What Has Sociology To Say to the Teacher." In C. Cazden, et al., eds., *Functions of Speech in the Classroom.* New York: Teachers College Press.

Forge, A., 1970, "Learning to See in New Guinea." In P. Mayer, ed., *Socialization.* London: Tavistock.

Frake, C. O., 1962, "The Ethnographic Study of Cognitive Systems." In S. Tylor, ed., *Cognitive Anthropology.* New York: Holt, Rinehart and Winston, Inc., 1969.

———, 1973, "How to Enter a Yakan House," unpublished ms.

Garfinkel, H., 1956, "Some Sociological Concepts and Methods for Psychiatrists," *Psychiatric Research Reports* 6:181–196.

———, 1963, "A Conception of, and Experiments with, 'Trust' as a Condition of Stable Concerted Actions." In O. Harvey, ed., *Motivation and Social Interaction.* New York: Roland Press.

Geertz, C., 1965, "The Impact of the Concept of Culture on the Concept of Man." In E. Hammel and W. Simmons, eds., *Man Makes Sense.* Boston: Little, Brown and Company.

Gibson, E., 1965, "Learning To Read," *Science* 148:1066–1072.

Goffman, E., 1963, *Stigma.* Englewood Cliffs, N.J.: Prentice-Hall, Inc.

Goodman, K., 1967, "Reading: A Psycholinguistic Guessing Game." In H. Singer and R. Ruddell, eds., *Theoretical Models and Processes of Reading.* Newark, N.J.: International Reading Association.

Gumperz, J., 1970, "Sociolinguistics and Communication in Small Groups," *Language-Behavior Research Laboratory Working Paper no. 38.* Berkeley, Calif.

———, and E. Herasimchuk, 1973, "The Conversational Analysis of Social Meaning." In R. Shuy, ed., *Sociolinguistics: Current Trends and Prospects.* Washington, D.C.: Georgetown University Press.

Hall, E., 1966, *The Hidden Dimension.* New York: Anchor Books.

———, 1971, "Environmental Communication." In H. Essor, ed., *Behavior and Environment.* New York: Plenum Press.

Holt, J., 1969, *The Underachieving School.* New York: Pitman.

Hostetler, J., and G. Huntington, 1971. *Children in Amish Society: Socialization and Community Education.* CSEC. New York: Holt, Rinehart and Winston, Inc.

Jackson, P., 1968, *Life in the Classroom.* New York: Holt, Rinehart and Winston, Inc.

Jensen, A., 1966, "Social Class and Perceptual Learning," *Mental Hygiene* 50:226–239.

———, 1969, "How Much Can We Boost I.Q. and Scholastic Achievement?" *Harvard Educational Review* 39:1–123.

Johnson, K., 1971, "Black Kinesics," *Florida FL Reporter* 9(1,2):17–20,57.

Kasamatsu, A., and T. Hirai, 1966, "An Electroencephalographic Study on the Zen Meditation," *Folia Psychiat, Neurolog, Japonica* 20:315–336.

Kendon, A., 1967, "Some Functions of Gaze-Direction in Social Interaction," *Acta Psychologica* 26:22–63.

———, 1970, "Movement Coordination in Social Interaction," *Acta Psychologica* 32:100–125.

———, 1973, "The Role of Visible Behavior in the Organization of Social Interaction." In M. von Cranach and I. Vine, eds., *Social Communication and Movement.* London: Academic Press.

Kohl, H., 1967, *36 Children.* New York: New American Library.

Labov, W., 1964a, "Phonological Correlates of Social Stratification," *American Anthropologist* 66(4, part 2):164–176.

———, 1964b, "Stages in the Acquisition of Standard English." In R. Shuy, ed., *Social Dialects and Language Learning.* Champaign, Ill.: National Council of Teachers of English.

———, 1969, "The Logic of Nonstandard English," *Florida FL Reporter* 7(1):60–75, 169.

———, P. Cohen, C. Robins, and J. Lewis, 1968, "A Study of the Nonstandard English of Negro and Puerto Rican speakers in New York City," Cooperative Research Project No. 3288.

———, and C. Robins, 1969, "A Note on the Relation of Reading Failure to Peer-group Status in Urban Ghettos," *Florida FL Reporter* 7(1):54–57, 167.

Largey, G., and D. Watson, 1972, "The Sociology of Odors," *American Journal of Sociology* 77(6):1021–1034.

Laver, J., 1968, "Voice Quality and Indexical Information," *British Journal of Disorders of Communication* 3:43–54.

Leonard, C., 1972, "A Method of Film Analysis of Ethnic Communication Style." Paper presented to the American Ethnological Society Meetings, Montreal, April 6.

Lewis, L., 1970, "Culture and Social Interaction in the Classroom," Language-Behavior Research Laboratory Working Paper no. 38. Berkeley, Calif.

Long, N., 1958, "The Local Community as an Ecology of Games." In N. Polsby, et al., eds., *Politics of Social Life,* 1963. Boston: Houghton Mifflin Company.

MacKay, D., 1972, "Formal Analysis of Communicative Processes," In R. Hinde, ed., *Nonverbal Communication.* London: Cambridge University Press.

Mackworth, J., 1972, "Some Models of Reading Process: Learners and Skilled Readers," *Reading Research Quarterly* 7:701–733.

Mackworth, N., and M. Bagshaw., 1970, "Eye Catching in Adults, Children and Monkeys. Perception and Its Disorders," *ARNMD* 48:201–203.

Makita, K., 1968, "The Rarity of Reading Disability in Japanese Children," *American Journal of Orthopsychiatry* 38:599–614.

McDermott, J., 1969, "Deprivation and Celebration: Suggestions for an Aesthetic Ecology." In J. Edie, ed., *New Essays in Phenomenology.* New York: Ballantine.

McDermott, R., 1974, "The Cultural Context of Learning To Read." In S. Wanat, et al., eds., *Extracting Meaning from Written Language.* Newark, N.J.: International Reading Association.

Melmud, R., 1971, "Black English Phonology: The Question of Reading Interference," Monographs of the Language-Behavior Research Laboratory. Berkeley: University of California.

Miller, G., E. Galanter, and K. Pribram, 1960, *Plans and the Structure of Behavior* New York: Holt, Rinehart and Winston, Inc.

Mitchell, R., 1967, *The Korean Minority in Japan.* Berkeley: University of California Press.

Montagu, A., ed., 1964, *The Concept of Race.* New York: Crowell-Collier and Macmillan.

Ninomiya, S., 1933, "An Inquiry Concerning the Origin, Development, and Present Situation of the *Eta* in Relation to the History of Social Classes in Japan," *Transactions of the Asiatic Society of Japan* (second series) 10:47–145.

Parsons, T., 1959, "The School Class as a Social System," *Harvard Educational Review* 29(4):69–90.

Pribram, K., 1969, "Neural Servosystem and the Structure of Personality," *Journal of Nervous and Mental Disease* 149(1):30–39.

———, 1970, "Looking to See. Perception and Disorders," *ARNMD* 48:150–162.

———, 1971, *Languages of the Brain.* Englewood Cliffs, N.J.: Prentice-Hall, Inc.

Rist, R., 1970, "Student Social Class and Teacher Expectations," *Harvard Educational Review* 40:411–451.

Roberts, J., 1970, *Scene of the Battle: Group Behavior in Urban Classrooms.* New York: Doubleday Company.

Rothblat, L., and K. Pribram, 1972, "Selective Attention: Input Filter or Response Selection," *Brain Research* 39:427–436.

Scheflen, A., 1960, Regressive One-to-one Relationships, *Psychiatric Quarterly* 23:692–709.

———, 1964, The Significance of Posture in Communication Systems, *Psychiatry* 27:316–331.

———, 1971, Living Space in an Urban Ghetto, *Family Process* 10(4):429–450.

Schutz, A., 1953, "Common-Sense and Scientific Interpretation of Human Action." In M. Natanson, ed., *The Philosophy of the Social Sciences,* 1963. New York: Random House.

Segall, M., D. Campbell, and M. Herskovits, 1966, *The Influence of Culture on Visual Perception.* Indianapolis: Bobbs-Merrill.

Shimahara, N., 1971, *Burakumin: A Japanese Minority and Education.* The Hague: Martinus Nijhoff.

Singer, H., and B. Beardsley, 1970. *Motivating a Disabled Reader,* Thirty-seventh yearbook of the Claremont College Reading Conference.

Sokolov, E., 1969, "Modeling Properties of the Nervous System." In M. Cole and I. Maltzman, eds., *Handbook of Contemporary Soviet Psychology.* New York: Basic Books.

Sommer, R., 1969, *Personal Space,* Englewood Cliffs, N.J.: Prentice-Hall, Inc.

Spindler, G., 1959, "The Transmission of American Culture." In G. Spindler, ed., *Education and Culture,* 1963. New York: Holt, Rinehart and Winston, Inc.

Taira, K., 1971, "Japan's Invisible Race Made Visible," *Economic Development and Cultural Change* 19(4):663–668.

Thompson, L., 1966, *Reading Disability.* Springfield, Ill.: Charles C Thomas.

Trubowitz, S., 1968, *A Handbook for Teaching in the Ghetto School.* New York: Quadrangle.

Valentine, C., 1971, "Deficit, Difference and Bicultural Models of Afro-American Behavior," *Harvard Educational Review* 41(2):137–158.

Wallace, A., 1965, "Driving to Work." In M. Spiro, ed., *Context and Meaning in Cultural Anthropology.* New York: The Free Press.

Wanat, S., 1971, "Linguistic Structure and Visual Attention in Reading," *Research Reports,* International Reading Association.

Watzlawick, P., J. Beaven, and D. Jackson, 1967, *Pragmatics of Human Communication.* New York: Norton.

Zimmerman, D., and M. Pollner, 1970, The Everyday World as a Phenomenon. In J. Douglas, ed., *Understanding Everyday Life.* Chicago: Aldine.

JOHN A. HOSTETLER/*Temple University*

6 *Education in Communitarian Societies—The Old Order Amish and the Hutterian Brethren*

In the United States it is generally assumed that every citizen, regardless of his personal values or ethnic membership, must be educated to the limit, that democracy will prevail when education is made available to all, and that the national goals should become the personal goals of everyone. Education is believed to be important not only for national life but also for personal fulfillment and a wide range of social and economic goals. "Ultimately," says *The Report of the President's Commission on National Goals* (1960:81), "education serves all of our purposes—liberty, justice and all our other aims. . . . The vigor of our free institutions depends upon educated men and women at every level of society. And at this moment in history free institutions are on trial." The goals of education in the United States tend to be in the direction of self-development and fulfillment of individual wants, development of rational powers, and the enhancement of personal freedom. Thus we read in a publication of the National Educational Association (Educational Policies Commission 1961:8) that

> A person with developed rational powers has the means to be aware of all facts of his existence. In this sense he can live to the fullest. He can escape captivity to his emotions and irrational states. He can enrich his emotional life and direct it toward even higher standards of taste and enjoyment. He can enjoy the political and economic freedoms of the democratic society. He can free himself from the democratic society. He can free himself from the bondage of ignorance and unawareness. He can make of himself a free man.

Within the United States there are "little" societies which are threatened by the sweeping effort to educate every citizen. They reject the premise that man "can make of himself a free man." The NEA statement of goals, for example, contrasts sharply with that of the Hutterian Brethren, who say:

> Our children are our noblest, highest, and dearest possession. We teach them from the beginning to know God, to humble and abase oneself before God, to bring the flesh into subjection, and to slay and kill it. We permit them not to go to other schools since they teach only the wisdom, art, and practices of the world and are silent about divine things. (Rideman 1965; 1938 ed.)

In reply to the question: What is a good education? an Amish bishop (Bontreger 1910:77) says:

> A good education does not mean simply book learning, or the acquiring of a great store of information, or a scholarship that has mastered the many branches of learning that are taught in the schools, colleges, and universities of this day. It does mean, however, a store of practical knowledge and skill, a knowledge that can discern between that which is good and useful and ennobling, and that which is a useless accumulation of learning in worldly arts and sciences.

The success of communitarian societies in evading the pervasive educational values of the "great" society, or of integrating some of the insights of public schooling into their indigenous educational system, varies greatly. Many traditional societies have been "swept out by the broom of our industrial and urban civilization," as Everett Hughes (1952:25) has put it. Communitarian societies are faced with the task of not only transmitting their distinctive culture but also maintaining their identity. They engage in what Siegel (1970:11) has aptly called "defensive structuring," defined as "a kind of adaptation that recurs with great regularity among groups that perceive themselves as exposed to environmental stress of long duration with which they cannot cope directly and aggressively."

Over a period of several years the writer has observed differences in the defensive structuring of two communitarian societies, the Amish (Old Order) and the Hutterites (Hutterian Brethren) with respect to education. In this chapter we shall discuss defensive structuring and relate it to community self-realization. At the outset we shall describe the world view and social structure of the two cultures, the areas of tension in relation to education, and then consider the differences in assimilation and disruption patterns. Generalizations dealing with education and the viability of the two cultures will conclude the chapter.

World View and Social Structure

Similarities in World View

Common to both Amish and Hutterites is the dualism of Christianity and of Anabaptism in particular. The doctrine of two kingdoms, the kingdom of God and the kingdom of Satan, light versus darkness, the carnal versus the spiritual, the perishable versus the eternal, and paradise versus wilderness are dominant themes in juxtaposition running through the indoctrination activity and the social structure of the subcultures.

The belief consistently set forth by the Anabaptists (Simons 1956) was that they, like the apostolic community, sought to be the blameless church consisting of those personally awakened and called by God. They believed that those who have been born again, and they alone, are brethren of Christ, because they, like him, have been created in spirit directly by God (Weber 1958:145). Taking the life of the first generations of Christians as a model and "avoiding the world"—in the sense of all unnecessary intercourse with "worldly" people—has been a cardinal principle with the Anabaptists wherever they have lived.

Thus an Amish or Hutterite person must live "unspotted from the world" and separate from the desires, intent, and goals of the outside or outer world. The literalness with which the basic doctrine of separation is practiced is evident in the symbolic systems of dress, in the taboos against forming economic partnerships or alliances with nonmembers, and in forbidding marriage with outsiders. Both groups view themselves—but in different ways, as "a chosen people," "a remnant people," and "a peculiar people." Because they considered infant baptism invalid and began baptizing only adults on confession of faith, they were called rebaptizers or Anabaptists and were greatly harassed by state churches in the sixteenth and seventeenth centuries. Both groups refuse to bear arms or serve in public office, practices which earned them the title of "radicals" during the Protestant Reformation (Williams 1962). Both have strong ascetic tendencies in Max Weber's sense, and in both persecution has been an important element in perpetuating a sense of distinctiveness. Each has an impressive record of martyrs.

The Old Order Amish today number about 60,000 persons. Their Swiss origin and history from the Rhineland to Pennsylvania and to other midwestern states has been well known. (Bachman 1942; Hostetler 1963). The Hutterian Brethren number about 20,000 persons. Like the Amish, they are a Germanic-speaking people but of Tyrol and Moravian origin who have subsequently migrated to Slovakia, Romania, the Ukraine, South Dakota and Montana, and Canada (Peters 1965; Bennett 1967). Hutterite and Amish groups have different dialects, but both use High German in their ceremonial activity. Both societies are communitarian in the sense of having an ideological emphasis on sharing and community, in limiting individual initiative, and in subordinating individual freedom and rationality to community values. The Hutterites are strictly communal, for their basic social unit is a colony, a social entity practicing the community of goods.

The Amish Community

The central integrating institution in Amish society is the ceremonial "preaching service" held every two weeks on Sunday in the home of one of the members. The Amish community consists of a number of farm households in proximity, bonded by a common tradition and faith, articulated in a local church district (congregation), and limited to a few square miles (due to their reliance upon horse-drawn vehicles). Amish and non-Amish farms are interspersed in the same region. The Amish do not own blocks of land as a corporation. Farm machinery, livestock, and individual household units are individually owned. The only property held in common in an Amish church district are the hymn books, and in some districts, the benches used for the church service which are rotated among the households. Sharing and mutual aid in times of fire, sickness, death, or catastrophe are highly characteristic but voluntary.

The authority of the Amish community is vested in the congregation of baptized members, headed by a bishop and several other ordained persons. The basis of all policy is the *Ordnung* (discipline) to which every individual gives assent on his knees when he takes the vow of baptism. The *Ordnung* embodies all that is distinctive of the group and includes common understandings taken for granted. Hence, these rules are unwritten, and most are learned and known only by being a participant member. The *Ordnung* is essentially a list of taboos, reflecting the peculiar problems and encounters of a local congregation. At the basis of any change in the *Ordnung* are the borderline or questionable issues. Any changes are recommended by the ordained and presented orally to the congregation twice each year just prior to the communion service. Each member is asked to approve any changes of the rules. A unanimous expression of unity and "peace" with the *Ordnung* is necessary before the congregation can observe communion. A member can be excommunicated at any time by violating one of the basic rules, but in the case of minor infractions, these must be reconciled before communion. Variations of rules from one congregation to another may be observed, but the most distinguishing rules among all Old Order in the United States are no electricity, telephones, central-heating systems, automobiles, or tractors with pneumatic tires. Required are beards but no moustaches for all married men, long hair (which must be parted in the center if parting is allowed at all), hooks and eyes on dress coats, and the use of horses for farming and transportation in the community. No formal education beyond the elementary grades is a rule of life.

For the Amish farmer who cannot assent to the *Ordnung* there are two means of mobility. Both are difficult and inconvenient. One way is to join a more liberal congregation, but the difficulty is that one may have to be shunned for life by his kin. The other way is to move the household to a community where there is a more compatible *Ordnung*. The *Ordnung* does not prevent a farmer from moving to another community or another state. This degree of freedom is constantly exercised by families who wish to move either because the *Ordnung* is too strict or not strict enough.

The Hutterite Community

A group of married families (from eight to twelve) and their children who live on a Bruderhof or colony constitute a Hutterite community (Hostetler and Huntington 1967). The family is assigned rooms in a long dormitory according to its size and needs. A colony may vary from 70 to 140 persons. With all its dwellings, communal kitchen, schoolhouse and kindergarten, livestock and poultry buildings, storage and machine buildings a colony may have up to a total of 70 buildings. A colony integrates not only religious ceremonialism but an economic enterprise, kinship, socialization processes, and property institutions. This basic community structure is very unlike the nucleated households of the Amish. From their beginning in 1528 the Hutterites equated communal living with the primitive and true expression of Christianity. They rejected as pagan the private ownership of property. Thus, land is owned by the colony corporation. Ownership of farm equipment and the purchase of all goods require the consent of the corporation. The colony is the self-sustaining unit within which the needs of all the members are met.

The authority of the colony is centered in the baptized men of the colony and is headed by a council of five to seven members, one of whom is a preacher. He is ordained by an assembly of preachers and is responsible for the moral leadership of a colony. Although a colony may make its own rules, it must also abide by the rules of a confederation of colones, the *Leut*. All executive functions of the colony are implemented by the council of five to seven men, headed by the preacher. The sale and purchase of goods is the responsibility of the steward who must give an accounting to the colony. From infancy the individual is socialized to be cheerful, to be submissive and obedient to the colony discipline, and never to display anger or hostility or precipitate quarrels. Individual initiative and self-development are deemphasized. Travel is limited but permitted among colonies, and there are occasional trips to trading centers. Respect for order, for authority, hard work and cooperativeness, and submission of the individual will to that of the colony are dominant in the life style of Hutterite personality. The individual never receives schooling outside of the colony. He attends kindergarten from ages three to five, the colony German school and the English school during the school years, and is baptized at the age of about twenty. Ultimate good is achieved by identification with the colony, its communal work and sharing of goods, and only in this way can God be worshipped and honored properly.

The Areas of Tension and Defensive Structuring

The conflict of the two communitarian groups with the state over educational policy has received widespread publicity. School officials view the problem as one of law enforcement. The Amish and Hutterites view the issue in religious terms and as one of survival. Lawyers interpret the problem in legal categories. Citizens of the community often view the conflict as a "fight" between the old and new sentiments of the community. From the viewpoint of anthropology we are interested in contrasting one culture with another, touching on the significant areas of culture contact, formal and informal, and in defensive structuring as manifested in the socialization process. By concentrating on the areas of greatest tension we may obtain knowledge about the defensive structuring and the consequences for the communities themselves.

Amish Education

Acquiring literacy and skills for their young without subjecting them to a change in world view confronts the Amish community with a fundamental human problem (Hostetler and Huntington 1971). "The Amish as a whole," as one Amish spokesman has pointed out, "are very much interested in teaching their children the three basic parts of learning: reading, writing, and arithmetic" (Kanagy in Stroup 1965:15). The Amish child typically grows up in a large family in a farm environment. His first formal schooling begins when he is six or seven years old. His first major task is to learn the English language. This is not a major problem with brothers or sisters in the same school. While attending school he is expected to assist with farm chores and related family responsibilities at home, as do other members of his family. After completing grade eight, the formal schooling period,—with some exceptions as noted below,—is over.

During the period when the American youngster is in high school, the Amish child is learning to identify with his culture. High school comes at a time in the life of the Amish child when isolation is most important for the development of personality within the culture. During this period he is learning to understand his own individuality within the boundaries of his society. As an adolescent he is learning for the first time to relate to a group of peers beyond his family. As with most adolescents, he is testing his powers against his parents and the rules of the community. It is important for the Amish community that his group of peers include only other Amish persons. If the child should acquire competence in the "English" (non-Amish) culture at this stage, he is likely to be lost to the Amish church. While the parents are loosening their direct control and the community has not yet assumed much control the period is too critical to expose the child to outside influences.

High school would break down this needed period of isolation by taking the youth away from the family farm and by teaching him to identify with non-Amish associates. This is what the Amish mean when they say that high school is "a detriment to both farm and religious life." The public high school also teaches ideas that are foreign to the Amish culture and not appreciated by the community. The "way of life" of the high school is feared perhaps even more than the curriculum itself. If the child is removed from the community for most of the working hours of the day there is virtually no chance that he will learn to enjoy the Amish way of life. The incentive to comprehend his individuality, to master the required attitudes and skills necessary to enjoy life as an Amish person, are achieved during adolescence within the context of family, kinfolk, and church-community.

The Amish family needs the help of its teen-aged children more than the typical American family. The child also feels the family's need of him. To know that the family needs his physical powers and to know that he is an economic asset to the welfare of the family is important to the individual. Quitting school after the elementary grades for greater identification with family and for the rewards of participation in adult society is normative. The typical Amish boy or girl who learns to enjoy his family and his way of life has little regret when leaving school. Rather than relying on authority as a means of controlling the child, the parents now exercise control by showing the adolescent clearly how much the family needs him. The young person who works on the farm can understand and feel the contribution he is making to his family.

The formal objections to public education are based on religious precepts such as "The wisdom of the world is foolishness with God" (I Cor. 3:19). The world is educated, the Amishman would point out, but is plainly corrupt. Education has produced scientists who have invented bombs to destroy the world and through education the world has been degraded. A "high" education is believed to militate against humility and obedience to Christ.

Given the educational goals of "practical knowledge and skills" and avoidance of "that which is a useless accumulation of learning in worldly arts and sciences" the rural elementary public school has from the viewpoint of the Amish been workable in the past. Parents fear a strong, progressive public school. They recognize that its aim is to make the child self-sufficient outside of the Amish community and perhaps moral, although not necessarily Christian. They fear what teachers they do not know are teaching their children. They resent the school for taking too much time away from the family and from the discipline of farm work. Learning, or reading, for purposes other than the goals of the culture are looked upon with suspicion. But in spite of the adverse influences the small public elementary school has had on the Amish child, it helped to make of the child a good Amish person. It provided enough contact with outsiders to enable the child to participate minimally in two worlds, and just enough indoctrination into the outer culture to make the child feel secure in his own family and community.

Until about 1937 the Amish generally accepted most of the legal school requirements. As consolidation became widespread, however, the Amish established private schools as a matter of policy. The intent was not so much to teach religion as to avoid the "way of life" promoted by consolidated school systems. The Amish prevailed upon the school boards to keep the one-room schools open. In the process of consolidation, the public school officials often regarded the strongly populated Amish areas as a "problem" in attaining votes for reorganization (Buchanan 1967). All states with Amish populations have attempted to compel the Amish to meet the minimum standards required by law.

Pennsylvania was the first state to attempt widespread enforcement of the school-attendance law affecting the Amish. The law required children to attend school until their seventeenth birthday, but children engaged in farm work were permitted to apply for a permit which excused them when they reached the age of fifteen. However, many had repeated the eighth grade and were still not old enough to apply for a farm permit. The conflict erupted when schools were no longer willing to tolerate the practice of allowing the Amish children to repeat grade eight. School officials tried withholding the farm permits. When the parents did not send their children to the consolidated high school, the parents were summoned to court and fined. They refused to pay the fines on grounds that this would admit to being guilty and were sent to jail. Anonymous friends and businessmen frequently paid the fines to release the parents from prison. Some were arrested as many as ten times. The Amish fathers and mothers took the position that compulsory attendance beyond the elementary grades interferes with the exercise of their religious liberty, and that the values taught in the public school are contrary to their religion. Attorneys and friends of the Amish who took the case to the courts found no legal solution. After many confrontations and embarrassments, Governor George Leader, in 1955, arranged a reinterpretation of the school code to legitimize a compromise plan, the Amish vocational school (Policy for Operation of Home and Farm Projects in Church-Organized Day Schools 1955). Amish lay leaders took the initiative in developing the vocational schools for those pupils who were not of legal age to obtain a farm permit. Under this plan, known as "The Pennsylvania Plan," the pupils perform farm and household duties under parental guidance, keep a daily journal of their activities, and meet a minimum of three hours per week until they reach their sixteenth birthday. The schools are required to teach certain subjects and to file attendance reports, but teachers are not required to be certified.

The showdown in Iowa between the Amish and the public school officials in 1965–1967 illustrates not only how intense the feelings can become in a rural community but also the social processes when coercion is used (Erickson 1969). In a small Amish settlement centering in Buchanan County, Iowa, school authorities forced their way into an Amish private school to transport the children to a consolidated town school. The press recorded the scene as frightened youngsters ran for cover in nearby corn fields and sobbing mothers and fathers were arrested for noncompliance with an Iowa school law.

A few public school districts have maintained country schools in the more heavily populated Amish areas, thus forestalling the establishment of private schools by the Amish. The boards of these schools seek teachers sympathetic to the Amish way of life, and in keeping with respect for cultural diversity, see that religious values of the pupils and parents are not offended. The few schools that are following such a policy have achieved remarkable results. The arrangement provides for state-certified teachers, more modern curricula and facilities than is possible in the private Amish schools, and for enlightenment that is fitted to the culture. The recent agreement between the Amish and the Department of Education of the State of Indiana (1967) is an attempt to use means other than the courts to solve differences in educational policy.

In summary, defensive structuring in the case of the Amish takes the following forms: The Amish will vote against school consolidation to protect their group solidarity and they establish private schools for the same reason. There is a conspicuous absence of formal dialogue between the Amish and the school officials (Buchanan 1967). The Amish are almost wholly dependent on verbal agreements with school officials which the Amish accept at face value. The turnover of school personnel at local and state levels often operates at a great disadvantage to the Amish. Amish parents will refuse to send their children to school even when it appears to school officials that no religious principle is involved. It seems ironic that the Amish are forming private schools not for teaching religion but for obtaining literacy and practical skills under conditions that enable the culture to survive. Pressure from local residents to make the Amish conform to school-attendance laws is often reinforced by longstanding antagonisms. When negotiations break down on the district level, state officials intervene and usually arbitrate either informally or in the courts. School administrators have, in many cases, not learned the difference between those issues on which the Amishman will "bend" and those on which he will not compromise.

Amish Controls Over the Socialization Process

The Amish have no control over the philosophy of education presented in the elementary public school and their response is to form private schools. In communities where Amish attend public school, the school experience is accepted as necessary but with great reservations. The attitude toward public schooling is defensive. Efforts are made to keep methods and ideology from changing. Schooling beyond the elementary grades is not approved and parents will go to prison if necessary to defend this position. An Amish youth who insists on going to high school or college becomes a deviant. The high school is viewed as a system that prepares the individual for living in the "world," not in the Amish community.

The elementary school experience is considered a normal part of life, but if the school is public, then it is regarded as a part of the domain of the outside world. The public school is outside of the central integrating activity of the Amish community. When the school is private, its activity is also carefully guarded so that in many Amish private schools it is not permitted to teach religion, for this would compete with the roles and function of church officials.

In selecting the curriculum, the Amish have no control over the materials selected by the public school. In the private school some of the older texts discarded by the public school are used. They are less objectionable because they have less emphasis on science, modern technology, and physiology. The need for texts appropriate to the private schools is keenly realized. A few have been written by the Amish and others are in preparation.

Typically the one-room school building is located in the country, somewhat central to the Amish farm community. Whether the school is public or private, the distance to school is essentially the same. Many of the Amish live within walking distance, although some hire buses to transport their children to private schools. The school building is midway between the community and the outside world and is least integrated with other Amish institutions.

Hutterite Education

The constitution of the Hutterian Brethren Church (1950) assures every child of an education in skills and in religious training. The initiative for formal training in school belongs to the colony and not to the nuclear family. At all levels in socialization, the family supports the colony. Hutterite society from its beginning has had a highly institutionalized and effective system of formal education for all the age-sets. The major levels of formal education are kindergarten *(Klein-schul),* German school *(Gross-schul),* and Sunday school *(Suntag-schul),* aside from the English or public school taught by an outside certified teacher (Hostetler and Huntington 1967).

When the group settled in the Dakota territories from 1874 to 1879, schools were formed on each of the three founding colonies and were taught by colony members. After 1889 the Hutterite teachers had to qualify for teaching certificates by written examinations. The first outside teacher was hired in 1909 in the Bon Homme colony (Deets 1939:40). By 1931 all the colonies were staffed by non-Hutterite teachers since few members were able to procure teaching certificates. When the Hutterites moved to Alberta in 1918 the establishment of an ungraded rural school in each of the colonies was acceptable to the province. The Alberta Department of Education appointed an official trustee for each school. When school districts were formed, the Hutterites refused to send their children to schools away from the colony grounds. Three private schools were founded as a result. However, in most of the 140 or more Canadian colonies today, the colony school is not a private school. The teacher is appointed and paid by the Department of Education (in consultation with the colony) and the building, heating, and maintenance is provided by the colony.

The agreement between divisional school boards and colonies in Alberta states that "if the colony insist that they shall have their own school apart from the schools for the division, the other rate payers of the division should not be asked to bear any of the cost of the school in the Hutterite Colony" (Knill 1958:86). Three acres, fenced, with an approved building and a residence for the teacher are to be supplied by the colony. The division appoints and supplies the salary of the teacher, supplies school equipment and books, but permits the building to be used by the colony for church activities. The Alberta School Act does not allow divisional boards the right to impose centralization on any school districts opposed to it. The Department of Education has thus far hesitated to enforce transportation of Hutterite pupils to schools outside their colonies. If this were done, Hutterites would exercise the option of establishing private schools. The Hutterites want and need the benefits of an outside teacher, and the Provincial authorities do not want to force the colonies into a situation where they would form private schools. Hutterites have also resisted forming a centralized school for several of the colonies. When the South Dakota colonies moved to Alberta the several Hutterites who had teacher's certificates were not approved for teaching in Alberta. The colonies permitted four of their young men to attend high school and Calgary Normal School to obtain teacher training. The experiment was considered a failure, for only one boy returned to become a teacher in the colonies. Through such attempts in the past some of their young men in both the Ukraine and in North America deserted the colonies. Although there are presently three college-educated Hutterite men teaching colony English schools, the practice is not favored with unanimity by the leaders. The reason as given by one spokesman is: "It is better to have the worldly school taught by a worldly person so that we can keep the lines straight."

The attitude toward English school is that it is important, especially in the early grades, for all children must know arithmetic and be able to use the language of the country. One leader said: "We expect our children to learn math, reading, and science as required by the Department of Education. We must learn English to understand the people around us." When asked what is most undesirable about the English school, these answers were given: "When the teacher does not cooperate with the German teacher or the preacher; taking pictures and then distributing them to the children or when dancing is held in the school, as it happened once. Learning the worldly ways would lead to their damnation. The old physiology books were all right, but the modern health books contain too much about dating, sex education and anatomy."

Aside from acquiring a good knowledge of arithmetic and reading, the only additional goal for Hutterites is that discipline be maintained in the English school. Teachers are expected and often encouraged to "lay down the law," and if they cannot maintain order, they are considered failures. A German teacher advised a new English teacher to "use the willow, for it's the only language they understand." A common complaint of teachers is that the children lack self-discipline and have less respect for an outside teacher than for the colony's German teacher. Greater respect for colony authority can be maintained if the English school also supports the prevailing authoritarian pattern. The English school on a colony becomes a disruptive force when social distance is not properly maintained. In its place, the school contributes to colony cohesion. Keeping the English school "in its place" is crucial, for here is where the ideology of the world and of the colony compete for the loyalty of the young minds. For the child who has not responded properly to colony indoctrination, the English school can become an important influence leading to possible desertion. In school the child can function as an individual and learn about the world outside his colony from his books and from his teacher. Intimacy between teacher and pupil can lead to defection. Friendships can lead to marriages with outsiders, to changes of denominational loyalties. In some instances, teachers have helped young Hutterites find jobs and leave the colony. Young single teachers, male or female, are greater risks than older teachers who are married and have children of their own.

All children of school age attend the English school of the colony. The colony makes a point of not interfering with the living pattern of the teacher, who may have a radio, a television, and even a separate mailbox. The home of the teacher is a potential source of worldly knowledge to colony people and a source of intrustion if not properly controlled.

The teacher is given moral encouragement in ways that aid the colony pattern, mainly as a strong supporter of discipline. The teacher cannot encroach on the child's colony time pattern by asking a child to stay after school, by staying during the lunch hour, or by homework assignments. A child may not be punished by depriving him of food. Discussion of a teacher's shortcomings in the presence of children limits his influence. Many of the colonies complain about receiving poor teachers. Indeed some are inferior as teachers, but there is evidence that many of the marginally good teachers like to teach in the colonies. Relatively inferior academic teaching is tolerated, and teachers are virtually free from the informal supervision of superiors. There is little pressure from parents for excellence and no parental interference in teaching. Unlike most school teachers, who must participate and relate to the wider activities of the community, the teacher in a colony enjoys a type of privacy and freedom from such demands. The formal relations between colony adults and teacher are cordial. Those with cooperative attitudes, including the poorer teachers, are more readily absorbed into the environment of the colony than teachers who are truly competent by outside standards and demand independent thinking of their pupils. Even then, there is little danger that the teacher will become a model for the children. When the teachers will emulate the colony pattern, in dress or by wearing a beard, disruption patterns are minimized and the children tend to show greater respect for the teacher.

Laws intended to raise the minimum attendance age, requiring children to take formal schooling through the ninth or tenth grades, are now adversely affecting colonies in some states and provinces. A few young Hutterites take correspondence courses from state colleges. Some of the teachers who are assigned to teach in the colony are willing to tutor or to give instruction beyond the elementary grades. Exploratory efforts have been made to establish high schools for Hutterite young people in regions where there are many colonies. All such efforts to take the pupils from the colony grounds have run counter to Hutterite religion. The consequences of having to attend school beyond the time when he is accepted as an adult in his society (age fifteen) adversely affects the pupil himself. At this age young people are given adult work privileges. They serve as apprentices to skilled adults under supervised conditions of learning. There is a tendency for the young Hutterite to feel deprived of his status as a growing person when forced to attend formal schooling beyond the age required by his culture.

The farther the child goes in school the less he is said to learn. From the colony's point of view this is correct, for once a child has mastered the basic skills, much of the rest of the subject matter learned has little relevance to their way of life. The colony German school teaches the children how to live, and the English school teaches facts, many of which are of little use to them. German school teaches proper ritual, the English school teaches worldly knowledge. The schools are clearly different, but both are regarded as necessary. In the ideal colony there is little conflict between the two schools, and the normal child receives an integrated learning experience from the viewpoint of his culture.

Hutterite Control Over the Socialization Process

While Hutterites have no formal control over the educational philosophy of the school, they exercise severe informal controls over the secular educational philosophy. They accept the benefits of the public school system and prefer it to operating their own private school. Leaders want their young to learn enough of the skills of arithmetic, writing, and English to become leaders among themselves in the future. While the "worldly" philosophy is brought into the colony, its influence is carefully guarded in a controlled informal environment.

The Hutterites tolerate the public school experience but reject the elements that are dysfunctional to the colony. Hutterites have a deliberate and well-formalized program of education for all the age-sets. The public school is only one of several "schools" in the life of the pupil and its effects are diminished. From the ages of two to five the child is in kindergarten daily to recite, sing, write, and think as required by the system. When he enters the English school on the colony he is already fortified against a foreign culture. During his school years he attends in the morning and often in the afternoon the colony's German school. This is the "real" school from the viewpoint of the pupil. The noxious effects of the public school are minimized by the German teacher. Instead of sending their children away to the English school as do the Amish, the Hutterites bring the English school into their environs and attempt to control the learning process.

The curriculum is selected by the divisional school boards and the Hutterites have no formal and direct control over text materials. Whether the school is private or public, the curriculum is similar to that in the rural schools. The physical proximity of the school to the colony allows for a great deal of informal visits and a strong degree of informal control over the teacher. This indirectly affects what is taught in the school. Teachers who are assigned to a colony for the first time are typically given a "lecture" by the preacher at the start or with the first offense against the colony. He outlines the colony's expectations of the teacher and sets the limits of practices which are "against our religion." The gifts in kind from the colony to the teacher and his family who reside on the colony may obligate the teacher to comply with the wishes of the preacher. Colonies prohibit the use of a radio, projected films, and the record players in the school rooms. Since the building is used for church in the evening, all art work and visual materials must be removed at the end of the day. Because the role of the teacher in the colonies is a very difficult one for these reasons, some of the most capable teachers by outside standards are not attracted to Hutterite colonies.

The school building is integrated within the colony layout. Its presence in the colony is symbolic of those aspects of schooling that are important to the colony. The colony accepts the English school complex but restrains its influence to serve colony ends. The school and teacherage are on the grounds, but they are oriented to one side of the colony and can function without major interference. The English school remains emotionally outside the colony. The time patterns, schedule, and colony holidays suggest superior loyalties. The first language learned and the first writing skills acquired are in German. German school is held at the start of the day, followed by English school. In effect, the English school is held in the visible presence of the elders, suggested by the council bench in front and the pews in the rear of the school. Thus the English school is encapsulated by the colony pattern, and ideally its influence cannot go beyond the bounds set by the culture.

Assimilation and Disruption Patterns

The type of controls exercised by communitarian societies over the educational offensive of the great society may be a significant variable for explaining why some "little" societies dissolve faster than others. The effectiveness of the controls (and defensive structuring) may be assessed in various ways. We have chosen to examine the extent of assimilation in the two cultures as reflected in the loss of members. A society with the least deserters would be one where we would expect a high degree of solidarity and one whose defensive mechanisms are effective.

Patterns of Mobility in Amish Society

In Amish society there is a constant movement from the orthodox to the more liberal groups of Amish-Mennonites. Individuals, family heads and their children, or entire congregations change their religious affiliation. Thus an Amish farmer who wishes to use a tractor for farming or drive an automobile instead of horses, will usually affiliate with a Mennonite denomination. In virtually all communities where there are Amish people there are also liberalized Amish or Mennonite groups. These groups form a continuum from conservative to liberal positions with respect to the rules of discipline (Fig. 6.1). Thus a deviating person may move from a conservative to a more liberal group without losing his identity as an Anabaptist. Although there are many divisions (as is evident from the different forms of dress and material culture), there is a common value orientation. The most orthodox groups lose the smallest number of members while the more liberal groups lose the most. The gains in the more progressive groups are a consequence of the secularization process and not the result of evangelistic activity. Most defectors from the Amish justify their change in affiliation for religious reasons. To turn against the moral training of early life, against kin, and the severe discipline learned in the formative years is not accomplished in the life of some defectors without cultural and religious shock. Religious revivalism, guilt, and conversion are important stages in the experience of the liberalizing Old Order Amish person.

An intensive study of defection in one Amish church in Pennsylvania revealed that 30 percent of the offspring did not join the church of their parents. Of all those who did not join the church of their parents, 70 percent

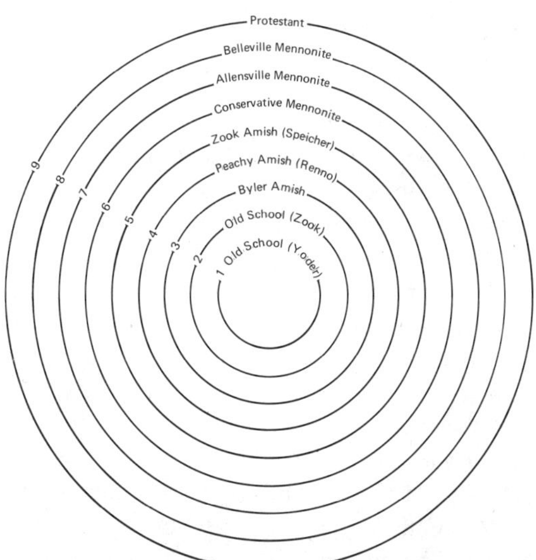

Figure 6.1. Cognitive orientation of Amish-Mennonite groups from "low" to "high" church in Mifflin County, Pennsylvania.

joined a Mennonite group and less than 10 percent joined other Protestant groups. In a study of religious mobility in the Mennonite Church, it was found that 24 percent of the converts came from Amish churches, while that denomination lost only 3 percent of its members to the Amish (Hostetler 1954:257). The loss of members varies considerably with affiliation, discipline, and church district.

The problem of land room is generally alleviated by the rather sizable number of persons who leave the orthodox groups. They then join the liberalized groups, who are usually engaged in occupations other than farming. The size of ceremonial affiliations is in many instances kept small by the disagreements over the discipline. Among groups who exercise the rigid form of excommunication and shunning, divisions are an alternative to migration. Migration to other rural areas is another alternative where social distance breaks down between the different groups. The assimilation patterns suggest that the Amish, who make the least use of formal education, whether indigenous or nonindigenous, are most vulnerable in terms of losing members.

Patterns of Mobility in Hutterite Society

In Hutterite society the loss of members is low. Some single boys leave the colony during the summer, but usually return in the fall. Of those who attempt to leave permanently, many return after they have "tried the world." The transition from the communal to individualistic style of living appears to be unnatural for them. Intensive moral indoctrination from kindergarten through adolescence helps to offset attractions in the world. Only 258 men and 11 women left the colony voluntarily from 1880 to 1951 (Eaton and Weil 1955:146), but over half returned.

Our study of Hutterite defection suggests that the communal socialization patterns are so effective that the small number who do abandon the colonies are those who were deprived of the normal communal training usually given a child (Hostetler 1965). The loss of members varies with "declining" versus "cohesive" colonies. A declining colony has chronic problems of internal leadership or dissension that have not been resolved. The rules of mobility do not permit a member to move from one colony to another of his choice. Of 38 defectors interviewed in depth, it was found that half had come from five nuclear families and all were located in declining colonies. In a few cases the school teacher was blamed for leading the young astray, teaching anti-Hutterite doctrine, and for finding jobs for them outside the colony. One colony girl eloped with the school teacher.

In Hutterite society there are no legitimate ways to become a non-Hutterite, not even Mennonite. Mobility is essentially blocked. Most male defectors interviewed tended to be indifferent to religion. They showed little interest in making distinctions between the vast number of denominations that are not Hutterite. The absolutist position of the Hutterite religion continues to structure the thinking patterns of those who defect permanently. The religion taught to them in childhood is basically respected by them in such statements as: "If I ever want religion, I know where to find it." One who had abandoned the colony forty years ago said that during the intervening years, "the little faith that you had was right there to sort of guide you. The guardian angel was always with you, it seemed like."

All colony roles are psychologically marked by strong elements of dependency, especially for women. Any woman who cannot accept the definition of the role given to her will have more difficulty than a man in finding alternative avenues of expression. Several groups of sisters who abandoned a colony gave us their reasons that the colony was no longer Christian. An underlying factor is that these sisters who found company in each other's misery rejected the submissive Hutterite role assigned to women. Their conversion to an individualistically oriented fundamentalist denomination permitted a rational way of escape.

Emphasis on individual self-development constitutes a disruptive influence in a communal society. It is rare that an individual will receive sufficient personal attention to develop adequate personal security to leave the protective environment of the colony. Parents who show favoritism to a child or entertain ambitions for a child beyond those sanctioned by the colony introduce dissident elements and increase the probability of defection. This relationship is understood by Hutterites. They say that if one is too good to a single child he is more likely to leave. The favored child who obtains attention and privilege above others in the family or in the colony acquires self-confidence above his peers. Interests are developed and needs are felt beyond what the colony can provide. A child that does not experience the same rejection as his peers will not be frightened by problems that require imagination and individual solution. A father who wanted his son to become an engineer (a goal not attained by others in the colony) entertained non-colony goals for him. A father who wanted his son to become the English school teacher on the colony entertained a vocation for him that led to defection. An able leader who exceeds the limits (usually intellectually) or engages in certain privileges may unwaringly pave the way for subsequent deviation by his children. When children are treated as separate personalities in the formative years, individualism tends to develop to such an extent that it constitutes a threat to the colony. The system works best when the preeminence of the collective welfare over individual welfare is cheerfully and unquestionably accepted by all the members. Although the Hutterites recognize real difficulties in maintaining the loyalty of their young, it will be observed that they have a different pattern of assimilation than do the Amish.

Conclusions

1. In American society it is assumed that the vigor of national life depends upon educated men and women at every level of society. The goals of education are directed toward self-development and fulfillment of individual wants,

the enhancement of rational powers and personal freedom. The two communitarian societies we have described emphasize submission of the individual to community goals and the subordination of personal freedom and rationality to community values. Individual fulfillment is realized primarily within the bounds of the culture rather than outside of it. Science, technology, and science-oriented education are held in moderation in order to preserve the social order.

2. While the American young person is in high school, the Amish and Hutterite adolescent is learning to identify with his culture. The task of acquiring the necessary attitudes and skills to enjoy life in the little society are achieved in the context of family, kinship groups, work, and community. Socially it is an age span when greater freedom is permitted. The vows of the church and the commitment to the moral values have not yet been assumed, and during this period the young person is allowed maximal freedom to voluntarily test his beliefs and find his identity. These communitarian societies recognize the danger of exposing their young people to an alien peer group during adolescence. The high school is recognized for what it is: an institution for drilling children in "values, preoccupations, and fears found in the culture as a whole" (Henry 1963:287). The extent to which the communitarian society can control the social patterns of interaction and fulfill the basic needs of personality during the adolescent period is directly related to its viability.

3. The differences in assimilation patterns between the Amish and the Hutterite groups are related to the differences in social structure and defensive structuring. Given the same religious background and values, the communitarian society with the most integrated educational experience has the least amount of assimilation. The individual as well as the family in the Amish society has greater freedom of mobility, where and when he will travel and where he will live, than does the individual in Hutterite society. Amish persons who leave their culture often associate with groups similar to their own in religious orientation. Hutterites often show little inclination for religious affiliation after defection. The Navaho and Zuni adaptations to culture change (Adair and Vogt 1949) appear to have some similarities to these two Anabaptist groups.

4. Hutterites maintain formal education through all ages to maturity. There are "schools" fitted to all ages. The Amish depend entirely on informal education except for the elementary school period. The effect of introducing one more formal system of education (public) in the Hutterite colony is minimal since there is already a great amount of formal instruction. The Hutterites rather than the Amish manifest the least apprehension in accepting certain aspects of public education. The Hutterites integrate certain aspects of public education into their system of total socialization in a manner that maximizes their communal life and neutralizes any noxious effects. Formally they accept the inevitability of public education but informally they "tame" its pagan influences.

5. The management of crises over educational policy in the Amish and Hutterite groups differ significantly. The conflict is felt more directly by the Amish child than by the Hutterite child who may not even know that a "school problem" exists. Amish children often know they are the objects of controversy. When a legal code is enforced against a Hutterite parent the government is faced with religious leaders who are also the school officials and the real defendants. An Amish parent who may be charged with a violation must appraise his own commitment to his church, seek informal support from his church officials, obtain legal counsel at his own expense, or defend his position in court without either legal aid or representation from his church. Social solidarity is thus best maintained in a communitarian society that institutionalizes its contacts with the great society in contrast to one where the individual must represent his own position in an alien culture.

This analysis has not dealt with the products or the personality types developed in the two communitarian societies. These topics are discussed in greater detail in two case studies (Hostetler and Huntington 1967 and 1971). Through internal discipline and community support, often in the face of court action and scant legal protection, the two communitarian societies have transmitted the skills and attitudes required by their culture. Both have been able to mitigate, at least temporarily, the onslaught of the large consolidated school and its associated values.

References

Adair, John, and Vogt, Evon, 1949, "Navaho and Zuni Veterans: A Study of Contrasting Modes of Culture Change," *American Anthropologist* 51 (1947): 547–461.

Bachman, Calvin G., 1942, *The Old Order Amish of Lancaster County, Pennsylvania.* Norristown, Pa.: Pennsylvania German Society. Reprinted 1961.

Bennett, John W., 1967, *The Hutterian Brethren: Agriculture and Social Organization in a Communal Society.* Stanford, Calif.: Stanford University Press.

Bontreger, Eli J., c. 1910, "What Is a Good Education?" In, J. Stoll, ed., *The Challenge of the Child.* Aylmer, Ontario, Pathway Publishing Company, 1967, p. 77.

Buchanan, Frederick R., 1967, *The Old Paths: A Study of the Amish Response to Public Schooling in Ohio.* Ph.D. dissertation, Ohio State University, Columbus, Ohio.

Deets, L. E., 1939, *The Hutterites: A Study of Social Cohesion.* Gettysburg, Pa., privately printed.

Eaton, J. W., and R. J. Weil, 1955, *Culture and Mental Disorders.* New York: The Free Press.

Educational Policies Commissions, 1961, *The Central Purpose of American Education.* Washington, D.C.: National Education Association.

Erickson, Donald A., 1969, *Public Controls for Non-Public Schools.* Chicago: University of Chicago Press.

Goals for Americans. 1960, *The Report of the President's Commission on National Goals.* Englewood Cliffs, N.J.: Prentice-Hall, Inc.

Henry, Jules, 1963, *Culture Against Man.* New York: Random House.

Hostetler, J. A., 1954, *The Sociology of Mennonite Evangelism.* Scottdale, Pa.: Herald Press.

———, 1963, *Amish Society,* revised 1968. Baltimore, Md.: The Johns Hopkins Press.

———, 1965, "Education and Marginality in the Communal Society of the Hutterites." University Park, Pa., mimeographed.

———, and Huntington, G. E., 1967, *The Hutterites in North America.* CSCA. New York: Holt, Rinehart and Winston, Inc.

———, 1971, *Children in Amish Society: Socialization and Community Education.* CSEC. New York: Holt, Rinehart and Winston, Inc.

Hughes, Everett C., 1952, *Where Peoples Meet.* New York: The Free Press.

Hutterian Brethren Church, 1950, *Constitution of the Hutterian Brethren Church and Rules as to Community of Property.* Winnipeg, Manitoba.

Indiana, Department of Public Instruction, 1967, Articles of Agreement Regarding the Indiana Amish Parochial Schools and Department of Public Instruction. Richard D. Wells, Superintendent.

Knill, William, 1958, *Hutterian Education.* M.A. thesis, University of Montana, Missoula, Mont.

Peters, Victor, 1965, *All Things Common, The Hutterian Way of Life.* Minneapolis: University of Minnesota Press.

Redfield, Robert, 1955, *The Little Community.* Chicago, Ill.: University of Chicago Press.

Rideman, Peter, 1965, *Account of Our Religion,* English edition 1950. London: Hodder and Stoughton, Ltd.

Siegel, Bernard J., 1970, "Defensive Structuring and Environmental Stress," *American Journal of Sociology* 76: (July) 11–32.

Simons, Menno, 1956, *The Complete Writings of Menno Simons.* Scottdale, Pa.: Mennonite Publishing House.

Stroup, J. Martin, 1965, *The Amish of the Kishacaquillas Valley.* Lewistown, Pa.: Mifflin County Historical Society.

Weber, Max, 1958, *The Protestant Ethic and the Spirit of Capitalism.* New York: Charles Scribner's Sons.

Williams, George, 1962, *The Radical Reformation.* Philadelphia: Westminster Press.

GEORGE D. SPINDLER/*Stanford University*

7 *Beth Anne—A Case Study of Culturally Defined Adjustment and Teacher Perceptions*

This case study of Beth Anne will demonstrate how culturally unsophisticated perceptions of children by teachers may damage the "successful" middle-class child as well as the academically "unsuccessful" minority child in the school. The situation is in many respects the reverse of those portrayed in the preceding chapters by Raymond McDermott and myself, but in all three chapters the basic theme is the influence of the teacher's culture and the school upon perceptions and interpretations of children's behavior. For this purpose I am using a case study carried out when I was one of three people working in a school system under the aegis of the Stanford Consultation Service, directed by Dr. Robert N. Bush.[1]

Our purpose as a service team was to perform various studies of whole classrooms, teachers, individual children, other groups in the school, and even of whole school systems, as well as top supervisory personnel. Unlike the practice in a usual field study, we shared the data we collected and the analyses of those data with our informants. By so doing we hoped to share any benefits that might result from our research and direct them toward the improvement of the schools and the professional competence of teachers and related staff.

In this particular school, which we will call Washington Elementary School, we had entered to work with the whole staff of twelve teachers and the principal. First, we asked the assembled staff what it was they would like to study. They proposed a study of the "adjusted"—rather than the maladjusted—child in the classroom and in interaction with teachers and peers. We accepted this novel idea enthusiastically and proceeded to set up a mechanism whereby "adjusted" children could be selected for study. After some discussion the teachers helped out by deciding upon several specific children. These children's classes were approached as a whole for volunteers for the study. Among the volunteers were the children picked out by the staff.

[1] Details of time and place are left ambiguous, certain minor details of fact are altered, and all personal references are disguised in order to protect all parties involved with the case study.

The studies were cleared with their parents and we proceeded over a period of about three months to collect data and periodically to discuss these data and our interpretations with the assembled staff of the school. Beth Anne, a fifth-grade pupil, is one of the children studied.

The Classroom and Beth Anne's Place in It

The fifth-grade class consisted of 35 children ranging in age from 9 years, 8 months to 11 years, 8 months. The I.Q. range as measured by the California Mental Maturity Test appropriate to this age level was 70–140 with a mean of 106. There were three reading groups in the room, highly correlated with I.Q. scores as well as with reading achievement scores.

The classroom consisted of 20 children who could be described as Anglos whose socioeconomic status ranged from upper lower to upper middle (using the scales drawn from the studies of H. Lloyd Warner and his associates). The other 15 children were from the minority groups represented in the community surrounding the school and included 3 blacks, 2 Filipinos, 3 Japanese-Americans, and 7 Mexican-Americans (the term "Chicanos" was not current at that time).

Beth Anne was 10 years and 3 months old, just 3 months below the average for the whole class. She was in the top reading group and at the 95th percentile with her I.Q. test score of 132.

Excepting for occasional minor illnesses Beth Anne was apparently in good health, according to her parents and to records from the school office. She was dark haired, clear skinned, well developed for her age, had regular features and almond-shaped brown eyes, and wore braces on her front teeth. She always came to school extremely well dressed and was polite and considerate in her relations with her teachers; she appeared to be slightly reserved but equally considerate with her peers. The members of the team as well as the teachers in the school were impressed with her appearance and manners and regarded her as an exceptionally nice-looking child of good background.

Beth Anne was described by the teachers as an "excellent student," one of "the best students in the school," one who is "extremely conscientious," "cooperates well," "never has caused trouble in any of her classes," and who is "well liked by the other children." Further comments from the faculty were elicited in discussions of Beth Anne and the other children selected for study before the studies began.

Her former first-grade teacher said, "She was a very bright little child, perhaps not too friendly. At first she didn't respond too readily to me, but gradually began to work well and by the end of the year appeared to have made an excellent adjustment." Her present fifth-grade teacher said that "Beth Anne has attended very regularly this year. She is very interested in her class work and activities and performs at top level in everything. She even does excellent work in arithmetic and she plays very well with the other members of the class and in general with children of her own age." The principal said, "Her home would certainly be classified in the upper-middle bracket. The parents are middle aged, having married late. They have a very nice home and provide every cultural experience for the children." She went on to say that "one of the things that has concerned me a little, however, is a kind of worried look that Beth Anne has sometimes. It seems that if she doesn't understand the very first explanation in class, she is all concerned about it. She hasn't seemed so much that way this year but I have noticed it a lot in the past." Another teacher said, "Well, the mother has always been very interested in her children and has worked to give them many advantages. Beth Anne and her brothers and her parents go to many things and places together." Another teacher agreed, "Yes, they go to symphonies, I know. And they all went to the football game at Orthodox U."

Several times, and in different ways, we asked the teachers whether they regarded Beth Anne as a "well-adjusted" child. There were no explicit reservations expressed except for the comment by the principal about her "worried look" and the comment by her first-grade teacher that at first "she didn't respond too readily." The teachers all expressed verbal agreement that she was indeed very well adjusted, both academically and socially. Several teachers went out of their way to say that she was not only accepted by her peers but was considered a leader by them.

The Evidence

The study consisted of weekly classroom observations, watching playground activities, interviewing teachers, and administering psychological and sociometric tests. After having established the conditions of our study, our first step was to explain to Beth Anne what we would be doing and why. With her apparent enthusiastic consent, we proceeded then to a first interview followed by administration of the Rorschach projective technique and the Thematic Apperception Test (TAT). Within the following two weeks we also administered a sociometric technique to the classroom group. This technique included the questions, "Whom would you like best to sit next to?" "Whom do you like to pal around with after school?" and "Whom would you invite to a birthday party if you had one?" The sociometric maps of the choices expressed by the children were made up from the results elicited by these questions. They were quite consistent with each other. The sociometric map (sociogram) resulting from the responses to the first question is shown in Figure 7.2. We also administered a status-reputation technique that included thirty-two statements such as, "Here is someone who fights a lot," "Here is someone who never has a good time," "Here is someone who does not play fair," "Here is someone who is good looking," "Here is someone who likes school," "Here is someone who plays fair," and so forth. The children were to list three names in rank order following every statement.[2] Following are summaries of these categories of data.

Observations

The reports by our three-man team of observers of Beth Anne's behaviors in the classroom and around the playground were monotonously similar. Beth Anne did not cause trouble. She was obedient, pleasant, and hard-working. She responded to questions in a clear voice and was noticeably disturbed when she was unable to provide the answer to a question in the arithmetic section. She read well and easily.

However, she interacted only infrequently with the other children in the classroom, either in the room or on the playground. She seemed quite reserved, almost aloof. Apparently she had a fairly strong relationship with one girl who looked and acted much as she did and who seems to have come from the same general social and cultural background.

Sometimes she chose to stay in the classroom when recess was called and would go out only at the urging of the teacher. She played organized games but not enthusiastically and seemed to find aggressive handling of a ball or other play equipment difficult.

Psychological Test Results

The Rorschach and the TAT were administered the day after the preliminary interview with Beth Anne and before any other observations or other methods of data collection had been implemented. Without becoming involved with the many problematic aspects of their interpretation, I will summarize the results of these psychological techniques. In general we found these projective techniques to be of considerable use in our studies of individuals, though we regarded them with a certain flexibility.

THEMATIC APPERCEPTION TEST ANALYSIS Most of the pictures in the TAT are of people engaged in social interaction and the subject is asked to tell a story about each picture. This story should state what the people are doing and thinking, what probably happened before the situation pictured, and what probably will happen. Beth Anne did not like to tell stories of this kind. Picking up the TAT pictures, she stated perfunctorily who the people were and what they were doing and then laid them down with what appeared to be an impatient air of finality. She was not able to say more upon probing, though

[2] With the wisdom of hindsight, I would not administer this technique again. It is potentially destructive to children's self-feelings and stimulates corrosive interpersonal evaluation.

she appeared to be at least superficially eager to comply. The TAT record is consequently rather sparse, though it is revealing.

The resistance to letting her imagination guide her to a creative solution to problems of human relationships as suggested by the pictures seems to be the most important feature of her protocol. She does not seem to like to be in a situation where she has to turn to her own creativity and utilize her emotions for interpretation. She does not seem to be able to empathize freely with the people in the pictures, even when she sees them as children. When asked what they might be feeling or thinking, she answered "I don't know," and if pressed by the interviewer, "How should I know?"

It is hard to pick out the most revealing instance of this aspect of her personality from the large amount of evidence in the TAT protocol. Upon seeing a picture of a little boy sitting in front of a log cabin she said, "It looks like he lives in a log cabin." ("What is he doing there?") "He's probably sitting there thinking about something." ("What is going to happen?") "Probably he is going to do what he is thinking about after a while." ("What is he thinking about?") "I don't know what he's thinking about. He's just thinking about all the things there are to think about!" In my experience with the administration of this technique with children her age, this is an unusual response. Most children as intelligent as Beth Anne seemed to embrace the task of telling the story about each picture with considerable spontaneity and creativity. Not so Beth Anne, who did not seem to be able to let herself go.

In another instance, when she was presented with a blank card and told to put a picture there by telling a story, she said, "There's nothing to make up that I can think of." That appeared to be literally true. She did not seem to be able to dip into any reservoir of imagination.

Beyond this prevailing feature in her TAT protocol, we can say that she shows some overt hostility toward authority. She also shows a certain amount of depression that is fairly rare for children her age, and she is made quite uneasy by symbols of open aggression.

There is no direct evidence of what could be called a pathological character development. What seems to be apparent is a lack of spontaneity and a refusal or inability to use her imagination to interpret the behavior of others.

RORSCHACH Beth Anne gives evidence in her Rorschach protocol of possessing superior intelligence. She produced forty-eight appropriate responses, a result which is not only well above the average for her age group but higher than most adults achieve. She exhibits a high regard for detail and specification, but does not embark upon any flights of fantasy nor does she often put the details together to form an integrated whole perception.

Both qualitatively and quantitatively her protocol suggests that she is more constricted emotionally and intellectually than her superior productivity would lead one to expect. She has a well-developed perception of the concrete world about her, but these perceptions seem to stop at the level of concrete detail.

There is some evidence that she feels herself to be at times overwhelmed by forces beyond her control. There is also evidence that she has strong feelings that are not channeled into manageable interpersonal relationships or self-development.

It may be misleading to say that she lacks "creativity," but there is little imaginative spontaneity and little use of emotions for interpretive purposes. Beth Anne is what is sometimes known as a "tightrope" walker who sees what it is safe to see. She seems to avoid aspects of the inkblots that may have strong emotional implications for her and does not go deeply within herself for responses that would be emotionally meaningful. She avoids entanglements in emotionally laden material.

Furthermore, she seems to be fairly restricted in her ability to empathize with human motives or feelings. She does not seem to be able to put herself into another person's shoes, possibly because she has suppressed many of her own drives and feelings. At times, this may affect her intellectual performance, since she appears to be led off into inconsequential details and fails to see the larger whole.

Beth Anne is not likely to be a trouble maker. She conforms even at her own personal cost. She says "Thank you" every time a Rorschach card is handed to her and "Oh, pardon me!" when she drops a card an inch onto the desk and it makes a little noise. She seems very concerned about performing adequately and asks continually if she has given enough responses.

There is evidence that there are some definite problems in the handling of emotions. Generally speaking, the emotions seem to be suppressed or avoided, but when they are confronted they seem overwhelming. Given this evidence within the context of a personality adjustment that can be described as constricted and at the same time achievement-oriented, one would predict the probability of some form of hysterical behavior, probably in the form of conversion to somatic disturbances or to chronic invalidism. We shall see later that this prediction was supported.

The Rorschach psychogram is reproduced here (Fig. 7.1). For those familiar with Rorschach interpretation, one can note the heavy emphasis upon the "m" response and upon the "F" category, the absence of textural or shading responses, the absence of controlled color responses, and the presence of several relatively uncontrolled color responses. This psychogram is accompanied by 6 percent whole responses, 51 percent large usual-detail responses, 20 percent small usual-detail responses, and 23 percent unusual-detail or white-space responses. Beth Anne's average reaction time for all responses was 11.5 seconds. As everyone who has worked with the Rorschach knows, not too much faith should be placed upon the formal psychogram. It happens in this particular case that the psychogram relates closely to interpretations that flow from the qualitative nature of the responses. This tends to support the interpretation but does not validate it.

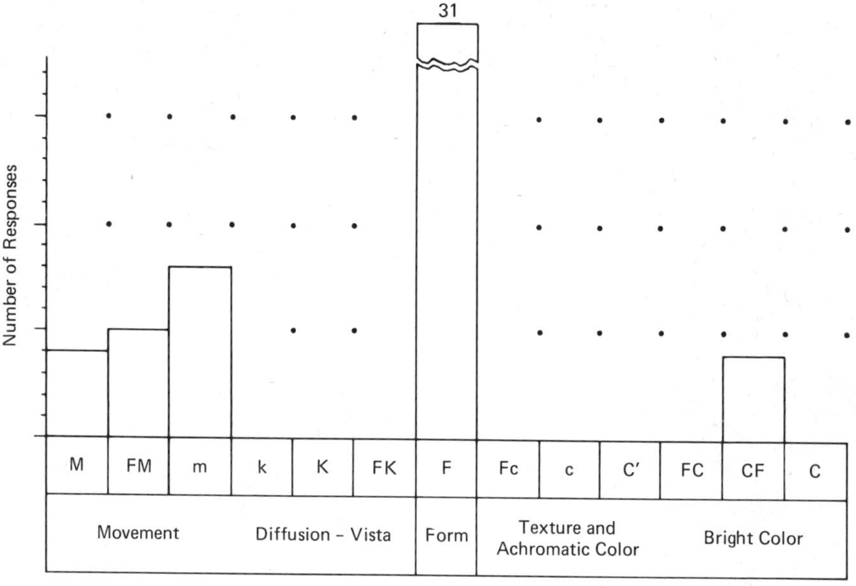

Figure 7.1. Beth Anne's Rorschach profile.

Sociometric Results

The sociogram (Fig. 7.2) maps the results of class responses to the question, "Whom would you like to sit next to?" Without attempting an analysis of the classroom as a whole, I will only say that as is not unusual at this age level, there is a definite separation between boys and girls. While the boys tend to cluster around certain leaders or "stars of attraction," the girls usually relate to each other in smaller cliques or even dyads.

Beth Anne's position in the classroom group insofar as these data show is extremely marginal. She is the second choice of a girl whom she considers (inferred from other data) to be her best friend. She made no choices herself. Her social situation is not significantly altered according to the social mapping of the results of the responses to the other two questions, "Whom would you like to pal around with after school?" and "Whom would you like to invite to a birthday party?"

Responses on the status-reputation test from the classroom group are impressively consistent with the results of the sociometric technique. Beth Anne is rated minimally: once for "Never having a good time" and once each for "liking school" and "Being good looking."

The results from both techniques indicate that Beth Anne is marginal in the classroom group. She is given very little attention—either favorable or unfavorable. It is almost as though she were not there at all. These results are consistent with direct observations made of her behavior and interactions with other children in the classroom and on the playground during recess.

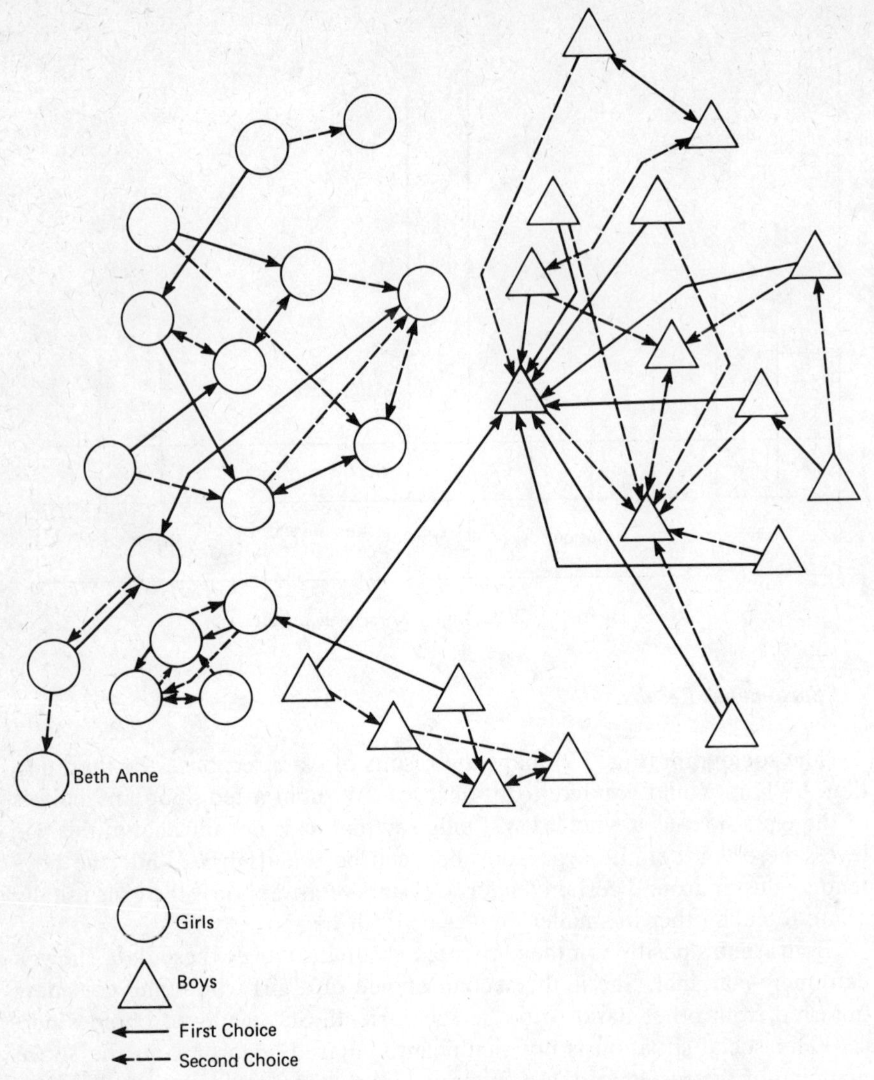

Figure 7.2. Sociogram for Beth Anne's fifth-grade class.

Home Visit and Parent Interview

Her parents were informed that the study of Beth Anne was under way. They had given their enthusiastic permission for the study when they were told, as was true, that Beth Anne was selected as a particularly well-adjusted child for special study. After the data collected above had been discussed within our team, an appointment was made to discuss the material with the parents and I was elected as the team representative. By that time the study had become primarily mine, although all three members of the team had engaged in observations and we had discussed the data as they came in during weekly seminar sessions.

Beth Anne's home was decidedly upper middle class in furnishings and exterior appearance. The interior appointments were luxurious and a two-car garage with a beautifully landscaped lawn completed the picture. Her father's occupation as the manager of a large building materials manufacturing company was appropriate to the socioeconomic status assignment.

When I entered the house Beth Anne's mother was waiting for me and said that her husband would come soon because he was very interested also. We discussed their recent trip to Alaska until Mr. Johnson arrived. Mrs. Johnson's attitude seemed very cooperative, and in fact she appeared pleased that the school had arranged to have a home visit and interview.

As soon as Mr. Johnson arrived we began a cordial discussion over coffee. I wished to make it clear at the very beginning that we were not dealing with Beth Anne as a "problem" case, so I reviewed the circumstances of the selection. We were working with the faculties of several schools in the community in an attempt to improve understanding of the adjustments of children at different grade levels—academically, socially, and emotionally. Having set the stage in this positive manner, I asked what aspects of our results they were particularly interested in. The father, a dynamic doer who wasted no time getting to the point, asked three questions as one, "What did you do, what did you find out, and what are you going to do about it?"

Rather than answer all these questions, I explained the techniques used in our study in some detail, including observations, sociometric materials, and projective tests. I explained why we used these techniques and what each contributed to a rounded picture of the child's adjustment. The parents seemed interested but obviously had some other concerns on their minds.

Mrs. Johnson queried, "Did you find that Beth Anne was temperamental or nervous at all?" I asked her to explain what she meant by that. She went on to explain that Beth Anne was "always complaining about her health. If any little thing is wrong with her, she wants to go to bed and she is always thinking that she is getting sick." She elaborated upon this at some length and then went on further to say, "She used to have a tic. . . . I guess that's what you would call it. When she was reading, and she reads a lot, she would draw her stomach up into a tight little knot and then let it go and the abdominal muscles would jerk back and forth." She continued, "I took her to the doctor, of course, and he said that she was tense and nervous but not to worry about it, that it was just an abdominal tic. He said that she would get over it eventually and as a matter of fact she is better now." This condition had apparently become obvious about a year ago.

Using this as leverage, I asked the parents if she were not rather a perfectionist—if she didn't seem to feel that everything she did, particularly at school, had to be done perfectly. Both parents agreed quickly and rather enthusiastically that this was the case. They appeared to regard my question as somewhat of a compliment. Possibly they could regard the pattern I described as evidence of a high achievement drive. They confirmed the observation implicit in the question with several examples concerning her behavior at home, in her room, her dress, and maintenance of personal possessions. After some minutes of this, I asked them if they thought this perfectionism might not cost her too much in tension and loss of spontaneity. While both parents nodded assent to this, they did not agree as wholeheartedly as they did when I asked them if she were not a perfectionist. They apparently could accept the definition of Beth Anne as an achievement-oriented youngster, but they could not bring themselves to accept the possibility that the standards of achievement could be so high as to make the cost so great. I did not press the point. When a silence in the conversation developed, I did nothing to fill it.

At this point Mr. Johnson said, "There's something else. . . . I'm not so concerned about it but Mary [the mother] is. . . ." And then the mother took up the cue, saying, "There are several junior high schools here [and she named them], now you have had a lot of experience in schools, could you tell us which one is the best?" I replied by asking her what she particularly wanted of the school selected. She said, "Well, we've been wondering whether or not we should move to a different neighborhood when Beth Anne is ready for junior high school. Washington School has been fine and we both appreciate all the things the teachers have done for Beth Anne, but you know there are all kinds of children over there—Mexicans, Italians, Chinese, Japanese, and even Negroes. Now, I believe in being democratic, but I feel that Beth Anne should associate with children that are, well . . . more her *equals!* [emphasis hers]. When she gets into junior high school this will be more important than it is now, but she feels it even now. She came home just the other day and said, 'Oh Mother, do I *have* to dance with them?' I think she should go to a school that doesn't have such a mixed group, where the children are all more her kind . . . don't you think so?"

In response I pointed out that the choice of a school was a decision that should be made by the parents in consultation with the child, and that what was important to one might not be important to another. Furthermore, it seemed to me that two points of equal importance in respect to a child's associates are, first, that the child be given a sense of belonging to a particular group and, second, that he or she should have broad experience with a wide variety of people from different backgrounds. This should enable the child to adjust well in any situation and to respect differences in others. When the parents pointed out that the two seemed contradictory I agreed, stating, however, that both could be accomplished if the parents' attitudes were supportive. To probe their attitudes a bit, I then suggested that they send their daughter to a private boarding school. Mrs. Johnson said that she wanted Beth Anne to be under her supervision, which would not be possible if she went away. However, she said, she wanted Beth Anne to be able to choose her own friends, with no attempt at reconciliation of the contradiction this posed with her other statements. I ended this phase of the discussion by saying that whatever the situation, Beth Anne's attitudes toward her classmates would reflect in significant degree what the parents thought.

I asked if there was any other specific topic they would like to discuss. The father asked how well Beth Anne was liked by her classmates. I replied, "She was not rejected more than a very few times by any other child; apparently they do not dislike her." While this did not tell the whole truth, it was at least in the direction of the truth, and I thought it was about as much as the parents could accept. I then asked if any of Beth Anne's friends were in her class, and Mrs. Johnson named three. My next statement was that Beth Anne was not chosen often either, and that in my opinion some of her classmates may have felt that she was critical of them. However, I told them also that the only negative trait on our status-reputation test was that she was rated as never having a good time. I could not explain the exact meaning of this, but assumed that it represented the children's feeling that she was serious about her school work. Before leaving I reassured them that "Beth Anne is a very excellent student and the teachers all like her a great deal." With reference to the points they had brought up, I told them that it might be important to see that she is encouraged to relax a little more and enjoy life as it comes. I said I thought her school work would keep up since she is very intelligent, even though her parents make this appear less important. I left thanking them for their cooperation and saying that it was a pleasure to talk with parents who were as cooperative as they were. They both uttered the usual pleasantries and said that they very much appreciated my coming to talk with them.

Teachers' Responses to the Evidence

By the end of our study period all of the evidence described above, plus many more details, had been shared with the staff. The teachers' responses could be described as ranging from surface compliance and agreement to deep covert resistance and resentment. I will draw a few representative comments from the tape taken during the final session with the faculty.

"I have her in art for 80 minutes a week where we try to bring out creative ideas, but actually she never offers any ideas. She usually looks at me as if to say, 'Well, what do I do next?'"

"I know Beth Anne and her family quite well and she knows this, but she is aloof with me. Does she impress the rest of you that way?"

"She reads so much. I should think this would aid her imagination. She reads stories about girls, camping, fairy stories, everything that children her age and even older read."

"She belongs to a group that went to camp last summer, but I don't think she went. She does have that little frown or worried look. I remember it bothered you, Mrs. Smith."

"I suppose that when a teacher has thirty-five children she tends to think of normal and adjusted in terms of how well they conform."

"Well they do have a very nice home. The parents just returned from a month's trip to Alaska and they hired a trained nurse to stay with the children. They have always been very thoughtful about their welfare."

"Well she has certainly done outstanding work academically, all the way through since kindergarten right up to the present in this school."

"She was always absent a lot in third grade and she never was particularly friendly. I always felt that she looked down her nose at the other children in the class who weren't quite up to her . . . I don't know whether she just didn't want to enter into things or whether she was fearful of making a mistake or what. Though she did good work, I always had a queer little feeling about her. I don't know just what it was."

"I don't think you have to worry about Beth Anne. She is going to arrive. Her family and their standing will see to that and she represents them very well."

"I agree. She'll be successful! She'll belong to a sorority."

"Well, anyway, she's a great reader!"

Interpretation

This case study virtually tells its own story and in that sense little interpretation is needed. Not all cases are as neat. This one was selected out of a much larger group—not for its representativeness but rather for its ideal-typical characteristics. It pulls together in one configuration dynamic processes that are present in some form in many other cases. It seems to be in part a reversal of the relationship between the teacher and the fifth-grade class and the counselor and his class that I have discussed elsewhere (1959). It is actually only a variation in this relationship. In all of these cases and in many others that we studied during our several years of field research and consultation, it became apparent that teachers, usually quite contrary to their expressed intentions and ideals, were selecting children for the fruits of success in our social system or for the ignominy of defeat and alienation on the basis of undeclared, and probably unknown, cultural biases.

Beth Anne was selected by the teachers by consensus as exceptionally well adjusted. It is difficult to know exactly what "adjusted" means to anyone, though it was a term used very widely in the fifties and sixties in American public schools. These particular teachers said during our preliminary consultations that adjustment meant "conformity to the rules and regulations of the classroom," "success at school work," "the ability to achieve according to the expectations of parents and teachers," "an ability to get along well with one's peers," "a person who is not too conflict-ridden when he or she attempts to get along with their work and play," and "a child who works and plays well with others." The teachers were clearly not all of a single mind concerning what adjustment meant, but their definitions tended toward an adaptation to the situation as defined by teachers, by rules, and, by the culture which the school represented. This is not unreasonable. In every cultural system those who accept the rules and achieve the goals laid down within the system are "adjusted" and those who do not are deviant, maladjusted, or criminal. The teachers' definitions do not pay much attention to what is inside Beth Anne's mind and, in fact, do not have much to do with Beth Anne at all. They have more to do with the school than with the child. This is understandable too.

However, we are faced with the fact that the teachers, even given their own criteria of adjustment, inaccurately perceived Beth Anne's situation. It is true that she achieved well according to the formal standards of academic performance. This achievement, however, was apparently at considerable psychic cost which was almost completely overlooked. Even more startling is the fact that the teachers misread the degree of her social adjustment. She did not "work and play well with others." In fact, she interacted with other children very little and was definitely marginal, really isolated within the classroom group.

Beth Anne's social marginality and isolation within the school was accompanied by severe internal distress in her own psychic system. She was compliant, a high achiever, but fearful of not achieving. She was unable to express her own emotions and had begun to evolve into a very constricted personality—all the more sad because she was such an intelligent girl. These processes had gone so far that a form of hysteric conversion had occurred. The prediction made on the basis of Rorschach evidence that the conversion would take the form of a somatic disturbance or possibly chronic invalidism was strongly supported. She wanted to stay in bed "on the slightest pretext" and suffered an "abdominal tic."

It would be easy to conclude that the teachers misperceived Beth Anne simply because she was academically successful—a high achiever in those areas where the teachers are directly responsible. This is, indeed, part of the cause for the misreading, but it is not a sufficient cause.

As I interpret the whole pattern of Beth Anne's adaptation and the perceptions of others of this adaptation, I see the teachers' perceptions as a self-sustaining cultural belief system. Beth Anne was selected not only because she was a high achiever but because in every other way she represented the image of what is desirable in American middle-class culture as it existed at the time of the study in the fifties and still exists today in slightly modified form. Beth Anne and her family represented success and achievement, the value of hard work, the validity of gratification delayed for future satisfaction, the validity of respectability and cleanliness, of good manners and of good dress as criteria for behavior. Beth Anne fit the criteria by means of which the teachers were selecting behaviors and children for the single channel of success and adaptation for which the school was designed as an institution representing the dominant mainstream culture.

I have characterized the belief in these values and selective criteria as self-sustaining because negative evidence was rationalized out of the system. Despite behaviors and attributes that any alert observer could have picked up in Beth Anne's case without the aid of outside experts or foreign instruments, Beth Anne was seen as one of the best-adjusted children in the school because she fit the belief system about the relationship between certain symbols, certain behaviors, and success as culturally defined.

This belief system, like most, can and does work. When belief systems stop working entirely they cease to exist, but they can continue to work partially for a very long time at great cost. In this case the cost to Beth Anne was profound. The culturally induced blindness of her teachers was in a certain real sense killing her and in ways no less painful than those in which minority children were and are being "killed" in many American schools.

Conclusion

I am not blaming teachers personally for what I have described in this case analysis. The teachers, the children, the administrator, and all of the other actors on the stage are acting out a cultural drama. What I am striving for as an anthropologist of education is an understanding of this drama as a cultural process. As an anthropologist teaching teachers I want to promote *awareness* of this cultural process. None of the teachers that I have described here or elsewhere in my writings (Spindler, 1959) are people of bad intent. Most teachers are idealistic, many are quite liberal in their political and social beliefs, but they *are products of their culture* and live within the framework of values and symbols that are a part of that culture. By being made aware of what they are and do they can be freed from the tyranny of their cultures; in turn, they will be able to free children from the damaging effects of premature, inaccurate, or prejudiced estimates and interpretations of their behavior that are culturally induced.

This awareness is not easily gained. Though the teachers were exposed to intimate details of Beth Anne's case as these details developed, and though we exercised responsible skill and sensitivity in the dissemination of this evidence in open and closed discussions, the resistance of the teachers to the implications of the evidence was profound. The educative process had some effect, probably, but I doubt that it was very significant as far as the future behaviors of the teachers is concerned. Nor is a course or two in anthropology the answer. A year's fieldwork in a foreign community where one's assumptions, values, and perceptions are profoundly shocked by raw experience would make a significant difference, but not always in a direction that would be useful in the classroom. Matters have improved since the study of Beth Anne, but they have not improved enough. In my opinion a substantial part of the energy and time devoted to training teachers should be devoted to learning how to cope with the kinds of problems that I have been discussing in this and other case studies.

We were somewhat more successful with Beth Anne and her family as individuals than we were with the teachers. We explicitly recommended that the standards of excellence be lowered somewhat for Beth Anne and that she be given to understand that such achievements were not all that was important. Beth Anne seemed considerably improved according to a short follow-up observation the next year. But we cannot be sure of what happened. It may be that doing the study had a positive effect. Beth Anne at least knew that someone else had found out what it was like to be Beth Anne, and her parents discovered that it was possible to face a problem that they intuitively felt to be there because an outside agency had detected the same problem.

Reference

Spindler, George Dearborn, 1959, *The Transmission of American Culture.* Cambridge, Mass.: Harvard University Press, for the Graduate School of Education.

GARY SCHWARTZ/*Institute for Juvenile Research, Chicago, Illinois*
DON MERTEN/*Institute for Juvenile Research, Chicago, Illinois*

8 *Social Identity and Expressive Symbols: The Meaning of an Initiation Ritual**

The Problem

This paper examines adolescent initiation rites in an urban context. Our analysis concerns the initiation rites of three high school sororities. Their members attend a public high school located in an upper-middle class residential area of a large Midwestern city.[1] The school also draws students from nearby stable working-class and lower-middle class areas.

The rites are elaborate and exotic: the meaning of many ceremonial activities appears obscure not only to outsiders but to the participants as well. The ritual also has a compulsive aspect, and, regardless of circumstances, these groups rigidly follow their ritual calendar. For instance, they presented *mock*[2] (a rite pervaded by exuberant buffoonery and grotesque ridicule) in a park the day after President Kennedy was assassinated. In our opinion, this did not reflect their callousness to the national sensibility or antipathy to the late President. Some of our informants recognized that their conduct appeared disrespectful to the rest of the community and felt guilty about it. Even though they might have preferred to postpone the proceedings, they felt that they could not violate the proper timing of the ritual sequence.

In many respects, these rituals are unlike adolescent rites of passage in tribal peasant societies. They do not involve transitions between basic social statuses for an entire age grade. Sorority initiation rituals include only some

*Reproduced by permission of the American Anthropological Association from the American Anthropologist 70(6), 1968: 1117–1131. We are indebted to Cal Cottrell for stimulating our interest in the general problem of expressive symbolism. See Schwartz and Merten (1967) for a brief discussion of our field methods. This paper reports on an on-going anthropological study of the youth culture in different types of urban communities that is supported by the National Institute on Mental Health, grant MH 12172-03.

[1] See Schwartz and Merten (1967) for a description of the salient socioeconomic characteristics of this community.

[2] We have italicized terms, on their first appearance, used with considerable frequency by our informants.

members of one social stratum and exclude all members of other social strata in the adolescent social system. Furthermore, adults do not supervise these rites, and it seems unlikely that these ceremonies occur in exactly the same manner elsewhere in the society. Finally, these initiation rites refer to symbolic movement between statuses within age categories rather than across age-category boundaries. Thus, the transformation of the initiate's social identity is recognized ordinarily only by his peers and not by his elders.

What bearing can such a parochial ritual have upon current anthropological theory that deals with the social implications of adolescent initiation rites? This paper argues that the meaning of this ritual illuminates two interrelated theoretical questions: (1) by what means do initiation rituals transform the initiate's self-image and social identity, and (2) what impact does this change have upon the social system? Here we follow Daniel Miller's (1963:673) definition of social identity as "the pattern of observable or inferable attributes [that] 'identifies' a person to himself and others; his identity is a socially labeled object which is of great concern and frequently reevaluated both by the person and others in the groups in which he is a member."

The first question probes assertions that initiation rites "express" or "dramatize" an individual's movement through the social structure (e.g., Gluckman 1962). While this is undoubtedly true, it hardly explains the source of their dramatic effect. That is, why are the participants convinced that their personal character is fundamentally altered by this ritual performance? In what way does this celebration of social virtues, which the initiate most likely has not demonstrated, bestow his new status upon him? More generally, if initiation ceremonies deal with the problem of shifts in an individual's social ties and allegiances, why should this form of symbolic communication supplant more mundane methods of discourse?

We propose that the kind of imagery that characterizes adolescent initiation rituals is responsible for this change in the participant's prosaic social identity. Those symbols Parsons (1951) terms "expressive symbols" transform social identities in a ritual setting.[3] Expressive symbols combine moral and aesthetic meanings. They not only represent one dimension of social

---

[3] Victor Turner has a similar approach. He says that:
"This term 'to grow' well expresses how many peoples think of transition rites. We are inclined, as sociologists—I have done so in this paper, and it is indeed a device which helps to understand many kinds of social interconnection—we are inclined to reify our abstractions and to talk about persons 'moving through structural positions in a hierarchical frame' and the like. Not so the Bemba and the Shilluk of the Sudan who see the status or condition embodied or incarnate, if you like, *in* the person. To 'grow' a girl into a woman is to effect an ontological transformation; it is not merely to convey an unchanging substance from one position to another by a quasi-mechanical force. . . . To arcane knowledge of *'gnosis'* obtained in the liminal period is felt to change the inmost nature of the neophyte, impressing him, as a seal impresses wax, with the characteristics of his new state. It is not a mere acquisition of knowledge, but a change in being. His apparent passivity is revealed as an *absorption* of powers which will become active after his social status has been redefined in the aggregation rites" [1965:11].

reality but also provide a source of immediate personal gratification. Expressive symbols reinforce the actor's experience of ethical achievement (i.e., he senses that he is the kind of person significant others esteem), and therefore they sustain his feeling of personal worth.

In initiation rituals, expressive symbols refer to personal qualities associated with membership in different social groups or statuses. The people who belong to these groups are thought to be certain types of persons; they are placed in moral categories. Expressive symbols metaphorically link the initiate's self-esteem to a set of moral categories that define various locations in a status system. As the initiate symbolically passes through the social hierarchy—to a status that is somehow "better," "higher," "nobler," etc. than the one he presently occupies—he discovers the significance this social transformation has for his personal character. He sees the kind of person he has become and likes what he sees. At the same time, he perceives some of the less benign implications of what he would have become or remained had he not completed this ritual journey.

The initiate, then, not only appreciates but also participates in expressive symbols in a ritual context. That is, their meaning resides both in what they say about him and do to him. As a newly confirmed member of a prestigeful social group, the initiate reveals those personal characteristics that his peers admire and applaud.

Expressive symbols have figurative meanings. On one level, the specific physical properties of an expressive symbol contain its meaning; they "convey some incorporeal or intangible states in terms of the corporeal or intangible" (Burke 1945:506). In one rite, the members of these sororities symbolically disfigured the initiates' appearances. The resultant image refers to the ritually imagined physiognomy of those persons who belong to a morally devalued and hence "degraded" social status in the adolescent social system.

On another level, expressive symbols act metaphorically. They organize the initiate's social experience in terms of the moral oppositions that underlie his passage through the status hierarchy. According to Kenneth Burke:

> Metaphor is a device for seeing something *in terms of* something else. It brings out the thisness of a that, or thatness of a this. If we employ the word "character" as a general term for whatever can be thought of as distinct (any thing, pattern, situation, structure, nature, person, object, act, role, process, event, etc.) then we could say that metaphor tells us something about one character as considered from the view of another character. And to consider A from the point of view of B is, of course, to use B as a *perspective* upon A (1945:504).

At once, the ritual establishes a symbolic perspective that refers to what the initiate is now (i.e., what status he occupies and what this implies about his personal character), what he shortly will become, and what he must not become. Here we agree with Black (1962:37) who says that "it would be more illuminating in some cases to say that the metaphor creates the similarity [between its literal or, in this case, social referent and its implied meaning] than to say that it formulates some similarity antecedently existing."

In this ritual complex, expressive symbols link the initiate's nascent or potential social identity to his achieved or ritually demonstrated social identity. In other words, those personal traits that made him a candidate for membership in these "exalted" social groups are now defined as proven and hence indelible aspects of his character. On the other hand, these symbols also point to a relationship of mutual exclusion between the initiate's new social identity and the personal attributes of members of morally-devalued categories. The ceremony claims that the initiate will never act in ways that identify the members of the latter categories, and, conversely, it suggests that these persons will never behave in ways that challenge the social pre-eminence of the dominant group in the adolescent community.

This symbolic complex enables the initiate ritually to transcend the future possibility of status contamination or loss; that is, he is now convinced that he never can become "like" the kind of people from whom he wishes permanently to disassociate himself. Since it is no longer possible for him to acquire these disreputable personal characteristics, his new social identity rests upon incontrovertible grounds.

The problem of the impact of adolescent initiation rites on the social system has generated considerable argument in the recent literature (Burton and Whiting 1961; Whiting 1962; Young 1962, 1965; Cohen 1964, 1966). While these investigators deal with male rites within a societal frame of reference, we believe that our approach reveals generic features of adolescent initiation rites obscured by methodological assumptions that unify these otherwise disparate studies. The issue, then, concerns an alternative method for interpreting the significance of adolescent initiation ceremonies.

Role Commitment and Group Solidarity

In spite of substantive methodological differences, these anthropologists presuppose that we can discover what the rites do to individuals once we know what they do for the community. From this perspective, the meaning of these rites ultimately resides in their functional implications for the society—the extent to which they contribute to the integration of the social system. Stated somewhat differently, they assume that there is an isomorphic relationship between the effect these rites have on the initiates' social identities and group solidarity; that is, the ceremony makes them the kind of persons they must become if the community is to function effectively.

Young (1965) argues that male initiation rites convey unequivocal definitions of appropriate sex-role behavior to the initiate. They fuse this essentially cognitive role discrimination with his desire to dramatize his increased status in the community. Therefore, according to Young, these rites create shared evaluations of sex-role performances, promote same-sex solidarity, and thereby strengthen cooperation in those activities vital to the community's welfare. Similarly, Cohen (1964) asserts that adolescent initiation rites (along with the earlier and more powerful practices of extrusion and brother-sister avoidance) weaken a youth's emotional identification with the members of his nuclear family, and, at the same time, define his social identity (i.e., establish his "socioemotional anchorage") in terms of his status in the larger corporate descent group to which he belongs. At this point, the adolescent realizes that under certain circumstances he is legally responsible to and for the members of this larger social unit. Thus, for Cohen, male initiation rites are part of a process that enables society to commit its members to accept the sometimes onerous burdens of adulthood.

Quite clearly, then, Young and Cohen subscribe to a role-commitment theory of adolescent initiation rites. But how does Whiting's work fit into this conceptual scheme? Young (1965) claims that Whiting's explanation of the function of male initiation rites rests upon "psychogenic" rather than "sociogenic" premises. That is, Whiting employs psychodynamic processes as the critical link between social structure and initiation rites and, moreover, views the latter as a means of resolving intrapsychic conflict rather than (as Young prefers) a means of creating attitudes that integrate the social system. Cohen (1966:358) characterizes Whiting's approach in similar terms; he remarks that the "individual as a system, and the effect on the individual of specifiable experiences" constitutes the basic unit of analysis for Whiting rather than the social system.

This vision of theoretical divergence (if not opposition) misconstrues Whiting's (Burton & Whiting 1961) argument. Specifically, it distorts the analytic significance of psychological variables in his explanation of adolescent initiation rites. Like the other investigators, Whiting is primarily interested in the integration of the social system. In particular, he wants to discover how a society induces its members to willingly accept their adult role responsibilities. As he phrases the question, how does a society make its members feel that the status they eventually must occupy is desirable as well as inevitable?

For Whiting, psychological variables reveal how individuals are integrated into an on-going social system. The process of identification and two derivative concepts, status envy and sexual identity, are the critical factors in his study: They bridge the gap between an individual's needs and desires and his enduring commitment to a particular social role. In fact, he defines identification as an emotional process that insures role commitment. An actor not only cathects but prepares to play a given role:

> The process of identification consists of the covert practice of the role of an envied status. Identification consists of learning a role by rehearsal in fantasy or play rather than by actual performance, and this rehearsal is motivated by envy of the incumbent of a privileged status (Burton and Whiting 1961:85).

Whiting assumes that a child identifies with those persons who command valued resources over which he desires but cannot gain complete control. In patrilocal societies that have exclusive mother-son sleeping arrangements, the male infant's early identification with the female role (i.e., with his mother) is later blatantly contradicted by the obvious power men exercise in community affairs. Hence, in these societies male adolescents experience sexual identity conflicts. Initiation ceremonies erase the youth's primary identification with the female role while instilling his masculine identity, and thus resolve structurally engendered sexual identity conflicts in the service of role commitment.

Whiting, therefore, shows how societies motivate individuals to strive to attain statuses for which they are ordained by the functional prerequisites of the social system:

> It is our thesis that the aim of socialization in any society is to produce an adult whose attributed, subjective, and optative identities are isomorphic: "I see myself as others see me, and I am what I want to be" . . . such isomorphism can only be achieved by passing through a stage in which there is status disbarment, status envy, and thus a discrepancy between one's optative and attributed identities (1961:87)

Though not explicit, it is clear that a society cannot survive for long if many of its members avoid or otherwise refuse to acknowledge their adult sex-role obligations.

The following analysis of these sorority initiation rites does not question the general validity of the role commitment thesis but this theory is not applicable to our data. On the other hand, Young (1965:10) remarks that while initiations into fraternities and similar organizations in our society are more abstract than those in simpler societies, they nonetheless "must appeal to general ideas of fraternal fellowship." However, in this instance, notions of fraternal fellowship and group cohesion are independent variables. For our informants, sorority *sisterhood* definitely implies solidarity. But they are well aware of the discrepancy between the ideal of loyalty among sorority *sisters* and the realities of a competitive, individualistic status system. In vital areas of interpersonal relationships such as rivalry over boys or gossip about *reputations,* one person's gain is another's loss. Thus, these girls are not likely to support others in the struggle for general esteem unless the other person is a *best* friend. Best friends are not restricted to the sorority to which one belongs, and, in any case, very few girls have more than one or two best friends.

Nor do these girls believe that this sort of solidarity is actually possible. These groups usually have no less than forty and often more than sixty members. The sorority includes what its members perceive as significant age differences that influence friendship patterns (i.e., sophomores, juniors, and seniors in the high school age-grading system). Furthermore, they regard factionalism as an inevitable though not desirable consequence of these informal friendship cliques.

These rites affirm the moral solidarity of persons who claim similar social virtues and who deny them to others. Hence, their function is specifically cultural (Parsons 1951). They support the ideology of groups that try to maintain their hegemony over the adolescent status system.[4]

Our approach reverses the methodological strategy of those who subscribe to the role commitment theory of adolescent initiation rites. Instead of looking at the effect these rites have upon the community, we focus on their impact upon the participant. To do this, we first discuss the meaning of sorority membership and then interpret this testimony in light of the cultural constructs adolescents use to evaluate their experience in the peer-group world.

The Culture Framework

Some studies of initiation rites rely upon native exegesis of ritual symbols and actions (Richards 1956, Turner 1962). Our informants were uniformly unable to offer even the most minimal rationale for the entire ritual complex, and they could not explain the significance of particular acts and symbols. Though emotionally involved in the ritual process, they were unintrigued by ritual symbolism. While we cannot explain this phenomenon, the fact that these ritual symbols invoke values that rest upon invidious comparisons with other strata in the adolescent community perhaps sheds some light on this issue.

In this community, the adolescents have an egalitarian ideology. Even informants situated at the apex of the status system said that no one is intrinsically superior to anyone else until proven otherwise. And though they argued that certain groups were inferior, they nevertheless did not feel that this contradicted their version of the American ethos of social equality: Given the proper "motivation" anyone can rise to the highest level of the adolescent social hierarchy. At the same time those personal traits that disqualified an adolescent from membership in the highest social circles were described in a biological idiom—as if these people were born with defective *personalities.* They were dull, ugly, shy, etc. Mobility in the status system, then, demands a change in what appears as innate personal characteristics.

Our informants agreed that one joins a sorority to demonstrate and validate one's ultimate *cool.* For these adolescents *coolness* and prestige are synonomous (see Schwartz and Merten 1967 for a discussion of the sources

---

[4] Though perhaps obvious, it is necessary to state that youth status hierarchies are by definition transitory (i.e., a person simply outgrows his status) and the dominant groups within them lack political and economic power. Those strata that gain social ascendancy in a particular area can only reinforce their position by the force of their interpretation of correct sex role behavior (i.e., by their conceptions of *coolness*). Authority in these social systems is solely moral, and therefore the stratification system rests on shared evaluations of the social attributes associated with the members of different social categories.

and meaning of coolness). Although coolness is a personal attribute, it is also a group property. In this context, the moral qualities ascribed to members of these groups influence their members' coolness and therefore prestige in the adolescent social system.

Our informants (here we are limiting our discussion to persons who belong or belonged to sororities and hence view the adolescent social universe from this perspective) use two sets of closely related categories to discriminate various groups in two different contexts.[5] As a guide to social reality, the first set of categories simply "describes" the relative rank and salient features of the strata of this status system. As a set of social standards that shape a person's willingness to associate with others, the second set of categories reveals the criteria that determine who is excluded from sororities. These sets of categories are not disparate "cognitive maps" but rather are models that organize native semantic distinctions made in existential and evaluative contexts.

When describing the social system, our informants saw two contrasting life-styles and three distinct strata. The *socialites* or *socies* occupied the top rung of the status system, and the *hoods* or *greasers* were situated at the bottom. Each stratum cultivated a life-style (i.e., modes of speech, dress, demeanor, and attitudes toward authority) that they believed opposed the values held by the other strata. They identified another stratum for which many did not have a specific label but which we called the conventionals. This stratum belonged to neither socie or hoody cliques but generally approved of socie styles and values. While this stratum occupies a middle position, none of our informants felt that there was anything like "middle-class respectability" in this social system.

When the grounds for membership in socie groups were discussed, this set of categories acquired different meanings. In this context, persons were located in groups according to their coolness. On this basis, our informants distinguished three strata: the *(socie) elites,* the *out-of-its* (which included hoods and anyone else whose very being evidenced a complete lack of coolness), and a group that was less frequently labeled by our informants but that some termed the *others.* One informant describes the latter group this way: "Well I suppose you can say the kids that aren't real popular or that you don't ever hear too much about or that aren't too intelligent." Whether an informant explicitly identified two or three lower strata was less important than the uniform emphasis on the line that divides those who properly belong to the socie world from those who do not. The critical social boundary for this group separates sorority members from all others. The following dialogue is instructive in this respect:

Q: What do you consider people who hang around with but don't belong to the sorority?

[5] This is a reformulation of an earlier model of the social system (Schwartz and Merten 1967).

A: Well, I don't know, now that I think about it, I can think of one girl that was just like that, Barbara; you know she hung around with ABCs.
Q: Who else?
A: Ah a couple of other kids, they were real close . . . but anyway Barbara hung around with them, and they were all ABCs, and they were real close and always had lunch together and everything, but when it came to being ABCs everybody still knew that Barbara wasn't one. And I think that she wanted to be one. She always wanted to be one and I think she tried to convince herself that she was an informal one, but still I don't think anyone else was convinced.

Thus, it is the latter set of cultural constructs (i.e., evaluative) that give sorority initiation rites their special meaning. As we shall see, ritual symbolism focuses on the implications of exclusion from the sorority, although specific rites employ imagery that refers to particular moral categories imagined to represent the antithesis of the sorority girl's personality. In sum, the primary significance of sorority membership resides in what it reveals about a member's social identity, that is, her coolness. As one informant put it:

Q: Well, when one becomes inducted into the sorority, are you leaving one category of people and entering another?
A: I think the members of the sorority and the pledges think of it that way.
Q: Which way?
A: As becoming . . . one of the cool. But it's funny, the way you face it, it just seems like rising above the crowd. I don't know if they think of it quite that way but I do know that they think well, you know now I am one of the in-crowd.
Q: So you are potentially cool?
A: Uh huh. They figure if you were potentially cool enough to be asked to pledge and pledge for a while, you're fairly cool.

The Ritual Cycle

This description of the sorority initiation ceremonies ignores minor variations in the procedures of different groups. The ritual is divided into named stages.

Rush

Early in the fall each sorority compiles a list of eligible girls; most are sophomores and a few are juniors. Those girls invited to the first *rush* party must be known by at least three members and have a few supporters willing to argue that they are worthy of the invitation. There are two kinds of rush parties given by each of the three sororities on three different days: a dessert and tea, and a quite lavish dinner party organized around a decorative motif. The inter-sorority council, comprised of officers from the three sororities, schedules these events.

The girls asked to these affairs are aware of the sort of inspection and evaluation they must undergo. Yet, these gatherings have an atmosphere of informal sociability; our informants wanted to get to "know" prospective members. Their personality assessments are based upon public presentations of self; they seek personal styles that indicate considerable facility in impression management. More concretely, a good prospect is supposed to be cool but not too cool, confident but not overbearing, sweet but not saccarine, deferential but not obsequious, gregarious but not self-assertive, demure but not shy, etc. Personal appearance is also carefully scrutinized. Our informants were likely to accept a girl who was very good looking and attractive to males but who lacked the social graces associated with feminine excellence. Conversely, they might *pledge* a girl they liked and admired but who was not physically attractive. Both were thought necessary to maintain the sorority's *image,* although girls who were successful in dating had a distinct advantage over those who were not. In general, they chose girls who exemplified complete adolescent virtue, that is, were both cool and *popular.*

BLACKBALL After the first rush party, the members discuss and vote on those who attended it. The discussion is termed *thinking of blackball,* at which time members who feel they will *blackball* the girl under consideration express their negative views. After those members who favor the girl try to convince those against her to change their opinions, blackball proper is held, which is secret. The outcome of each vote is held until all girls have been voted on. Five blackballs denies a girl an invitation to the second rush party. Usually thirty to forty girls remain on the second rush list. At the second rush party, the rushees are scrutinized especially closely. After the party, blackball is held again. Since this is the last opportunity for a member to vote against a rushee, the discussion of the merits of particular girls is much more heated than at earlier stages. It takes three blackballs to keep a girl from being asked to pledge. Those persons to whom pledge invitations are offered usually number between twenty to thirty. These invitations are delivered to the homes of prospective pledges by the sorority members.

For those who aspire to sororities and have survived the first blackball this is a critical moment in the ritual cycle. The meaning of being chosen or ignored is evident in the following statements:

Q: You got into ABC [often reputed to be the best of the three sororities] didn't you?
A: To this day I don't know [how she got in] because I didn't know, I knew maybe four kids in the sorority and I was asked to the first rush party and then I was asked to the second rush party and both of those invitations were delayed. They didn't come . . . they had the wrong address and it was kind of, you know you feel . . . I know how it feels because the night before one of the rush parties the girl brought it over and I didn't get it in the mail that day. I was just heartbroken and then she brought it over and it made me feel very good, and then it's really great when they deliver the pledge invitations personally because there's a big, long line of cars

and they all stop in front of your house and start singing one of their songs, usually the peppiest. And they all come into your house. And the first one that came was ABC and I was so happy. I was spoiled because I knew that was the one I wanted and oh, it's so great to see all these kids out there and you know, it's just really great. And then the other ones came and you try to be happy but it's not the same.

Another girl described her experiences thusly:

Q: You once said that making sorority was a sort of pivotal point in your life.

A: Yeah, because I was kind of jerky. It kind of makes me confident and it's about the only thing that would. I kind of fall back on it. If I hadn't gotten into sorority I would have been very self-conscious of my inadequacies. Maybe I would have come back up but I don't know . . . With some kids in A Cappella [a high school choral group] that's all they have. If they hadn't made it, it would have left them with absolutely nothing and shattered everything. They would really have no confidence in themselves. For me it wasn't the only thing I had [i.e., she was a sorority member].

Q: Do you think that if you had not pledged ABC, it would have changed your high school career appreciably?

A: Yes, but I don't know how . . . I probably would have walked along the side of the wall with my head down. . . . I remember the day after we got in—I was hysterical—you try to take it with a facade of calmness like you knew it all along and actually I had a case of hysterics the night before. But the next day a lot of girls took it kind of funny. They were almost mad at the ones that made it. I remember Sandra gave me the filthiest look. She probably figured that she should have made it and not me. I think it hurts them for a while but after a while I imagine they're still kind of conscious of it, and it's still a sore point but most kids take it real well and figure that they weren't the type. I wish I could have thought of it that way that night—that maybe I wasn't right for them. There's nothing wrong with me but I'm not right for them but it's kind of hard to think of it that way.

Pledging

Pledging lasts seven to nine weeks and includes distinct, named rites. Pledging begins with a formal tea. At this time *pledges* are given their bows (i.e., hair ribbons in the sorority colors). Each pledge is assigned to a *pledge mother,* a member who is supposed to help the pledge through the difficult period to follow.

Outside the immediate precincts of the school, a pledge must acknowledge a member's presence with a curtsey and a complimentary greeting such as "good morning, your royal highness." During the day, pledges provide menial services for members. More significantly, pledges are made to do foolish and childish stunts in the vicinity of the school, such as asking boys to marry them, proposing to a mail box, etc.

Pledges are segregated from the members in another room during sorority meetings. They are subjected to minor harassment and must entertain the members. Then they are individually brought into the members' room for *yelling.* The members literally scream at pledges for real or assumed failures, that is, the pledge is chastised for letting the sorority down. She has to supply personal information about each of the members of the sorority, and if her answers are not satisfactory, the yelling intensifies. Though the specific insults vary, the members try to convince the pledge that she is in some way unworthy of her present status. That is, the members imply that by chance the sorority overlooked some grave personal deficiency and that the pledge must now strive to make her character consonant with the sorority image. For these girls, then, the *raison d'être* of the sorority arises out of its collective personality.

HELL NIGHT On Wednesday night of the last week of pledging the pledges come to the meeting dressed in shorts and tennis shoes and bearing lipsticks. The members freely decorate the pledges with these lipsticks, emphasizing personal insignias such as their boy friends' names. Yelling reaches its peak at this meeting. Questions touch on primary identity issues: "Why do you want to be an XYZ?" And they focus on personal traits that the members feel demean the sorority: "Why do you date that creep?" "Why are your legs skinny?" Finally, the pledge is asked, "Will you do anything for your sorority?" Then she is told to cry. If she cannot, members scream at her until she does. However, there are cases where a pledge simply cannot cry, and in these very rare cases she is *depledged:*

Q: How can you cry?
A: Out of the clear blue sky?
Q: Yes.
A: It's easy, because you're scared, you know . . . you're not terrified but you're a little scared . . . it's not hard . . . some kids couldn't . . . Carole couldn't . . . Oh she just could not cry . . . she was scared too, but she couldn't cry for some reason. You know, if you don't cry they burn your pledge bows . . . And that's it . . . I mean it's a definite thing, you don't cry you don't get pinned . . . Unless they make a very, very rare exception and I mean a very, very rare exception.
Q: Did they do this in Carole's case?
A: No, they burned her pledge bows and then they said, "All right Carole, we're taking you home . . . there's nothing else we can do," and they started taking her home and she said, "No, I won't go home." She wanted to cry . . . It wasn't that she was being stubborn, but she just couldn't and then . . . when she ran back downstairs she knocked out her contact [lens], and I don't know if that shocked her or what because she cried as soon as it came out . . . she cried, and it wasn't because she lost it because she found it right away, she cried then, so then it was all right.

Crying prepares the initiate for the transformation of her social identity; she now realizes that through this ritual process she can resolve her character flaws and thus become truly worthy of her new status. Crying is also taken as the most concrete sign of commitment to the sorority. And this is a crucial element of pledging:

Q: Well, is being compliant enough to make you a good pledge?
A: You have to well . . . you have to be compliant but you have to show enthusiasm and that you want to be a member.

Genuine concern for one's acceptability to the sorority is one of the aims of pledging:

Q: What sort of things do bad pledges not do?
A: A pledge is sort of expected to be scared of members. And a bad pledge is kind of —the one we had in our lunch period, the only one—insolent. It didn't seem like she really wanted it, and she just didn't know when to bow [curtsey] and all this. There is really nothing that makes them good or bad except the way they act because you remember the way you had to act and oh we had hard members around then. You also take into consideration whether they act like they want it or whether they act like they don't care. If they act like it's a big mock; because if they think that then you're going to take offense to them right away.

For this stratum of the adolescent community, "sincerity" is a vexing problem in interpersonal relations. Both our socie and nonsocie informants believe that one of the great virtues and vices of the socies was their ability to appear friendly and gregarious in any social situation. Hence, role playing, the capacity to seem as if one truly cares about the outcome of social interaction in a given setting, is seen as problematic: No one is certain to what extent another is involved in or committed to a particular relationship. Therefore, the members of the sorority search for subtle clues to an initiate's true sentiments about her imminent membership. Crying, then, is perceived as an "involuntary" expression of emotion; it is a response to this critical status transition that cannot be dissimulated even though it is obviously induced by peer-group pressure.

SILENCE DAY Silence day begins the next morning in school. The initiate cannot speak to anyone besides parents, teachers, and sorority members. She is, to use Van Gennep's (1960) terminology, in a heightened state of ritual segregation while ostensibly participating in the normal activities prescribed by the adult community. Moreover, she is not allowed to set her hair the night before or to wear make-up to school that day. Since for socie girls dress and physical appearance identify the members of a morally devalued group, the hoody girls, this is more than a mild form of harassment.

TURNABOUT Turnabout occurs the next day; it involves role reversal. The members assume the subordinate position of initiates and the initiates take the superordinate role of the member. Though the members retain the right to refuse to obey the orders of the pledges, they carry out instruction with alacrity: the members try to impress the pledge with the seriousness of pledging. These seemingly absurd obligations prepare the initiate for something of utmost importance: the exchange of temporary personal discomfort for the lasting security of a socie identity.

MOCK On hell night each pledge gets a *mock* summons contained in an outrageously contrived package that requires some ingenuity to open. The message is a complex puzzle the initiate must solve in order to know what she must wear and bring to mock. Mock begins early in the morning when all of the members and pledges who belong to these three sororities assemble in a public park. Some of the friends and acquaintances of those involved in the proceedings come to view the spectacle. The pledges arrive in the garb prescribed by their summons. In our opinion, their dress on this occasion reveals one of the underlying concerns of this ritual complex: the social identities that the initiate presently will define as antithetical to their very being, that of the hoody girl and of the other.

Each girl is given a somewhat different appearance at mock but all have their usual mode of presentation of self radically altered. Normally, socie girls dress in very similar clothes, and they feel strongly that certain hair and make-up styles and clothing preferences are the most tangible and reliable indicators of a hoody identity. In their opinion, dress alone is not enough to determine whether a person is a socie but it certainly reveals commitment to a hoody way of life. Moreover, certain dress styles are believed to identify those others who are so removed from the fashions of the adolescent world that they cannot perceive the significance of dress. Dress identifies those who either reject socie values or who are insensitive to their standards.[6] One informant eloquently describes the meaning of dress:

Q: Would you say that your nonsorority friends made an effort to maintain the friendship?

A: Yes. I've stayed friends with Alice because Alice is really friendly with them all. You can't help but stay friendly with her because she shares a lot of interests but I didn't stay friends with a lot of them because you think that maybe the girls will look down on you if you hang around with so and so because she's not good looking or she's not that type. When you're in a sorority the other girls try to mold you and they [girls who are not in a sorority] get the wrong idea of what it is they [the sorority] want you to be. They want to be just like you when you're in a sorority. They think it's a lot of loud talk and they embarrass you. They try to dress like you and they try and act like you but they don't know how to do it. You've got to be trained by the experts and the experts are the girls. After watching them at

[6] Incidentally, this concern with the negative identity of the hoody girl is partly explicable if one understands some of the covert attractions this way of life has for a society girl. In their view, hoody girls are promiscuous, which at once makes them morally contemptible and gives them an "unfair" advantage in the dating system.

the meetings and watching how they act you're trained after six to eight weeks of pledging and you know just what to do. It's like a period of training.

Q: And other people try to emulate this but do it imperfectly?

A: They try and some will catch on but some are really pitiful. They're worse and they'll wear some of the clothes and some of a different kind and mix them together. Some of the time they'll act like sorority girls and some of the time they'll act like the others—like the middle group would.

Q: What would a person wear that was mixing the styles?

A: What really looks silly is they'll wear the right clothes but wear a big bouffant hair-do. Loafers look funny with a dress. Just little things like purses or jewelry. They all have to blend together to get a perfect picture. You wear a dress with flats and stockings, not with loafers and knee socks. Then you also have to have the real leather purses and the real expensive shoes and they'll go out and get the cheaper imitations of it. Sometimes you can get away with it but most of the time you can't and it looks funny. They [purses and shoes] start falling apart. But you've got to give them some credit for trying. I feel sorry for them and feel sorry for the girls in the sorority . . . They think they're better than anyone . . . I feel sorry for the kids because although they're just as nice, they can't be in because they don't have the looks and money. They're cheated. They'll [the sorority girls] look at one and say, "Isn't she a wierdo?"

Early Saturday morning all pledges arrive at the park in bizarre and exotic dress. Though it is difficult to capture the impression they make assembled at this park, perhaps a "typical" example might convey the visual impact of this gathering. A girl wears a bathing suit over men's pajamas and has a woman's stocking on one leg with a high-heeled shoe and a sock on the other foot with a flat-heeled shoe. Her hair is separated into many braids to which balloons are attached, and she wears a necklace composed of onions and sardines. She has a rope belt from which tin cans are hanging. Her face is painted in unmistakably strange patterns, perhaps one side is red and the other is black. No one sees this as a costume in the usual sense of the word. While it is obviously absurd and obtrusive, it nevertheless exaggerates dress styles socies see as common to other strata of the adolescent community. In addition to this garb, pledges are required to bring catsup, eggs, garlic salt, chocolate syrup, shaving cream, and the like with them to the park.

When all the pledges from these three sororities are present, they begin a race for six blocks to another park where the final phase of mock begins. The members drive to the other park shouting encouragement to their pledges who run along one of the main streets of the community. The pledge who arrives at the park first "wins" for her sorority although there is no special recognition of this accomplishment. Each sorority takes its pledges to a separate section of the park and starts to cover them with an amazing assortment of difficult to remove substances. The aim of this activity is to smear the pledge so that she looks as messy as possible. Special attention is paid to their hair. The substances are hand-rubbed (by the pledges) into the hair, and those who have been through this ritual claim that it takes weeks to completely remove all the odor and traces of this treatment. The official rationale for this event is that it is fun. Though the members engage in considerable hilarity, they also do a thorough job and work in a rather systematic fashion on each pledge. While the treatment is going on, the pledges are made to play in the sand or on the slides. After thirty to forty minutes have elapsed, the pledges are driven home in the open trunks of cars and mock has ended.

Induction

Until the next sorority meeting, the pledges remain in a transitional state; they are no longer pledges but are not yet members. Before the formal rite of induction, pledges exchange gifts with their pledge mothers. These gifts are sorority paraphernalia such as rings with the sorority seal. After this gift exchange, pledges retire to another room where they wait until the regular sorority meeting is over. Each pledge then is brought down into the room where she is told the secret password of the sorority, and for the first time sorority members address her by her first name. She now is blindfolded and gives the password before she passes through the door. The blindfold is removed and she approaches the sorority president. She then kneels on a pillow set before a table where the president is seated. Before inducting the pledge, the president asks the members if anyone has any objections and there never are. The pledge then reads a statement about her obligations to the sorority while the members gather around her and softly sing a song reserved for this occasion. After everyone is inducted, the members and pledges have a small party.

Interpretation

To understand this ritual, it is necessary to distinguish between an individual's personal and social identity. Goodenough (1966:178) says that "we must bear in mind that a person's identity as he perceives it, his self-image, does not necessarily coincide with his identity as perceived by others." Though formed out of the reactions of significant others, an individual's personal identity is never the simple sum of these judgments because it is not only subject to but can transcend the vicissitudes of time and place. Each person has a history that both places limits on and, at the same time, offers opportunities for new self-definitions. Goffman describes the historical aspect of personal identity in these terms:

> By *personal identity,* I have in mind only the first two ideas—positive marks or identity pegs, and the unique combination of life history items that comes to be attached to the individual with the help of these pegs for his identity. Personal identity, then, has to do with the assumption that the individual can be differentiated from others and that around this means of differentiation a single contin-

> uous record of social facts can be attached, entangled, like candy floss, becoming then the sticky substance to which still other biographical facts can be attached (1963:56).

A person's public record of achievements and failures, as well as his relatively stable attributes, provide the basis upon which others assign him to moral categories and hence shape his social identity. Along with his current roles and statuses, these judgments about his personal character constitute his social identity. And what has happened or what others imagine has happened in his past discloses the kind of person he is now. Thus, a person's known past can either qualify him for membership in valued groups or can discredit him regardless of his present performance.

According to socie ideology, a girl's social identity resides most visibly in her current role-playing ability, whether she is cool or not. This judgment, however, rests upon rather global assessments of her personal identity. Her personal identity is predicated upon enduring moral qualities that, in turn, are evident in her adherence to one of two opposing life-styles.

For socie girls, those who subscribe to the adolescent version of a middle-class way of life are morally acceptable; girls who follow the adolescent variant of a working-class way of life are morally contemptible. All of our socie informants felt that hoody girls tended to be promiscuous, sloppy, stupid, and unfriendly. In short, they were seen as perversely unfeminine. This opposition between socie and hoody morals supplies part of the impetus for the identity transformation that gives this ritual its meaning.

This vision of the sources of a girl's moral character does not refer to her social origins. Rather, it is based on value commitments that are manifest in a mode or presentation of self. The socie style of unqualified public sociability (whatever one's private sentiments toward others) contrasts vividly with the hoody ethos of interpersonal integrity, that is, one is friendly only to those whom one likes.

The imagery of female excellence has another dimension grounded in ideas about interpersonal competence. One of the essential elements of a socie identity depends upon a girl's ability to manage relationships with others so that her circle of friends and acquaintances is as wide as possible, and she must impress others as vivacious and genuinely interested in them. This sort of role performance is thought to rest partly on inherited characteristics, a girl's physical attractiveness. Socies believe that there is a high though not perfect correlation between coolness and *cuteness.*

At this point, the opposition shifts away from hoody moral impurity to one where positive social virtues distinguish those who deserve general acclaim from those who deserve to exist anonymously in this adolescent community. In other words, the hoody/socie opposition is one of notoriety versus propriety whereas the other/socie contrast is one of obscurity versus renown. That is, those girls who are known and personally recognized by many are thought to be "somebody" whereas those girls who are known and personally recognized by a few are thought to be "nobody." This opposition between an other and a socie provides the second stimulus for the social transformation that gives this ritual its meaning.

A girl's social identity potential is partly a function of her previous peer-group affiliations. Those she has known and who have known her are taken as a reliable index of her personal identity. She shares the presumed moral virtues and vices of her past as well as her present associates, and thus her desire to claim and demonstrate a new social identity is always tempered by her past. Therefore, mobility beyond the earliest stages of a girl's high school career, which involves a radical transition from either the hoody or other to the socie category, is relatively rare. But, looked at from another vantage point, the criteria that determine one's status are purely subjective inasmuch as there are no objective economic, jural, or political means with which the incumbent can compel another to render deference and respect. Except for the collective act of sorority initiation, there is an essential ambiguity in a person's status in this social system. Our informants constantly stress the crucial importance of simply being able to say to oneself and to others, "I am an ABC."

In this light, the fundamental meaning of sorority initiation rites in this community is obvious. They validate and legitimize a girl's social identity as a socie and hence make her self-image a viable guide to interaction with others. It enables her to eliminate any doubts about her essential worth and thus places her role performances on solid ground. What remains in this analysis is to examine the symbolic elements of the ritual process to see how this identity transformation is accomplished.

This ritual relies on two processes associated with the development of a personal identity, that is, a self the individual and others recognize as relatively constant amidst her various involvements and activities. Instead of appealing directly to ideal values that transcend the limits of the peer-group world, this ritual relies upon the notion of a negative identity. Goodenough remarks:

> To identify with people as the incarnations of our own identity ideals is not the only way in which we use others as models. Instead of trying to identify with another, for example, we may do the very opposite and try to dissociate ourselves from him by acquiring as few features of identity in common with him as possible (1966:206).

And Erikson notes that "each *positive* identity is also defined by *negative* images. . . ," (1966:154) and that:

> The human being, in fact, is warned *not* to become what he often had no intention of becoming so that he can learn to anticipate what he must avoid. Thus, the positive identity (far from a static constellation of traits and roles) is always in conflict with the past which is to be lived down and by that potential future which is to be prevented [1966:155].

The second identity process, which concerns one aspect of what Erikson (1959) labels identity diffusion, involves experiences of shame and embarrassment (Lynd 1961), and in this instance is induced by ritual stigmatization (Goffman 1963). Using these processes, the initiation rites prepare the initiate for an identity transformation. Although she may feel that the ritual will only make her the kind of person she already senses herself to be, it nonetheless provides the concrete evidence that confirms this intuition and also denies that her social identity could have developed in other less praiseworthy directions—that she could have become or remained other than what she is now.

This ritual uses hazing to embarrass the initiate before her peers. This heightens any doubts she may have about whether she is in fact *sorority material* and deserves the honor about to be bestowed upon her. Although selection as a pledge is presumptive evidence of inherent coolness, it does not constitute positive proof. Moreover, this aspect of the ritual removes some of her certainty about what she has assumed was her superior ability to manipulate interpersonal relations. She becomes gauche. By placing her in awkward situations, the ritual creates a sense of shame. It raises questions about the solidity of her personal identity and thereby opens her to the experience of a radical reintegration of self (Lynd 1961:43, 46, 47). If this is not enough to weaken her confidence that she possess the inner qualifications for the socie status, yelling wears down her capacity to maintain the open, friendly, and composed demeanor that identifies a socie girl. Our informants recognized the importance of this aspect of the ritual insofar as they felt that the only sign of a bad pledge was arrogance, an unwillingness to invest one's self in the ceremonies. In sum, this part of the ritual induces identity diffusion, disrupts previous continuities in the perception of self, increases the initiate's emotional receptivity to the transition to the socie identity in the rites that follow, and thus makes it credible.

The rites of hell night and mock occur in the context of mild identity diffusion where the initiate no longer relies on her capacity to impress others as she ordinarily does. The injunctions of an earlier rite, silence day, are the first indications that this ritual depends upon negative identity images, that is, communicates what the initiate has become by stressing what she is not. On this occasion she is not allowed to wear makeup or set her hair. She is temporarily denuded of those attributes that distinguish her from hoody and other girls—her sophisticated cosmetic style. On turnabout day, the pledge vicariously experiences the social mastery and dominance implicit in the socie identity. Hell night and mock reverses this sensation; she is symbolically stigmatized with the attributes of the morally devalued hoods and others.

The latter rites are a special case of what Garfinkel (1956) has called degradation ceremonies. As its title implies, mock applies to those who do *not* go through the ritual. These rites seize what these girls fear are latent possibilities in their character and project them onto highly stigmatized and stereotyped images of others and hoods. The act of smearing pledges with lipsticks on hell night is a veiled reference to what socies believe is a most salient feature of the hoody cosmetic style, the use of makeup in ways that resemble the appearance of a slut. Mock exaggerates this image and introduces new elements into the process. Not only are the initiates painted in the most absurd fashion, which stresses the lack of taste as well as the obscenity of the hoody visage, but mock concentrates its ridicule on their hair. Socies interpret hoody hair styles, in which the hair is worn massed on top of the head and is held together by a liberal application of hair spray, as a sign of lack of sexual restraint, and, incidentally, there is some cross-cultural evidence that supports this view (Leach 1958). In contrast, socie hair styles emphasize neatness, and mock carries its stigmatization of the hoody hair style to extremes. The initiate is literally made to feel dirty, messy, and ugly, and it does not require too much imagination to guess the relief they feel when they realize that this is a transient experience.

The garb pledges are compelled to wear burlesques what socies perceive as the ludicrous incongruities of the others' style or, more properly, their lack of one. This rite carries their perception of the others' lack of savoir-faire to its logical conclusion. Nothing is in the current fashion and nothing matches. Moreover, there is something childish about the appearance of the pledge with braids and balloons. The comical effect results not only from the juxtaposition of particular items of clothing and adornment but also from the recognition that others are insensitive to even the externalities of the socie style. Playing in the sand and on the slides refers to the underdeveloped nature of the other's social personality. Socies carefully discriminate between *goofing around* (see Schwartz and Merten on the meaning of *idiot* behavior) and playing as a child would. The former reveals a certain inner freedom from adult constraints and the ability to mildly ridicule one's previous childish concerns whereas the latter reflects the others' inability to perceive that they are no longer children.

After the pledges return home, they wash up and dress in the normal clothes. Now, they are forever cleansed of any possible latent moral impurities, and their social identities as socies are publicly confirmed. They are ready for induction into the sorority and are properly prepared to take their place on the top of the social pyramid in this adolescent social system.

Summary

In this paper we have shown how expressive symbols formulate the meaning of the identity transformations implicit in these and perhaps in other adolescent initiation rites. Further, they delineate the kinds of characterological changes inherent in these status transitions; that is, they reveal the kind of person who occupies the new status. And they mobilize the initiate's deepest emotional interest, his self-esteem, in ways that endow dramatic performances with an aura of social reality. Though we agree that initiation rites create solidarity, in this instance and perhaps in others the solidarity resides not primarily in greater social cohesion but rather in the felt validity of the perception of one's self and similar others as sharing the same social identity. Functionally, then, this rite strengthens the social implications of the moral categories that define the status system, and therefore it ultimately sustains the social hierarchy in this adolescent community. In conclusion, we agree with Lynd (1961:250) who says that "only a language of symbols, of paradox, of abundant meaning can communicate the deeper and more elusive ranges of human experience."

References

Black, Max, 1962, *Models and Metaphors.* Ithaca, N.Y.: Cornell University Press.

Burke, Kenneth, 1945, *A Grammar of Motives.* Englewood Cliffs, N.J.: Prentice-Hall, Inc.

Burton, Roger and John Whiting, 1961, "The Absent Father and Cross-Sex Identity," *Merrill-Palmer Quarterly* 7:85–95.

Cohen, Yehudi, 1964, "The Establishment of Identity in a Social Nexus: The Special Case of Initiation Ceremonies and Their Relation to Value and Legal Systems," *American Anthropologist* 66:529–552.

———, 1966, "On Alternative Views of the Individual in Culture-and-Personality Studies," *American Anthropologist* 68:355–361.

Erikson, Erik, 1959, "The Problem of Ego Identity." In *Identity and the Life Cycle. Psychological Issues* 1:101–164.

———, 1966, "The Concept of Identity in Race Relations: Notes and Queries." *Daedalus* 95:145–171.

Garfinkel, Harold, 1965, "Conditions of Successful Degradation Ceremonies," *The American Journal of Sociology* 61:420–424.

Gluckman, Max, 1962, *"Les rites de passage."* In M. Gluckman, ed., *Essay on the Ritual of Social Relations.* Manchester: University of Manchester Press.

Goffman, Erving, 1963, *Stigma.* Englewood Cliffs, N.J.: Prentice-Hall, Inc.

Goodenough, Ward, 1963, *Cooperation in Change.* New York: John Wiley & Sons, Inc.

Leach, E. R., 1958, "Magical Hair," *Journal of the Royal Anthropological Institute* 88:147–164.

Lynd, Helen, 1961, *On Shame and the Search for Identity.* New York: John Wiley & Sons, Inc.

Miller, Daniel, 1963, *"The Study of Social Relationships: Situation, Identity and Social Interaction."* In S. Kock, ed, *Psychology: A Study of a Science,* vol. 5. New York: McGraw-Hill Book Company, Inc.

Parsons, Talcott, 1951, *The Social System.* New York: The Free Press.

Richards, Audrey, 1956, *Chisungu: A Girl's Initiation Ceremony among the Bemba of Northern Rhodesia.* London: Faber and Faber.

Schwartz, Gary, and Don Merten, 1967, "The Language of Adolescence: An Anthropological Approach to the Youth Culture," *American Journal of Sociology* 72: 453–468.

Turner, Victor, 1962, "Three Symbols of Passage in Ndembu Circumcision Ritual: An Interpretation." In M. Gluckman, ed., *Essays on the Ritual of Social Relations.* Manchester: University of Manchester Press.

———, 1964, "Betwixt and Between: The Liminal Period in *Rites de Passage,"* In J. Helm, ed., *Symposium on New Approaches to the Study of Religion.* Seattle: American Ethnological Society.

Van Gennep, Arnold, 1960, *The Rites of Passage.* Chicago: University of Chicago Press.

Whiting, John, 1962, "*Comments on* The Function of Male Initiation Ceremonies," *American Journal of Sociology* 67:391–394.

Young, Frank, 1962, "The Function of Male Initiation Ceremonies: A Cross-Cultural Test of an Alternative Hypothesis," *American Journal of Sociology* 67:379–391.

———, 1965, *Initiation Ceremonies.* Indianapolis: Bobbs-Merrill.

HARRY F. WOLCOTT/*University of Oregon*

9 *The Elementary School Principal: Notes from a Field Study**

"Harry, you ought to watch the company you keep," quipped a colleague from the university when he encountered me at lunch one day with a group of five elementary school principals. "He does!" came the immediate retort from the principal sitting next to me.

The principals had just completed an all-morning meeting at the school district central office, where they had been appointed to serve as a Principal Selection Committee for the school district. As such, they were to interview and recommend candidates to fill new positions as elementary school principals for the following school year. I had been present at their morning session in the role of an ethnographer inquiring into the life and work of the elementary school principal from an anthropological perspective.

This chapter draws upon a larger study designed to provide an ethnographic-type account of the elementary school principalship by means of an extensive case study of one principal (Wolcott 1973). In the present chapter, I have selected from the field notes an episode in which attention is drawn to the behavior of a small group of principals rather than to the behavior of an individual. The context of this episode is the proceedings of the Principal Selection Committee. A major portion of the chapter is devoted to a descriptive account of the proceedings of this committee and a discussion and comment based on the data presented. The chapter begins with an overview of the perspective and methods basic to the entire field study.[1]

*The author is professor of education and anthropology and a research associate at the Center for the Advanced Study of Educational Administration (CASEA) at the University of Oregon. The author wishes to acknowledge the support of CASEA during a portion of his time devoted to the preparation of this chapter.

Grateful acknowledgment is expressed to Max Abbott, Norman Delue, Joanne M. Kitchel, and George D. Spindler for critical comment and editorial assistance in the preparation of this material.

[1] A discussion of the methodology employed here has also appeared in *Human Organization* (Wolcott 1970). A more thorough discussion appears as Chapter 1, "A Principal Investigator in Search of a Principal" in the completed monograph (Wolcott 1973).

The Ethnographic Approach

The apparent neglect of attention to the *actual* behavior of school administrators in the literature on educational administration led to the proposal for conducting this research. That literature could well be augmented by a series of detailed ethnographic-type accounts of the actual behavior of people occupying roles in professional education, contextualized not only in terms of the formally organized institution in which they work but also in terms of their lives as human beings interacting within the context of a broader cultural milieu. This study was designed specifically to provide such data about the elementary school principalship.

The ethnographer's task is the recording of human behavior in cultural terms. The standard ethnography provides an account of some cultural process, such as law or divorce, or the way of life of some particular group of people, such as the Tikopia or the Children of Sanchez. This study is ethnographic to the extent that the principal who provides the focus for it is seen as an interacting member of a cultural system. Because the study is social and cultural rather than psychological in orientation, its scope includes not only the behavior of the principal himself but also the behavior of those with whom a principal interacts in the course of his professional life. This includes to some degree his spouse, his family, and his friends, and to a greater degree teachers, other administrators, parents, and pupils. These roles, and the interaction of the people filling them, are the human elements of a cultural system, the school system of one community. To the extent that the cultural system involved in this study is similar to other cultural systems serving the same purpose, this ethnography of a single principal should produce knowledge relevant to the understanding of such roles and cultural systems in general.

There are other ways one might proceed in studying a school administrator, one of which would be for the ethnographer to obtain such a position. In prior fieldwork, however, I had become acutely aware of the limitations on one's ability to observe objectively processes in which he is deeply involved as a participant (Wolcott 1967).

The literature dealing with school administration might have been expected to serve as a source of information about administrative behavior, but that body of writings is susceptible to several of the limitations which characterize the literature of professional education more generally. One such limitation is that much of the literature is hortatory or normative in content. It tells principals (or teachers, or superintendents) how they *ought* to act. It is prescriptive rather than descriptive. Literature of this type can provide a source for inquiring into the *ideal* world of formal education (Lee 1963), but it fails to provide an account of what actually goes on or how the ideals are translated into real behavior. The literature that *is* empirically based, on the other hand, provides factual data which tend to tell too little about too much. Such data prove valuable as a source of census information; for example, we can readily obtain a description of the "average" American elementary school principal (DESP 1968):

> a male
> married
> between the ages of 35 and 49
> has had 10 to 19 years total experience in schools
> was an elementary classroom teacher just prior to assuming his administrative post.

This description fits the case-study principal perfectly. Yet the data provide little insight into how one becomes a principal, how a principal acts, or what he finds satisfying and perplexing about his role.

The barrage of questionnaires that confront public school personnel to inventory their training, habits, and preferences might also be expected to provide data about the principalship. However, the people who compose these questionnaires have frequently failed to do careful preliminary field-work. The information obtained in answer to questions like "Should a principal attend church regularly?" may reveal little more than the tendency of school administrators to give "expected" responses. Such studies seem to ignore the consequence that if the questions one asks are not crucial, differences in responses are not crucial either.

The nearest approximation we usually get to the actual behavior of administrators is from data based on self-reporting techniques. These techniques have frequently been employed in studies of school principals. Although self-reporting is somewhat comparable to one of the standard methods by which ethnographic accounts have been obtained—intensive interviews with a single or a few selected informants—it is far more subject to problems of informant reliability than is the method of intensive interviewing employed as one of a number of data-gathering techniques in the ethnographer's multi-instrument approach.

The ethnographic approach taken in this study has not been widely employed in conducting research in school settings. To my amazement I have occasionally been asked, "Did the principal know you were making the study?" I spent weeks searching for a suitable and willing subject, and I did not request formal permission from the school district to conduct the study until I had the personal permission and commitment of the selected individual. His family, his faculty and staff, his fellow principals, and many visitors to the school knew something about the research project. The faculty assigned me the nickname "The Shadow" as a way to jokingly acknowledge my presence and purpose at their school, and the name was learned by some of the pupils, too.

In order to learn how it is to be a principal, every aspect of the principal's life had some potential relevance for the study. I was once asked (somewhat facetiously, I suppose) whether I planned to take the principal's temperature each day. I replied, not at all facetiously, that were it readily available I would have recorded that information, just as it might be interesting to know what the principal and his family ate at each Sunday dinner, but I would obviously need priorities in my data gathering. My attention has been drawn primarily to such aspects of the principal's life as the who, what, where, and when of his personal encounters, the cultural themes manifested in his behavior and in his attempts to influence the behavior of those about him, and the problems and paradoxes inherent in the role of the principal. Although the behavior of one principal served as the focus of the study, the fieldwork provided extensive opportunities for observing many principals, ranging from the rather frequent and often informal contacts of the case study principal with administrators at nearby schools to his participation in the official sessions and formal meetings of his school district and his memberships in county, regional, and state organizations of elementary school principals.

Methods in Fieldwork

An "ethnographic approach" implies commitment to a perspective in both the methods of field research and the handling of data in subsequent writing, but it does not explicate the methods for doing either. Whenever it has been expedient to describe my research methodology by a brief label I have leaned to the term "field study." Zelditch (1962) has stated a case for the merits of the participant-observer approach in the field study without going to the extreme of insisting that participant-observation entails only participating and observing. He argues, "a field study is not a single method gathering a single kind of information" (1962:567); rather, the participant-observer employs three different modes in his research: "enumeration to document frequency data; participant observation to describe incidents; and informant interviewing to learn institutionalized norms and statuses" (566). I shall use these three categories—enumeration, participant-observation, and interviewing—to describe the specific techniques employed during my fieldwork.

Enumeration and Census Data

1. Collecting copies of official notices sent to and from school to pupils, parents, or faculty (greatly facilitated by having a faculty mailbox in the office and by a school secretary who did not mind making an extra carbon of routine reports and correspondence).
2. Collecting copies of records (or, at the end of the year, the records themselves) of enrollments, reports, the principal's personal log of events, and daily notices written in a faculty notebook.
3. Collecting "time and motion" data by noting, at 60-second intervals over a

carefully sampled period of two weeks at school, what the principal was doing, where he was, with whom he was interacting, and who was talking.

4. Mapping and photographing the school and neighborhood.[2]

Participant Observation

The primary methodology used at the beginning of the study was that of participant observation. Customarily the principal introduced me by saying, "This is Harry Wolcott. He is from the university and doing some research in which I'm involved." This brief introduction seemed to serve as a sufficient explanation of my presence to all but the most curious, but anyone who asked was welcome to a fuller description. The principal and staff were remarkable in their capacity for allowing me to observe and record without insisting that I become an active participant in their conversations and activities. Although simply "keeping up" with a busy principal precluded the possibility of my ever being a totally passive observer, my active participation at school was limited primarily to engaging in the social banter of the faculty-room during lunch or at coffee breaks.

I made it a practice to carry my notebook with me and to make entries in it almost continuously. My intent was to create a precedent for constant note-taking so that the people would feel it was natural for me to be writing regardless of the topics or events at hand. Notes were taken in longhand in complete and readable form whenever possible. When I could not make complete notes and still remain present as observer, I jotted brief notes in the margins of my notebook and completed the full account later, often before leaving the school building. I never returned to the school until a complete account from a previous period of observation was finished. Nothing was gained by my mere presence as an observer; until the notes from one visit were a matter of record, there was no point in returning to school and reducing the impact of one set of observations by imposing a more recent one. Ultimately the longhand entries were transcribed onto 5 by 8 papers, each entry describing a single event, whether a lengthy transcription such as that containing my notes of the three meetings of the Principal Selection Committee or brief entries such as

> The principal said that when he called his wife to tell her he would be home by 5:30 this evening she replied, "So early! Why—what's wrong?"

> As the principal is trying various keys in the lock [he had just received some duplicates from the central office but did not know which doors they fit] a little

[2] This part of the research was conducted by my research assistant, an experienced geographer, who developed a socioeconomic map of the school-attendance area (Olson 1969). Although I carried out the balance of the field research, it was invaluable to have assistance in the analysis of enumeration and interview data by someone less closely connected with the school setting and thus presumably more able to restrict his analysis to the data at hand.

girl from grade two comes up quietly behind him, pokes him gently in the ribs, and says, "Boo." "Oh, my," he says. The little girl continues happily down the hall.

One of the objectives of this research was to see the principal in as many different settings appropriate to an ethnographic study as possible. It was easier, of course, to intrude on his professional life in connection with his work as a school administrator than to intrude into his personal life. At the school I was excluded, by prior arrangement, only from a few "touchy" parent conferences. Although more symbolic than functional, a table and chair were moved into the principal's office for my use. My observation extended to such settings as any school or school district activity or meeting; meetings of local, regional, and state educational organizations; formal and informal staff gatherings; in-service programs; and traveling to meetings with groups of principals.

In reviewing plans for the fieldwork with colleagues, I had been cautioned against becoming "overidentified" with the principal, particularly since he was the formally appointed status leader of the school. I visited often with teachers and staff members, including visits at school on days when I knew the principal was away. "Oh, checking up on us, eh?" someone would inevitably joke, leading me to feel that the caution against being overidentified with "the boss" had been well given.

My apprehension about being overidentified with the principal did not extend to those settings where he was away from his school. However, there are few guidelines for a researcher in accompanying a subject to see about a new battery for his automobile or to attend a service club luncheon. I was able to include within the scope of my observations such settings as the principal's home and family, business meetings at his church and the Sunday School class he teaches, trips to local businesses for school and personal reasons, Kiwanis luncheons, a family wedding and reception, and brief meetings with friends and neighbors.

Informant Interviewing

These interviews were of several types. First were taped interviews of approximately one hour duration, structured but open-ended, which provided excellent data concerning the principal's family life (interviews with his wife and mother) and the perceptions of him as a school administrator (interviews with thirteen faculty and two staff members). The interviews took time to arrange and conduct, and they seemed to take an eternity to transcribe, but they proved extremely valuable for uncovering the range of perceptions and the extent of the affective content expressed by the teachers regarding their work and the people with whom they associated professionally. The fact that I requested each interview as a personal favor and that no interviewing was done until I had spent over half a year at the school undoubtedly contributed to the extensive and useful data gathered via this method.

Another approach was to ask all the pupils in each fifth- and sixth-grade classroom to write briefly (and anonymously) what they thought they would remember about the principal. The phrases which I suggested to them to start their writing were, "What kind of a principal is he?" "Pleasant memories are . . ."; and "One time I won't forget. . . ." The comments I received ran the gamut of opinion, from the succinct response from a boy who wrote that his principal is "a Dam stopit one" to the reflection by a sixth-grade girl that "He is the kind of a principal who helps you figure it out." One boy wrote: "I won't fore get the time when my freind and I were blamed fore bilding a fire in the bath room."

The principal himself served as a primary informant, as he was not only the focus of the research but was to some extent a co-worker as well. I was never too explicit about what data I was gathering, nor did I often share my hunches or tentative analyses with him, but he correctly assumed that a brief recounting of what had occurred at school since my last visit would be helpful to the study. He enjoyed talking and visiting (I found that he did the talking one-third of the total school day during the "time and motion" study), so this self-appointed task came easily to him. At times he reflected on his personal feelings and philosophy and these statements provided valuable insights into his "ideal world." The juxtaposition of actual behavior and ideal behavior provides an excellent means for describing and analyzing a cultural system, and I was fortunate in having an informant who talked easily about aspects of his ideal world.

On a few occasions I emphasized the informant role and asked the principal to relate specific accounts. Plans were always discussed in advance when these sessions were to be taped. Important tapes included a session in which the principal summarized the opening of school and gave a forecast of the coming year, a session in which I asked him to review the wedding list and chat about the people who had been invited to his daughter's marriage and reception, and a session recorded in my automobile as we drove through the school-attendance area while the principal described the neighborhood to three new teachers who accompanied us.

A ten-page questionnaire designed for the study was distributed to all the faculty and staff at the end of the fieldwork. The questionnaire was particularly valuable in enabling me to obtain systematic data about the staff, as I could see no point in holding a long taped interview with each of the twenty-nine members of the regular and part-time staff. This questionnaire provided standard census data and information concerning each teacher's perceptions of the school, community, and classroom. It also provided an opportunity for all staff members to state their feelings about an "ideal" principal.

The use of the questionnaire provided me with a chance to thank the staff for their patience and help during the study. I felt that the questionnaire might also give me an opportunity to elicit staff reaction to the research project, and the last statement of the questionnaire was, "Some things the researcher may never have understood about this school are. . . ." The question did not evoke much response, but it was flattering to read "I think you probably understand more than we may think." I delighted in the humor of one teacher who assumed (correctly) that I did not know "There is no Kotex dispenser in the [women's] restroom."

My presence in the school district throughout the study was, I suppose, viewed as a mixed blessing. The mild but constant surveillance produced little overt strain that could not be alleviated by joking, but I provided so little feedback that there was no "payoff" for the many people who shared their perceptions and feelings with me. Still, a sympathetic and nonevaluative listener can provide an unusual opportunity for emotional catharsis, and I was amazed at how often teachers and principals seemed to appreciate an opportunity to "speak their minds." In this regard I feel that my position as observer and information-getter was considerably enhanced by the fact that, like the teachers and administrators who were the subjects of the study, I spoke the "language" of educators and had been "on the firing line" as a classroom teacher. I believe the case-study principal also found some comfort in having a part-time cohort with whom he could share something of the nature, complexity, and extent of problems which confronted him in the course of his daily work.

From the Field Notes: Proceedings of the Principal Selection Committee

Any number of episodes recorded during the course of the fieldwork could have been drawn upon here to illustrate aspects of a principal's professional life. Many would call attention to the routine of a typical day and to the incessant questions, problems, and meetings that seem to make constant demands on a principal's time and resources. I have chosen instead to draw upon a rather unique set of events, the proceedings of the Principal Selection Committee. This committee met three times during one month in the spring of 1967. These meetings provided a special setting in which the principals appointed to an *ad hoc* screening committee found themselves compelled to review and define—for the purpose of evaluating candidates—the critical attributes and qualifications of their role. This charge to interview and endorse certain candidates to join their ranks, though directed only to the principals appointed to the committee, served as an annual renewal ceremony for all the elementary school principals of the district. The fact of their appointment and task, and the results of their interviews and deliberations, served to reaffirm publicly the standards and responsibilities of their office.

The necessity for adding new members to their ranks occasioned a time when, like the elders among North American Indian tribes, the principals were obliged to "review, analyze, dramatize, and defend their cultural heritage" (Pettitt 1946).

The circumstances underlying the committee's existence—who appointed it, the task it was given, how binding its recommendations would be—provide clues about the formal context in which it worked. As the committee convened, for example, no one explained nor questioned why it had five principals (among the twenty-seven elementary school principals in the district), how or why the four new members had been selected by the director of elementary education and why one member had been retained from the prior year (especially after the director commented, "I tried to eliminate people who had ideas from the past"), how many vacancies or at which schools they would occur ("We will need two people, maybe three. We should pick our best people, not for [specific] positions but for ability, because we don't know where they will go"), or how binding the committee's actions would be on the ultimate recommendation which the superintendent would make to the school board. It was customary in this school district for the director of elementary education to appoint committees of varying sizes and varying purposes, and it was part of her job to "know" when she had sufficient authority to make appointments on her own or when she, in turn, needed the approval of the assistant superintendent or superintendent. The principals seemed to assume that she would be present during their meetings, and she slipped easily into the role of informal chairperson of the group.

For the principals appointed to the committee, to select "two, maybe three" candidates apparently provided sufficient parameters for their task, since in their ultimate decision they ranked the most "controversial" of the acceptable candidates as number four. No one pressed to learn why the number of vacancies was ambiguous. Two new schools were to be opened in the fall. If "maybe three" vacancies were to occur, there was more than mere conjecture about which principals might be in disfavor among the powers in the central office. (The third vacancy proved later to be due to an as yet unannounced plan for administrative reorganization which required the full-time services of one elementary school principal in the central office.)

Although the recommendation of the committee could be ignored by the superintendent, it did not necessarily mean that it would be. The new members checked with the principal who had already served on the committee to reassure themselves that recommendations made the previous year had been honored. The confidence expressed in the superintendent was formal and reciprocal. The committee showed no inclination to test the extent of its power or to threaten the power of the superintendent by making radical or unexpected recommendations. Attention was addressed specifically to assessing each candidate's standing "in the eyes of the superintendent" during discussions prior and subsequent to the interviews. In turn, official recognition was accorded to the committee through brief appearances before and during its sessions by the director of personnel, the assistant superintendent, and the superintendent.

During the total twelve hours of interview and discussion through which members of the Principal Selection Committee sat, fourteen possible candidates were reviewed. A brief profile of the candidates as a group showed them to include male and female applicants from within and outside the district, all holding a master's degree and all experienced elementary school teachers. In age they ranged from thirty-one to sixty-one. Their total experience in professional education varied from eight to thirty-nine years.

The extent of significant variation among the candidates is less than this description implies. One applicant who was not seriously considered and who was not invited for an interview accounted for most of the variation. She was the only female applicant and had served in an administrative capacity for only one year some fourteen years previously. In age and teaching experience she had thirteen more years than the next most senior applicant. The committee shared the feelings of one principal who summarized, "I think she's a wonderful gal and a fine teacher, but I question anyone going into this at 61." While age provided the immediate basis for a decision not to consider her further, it is likely that sex would have been the critical issue had she been younger. Three of the district's twenty-seven elementary schools were administered by women. As one male principal had candidly remarked on a prior occasion, "It's going to be a long time before we put in another woman."

Some candidates were dropped after only a brief comment as the committee sought ways to reduce the number of people who were to be accorded interviews and serious consideration. Regarding a relatively young newcomer in the district who had asked to be considered, for example, no one added any further comment after one principal expressed the opinion, "I see too many people ahead of him." Someone added, "The same with so-and-so." A third principal immediately suggested dropping both their names. Consideration of another applicant, an administrator from outside the district, was summarily ended when the personnel director, during a brief preview of the slate of candidates, recalled that this applicant had "already been hired [i.e., offered a contract] once in this district" and certainly should not have the opportunity to turn them down again. The committee agreed that there was no point in retaining names of people who were not going to be considered among the top eligible candidates, and they expressed concern over the problem of "getting the hopes up" among candidates called in for interviews. Yet any time a candidate's name was about to be dropped permanently, there was some hedging about giving everyone a chance. The frequent statement, "Let's just leave his name on for now" revealed a reluctance to take decisive and final action (eliminating a candidate) when less decisive action (ranking eight "top" candidates for three positions) accomplished the same purpose without requiring the ultimatum.

As the preliminary discussion of the candidates continued, based on the perusal of each candidate's folder of letters and recommendations, two procedural questions were discussed. The first was whether candidates would be selected only from within the district. The assistant superintendent observed that no outsider had been appointed to an elementary school principalship for many years. "We shouldn't overlook good people from outside, but in the past when things have been equal we have given preference for 'in-district.'" The tradition of selecting applicants from within the district was reaffirmed in the final recommendation made by the committee, although two out-of-district candidates were called for interviews. The rationale for interviewing "outsiders" was that the district did not wish to foster the impression that promotions to administrative positions were made only from within the ranks. To reaffirm among themselves that good candidates were always being sought, one principal recounted how an outstanding principal from California had "almost" been hired in a previous year. Another principal reminded the committee that any candidate "might come teach with us first" and work up into a principalship through promotion within the system.

The other procedural question dealt with the manner of conducting the interviews. The alternatives considered were to hold informal interviews, to ask candidates a set of prearranged questions (e.g., "What do you see as the role of the principal?" "How can the principal make the best use of teacher competencies?") or to guide the interview by using either an "in-basket"[3] or a problem approach. The pros and cons of each approach were discussed briefly. When the director of elementary education recalled that in a prior year one of the present applicants had been interviewed by using a structured interview technique, interest in that approach quickly subsided. Though never formally resolved, the actual procedure followed in the interviews was unstructured and was oriented primarily to getting a candidate to talk freely about his experiences, his beliefs about teaching, and his thoughts about the role of the school and the role of the principal.

Excerpts from the interviews and discussions are presented below. I have rearranged the actual order of interviews and have presented the candidates here according to the final rank order decided upon by the committee. The name of each candidate's ordinal position in the final ranking is used as a pseudonym.

Mr. Seventh

Mr. Seventh, age forty-eight, was an out-of-district candidate. Off and on he had been working toward a doctorate in education at the local university. He had served in administrative capacities, first as a principal and more

[3] The in-basket approach (cf. Hemphill et al. 1962) presents a series of hypothetical problems typical of those which require the attention of an administrator, presented in the form in which they might come across his desk in notes, memoranda, notices, letters. A whole set of simulated materials has been developed for use in graduate courses in elementary school administration (UCEA 1967, 1971).

recently as an assistant superintendent, for twenty-two of his twenty-five years in education. At the beginning of his brief interview he was asked whether he would plan to stay in the district if he completed his doctorate. He said that even with a doctorate he felt he might be able to advance sufficiently in a district of this size (over 20,000 students) to keep him there. He added that he might not finish his doctorate anyway. One principal joked with him about wanting to "go beyond" the principalship: "Isn't the principal about the best thing you can be?"

One of the interviewing principals had served years before as a teacher in a school where the candidate was principal, and he later said of him, "I think he'd be a pretty good candidate—he's pretty strong." At age forty-eight, however, the committee seemed reluctant to endorse him. Their reservations were reinforced by their suspicion that he wanted to get into their school district only because of its proximity to the university so he could complete his graduate work. When it finally came time to draw the line on candidates, Mr. Seventh's presumed lack of commitment to the principal role and his potential mobility, especially were he to complete his graduate studies, served as the basis for a low ranking. As one principal summarized, "I would have ranked Seventh higher, but I think of the elementary principalship as a career. He's a stronger candidate than some of the others, but I just don't think he's going to stay—he'll stay about four or five years and use us as a stepping stone."

Mr. Fifth

Mr. Fifth, 39, also from outside the district, had been principal of a large elementary school in a growing but still rural community for the previous five of his twelve years in public school work. In spite of his long tenure, his experience, which was confined primarily to rural schools, was regarded as a serious handicap. "Coming from those rural communities, he will be facing a real change if he comes here to be an elementary school principal," noted one committee member. "Would he be willing to come here as a *teacher?"* asked another. At the time they decided to invite him for an interview, members of the committee also tacitly assumed that his age and experience had probably narrowed the range of positions he would accept to that of a principalship. They found themselves in agreement that his rural-conservative school experience had probably failed to provide him with a sufficiently "exciting" background from which he might make a contribution to their own schools (thus rather subtly reinforcing the explicit preference for candidates who have worked in their own district, one they perceive as a school system in which the program *is* exciting).

Committee members were cordial in their greetings and introductions when Mr. Fifth appeared for his interview. He was directed to choose one of the (few) comfortable chairs in the meeting room, prompting the personnel director to joke, "It won't be this comfortable again." After a folksy prelude, the director of elementary education asked, "What things have you been doing and how have you been involved?"

MR. FIFTH: Ma'am?
DIRECTOR OF ELEMENTARY EDUCATION: Well, if you were a principal, what kinds of changes would you want to make?
MR. FIFTH: It would depend on what I found. If I found some needs, I would move in and meet those needs.

INTERVIEWING PRINCIPAL: How do you see the role of the counselor in relation to the principal?
MR. FIFTH: I see the principal as a sort of mediator—right in the middle—if there is a middle.

He described a two-stage role for the principal, first in getting the cooperation of the staff, then in a "selling" role to convince the parents. To illustrate, he elaborated upon an experimental "group counseling situation" recently set up at his school, a topic of immediate interest to the interviewing principals because of district-wide efforts to develop a counseling program at each elementary school.

INTERVIEWING PRINCIPAL: How were the children selected for your group counseling?
MR. FIFTH: Well, being in the school for four years, I pretty well knew which children needed help. Our goals were to help Bill Jones get some subjects so he could do his doctorate. But of course if I was setting up a [real] program, I would identify which kids needed certain things.

INTERVIEWING PRINCIPAL: How have you gotten teacher involvement in curriculum development in your district?
MR. FIFTH: We gave them their choice: "Do you want math or do you want social studies?" You see, they had a choice of what they would do. [There was some laughter at this. One interviewer asked, "No third choice?" Another joked, "Oh, there's a third choice, all right."]
INTERVIEWING PRINCIPAL: Is everyone on one of the two committees?
MR. FIFTH: Yes.
INTERVIEWING PRINCIPAL: Why do you say you like autonomy?
MR. FIFTH: I like to be an individual, just like you do.
INTERVIEWING PRINCIPAL: Do you like your teachers to be individuals, too?
MR. FIFTH: Yes. As a matter of fact, I encourage it.

INTERVIEWING PRINCIPAL: What do you feel is the role of the departmentalized program in the elementary school?
MR. FIFTH: We have "self-contained,"[4] yet I guess there are more exceptions than

[4] "Self-contained" refers to the organizational program of a school in which one teacher remains with the same group of pupils throughout the day.

the rule. [He described his reading program, a one-hour uninterrupted period during which the children are regrouped] It's a sort of modified Joplin plan. . . . We have Bible class but we don't let it interfere with reading.

His discussion of the reading program prompted him to comment about the extensive "help" received at his school from a nearby teacher's college:

MR. FIFTH: So much help can be a problem. For example, in our building we have fourteen teachers, two aides, nine high school cadet helpers, twenty-eight teacher trainees (ranging from part-time observers to student teachers), plus our own music and special education people, plus five more coming in doing research from the college. After describing how many people are in and out of the building, you could see why I would want to leave.

INTERVIEWING PRINCIPAL: It's not so rare here, either. This morning I had thirteen visitors, four teacher trainees, seven students observing from the university, and three policemen, plus the regular faculty.

The question of salary was introduced as a point of information by one of the interviewing principals, who explained that in the district an administrator's salary is not dependent upon school size but on tenure. The personnel director explained the administrative salary schedule in some detail: "Roughly, a principal gets one-fifth above the teaching schedule. So in your case, the teaching salary of $8,000 for a teacher with a master's degree and ten years of experience [the maximum years of nondistrict experience acceptable in the school district for purposes of salary evaluation] plus one-fifth is about $11,000 for ten months. A total of 205 days; $11,000." Mr. Fifth said that at present he was on an eleven-month contract. "You gain a month there," was the reply. He was informed that many school personnel work for the school district in the summer, writing curriculum or teaching summer school, "but not on the administrative [salary] schedule, of course."

Following the interview, committee members chatted as they watched Mr. Fifth walk out onto the parking lot, get into his pick-up truck, and drive away. "My wife once applied for a teaching position in that district," commented one principal. "It was *very* conservative!!"

In the review of the candidates at the conclusion of all the interviews the following comment of one interviewing principal seemed to summarize the reaction to Mr. Fifth: "We're doing *so much* here for boys and girls. We've gone about as far as we can. These fellows from outside have a real disadvantage, because they're still talking about getting kids in and out of rooms, holding ball games, and so on. I think he'd come along pretty well in a couple of years. He'd know our lingo and he'd be doing a good job. It might just take him a little longer."

A second principal concluded the discussion: "The more he talked, the farther I got from him."

Mr. Fifth, Mr. Seventh, and, in all, the names of ten applicants were excluded from the list of candidates recommended to the superintendent. Slight as the variation was among the original panel of fourteen candidates, the variation among the final four candidates chosen was even less. The four were married males between the ages of thirty-one and thirty-four. They had been in professional education from eight to twelve years, had all taught in the upper elementary grades, and all held degrees received five to ten years earlier at the master's level. Each candidate had been with the district from five to ten years. Although they held somewhat different positions at the moment (administrative intern, teacher on leave to pursue a doctoral program, resource teacher, junior high vice principal), each candidate had managed to alter his status from that of the full-time elementary classroom teacher he had once been; none now had direct teaching responsibilities. With the exception of the resource teacher (an extra teacher assigned full-time to a school to provide instructional assistance to the staff), all had held positions specifically entailing administrative duties. All four were considered eminently qualified to assume a principalship. Each candidate had achieved his present visibility *within* the district. With the exception of Mr. Fourth, each had achieved this visibility without stepping on the wrong toes.

Mr. Fourth's problem, at least in part, was that he had run head-on into a not-unknown obstacle in the path of a young man heading for the elementary principalship—the female administrator. A brief comment here concerning the different roles played by men and by women in the hierarchy of the elementary school, particularly in the professional relationship of the administration-bound male vis-à-vis the authority-holding female, may help put Mr. Fourth's problems as a candidate into perspective.

At the teaching level, the world of the elementary school is a world of women. At the administrative level the ratio of men to women is almost exactly reversed: 85 percent of the elementary school teachers are females (NEA Research Report 1967: 14); 78 percent of the elementary school principals are males (DESP 1968:11). The administration-bound male must obviously be able to survive in a predominantly female setting among his teacher colleagues. In addition, he must be able to survive in such relationships as that of student teacher–master teacher, or teacher–supervisor, where his immediate superior is most frequently a woman. And finally, there is a considerable likelihood that among the principals under whom he serves as a teacher he will be assigned to a "woman principal"[5] at least once—an assignment which probably exceeds random chance because female administrators seem particularly sensitive about securing teachers with whom their male pupils can "identify." Thus while women administrators do not exert a majority influence in the formal organization of their peers (indeed, in that era just

[5] In this regard note how the term "principal" is often qualified with the adjective "woman" if the role occupant is female, just as the term "teacher" is usually qualified with the term "man" when the role occupant is male, particularly in referring to teachers at the elementary school level.

prior to Women's Lib, I believe I detected a tendency among male principals to keep their few female colleagues "in their place" in their professional organizations by relegating to them such assignments as taking charge of table decorations, sending out invitations and thank-you letters, and performing minor bookkeeping tasks), the women exert a powerful influence as gatekeepers to the principalship.

Among the fourteen candidates reviewed by the Principal Selection Committee the only two whose current dossiers contained overtly negative statements were two candidates working with female principals. Both had already achieved nonteaching assignments at their schools as resource teachers, and both maintained high involvement in the activities of the local teacher association. It was their active participation in the teacher association that provided the basis for some of the criticism which each candidate received in his evaluation. One principal noted two complaints in her written evaluation: one, that the candidate was "traditional" in his approach to teaching (an implied criticism and a somewhat irrelevant one since he was neither serving as a classroom teacher nor being considered for a teaching position); and two, that he conducted too much of the business of the teacher association at school, thus detracting from his responsibility as a resource teacher to assist the teaching faculty. "First things should be first," the principal had admonished in summary.

"In other words," the personnel director commented after the evaluation was read aloud to the committee, "the teachers aren't getting the help they need."

"That's the only man left on her staff," observed one principal. "As I recall, she wasn't satisfied with the only other guy on her staff last year, either."

Mr. Fourth

Mr. Fourth had been highly regarded as a candidate the previous year. His candidacy was critically reviewed because members of the committee expressed some hesitation about his present status, particularly concerning a prevalent rumor that Mr. Fourth and his principal were not getting along very well. Differences between Mr. Fourth and his woman principal were more than hinted at, they were openly aired by committee members. The candidate himself commented of their relationship during his interview, "She's not too good for a man's ego—especially if you're a little inefficient like I am."

Unlike the procedure followed with any other candidate, Mr. Fourth's principal was invited to meet with the committee to share her views about his candidacy. Her discussion began with these comments:

> I think his one big problem is relating to people, because he tends to want to move too fast. . . . One thing he feels inadequate about is making small talk that makes people feel comfortable when they come to school. . . . I think he is better with

men than women. I've talked to him about how as an administrator he will be working mostly with women, and he'll have to observe certain amenities.

To the direct question, "Do you think he should be an administrator—say, for example, in a smaller school or some special setting?" she replied, "If I had my druthers, I'd like to have him in a situation where he could get some help—especially in human relations. I think we need to realize he's been in a very difficult position this year, working with a woman. . . . He has told me, 'It hasn't been any morale boost to work *with you.*'"

Immediately after the conference with Mr. Fourth's principal, one principal said, "Well, she hasn't changed my ideas any. We talked last year about his impulsiveness and these other problems." Another principal said, "There's no question of his ability. But I do feel some reservations about him." Another added, "A member of my staff said he walked right by her the other day without speaking. She felt badly about it. Of course, that doesn't pertain here."

Mr. Fourth's position as a former favorite was altered only slightly, but it was sufficient to put him out of the running. One committee member noted that no doubt the outcome would have been different had Mr. Fourth still been assigned to his former school, working with a male principal who had helped both to groom and to sponsor him for the step into administration.

Mr. Third

Mr. Third was less well known among committee members than any other in-district candidate. He had the briefest tenure in the district (five years), and this was his second consecutive year on leave in order to pursue graduate study toward a doctoral degree at the university. He helped reestablish his longevity by remarking to the committee as he entered for his interview, "I sat *here* last year," but the committee had already been reminded by the holdover member that Mr. Third had been "high on our list" the year before.

The search for topics to discuss was more difficult with a candidate who had not been active in the district for the past year and a half. As Mr. Third noted, "I've sort of lost track of some of these different programs." The discussion soon turned to the candidate's observations on the doctoral program at the university. The committee was receptive to his criticism that the "whole question of curriculum and administration at the university is all geared to secondary school." He told them that the set of qualifying examinations he had just written were all of the order, "Imagine yourself the principal of a *secondary school.* What would you do if. . . ."

One interviewing principal asked how Mr. Third's previous school district compared with this one.

MR. THIRD: The principals in this school district have a little more autonomy in the selection of staff.

INTERVIEWING PRINCIPAL: Is this autonomy a good thing?

MR. THIRD: I think this situation is good.
INTERVIEWING PRINCIPAL: Why do you?
MR. THIRD: So a staff can develop its abilities to the maximum. For example, maybe one staff can do more with "flexibility" than another.

Several times during the interview Mr. Third reaffirmed his belief in the importance of the elementary school principalship. In his concluding remarks he summarized, "I think the elementary principalship is a great challenge and quite different from other areas. You are working closely with individuals and different programs. . . . I've been an assistant principal, and now I'd like to try another notch up the ladder."

Mr. Third seemed to have made a good impression among the members of the committee. Their favorable reaction created some dilemmas which they discussed following his interview. One problem was his brief tenure: "He's the least experienced." Although his experience prior to coming to the district included two years as a teaching vice-principal, it was noted that he had held no position other than classroom teacher in his three active years in the district. An earlier bias expressed in the case of Mr. Seventh, who had been suspected of planning to come to the district in order to pursue a doctoral program at the university and then "moving on," was reinterpreted to differentiate between in-district candidates and out-of-district ones. "It's different in using the district if you've come up through the ranks or from outside it," suggested one principal. Mr. Third "might just be willing to stick around," posited another.

Mr. Third's recent efforts as a conscientious and effective supervisor of student teachers, fulfilling a part-time position on the university staff along with his program of studies, were duly noted by principals who had seen him in action: "Often these guys on a degree program don't have time to spend in supervising, but that's not the case here." Another principal added, "We've had some supervisors from the university who have missed a whole term."

Someone questioned, "We don't have anything on the salary schedule for a Ph.D. Couldn't he do better somewhere else?"

"He's told us he likes this district and wants to stay here," assured the assistant superintendent. "He doesn't want to be a professor."

I am quite sure I was the only person at the meeting who did not realize that the candidate was the superintendent's son-in-law.

Mr. Second

Enthusiastic support of Mr. Second's candidacy was expressed before, during, and after his formal interview. His excellent performance as a teacher and resource teacher, that he "dealt with difficult situations very well" as an active member of the local teacher organization, his "energy and interest," his active role in church work, even that his father had been a principal—all were duly reviewed before the interview began. If there was any reservation expressed at all, it was only to suggest that a promotion to the principalship might be a bit premature at present. While comments like "he was highly considered last year" and "I think he has matured greatly" tended to dispel such reservations among committee members, one principal reminded the committee, "He'll be around another year."

Mr. Second's interview began with the suggestion that he describe his "present situation," his experience, and the new programs he was working on. He launched easily into a fifteen-minute description of the educational program in the school where he was presently assigned. The following discussion was precipitated by his account of that program.

INTERVIEWING PRINCIPAL: I think we've heard a lot about the program at your school, and it's been a real good education. Now let's hear about how you think of *yourself* in a program—what do *you* want in a program?

ANOTHER INTERVIEWING PRINCIPAL: Yes, what do you think is the unique role of the elementary school?

MR. SECOND: I think it is to take each child where he is and take him as far as he can go. But that isn't unique to the elementary school. It's also junior high, isn't it? Yet I'm not qualified for the junior high.

ANOTHER INTERVIEWING PRINCIPAL: Who has the responsibility for making improvements in a school's program?

MR. SECOND: That's the principal's job—along with the whole faculty, of course. As an administrator, you should be the last one to take the glory.

To signal the start of the closing ritual during the interviews each candidate was asked if he had questions to address to the members of the committee. No candidate seemed to have a crucial question he wanted to ask, but none forfeited the implicit challenge to be able to ask *something.* The out-of-district candidates wondered which position they were being interviewed for. The in-district candidates already knew that this information was not yet available and that the decision about the annual "administrator shuffle" had not been announced and probably had not been made. Their questions concerned the dates when appointments were to be announced or the types of appointments to be made. The top two candidates expressed their concern about appointments to smaller schools, since the word was out that one of the new appointments might be for a "two-role" person (e.g., principal of two smaller schools, or principal plus some other assignment in one school). Mr. Second's query set off the following series of remarks in this regard.

MR. SECOND: I've been curious as to just how the joint principalships between two schools work out?

INTERVIEWING PRINCIPAL ONE: I've worked with it and it leaves a lot to be desired.

INTERVIEWING PRINCIPAL TWO: I think we took a step backward when we went to it.

INTERVIEWING PRINCIPAL ONE: I think it is better to combine a half-time principal and a half-time resource teacher in *one* school.

INTERVIEWING PRINCIPAL THREE: That looks good on paper, but it never seems to work out.

INTERVIEWING PRINCIPAL TWO: Of course, you know which one will give—just like when we principals have a conflict between supervision and administration.

INTERVIEWING PRINCIPAL ONE: There are no half-time jobs.

INTERVIEWING PRINCIPAL FOUR: How about combining the role of principal and the role of counselor?

INTERVIEWING PRINCIPAL ONE: With the role we're trying to create for the counselor, those two roles are not always compatible. When the axe has to fall, I'm the one who has to do it.

Mr. First

Presently serving in his second year as a full-time junior high school vice-principal, Mr. First had already established himself in an administrative niche. His request to get "back" into the elementary schools was met with a pose of suspicion by members of the committee which masked (but just barely) the significance they attributed to his application as a reaffirmation of the importance of the role of the elementary school.

The discussion prior to Mr. First's interview included the following comments:

ASSISTANT SUPERINTENDENT (reviewing his record): He's been a junior high vice-principal two years, but it only took one year to make him want to come back.

INTERVIEWING PRINCIPAL ONE: He's been so nice to work with over there that for selfish reasons I'd like to see him stay at the junior high level. How did he happen to get put into junior high?

DIRECTOR OF ELEMENTARY EDUCATION: They talked him into it one summer when I was away. They desperately needed a junior high vice-principal. He didn't know what his chances were for an elementary school position, so he took it.

INTERVIEWING PRINCIPAL ONE: Should he stay at junior high? Can he do any good there? Can he move up?

INTERVIEWING PRINCIPAL TWO: I think we should interview him and find out his feelings about junior high, whether he wants to get back into elementary, and if so, why.

INTERVIEWING PRINCIPAL THREE: How often do we ask people to do things in the district because it will be good for the district rather than for them? I'm not sure we're even doing these guys a favor.

ASSISTANT SUPERINTENDENT: Do you think that First's role on the Teacher-School Board Salary Committee has made a difference in how the Board might regard him? When we bring names to the Board, they react.

INTERVIEWING PRINCIPAL ONE: It might, but it shouldn't.

Mr. First's interview got off to a late but jovial beginning—he had thought his appointment was 11:40 A.M. instead of 10:40 A.M. and had to be telephoned at his school. His arrival precipitated the exchange of a few moments of raillery among those present. He knew everyone on the committee.

INTERVIEWING PRINCIPAL: What makes you think you want to be in a gang like this?
MR. FIRST: Are you serious? Do you want me to answer?
INTERVIEWING PRINCIPAL: Yes. That's really why we are all here.
MR. FIRST: Well, this is where I belong. This is where my training and my interest is.

Mr. First described programs and problems at his junior high school. He explained how he had tried to break down the resistance of those parents who "have the attitude that the school only calls once a year and that's when the kid is in trouble." He cited several aspects of secondary school administration which he disliked: "I don't like the sports emphasis in high school, the problems with buses and scheduling, the court cases. Last year I spent one day out of every two weeks in court. I'd rather be working with kids earlier in their lives, not in the kind of conference I sat in recently with a parent when a doctor told the mother her alternatives are either to give the daughter 'The Pill' or lock her up in a cage."

Another question gave him an opportunity to remind the committee of both his prior experience as a school administrator ("When I was an elementary principal in the Midwest," he began, "we had this problem. . .") and of an early encounter he had had with administrative rigidity. He described the attendance area of that school, a predominantly black slum area in a large city, as a "third-generation ADC neighborhood."[6] He discussed the program he had tried to initiate at the school: "It was a very peculiar nongraded program for a very peculiar neighborhood, a program for which the teachers and I were ready but the administration was not. I felt like I'd been kicked real hard when they turned down the program. That was about the time the director of elementary education came through recruiting teachers for this district. That's how I happened to come here."

INTERVIEWING PRINCIPAL: When you went back to the classroom after being an administrator, what were some of the problems?
MR. FIRST: Unwinding!! Not worrying so much about 50-minute programs.

MR. FIRST: One of my goals once was to go into teacher education. I used to think you could do the most good there, but I think now that's too far removed. You can do more good in the public schools—you're closer there. But it has some distasteful parts, too, like worrying over school budget elections or hasseling with the school board over a $100 raise.

---

[6] An ADC, or Aid to Dependent Children, neighborhood, i.e., a neighborhood with many families on welfare.

Final Deliberation

Members of the Principal Selection Committee deliberated for almost an hour after interviewing the last of the candidates before reaching a decision on their recommendation to the superintendent. One principal suggested a straw vote to rank all candidates and "see how near we are to one mind." The director of elementary education proposed that they identify and rank the top five candidates. Selecting a panel of five candidates for a maximum of three positions followed the earlier recommendation of the personnel director who had suggested they rank more candidates than needed because "someone might not take it." When the straw ballot was taken, four "favorite" in-district candidates topped the list. That number was informally adopted as the number of candidates the committee would recommend. Another straw vote was taken which reaffirmed the original ranking of the top candidates but revealed that one committee member was disrupting what was an otherwise highly agreed upon rank order.

INTERVIEWING PRINCIPAL ONE: There's someone who is ranking a top candidate low. I wonder if there is something we should have talked about?

INTERVIEWING PRINCIPAL TWO: I'm the one voting him low. Not because I have anything against him, but I still feel we have an obligation to another candidate. So I'm voting higher for him than I really feel about him. Yet I don't know if that's right, either.

Discussion, without further voting, revealed that all the members were satisfied with the composite results of the ranking and with the specific recommendation of the top candidates, as agreed upon from Mr. First to Mr. Fourth. The director of elementary education summarized: "I'll give these results, and our first vote, to the assistant superintendent. I'll tell him that before we would recommend anyone besides these top four we would want to discuss it."

The meeting, and the Principal Selection Committee itself, disbanded. "I'd much rather interview teachers," commented the case study principal. "So would I," added the director of elementary education.

Discussion and Comments

The proceedings of the Principal Selection Committee were presented here because that event, though well removed from the daily routine of any principal, brought into bold relief several aspects central to the professional life of the case study principal and to the principals with whom he worked. The present discussion is limited to three interrelated dimensions of the principalship which seem to pervade the life and work of a principal and which are substantially reflected in the data presented. These dimensions are (1) the lack of professional knowledge associated with the role, (2) an esteem for personal feelings, and (3) a proclivity toward variety-reducing behavior.

Lack of Professional Knowledge Associated with the Role

Throughout my fieldwork I was struck with the number of occasions in which principals communicated to each other uncertainties about what they "should" be doing and what is their "real" role. To any outsider, whether teacher, pupil, parent, or even researcher, the principals I met were always ready to describe and defend the importance of the elementary school and their contribution to its mission. In their own gatherings, however, free from their usual audiences and oblivious to the observer, they probed constantly for guidelines to answer one common and basic question, "What is the role of the principal?"

The role uncertainty of the principalship seems due in part to the problem of the lack of any professional (i.e., private and/or technical) knowledge or skill which clearly distinguishes the administrator from those administered. This problem is referred to broadly in the field of educational administration as that of working from a "limited knowledge base." Evidence of the limited knowledge base is illustrated in two ways in the proceedings of the Principal Selection Committee. First, in examining dialogue recorded during the committee's proceedings, one becomes aware of the absence of an esoteric technical vocabulary which might have been expected in other settings in the deliberations of such a "board of examiners." Except for Mr. Fifth's use of the terms "self-contained" and "a sort of modifed Joplin plan" the vocabulary evident throughout the proceedings reflects the ambiguous and general terms that characterized the professional language of administrators observed throughout the study: "real challenge," "meeting needs," "good situation," "involvement," "more autonomy," "unique program," "doing so much for boys and girls," and so forth. Indeed, to the extent that there is an esoteric language shared among professional educators (a language sometimes referred to jokingly within their circles as "pedagese"), principals express concern with their own ability to keep up with the latest changes in techniques or terminology. One principal observed, "You hire one or two new teachers and listen to them and you don't even know what they're talking about."

A second example of the problem of a limited knowledge base is suggested by the lack of systematic procedures by which the principals made evaluations necessary for ranking candidates. Having to make judgments which result in identifying one person as superior to another or which distinguish qualified from unqualified personnel can be a difficult and for some people a distasteful business. Nonetheless, the work of the schools is inexorably bound up with evaluating the performance of both staff and pupils. One of the crucial aspects of the principal's job in this school district, as it is elsewhere, is the annual process of preparing evaluative recommendations regarding personnel, particularly for those on probationary status. The lack of special skill or knowledge available to principals in performing this evaluative function was reflected collectively by the Selection Committee in the haphazard approach they took in interviewing and assessing candidates for the principalship. Whatever specific criteria each member of the committee used as a basis for judgment seemed to be assiduously avoided as a topic for mutual discussion and concern. One senses that each principal felt that regardless of the criteria he or his cohorts used, ultimately the group would reach substantially the same decisions regarding the selection and ranking of the candidates at hand. It should be pointed out in this regard that the final decision of the Committee did reflect just such a consensus.

An Esteem for Personal Feelings

The case-study principal and his colleagues seemed to share a distaste for formal evaluative tasks. Their reluctance was particularly apparent in the comments and jokes they made throughout the year about preparing their formal "teacher evaluations" and by the collective anxiety they exhibited as the deadline neared for submitting those reports to the central office. The same distaste was apparent throughout the meetings of the Principal Selection Committee as they spoke of "getting this over with." But their lack of regard for the formality of evaluation *procedures* should not be confused with their regard for the personal feelings of those whom they were evaluating. Their esteem for the feelings of the candidates, for the feelings of each other, and for their own feelings and intuitions as part of the assessment task, are repeatedly revealed in the dialogue. If the role of the principal can be characterized by a lack of professional knowledge, as suggested above, a compensating behavior of those who serve in it may be to give the affective domain considerably more importance than one generally associates with the processes of administration.

All candidates were interviewed graciously under circumstances in which the formalities inherent in the setting, such as meeting by a tight schedule of appointments at the central office, or holding most interviews seated around a large conference table in the formally designated Board Room, were consciously underplayed. The interviewers attempted to engage candidates in light social banter as they arrived for interviews. They asked open-ended questions, starting always with a question intended to put each candidate at ease and let him "tell something about himself." No question addressed to or response of a candidate was treated with the air of a grueling interrogation. Concern was expressed about interviewing any candidate for whom an invitation to appear for an interview might serve inappropriately to arouse his hopes. At the same time, the names of persons whom the committee never intended to consider as serious candidates were gently retained rather than summarily dropped. The only candidate really "rejected," and this primarily at the suggestion of the personnel director, was an out-of-district candidate who had once accepted and then rejected a contract offered him by the school district.

The personal feelings of the interviewing principals also made their way into the discussion of literally every candidate. Some of the statements regarding personal feelings were quite explicit: "I think I know him less well than some of the others, but I have a better feeling about him"; or, "I feel some reservations about how he relates to kids, but there's no question of his ability."

Not only were feelings of the interviewers introduced into the discussions, so also were feelings imputed to the candidates themselves. Most often such descriptions put the candidate in a favorable light or showed concern for his own feelings: "He has as good a feeling about children as anyone I know." "I think it would be a terrible blow to him if he didn't get a principalship."

Under conditions in which most comments are favorable, however, even the least hint of negativism served as a signal of caution: "He may be a bit bitter about education. He's talked to me about changing jobs and about being an administrator." [This comment brought a retort from another principal: "If he's somewhat bitter now, this would be the worst possible thing for him."]

A Proclivity toward "Variety-Reducing" Behavior

The proceedings of the Principal Selection Committee reveal a tendency among the principals to engage in what might be described as "variety-reducing" behavior.[7] This terminology comes from the field of general cybernetic systems. In the present case it draws attention to the fact that when the principals had to express preferences or to exercise choices which might be expected either to generate or to reduce the variation in certain aspects of the schools, their behavior reveals an inclination to reduce and to constrain. Their attention was directed toward keeping things "manageable" by drawing upon and reinforcing the existing system rather than by nurturing or even permitting the introduction of variation. This behavior is exemplified most clearly in the results of the major task confronting them, identifying candidates to receive official sanction. In that gentle but effective culling a panel of fourteen applicants was reduced to a final trio in which the successful members appeared so similar as to be virtually interchangeable. Whatever potential for variation extant among that original panel in terms of age, sex, background, recent experience, type and amount of formal education, marital status—in this instance even height, weight, and manner of speech and

[7] I am indebted to anthropologist Alfred G. Smith for suggesting to me the concept of variety-reducing versus variety-generating behavior as a means of analyzing administrative strategies.

dress—was successfully narrowed in the final selection. And while this process was going on, the principals also lent whatever support they could to reducing the potency of other variety-generating agents with whom their work brings them into continual contact, such as local colleges and universities, or central office administrators ready to saddle the principalship with a double role.

That the behavior of the principals in the episode gives such overt evidence of variety-reducing behavior is, in one sense, hardly surprising. The task to which they were assigned was by definition a variety-reducing task: there were almost five times as many aspirants as positions to be filled. Further, the very terms which the concept of "variety-reducing" calls to mind are terms which are descriptive of management processes: organize, systematize, categorize, constrain, control. What may be unusual is the extent to which variation was so thoroughly and systematically reduced, albeit this seemed to be neither an immediate nor a conscious concern of any of the principals on the committee.

Conclusion

I would like to conclude with a note of reflection relating the role of the principal to the emphasis placed on "change" in the public schools. This observation relates particularly to the preceding discussion on the phenomenon of variety-reducing behavior observed during the proceedings of the Principal Selection Committee.

The public schools have a seeming penchant for change. School people write, read, and talk constantly of new programs, new "hardware," new approaches, One can gather the impression from educators that anything "old" is suspect and that "changed" is automatically assumed to be "improved." In the last decade a whole vocabulary of change, including terms particularly familiar to students of cultural dynamics like "change agent," "acculturation," "innovation," and "diffusion," became the vogue in educational circles.

The school principal, charged directly with the role of being the instructional leader of his school, is often described as both instrumental and essential in the continuing process of introducing change into the school. The case study principal and his colleagues recognized this charge and responsibility. They acknowledged not only their formal obligation but their personal commitment to fostering change in the interests of a better education for children.

In looking at the totality of a typical "live" elementary school as the person charged with administering it might do, rather than at what is going on in any particular setting within it, one can appreciate that a school is a very dynamic institution. An elementary school is in a constant state of change without anyone having to do anything to induce or encourage the process. More than 500 people moved constantly into, out of, and within the school in this case study each day. New pupils, parents, teachers, substitutes, specialists, solicitors, sales- and servicemen, and visitors arrived constantly to replace former ones or to swell the ranks of those already present. New problems, programs, and personnel are introduced constantly in schools as pupils graduate or move away, teachers "turn over," or interest groups demand and governmental agencies offer to subsidize new curricula and services.

Regardless of what he *says* about the desirability of creating a climate for change, the principal already lives with incessant change as a way of life. If an occasional principal demonstrates such a tolerance of or personal need for change that he actually becomes an innovator who induces significant change into his own school, really creating something new or introducing new degrees of freedom into the setting (rather than simply manipulating or restructuring what was already present) I would think he would be a rare principal indeed. I do not believe I encountered such people among the career administrators with whom I came in contact during my fieldwork. The life of innovative programs or schools, and the tenure of innovative administrators, is frequently short-lived (see Fleming 1967; Miles 1964; Redefer 1950; Rogers 1962; Smith and Keith 1971).

Faced as he is with the inevitability of change as an inherent and major aspect of his task, even though he may not recognize it as such, the school principal is successful in his work as he is able to contain and to constrain the ever-changing group which he is assigned to administer. If his survival in that role necessitates his constant effort at variety reduction, we may have an important clue in helping to explain why certain dimensions of public school education remain so relatively unchanged in spite of the constant attempts to change them both from within and from without. For it may be that the only way one can hope to maintain any control in a system which is inherently so volatile and constantly changing in some dimensions—in this case, its personnel—is to exert all the influence one can in reducing the potential variety which might enter the system via routes more amenable to restraint. Although it presents a curious paradox between their ideal and actual roles as "agents of change" if principals actually serve to constrain rather than to facilitate the dynamic aspects of formal education, that is exactly the paradox which I am suggesting here.

The paradox may be explained by reanalyzing the extent to which managing change is already an inherent and significant part of the principal's role. Change comes in the form of a constantly changing population, both in the local community of parents and children and, perhaps even more, in the day-to-day composition of the adult cadre present at school. How long does it take to orient a new substitute teacher so that her day at school will not be a fiasco? What amenities are required for meeting a parent new to the community or orienting a relief custodian or secretary new to the school? How much more variation might a principal be expected to seek out per day after spending a not-so-unusual two hours orienting "thirteen visitors, four teacher trainees, seven students observing from the university, and three policemen" plus handling the new problems generated by over 500 pupils and staff members already part of the daily complement?

Programmatically the public schools may still warrant the assertion made by Willard Waller years ago that they are "museums of virtue" (Waller 1932:34), but while the air of virtue about them may have remained, the characteristic of "museum-ness" has not. Most urban elementary schools today are large, bustling institutions. The people who manage them live their professional lives among a constantly changing and volatile group of children and adults in which everyone, including themselves, has only relatively temporary status. The irony for the elementary school principal is that the extent of change with which he lives is neither acknowledged by those about him nor even necessarily recognized by himself. Indeed, he listens to the cries for change and often joins ritually with those who attempt to bring it about. Yet ultimately his own actions, in a constant press to keep the institution manageable at all, may tend to reduce the variation with all the ploys and powers characteristic of administrators in general and an elementary school principal in specific: "We'll have to see about that"; "Mrs. X has some good qualities as a teacher, but she and I just aren't seeing eye to eye. I'm going to have to suggest that she either transfer or resign"; "It's a grand idea, but there's no money in the budget for it"; "These fellows from outside have a real disadvantage. . . . I think he'd come along pretty well in a couple of years. He'd know our lingo and be doing a good job."

Could it be that those people who seek to become and are able to survive as principals, through a perhaps inadvertent but apparently critical and essential proclivity toward variety-reducing behavior, have their greatest impact on education not as agents of change but rather as advocates of constraint? If so, we may be better able to account for the remarkable stability and uniformity that has characterized American elementary schools in spite of the forces for change swirling constantly about them.

References and Further Reading

Department of Elementary School Principals, NEA, 1968, *The Elementary School Principalship in 1968*. Washington, D.C.; Department of Elementary School Principals, National Education Association.

Fleming, Emett E., 1967, "Innovation Related to the Tenure, Succession and Orientation of the Elementary Principal," Northwestern University, unpublished doctoral dissertation.

Fuchs, Estelle, 1966; *Pickets at the Gates*. New York: The Free Press.

———, 1969, *Teachers Talk: Views from Inside City Schools*. New York: Anchor Books, Doubleday & Company.

Griffiths, Daniel E., Samuel Goldman, and Wayne J. McFarland, 1965, "Teacher Mobility in New York City," *Educational Administration Quarterly* 1:15–31.

Hemphill, John K., Daniel E. Griffiths, and Norman Frederiksen, 1962, Administrative Performance and Personality. New York: Bureau of Publications, Teachers College, Columbia University.

Lee, Dorothy, 1963, "Discrepancies in the Teaching of American Culture." *In* George D. Spindler, ed., *Education and Culture: Anthropological Approaches.* New York: Holt, Rinehart and Winston, Inc.

Miles, Matthew B., ed., 1964, *Innovation in Education.* New York: Bureau of Publications, Teachers College, Columbia University.

National Education Association Research Report, 1967, "Estimates of School Statistics 1967–1968." *Research Report 1967 R-19.* Washington, D.C.: National Education Association.

Olson, John A., 1969, "Mapping: A Method for Organizing Data about Your School Attendance Area," *Oregon School Study Council Bulletin,* vol. 12, no. 7.

Pettitt, George A., 1946, *Primitive Education in North America."* Berkeley: University of California Publications in Archaeology and Ethnology 48 (Excerpted in Walter Goldschmidt, ed., *Exploring the Ways of Mankind.* New York: Holt, Rinehart and Winston, Inc., 1960).

Redefer, Frederick L., 1950, "The Eight Year Study . . . After Eight Years," *Progressive Education* 18:33–36.

Rogers, Everett M., 1962, *Diffusion of Innovations.* New York: The Free Press.

Sarason, Seymour B., 1971, *The Culture of the School and the Problem of Change.* Boston: Allyn and Bacon.

Smith, Louis M., and Pat M. Keith, 1971, Anatomy of Educational Innovation: An Organizational Analysis of an Elementary School. New York: John Wiley & Sons, Inc.

Spindler, George D., 1963, "The Role of the School Administrator," in George D. Spindler, ed., *Education and Culture: Anthropological Approaches.* New York: Holt, Rinehart and Winston, Inc.

University Council for Educational Administration, 1967, *The Madison Simulation Materials: Edison Elementary Principalship.* Columbus, O.: University Council for Educational Administration.

———, 1971, *The Monroe City Simulations: Abraham Lincoln Elementary School.* Columbus, O.: University Council for Educational Administration.

Waller, Willard W., 1932, *The Sociology of Teaching.* New York: John Wiley & Sons, Inc. (Science Edition, 1965.)

Wolcott, Harry F., 1967, *A Kwakiutl Village and School.* CSEC. New York: Holt, Rinehart and Winston, Inc.

———, 1970, "An Ethnographic Approach to the Study of School Administrators," *Human Organization* 29:115–122.

———, 1973, *The Man in the Principal's Office: An Ethnography.* CSEC. New York: Holt, Rinehart and Winston, Inc.

Zelditch, Morris, Jr., 1962, "Some Methodological Problems of Field Studies," *American Journal of Sociology* 67:566–576.

MARION LUNDY DOBBERT/*University of Minnesota, Social and Philosophic Foundations of Education*

10 *Education, Schools, and Cultural Mapping**

The main aim of this chapter is to show that university and college student analyses of the role and purposes of postsecondary education are incorrect and do not account for the facts at hand. First, I will examine these analyses in some detail in order to show their weak points, and then offer an alternative explanation.

The necessary research into the facts has been carried out at length by historians, sociologists, and anthropologists. What needs to be done here is to show which relationships are relevant to education.

Student comments upon the roles and purposes of universities and colleges are, in the opinion of the author, similar to sociological analyses of higher education as seen in such works as Havighurst and Neugarten's *Society and Education* (1968) or Halsey, Floud, and Anderson's *Education, Economy and Society* (1961). Thus this paper is also indirectly a criticism of sociological analyses of education.

Complex systems such as the culture of the United States, the system with which we will be dealing here, may be analyzed into numerous subsystems. This chapter will deal with three analytically separable subsystems of U.S. culture: 1. the university and college system, 2. the U.S. socioeconomic system, and 3. the basic philosophical system of U.S. citizens.

The socioeconomic, philosophical-scientific, and educational aspects of the U.S. cultural system are reciprocal, mutually supporting subsystems, which are so closely interwoven that an attempt at explanation of only one aspect, here the educational aspect, is fruitless unless accompanied by an analysis of interrelationships with the other two aspects. We constantly make use of such interrelationships in explaining, for example, the culture of Mesopotamia, showing how economy, writing, and ciphering on the one hand and political-religious hierarchy on the other are interwoven, but I have found this holistic assumption frequently lacking in analyses of U.S. culture and education, though the relationships of economy to education are often discussed.

---

*This chapter was presented in brief form at a Council on Anthropology and Education session at the meetings of the American Anthropological Association in November 1970.

The Research and Its Results

Thirty-eight students were interviewed in an informal but planned manner in order to pin down the writer's impressions of what students think. The writer is widely acquainted with students from many campuses, having been a student herself not too long ago. Thus in a sense this chapter is based on studies of hundreds of students. The thirty-eight interviews confirmed the impressions of years. In addition, student writings and speeches were examined as well as studies about students and their ideas. But the number of students interviewed and read about is not crucial to the point of the research, since its object was to determine the gamut of the responses.

Students' analyses of education recognize that school provides U.S. citizens with a set of statuses. Deriving a status from education is called "getting an education," a phrase which has two meanings. The first is expressed in the phrase "getting a *broad* education"—holders of the broad education point of view see undergraduate schools very much as the upper-class English of the nineteenth century saw prep schools. They are a place to which one goes for the experience because it "socializes, finishes, or broadens." This strikes me as much like the statement that prep school "forms your character." Some students analyze the university as failing in this capacity. The pressure of having to get grades turns the experience sour and causes some to drop out. Further, it is felt that the university is too bureaucratic and impersonal, a problem which stems from the highly programmed nature of courses, overenrollment and the wish of the faculty to do research instead of teach. Others feel that the university and colleges are reasonably successful in this purpose because by their very nature they bring together diverse students and diverse professors and provide a variety of activities.

Students recognize another type of status derived from education in the phrase "getting a *liberal* education." They see the educated person as one with a better way of looking at problems of life. In their minds the purpose of a university or college is to teach students to ask "why" and to tell them how to seek answers in a broad spectrum of sources. Through this, in the students' point of view, persons escape being bound by society. Some feel that the university fulfills this purpose. Again the very nature of the university or college is felt to help achieve this goal. Others feel that grades, set courses, poor or disinterested professors, and insistence on memorization prevent the university from imparting liberal education.

Many other students feel that the main purpose of colleges is to prepare students for adult occupations. These students are also divided in their assessment of the success with which colleges and universities achieve this aim. Some feel that they are quite successful and provide just what is needed—a certificate entitling the graduate to a job. Others feel that colleges and universities are failures. One reason is that they do not teach practical application and problem-solving, but require memorization of facts and theories which turn out to be totally useless for a person out in the world. Another is that universities do not provide careful occupational counseling services.

Most students recognize that the university has more than one role and that students come for different purposes. But each student has his own favorite purpose and feels that the other purposes cause the university to fail to achieve its "higher" purpose. Thus the persons who feel that the university is there to provide an experience resent the competition which it has set up to weed out the intellectually and/or occupationally incompetent. The occupationally oriented student resents the liberal education he is required to get as an undergraduate and feels that only courses related to needs should be required. Liberal-education–oriented students feel that the party and football atmosphere of the former and union card orientation of the latter create an atmosphere in which intellectual exchange is all but impossible. However, the dissatisfied members of all camps agree that a course structure causing memorization and grade competition is an evil.

The sociologically recognized role of the universities in keeping persons off the labor market is not recognized as such by most students. Some students mention that they personally came to college to avoid working or avoid the draft (the alternative form of relieving pressure on the labor market), but the university and college role is not conceived of in terms of the labor market's overpopulation. This gives us, I believe, a very complete picture of what we might call the folk-ethnographic view of colleges and universities as held by students originating from approximately the upper-lower social class through the upper middle.

Society, its occupations and life-styles, and the schools are seen in folk ethnography as organized in ascending parallel steps in which the proper schooling is necessary for entering each next higher step. (See Fig. 10.1.) These steps are thought of in terms of occupation, life-style, or ability to think and lead a questioning and open life. The strange thing about this mapping of the roles and purposes of universities and colleges is that even those students who do not believe that the university is accomplishing its purposes believe in this set of relationships between education and society. To them these are the relationships that ought to exist, but do not because the universities and colleges have too many other functions that interfere with the right and proper function which the student has in mind when he evaluates the university.

The students' understandings of the roles of universities are not necessarily incorrect, but they do not explain all of the facts. First, none explain why, in a social sense, university-level education continues to fulfill mutually exclusive functions which interfere with each other. Second, the explanation that the university is a broadening institution is inadequate; it does not explain why students are graded when grading is irrelevant to the finish imparted by a college education. Third, the idea that universities and colleges give people the necessary skills for jobs is not completely correct, as the above cited student complaints indicate; students just do not receive realistic

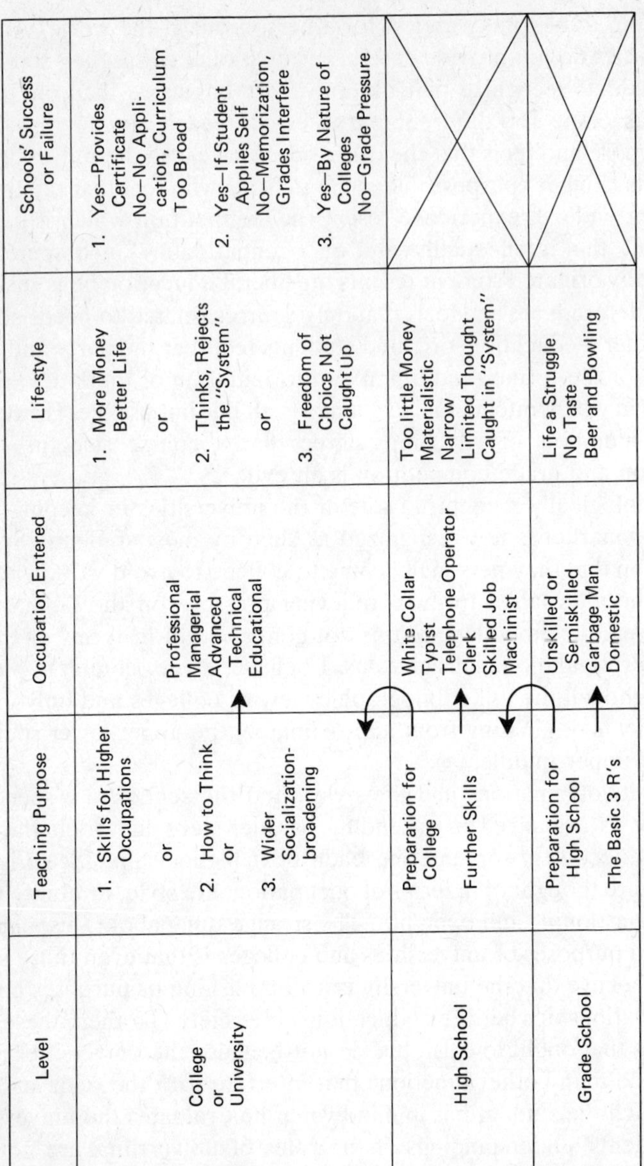

Level	Teaching Purpose	Occupation Entered	Life-style	Schools' Success or Failure
College or University	1. Skills for Higher Occupations or 2. How to Think or 3. Wider Socialization-broadening	Professional Managerial Advanced Technical Educational	1. More Money Better Life or 2. Thinks, Rejects the "System" or 3. Freedom of Choice, Not Caught Up	1. Yes—Provides Certificate No—No Application, Curriculum Too Broad 2. Yes—If Student Applies Self No—Memorization, Grades Interfere 3. Yes—By Nature of Colleges No—Grade Pressure
High School	Preparation for College Further Skills	White Collar Typist Telephone Operator Clerk Skilled Job Machinist	Too little Money Materialistic Narrow Limited Thought Caught in "System"	
Grade School	Preparation for High School The Basic 3 R's	Unskilled or Semiskilled Garbage Man Domestic	Life a Struggle No Taste Beer and Bowling	

Figure 10.1. Summary: student views of education.

occupational training; and jobs are not distributed according to type of degree or academic standing. Fourth, the idea that colleges exist to provide liberal education is also inadequate. This explanation does not account for the need to give grades and to structure curricula or account for the close correlation between education and occupational type. The idea that college holds students off the labor market is of course correct, but again does not account for the contradictory features discussed here nor is it so much a part of folk beliefs as it is of social science.

Rejection of the Folk Explanation

Where in this confusion do we turn to seek an anthropological explanation of the roles of universities and colleges in American life? We should, I believe, turn to the same method used to solve problems we do not understand in dealing with other societies. That is, we should consider the United States and the colleges and universities within it as an integrated adaptive system. This I do in a nonspecific way in Figure 10.2, which shows the American habitat and the arrangement of personnel used in its direct exploitation.

This diagram is revealing. When we consider the persons involved directly—using their hands or power tools in the immediate tasks of the basic exploitation of our habitat—we find that the average amount of education is low. It should be well below the 10.6 years of education average for the nation in 1960. The only group of highly educated persons involved directly in handling our environment is the medical personnel. By my calculations from the Detailed Occupation Table of the 1960 U.S. census, 56 percent of our

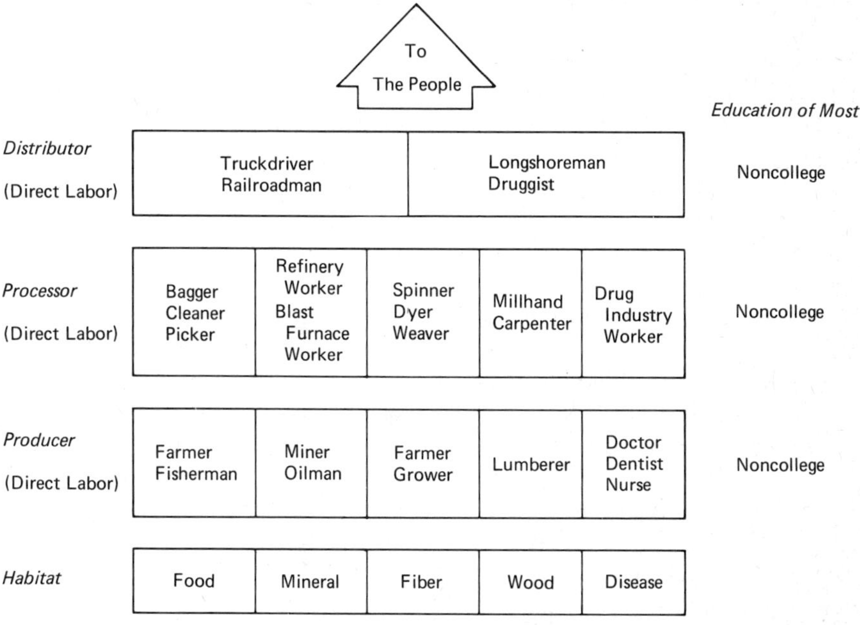

Figure 10.2. Direct labor (uses hands).

working population is involved in the types of occupations which provide for our basic needs.

What about the other 44 percent of the working population? These are persons engaged in management, law, government, clerical occupations, research, schooling, and so on. Certainly some managers, supervisors, and clerical personnel are necessary to continue production and some specialists in government and education are needed, but it would be difficult to argue that the society could not exist with less than 44 percent of its persons involved in such activities. If we compare this percentage with the percentage of persons involved in full-time activity keeping them out of direct production in non-Western complex societies, we find the non-Western percentages appear to be much lower. Let us calculate the percentage for a non-Western complex culture, the Yoruba Kingdom of Ifẹ in 1921. Forde (1951) gives the Ifẹ subtribe population as 23,213. If we assume that one third of these persons are in the labor force, and that of these 600 are directly involved in nonproductive occupations, which is to say the government of the kingdom, we find that slightly less than 8 percent of the working population is not involved directly in the exploitation of the habitat. The Yoruba bureaucracy provided one manager or official for each 38 persons by the above figures or even if we are off in population figures by a factor of 3, one for each 114. Our own society, on the other hand, provides one manager, governing official, lawyer, or teacher for each seven persons. Human society just does not need that many overseers to function.

Figure 10.3, which is the same as Figure 10.2 but expanded to bring in the total labor force, illustrates another important related point: how little education is actually needed to maintain our physical adaptation to our environment, far less than the amount of education represented! Of the jobs related directly to adaptation we easily can conceive of the great majority being carried out adequately by nearly illiterate or completely illiterate persons, which is how they have been carried out in the past in our own nation. Indeed, one can argue that most actual job skills are learned on the job itself, formally during an on-the-job training program or informally during a breaking-in period, and that education in schools is generally irrelevant to job performance, even for doctors. We might like to give a little education to managers and record keepers, but vast distributive systems have flourished in the past with the benefit of little or no writing. My conclusion is that we must reject any notion that schools, especially high schools and colleges, provide most of the essential skills that keep our economy functioning at its present level.

We must also reject the notion that higher education is the primary factor which gives differential access to various occupational and/or socioeconomic class levels, since research has shown that in the majority of cases, 70–80 percent (Havighurst and Neugarten 1968) of the people are found in the same class as were their parents. In other words, we must reject the idea that education affects the placement of the majority in particular occupations. There

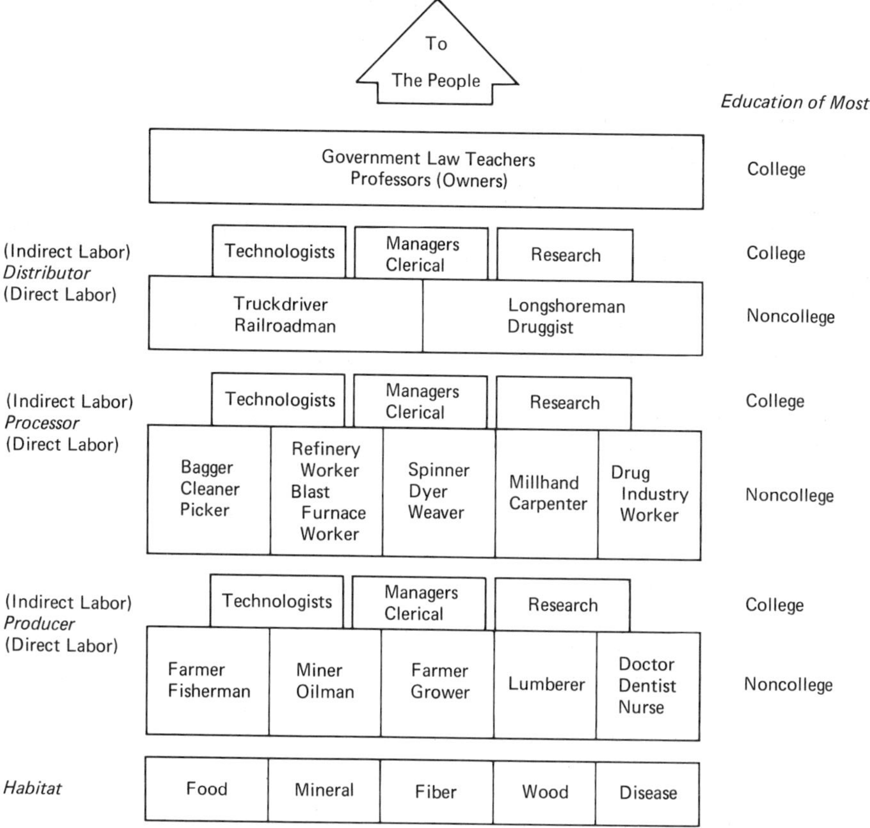

Figure 10.3. Other labor.

are, of course, exceptions to this rule in the cases of doctors, researchers, and professors, but it is these exceptions, as I will explain later, that prove the case for the anthropological point of view as I am advancing it.

I will now advance this explanation of the school's functions. Figure 10.3 shows how this society relates to its environment with respect to satisfying basic needs, but it does not show how the system is integrated. If we are to consider universities and colleges in context, we must certainly place them somehow within the economic structure, since the parallel between education and economy must have some meaning. This meaning, however, is not the one the natives think it is.

There are, as might be expected, several modes of integration. A primary one is economic. My view of the way in which this economic integration works follows Lundberg (1946) and Domhoff (1969). They have shown that the system is integrated economically through the existence of a small governing class. This class controls the U.S. economy through effective, though not necessarily actual, ownership, of the country's resources and means of production. Effective control is achieved through monopolizing the decision-making positions in the economic realm and in the federal government. This view of U.S. economic integration has withstood severe criticism from Parsons, and Domhoff and others have adequately answered criticism directed against it (Domhoff 1969).

I will thus accept this analysis and view the United States as a gigantic pyramidal bureaucracy with the governing class on top, with lines of communication or of vertical integration flowing down from owners to upper management to middle level management, to foremen and supervisors, and finally to the people engaged directly in the work of production, processing and distribution. Basic horizontal integration is achieved through interlocking and overlapping at the governing class level. It should be noted at this point that many prominent universities, colleges, and prep schools fit directly into this economic mapping because it is the governing class which controls their boards of regents or trustees.

This is not to say of course that all U.S. business and all U.S. universities and colleges are integrated into one huge pyramidal economic structure by a direct chain of command stemming from the governing class. We have many independent businesses owned by the middle class, many colleges and universities governed by middle-class boards, and much government at the state and local levels in the hands of the middle class. In other words, the economic or directly adaptive mapping of the habitat does not explain all of the facts about U.S. society. The United States is not completely integrated around its arrangements for physical adaptation to the habitat. We must look for another horizontal integrator. The mechanism which integrates the economically independent entities with the total structure of the U.S. is one familiar to all anthropologists—religion—that proverbial supporter of the social structure in nonwestern societies.

I would like to argue that religion is also a primary integrator in the U.S. However, we have failed to notice this because in modern English there is no word corresponding to what anthropologists mean by religion. Also, like most of the people anthropologists describe, U.S. citizens do not separate religion, in the anthropological sense, from everyday life.

The first step in the explication of this point of view is a definition of religion. I shall use Clifford Geertz's definition: "a religion is: (1) a system of symbols which acts to (2) establish powerful, pervasive, and long lasting moods and motivations in men by (3) formulating conceptions of a general order of existence and (4) clothing these conceptions with such an aura of factuality that (5) the moods and motivations seem uniquely realistic" (1966:4). It follows from this definition that science or scientific explanation may be considered as the religion of the United States. Science provides an interpretation of reality or existence that seems to satisfy contemporary Americans, whereas the folk-ethnographically defined religions stemming from the Judeo-Christian traditions fail, for the most part, to do so.

A further argument for this point of view is that historically science stems directly from the Judeo-Christian outlook and its philosophical traditions. In fact, Whitehead (cited in Cardwell 1965) finds the inspiration for the development of science in the medieval insistence upon a rational deity and a consequently rational universe. In addition, Whitehead notes that the religiously based medieval universities built the earliest corpuses of knowledge.

Following this train of thought, I maintain that the universities began as religious institutions and still are religious institutions charged with the advancement and preservation of a basic world view. In the tradition of Whorf and Kluckhohn and following Geertz's (1966) notion that religion formulates general conceptions of the order of the world, thus providing a model of and for reality, let me attempt to identify the basic world view of the religion called "science."

I see science as having several major premises, none of which are prior to the other. One of these is that the universe is extraordinarily vast, not only in the sense of size but also in the sense of complexity. Because it is so vast, it may be subjected to endless analysis without exhausting its possibilities. Second, all of this vastness is interdependent, a fact which is especially clear to scientists who find it difficult to conduct uncontaminated experiments or to measure just one thing at a time. Third, this vastness and its integration is lawful and regular, not chaotic. This has led to the creation of scientific laws and to the realization that prediction is possible. Fourth, the entire universe has a movement which is unceasing, whether it be conceived of as linear or circular movement.

A main expression of this religious philosophy is through a set of practitioners commonly known as scientists. The everyday use of the word "scientist" implies the inclusion of all persons specializing in physical studies such as physics, chemistry, biology, medicine, and so on, and all specialists in social studies such as geography, sociology, psychology, and so on. I could argue my point using this limited definition, but it is, again, a folk-ethnographic category and does not conform to the social facts seen by an analyst specializing in the dissection and explication of the workings of society. I feel that the practices and persons involved in engineering, management, law, ministry, and teaching should be included within the scope of science. The life pathway and training that such people follow is very similar to that of the ordinarily defined scientists—all pass through at least four years in a university or college and thus all share a good deal of actual training in basic required courses, share in socialization, and share the identity of having a college education.

Not only is the training of these persons similar to that of the ordinarily defined scientists, but also their functions are similar; they too are in positions of leadership and of social validation. Ordinary scientists such as physicists and chemists validate and support U.S. society by improving its technology or developing weapons to fend off other nations with other ways of life. Psychological studies prove the superiority of democracy (Lewin, Lippitt, and White 1960). Scientific commissions are called to make investigations that end up supporting what the government does or is planning to do about welfare, migrants, Indians, or education. Similarly the lawyer validates a law by applying it to given circumstances and showing that it is good and workable; or he may show that it is irreconcilable with the total body of law which is then validated by rejection of the one law. Lawyers working on cases consult psychologists and doctors. The teacher validates the whole of society to a new generation. Managers make use of sociological studies about personnel and of technical studies on industrial processes. For purposes of this chapter, then, I will expand the word scientist to include all of these persons and one further group of persons which I add to the group last and separately merely for emphasis. That group consists of persons involved in the higher levels of state and federal governments. The argument for inclusion is the same.

The major question that remains to be answered is how this scientific-religious structure supports the existence of the social pyramid described earlier and integrates the independent middle-class businesses, schools, and governments. Some of the simple, easily identified types of support were just mentioned, but even more important is the fact that the scientific world view itself is supportive of the existing society. This needs some elaboration.

Like all men in this world, the scientifically oriented man is insecure in a universe he does not understand. His insecurity stems from his knowledge of its vastness and from the fact that he knows that the universe moves on regardless of him or his desires. Further insecurity stems from his knowing that this heedless, ongoing vastness is integrated in a way that he cannot fully comprehend. The security of the scientifically oriented person rests in his faith in the logical nature of the universe and in his faith in human ability to attack it and overcome it in the piecemeal fashion used in the past. The ordinary person in U.S. society does not expect to participate in this attack himself, and therefore delegates this job to his shamans—a practice common in all parts of the world. These shamans, in this case called scientists, are like all shamans in that they are thought to understand much more about the underlying nature of the universe than the ordinary man. Like all shamans, they do mysterious and possibly dangerous things that ordinary men cannot comprehend.

Most mysterious is the way in which scientists attempt to understand the order of the universe. This particular order is potentially expressible in infallible laws which can be written with mathematical formulas, or in the common man's terms, in numbers. An extremely important consequence of this manner of expressing order is that the ordinary person does not learn the basic means of expressing the structure of the universe and is therefore unable to participate in its study or manipulation. Study and manipulation are left to persons considered extraordinarily intelligent and capable of grasping the mathematical mode of expression and the vast schemes of which they are a part.

This same scientific world view is used to look at U.S. society. It is seen as vast and basically not understandable as a totality. Some aspects, though, have become understandable through the diligent efforts of social scientists who have pecked away and discovered various elements of society, such as orderly social classes. Just as the universe is lawful, U.S. society is thought to be logically ordered, running by law. This law is partially understandable and created by man through the Constitution and statutes and partially an aspect of "the nature of things," for example, the laws of economics. The ordinary man knows that the U.S. social system is rational. He learns to understand small parts of it in civics classes, and consequently he is reasonably secure even though he does not understand everything. What is important here is the fact that he feels things are rational.

This world view supports the ruling class by presenting the society as a vast given, proceeding on rules of its own and relatively invulnerable to the attacks of individuals or small groups. Furthermore, society is presented as mostly unintelligible due to its vastness, which means that it can be manipulated only by experts, namely, scientists. Not only do these two assumptions point to the uselessness of attempting change, but they go even further in that scientists are pictured as the persons in charge of improving the world around us, should it grow unbearable. Whether it be the poverty of migrant workers or the injustices of segregation, the ordinary person feels that the problems can assuredly be attacked by the scientists and after long and arduous research be resolved. He knows that the problems are being attacked because he reads about research in newspapers. The governing class has recognized the value of this outlook and has ceased buying time and patience through large charitable foundations as it did in the past. It now supports benevolent scientific organizations such as the Ford Foundation which have funded a great deal of social research (Price 1965).

We can conclude, then, that the religion of science supports the existing social order in various overt and covert ways. The one problem which remains is to show how the educational system is articulated with the integrated hierarchical governmental and economic system. The integrating factor here also is the scientific world view. It is clear in the first place that using my broad definition of science, the schools concentrate upon providing students with the scientific world view. Some of the time in schools is given to imparting reading, arithmetic, and English skills and for direct socialization activities, but in formal outline schools concentrate upon teaching the scientific world view beginning with natural science and social studies and advancing to more specific and sophisticated aspects of these fields as the student progresses. I see the function of education at the elementary level as providing the basic framework of the scientific viewpoint. It functions in the same way that the telling of myths and legends and the viewing of public religious ceremonies function in other societies. Elementary education creates the necessary, society-supporting, common world view and does it in such a way that its production is not left to chance.

I see secondary education as imparting further scientific information in order to create a group of specialists—particularly clerical workers and skilled workers or foremen. These persons are, along with many technologists who often take two further years of education, the persons who correspond to potters, weavers, and smiths in other societies. These specialists are in a better position to understand and consequently change society, because they are more directly involved in the technology which is the backbone of the U.S. adaptation. These persons must therefore have a deeper understanding of science and of the consequent orderliness and unchangeableness of society if the use of their skills is to be socially controlled.

At the third level of education, the college and graduate school level, we train the group of persons whom I have labeled scientists; we could just as well label them priests, or system-maintenance specialists. Three different grades of these persons are produced, each grade having a different function. The first grade is that of teachers whose function as system-maintenance persons is self-evident. They must, of course, know a great deal of science as they are its primary public apologists with relation to the new generations. It is also important to note that teachers are taught to educate children scientifically, applying the latest insights from psychology and sociology. In universities, education departments or colleges stand prominently next to physics departments and engineering colleges as their scientific equals in the university's structural arrangements.

The second class is what we might call the scientific shamans who specialize in system maintenance through system adjustment. In this category I would include persons who could be administrators, managers, lawyers, or politicians. These persons oversee the smooth functioning of already ordered social arrangements, order new economic and social arrangements, and change social arrangements when the order is not functioning smoothly. Again, if this is to be carried out in such a way as to promote social continuity, these persons need clear knowledge of the basic principles of the scientific viewpoint, lest their adjustments be haphazard and lead to disorder. The independent adjustments of the numberless persons in this category must have direction and coherence and, of course, limits. If these shamans' adjustments were not controlled by a deeply held, well-interiorized view that only minor changes are possible within the vast given order of society, they could try revolutionary changes. At this point let me emphasize that the structural position of higher governmental officials in the United States is in this second class of priests.

The third class of priests, which I shall call the high priests, is trained via the initiation ordeal of the Ph.D. This is a class of priests who are thought to possess the real insight into the order of the universe. Their primary occupation is to pass this insight down to future generations to improve upon the insight if possible, and to provide the rulers of the people with aspects of this knowledge needed in making decisions and formulating workable policies. It strikes me that they function almost exactly in the same way as have astrologers in general, by telling the rulers which actions are propitious and likely to succeed with relation to the basic religious structures of the universe.

Before concluding this argument, I must cover one minor point explicitly, though it has implicitly been answered. This has to do with the function of grades in education and of their structural equivalent in the world of work, money. I see both grades and money as social equations that follow from the fact that the social universe is orderly and that order may be expressed in number. Basically, both function as visible social integrators because they openly declare what the nature of this social orderliness is, an hierarchical orderliness. Thus grade, wages, and occupational classes are closely correlated, as they are three different expressions of the same social-order facts.

Closing Remarks

The main thrust of this chapter is that neither students nor educators really understand what the colleges and universities are. They are actually the places which specialize in giving an identity to the priestly class of U.S. society. It strikes me that this is the only theory about the functions and roles of universities and colleges that can explain all the social facts. The relevant social facts I see as (1) the great social class differential in availability of education; (2) the limited socioeconomic class mobility; (3) the historical connection between religion, schools, and the upper classes in the Western European tradition; and (4) the connection between higher education and the professional, or scientific jobs.

I feel that those students who are satisfied with their university or college experience intuitively understand and accept the perpetuation functions of the universities and will easily take their places in the priestly class. They do not, of course, state things in these terms but explain the functions of universities with relation to giving education, job skills or socialization as stated earlier, all verbally consistent with democratic ideals. Thus they say that "normal" persons get what they want in the university—better material life, wider socialization, and "education" through the very nature of the schools.

On the other hand, those who are dissatisfied do not accept the perpetuation functions of colleges and universities. This function is contrary to widely stated U.S. values of equality and democracy. Many students who are dissatisfied with colleges explain their proper functions in terms of democratic values: Persons in universities and colleges should have equal access to both education and occupations; and grading, required courses, and traditional subject matters are seen as limiting equality of opportunity, as they most likely do. Some dissatisfied students, those with socialistic ideals, do analyze U.S. society in terms of a conflict between a ruling class and the working class. But they do not analyze colleges as places producing priests and rulers from sons of the priestly or ruling class. Their detailed criticisms of the universities are stated in the same democratic terms as those of other students. Were this not the case, they would be forced in all honesty to withdraw, as perhaps a few have. But if the university *ought* to be a place of opportunity for all, then withdrawal is unnecessary though reform may be necessary.

In closing, let me say that this analysis is difficult to swallow as it places all of us right in the center of a priestly ruling class, a notion which revolts us, since we have been socialized in the American value system; and which, if we were to take seriously, would place us in a dilemma. Suppose we really are part of the priestly ruling class. Possibly we accept that with an anthropological philosophy saying that most societies have ruling classes and that men have to live in the cultures where they are born. Or, do our American value-trained consciences require some action of us? The easiest thing to do is ignore the whole problem.

References and Further Reading

Becker, H., Geer, B., and Hughes, E., 1969, *Making the Grade.* New York: John Wiley & Sons, Inc.

Bertalanffy, Ludwig von, 1968, *General System Theory.* New York: George Braziller, Inc.

Bureau of Census, 1963, *U.S. Census of Population 1960.* Washington, D.C.: Department of Commerce.

Cardwell, D. S. L., 1965, "Science and Society." In N. Kaplan, ed., *Science and Society.* Chicago: Rand McNally.

Domhoff, G. Wm., 1969, *Who Rules America?* Englewood Cliffs, N.J.: Prentice-Hall, Spectrum.

Forde, D., 1951, *The Yoruba-Speaking Peoples of South-West Nigeria.* London: International Institute of Africa Studies.

Geertz, Clifford, 1966, "Religion as a Cultural System." In M. Banton, ed., *Anthropological Approaches to the Study of Religion.* London: Tavistock.

Halsey, A. H., Jean Floud, and C. Arnold Anderson, 1961, *Education, Economy and Society.* New York: The Free Press.

Havighurst, R. J., and Neugarten, B. L., 1968, *Society and Education.* Boston: Allyn and Bacon, Inc.

Lewin, K., Lippitt, R., and White, R. K., 1960, *Autocracy and Democracy: An Experimental Inquiry.* New York: Harper & Row.

Lundberg, Ferdinand, 1946, *America's 60 Families.* New York: Citadel Press. Inc.

News from Nowhere, 1969–70. Various issues. Student underground newspaper at Northern Illinois University.

Price, D. K., 1965, "The Scientific Establishment." In N. Kaplan, ed., *Science and Society.* Chicago: Rand McNally.

Students, Northern Illinois University 1969–1970. Various leaflets.

U.S., 1963. "Occupational Characteristics." *U.S. Census of Population: 1960.* Subject Reports, Pt. 7. Washington, D.C.: Government Printing Office, see Table 2.

THOMAS P. ROHLEN/*University of California at Santa Cruz*

11 Seishin Kyōiku *in a Japanese Bank: A Description of Methods and Consideration of Some Underlying Concepts**

During the last few years, Japanese newspapers, television, and other media have given considerable attention to the startling increase of company training programs devoted at least in part to *seishin kyōiku,* a manner of training commonly translated as "spiritual education." These accounts have been impressionistic and generally critical of such programs as unwanted and unwarranted echoes of Japan's prewar education, universally condemned until recently as militaristic, nationalistic, and stultifying. The fact that many, perhaps as many as one-third of all medium and large Japanese companies, now conduct some sort of *seishin kyōiku* program may be considered strong evidence of a reaction in business quarters to the "excesses" of Western influenced progressive education and a desire to supplement, at least for their own employees, the education received in the public-school system with some traditional education. The occasional assertion that company *seishin kyōiku* echoes prewar militarism and represents a growing reactionary storm is certainly unwarranted at present, but, it is a sign of the arrest, if not the reversal, of the twenty-year trend in the decline of particularly Japanese forms of education.

In this paper I wish to describe one such company spiritual training program in which I was a participant for its three-month duration in 1969. The patterns underlying the various activities will be summarized since they provide for the non-Japanese something of a definition of the meaning of *seishin* and the educational concepts underlying *seishin kyōiku.*

Training sessions lasted between ten and sixteen hours per day, six days a week. The time devoted to *seishin* education was estimated by the training staff to be about one-third of the entire introductory program. The remaining two-thirds was devoted to training new bank members in the numerous

---

*Reprinted from the Council on Anthropology, and Education *Newsletter.* Vol. 2, No. 1, February 19, 1971, with permission.

For Harmony and Strength: Japanese White-collar Organization in Anthropological Perspective (Berkeley: University of California Press, in press) by Thomas P. Rohlen contains broad background information for the study reported in this chapter.

technical skills expected of them in their job; however, this estimate of the division of time between spiritual training and technical training ignores the fact that a *seishin* orientation was often given to technical training activities. The atmosphere surrounding the trainees throughout each day was strongly colored by *seishin* concepts. Here and there in the institute, for example, slogans carrying *seishin* messages were posted. Individual performance in the task of learning banking skills was commonly interpreted according to *seishin* concepts and even many aspects of recreation, such as the songs the group sang, were in fact vehicles for *seishin* messages.

While unquestionably this bank's program varies in many details from the *seishin* training of other companies, conceptually the goals and methods are essentially the same according to my experience and inquiry. The underlying similarities among them are the patterns and concepts of *seishin kyōiku*, which this paper will attempt to clarify.

My experience with Japanese who have had no personal contact with company *seishin kyōiku* is that they tend to associate it with the moral education *(shūshin kyōiku)* practiced in the public schools before the war. In a very much altered form, moral education does survive in contemporary *seishin* training programs. The morality is considerably altered in content and presentation. Today, the institution sponsoring the training is the prime focus of morality, whereas before, the nation, in the person of the emperor, was central. Instead of rituals of nationalism the bank today draws attention primarily to its own symbols. Through such daily actions as singing the bank song, reciting its motto, learning of its history, being told of the "company spirit," and hearing inspirational messages from its leaders, the trainees are taught pride and respect for their bank. The nation is not ignored, but rather the company stresses the service given to Japan by the bank and urges its trainees to fulfill their responsibilities to the nation through loyalty to their bank. It is not uncommon that service to the bank even be characterized as service to the entire world and to world peace, so organic is the model of social life taught by the bank. No matter what the ultimate benefit, however, the message is that the moral man is the man who works hard for his own company. The bank and all other institutions, according to this view, serve as intermediaries between individual intentions to aid the greater society and the actual realization of national well-being. The bank, by virtue of this position, regards itself as an interpreter and defender of social morality and when it practices moral education it does so not only for the good of the bank but also for the entire society.

It is an oversimplification, however, to describe the moral education of the bank exclusively in terms of a narrow focus on loyal role fulfillment in the bank. The content of the program includes many quite fascinating elements borrowed from the pool of inspirational stories of other countries. The diary of a missionary's medical work in Vietnam, the pronouncements of President Kennedy, and the opinions of the Ethiopian Olympic marathon champion are among the instructional materials drawn from foreign sources. Such a selection is especially effective for without this contextual sleight of hand, the moral of the story might well be rejected as old-fashioned or militaristic if the example was Japanese. "Foreigners do this," or "abroad the custom is such and such," are common and powerful arguments in the bank's moral instruction program.

In addition to foreign influence, the bank's program utilizes the prestige of scholarship and science, whenever convenient. Writings of famous professors which are consistent with the bank's message are found on the required-reading list for trainees and teachers from the regional university lecture occasionally at the institute.

Yet the overall aim of the moral instruction program is not to "brainwash" or greatly manipulate the thinking of the trainees. This would be an impossibility. What is intended is that the trainees 1. be familiar with the point of view of the bank, its competitive circumstances and its intention to contribute to the social good, and 2. that this moral perspective strengthen their will to perform their work properly in the future. In this way moral education, which is almost exclusively verbal in nature, fits into the overall *seishin* program where the emphasis is primarily on learning taking place through experience.

Keeping in mind that the program included many lectures and assigned readings, we may turn to the activities designed to provide direct lessons in matters of *seishin* for the trainees. These were clearly the heart of the program and provided the most interesting moments during the entire three-month period. The lectures, in contrast, were often sources of boredom for the trainees. What follows is an account of some of the training activities, often in the form of a personal narrative since my experience in taking part in these activities is an important element in my analysis.[1]

Rōtō

For two days during the latter part of the second month of training we stayed at a youth center sponsored by the Japanese government. This center, located on a mountainside, overlooks a large agricultural valley and just below is the market town for the area. Early in the morning after our arrival, we were instructed to go down into that town and there find work from the residents. Our instructions were to go singly from house to house offering to work without pay. We were to do whatever the host wished us to do. It was strongly emphasized that this was not to be a group operation. Each was to go alone and work alone for the entire day. In addition the trainees were

[1] *Editor's Note:* Accounts of participation in Zen meditation, visits to military bases, and a weekend outing have been deleted from this presentation because of limitations on space.

disallowed from making any explanation for themselves or their reasons for volunteering to work. They could offer no more than their name and their willingness to work. We dressed for the exercise in white nondescript athletic uniforms common throughout Japan. Without benefit of a social identity or a reasonable explanation for ourselves, we were sent out to make a most unusual request of strangers. Our reliability would not be vouched for by our relationship to a known institution like the bank. We were dependent on the good will of the people we met and on their willingness to disregard their own distrust of strangers.

This form of situation, difficult as it would be anywhere, is of particular difficulty in Japan where as a rule strangers ignore one another and social intercourse between them is unusual and suspicious. Approached by an unknown person with a request like this, the common response would be a hurried and not very polite refusal. People doing *rōtō* in Japanese cities have met refusals perhaps four times out of five. It was with considerable consternation that the trainees left for the town below.

I followed the young men into the town and watched them as they wandered about from house to house. They were very reluctant to leave their friends and go alone to the front gate of some house. In the case of some groups, they walked several blocks together before anyone was able to muster the courage to make his first approach to a house, but gradually the groups dispersed. The common experience was to be refused two or three times before finally finding someone who would allow them in and give them work. All agreed to having been very careful and worried about the first approach, but the second and then the third were easier to make. People who did take them in were regarded as warm and understanding people for whom they were very happy to work hard. The common pattern was to volunteer to do things which even the host would not have thought to ask in order to avoid going out again and seek another accommodating house. Boys who had been raised on farms tended to go to the edge of town seeking familiar work from farming families there. The majority found work in various small shops. One helped sell toys and another assisted a mat maker, a third delivered groceries and another pumped gas, for example. One rather clever young man found work in a small roadhouse by the bus station which served coffee, snacks, and drinks. He quickly established himself as more than just a dishwasher by showing his skill in mixing cocktails. When one of the instructors happened to notice him working there, he was angered by the lack of seriousness with which this trainee regarded the day's exercise. The offender was told he had selected an inappropriate place and instead of doing service for some respectable family, he was busy swapping jokes with the customers and waitresses of a roadhouse. He was sent away from the place and told to find other work. Later he was roundly criticized for taking *rōtō* lightly.

When the group had all returned sometime in mid-afternoon, a general discussion of the day's experience was held in the auditorium. When it was apparent that comments from the floor would not be forthcoming, the instructor in charge had each squad talk over their impressions and then discuss the relevance of the day's experience to the question, "What is the meaning of work?" As usual a variety of opinions emerged. Many trainees seemed to have had such a pleasant time with their hosts that they were unaware of the fact that they had enjoyed doing tasks which they would normally label work. The discussions did often contain the observation that enjoyment of work has less to do with the work performed than it does the attitude the person takes toward it. The bank's major reason for utilizing *rōtō* centers on establishing this lesson.

The original intent of *rōtō,* however, is somewhat different. A Kyoto temple developed it as a method of shocking people out of spiritual lethargy and complacency. The word actually means something like "bewilderment" and refers to the state of insecurity established when the individual is divorced from his comfortable social place and identity. In the course of begging for work, that is, begging for acceptance by others, he learns of the superficial nature of much in his daily life. His reliance on affiliations, titles, ranks, and a circle of those close to him is revealed clearly and, perhaps for the first time, he begins to ask who he really is. *Rōtō* also provides a unique opportunity for a trusting and compassionate interaction between strangers. After a *rōtō* experience, it is very unlikely that a person will continue to disregard the humanity of others no matter how strange they are to him in terms of social relationship. It is hoped that a greater warmth and spontaneity will develop in the individual from this experience.

From the point of view of the bank, there is an additional purpose which they hope this training will fulfill, which helps explain why *rōtō* is included in a training program for new bankers. It has been the experience of many people from the bank who have done this both in Kyoto and under the auspices of the bank itself that "the meaning of work" and "attitudes toward work" have changed after doing *rōtō.* The anxiety of rejection and isolation mounts with each refusal until finally, when some kindly person takes them in and gives them work, there is a cathartic sense of gratitude to being accepted and allowed to help. No matter what it is, even cleaning an outhouse, the sense of relief makes the work seem pleasant and satisfying. Work normally looked down upon is in this circumstance enthusiastically welcomed.

After such an experience, it is difficult to deny the assertion that any form of work is neither intrinsically good nor bad, satisfying or unsatisfying, appropriate or inappropriate to the person, but rather that the result varies according to the subject's attitude and circumstances. Failure to enjoy one's work becomes essentially a question of one's attitude toward it. The experience of *rōtō,* according to the people in the bank, teaches that any work can be enjoyable with a positive attitude. Since it must assign rather dull and methodical tasks to many of its employees, the bank finds this lesson of obvious value. Instead of taking this cynically as evidence of deceit on management's part, we should acknowledge the bank's very great concern that work be enjoyable for all members of the organization.

Endurance Walk

Ever since our first day, we had heard about the twenty-five-mile endurance walk sometime near the end of the training period. Our daily early-morning mile run routine and the many other climbing and hiking activities we had undergone served as preparation for this event. On the morning we were actually to begin our endurance walk, there seemed to be a high level of anticipation and readiness to try it even among the weaker and less athletic trainees.

The program was simple enough. We were to walk the first nine miles together in a single body. The second nine miles were to be covered with each squad walking as a unit. The last seven miles were to be walked alone without conversation. All 25 miles were accomplished by going around and around a large public park in the city. Each lap was approximately one mile, so in total we were to go around the park 25 times. There were a number of rules established by the instructors. We were forbidden to drink water, soda pop, or take any other refreshment. During the second stage, each squad was to stay together for the entire nine miles and competition between squads was not encouraged. Finally, we were strictly forbidden from talking with anyone else when walking alone during the last stage. The training staff also walked the 25 miles but they went in the opposite direction, thus passing each of us each lap. Some dozen or so young men from the bank, recent graduates of previous training programs, were stationed along our route and instructed to offer us cold drinks, which we, of course, had to refuse. This was the program, and there was no emphasis at all placed on one person finishing ahead of another. We were told to take as much time as needed as long as we completed the entire 25 miles. We began around 7:30 a.m. and generally finished around 2 p.m. There was no time limit placed on us.

On the surface, this program was simple enough, but in retrospect it seems to have been skillfully designed to maximize certain lessons related to *seishin.* When we began, the day was fresh and cool, and we felt as though we were beginning a pleasant stroll. Walking together in one large group, we conversed, joked, and paid very little attention to the walk itself. The first 9 miles seemed to pass quickly and pleasantly. The warnings about not drinking water and the severe physical hardship that we had been expecting seemed remote.

As we were forming up in our squad groups at the beginning of the next 9 miles, we were reminded again not to compete with other squads, but discovering squads close before and behind us, we began escalating the pace.

The result was an uproarious competition that involved all but a few squads. Each time a team would come up from the rear, the team about to be overtaken would quicken its pace, and before long we found ourselves walking very fast, so fast that those with shorter legs had to jog occasionally to keep up. There was much yelling back and forth within each squad. The slower and more tired cried out for a reduction in speed, with the others urging them to greater efforts. A common solution was to put the slowest person at the head of the squad. This not only slowed the faster ones down, but forced the slow ones to make greater effort. The competing squads were so fast that within four or five miles they had already begun to lap those squads which chose not to compete. By the end of the second 9 miles, the toll on the fast walkers was obvious. Many, besides suffering from stiff legs and blisters, were beginning to have headaches and show evidence of heat prostration. It was noon by that time, and the full heat of a mid-June sun was baking down on our heads.

Any gratification the leading squad got in their victory was soon forgotten. At the finish line there was no congratulation and no rest. Squads were instructed to break up and continue walking, this time in single file and in silence. Soon a long line of trainees stretched over the entire circumference of the course. Having already covered eighteen miles, the last nine at a grueling pace, we were very tired. Suddenly everything was transformed. The excitement and clamor of competition was gone. Each individual alone in a quiet world was confronted by the sweep of his own thoughts and feelings as he pushed forward.

My own experience was to become acutely aware of every sort of pain. Great blisters had obviously formed on the soles of my feet; my legs, back, and neck ached; and at times I had a sense of delirium. The thirst I had expected to be so severe seemed insignificant compared to these other afflictions. Over and over in my mind I counted the laps still remaining. After accomplishing each lap, instead of feeling encouraged, I plunged into despair over those remaining. My awareness of the world around me, including the spectators in the park and the bank employees tempting us with refreshments, dropped almost to zero. Head down, I trudged forward. Each step was literally more painful than the one before. The image of an old prospector lost on the desert kept recurring in my mind. The temptation to stop and lie down for a while in the lush grass was tremendous and many times near the end I walked for a minute or two and then rested for much longer. The others around me seemed to be doing the same thing. It was so difficult to stand and begin again after one of these rests, however, that I was constantly telling myself not to stop, but just as often giving in to a persistent internal demand that I escape the agony. For some reason, it was heartening to discover that six or eight of the other trainees had fainted and were lying prostrate under a shady tree at the finish line where they were receiving some medical attention. I too wanted to lie there with them and yet I felt encouraged by the fact that

I had not yet fallen. "I was stronger, I could make it" I thought to myself as I passed by. Feverish dreams of somehow sneaking away presented themselves often during the final laps. I reasoned no one would notice if I slipped out of the park and returned just when the event was closing. Bushes became places I could hide behind and rest until the group was ready to go home. I kept going, I suppose, because I feared discovery. Though I was in a feverish state, I was in some sense quite capable of objectively looking at my response to this test of endurance. The content of lectures about *seishin* strength came back to me. I could see that I was spiritually weak, easily tempted, and inclined to quit. Under such stress, some aspects of my thought were obviously not serving my interest in completing the course. Whatever will power I had arose from pride and an emerging almost involuntary belief in the *seishin* approach. If I was to finish, I needed spiritual strength. It angered and amused me to realize how cleverly this exercise had been conceived. I vowed over and over never to get involved in such a situation again, and yet, within days, when the memory of the physical pain had dimmed, I was taking great pride in my accomplishment and viewing my completion of the twenty-five-mile course as proof that I could do anything I set my mind to.

Some Considerations for the Anthropology of Education

First, it might be useful to review some of the characteristics of *seishin* education as they differ from the philosophy of American-inspired contemporary public education in Japan. This is not only an interesting exercise—the comparison is one Japanese educators and their critics are making when they evaluate today's educational system, particularly in the light of student turmoil and popular dissatisfaction with the liberality of youth. Considering the history of Japanese education since the Meiji Restoration, it is not difficult to see official policy make pendulum-like swings back and forth between "Western" progressive and "Japanese" *seishin* approaches.

1. In *seishin* education, emphasis is placed on nonverbal forms of behavior. A well-behaved, but silent class, for example, is not necessarily an indication of lethargy, stupidity, or the failure of the teacher. It is likely to be interpreted as evidence that students are well-disciplined, receptive, and respectful. In some instances, a *seishin* orientation may take a somewhat skeptical view of verbal logic and its forms of understanding, favoring experience as the basis of knowledge instead.

2. Rather than viewing difficulties and hardships the students face as barriers to education and therefore things to be overcome by better facilities or improved methods of instruction, *seishin*-based education is liable to regard problems in the educational situation as valuable assets to the training process itself. They are tests and therefore means of furthering spiritual training.

3. A knowledge of self and reflection on oneself *(jikaku)* will be stressed in *seishin* training. And in the former case, the blame for difficulties or failure, individual or social, will be placed most heavily on spiritual weakness rather than on social organization. This educational approach to social betterment would give precedence to spiritual reform over social reform. Schools are certainly instruments of change and improvement, but their influence should be over individual character rather than over the shape of society.

4. Rather than encouraging students to consider themselves as different from one another and sponsoring individualistic thought and creativity, *seishin* education sponsors outward conformity to teachers' examples and group standards. Conforming behavior reflects not only self-discipline, but it also contributes to the basic unity of the group. Nonconformity, on the other hand, is disruptive of that unity and a sign of character weakness. It is thought that conformity is made from conviction, not dullness, and that to conform to the group is difficult, rather than easy. Consistent with this is the idea that creativity results from long-practicing patterns taught by a teacher. When the patterns are mastered and the barrier of an extended apprenticeship passed, the individual will emerge creative and his art (in the widest sense) will reflect his spiritual development.

5. *Seishin* education aims to allow the individual to achieve contentment based on the development of an ordered and stable psyche free from confusion and frustration. This is to be through the gradual conquest of *waga* or *ga* (one's primitive self, or in freudian terms, id). The phrase expressing this process, *waga o korosu* (literally "kill one's self"), is the extreme opposite of the emphasis in progressive education on teaching a person skills which will advance his career in the external world and intensify his need for gratification of self.

6. Whenever possible, competition will be organized along group rather than individual lines and many events will have no obvious competitive quality. This will not be because competition hurts feelings, but because it disrupts group unity and because the real competition takes place inside each individual.

7. The unchanging nature of spiritual problems and their solutions is another fundamental tenet of the *seishin* approach, rather than emphasis being placed on the changing nature of knowledge as taught in conventional education. Teachers, parents, and senior students are, by virtue of greater experience and training, spiritually more advanced, more knowledgeable, and therefore worthy of respect and authority. Since age is not a sign of outdatedness, intergenerational continuity and concord are more possible.

8. Teachers with a *seishin* point of view, though they know the course of spiritual development in great detail, may often choose not to be explicit about the outcome of their methods when instructing their students, choosing to let them find out directly from the experience itself. They may provide hints and indicate complete understanding by successfully predicting certain

developments, but as a rule they let experience happen, rather than talking overly much about it. The instruction in progressive education (except science) by comparison, seems quite explicit and abstract with the teacher having the role of verbal transmitter rather than that of one who only points the way for students. In some sense the *seishin* teacher conducts experiments in human nature and lets the results speak for themselves.

Turning from questions which focus exclusively on Japanese education, I would like to offer some observations on the significance of this material to the emerging field of the anthropology of education. I have no special expertise in this area and my observations depend on my impression of what are the major directions in the field.

1. The bank example represents a kind of education which to date has received very little attention. It is not centered in a school system, it involves adults, it is not universal for the society, and it is operated by a kind of institution which in other societies may have no direct interest in education at all. Such conditions would hardly attract the attention of anthropologists about to study education, and yet, at least in the case of Japan, such forms of education, training, socialization, or whatever are very significant social forces, and deserve much greater coverage than they have received. It is my impression that relatively far too much attention is devoted to studies of schooling, schools, and school systems and not enough is devoted to religious education, sports training, military indoctrination and the countless other kinds of more subtle and perhaps more effective ways societies improve and integrate their members.

2. The similarity between the bank's program, and processes and methods found in psychiatric therapy of the *Morita* type. Zen training, and religious conversion in Japan illustrates a simple lesson, namely, that educational efforts which seek some kind of character change or improvement are perhaps best studied within a single theoretical framework which will also adequately account for other kinds of psychological transformations. At various points in the *seishin kyōiku* activities, for example, anxiety or deprivation was artificially intensified and then reduced creating a strong sense of relief and catharsis which served to strengthen certain intended directions of change in a trainee's view of himself and of his relationships with the society around him. The parallels between education and such processes as initiation, therapy, and conversion would deserve more attention.

3. Whether the bank's program is education, socialization, or therapy is not a profitable question to ask, but it does raise one important issue. What, in fact, do we mean by education, and how does it differ from or relate to learning and socialization? Again, in my opinion, there is in the West a strong inclination to understand education as verbal instruction leading to (a) the storage, and (b) the manipulation of symbolic information. This is what explicitly happens in schools. Yet, learning, intelligence, knowledge, social-

ization, and other concepts normally related to education progress by many means, not just verbal instruction, and may be grasped and retained without exclusive reliance on symbols. *Seishin kyōiku* emphasizes experience and the development of spiritual strength. There are, no doubt, many other valued avenues of human growth which are as unlike Japanese spiritual education as they are unlike classroom instruction. The use of various halucinogenic drugs to educate religious initiates and train practitioners is one widespread example.

Just as the study of kinship began to make real headway only after considerable skepticism arose about the ethnocentricity of the concerns and impulses which originally gave it momentum, so the anthropology of education could benefit greatly from a reexamination of its implicit understanding of education.

GEORGE D. SPINDLER/*Stanford University*

12 *Schooling in Schönhausen: A Study in Cultural Transmission and Instrumental Adaptation in an Urbanizing German Village**

The purpose of the study reported in this chapter is to discover how the culture transmitted in an elementary school in an urbanizing area influences the cognitive organization and identities of the children attending the school. This purpose narrows to two major questions. First, does the culture transmitted by the school constrain choices children make of urban life styles and the means to them? This question is of special significance, since children in the situation to be described, as they grow to maturity, must make choices of life styles and means to them that are more relevant to an urbanized and industrialized society than those available to their parents and teachers. Second, does the school provide a common identity for children of diverse origins? The parents of children in the school come from various parts of Germany and her outlying prewar settlements as well as from the local community. They speak dialects that are often mutually unintelligible (as well as High German), some are Protestant and others Catholic, and their regional cultures vary considerably. Their presence in the area served by the school is the result of the great post-World War II migration to Western Germany.

*This chapter was written with the assistance of Erika Lueders-Salmon, who was a graduate student in the sociology of education at Stanford University at the time these data were analyzed. She did the computerizing of all I.A.I. data and the content analysis of I.A.I. protocols. She is a native of the region studied. Her insights and criticisms have been of inestimable importance. I also wish to express my appreciation to Henry Burger, Bruce Grindal, Ethel Nurge, and especially to Evelyn Rohner, for meticulous readings and criticisms. Naturally, all the errors are mine.

Readers will find Richard Warren's study of *Rebhausen* (1967) extremely relevant to the analysis to be presented, as it analyzes cultural transmission in a village in southern Germany. *Burgbach: Urbanization and Identity in a German Village,* by G. Spindler (1973), provides broad background for the study reported in this chapter.

Under these circumstances, one of the important functions of the elementary school could be to provide common reference points for the children.

In order to answer these questions it is necessary to describe the culture being transmitted in the school and how it is transmitted. Data provided by participant-observation, interviews with teachers, children, and parents and analysis of curricular materials are used as the basis of this ethnography. But we must go beyond ethnography. We must find a way to detect the influence of the school upon the cognitive organization and identities of the children, as relevant to the environment they are growing up in. For this purpose a technique, the Instrumental Activities Inventory (henceforth I.A.I.) developed by the Spindlers for use in the study of culture change, was especially modified for this study and applied to a sample of children in the elementary school and an advanced school in the area attended by children from the elementary school and to a sample of their teachers and parents.

Though this is a case study of one school and its locale, its methodology and theoretical model are applicable elsewhere. Since they are somewhat novel, they are explained in some detail. The results of the study should also parallel those obtainable from situations where rapid culture change and urbanization are occurring and where the school is an agent of continuity. The specific locale of this study will now be described.

The Setting

Until the beginning of World War II, Schönhausen, a village in southern Germany and the setting of the study, was almost entirely devoted to the cultivation of wine grapes and subsistence farming. It is near a large city and is part of a rapidly urbanizing area, the Rems River Valley (henceforth Remstal) in Baden-Württemberg, Federal Republic of Germany. More than twenty separate villages and small towns of the Remstal are coalescing now into one more or less continuous urban complex. At present Schönhausen is one of several smaller villages with a total population of around 2500, an increase from a pre-World War II population of about 1300. Two kilometers in a northeasterly direction separate it from the next village and one kilometer in a southwesterly direction from a town of about 7000. Schönhausen is surrounded by terraced hillsides where nine different varieties of wine grapes are grown. Grains and vegetables are grown in the valley flat lands. There are also factories and machine shops within a short distance built on what was until recently agricultural land. Custom furniture, machine parts, women's sandals, map globes, metal cabinets and cases, electrical equipment, soft drinks, leather goods, and many other items, not to mention thousands of liters of bottled wine, are produced in these factories and shops. Most of the operations involved in this production require skilled labor. Though

Schönhausen is part of this rapidly urbanizing and industrializing complex, it has retained a fairly traditional appearance. The ancient *fachwerk* houses are protected by law from significant exterior change, and new houses, apartments, and other buildings have been constructed so as to blend harmoniously with existing structures. A number of large houses, some very old, shelter both human beings and animals—cows, pigs, rabbits, and fowls—under one roof.

The rather traditional appearance of Schönhausen can be misleading. The village has increased almost 100 percent in population since before World War II, due largely to a massive influx of population resettled in West Germany from 1945 through the fifties. Before the war the village was almost entirely agricultural, of the type known as *ausgesprochener Weinort* (a village devoted to the cultivation of grapes and the making of wine). It was almost entirely Protestant and almost entirely composed of people born in the area who spoke the Schwäbisch dialect as their native language, though they learned standard High German in school. Today Schönhausen is still a Weinort (a place where wine grapes are grown), but only a small minority of people are full-time Weingärtner (vintners).[1] Most of its inhabitants work in nearby factories built since 1950 or in the nearby city. Some maintain small plots of land and are part-time Weingärtner, even though they work for wages. Only a bit more than half are natives and speak the Schwäbisch dialect—the rest are migrants from what was the east zone (now the German Democratic Republic) or from the outlying prewar German minorities, such as the Sudetenland and Bessarabia, or from other parts of Western Germany. There is also a group of *Gastarbeiter* (workers from other countries).

Until recently, Schönhausen was a homogeneous agricultural folk community. Today it is a heterogeneous, only partly agricultural, largely suburban community. Some of its people are Catholic, many do not speak the native dialect (but have dialects of their own representing the linguistic diversity of Germany), and only a few work the soil. Schönhausen is being incorporated, both physically and symbolically, into the emerging metropolis, though this process will take more than a decade.

It is precisely these conditions that make Schönhausen a significant site for a study of the role of the school as a culture-transmitting agency in a rapidly changing community. The community is changing from folk to urban, and the divergencies in backgrounds between natives and newcomers set the stage for potentially explosive confrontations. This is especially true since the newcomers were at first simply assigned to various homes in Schönhausen (as in other communities) during the resettlement, until new housing could be constructed, and were then given various advantages, among them loans at relatively low interest rates, in order to help them recoup the losses incurred by fleeing the east zone or occupied lands. The children of these

[1] All German terms are defined in the Glossary at the end of this chapter. No case endings are observed in order to avoid confusing the reader who does not know German.

people are now, and have been for some time, in the Schönhausen School, as well as in the more advanced schools to which the children from Schönhausen, and elsewhere, graduate. All the children in the village attend the Schönhausen School for four years. This attendance is irrespective of the eventual educational and occupational routes they will take after finishing the first four grades. It is also irrespective of their origins—whether native or newcomer, born of parents whose work ties them to the land or to parents whose work takes them to the city or whether their families migrated from an urban or a rural area. Particularly intriguing is the fact that on the whole this great influx of diverse (though Germanic) population was assimilated without any apparent disturbance. The low incidence of crime, suicide, and juvenile delinquency suggests that there has been no substantial increase in the social and psychological ills that often accompany rapid urbanization. Schönhausen and the area around it give every appearance of social and economic health.

Methods of Study (Exclusive of the I.A.I.)

The study in Schönhausen was carried on from March through June 1968,[2] with return visits in the spring of 1970 and the winter of 1971. Data on urbanization, industrialization, and culture change in several communities in the Remstal, including Schönhausen, had been collected by the author and his students at nearby Stanford in Germany before the study began.

The first step in the study in Schönhausen was to make direct contact with my potential instructors. This meant establishing contact with and being accepted by the staff and students of the Schönhausen School. It was also necessary to establish contacts with faculty and school system personnel and students in the *Hauptschule,* one of the advanced schools to which the children from the Schönhausen School graduated, as well as with villagers and townspeople.

This contact was established simply and directly. My wife and I were introduced to the *Oberlehrer* (senior or master teacher) by mutual friends. After some pleasant hours sipping wine and eating delicious *Kuchen* I asked permission to observe in the school for an indeterminate period of time. This request was granted graciously, and with no apparent anxiety or hesitation. I began my observations the next day. In order to give myself a home base I began each day with the third-grade class and stayed with it through some significant portion of its daily cycle of activities.[3] I usually sat among the children toward the back of the room.

---

[2] Supported by NSF grant GS-2106 and by Faculty Research Funds, School of Education, Stanford University. This help is acknowledged with gratitude.

[3] Our sample starts with the third grade because children in grades lower than this cannot respond to the I.A.I. effectively in written form (though they are productive in oral administrations).

Insofar as possible I did the lessons the children did. The children soon realized that I was unable to speak or understand the Schwäbisch dialect, and even that I could not always follow the High German. They became solicitous, often helping me with my lessons. It seemed to be quite understandable to them that if I wanted to know how German children got along in school and what they learned I should participate in their activities. Knowing this was my purpose they also went out of their way to explain what they were doing and what they thought about school, their teachers, and their classes. I "interviewed" in this way about half of the children in the third, fourth, and fifth grades. Although this could have constituted a threat to teachers, all but the youngest and most inexperienced teachers did not act as though they felt threatened. However, it took the teachers longer than it did the children to accept me in the classroom as a learner with little status rather than as an expert with status. This is quite understandable, since they had longer experience with the German status system. In addition, they had a status of their own to defend, which I was implicitly violating by not acting as they anticipated a university professor would act. On the whole, however, both the teachers and the children accepted my presence with remarkable equanimity.

At first I carried nothing but occasional school books and a notebook and pencil. I had the teachers' consent to take notes in class, and I tried to keep running notes on classroom activities. I also sketched the layout of each classroom, made notes on individual comments or behaviors, and, as I have said, did some of the lessons the children did. I went on all regular third- and fourth-grade excursions. These sometimes lasted all day while we tramped over the countryside learning firsthand about geography, nature, and ecology, or for only an hour or two as we visited some local monument or building with historical or social significance. These excursions were a part of *Naturkunde* (learning about the land and nature), and *Heimatkunde* (learning about the homeland, or local area), to which regular hours and instruction were devoted each week in the classroom. This part of the curriculum is a bone of contention among German educators and is of particular significance for our study. The older teachers tend to regard these subjects as being of great signficance during the early school years. Other educators regard these subjects with some suspicion because of the "land," "folk," and "blood" emphases of the Hitler period, and perhaps more importantly, as being inappropriate to the fast-developing urban-industrial society of modern Germany.

After about three weeks in school I requested permission to use a tape recorder to record classes, conversations, lectures, noise, and so forth. I used a simple battery-powered machine which I carried about constantly in a regular plastic grocery carrying bag, with the microphone in my pocket. I always told people when they were being taped. By keeping the machine in the bag and the microphone in my pocket, however, I seemed to keep the recorder out of mind as well as out of sight. I taped formal interviews, informal conversations, class periods and lessons, and verbal instructions on excursions. I also kept running observational notes on whatever was happening when I was doing the recording, with times for specific events recorded so I could match my observations with tapes later.

After the sixth week I began to use a camera in the classroom. I had not introduced it earlier because I felt people would become self-conscious before I had a chance to observe them while they were relatively unself-conscious. I used 35 mm. color slide film with an ASA of about 400, which permitted me to take pictures indoors without a flash. These slides have supplied me with important illustrative material for teaching at Stanford. I have also learned a great deal about interaction patterns, room layout, distribution of instructional materials and activities, nonverbal communication, and room decorations. (Those who would like to pursue the use of photography in anthropological fieldwork will find the methods study by John Collier (1967) instructive.)

There was a small room where teachers gathered before classes and where they ate mid-morning snacks and lunch. I made it a point to be there as often as I could in order to facilitate informal interaction. My wife and I also gave several parties and had many informal out-of-school contacts. My wife, who is an experienced anthropologist, contributed invaluable observations of her interaction on these occasions. I formally interviewed each teacher several times. The two senior teachers with whom I spent the most time were "interviewed" virtually every day as we talked casually about events, teaching techniques, educational philosophy, the children, and, in a limited way, about the other teachers. They might have been pressed further in the latter dimension, but interpersonal relations were good, and though there were some strains and interpersonal stresses, most of the staff preferred keeping comments about each other at a very objective and fairly impersonal level. This seemed to be a sensitive area in which I could create problems by probing or even seeming to be interested, and therefore I never pushed the subject. Staff members did, however, talk quite frankly about their estimates of superiors and other professionals outside of the school. But even here an attempt to be objective seemed to be the rule. I also administered the same Instrumental Activities Inventory to the teachers which an assistant and I administered to all of the children in grades three through five in the Schönhausen School, to a sample of students in the Hauptschule, and to a sample of Schönhausen parents.[4]

Besides the collection of classroom observations aided by tape and camera, interviews with children and teachers, informal "participant-ob-

---

[4] I am grateful to Mr. Robert Stiles for his assistance in the field, and to Herr Steinhardt, an Oberlehrer at Schönhausen School, for administering the I.A.I. to the parents, and to Herr Steinhardt and Frau Muller for countless personal kindnesses.

server" observations in and out of school and the application of the I.A.I. to children, teachers, and parents, there were also curriculum content and children's products to sample. I collected the books and manuals currently used in the third and fourth grades and several of those which were to be used in the coming year when the old texts were to be largely replaced by others considered more modern. I collected similar materials from the advanced classes. I also collected lesson plans when I could and a few teacher plans for whole subject areas, especially Heimatkunde and Naturkunde. I collected children's drawings and paintings, decorations for the walls of the classrooms, and themes or essays. I wish I had collected more of everything than I did. There is virtually nothing produced or used by the teachers or pupils that is not relevant to understanding what is being transmitted in the school. Such materials also have the virtue of keeping their form after they are collected without bias from the collector so they can be examined again and again for different purposes.

The results of these data-gathering activities can be grouped under six headings: (1) curriculum content; (2) personnel; (3) classroom observations; (4) interpersonal perceptions; (5) children's products; and (6) I.A.I. data.

Research results in categories 1, 2, 3, and 6 are discussed in this paper. The rationale for the I.A.I. will be presented immediately before the results of its application are analyzed.

I now turn to a synoptic ethnography of some of the most important features of the cultural system of the Schönhausen School under the two headings "Curriculum" and "Classroom Observations." The purpose here is to identify what culture is being transmitted in the school and how it is transmitted. After examining this, we can turn to the I.A.I. data, which show us what effect the culture and its transmission had upon the children.

Curriculum

The Schönhausen School offers a curriculum broadly equivalent in its formal coverage to that of the public elementary school in the United States: reading, writing, arithmetic, nature study, and the arts. The objective is to supply a basic education from which it is then possible to go in various directions within the German educational system and later into the society. There are distinctive differences between German and American teaching methods and educational philosophy. On the whole, my impression is that the expectations for performance in most of the basic skills, particularly in reading and writing, are significantly higher for younger children in the Schönhausen School and in other comparable schools in the Remstal of which I have some knowledge than in schools in the United States.

For the purposes of this chapter I will concentrate on Heimatkunde and Naturkunde and upon a principle called "integrated learning" to which all of the teachers in the Schönhausen School were committed. Revision of the educational philosophy and of the elementary curriculum texts and other materials is underway, stemming mainly from the centralized administration of schooling in Baden-Württemberg as well as from the federal level.[5] Although the curriculum underwent some change the year after the first part of the field study was done, the children whom I observed at all grade levels and who responded to the I.A.I. had experienced the established curriculum texts that are described later in this chapter.

The principle of integrated learning, as well as the emphasis upon Heimat and Natur, can be demonstrated by describing relevant aspects of three experiences: a *Wanderung* (an expedition outside of the classroom by the class and teacher); a classroom lesson on migrations out of Germany in general but Schönhausen in particular to America, Australia, Canada, and elsewhere; and a class presentation about the great bells in the nearby community church, followed by a trip to see and hear them. I will draw selectively from my field notes to demonstrate each.

The Wanderung

Today I went on a Wanderung with Herr Steinhardt's fourth-grade class. We left at 8:05 A.M. and returned at 2:35 P.M., having walked in a circle route from Schönhausen, along the ridge of the valley and back. We walked almost entirely on small paths through forest, *Weinberg,* and meadow, for nearly 18 kilometers (about 12 miles). The purpose of this expedition as described to the class was very general—to observe firsthand the geography, plants, animals, and economy of the area and to see some local historical sites; in short—anything of interest.

We walked at a brisk clip all day with short breaks for a snack, lunch, and brief stops to examine things of interest. The children showed no fatigue. At the end of the day they were still talking excitedly and jumping into any intriguing place they found along the way. Herr Professor was not as fresh, though Oberlehrer Steinhardt seemed just fine. I cannot imagine a fourth-grade class in the United States that would be able, much less willing, to make this hike.

The children had a high degree of freedom. They walked in their own groups, sometimes at a considerable distance from the main body, or alone (a few did). They climbed to what seemed to me to be dangerous heights, especially on a tower overlooking the valley that we visited, and crossed highways and roads on their own. The teacher said that although he would be legally responsible for an accident he did not feel there was any point to the expedition if the children were too tightly controlled. He had spent considerable time, however, in his classroom preparation for the trip explaining to the children what the hazards were, and the extent of his responsibility. When one or two of the boys did something really dangerous he called sharply to them and they desisted immediately.

The freedom extended to personal relations among the children, and in certain ways, to their relations to the teacher. He was constantly called from every side,

[5] This concern in its most intellectual dimensions and as particularly relevant to this chapter is exemplified in *Das Bild Der Heimat im Schullesbuch,* Jorg Ehni, 1967.

usually in a contraction of his name to something like "Herrhardt." Children, especially girls, walked in twos and threes with him and frequently with one on each side holding his hand. The handholders took turns. I was offered the same treatment after awhile, and found it very touching.

The instructional values of the walk were obtained without explicit effort. When we came across a small pond with frogs and salamanders in various stages of metamorphosis, specimens were caught and retained in bottles for later observation, and the teacher reviewed their growth cycle, which had been gone over in detail in the classroom. Several species of trees were identified, and reference made to their growth characteristics, their distribution, and their economic uses. This material was also familiar to the children from classroom work and reading. When we climbed the tower overlooking the Remstal the teacher pointed out each of the communities in the valley below, their relation to the waterways, and to the city visible in the distance. He commented on the very apparent zones of forest, Weinberg, and flat garden land, and the new apartment buildings and industries plainly identifiable in the valley. In Erdbunde lessons the children had examined in detail a map of the area and had learned in the class all of the things the teacher talked about. Their interest, as they peered about from the very top of the tower, which was about 100 feet high and on the crest of the ridge above the valley, was acute. One had the feeling that the images of map and actuality were vividly superimposed. They asked many excited questions about things they could see spread out below them. For most of the children this was the first visit to the tower. Herr Steinhardt said that parents rarely took their children on local expeditions, though many went fairly far afield on annual vacations (to Spain, Italy, the North Sea). In families that did not take trips free time was usually spent visiting relatives. He felt that the real value of the Wanderung was to "just explore the local area, and to do something interesting together."

When we came unto a large open meadow circled by forest not far from the tower, it was almost filled by a vast flock of sheep. Though the area was bisected by two small black-topped roads and there was considerable traffic, one man and two very busy dogs kept the entire flock under control. The children walked through the flock. One or two minor indiscretions by adventurous boys were brought sharply under control by the teacher. We stopped to talk with the shepherd, a somewhat unsocial man who spoke very thick dialect but answered questions from the teacher effectively enough. He spoke (insofar as I could understand him) about how the flock was controlled, where the dogs came from, and who trained them, when the sheep were sheared, and the problem of disease.

During the trip I noted that the schwäbisch dialect was spoken by all the children, including offspring of migrants, when they spoke with each other. When they addressed me they used High German, but sometimes responded to the teacher in Schwäbisch. The bilingualism seemed to cause no distress, and seemed to be taken for granted. I could not help but reflect that there was no reason why bilingualism should be an issue either in Germany or the United States, and yet it is widely considered to be a source of serious educational problems and identity conflict in our society. (See Fishman and Lueders-Salmon [1971] for a discussion of the implications of teaching a standard language to dialect-speakers in the classroom.)

The Lesson on Migrations

> Today the teacher [Herr Steinhardt] has a large map of the world hung before the class on one side and a huge colored photo of New York City hung up on the other side. The children are attentive, but noisy as usual. The teacher starts with me! Where does Professor Spindler live? (Children answer, but most don't say California, and the teacher points to California and to the vicinity of San Francisco on the map.) When did Professor Spindler's ancestors come to America? (He knows that one side of my family had come from Holland, and probably before that from Germany. Children are startled and give various answers. Teacher asks me to tell them, which I did.) What does Professor Spindler have left of his German heritage? (The children name all sorts of things such as clothes, appearance, my Volkswagen, and several said "his German." The teacher corrected all of these. When finished, all I have left is my name. The teacher had made his point.) The presentation becomes less personalized. During the past 100 years 1032 people migrated out of Schönhausen. Where did they go? (Gives breakdown; to the United States, to South America, Australia, Canada, and several other places.) Why did they go? (Teacher shows how periods of drought and war relate to migrations, so economic survival is one motivation. Other motivations are the lure of adventure, new opportunity, good luck, and the fear of religious and political persecution. The focus of the discussion is the United States, since the bulk of the migrants did go there. Teacher discusses the westward movement in America and the participation of migrants in it. Reads letters from two German friends who visited Indian reservations in the United States and report on the conditions there.) Herr Steinhardt closes the lesson with a question: How many present have relatives in the United States? (Of thirty-three in the class, fourteen raise their hands.) The lesson has many dimensions, some explicit, other implicit. The United States in particular, Canada and Australia less so, are seen as places of opportunity, space, and freedom. When life became unbearable or impossible in Schönhausen, one migrated to *Amerika*. The United States is *huge,* compared to Germany (the spatial dimensions as seen on standard maps are startling). When people migrate they become like the people in the country to which they go. (All that Professor Spindler has left of his German heritage is his name!) Schönhausen, like Germany, is comparatively small, but important. It has influenced the history of the rest of the world. People from Schönhausen have been participants in the great movements of history.

The children are shown that a way of life is a mutable process, not a final given, that people are frequently threatened by forces over which they have no control, and that they escape and survive as best they can. They also learn considerable geography and history. The teacher was dissatisfied with the lesson, feeling that his presentation was too formal. Indeed it may have been relatively formal, for when this same lesson was observed in another class the teacher started by interviewing various children in the class about their relatives in other parts of the world. She had such extensive knowledge of the families of the Schönhausen children that she could name some relatives in the United States, South America, or Africa that the children themselves apparently did not know about. But I felt that Herr Steinhardt presented the lesson very effectively and in conversations with the children afterward found evidence that it was enjoyed by them and that it did influence their perceptions and thinking.

The Bells

The last experience upon which I will report occurred in the third grade. The teacher, a very gifted, expressive, talkative, intelligent, older woman, was a regional historian who had written a definitive history of Schönhausen and wrote poetry with a special flair. She captured the attention of her class with stories, drawn from her own experience, or from chronicles she had studied. To illustrate her points she leaped about, sang, changed voices, played her violin, gestured, acted out, and imitated animals and sounds made by bells, whistles, and screeching wheels. I have never been so entertained and intrigued by any public or private performance as I was almost every time I visited her classroom. In addition, she shook my stereotypes about German schoolrooms by grouping the children at tables in working and talking groups. Her classroom, except when she was performing, was among the noisiest I have visited in Germany or the United States. The children moved about with apparently complete freedom, talking to one another incessantly, even when the teacher was shouting instructions about the lesson they were doing. To my question as to whether the noise bothered her she said, "Yes, sometimes, but children must talk to learn. Their talking is positive [positivschwätzen]. When it is not, I stop them from talking." Indeed, most of the talking I heard was positive—concerned with the task, or at least not disruptive of it. Indeed, the children produced well—in lessons accomplished, in group performances of skits and acting out of dramatizable lessons, in music hour participation (with singing, triangles, cymbals, flutes, a xylophone, rhythm sticks, and hand-clapping), and in art products. Among the latter were crayon drawings and water paintings of impressive complexity and style drawn of the center of Schönhausen, as one might see it on a medieval map. I will draw again from my field notes to describe a specific experience.

> This morning the lesson is about the history of our four great bells in the tower of the Protestant church in Schönhausen, which is near the school. Teacher shows pictures of the tower and the bells at various periods of history. She draws the four bells, each of which has a different history, on the board, and identifies the parts. Describes each bell in detail; exactly when they were cast, when melted down for armaments, when and by whom recast, and what tones they produce. She gives this history without pathos. The children seem impressed by the fact that the bells have served for both war and peace, and that the form of something may stay the same even though its constituting materials change completely. Teacher then explains, with some expressiveness, why the bells ring, and how these functions have changed over time, and change now, as they did then, over

the seasons: to awaken people, to tell them to go to bed, to call to vespers, to announce weddings, to give notice of invading armies, and as a call to arms. She gives vivid details on how the church and the community made different demands upon its members and citizens in medieval times and during the late nineteenth century, in contrast to the present, and how these demands are reflected in the times and ways the bells ring. The bells are the voice of the community in both its sacred and secular dimensions. The children "oooh" and "aaaaah" during the presentation. [Some of this response seems a little "put on" to me, but after talking with the children about it I decided that this was my projection.] The teacher ends the classroom lesson with a song with a "ding-dong" theme. She plays it once on the flute, then sings it, then has the children sing it with the flute accompanying.

Then we all get up and walk over to the church tower, a short distance. We climb up the several flights of rough wooden stairs (actually almost ladders) covered with pigeon leavings to the loft where the bells are. The last ten feet are especially difficult to negotiate, so the teacher goes first (she is near retirement!), then helps each child up through the narrow opening at the top of the "stairway." The bells are enormous, each weighing more than a ton, suspended on huge beams, and run by a very sturdy electrically powered and timed mechanism. Each bell is identified and children are reminded of things the teacher has said about them. While we are still in the loft the mechanism begins to whirr and clank, and the bells start ringing. The noise is total. The children cover their ears and shriek, both of which are probably good protection against deafness. The teacher laughs (while holding her ears). She planned it that way. We all leave the loft. None of us will ever forget our visit to see (and hear) the bells of the evangelischen Kirche in Schönhausen. I believe that the children will also remember what Frau Müller taught them about the history of the community and the role of the bells.

It was my impression that each of these three learning experiences was successful on the teacher's own terms. All three communicated specific content as well as generalized attitudes about the history of the area, about Schönhausen itself, and in the first expedition, about nature and people's relation to it. The principle of integrated learning was always evident. The teachers planned each lesson to teach more than one kind of thing at a time, and the emphasis was on the local area, places the children could directly see and experience. I view these as the kinds of learning experiences that should lead to a commitment to the credibility of instrumental linkages productive of satisfaction within the local cultural system (in its more tradition-oriented than "modern" form). However, many dimensions of these experiences (the observation of the spreading urbanization and industrialization of the Remstal visible from the tower; the changing functions of the bells and the community needs, and so forth) prepared the children for instrumental choices which move well beyond a traditional frame of reference, even though some form of identity relevant to Schönhausen was retained. In the process, identities were being reinforced, while specific knowledge and attitudes were being acquired. The locus of the identities is the local community, its history, and its immediate area, but this locus is not an absolute. It seems transferable and enlargeable.

Learning Materials

Besides classroom and extraclassroom experiences one must consider the materials of instruction if the purpose is to describe the school as a culture-transmitting process. I collected examples of the various categories of all published books, manuals, lesson guides, and so forth, used by the teachers in the Schönhausen School. I will give examples from two texts, both for the third school year and both "reading books" (Lesebücher). The first, *Haus in der Heimat* (House in the Homeland,) was published in 1957 and was still in use in 1968 when I did the largest part of the study. The other, *Schwarz auf Weiss* (Black on White), was published in 1967 and is still being used now. It should be noted that neither of these books is directly associated with either Heimatkunde or Naturkunde; they are prepared for the teaching of reading.

I will first paraphrase a selection from *Haus in der Heimat,* titled "Frühling in der Grosstadt" (spring in the Big City, p. 5).

> In the middle of the great city, between tall, gray houses and the autos, streetcars, and people, stood a woman with a basket of spring blossoms. The blossoms had only this morning come in from the country on the early train and they were very lonesome. In the country the sky is very wide and blue, the air very fresh, and the earth wonderfully green. One hears nothing there but singing birds, the brook, and now and then a murmur from the village. One sees only the sky, the forest, the paths, and the garden with its many, many colorful blooms.
>
> "I am dizzy, and I've got dust in my eyes" said the violet and sank her head.
>
> "And not a butterfly is there to see or to fly over my yellow dress," the narcissus complained.
>
> The bushroses were not satisfied either. "Here there is no wind to flutter our white skirts," they said.
>
> The story goes on, each of the flowers with a specific complaint directed at conditions in the great city. The woman keeps trying to sell the flowers, but everyone hurries past, intent upon their business. Only a little girl stops. A bouquet would make her mother happy, so she chooses some of the blossoms that would please her the most and takes them home. "Oh! how happy the little flowers were, as they stood on the table, explaining about the forests and meadows, the stars and the sky. They described everything so beautifully that everyone in the room believed they sat outside in the lovely spring. Instead, they sat in the huge city."

The book contains fairy tales, stories, poems, descriptions of nature, short essays on the garden, the first *Maikäfer* (a plant-eating beetle that occupies a special place in the literature of the Grundschule), the zoo, fire station, annual seasons, and ceremonies. Frequently presented features include personification of plants and animals; magical events, people, places, animals; the idea that nature, land, garden, village are clean, friendly, fun, and warm—the city is the converse of these; the idea of God as a protector who made everything, particularly nature, beautiful; and the notion that parents take care of their children and ask nothing in return.

What the text implies is the existence of a secret, wonderful world of childhood where adult realities do not intrude. In general there is considerable sentimentality centering upon mother love, home, God, comrades, animals, and plants and the beauties of country, nature, and garden. There is only one story set in the city, "Die Stadt Erwacht" ("The City Awakens"), and one poem about the railroad station. The book is beautifully illustrated with tasteful, imaginative watercolor paintings.

The orientation of reading books for the lower grades has been the subject of commentary by German educationists and social scientists. As Ehni concludes, "The Heimat as the essence of cultivated feelings, of the internalization of the world, and of retrospective sentimentality has become questionable, and is no longer useful as a pedagogical goal" (1967:241). This conclusion should be modified in light of the realization that there are values that the Heimat orientation was designed to communicate that should not be overlooked in the reorganization of schoolbooks and curricula. The heavy sentimentality and the unreality are the targets of objections, not the values themselves.

In fairness to the teachers of Heimatkunde, Naturkunde, and Erdkunde ("geography") at Schönhausen School, it must be emphasized that the total range of lessons and experiences covering these subjects moves far beyond the rather heavy and essentially nonintellectual sentimentality of some of the readings. When Herr Steinhardt demonstrated the geography, demography, and ecology of the Remstal by taking his pupils to the top of a tower overlooking the valley and pointing out things they had already learned about in the classroom, he was not merely perpetuating the picture of the Heimat represented in school reading books. When Frau Müller took the children to see the bells in the church and contextualized this event in a solid presentation of local history and a functional analysis of the community and its demands upon its members, she was not merely transmitting sentimentality. Both teachers *used* sentiment to communicate the content of the lesson units. This must be done by all educators if children are to accept the credibility of the content.

Part of the problem (for German educators) is that with the current movement against Heimatkunde and its associations the implicit values of this subject matter and the learning process associated with it may be destroyed or at least seriously weakened. This could have unfortunate consequences. The configuration that has been described may have been influential in the development of a common identity among children from diverse backgrounds, and to the extent a local identity could be shared by their parents it may have been a signficant factor in the assimilation of the great new population, and in the relatively smooth ongoing transition from an essentially folk community to an essentially urban way of life in the Remstal.

It is difficult to predict what will happen as the curriculum changes, but the new reading book gives us some clues. I paraphrase a story from *Schwarz auf Weiss* (1967). The scene is China (p. 10).

> Little Pear stands by the river that goes past his village. His mother has told him to be very careful and not fall in. But he does, just as a houseboat, with a family, including three children, goes past. He almost drowns, but is saved. They go downstream to the next dock, perhaps a mile or two. Little Pear talks to the children while they drift along. They ask him about his village, family, fields, animals, etc. All their lives they have been on the boat. He gets out at the dock, finally, and runs and runs toward his village and home. He is so glad to see it in the distance, and even happier when he is embraced by his mother, father, grandparents, and siblings.

Perhaps the change in emphasis between the old and new reading books is not so great as it at first seems or as it is intended. Although the scene has shifted, the village and its associations (family, fields, animals) are still presented in familiar terms and as positive values. But as one Schönhausen teacher said, "Why do we have to start with strange and far-off places? Why can't the children be taught to value their own surroundings first, then be led to an understanding of the rest of the world?" Indeed, the educational theory standing behind Heimatkunde is familiar to American elementary school teachers—it is sometimes called the "concentric ring" theory—that experience should begin with the familiar and widen out to the unknown.

Schwarz auf Weiss appears to have changed the scene in this story, but not the theme. The consequences of this kind of change in reading materials are indeed difficult to foresee, but one sympathizes with the teachers who know their local area well and who regard it as a resource in the transmission of a unified view of reality. However, in fairness to the new books and other curricular materials I must point out that *Schwarz auf Weiss* is less heavily sentimental, there is less emphasis on the small village and cozy valley, less personification of plants and animals, fewer explicit moral lessons, and more straightforward descriptions of places and events than in the old reading books. The locale shifts about from China to Italy to Siberia to India to Eskimoland and often to generalized Germanic locales. There are also some classic fairy tales and thirty-five poems (of which eighteen are about nature or animals). There are some very flat-footed descriptions of events, that would be unlikely in a third-grade reading book in the United States, such as the abrupt death of a migrant worker who tries to cross a busy city street against a red light and is run down. In general, also, I cannot help but make the comment that both of the reading books for the third grade described in this chapter are considerably advanced over anything comparable with which I am familiar in U.S. schools. The sentences are long and complicated, the vocabulary large, the ideas quite sophisticated, the illustrations superb, and the food for the imagination is very rich.

Although it seems there will be a shift in emphasis in the elementary school curriculum, there probably will be enough continuity for some time, so that the major conclusions of this study will remain viable, despite urbanization, for that part of the Remstal represented by Schönhausen.

Classroom Observations

I have already given some of the pertinent results of classroom observation, and I will not attempt to produce in this chapter an adequate sampling of these observations. However, one theme particularly worth discussing is that of freedom and constraint.

I had visited all the school's classrooms, and found them all to be closer to the "free" end of a continuum of explicit freedom and constraint. None of them supported the authoritarian characterization that is suggested by stereotypes of German schools. Some of the rooms were often close to bedlam though I never saw a classroom out of control. In general, the more experienced and secure teachers permitted a higher degree of freedom in the classroom. It was only the younger and relatively inexperienced teachers who made an attempt to keep the classroom quiet much of the time, whether or not this was necessary or even relevant to the learning process presumed to be taking place.

After the first few visits to the more free classrooms, I was left quite puzzled and unable to understand how order could ever be maintained or how any kind of intervention for control could take place. Herr Steinhardt expressed the school's philosophy in words similar to those used by leading personnel of "free schools" in the United States, "This school is not based upon fear, it is based upon love. Children do not learn well when they are anxious. They must feel free." At first that is the way it seemed to be in the Schönhausen School. But there is a difference.

One day while I was standing outside the door of the school at the dismissal of the classes, a line of fourth-graders rushed past one of the senior teachers, in their usual hurry to get outdoors. The teacher smiled as usual, but there was something additional in his look. Suddenly, as one of the boys went past, the teacher reached out to cuff him on the side of the head. The boy barely flinched, though it was a goodly cuff, and continued out the door with his face set and somewhat reddened. I was astounded, and as soon as I could, asked the teacher what that was all about. The teacher said, "That boy knew what I would do. He sat in class for the past hour pestering the girl sitting in front of him. I suggested he stop it, but he chose not to do so. I don't like to make issues of such things during class time, so I punished him as he left the school." I watched the boy carefully afterwards for overt signs of resentment against the teacher or the school, but saw none. Nor did I see any change in the teacher's behavior toward him. It was a normal incident. The punishment was abrupt, direct, and was apparently considered deserved.

With this experience behind me I began to look closely at the problem of freedom and constraint. I observed numerous incidents that could be described as "the use of force." On one occasion, a young but experienced teacher called up, without warning as far as I could see, a rather large boy from the back to the front of the room and gave him a resounding whack on the face with open palm as soon as he arrived. The boy stiffened, set his expression, and returned to his seat without a word. My attention was diverted from him for a few minutes, until a little later, again without warning, the act was repeated. I inquired of the teacher. "He was playing around. He hasn't done any real work for three weeks." I asked why she hit him the second time. "He didn't get back to work." I talked with the boy. He was laconic, but said, in effect, "Fraulein Scherdt is O.K. I like her. I should work harder." The punishment simply did not have the meaning of chagrin, embarassment, and personal degradation that I was projecting as I viewed the incidents. Still, no one really enjoys an *Ohrfeige,* and insofar as possible they are avoided.[6] The threat of one is always present, but it is a simple, direct threat. I don't believe that the children in these classrooms became neurotic or unduly fearful because of these punishments.

Other techniques are used that can be described as "patterned warning interventions." For example, when classes start to get out of hand, shouting and shuffling about, the teacher may suddenly command attention, and have the children sit down quietly. Then suddenly the teacher shouts, "Stand up!" then, "Sit down!" then up and down several times, include a few "Remain seated!" or "Remain standing!" In this way the teacher reestablishes command. The noise level quickly goes back up, but the children are reminded that the teacher is ultimately in charge and that there are limits.

The limits of behavior are known, and the punishments for exceeding them are usually predictable. Within those limits teachers tolerate a wide range of behaviors. The situation in schools elsewhere in Germany doubtless varies. We have some data on other classrooms in nearby schools, and something of the same balance of freedom and constraint seems to operate, though some of the classrooms are more strictly controlled than was the rule in the Schönhausen School. Rebhausen classrooms (Warren 1967) are somewhat similar, though the classrooms there seem more constrained than in Schönhausen.

I have not described all the mechanisms of constraint. The teachers tend, for example, to lay out tasks very carefully, and with considerable emphasis

[6] See Warren 1967 for the use of the Ohrfeige in Rebhausen.

on the right order. When pictures are drawn they represent certain subject matter, and certain criteria, mostly having to do with representation of reality, are applied. Themes are written in a certain hand with certain spacing. Children are expected to accomplish tasks at their own speed, with freedom to move about, ask questions, make small innovations, but the task is defined for them, and the criteria applied are the teacher's. The teacher does not let go of the class at any time, even though to the foreign observer it may seem at first that most teachers have no control at all over what the children are doing. When any lesson is being worked out by children at their desks, whether in free discussion groups or individually, the teacher walks about, examines the work, comments on progress, sometimes placing a hand with a certain amount of pressure on a child's head to direct his or her attention to the task or lightly rapping the child's hand or head. These touches seem almost like caresses, and they are very light, but the distance between this kind of caress and an Ohrfeige is not as great as one might think.

The combination of freedom and constraint seems effective. The children have the security of knowing what they are expected to do and how far they can deviate. Within these known limits the authority figures are beneficent, responsive, very human, and they are good communicators of information and skills. They are very effective teachers.

Schönhausen School apparently transmits a culture which is oriented to the local environment in both its manmade and natural forms. The orientation is transmitted by what appears to be highly effective methods involving classroom interaction, excursions, and the use of attractive instructional materials. The principle of integrated learning appears to be a central theme in the transmission process. The balance of freedom and constraint is maintained quite differently than in schools in the United States and the methods of doing so appear to reinforce the culture-transmitting process.

With essential features of the culture transmitted in Schönhausen School and the processes of its transmission outlined, the next step is to describe the Instrumental Activities Inventory and present the rationale for its use.

The I.A.I.

The I.A.I. developed for our research in Germany consists of a total of thirty-seven line drawings of thirty-seven activities. These activities are instrumental to the attainment of goals that are integral parts of life-styles in the cultural system. In our study this meant the urbanizing, industrializing Remstal with its baseline of culturally conservative, long-established, land-oriented communities. The technique elicits respondents' preferences for certain instrumental activities and goals and their rationale for these preferences. The activities are not only occupations (such as working in a factory or being a chemist), but include having a dinner for friends at home, going to a lively party in a public place of entertainment, going to church, living in a particular kind of house, attending school, and commuting to work. The goals are to be thought of as not only specific attainments, such as a certain income or possession of a certain object, but as life styles or conditions of being which may subsume a number of specific preferences and instrumental activity-goal linkages. Rather than being a personality test, the I.A.I. is a technique for eliciting responses that express the perception of social reality.

The rationale for the technique is furnished by an instrumental model of a cultural system which we have already begun to describe. The model, incomplete in its present form, draws from functionalist, systems, and cognitive theory. The notion of instrumental acts or behaviors is not in itself new. To my knowledge, however, the specific model and its application developed in this paper are unique. It is possible to understand the analysis of the I.A.I. results at one level without this model, and some readers may want to go directly to the results. The statements following are formulated at a level of abstraction that permits their application to any cultural system.

A cultural system operates so long as acceptable behaviors usually produce anticipated and desired results and unacceptable behaviors usually produce anticipated and undesired results. These behaviors can be thought of as *instrumental activities,* and the results as goals or satisfactions. Beliefs that are part of the cultural tradition support the accepted relationship between activities and satisfactions. The relationships are *credible.* The credibility of the instrumental relationships is an essential attribute of the system and one that schooling is designed to support. Both goals and the activities instrumental to them are socially sanctioned. These may not involve a consensus of all the members of a cultural system: various subgroups, classes, or cliques within the larger system have their own goals, instrumental activities, and sanctions. The relationship between given activities and the goals or end-states to which they are instrumental may be thought of as instrumental activity-goal linkages, or, for efficiency in communication, as *instrumental linkages.* Activities may also become goals in themselves in that they may become so satisfying that the original goal to which they are linked assumes secondary importance. The linkages are dynamic. *Social control* may be defined as sanctioned intervention in the operation of the instrumental linkages for members of a cultural system by other members. *Social organization* may be thought of as the organization of personnel (and, if necessary, of materiél) and their roles in relation to each other, so that the linkages can function. Education as *cultural transmission* may be defined as means employed by established members of a cultural system to inform new members coming into the system of the sanctioned instrumental linkages, to communicate how they are ranked and organized, and also to commit these new members to the support and continuance of these linkages and the belief system that gives them credibility. Educational institutions therefore serve mainly functions of reaffirmation, system maintenance, and recruitment so long as the cultural system is in a steady state.

The resulting *cognitive structure* in individual minds consists partly of this organization and related commitments, insofar as cognitive structure is relevant to perception of social reality. *Cognitive control* as socially relevant is the ability of an individual to maintain a working model, in his mind, of relevant and at least potentially productive instrumental linkages and their organization. When I.A.I. data are analyzed, I will refer to *supporting values.* By this I will mean specific conditions of being or specific attributes of situations or events as end-products (attained goals) or as associations with an instrumental activity itself that are used by respondents to justify (i.e., "support") expressed instrumental preferences. All acceptable activities and end-products have "value," but some have more than others. Unacceptable or negatively sanctioned activities and goals may be said to have negative value. *Identity* may be defined as individual commitments, often at an ideal level, to certain configurations of instrumental linkages and supporting values and to symbols representing them. To a degree, these commitments can be verbalized.

As presented above, the model applies to cultural systems at times of relative stability. It is, however, open and it provides for change. During rapid urbanization established instrumental linkages are challenged both ideologically and pragmatically by new information and by alternative behavior models. The credibility of the established linkages is weakened and their operational viability declines. Alternative linkages are recognized, acquire credibility, and become operable. The individual's range of alternative instrumental linkages increases, but the total range will include a number of conflicting choices. Cognitive control becomes more difficult. Attempts to maintain cognitive control under conditions of radical cultural confrontation between incongruent cultural systems may result in exclusion of conflicting instrumental linkages, reaffirmation of some, synthesis of selected elements, or segmentalized adaptation (Spindler 1968). Some or all of these processes will take place during rapid urbanization. In studies of culture change or urbanization, one may be concerned with either the culture-system processes (including economic, technological, political) that result in new instrumental linkages or with the perception and cognitive ordering of alternative linkages. In this chapter I am concerned almost solely with perception and cognitive ordering of alternative linkages as affected by schooling.

Schooling—that aspect of the total educational process carried out in school—influences the perception, selection, and cognitive ordering of alternative instrumental linkages by school children. In this study we want to find out whether children in Schönhausen with different backgrounds choose the same or different instrumental activities, anticipate the same ends, and rationalize their choices similarly or differently. We want to identify the elementary school's influence on these choices, particularly how the transmission of culture by the school may act as a constraint upon urban-oriented instrumental perceptions and choices. We are also interested in changes that may occur as children mature, and in sex differences.

Our method was to present to respondents in a situation where rapid urbanization and industrialization is occurring pictorial representations of activities selected from the total range of possible instrumental activities. The respondents are asked to tell us what these activities are and, as they see them, what satisfactions they produce. We do this in the form of line drawings, which when assembled for purposes of eliciting responses we call an "inventory" of instrumental activities. We use drawings rather than verbal descriptions because the drawings are more concrete and less ambiguous. The essential aspects of the activity are easily portrayed in a drawing, and they appear to be more easily grasped and to stimulate more complex associations.

The drawings must be clear, technically accurate, and culturally appropriate. The I.A.I. is culture-specific, though the underlying principles of construction, application, and interpretation of results are transcultural. The pictures cannot be as ambiguous as the Thematic Apperception Test developed by Henry Murray or the Rorschach Projective Technique (the "inkblot test"). The respondent must recognize what it is the drawing is intended to represent so that he can choose or discard that activity. For our purposes the pictures cannot be as contextualized or as personalized as photographs because respondents tend to get involved with irrelevant background details or personal implications and do not deal as directly with the instrumental activity or its linked goals. For other, related purposes, photographs serve better (Collier 1967). We (Louise and George Spindler) have used this technique with the Blood Indians of Alberta, Canada (Spindler 1965), and with the Cree Indians of Mistassini Post, Quebec, as well as in Germany. In each case we had the pictures drawn from carefully selected photographs. In selecting the activities to be drawn, and in evaluating the pictures themselves, we consulted with people who were members of the cultural systems for which they were designed (among the Blood and in Germany), or with someone who had done ethnographic fieldwork in the area (for the Cree). This insured that we were not making choices biased by the anthropological subculture or by our own perceptions.

The technique is administered to individual respondents by telling them, after their consent and cooperation is secured, that we are going to show them some drawings of activities that they might choose to engage in. The respondent is handed the whole set of drawings (our sets range from twenty-four to thirty-seven drawings) and is asked to choose his or her three favorite and three least favorite. The respondent is then asked to tell the interviewer what he chose and why he chose it. After this phase is completed the interviewer can either ask the respondent to repeat this procedure with the remaining drawings, until the choices are exhausted, or ask him to identify each drawing and explain what he thinks about it and how desirable or undesirable it is. In either case it is possible then to probe further by asking for choices between various pairs of drawings and requesting further clarification of the rationale for these choices, often in the light of potentially contradictory preferences already expressed by the respondent. A complete protocol can usually be collected in from a half hour to two hours. We had a number of interviews among the Blood that lasted all afternoon. The richness of material that pours forth is sometimes unbelievable to one accustomed to working with laconic respondents.

It is essential that the technique not be regarded as a "test" or that rigid procedures be adhered to despite variance in conditions and respondents. We have run into a number of respondents, though not in Germany, who would not make choices at our request, but who would go through the whole deck making comments, often lengthy ones, about each activity. After this process had been finished to the respondents' satisfaction we were sometimes successful at getting them to make explicit choices. Occasionally we had to be satisfied with inferences from the evaluative comments made. Usually this is not too difficult. This type of response seems more likely to occur among non-Western peoples, and a number of our Blood Indian respondents acted in this way.

In the research in Germany we introduced a variation in the procedures. First, my student assistant and I administered thirty individual I.A.I. interviews, using the whole array of thirty-seven line drawings developed for the study. On the basis of this experience, we picked seventeen pictures for group administration. These seventeen drawings were selected as particularly diagnostic of different orientations with respect to the process of urbanization, and as relevant to our sample, which did not include those advanced schools preparing children for high-level professional or business careers. We had 35 mm. slides made from these pictures and used two slide projectors simultaneously to show seven pairs of pictures. The respondents were asked to make choices from these pairs as well as from three pictures shown singly that they were asked to evaluate. A data sheet filled out by each respondent included such items as birthdate, birthplace, father's occupation, and birthplace of each parent. A two-page form is provided each respondent with appropriate space to write down choices and rationales. The drawings shown in this manner included the following:

1. *Fachwerkhaus* (traditional house) verses modern *Einfamilienhaus* (single family home)
2. *Weingartner* (one who grows wine grapes) versus *Angestellter* (white collar worker)
3. *Fabrikarbeiter* (workers changing shifts at a factory) versus *Selbständiger* (an independent owner of small shop)

4. *Bauer* (a farmer, his wife, and child working with a small tractor on flatland) versus *Maschinenarbeiter* (a machinist working at a lathe)
5. *Schule* (a picture of an elementary school with children going into it)
6. *Alte Kirche* (a traditional church, with medieval structures) versus *Moderne Kirche* (a rectangular, very modern church)
7. *Grossbauer* (a farmer or a forester and his helper working with a very large tractor plow) versus *Technischer Zeichner* (technical draftsman)
8. A large and very modern *Bauernhaus* (a farmer's dwelling, with stalls for stock, loft for hay, machinery, etc., combined with the family's house)
9. A *Fest Daheim* (a dinner table with party-style settings at home) versus *Party* (a very lively "Faschings"-type party in a public place)
10. *Weinlese* (the grape harvest showing a wagon and several people, including children, pouring grapes into it)

The drawings were shown in this sequence in nine classrooms ranging from the third to the ninth grade. They were shown to 282 children, of whom 278 responded adequately enough to allow analysis. Probably in many American schools it would not be possible to get adequate responses from third- and fourth-, and perhaps even many fifth- and sixth-graders. The children in the Schönhausen School and in the nearby Hauptschule (grades five through nine) provided more than adequate responses, in most cases writing rather complex rationales for their expressed preferences.

On our data and response sheets we also included two statements and asked respondents for short paragraphic essays about them. The first was (translated) "Life in a big city is better than life in a little village. Do you agree or not?" The second was "The life of a *Weingärtner* is better than the life of a factory worker. Do you agree or not?" The second one was included only on forms for the sixth to ninth grades, for we did not want to tire out the younger children before they got to the I.A.I. pictures. Responses to these stimuli were adequate for our purposes and the children in grades six through nine often wrote rather complex statements explaining and defending their positions. But the children in grades three, four, and five responded well to the first essay question, many with complex, complete sentences. These questions were included in order to elicit self-conscious, explicitly rationalized responses relevant to broad value-oriented life-style preferences. We regarded the responses as indicative of identity at one level of cognitive organization. The statements also presented global concepts that could hardly be portrayed in pictures. The essay and the pictorial elicitation complemented each other.

In order to answer the questions properly it was necessary to extend our sample and observations beyond the elementary school years. Though our case study focuses on the Schönhausen School, we collected responses to the I.A.I. and made limited classroom observations in grades six through nine in the *Hauptschule* near Schönhausen. In 1968, the year the I.A.I. data were collected, 69 percent of the children finishing the first four grades in the Schönhausen School went on to the *Hauptschule,* 24 percent to the

Gymnasium,[7] and the remainder to the *Realschule* (see Appendix). The Hauptschule sample was essential to the study because it enabled us to see whether the effect of the elementary school persisted beyond the time the children attended it, and also because we could see if there were changes in instrumental choices as children approached entrance into adult roles.

We can now turn to the I.A.I. data for the 278 children in the third through ninth grades in the classes of the Schönhausen School and the nearby Hauptschule, a sample of their parents, and the teachers in the Schönhausen School. It is important to remember at this point that the reason for collecting I.A.I. data is to find out how the culture transmitted by the school affects the cognitive organization and identities of children as pertinent to choices of life-styles and means to them in an urbanizing environment.

The I.A.I. Data

The Sample

The characteristics of the sample must be further clarified. The 278 children are distributed more or less evenly over nine classes, including two fifth-grade classes retained in the Schönhausen School, two sixth grades, and an eighth- and a ninth-grade class in the Hauptschule. Fifty-three percent of the children's fathers were born within the Remstal, the remainder outside. Fifty-seven percent of the children were born in the Remstal. Seventy-two percent of the fathers were born in villages or small towns under 5076 in population, and the rest in towns and cities of 5077 or more.[8] Fathers' occupations represent 24 percent labeled "inside" (including white collar and menial desk jobs and professional) and 76 percent as "outside" (including Weingärtner, farmer, and highly skilled "outside" jobs such as mason). Forty-four percent of the respondents were male. The age range was eight years eight months to fifteen years nine months.

We also administered the I.A.I. to a sample of thirty-one parents of children attending the Schönhausen School. Eighteen of the parents were from the Remstal, thirteen from outside. Fourteen were born in Schönhausen, in towns or cities of over 5077 in population, and the remaining six in villages. The occupational range (husband's or own) included twelve Weingärtner, thirteen skilled craftsmen, and six white collar workers. Six of the sample were males. The age range was twenty-six to forty-eight years.

---

[7] The I.A.I. was also applied as a "pilot" run to one ninth-grade *Gymnasium* class, but the techniques used were different enough to make statistical comparisons problematic. A qualitative examination of the responses suggests that this class did not produce responses widely divergent from those produced by the ninth-grade Hauptschule class. A larger sample, however, might produce quite different results.

[8] We determined the boundaries of population categories by the population figure of an actual town at a relevant cut-off point, hence the odd figure.

All of the six teachers in Schönhausen School responded to the I.A.I. They ranged in age from twenty-five to sixty-five years, with four of the six under thirty. Two were born in what is now the German Democratic Republic (the former east zone). The other four were born within the area where the Schwäbisch dialect is spoken. Three were born in towns of over 5076 population but none in cities of over 20,000. Three were born in villages in the Remstal (under 5076 population).

Presentation of Data

We must now describe the overall distribution of instrumental choices with their associated values and the statistically significant differences (using chi-square) appearing within the sample as background variables are taken into account. These two steps will be combined in the discursive presentation following. The preference data were computerized using the already programmed Stanford Statistical Package for the Social Sciences. Only the results directly applicable to the present research questions are cited. We also content analyzed all responses to get modalities and distributions of specific supporting values. The consistency of these values within major instrumental preference categories makes it meaningful to state the modal-specific values supporting each major preference category.

Table 12.1 presents distributions of instrumental preferences for the sample including all grades of children, thirty-one parents, and six Schönhausen teachers. All figures in the cells are in percentages. In the interests of simplicity only the percentages for the preference expressed by the majority of all respondents for each choice set are given. Except for a few neutral responses all other responses in each choice set are for the other preference, totaling 100 percent altogether. (Example: Picture Choice 1, third grade—the modern house is chosen by 56 percent of the respondents, the rest chose the traditional Fachwerkhaus or were neutral.) Pictures 5, 8, and 10 were presented singly and children were asked to express like or dislike (or neutrality) and explain why they felt that way. It should be clear that the table represents only a small portion of the data and the variables to be taken into account in the analysis. Gross choices by grade are included, and therefore by age, but sex, place of origin, urbanization, and occupational background are not represented, nor are values declared by respondents in support of their choices included.

The statistically significant differences in the distribution of instrumental preferences in relationship to the named background variables and the supporting values for these preferences will now be discussed.

When the term "tendency" is used the probability of the particular distribution in question occurring by chance alone (using χ^2) is .10 or less and greater than .05. When "significant" or "more frequently" is used the probability is .05 or less. The number of teachers is too small to permit reliable calculation of statistical significance, and I therefore have used the terms "consistent" and "divergent" to describe their relationship to all or part of

Table 12. Distribution of I.A.I. Responses (in percent)

	Essay		*Picture Choice*									
Grade	*1. Prefer Village*	*2. Prefer Wein-gärtner*	*1. Prefer modern*	*2. Prefer angestellt.*	*3. Prefer Selbst.*	*4. Prefer Maschin.*	*5. Like school*	*6. Prefer old church*	*7. Prefer Zeichner*	*8. Like Bauernhf.*	*9. Prefer at home*	*10. Like Weinlese*
Third	97	–	56	62	50	26	79	41	56	71	85	97
Fourth	70	–	46	73	70	58	100	64	55	58	64	97
Fifth	75	–	68	68	61	46	53	68	58	53	65	94
Sixth	90	91	43	56	69	40	74	71	55	70	33	92
Seventh	78	83	62	78	57	51	30	43	84	38	35	81
Eighth	60	73	33*	91	70	58	67	58	70	27	21	88
Ninth	39	83	77	81	58	81	42	48	87	29	32	97
Parents	86	Ques. not included	36	74	71	40	59	82	72	65	72	76
Teachers	67	67	67	33	100	18	82	100	0**	67	100	100

* In grade eight, 58 percent of the responses were mixed and were not classified as either preference for the *Fachwerk* or for the modern dwelling.

** Three teachers chose Grossbauer. The other three made no choice.

the rest of the sample. First I will present data on the essay-elicitation questions, then on the I.A.I. drawings. I provide a separate analysis of the teachers' responses at the end of this section, since they are the culture transmitters in the school.

ESSAY 1 "Life in a big city is better than life in a little village." All classes, together with parents and teachers, prefer the village except the ninth-graders, who strongly prefer the city. Modal values supporting village life include: fresh air, less traffic, quietness, nearness to nature, friendliness, and availability of fresh fruits and vegetables. City life is noisy and dangerous, there is no place to play or walk, the air is bad, and life impersonal. Girls and older children prefer city life significantly more frequently than boys and younger children. Children whose fathers were born outside the Remstal prefer the city more frequently, as do girls whose fathers were born in towns and cities with a population of over 5076. Supporting values for city life are: more activities, especially theater, film, and arts, more varied shopping, cheaper goods, more anonymity. It should be remembered that the *majority* ($\overline{M}$ 73 percent) of all respondents remain loyal to the village, but that there is significant differentiation by age, sex, regional origin, and degree of urbanization. Parents and teachers are not differentiated by these factors and tend to be more village-oriented than the older children in grades eight and nine and girls.

ESSAY 2 "The life of a Weingärtner is better than the life of a factory worker."

Classes six through nine heavily favor Weingärtner, as do the teachers. (This essay question was not included on the form for parents. Their time was limited and we sacrificed this question in favor of the pictures.) There are no significant differences created by dividing the sample by origin, father's occupation, urbanization of family of origin, or age. Girls, however, choose the life of the factory worker significantly more frequently than do boys, even though the majority of girls still choose Weingärtner. Supporting values for Weingärtner include: self-determination and independence, near nature, fresh air, healthier work, ownership of land. Supporting values for factory work include: earns more for time put in, regular hours, vacations, less hardship.

PICTURE CHOICE 1 FACHWERKHAUS VERSUS MODERN EINFAMILIENHAUS The distribution of responses on this first picture choice is less clear-cut than on the essays. Moderate preference is expressed for the modern dwelling in the total sample, though not by a majority of the fourth-, sixth-, and eighth-graders. The parents prefer the fachwerk style. Supporting values for the modern apartment are: more convenient, luxuries (e.g. the balcony), more practical, more light inside, easier upkeep. Supporting values for the fachwerk style are: more beautiful, more romantic, larger. Girls more frequently

choose the modern house than do boys, and there is a tendency for the younger children to prefer the Fachwerkhaus. Regional origin, urbanization, and occupation are not significant differentiating factors.

PICTURE CHOICE 2 WEINGÄRTNER VERSUS ANGESTELLTER Preference for white collar office work is expressed in all grades and by parents, but teachers favor the Weingärtner way of life. Specific values supporting the Angestellter are: regular hours of work and free time, more regular pay, cleaner work, not

such hard work, more pay per hour, independence from the weather. Values supporting the Weingärtner are: fresh air, bodily movement, can grow own food, own boss, healthier, near to nature. Many respondents choosing the Angestellter explicitly acknowledge the supporting values for the Weingärtner, but choose the white collar activity for pragmatic reasons. The younger children and boys prefer the Weingärtner activity more frequently, in agreement with the teachers. Girls choose the Angestellter more frequently. No other factors are significant.

PICTURE CHOICE 3 FABRIKARBEITER VERSUS SELBSTÄNDIGER All categories of respondents prefer the independent owner to the factory job. Supporting values include: being one's own boss, better money, owning one's own shop and equipment, less noise, fewer people. Independence of rules, hours, goals set by others is the most frequently cited value. The values supporting factory work are: regular pay, regular vacations, contact with more people, possibility of advancement within an organization. There are again significant differences between girls and boys, with the girls more frequently preferring factory work because of its security and regularity. Girls whose fathers work outdoors also prefer the Selbständiger more frequently than those whose fathers work inside. The latter choose factory work more frequently. ("Inside" and "outside" work was another way we "cut" the sample to see if significant differences regarding occupation of father would appear.)

PICTURE CHOICE 4 BAUER VERSUS MASCHINENARBEITER The moderate preference among children is for the Maschinenarbeiter. Parents, teachers, and younger children are divergent from the older children and choose the Bauer more frequently. Among other factors only boys whose fathers work outside proved significant—they more frequently choose the Bauer. Supporting values for the Maschinenarbeiter include: secure and regular job and pay, physically easier work, cleaner work. Supporting values for the Bauer are: fresh air, exercise, independence, relation to nature, togetherness with family, produce own food, less precise work, and more variety.

PICTURE CHOICE 5 LIKE OR DISLIKE SCHOOL All but the seventh- and ninth-grade classes like school more often than they dislike it, and parents and teachers agree with the majority of the children. Supporting values for school include: specific subjects and teachers enjoyed, its necessity for the future,

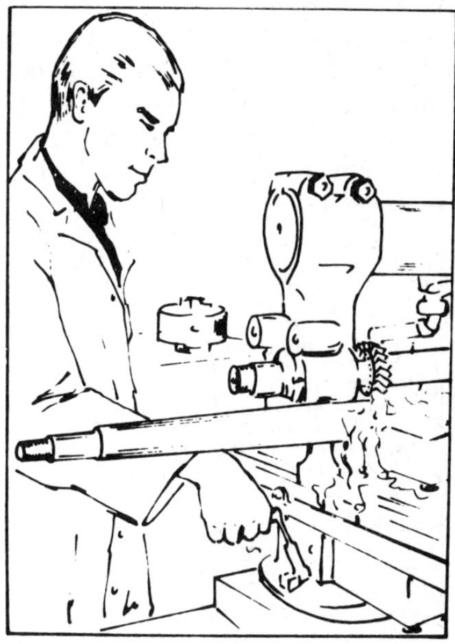

and just "like it." Many responses are qualified in what we have come to regard as a typical swabian way; "almost all, but not all, go gladly," "many are enthusiastic, some not." Those not liking school name: punitive homework, perceived injustices, feelings of powerlessness, confinement, boredom. Among the older children there is a tendency to dislike school more frequently than among the younger ones.

PICTURE CHOICE 6 OLD VERSUS NEW CHURCH Parents, teachers, and the majority of the children prefer the old church. Supporting values include: references to age, history, tradition, and beauty. Values supporting the new church are mostly utilitarian: heated better, cleaner, more comfortable, and modern appearance. Girls prefer the new church more frequently than do boys. Other factors are not significant. This is a troublesome choice because

the old church resembles the Protestant church in a nearby town, and the modern one resembles a Catholic church. Aware of this, we cautioned the respondents to "think only of the style and appearance." Doubtless both the resemblances and the cautions influence choices. However, a check of individuals whose religious affiliation was known reveals no persistent bias, and in some classes where the majority of children were Protestant, the majority choose the new church (grades three, seven, and nine).[9]

PICTURE CHOICE 7 GROSSBAUER (OR FORSTER) VERSUS TECHNISCHER ZEICHNER The majority of parents and children in all grades choose the technical draftsman over the large-scale farmer or forester. The teachers are divergent, choosing the latter. Supporting values for the draftsman cited by children include: good pay, pleasant kind of work, independence of weather, clean work, not such hard physical labor (as farmer), free evenings, regular vaca-

[9] Due to overestimating the respondents' sensitivity in regard to religious affiliation we did not include this factor on the form. Religious affiliation was checked with the teachers for the classes as a whole and for some individuals. I do not think it is a significant variable in relation to the instrumental choices researched in this study.

tions. Values supporting the Grossbauer are: fresh air, independence, ownership of land and machines, and working with large powerful machines. There is a tendency for the younger children and for boys whose fathers work outdoors, to more frequently prefer the Grossbauer.

PICTURE CHOICE 8 BAUERNHAUS Respondents were asked, "Would you like, or not like, to live in this house?" Fifty-one percent of the children say they would like to live in it. The supporting values are: lots of space, modern,

it is better for children to live near animals, outdoor space, interesting things going on, like to work as a farmer, living in fresh air, living in village or out in the country. Negative values given include: the animal stalls smell, flies, manure pile out front, too much work. Younger children like the Bauernhaus more frequently than do older ones. Parents and teachers agree with the younger children. Girls reject the Bauernhaus more frequently than do boys. Other factors are not significant except that more boys whose fathers have outdoor jobs rate the Bauernhaus more positively than those whose fathers work indoors.

PICTURE CHOICE 9 FEST DAHEIM VERSUS PARTY A majority of the children choose the affair at home over the party in a public place, but there is a sharp differentiation between the younger and older respondents, with the former

choosing the affair at home more frequently. Parents and teachers agree with the younger children. Girls choose the party outside more frequently. Girls with fathers who were born in towns or cities of over 5076 in population also choose the party more frequently than girls (or boys) with fathers born in villages smaller than this. Supporting values for the affair at home include: quieter, more control over what happens, less expensive, more *gemütlich,* family-oriented, not so wild. Supporting values for the party outside the home include: more to drink, get to meet some members of opposite sex, gay atmosphere, singing, dancing.

PICTURE CHOICE 10 WEINLESE Teachers and children in all grades overwhelmingly support the idea of participating in the grape harvest. The majority of parents are enthusiastic, though 24 percent are neutral about it. Girls are more frequently negative or neutral about participating in the Weinlese than boys, and more girls whose fathers were born in towns or cities of over 5076 are negative than girls whose fathers were born in villages smaller than that. Values evoked in support of enthusiasm for the grape harvest include: it is just fun, one can eat grapes, good kind of work, enjoy nice early fall

weather, be with friends and relations, be out in nature. Negative expressions about Weinlese are supported by: hard work, prefer playing, don't care for grapes.

The Teachers

The teachers responded to the same questions and I.A.I. drawings. In response to the essay question "Life in the big city is better than life in a little village," four disagreed, opting for the village. The other two gave qualified approval to the city, citing greater cultural and personal opportunities there, but granted that village life was quieter, friendlier, and that the air was better. Those choosing the village way of life cited these same values, but in all cases indicated that the city had enough advantages of the type mentioned to make it highly desirable that the village be in the vicinity of a city. In other words, they wanted a suburban village.

In response to the essay question, "The Life of a Weingärtner is better than the life of a factory worker," the same split occurred, four choosing Weingärtner with some reservations. The Weingärtner is his own master *(sein eigener Herr),* he works close to nature, out in the fresh air, his work is not boring, but natural catastrophes can wipe him out, and the work is very hard and demanding.

The teacher's responses to the I.A.I. pictures were consistent with these first choices. Four chose the old-, two the new-style house, but the first group insisted upon modernization of the old. Despite its more tasteful, romantic, traditional appearance (as they saw it), they felt that to be a fitting habitation it should have modern heating, good lighting, plumbing, and tasteful, comfortable furnishings. The other two granted the romantic quality of the old house and its more beautiful appearance, but said that living was more comfortable in the new structure. Five chose the old church for its traditional qualities.

Four chose Weingärtner rather than white collar office work, one chose the latter, and one did not respond. The most frequently cited positive value associated with Weingärtner was that this activity provided opportunity for initiative, movement, and free will, while the Angestellter was *bewegungsarm* (limited in movement) and his work *eintönig* (monotonous). But the cleanliness of work and financial security of the Angestellter was acknowledged.

All respondents chose the independent owner *(Selbständiger)* over the factory worker. Values associated with this choice were independence, being one's own boss, direct contact with products of one's labor, *"Fabrikarbeit totet den Geist"* (factory work kills the spirit), wrote one respondent.

Four chose *Bauer,* one *Maschinenarbeiter,* one was undecided, and one made no choice. Values associated with the first instrumental preference (Bauer) were: healthier, outside work, more direct contact with nature, and many-sided activities. One said, "I would rather have nature around me than walls." The same split occurred with Grossbauer verses technical draftsman.

I asked them to respond to the picture of the school as they remembered themselves feeling in the fourth or fifth grade. All but one remembered school positively, though qualified by memories of specific teachers and experiences. One teacher said the "deadly obedience and spirit of my school" was hateful to him, and he became a teacher in order to make the school better for future children.

The rest of the responses fall into categories similar to those already described. Choices tend to favor a village-rural-folk-nature orientation, but qualified by various considerations stemming from an interest in the wider world, concern for technological efficiency, and a comfortable manner of living. All chose the quiet dinner at home rather than the lively evening out "on the town." Specific values associated with this instrumental preference were that one could control better what happened, that one could enjoy conversation more, that the dinner at home is more *gemütlich* (that elusive, ever-used word!), more personal, quieter. All enthusiastically professed to enjoy the Weinlese (grape harvest) as a special time of enjoyment, fulfillment, and general good feeling. All but one had actually helped harvest the grapes at various times at the invitation of friends or relatives. Four said they would like to live in the Bauernhaus. The other two would not object, but preferred a strictly modern house or apartment.

I also showed one drawing of a tiny weekend house with a fence around it and a man working in the garden. All respondents said they would enjoy owning such a house (none did) and spoke of what they would do there if they did—plant some fruit trees, have a vegetable garden, flowers, and a grassy place to play games with friends and family.

The results of the I.A.I. applied to the teachers are consistent with data collected in interviews and observations. The teachers are strongly on the side of Natur and Heimat. Their adult perspective leads them to reservations and qualifications relevant to the pragmatics of the modern world. No teacher produced consistently prourban, contravillage, folk, land-oriented responses, and none denied all value to urban life and urban activities. But the weight of these preferences and the pattern of supporting values is on the side of village and nature.

Interpretation

There is diversity within the sample in expressed preference for instrumental activities and their associated supporting specific values. This diversity is largely a function of age and sex, rather than of differences in occupation of father, regional origin, or urbanization of place of origin. Occupation of father and urbanization of place of origin do produce some significant differences when controlled for sex of respondent, but compared to age or sex alone these are weak variables. Girls and older children are more frequently urban-oriented than boys and younger children.

The pattern of majority agreement is more impressive. This pattern of explicit preference agreement is not consistently rural-nature-village in orientation. It is an interesting mixture of idealization, romanticism, and pragmatism. This is clearly expressed both in the preferences and in the supporting values.

When children are asked to choose between village or city life in response to the first essay question they elect village life and support this choice with values that seem to be a direct extension of the Heimat and Natur lessons we observed in the Schönhausen School and of the preferences expressed by the teachers when they took the I.A.I. The same process occurs when the children choose between being a Weingärtner and being a factory worker. The syndrome of values—fresh air, independence, quiet life, closeness to nature, ownership of land, availability of fresh fruits and vegetables, friendliness of people—is invoked in variable combinations but with overall consistency in the responses to these first two essay questions. They reappear consistently as the village-folk-nature preferences are supported throughout the entire range of instrumental choices presented in the pictures. A reciprocal set of negative values concerning urban life and related activities is also invoked, though not as consistently. City life is noisy, dangerous, and impersonal.

The choices with which respondents are faced in the essay questions are global and idealized and do not require finite, pragmatic judgments of an instrumental nature. They make it possible for respondents to express their generalized, idealized value orientations. The pattern of responses to these two statements suggests a sentimental identification with the village and its associated supporting values.

What is the cognitive depth of this identity? The responses to the I.A.I. pictures seem only partly governed by this identity.[10] Pragmatic considerations seem to become important when respondents are faced with finite instrumental choices. The village-land-nature identity, then, may be regarded as idealized, perhaps even as "spurious" in that it cannot be applied consistently in the real choices presented in an urbanizing environment. Nevertheless, this idealized identity could be important as a cohesive force binding together apparently divergent elements of the total population.

That this unifying though "spurious" identity is consistent with the emphases in the school curriculum, teaching materials, and classroom and outside of classroom experiences, and with the teachers' explicit biases, does not prove that the Schönhausen School produced it. Despite diverse origins, the majority of the parents also share this idealized identity. School and home are consistent with each other, so far as our present sample of parents indicates and insofar as we are concerned with the idealized identity configuration. They both apparently transmit the same messages. Parents who live in small villages seem to like their way of life, or at least believe they do. Then again, perhaps only people who like village life remain there. These are variables that at present we cannot control with the scope of our data. But the fact remains that the school appears to transmit an identity and supporting values that are oriented toward the Weingärtner and the village way of life. The children appear to have accepted these values and this identity at one level of cognitive organization.

When during the presentation of I.A.I. pictures the children are faced with finite choices that force them to express a preference for a more village-nature-land or a more urban-linked instrumentality they tend to choose the latter. The majority prefer modern apartment houses, white collar office work, and working as a machinist or as a technical draftsman to alternatives that are clearly village- and land-oriented. The supporting values for these choices are very pragmatic: better pay, more security, regular hours, inde-

[10] One of the more interesting writings on identity processes is by Treiner (1965), whose research indicates that identification with a given place is the consequence of membership (at some time) in a social system that is closely bound to that place and that is symbolized by place names capable of eliciting complex emotional reactions—feelings of "identity," or place reference. Something of this nature may be operating in the identification as "villagers" by respondents who express various urban-oriented instrumental preferences. "Place consciousness" and "place belongingess" are highly developed in the nonurban areas of southern Germany, and probably in other parts of Germany as well, and involve quite different self-reference (my observation) than in North America. Herbert Schwedt (1968) discusses similar processes of place identity for an area of Baden-Württemburg not far from Schönhausen.

pendence of the caprices of nature, guaranteed vacations, and cleaner and less physically exhausting work.

A substantial minority of children consistently choose the village- and land-oriented instrumentalities of Weingärtner, Bauer, and Grossbauer, and when they do they invoke the same supporting values as they did in their more generalized and idealized essay choices. Approximately one half of the children who make the more urban-oriented choices also acknowledge explicitly the other set of values but self-consciously make pragmatic choices and defend them pragmatically. The identification with village and land also shows clearly in the enthusiasm of the younger children for the Bauernhaus, but this enthusiasm wanes as the respondents mature, and in any case, the supporting values for the Bauernhaus also emphasize pragmatic considerations such as space and modernity.

One instrumental choice that combines idealized village values with pragmatics—Selbständiger versus factory worker—results in a clear majority for the former, and the supporting values of being one's own boss, owning equipment and a shop, and dealing with a quieter social environment appear to be a translation of similar values supporting the choice of Weingärtner. Being an independent small machine shop owner and operator is pragmatically productive in the emerging urban environment. It also represents traditional values and identities and thus is a very popular choice.

When "romantic" instrumentalities uncomplicated by pragmatic realities are presented to the children—the old versus the new church and the Weinlese—the majority express preferences in a traditional village- and land-oriented direction. There is clear preference for the beautiful old church and enthusiastic interest in the grape harvest. Possibly the school is also supported as a part of this configuration, since the school and village are closely related. These choices do not challenge pragmatic orientations and are a logical extension of the idealized identity revealed in preference for small village life and the Weingärtner occupation expressed in the essay responses. This identity survives where it does not conflict with practical considerations.

The cognitive organization of the majority of children in our sample, insofar as relevant to our research problem, is therefore comprised of three parts: (1) the idealized identity—villager and Weingärtner, with supporting values: independence, quiet fresh air and sunshine, friendliness, love of nature, and fresh natural foods; (2) the pragmatic instrumental preference system—modern house and white collar and technical work—together with supporting values such as comfort, regular income and hours, security, less hardship, and cleaner work; and (3) the romanticized, instrumental preferences—traditional church, Weinlese, fachwerk house—with supporting values such as beauty, representation of the past, freedom, and health. The majority of the children appear to maintain cognitive control over these three potentially conflicting dimensions, perhaps because pragmatism has priority in critical areas of choice. In reality a compromise is possible, since one can live in a small village and commute to a nearby city to work. The older children, closer to full instrumental participation in society, tend to choose more pragmatically and are more urban-oriented. Conversely, the younger children are more frequently village-land-nature–oriented in their choices. As the time of entry into the adult instrumental structure nears, the choices become more pragmatic.

It is of considerable interest that the teachers definitely and the parents somewhat less so are more oriented toward village-land-nature, and are more "romantic," than are the older children. The teachers are not faced with the necessity of making the same practical instrumental choices as the older children. They can allow the idealized identity that is present somewhere in the responses of almost everyone in the sample to dominate their cognitive organization. The fact that the children seem capable of making pragmatic choices that are divergent from those of their teachers (and often their parents), particularly as they grow older, suggests that neither the school nor the home as culture-transmitting agencies act as powerful constraints. Possibly the Heimat and Natur lessons in the Schönhausen School are broad and realistic enough to provide means by which children can come to grips with the practicalities of life in the urbanizing Remstal, and the parents themselves are pragmatists as well as romanticists.

Apparently the school helps provide an idealized identity that is not a barrier to full participation in a changing cultural system. This identity may serve useful functions. If identity is as significant as many social scientists claim, then the result has been positive. A common framework of communication is created and sustained. That the identity is spurious in the sense that it does not permit prediction of pragmatic choices is unimportant. Keeping a village-land-nature identity intact in the midst of an expanding urban complex may have helped the Remstal avoid the disasters that seem inevitable in analagous situations in the United States.

Conclusion

The two primary questions posed at the beginning of this paper have been answered. Many others have emerged and have been answered during the course of the analysis, but it may be worth referring back to these two questions for closure, even though such repetition and simplification seem anticlimactic.

1. Does the culture the school transmits constrain instrumental choices by children relevant to the urbanizing environment?

The culture transmitted by the school is more traditional than urban in orientation. This orientation is apparently represented in an idealized identification by children with the land, village, and Weingärtner way of life. Instrumental choices, however, relevant to an adaptation to an urban environment appear to be governed by pragmatic considerations. This is most apparent among the older children, but it appears at all age levels. The school does not appear to constrain choices at the critical stage in growing up where adult roles and life-styles are seriously anticipated.

2. Is a common identity for children of diverse origins provided by the school?

The idealized identity referred to above is common to all groups whether native or newcomer. It is reasonable to hold the school responsible for some of this effect, but it is important to remember that parents and teachers are closer to each other than to the children in instrumental choices and supporting values and that they are land-village-Weingärtner in orientation. Home and school appear to be transmitting facets of the same culture insofar as we are concerned with the range of instrumental choices described in this study. With these reservations the question is answered in the affirmative.

The hypothesis was advanced that the idealized identification with the land-village-Weingärtner way of life had provided a common orientation and a base for communication for heterogeneous groups and that this has helped to avoid some of the corrosive effects of rapid culture change and organization. We cannot test the hypothesis adequately with the present scope of the study. Given our data it seems plausible. In any event the purpose of such an identity has been served. A new generation is already making its choices and in directions divergent from an idealized common base. The question we are left with is, Where did the children acquire this new outlook? Why do they make instrumental choices that are different than those of their parents and teachers? Part of the answer is that their teachers and parents are pragmatists as well as idealists. They have taught their children to adapt to reality. Another part of the answer lies in processes of cultural transmission that were beyond the scope of the study, such as cultural diffusion in the peer group and transmission via the mass media, particularly television. These processes are major interventions in the cultural-transmission process in established cultural systems world-wide. They challenge the credibility-maintaining functions of conventional educational institutions in all cultural systems in contact with the wider world today.

References

Collier, John, Jr. 1967, *Visual Anthropology: Photography as a Research Method.* SAM. New York: Holt, Rinehart and Winston, Inc.

Ehni, Jörg, 1967, *Das Bild der Heimat im Schullesebuch.* Volksleben, vol. 16. Tübingen: Tübinger Vereinigung für Volkskunde.

Fischman, Joshua, and Erika Lueders-Salmon, 1971, "What Has the Sociology of Language To Say to the Teacher?" C. B. Cazden, V. John, and D. Hynes, eds., *Functions of Language in the Classroom.* New York: Teachers College Press.

Haus in der Heimat, Lesebuch für das dritte Schuljahr der Volksschulen in Baden-Württemberg, 1957. Karlsruhe: Gemeinschaftsverlag.

Schwarz auf Weiss: Ein neues Lesebuch für Baden-Württemberg, Drittes Schuljahr. 1967. Darmstadt-Hanover: Herman Schroedel Verlag KG.

Schwedt Herbert, 1968, *Kulturstile Kleiner Gemeinden.* Tübingen: Tübinger Vereinigung für Volkskunde. Volksleben 21.

Spindler, George and Louise, 1965, "The Instrumental Activities Inventory: A Technique for the Study of the Psychology of Acculturation," *Southwestern Journal of Anthropology* 21 (1):1–23.

Spindler, George D., 1968, "Psychocultural Adaptation." In E. Norbeck, et al., eds., *Personality and Culture, An Interdisciplinary Appraisal.* New York: Holt, Rinehart and Winston, Inc.

Spindler, George D., 1973, *Burgbach: Urbanization and Identity in a German Village.* CSCA. New York: Holt, Rinehart and Winston, Inc.

Treinen, Heiner, 1965, *Symbolische Ortsbezogenheit: Eine soziologische Untersuchung zum Heimatproblem.* Inaugural-Dissertation. Köln and Opladen: Westdeutscher Verlag. (Also published in the Kölner Zeitschrift für Soziologie und Sozialpsychologie, Heft 1/2, 1965.)

Warren, Richard, 1967, *Education in Rebhausen: A German Village.* CSEC. New York: Holt, Rinehart and Winston, Inc.

Glossary

Angestellter	white collar desk worker
Bauer	farmer
Bauernhaus	a farmer's dwelling, with stalls for stock, loft for hay, machinery, and so on
Bewegungsarm	limited in freely moving around
Einfamilienhaus	modern house big enough for one family
Einheimische	people born in the area
Eintönig	monotonous
Erdkunde	geography
Evangelische Kirche	Protestant church
Fabrikarbeiter	shift worker in a factory
Fachwerk	a combination of open structural beams and stucco
Fasching	carnival in February before Lent
Fachwerkhäuser	houses built with a combination of open structural beams and stucco
Förster	forester
Gastarbeiter	workers from other countries
gemütlich	cozy, easygoing
Grossbauer	farmer with enough land to employ helpers

Grundschule	classes one through four of the elementary school; all children are attending the same school for these grades
Gymnasium	school which leads to the university; nine school years, starting with fifth grade
Hauptschule	school which leads to nonacademic jobs and apprenticeships; four school years, starting with fifth grade
Heimat	homeland
Heimatkunde	learning about the homeland
Hochdeutsch	High German, standard German
Katholisch	Catholic
Kirche	church
Kuchen	a form of cake, usually with a fruit topping
Lesebuch	reading book
Maikäfer	May-bug
Maschinenarbeiter	machinist
Natur	nature
Naturkunde	learning about the land and nature
Oberlehrer	master teacher
Ohrfeige	box on the ear, cuff
Realschule	school which leads to white collar jobs but not to the university; six school years starting with fifth grade
Selbständiger	owner of a small shop
Schule	school
Schwäbisch	Swabian, the native dialect
Technischer Zeichner	technical draftsman
Wanderung	hike
Wein	wine
Weinberg	hill (usually terraced) on which wine grapes grow
Weingärtner	one who grows wine grapes
Weinlese	grape harvest
Weinort	village devoted to the cultivation of grapes and the making of wine
Zugezogene	people living in the area who are not native to the area

PART III

Education and Cultural Process in Traditional and Modernizing Societies

PREVIEW

The chapters in this section are closer to the traditional concerns of anthropologists in that they deal with cultural systems that are either nonliterate or recently nonliterate. Of these cultures some are reported in their traditional form and others as they are being affected by modernization.

The first chapter demonstrates how education as cultural transmission occurs in a variety of cultural systems. The cultures discussed include those of the Palauans in the South Pacific, the Dusun of Borneo, the Tewa-Hopi of the Southwest, the Ulithians of Micronesia, the Tiwi of North Australia, Gopalpur—a village in South India, Guadalcanal, and Demirciler, an Anatolian village. Gopalpur and Demirciler are villages within a complex society; the others are tribal communities. Both village and tribal community, however, exhibit some of the same features of educational process. My interest in this chapter is to demonstrate various cultural processes where the leveling effects of modernization have not yet taken place. Therefore, I have treated the cultural systems and educational processes of the culture cases in the first part of this chapter as though no major interventions from the outside had occurred. I have stressed how initiation rites serve educational functions in many cultures, and how processes of cultural compression, cultural continuity, and cultural discontinuity produce adults who want to act in ways that will maintain the cultural system. The maintenance and recruitment functions of education and cultural transmission, not the innovative or change functions, are stressed until we reach that section of the chapter which is devoted to modernizing cultures. Here a new form of cultural discontinuity is introduced, one which is a product of intervention from the outside. This form of intervention and following discontinuity results in damage to the maintenance and recruitment functions of the educational process as relevant to the established traditional culture system, a process which seems inevitable where whole cultural systems are modernizing.

Dorothy Eggan's article on the Hopi focuses on cultural continuity and how the traditional Hopi obtained it through the skillful manipulation of instruction and experience. She clearly demonstrates the ways in which what appears to be cultural discontinuity in a stable system actually functions to reinforce the continuation of the existing culture.

In his chapter on the enculturation of Mistassini Cree children, Peter Sindell discusses discontinuities of a type that are created by the establishment of Western schools in non-Western societies. He shows how prolonged residential school experience makes it virtually impossible for these Cree children to participate effectively in the hunting-trapping life of their parents, for the values, attitudes, and behavior expectations which motivate dormitory counselors and teachers in their interaction with the children differ dramatically from those of Mistassini Cree parents. There are, of course, parallels between the situation of the Mistassini Cree and other societies. For example, John Collier, Jr., reports on Alaskan Eskimo education (1973), and Nancy Modiano describes education among the Indians of the Chiapas Highlands (1973). Both studies provide useful insights into these extremely important relationships.

C. W. M. Hart's article on prepubertal and postpubertal education is a classic of its kind. Though highly speculative in the sense that Hart goes well beyond his data in his interpretation and generalization, the article is solidly based upon the ethnography of a single case, the Tiwi of Northern Australia (Hart and Pilling 1960). In this chapter Hart makes a bold proposition—the educational experience that takes place at adolescence is more determinative of the culturally influenced aspects of character and behavior than are early childhood educational experiences. This reverses much of what childhood education, psychiatry, and psychoanalysis have to say. These schools of thought are not wrong, but they are interpreting processes from a quite different perspective. Hart's perspective is cultural rather than psychological. His essay contains many implications for the relationship between primary and secondary school education in our own and other modern societies. It is, however, important to remember that the differences between postpubertal and prepubertal education described for the Tiwi are similar to those described for the Hopi. They tend to reinforce and support the continued existence of the cultural system as a whole. The initiation ceremonies serve functions of recruitment and maintenance. Again, this is a different kind of discontinuity from that which occurs as a result of the intervention of one cultural and educational system into the affairs and processes of another.

Bruce Grindal in his chapter on students' self-perceptions among the Sisala of Northern Ghana takes the matter of discontinuity and cultural confrontation further. He shows how there seem to be two Africas in Ghana: one is a type of Western overlay and the other the traditional culture continuing up into the present. With this discontinuity as a backdrop, he treats the manner in which the Sisala schoolboy views himself and his future role as an adult. Grindal seeks to understand the schoolboy imagery as a product of his experiences with the modern educational process and his experiences within the traditional educational context of family, village, and tribe. The study by Grindal in the Education and Culture Series, *Growing Up in Two Worlds* (1972), is a valuable companion to this chapter.

In his chapter on culture and cognition Joseph Glick raises issues that continue to perplex and confound educators and researchers on cognitive process. He points out that the Kpelle of North Central Liberia solve problems in particular contexts but without context-free algorithms for their solution, and he goes on to discuss the complexities and uncertainties involved in taking even this interpretive position. As anthropologists of education, we are concerned with ways in which the cognitive structures and processes standing behind Western education may be different from those functioning in non-Western and particularly in nonliterate cultural contexts. This question has become loaded with political implications. One extreme view is that these differences are solely a function of testing situations or of the ethnocentricism of the observer. Some workers view even the acknowledgment of the possibility of cognitive differences as a form of racism or colonialism. It is true that the urban work on the "culturally deprived" child in U.S. society tended to be ethnocentric, and cross-cultural work has certainly not been free of it. The order of cultural-cognitive differences Glick is discussing, however, is much sharper than that found between social classes or ethnic groups in our society and is not necessarily related to poverty or deprivation. The traditional liberal position continues to be that there may be significant culturally produced differences in abilities to solve certain types of problems, particularly those involved with a technological and scientifically rationalized world. However, there are no *inherent* differences between normal human populations in the ability to do any form of thinking, given appropriate experience. Still, this position is little more than a statement of faith and does not solve the problem of how culture affects cognition. As experience occurs within a culturally construed semantic environment we are back at our starting point. The problem is whether experience in a given culturally construed semantic environment makes people think differently—not merely because they have different attitudes, values, cultural content, or world views to think with and through, but whether the *process* of their thinking is different. The crux of the issue is pinpointed by Michael Cole and John Gay in "Culture and Memory" (1972), as well as in Joseph Glick's chapter, which opens up a very important problem area for discussion. Readers will receive further help from Gay and Cole (1967) and from Cole et al. (1971).

References

Cole, Michael, and John Gay, 1972, "Culture and Memory," *American Anthropologist* 74:1066–1084.

Cole, Michael, John Gay, Joseph Glick, and Donald W. Sharp (in association with Thomas Ciborowski, Frederick Frankel, John Kellemu, and David F. Lancy),

1971, *The Cultural Context of Learning and Thinking: An Exploration in Experimental Anthropology.* New York: Basic Books.

Collier, John, Jr., 1973, *Alaskan Eskimo Education: A Film Analysis of Cultural Confrontation in the Schools.* CSEC. New York: Holt, Rinehart and Winston, Inc.

Gay, John, and Michael Cole, 1967, *The New Mathematics and an Old Culture: A Study of Learning among the Kpelle of Liberia.* CSEC. New York: Holt, Rinehart and Winston, Inc.

Grindal, Bruce, 1972, *Growing Up in Two Worlds: The Sisala of Northern Ghana.* CSEC. New York: Holt, Rinehart and Winston, Inc.

Hart, C. W. M., and Arnold Pilling, 1960, *The Tiwi of North Australia.* CSCA. New York: Holt, Rinehart and Winston, Inc.

Modiano, Nancy, 1973, *Indian Education in the Chiapas Highlands.* CSEC. New York: Holt, Rinehart and Winston, Inc.

GEORGE D. SPINDLER/*Stanford University*

13 *The Transmission of Culture**

This chapter is about how neonates become talking, thinking, feeling, moral, believing, valuing human beings—members of groups, participants in cultural systems. It is not, as a chapter on child psychology might be, about the growth and development of individuals, but on how young humans come to want to act as they must act if the cultural system is to be maintained. A wide variety of cultures are examined to illustrate both the diversity and unity of ways in which children are educated. The educational functions that are carried out by initiation rites in many cultures are emphasized, and the concepts of cultural compression, continuity, and discontinuity are stressed in this context. Various other techniques of education are demonstrated with selected cases, including reward, modeling and imitation, play, dramatization, verbal admonition, reinforcement, and storytelling. Recruitment and cultural maintenance are analyzed as basic educative functions. The chapter is not about the whole process of education but about certain parts of that process seen in a number of different situations.

What Are Some of the Ways That Culture Is Transmitted?

Psychologists and pediatricians do not agree upon the proper and most effective ways to raise children. Neither do the Dusun of Borneo, the Tewa or Hopi of the Southwest, the Japanese, the Ulithians or the Palauans of Micronesia, the Turkish villagers, the Tiwi of North Australia, the people of Gopalpur, or those of Guadalcanal. Each way of life is distinctive in its outlook, content, the kind of adult personalities favored, and the way children are raised. There are also many respects in which human communities are similar that override cultural differences. All major human cultural systems include magic, religion, moral values, recreation, regulation of mating, education, and so forth. But the *content* of these different categories, and the ways the content and the categories are put together, differ enormously. These differences are reflected in the ways people raise their children. If the object of cultural transmission is to teach young people how to think, act, and feel appropriately this must be the case. To understand this process we must get a sense of this variety.

*Reprinted with minor revisions from *Culture in Process,* second edition, by Alan R. Beals, George D. Spindler, and Louise Spindler. Copyright © 1967, 1973, by Holt, Rinehart and Winston, Inc. Reprinted by permission of Holt, Rinehart and Winston, Inc.

This Is How It Is in Palau

Five-year-old Azu trails after his mother as she walks along the village path, whimpering and tugging at her skirt. He wants to be carried, and he tells her so, loudly and demandingly, "Stop! Stop! Hold me!" His mother shows no sign of attention. She continues her steady barefooted stride, her arms swinging freely at her sides, her heavy hips rolling to smooth the jog of her walk and steady the basket of wet clothes she carries on her head. She has been to the washing pool and her burden keeps her neck stiff, but this is not why she looks impassively ahead and pretends not to notice her son. Often before she has carried him on her back and an even heavier load on her head. But today she has resolved not to submit to his plea, for it is time for him to begin to grow up.

Azu is not aware that the decision has been made. Understandably, he supposes that his mother is just cross, as she often has been in the past, and that his cries will soon take effect. He persists in his demand, but falls behind as his mother firmly marches on. He runs to catch up and angrily yanks at her hand. She shakes him off without speaking to him or looking at him. Enraged, he drops solidly on the ground and begins to scream. He gives a startled look when this produces no response, then rolls over on his stomach and begins to writhe, sob, and yell. He beats the earth with his fists and kicks it with his toes. This hurts and makes him furious, the more so since it has not caused his mother to notice him. He scrambles to his feet and scampers after her, his nose running, tears coursing through the dirt on his cheeks. When almost on her heel he yells and, getting no response, drops to the ground.

By this time his frustration is complete. In a rage he grovels in the red dirt, digging his toes into it, throwing it around him and on himself. He smears it on his face, grinding it in with his clenched fists. He squirms on his side, his feet turning his body through an arc on the pivot of one shoulder.

A man and his wife are approaching, the husband in the lead, he with a short-handled adz resting on his left shoulder, she with a basket of husked coconuts in her head. As they come abreast of Azu's mother the man greets her with "You have been to the washing pool?" It is the Palauan equivalent of the American "How are you?"—a question that is not an inquiry but a token of recognition. The two women scarcely glance up as they pass. They have recognized each other from a distance and it is not necessary to repeat the greeting. Even less notice is called for as the couple pass Azu sprawled on the path a few yards behind his mother. They have to step around his frenzied body, but no other recognition is taken of him, no word is spoken to him or to each other. There is no need to comment. His tantrum is not an unusual sight, especially among boys of his age or a little older. There is nothing to say to him or about him.

In the yard of a house just off the path, two girls, a little older than Azu, stop their play to investigate. Cautiously and silently they venture in Azu's direction. His mother is still in sight, but she disappears suddenly as she turns off the path into her yard without looking back. The girls stand some distance away, observing Azu's gyrations with solemn eyes. Then they turn and go back to their doorway, where they stand, still watching him but saying nothing. Azu is left alone, but it takes several minutes for him to realize that this is the way it is to be. Gradually his fit subsides and he lies sprawled and whimpering on the path.

Finally, he pushes himself to his feet and starts home, still sobbing and wiping

> his eyes with his fists. As he trudges into the yard he can hear his mother shouting at his sister, telling her not to step over the baby. Another sister is sweeping the earth beneath the floor of the house with a coconut-leaf broom. Glancing up, she calls shrilly to Azu, asking him where he has been. He does not reply, but climbs the two steps to the threshold of the doorway and makes his way to a mat in the corner of the house. There he lies quietly until he falls asleep.
>
> This has been Azu's first painful lesson in growing up. There will be many more unless he soon understands and accepts the Palauan attitude that emotional attachments are cruel and treacherous entanglements, and that it is better not to cultivate them in the first place than to have them disrupted and disclaimed. Usually the lesson has to be repeated in many connections before its general truth sinks in. There will be refusals of pleas to be held, to be carried, to be fed, to be cuddled, and to be amused; and for a time at least there will follow the same violent struggle to maintain control that failed to help Azu. For whatever the means, and regardless of the lapses from the stern code, children must grow away from their parents, not cleave to them. Sooner or later the child must learn not to expect the solicitude, the warm attachment of earlier years and must accept the fact that he is to live in an emotional vacuum, trading friendship for concrete rewards, neither accepting nor giving lasting affection (Barnett 1960:4–6).

Is culture being transmitted here? Azu is learning that people are not to be trusted, that any emotional commitment is shaky business. He is acquiring an emotional attitude. From Professor Barnett's further description of life in Palau (Barnett 1960) we know that this emotional attitude underlies economic, social, political, even religious behavior among adult Palauans. If this happened only to Azu we would probably regard it as a traumatic event. He might then grow up to be a singularly distrustful adult in a trusting world. He would be a deviant. But virtually all Palauan boys experience this sudden rejection (it happens more gradually for girls)—not always in just this particular way—but in somewhat the same way and at about the same time. This is a culturally patterned way of getting a lesson across to the child. This culturally patterned way of treating the child has a more or less consistent result—an emotional attitude—and this emotional attitude is in turn patterned, and fits into various parts of the Palauan cultural system. What is learned by Azu and transmitted by his mother is at once a pattern of child training (the mother had it and applied it), a dimension of Palauan *world view* (Palauans see the world as a place where people do not become emotionally involved with each other), a modal personality trait (most normal adult Palauans distrust others), and a pattern for behavior in the context of the many subsystems (economic, political, religious, and so forth) governing adult life.

Azu's mother did not simply tell him to stop depending upon her and to refrain from lasting emotional involvements with others. She demonstrated to him in a very dramatic way that this is the way it is in this life (in Palau at least). She probably didn't even completely rationalize what she did. She did not say to herself, "Now it is time for Azu to acquire the characteristic Palauan attitude that emotional attachments are not lasting and the best way to teach him this is for me to refuse to carry him." Barnett says that she "resolved not to submit to his plea." We cannot be sure that she even did this, for not even Homer Barnett, as well as he knows the Palauans, can get into Azu's mother's head. We know that she did not, in fact, submit to his plea. She may well have thought that it was about time for Azu to grow up. Growing up in Palau means in part to stop depending on people, even your very own loving mother. But maybe she was just plain tired, feeling a little extra crabby, so she acted in a characteristically Palauan way *without thinking about it* toward her five-year-old. People can transmit culture without knowing they do so. Probably more culture is transmitted this way than with conscious intent.

Discontinuity between early and later childhood is apparent in the Palauan case. Most cultures are patterned in such a way as to provide discontinuities of experience, but the points of time in the life cycle where these occur, and their intensity, differ widely. Azu experienced few restraints before this time. He did pretty much as he pleased, and lolled about on the laps of parents, kin, and friends. He was seldom if ever punished. There was always someone around to serve as protector, provider, and companion, and someone to carry him, usually mother, wherever he might go. Much of this changed for him after this day at the age of five. To be sure, he is not abandoned, and he is still shielded, guided, and provided for in every physical sense, but he finds himself being told more often than asked what he wants, and his confidence in himself and in his parents has been shaken. He no longer knows how to get what he wants. The discontinuity, the break with the ways things were in his fifth year of life, is in itself a technique of cultural transmission. We will observe discontinuities in the treatment of children and their effects in other cultures.

How Is It Done in Ulithi?

The Ulithians, like the Palauans, are Micronesians, but inhabit a much smaller island, in fact a tiny atoll in the vast Pacific, quite out of the way and fairly unchanged when first studied by William Lessa in the late forties (Lessa 1966). The Ulithians educate their children in many of the same ways the Palauans do, but differently enough to merit some special attention.

Like the Palauans, the Ulithians are solicitous and supportive of infants and young children.

> The infant is given the breast whenever he cries to be fed or whenever it is considered time to feed him, but sometimes only as a pacifier. He suckles often, especially during the first three to six months of his life, when he may average around eighteen times during the day and night. The great stress placed by Ulithians on food is once more given eloquent expression in nursing practices. Thus, if both the mother and child should happen to be asleep at any time and it seems to someone who is awake that the baby should be fed, both are aroused in order to nurse the baby. . . .

> The care of the baby is marked by much solicitude on the part of everyone. One of the ways in which this is manifested is through great attention to cleanliness. The infant is bathed three times a day, and after each bath the baby is rubbed all over with coconut oil and powdered with tumeric. Ordinarily, bathing is done by the mother, who, as she holds the child, rocks him from side to side in the water and sings:
>
> Float on the water
> In my arms, my arms
> On the little sea,
> The big sea,
> The rough sea,
> The calm sea,
> On this sea.
>
> [three sentences omitted]
>
> An infant is never left alone. He seems constantly in someone's arms, being passed from person to person in order to allow everyone a chance to fondle him. There is not much danger that if neglected for a moment he will harm himself (Lessa 1966:94–96).

Unlike the Palauans, the Ulithians do not create any special discontinuities for the young child. Even weaning is handled with as little disturbance as possible.

> Weaning begins at varying ages. It is never attempted before the child is a year old, and usually he is much older than that. Some children are suckled until they are five, or even as much as seven or eight. Weaning takes about four days, one technique being to put the juice of hot pepper around the mother's nipples. Physical punishment is never employed, though scolding may be deemed necessary. Ridicule, a common recourse in training Ulithian children, is also resorted to. The child's reaction to being deprived of the breast often manifests itself in temper tantrums. The mother tries to mollify the child in a comforting embrace and tries to console him by playing with him and offering him such distraction as a tiny coconut or a flower (Lessa 1966:95).

Apparently this technique, and the emotional atmosphere that surrounds it, is not threatening to Ulithian children. We see nothing of the feelings of deprivation and rejection suffered by Azu.

> The reactions to weaning are not extreme; children weather the crisis well. In fact, a playful element may be observed. A child may quickly push his face into his mother's breast and then run away to play. When the mother's attention is elsewhere, the child may make a sudden impish lunge at the breast and try to suckle from it. After the mother has scolded the weanling, he may coyly take the breast and fondle it, toy with the nipple, and rub the breast over his face. A man told me that when he was being weaned at the age of about seven, he would alternate sleeping with his father and mother, who occupied separate beds. On those occasions when he would sleep with his father, the latter would tell him to say goodnight to his mother. The boy would go over to where she was lying and playfully run his nose over her breasts. She would take this gesture good-naturedly and encourage him by telling him he was virtuous, strong, and like other boys. Then he would go back to his father, satisfied with his goodness (Lessa 1966:95).

We also see in the above account of Ulithian behavior that transmission of sexual attitudes and the permissiveness concerning eroticization are markedly different than in our own society. This difference, of course, is not confined to relations between young boys and their mothers, but extends through all heterosexual relationships, and throughout the patterning of adult life.

Given the relaxed and supportive character of child rearing in Ulithi, it is small wonder that children behave in a relaxed, playful manner, and apparently grow into adults that value relaxation. This is in sharp contrast with the Palauans, whom Barnett describes as characterized by a residue of latent hostility in social situations, and as subject to chronic anxiety (Barnett 1960: 11–15).

> Indeed, play is so haphazard and relaxed that it quickly melts from one thing to another, and from one place to another, with little inhibition. There is much laughter and chatter, and often some vigorous singing. One gains the impression that relaxation, for which the natives have a word they use almost constantly, is one of the major values of Ulithian culture (Lessa 1966:101).

Particularly striking in the transmission of Ulithian culture is the disapproval of unusually independent behavior.

> The attitude of society towards unwarranted indpendence is generally one of disapproval. Normal independence is admired because it leads to later self-reliance in the growing individual, dependence being scorned if it is so strong that it will unfit him for future responsibilities. Ulithians talk a lot about homesickness and do not view this as improper, unless the longing is really for a spouse or sweetheart, the suspicion here being that it is really sexual outlet that a person wants. Longing of this sort is said to make a person inefficient and perhaps even ill. Homesickness is expected of all children and not deprecated. I was greatly touched once when I asked a friend to tell me what a man was muttering about during a visit to my house. He said he felt sad that I was away from my home and friends and wondered how I could endure it. Ulithians do not like people to feel lonely; sociability is a great virtue for them (Lessa 1966:101).

The degree and kinds of dependence and independence that are inculcated in children are significant variables in any transcultural comparison of cultural transmission. Palauan children are taught not to trust others and grow to adulthood in a society where social relationships tend to be exploitative and, behind a facade of pleasantness, hostile. Palauans are not, however, independent, and tend to be quite dependent for direction upon external authority (Barnett 1960:13, 15–16). The picture is confused in Palau by the greater degree of acculturation (than at Ulithi) and the threatening situations that the Palauans have experienced under first German, then Japanese, and now American domination. In American society, middle-class culture calls for independence, particularly in males, and independence training is stressed from virtually the beginning of childhood. But adolescent and adult Americans are among the most sociable, "joiningest" people in the world. Ulithian children are not taught to be independent, and the individual who is too independent is the object of criticism. Palauan children are taught a kind of independence—to be independent of dependency upon other people's affection—by a sudden withdrawal of support at about five years of age. But which is really the more "independent" adult? Palauans are independent of each other in the sense that they can be cruel and callous to each other and exploitive in social relationships, but they are fearful of independent action and responsibility, are never originators or innovators, and are dependent upon authority for direction. Ulithians are dependent upon each other for social and emotional support, but do not exhibit the fearful dependency upon authority that Palauans do.

This does not mean that there is no predictable relationship between the training of children in dependency or independence and the consequences in adulthood. It does mean that the relationship is not simple and must be culturally contextualized if it is to make sense.

Every society creates some discontinuities in the experience of the individual as he or she grows up. It seems impossible to move from the roles appropriate to childhood to the roles appropriate for adulthood without some discontinuity. Societies differ greatly in the timing of discontinuity, and its abruptness. The first major break for Azu, the Palauan boy, was at five years of age. In Ulithi the major break occurs at the beginning of young adulthood.

> The mild concerns of ordinary life begin to catch up with the individual in the early years of adulthood and he can never again revert to the joyful indifference of his childhood.
>
> Attaining adulthood is marked by a ritual for boys and another for girls, neither of which is featured by genital operations. The same term, *kufar,* is used for each of the initiations. . . .
>
> The boy's *kufar* is much less elaborate and important. It comes about when he begins to show secondary sex characteristics and is marked by three elements: a change to adult clothing, the performance of magic, and the giving of a feast. All this occurs on the same day. . . .
>
> The outstanding consequence of the boy's ritual is that he must now sleep in the men's house and scrupulously avoid his postpubertal sisters. Not only must he not sleep in the same house with them, but he and they may not walk together, share the same food, touch one another's personal baskets, wear one another's leis or other ornaments, make or listen to ribald jokes in one another's presence, watch one another doing a solo dance, or listen to one another sing a love song (Lessa 1966:101–102).

Brother-sister avoidances of this kind are very common in human societies. There is a whole body of literature about them and their implications and consequences. The most important thing for us to note is that this is one of the most obvious ways in which restrictions appropriate to the young adult role in Ulithian society are placed on the individual immediately after the kufar. Transitional rites, or "rites of passage," as they are frequently termed, usually involve new restrictions of this sort. So, for that matter, do the events marking important transitions occurring at other times in the life experience. Azu lost the privilege of being carried and treated like an infant, and immediately became subject to being told what to do more often than demanding and getting what he wanted. One way of looking at Azu's experience and the Ulithian kufar is to regard them as periods of sharp discontinuity in the management of cultural transmission. Expressed most simply—what cultural transmitters do to and for an individual after the event is quite different in some ways from what they did before. Another way of looking at these events is to regard them as the beginning of periods of cultural compression. Expressed most simply—cultural compression occurs when the individual's behavior is restricted by the application of new cultural norms. After the kufar, the Ulithian boy and girl cannot interact with their mature opposite-sex siblings except under very special rules. Azu cannot demand to be carried and is told to do many other things he did not have to do before.

In Ulithi the girl's kufar is much more elaborate. When she notices the first flow of blood she knows she must go immediately to the women's house. As she goes, and upon her arrival, there is a great hullabaloo in the village, with the women shouting again and again, "The menstruating one, Ho-o-o!" After her arrival she takes a bath, changes her skirt, has magic spells recited over her to help her find a mate and enjoy a happy married life, and is instructed about the many *etap* (taboos) she must observe—some for days, others for weeks, and yet others for years. Soon she goes to live in a private hut of her own, built near her parent's house, but she still must go to the menstrual house whenever her discharge begins (Lessa 1966:102–104).

The discontinuity and compression that Ulithian young people experience after the kufar are not limited to a few taboos.

> Adolescence and adulthood obviously come rushing together at young Ulithians, and the attitude of the community toward them undergoes a rapid change. The boy and the girl are admitted to a higher status, to be sure, and they are given certain rights and listened to with more respect when they speak. But a good deal is expected of them in return. Young men bear the brunt of the heaviest tasks assigned by the men's council. For their own parents they must help build and repair houses, carry burdens, climb trees for coconuts, fish, make rope, and perform all the other tasks commonly expected of an able-bodied man. Young women are similarly called upon to do much of the harder work of the village and the household. Older people tend to treat these very young adults with a sudden sternness and formality lacking when they were in their childhood. The missteps of young people are carefully watched and readily criticized, so that new adults are constantly aware of the critical gaze of their elders. They may not voice strong objections or opinions, and have no political rights whatsoever, accepting the decisions of the men's and women's councils without murmur. Altogether, they are suddenly cut off from childhood and must undergo a severe transition in their comportment towards others about them. Only in the amatory sphere can they find release from the petty tyranny of their elders (Lessa 1966:104).

What Is It Like To Be Initiated in Hano?

Like the Hopi, with whom they are very close neighbors on the same mesa in Arizona, the Hano Tewa hold an initiation ceremony into the Kachina[1] cult at about nine years of age. In fact, the Tewa and Hopi share the same ceremony. Further examination of this occasion will be instructive. Up until that time Tewa children are treated about the way the Hopi children are. They are kept on a cradleboard at first, weaned late, by middle-class American standards, and on the whole treated very permissively and supportively by mothers, mother's sisters, grandparents, fathers, older siblings, and other people in and about the extended family household, admonished and corrected by the mother's brother, and half scared to death from time to time when they are bad by the Kachinas, or the threat of Kachinas. Of course nowadays the continuity of this early period is somewhat upset because children must start in the government day school at Polacca when they are about seven, and the teachers' ideas of proper behavior are frequently at variance with those maintained by Tewa parents. Excepting for school, though, Tewa children can be said to experience a consistent, continuous educational environment through the early years.

Things change when the initiation takes place at about age nine. A ceremonial father is selected for the boy, and a ceremonial mother for the girl. These ceremonial parents, as well as the real parents and for that matter everyone in the pueblo, build up the coming event for the child so that he or she is in a tremendous state of excitement. Then the day comes. Edward Dozier reports the initiation experience of one of his informants.

> We were told that the Kachina were beings from another world. There were some boys who said that they were not, but we could never be sure, and most of us believed what we were told. Our own parents and elders tried to make us believe that the Kachina were powerful beings, some good and some bad, and that they knew our innermost thoughts and actions. If they did not know about us through their own great power, then probably our own relatives told the Kachina about us. At any rate every time they visited us they seemed to know what we had thought and how we had acted.
>
> As the time for our initiation came closer we became more and more frightened. The ogre Kachina, the Soyoku, came every year and threatened to carry us away; now we were told that we were going to face these awful creatures and many others. Though we were told not to be afraid, we could not help ourselves. If the Kachina are really supernaturals and powerful beings, we might have offended them by some thought or act and they might punish us. They might even take us with them as the Soyoku threatened to do every year.
>
> Four days before Powamu our ceremonial fathers and our ceremonial mothers

[1] This word is sometimes spelled Katcina, sometimes Kachina. Voth, used as the source for the description of the Hopi ceremony, spells it Katcina. Dozier, used as the source for the Hano Tewa, spells it Kachina. Either is correct.

took us to Court Kiva. The girls were accompanied by their ceremonial mothers, and we boys by our ceremonial fathers. We stood outside the kiva, and then two whipper Kachina, looking very mean, came out of the kiva. Only a blanket covered the nakedness of the boys; as the Kachina drew near our ceremonial fathers removed the blankets. The girls were permitted to keep on their dresses, however. Our ceremonial parents urged us to offer sacred corn meal to the Kachina; as soon as we did they whipped us with their yucca whips. I was hit so hard that I defecated and urinated and I could feel the welts forming on my back and I knew that I was bleeding too. He whipped me four times, but the last time he hit me on the leg instead, and as the whipper started to strike again, my ceremonial father pulled me back and he took the blow himself. "This is a good boy, my old man," he said to the Kachina. "You have hit him enough."

For many days my back hurt and I had to sleep on my side until the wounds healed.

After the whipping a small sacred feather was tied to our hair and we were told not to eat meat or salt. Four days later we went to see the Powamu ceremony in the kiva. As babies, our mother had taken us to see this event; but as soon as we began to talk, they stopped taking us. I could not remember what had happened on Powamu night and I was afraid that another frightening ordeal awaited us. Those of us who were whipped went with our ceremonial parents. In this dance we saw that the Kachina were really our own fathers, uncles, and brothers. This made me feel strange. I felt somehow that all my relatives were responsible for the whipping we had received. My ceremonial father was kind and gentle during this time and I felt very warm toward him, but I also wondered if he was to blame for our treatment. I felt deceived and ill-treated (Dozier 1967:59–60).

The Hano Tewa children are shocked, angry, chagrined when they find that the supernatural Kachinas they have been scared and disciplined by all their lives up until then, and who during the initiation have whipped them hard, are really men they have known very well in their own community, their clans, their families. To be treated supportively and permissively all of one's life, and then to be whipped publicly (or see others get whipped) would seem quite upsetting by itself. To find out that the awesome Kachinas are men impersonating gods would seem almost too much. But somehow the experience seems to help make good adult Hano Tewa out of little ones.

If the initiate does not accept the spiritual reality of the Kachina, and will not accept his relatives' "cruel" behavior as necessary and good for him (or her), he can stop being a Tewa. But is this a real choice? Not for anyone who is human enough to need friends and family who speak the same language, both literally and figuratively, and whose identity as a Tewa Indian stretches back through all of time. Having then (usually without debate) made the choice of being a Tewa, one is a *good* Tewa. No doubts can be allowed.

There is another factor operating as well. Children who pass through the initiation are no longer outside looking in, they are inside looking out. They are not grown up, and neither they nor anyone else think they are, but they are a lot more grown up than they were before the initiation. Girls take on a more active part in household duties and boys acquire more responsibilities in farming and ranching activities. And it will not be long before the males can take on the role of impersonating the Kachinas and initiating children as they were initiated. The ceremonial whipping, in the context of all the dramatic ceremonies, dancing, and general community uproar, is the symbol of a dramatic shift in status-role. The shift starts with just being "in the know" about what really goes on in the kiva and who the Kachinas are, and continues toward more and more full participation in the secular and sacred life of the community.

Dorothy Eggan sums it up well for the Hopi when she writes:

> Another reorganizing factor . . . was feeling "big." They had shared pain with adults, had learned secrets which forever separated them from the world of children, and now they were included in situations from which they had previously been excluded, as their elders continued to teach intensely what they believed intensely: that for them there was only one alternative—Hopi as against Kahopi.
>
> Consistent repetition is a powerful conditioning agent and, as the youngsters watched each initiation, they relived their own, and by again sharing the experience gradually worked out much of the bitter residue from their own memories of it, while also rationalizing and weaving group emotions ever stronger into their own emotional core—"It takes a while to see how wise the old people really are." An initiated boy, in participating in the kachina dances, learned to identify again with the kachinas whom he now impersonated. To put on a mask is to "become a kachina," and to cooperate actively in bringing about the major goals of Hopi life. And a girl came to know more fully the importance of her clan in its supportive role. These experiences were even more sharply conditioned and directed toward adult life in the adult initiation ceremonies, of which we have as yet only fragmentary knowledge. Of this one man said to me: "I will not discuss this thing with you only to say that no one can forget it. It is the most wonderful thing any man can have to remember. You know then that you are Hopi. It is the one thing Whites cannot have, cannot take away from us. It is our way of life given to us when the world began" (Eggan 1956:364–65).

In many ways the preadolescent and adolescent period that we have been discussing, using the Ulithian kufar and the Hano Tewa initiation ceremonies as representative cases, is the most important of all in cultural transmission. There is a considerable literature on this period, including most notably the classic treatment given by Van Gennep (1960, first published in 1909) and the recent studies by Frank Young (1965), Yehudi Cohen (1964), Gary Schwartz and Don Merten (1968), and Whiting, Kluckhohn, and Albert (1958). Judith Brown provides a cross-cultural study of initiation rights for females (Brown 1963). But these studies do not emphasize the educational aspects of the initiation rites or rites of passage that they analyze.

One of the few studies that does is the remarkable essay by C. W. M. Hart (reprinted in this text in Chapter 16), based upon a single case, the Tiwi of North Australia, but with implications for many other cases. Hart contrasts the attitude of cultural transmitters toward young children among the Tiwi to the rigorous demands of the initiation period.

> The arrival of the strangers to drag the yelling boy out of his mother's arms is just the spectacular beginning of a long period during which the separation of the boy from everything that has gone before is emphasized in every possible way at every minute of the day and night. So far his life has been easy; now it is hard. Up to now he has never necessarily experienced any great pain, but in the initiation period in many tribes pain, sometimes horrible, intense pain, is an obligatory feature. The boy of twelve or thirteen, used to noisy, boisterous, irresponsible play, is expected and required to sit still for hours and days at a time saying nothing whatever but concentrating upon and endeavoring to understand long intricate instructions and "lectures" given him by his hostile and forbidding preceptors. [sentence omitted] Life has suddenly become real and earnest and the initiate is required literally to "put away the things of a child" even the demeanor. The number of tabus and unnatural behaviors enjoined upon the initiate is endless. He mustn't speak unless he is spoken to; he must eat only certain foods, and often only in certain ways, at fixed times, and in certain fixed positions. All contact with females, even speech with them is rigidly forbidden, and this includes mother and sisters (1963:415).

Hart goes on to state that the novices are taught origin myths, the meaning of the sacred ceremonials, in short, theology, ". . . which in primitive society is inextricably mixed up with astronomy, geology, geography, biology (the mysteries of birth and death), philosophy, art, and music—in short the whole cultural heritage of the tribe"; and that the purpose of this teaching is not to make better economic men of the novices, but rather ". . . better citizens, better carriers of the culture through the generations. . ." (Hart 1963:415). In this view Hart agrees (as he points out himself) with George Pettit, who did a thorough study of educational practices among North American Indians, and who writes that the initiation proceedings were ". . . a constant challenge to the elders to review, analyze, dramatize, and defend their cultural heritage" (Pettit 1946:182).

Pettit's words also bring into focus another feature of the initiation rituals implicit in the description of these events for the Ulithians, Hano Tewa, and the Tiwi, which seems very significant. In all these cases dramatization is used as an educational technique. In fact a ceremony of any kind is a dramatization, sometimes indirect and metaphoric, sometimes very direct, of the interplay of crucial forces and events in the life of the community. In the initiation ceremonies dramatization forces the seriousness of growing up into the youngster's mind and mobilizes his emotions around the lessons to be learned and the change in identity to be secured. The role of dramatization in cultural transmission may be difficult for American readers to appreciate, because the pragmatization of American schools and American life in general has gone so far.

These points emphasize the view of initiation proceedings taken in this chapter—that they are dramatic signals for new beginnings and, at various times before and throughout adolescence in many societies, the intensification of discontinuity and compression in cultural transmission. Discontinuity in the management of the youngsters' learning—from supportive and easy to rigorous and harsh; compression in the closing in of culturally patterned demand and restriction as the new status-roles attained by successfully passing through the initiation period are activated. Of course this compression of cultural demand around the individual also opens new channels of development and experience to him. As humans mature they give up the freedom of childhood for the rewards to be gained by observing the rules of the cultural game. The initiation ceremonies are dramatic signals to everyone that the game has begun in earnest.

What Happens in Gopalpur?

In the village of Gopalpur, in South India, described by Alan Beals, social, not physical, mastery is stressed.

> Long before it has begun to walk, the child in Gopalpur has begun to develop a concern about relationships with others. The period of infantile dependency is extended. The child is not encouraged to develop muscular skills, but is carried from place to place on the hip of mother or sister. The child is rarely alone. It is constantly exposed to other people, and learning to talk, to communicate with others, is given priority over anything else that might be learned. When the child does learn to walk, adults begin to treat it differently. Shooed out of the house, its training is largely taken over by the play group. In the streets there are few toys, few things to be manipulated. The play of the child must be social play and the manipulation of others must be accomplished through language and through such nonphysical techniques as crying and withdrawal. In the play group, the child creates a family and the family engages in the production of imaginary food or in the exchange of real food carried in shirt pockets (1962:19).

Children in Gopalpur imitate adults, both in the activities of play and in the attempts to control each other.

> Sidda, four years old, is playing in the front of his house with his cousin, Bugga, aged five. Sidda is sitting on the ground holding a stone and pounding. Bugga is piling the sand up like rice for the pounding. Bugga says, "Sidda, give me the stone, I want to pound." Sidda puts the stone on the ground, "Come and get it." Bugga says, "Don't come with me, I am going to the godhouse to play." Sidda offers, "I will give you the stone." He gives the stone to Bugga, who orders him, "Go into the house and bring some water." Sidda goes and brings water in a brass bowl. Bugga takes it and pours it on the heap of sand. He mixes the water with the sand, using both hands. Then, "Sidda, take the bowl inside." Sidda takes the bowl and returns with his mouth full of peanuts. He puts his hand into his shirt pocket, finds more peanuts and puts them in his mouth. Bugga sees the peanuts and asks, "Where did you get those?" "I got them inside the house." "Where are they?" "In the winnowing basket." Bugga gets up and goes inside the house returning with a bulging shirt pocket. Both sit down near the pile of sand. Bugga says to

> Sidda "Don't tell mother." "No, I won't." Sidda eats all of his peanuts and moves toward Bugga holding his hands out. Bugga wants to know, "Did you finish yours?" "I just brought a little, you brought a lot." Bugga refuses to give up any peanuts and Sidda begins to cry. Bugga pats him on the back saying, "I will give you peanuts later on." They get up and go into the house. Because they are considered to be brothers, Sidda and Bugga do not fight. When he is wronged, the older Bugga threatens to desert Sidda. When the situation is reversed, the younger Sidda breaks into tears (Beals 1962:16).

In their play, Bugga and Sidda are faithful to the patterns of adult control over children, as they have both observed them and experienced them. Beals describes children going to their houses when their shirt pockets are empty of the "currency of interaction" (grain, bits of bread, peanuts).

> This is the moment of entrapment, the only time during the day when the mother is able to exercise control over her child. This is the time for bargaining, for threatening. The mother scowls at her child, "You must have worked hard to be so hungry." The mother serves food and says, "Eat this. After you have eaten it, you must sit here and rock your little sister." The child eats and says, "I am going outside to play, I will not rock my sister." The child finishes its food and runs out of the house. Later, the child's aunt sees it and asks it to run to the store and buy some cooking oil. When it returns, the aunt says, "If you continue to obey me like this, I will give you something good to eat." When the mother catches the child again, she asks, "Where have you been?" Learning what occurred, she says, "If you bought cooking oil, that is fine; now come play with your sister." The child says, "First give me something to eat, and I will play with my sister." The mother scolds, "You will die of eating, sometimes you are willing to work, sometimes you are not willing to work; may you eat dirt." She gives it food and the child plays with its sister (1962:19).

This is the way the child in Gopalpur learns to control the unreliable world of other people. Children soon learn that they are dependent upon others for the major securities and satisfactions of life. The one with a large number of friends and supporters is secure, and they can be won and controlled, the individual comes to feel, through the use of food, but also by crying, begging, and working.

And among the Eskimo?

Eskimo children are treated supportively and permissively. When a baby cries it is picked up, played with, or nursed. There are a variety of baby tenders about, and after the first two or three months of life older siblings and the mother's unmarried sisters and cousins take a hand in caring for it. There is no set sleeping or eating schedule and weaning is a gradual process that may not be completed until the third or fourth year.

How is it then that, as white visitors to Eskimo villages often remark, the Eskimo have managed to raise their children so well? Observers speak warmly of their good humor, liveliness, resourcefulness, and well-behaved manner.

They appear to exemplify qualities that Western parents would like to see in their own children (Chance 1966:22). American folk belief would lead one to surmise that children who are treated so permissively would be "spoiled." Norman Chance describes the situation for the Alaskan Eskimo.

> Certainly, the warmth and affection given infants by parents, siblings, and other relatives provide them with a deep feeling of well-being and security. Young children also feel important because they learn early that they are expected to be useful, working members of the family. This attitude is not instilled by imposing tedious chores, but rather by including children in the round of daily activities, which enhances the feeling of family participation and cohesion. To put it another way, parents rarely deny children their company or exclude them from the adult world.
>
> This pattern reflects the parents' views of child rearing. Adults feel that they have more experience in living and it is their responsibility to share this experience with the children, "to tell them how to live." Children have to be told repeatedly because they tend to forget. Misbehavior is due to a child's forgetfulness, or to improper teaching in the first place. There is rarely any thought that the child is basically nasty, willful, or sinful. Where Anglo-Americans applaud a child for his good behavior, the Eskimo praise him for remembering. . . .
>
> Regardless of the degree of Westernization, more emphasis is placed on equality than on superordination-subordination in parent-child relations. A five year old obeys, not because he fears punishment or loss of love, but because he identifies with his parents and respects their judgment. Thus he finds little to resist or rebel against in his dealing with adults. We will find rebellion more common in adolescents, but it is not necessarily a revolt against parental control.
>
> By the time a child reaches the age of four or five, his parents' initial demonstrativeness has become tempered with an increased interest in his activities and accomplishments. They watch his play with obvious pleasure, and respond warmly to his conversation, make jokes with him and discipline him.
>
> Though a child is given considerable autonomy and his whims and wishes treated with respect, he is nonetheless taught to obey all adults. To an outsider unfamiliar with parent-child relations, the tone of Eskimo commands and admonitions sometimes sounds harsh and angry, yet in few instances does a child respond as if he had been addressed hostilely. . . .
>
> After the age of five a child is less restricted in his activities in and around the village, although theoretically he is not allowed on the beach or ice without an adult. During the dark winter season, he remains indoors or stays close to the house to prevent him from getting lost and to protect him from polar bears which might come into the village. In summer, though, children play at all hours of the day or "night" or as long as their parents are up. . . .
>
> Although not burdened with responsibility, both boys and girls are expected to take an active role in family chores. In the early years responsibilities are shared, depending on who is available. Regardless of sex, it is important for a child to know how to perform a wide variety of tasks and give help when needed. Both sexes collect and chop wood, get water, help carry meat and other supplies, oversee younger siblings, run errands for adults, feed the dogs, and burn trash.
>
> As a child becomes older, more specific responsibilities are allocated to him, according to his sex. Boys as young as seven may be given an opportunity to shoot

a .22 rifle, and at least a few boys in every village have killed their first caribou by the time they are ten. A youngster learns techniques of butchering while on hunting trips with older siblings and adults, although he is seldom proficient until he is in his mid-teens. In the past girls learned butchering at an early age, since this knowledge was essential to attracting a good husband. Today, with the availability of large quantities of Western foods, this skill may not be acquired until a girl is married, and not always then.

Although there is a recognized division of labor by sex, it is far from rigid at any age level. Boys, and even men, occasionally sweep the house and cook. Girls and their mothers go on fishing or bird-hunting trips. Members of each sex can usually assume the responsibilities of the other when the need arises, albeit in an auxiliary capacity (1966:22–26).

Apparently the combination that works so well with Eskimo children is support—participation—admonition—support. These children learn to see adults as rewarding and nonthreatening. Children are also not excluded, as they so often are in America, from the affairs of adult life. They do not understand everything they see, but virtually nothing is hidden from them. They are encouraged to assume responsibility appropriate to their age quite early in life. Children are participants in the flow of life. They learn by observing and doing. But Eskimo adults do not leave desired learning up to chance. They admonish, direct, remonstrate, but without hostility.

The Eskimo live with a desperately intemperate climate in what many white men have described as the part of the world that is the most inimical to human life. Perhaps Eskimo children are raised the way they are because a secure, good-humored, resourceful person is the only kind that can survive for long in this environment.

In Sensuron?

The people of Sensuron live in a very different physical and cultural environment than do the Eskimo. The atmosphere of this Dusun village in Borneo (now the Malysian state of Sabah) is communicated in these passages from Thomas Williams' case study.

Sensuron is astir an hour before the dawn of most mornings. It is usually too damp and cold to sleep. Fires are built up and the morning meal cooked while members of the household cluster about the house fire-pit seeking warmth. After eating, containers and utensils are rinsed off with water to "keep the worms off" and replaced in racks on the side of the house porch. Older children are sent to the river to carry water home in bamboo containers, while their mother spends her time gathering together equipment for the day's work, including some cold rice wrapped in leaves for a midday snack. The men and adolescent males go into the yard to sit in the first warmth of the sun and talk with male neighbors. The early morning exchange of plans, news, and recounting of the events of yesterday is considered a "proper way" to begin the day. While the men cluster in the yard center, with old shirts or cloths draped about bare shoulders to ward off the chill, women gather in front of one house or another, also trading news, gossip, and work plans. Many women comb each other's hair, after carefully picking out the lice. It is not unusual to see four or more women sitting in a row down the steps of a house ladder talking, while combing and delousing hair. Babies are nursed while mothers talk and small children run about the clusters of adults, generally being ignored until screams of pain or anger cause a sharp retort of *kAdA!* (do not!) from a parent. Women drape spare skirts about their bare shoulders to ward off the morning chill. About two hours after dawn these groups break up as the members go off to the work of the day. The work tasks of each day are those to be done under the annual cycle of subsistence labor described in the previous chapter. . . .

Vocal music is a common feature of village life; mothers and grandmothers sing a great variety of lullabies and "growth songs" to babies, children sing a wide range of traditional and nonsense songs, while adults sing at work in the fields and gardens during leisure and social occasions and at times of ritual. Drinking songs and wedding songs take elaborate forms, often in the nature of song "debates" with sides chosen and a winner declared by a host or guest of honor on the basis of "beauty" of tone, humor, and general "one-upmanship" in invention of new verse forms. Most group singing is done in harmony. Adolescents, especially girls, spend much of their solitary leisure time singing traditional songs of love and loneliness. Traditional verse forms in ritual, and extensive everyday use of riddles, folktales, and proverbs comprise a substantial body of oral literature. Many persons know much ritual verse, and most can recite dozens of stylized folktales, riddles, and proverbs.

Village headmen, certain older males, and ritual specialists of both sexes are practiced speechmakers. A skill of "speaking beautifully" is much admired and imitated. The style used involves narration, with exhortation, and is emphasized through voice tone and many hand and body gestures and postures. Political debates, court hearings, and personal arguments often become episodes of dramatic representation for onlookers, with a speaker's phrase listened to for its emotional expressive content and undertones of ridicule, tragedy, comedy, and farce at the expense of others involved. The verse forms of major rituals take on dimensions of drama as the specialist delivers the lines with skillful impersonations of voices and mannerisms of disease givers, souls of the dead, and creator beings.

By late afternoon of a leisure day people in the houses begin to drift to the yards, where they again sit and talk. Fires are built to ward off the chill of winds rising off the mountains, and men and women circle the blaze, throwing bits of wood and bamboo into the fire as they talk. This time is termed *mEg-Amut,* after the designation for exchange of small talk between household members. As many as 20 fires can be seen burning in yards through Sensuron at evening on most leisure days and on many evenings after work periods. Men sit and talk until after dark, when they go into houses to take their evening meal. Women leave about an hour before dark to prepare the meal. Smaller children usually eat before the adults. After the evening meal, for an hour or more, the family clusters about the house firepit, talking, with adults often engaged in small tasks of tool repair or manufacture. By 8 or 9 P.M. most families are asleep; the time of retiring is earlier when the work days are longer, later on rest days (1965:78–79).

Children in Sensuron are, like Eskimo children, always present, always observers. How different this way of life is from that experienced by American children! Gossip, speech-making, folktale telling, grooming, working, and playing are all there, all a part of the stream of life flowing around one and with which each member of the community moves. Under these circumstances much of the culture is transmitted by a kind of osmosis. It would be difficult for a child *not to* learn his culture.

The children of Sensuron do not necessarily grow up into good-humored, secure, trusting, "happy" adults. There are several factors that apparently interact in their growing up to make this unlikely. In the most simple sense, these children do not grow up to be like Eskimo adults because their parents (and other cultural transmitters) are not Eskimo, Dusun cultural transmitters (anybody in the community that the child hears and sees) act like Dusun. But cultural transmitters display certain attitudes and do certain things to children as well as provide them with models. In Sensuron, children are judged to be nonpersons. They are not even provided with personal names until their fifth year. They are also considered to be ". . . naturally noisy, inclined to illness, capable of theft, incurable wanderers, violent, quarrelsome, temperamental, destructive of property, wasteful, easily offended, quick to forget" (Williams 1965:87). They are threatened by parents with being eaten alive, carried off, damaged by disease-givers. Here are two lullabies sung to babies in Sensuron (and heard constantly by older children):

Sleep, Sleep, baby,
There comes the *rAgEn* (soul of the dead)
He carries a big stick,
He carries a big knife,
Sleep, Sleep, baby,
He comes to beat you!

or, as in this verse,

Bounce, Bounce, baby
There is a hawk,
Flying, looking for prey!
There is the hawk, looking for his prey!
He searches for something to snatch up in his claws,
Come here, hawk, and snatch up this baby!
(Williams 1965:88).

None of the things that the adults of Sensuron do to, with, or around their children is to be judged "bad." Their culture is different from Eskimo culture, and a different kind of individual functions effectively in it. We may for some reason need to make value judgments about a culture, the character of the people who live by it, or the way they raise children—but not for the purpose of understanding it better. It is particularly hard to refrain from making value judgments when the behavior in question occurs in an area of life in our own culture about which there are contradictory rules and considerable anxiety. Take, for instance, the transmission of sexual behavior in the village of Sensuron.

> In Sensuron people usually deal with their sex drives through ideally denying their existence, while often behaving in ways designed to sidestep social and cultural barriers to personal satisfaction. At the ideal level of belief the view is expressed that "men are not like dogs, chasing any bitch in heat," or "sex relations are unclean." Some of the sexuality of Dusun life has been noted earlier. There is a high content of lewd and bawdy behavior in the play of children and adolescents, and in the behavior of adults. For example, the eight-year-old girl in the house across from ours was angrily ordered by her mother to come into the house to help in rice husking. The girl turned to her mother and gave her a slow, undulating thrust of her hips in a sexual sign. More than 12 salacious gestures are known and used regularly by children and adults of both sexes, and there are some 20 equivalents of "four-letter" English terms specifically denoting the sexual anatomy and its possible uses. Late one afternoon 4 girls between 8 and 15 years, and 2 young boys of 4 and 5 years were chasing about our house steps for a half hour, grabbing at each other's genitals, and screaming, *uarE tAle!* which roughly translated means, "there is your mother's vulva!" Adult onlookers were greatly amused at the group and became convulsed with laughter when the four-year-old boy improvised the answer, "my mother has no vulva!" Thus, sexual behavior is supposed to be unclean and disgusting, while in reality it is a source of amusement and constant attention. . . .
>
> Children learn details of sexual behavior early, and sex play is a part of the behavior of four-to-six-year olds, usually in houses or rice stores while parents are away at work. Older children engage in sexual activities in groups and pairs, often at a location outside the village, often in an abandoned field storehouse, or in a temporary shelter in a remote garden (Williams 1965:82–83).

We can, however, make the tentative generalization that in cultures where there is a marked discrepancy between ideal and real, between the "theory" of culture and actual behavior, this conflict will be transmitted and that conflicts of this kind are probably not conducive to trust, confidence in self and in others, or even something we might call "happiness." We are like the people of Sensuron, though probably the conflicts between real and ideal run much deeper and are more damaging in our culture. In any event, the transmission of culture is complicated by discrepancies and conflicts, for both the pattern of idealizations and the patterns of actual behavior must be transmitted, as well as the ways for rationalizing the discrepancy between them.

How Goes It in Guadalcanal?

Many of the comments that have been made about child rearing and the transmission of culture in other communities can be applied to the situation in Guadalcanal, one of the Solomon Islands near New Guinea. Babies are held, fondled, fed, never isolated, and generally given very supportive treatment. Weaning and toilet training both take place without much fuss, and fairly late by American standards. Walking is regarded as a natural accomplishment that will be mastered in time, swimming seems to come as easily. Education is also different in some ways in Guadalcanal. There is no sharp discontinuity at the beginning of middle childhood as in Palau, nor is there any sharp break at puberty as in Ulithi, or at prepuberty as among the Hano Tewa or Hopi. The special character of cultural transmission in Guadalcanal is given by Ian Hogbin:

> Two virtues, generosity and respect for property, are inculcated from the eighteenth month onward—that is to say, from the age when the child can walk about and eat bananas and other things regarded as delicacies. At this stage no explanations are given, and the parents merely insist that food must be shared with any playmate who happens to be present and that goods belonging to other villagers must be left undisturbed. A toddler presented with a piece of fruit is told to give half to "So-and-so," and should the order be resisted, the adult ignores all protests and breaks a piece off to hand to the child's companion. Similarly, although sometimes callers are cautioned to put their baskets on a shelf out of reach, any meddling brings forth the rebuke, "That belongs to your uncle. Put it down." Disobedience is followed by snatching away the item in question from the child and returning it to thc owner.
>
> In time, when the child has passed into its fourth or fifth year, it is acknowledged to have at last attained the understanding to be able to take in what the adults say. Therefore, adults now accompany demands with reasoned instruction. One day when I was paying a call on a neighbor, Mwane-Anuta, I heard him warn his second son Mbule, who probably had not reached the age of five, to stop being so greedy. "I saw your mother give you those nuts," Mwane-Anuta reiterated. "Don't pretend she didn't. Running behind the house so that Penggoa wouldn't know! That is bad, very bad. Now then, show me, how many? Five left. Very well, offer three to Penggoa immediately." He then went on to tell me how important it was for children to learn to think of others so that in later life they would win the respect of their fellows.
>
> On another occasion during a meal I found Mwane-Anuta and his wife teaching their three sons how to eat properly. "Now Mbule," said his mother, "you face the rest of us so that we can all see you aren't taking too much. And you, Konana, run outside and ask Misika from next door to join you. His mother's not home yet, and I expect he's hungry. Your belly's not the only one, my boy." "Yes," Mwane-Anuta added. "Give a thought to those you run about with, and they'll give a thought to you." At this point the mother called over the eldest lad, Kure, and placed the basket of yams for me in his hands. "There, you carry that over to our guest and say that it is good to have him with us this evening," she whispered to him. The gesture was characteristic. I noted that always when meals were served to visitors the children acted as waiters. Why was this, I wanted to know. "Teaching, teaching," Mwane-Anuta replied. "This is how we train our young to behave" (1964:33).

It appears that in Guadalcanal direct verbal instruction is stressed as a technique of cultural transmission. Hogbin goes on to describe the constant stream of verbal admonition that is directed at the child by responsible adults in almost every situation. And again and again the prime values, generosity and respect for property, are reinforced by these admonitions.

The amount of direct verbal reinforcement of basic values, and even the amount of direct verbal instruction in less crucial matters, varies greatly from culture to culture. The people of Guadalcanal, like the Hopi, keep telling their children and young people how to behave and when they are behaving badly. In American middle-class culture there is also great emphasis on telling children what they should do, explaining how to do it, and the reasons for doing it, though we are probably less consistent in what we tell them than are the parents of Guadalcanal. Perhaps also in our culture we tend to substitute words for experience more than do the people of Guadalcanal, for the total range of experience relevant to growing up appropriately is more directly observable and available to their children than it is to ours.

> Girls go to the gardens regularly with their mother from about the age of eight. They cannot yet wield the heavy digging stick or bush knife, but they assist in collecting the rubbish before planting begins, in piling up the earth, and weeding. Boys start accompanying their father some two or three years later, when they help with the clearing, fetch lianas to tie up the saplings that form the fence, and cut up the seed yams. The men may also allocate plots to their sons and speak of the growing yams as their own harvest. The services of a youngster are of economic value from the time that he is pubescent, but he is not expected to take gardening really seriously until after he returns from the plantation and is thinking of marriage. By then he is conscious of his rights and privileges as a member of his clan and knows where the clan blocks of land are located. As a rule, he can also explain a little about the varieties of yams and taro and the types of soil best suited to earth.
>
> At about eight a boy begins to go along with his father or uncles when the men set out in the evening with their lines to catch fish from the shore or on the reef. They make a small rod for him, show him how to bait his hook, and tell him about the different species of fish—where they are to be found, which are good to eat, which are poisonous. At the age of ten the boy makes an occasional fishing excursion in a canoe. To start with, he sits in the center of the canoe and watches, perhaps baiting the hooks and removing the catch; but soon he takes part with the rest. In less than a year he is a useful crew member and expert in steering and generally handling the craft. At the same time, I have never seen youths under the age of sixteen out at sea by themselves. Often they are eager to go before this, but the elders are unwilling to give permission lest they endanger themselves or the canoe (Hogbin 1964:39).

The children of Guadalcanal learn by doing as well as learn by hearing. They also learn by imitating adult models, as children do in every human group around the world.

> Children also play at housekeeping. Sometimes they take along their juniors, who, however, do not remain interested for long. They put up a framework of saplings and tie on coconut-leaf mats, which they plait themselves in a rough-and-ready sort of way. Occasionally, they beg some raw food and prepare it; or they catch birds, bats, and rats with bows and arrows. Many times, too, I have seen

> them hold weddings, including all the formality of the handing-over of bride price. Various items serve instead of the valuables that the grownups use—tiny pebbles instead of dog's and porpoise teeth, the long flowers of a nut tree for strings of shell discs, and rats or lizards for pigs. When first the youngsters pretend to keep house they make no sexual distinction in the allocation of the tasks. Boys and girls together erect the shelters, plait the mats, cook the food, and fetch the water. But within a year or so, although they continue to play in company, the members of each group restrict themselves to the work appropriate to their sex. The boys leave the cooking and water carrying to the girls, who, in turn, refuse to help with the building (Hogbin 1964:37–38).

Children seem to acquire the culture of their community best when there is consistent reinforcement of the same norms of action and thinking through many different channels of activity and interaction. If a child is told, sees demonstrated, casually observes, imitates, experiments and is corrected, acts appropriately and is rewarded, corrected, and (as in the Tewa-Hopi initiation) is given an extra boost in learning by dramatized announcements of status-role change, all within a consistent framework of belief and value, he or she cannot help but learn, and learn what adult cultural transmitters want him or her to learn.

How Do They Listen in Demirciler?

In Demirciler, an Anatolian village in the arid central plateau of Turkey, a young boy, Mahmud, learns by being allowed in the room when the adult men meet at the Muhtar's (the village headman) home evenings to discuss current affairs.

> Each day, after having finished the evening meal, the old Muhtar's wife would put some small earthenware dishes or copper trays filled with nuts or chick-peas about the room, sometimes on small stands or sometimes on the floor, and the old man would build a warm fire in the fireplace. Soon after dark the men would begin to arrive by ones or twos and take their accustomed places in the men's room. This was the largest single room in the village and doubled as a guest house for visitors who came at nightfall and needed some place to sleep before going on their way the next day. It had been a long time since the room had been used for this purpose, however, because the nearby growing city had hotels, and most of the modern travelers stayed there. However, the room still served as a clearing house for all village business, as well as a place for the men to pass the cold winter evenings in warm comfort.
>
> The room was perhaps 30 by 15 feet in size, and along one side a shelf nearly 15 inches above the floor extended about 2 feet from the wall and covered the full 30 feet of the room's length. The old Muhtar sat near the center of the shelf, waiting for his guests to arrive. As the men came in, the oldest in the village would seat themselves in order of age on this raised projection, while the younger ones would sit cross-legged on the floor. No women were ever allowed to come into this room when the men were there. The Muhtar's wife had prepared everything ahead of time, and when additional things were occasionally needed during the evening,

one of the boys would be sent out to fetch it. Opposite the long bench was a fireplace, slightly larger than those in the kitchen of the other village homes, in which a fire burned brightly spreading heat throughout the room. The single electric bulb lighted the space dimly and so the shadows caused by the firelight were not prevented from dancing about the walls.

Mahmud would have been happier if the electric bulb had not been there at all, the way it used to be when he had been a very small boy. Electricity had been introduced to the village only a year ago, and he remembered the days when only the glow of the fire lighted these meetings.

As the gatherings grew in size, Mahmud heard many small groups of men talking idly about all sorts of personal problems, but when nearly all of the villagers had arrived, they began to quiet down.

The Hoca posed the first question, "Muhtar Bey, when will next year's money for the mosque be taken up?"

"Hocam, the amount has not been set yet," was the Muhtar's reply.

"All right, let's do it now," the Hoca persisted.

"Let's do it now," the Muhtar agreed.

And Mahmud listened as the Hoca told about the things the mosque would need during the coming year. Then several of the older men told how they had given so much the year before that it had been hard on their families, and finally, the Muhtar talked interminably about the duty of each Moslem to support the Faith and ended by asking the head of each family for just a little more than he knew they could pay.

Following this request there were a series of discussions between the Muhtar and each family head, haggling over what the members of his family could afford to give. Finally, however, agreement was reached with each man, and the Hoca knew how much he could count on for the coming year. The Muhtar would see that the money was collected and turned over to the Hoca.

The business of the evening being out of the way, Mahmud became more interested, as he knew that what he liked most was to come now. He had learned that he was too young to speak at the meetings, because he had been taken out several times the year before by one of the older boys and told that he could not stay with the men unless he could be quiet, so he waited in silence for what would happen next. After a slight pause one of the braver of the teen-aged boys called to an old man.

"*Dedem,* tell us some stories about the olden times."

"Shall I tell about the wars?" the old man nearest the Muhtar asked.

"Yes, about the great war with the Russians," the youth answered.

"Well, I was but a boy then, but my father went with the army of the Sultan that summer, and he told me this story" (Pierce 1964:20–21).

Is there any situation in the culture of the United States where a similar situation exists? When America was more rural than it is now, and commercial entertainments were not readily available for most people, young people learned about adult roles and problems, learned to think like adults and anticipated their own adulthood in somewhat the same way that Mahmud did. Now it is an open question whether young people would want to listen to their elders even if there was nothing else to do. Possibly this is partly because much of what one's elders "know" in our society is not true. The verities change with each generation.

At the end of the "business" session at the Muhtar's home an old man tells a story. The story is offered as entertainment, even though it has been heard countless time before. Young listeners learn from stories as well as from the deliberations of the older men as they decide what to do about somebody's adolescent son who is eyeing the girls too much, or what to do about building a new road. Storytelling has been and still is a way of transmitting information to young people in many cultures without their knowing they are being taught. Any story has either a metaphoric application to real life, provides models for behavior, or has both features. The metaphor or the model may or may not be translated into a moral. The elders in Demirciler do not, it appears, make the moral of the story explicit. In contrast, the Menomini Indians of Wisconsin always required a youngster to extract the moral in a story for himself. "You should never ask for anything to happen unless you mean it." "He who brags bites his own tail." A grandparent would tell the same story every night until the children could state the moral to the elder's satisfaction (Spindler 1971). People in different cultures vary greatly in how much they make of the moral, but stories and mythtellings are used in virtually all cultures to transmit information, values, and attitudes.

What Does Cultural Transmission Do for the System?

So far we have considered cultural transmission in cases where no major interventions from the outside have occurred, or, if they have occurred, we have chosen to ignore them for purposes of description and analysis. There are, however, virtually no cultural systems left in the world that have not experienced massive input from the outside, particularly from the West. This is the age of transformation. Nearly all tribal societies and peasant villages are being affected profoundly by modernization. One of the most important aspects of modernization is the development of schools that will, hopefully, prepare young people to take their places in a very different kind of world than the one their parents grew up in. This implies a kind of discontinuity that is of a different order than the kind we have been discussing.

Discontinuity in cultural transmission among the Dusun, Hopi, Tewa, and Tiwi is a process that produces cultural continuity in the system as a whole. The abrupt and dramatized changes in roles during adolescence, the sudden compression of cultural requirements, and all the techniques used by preceptors, who are nearly always adults from within the cultural system, educate an individual to be committed to the system. The initiation itself encapsulates and dramatizes symbols and meanings that are at the core of the cultural system so that the important things the initiate has learned up to that point, by observation, participation, or instruction, are reinforced. The discontinuity is in the way the initiate is treated during the initiation and the different behaviors expected of him (or her) afterward. The culture is maintained, its credibility validated. As the Hopi man said to Dorothy Eggan, "I will not discuss this thing with you only to say that no one can forget it. It is the most wonderful thing any man can have to remember. You know then that you are Hopi [after the initiation]. It is the one thing Whites cannot have, cannot take from us. It is our way of life given to us when the world began." (See p. 328.) This Hopi individual has been *recruited* as a Hopi.

In all established cultural systems where radical interventions from outside have not occurred, the major functions of education are *recruitment* and *maintenance.* The educational processes we have described for all of the cultures in this chapter have functioned in this manner. Recruitment occurs in two senses: recruitment to membership in the cultural system in general, so that one becomes a Hopi or a Tiwi; and recruitment to specific roles and statuses, to specific castes, or to certain classes. We may even, by stretching the point a little, say that young humans are recruited to being male or female, on the terms with which a given society defines being male or female. This becomes clear in cultures such as our own, where sex roles are becoming blurred so much that many young people grow up without a clear orientation toward either role. The educational system, whether we are talking about societies where there are no schools in the formal sense but where a great deal of education takes place, or about societies where there are many specialized formal schools, is organized to effect recruitment. The educational system is also organized so that the structure of the cultural system will be maintained. This is done by inculcating the specific values, attitudes, and beliefs that make this structure credible and the skills and competencies that make it work. People must believe in their system. If there is a caste or class structure they must believe that such a structure is good, or if not good, at least inevitable. They must also have the skills—vocational and social—that make it possible for goods and services to be exchanged that are necessary for community life to go on. Recruitment and maintenance intergrade, as you can see from the above discussion. The former refers to the process of getting people into the system and into specific roles; the latter refers to the process of keeping the system and roles functioning.

Modernizing Cultures: What Is the Purpose of Education?

In this transforming world, however, educational systems are often charged with responsibility for bringing about change in the culture. They become, or are intended to become, agents of modernization. They become intentional agents of cultural discontinuity, a kind of discontinuity that does not reinforce the traditional values or recruit youngsters into the existing system. The new schools, with their curricula and the concepts behind them, are future oriented. They recruit students into a system that does not yet exist, or is just emerging. They inevitably create conflicts between generations.

Among the Sisala of Northern Ghana, a modernizing African society, for example, there have been profound changes in the principles underlying the father-son relationship. As one man put it:

> This strict obedience, this is mostly on the part of illiterates. With educated people, if you tell your son something, he will have to speak his mind. If you find that the boy is right, you change your mind. With an illiterate, he just tells his son to do something. . . . In the old days, civilization was not so much. We obeyed our fathers whether right or wrong. If you didn't, they would beat you. We respected our fathers with fear. Now we have to talk with our sons when they challenge us (Grindal 1972:80).

Not all of the Sisala have as tolerant and favorable a view of the changes wrought by education, however:

> When my children were young, I used to tell them stories about my village and about our family traditions. But in Tumu there are not so many people from my village and my children never went to visit the family. Now my children are educated and they have no time to sit with the family. A Sisala father usually farms with his son. But with educated people, they don't farm. They run around town with other boys: Soon we will forget our history. The educated man has a different character from his father. So fathers die and never tell their sons about the important traditions. My children don't sit and listen to me anymore. They don't want to know the real things my father told me. They have gone to school, and they are now book men. Boys who are educated run around with other boys rather than sitting and listening to their fathers (Grindal:83).

That these conflicts should flare up into open expressions of hostility toward education, schools, and teachers is not surprising. A headmaster of a primary school among the Sisala related to Bruce Grindal what happened when a man made a trip to a village outside Tumu.

> He parked his car on the road and was away for some time. When he returned, he saw that somebody had defaced his car, beaten it with sticks or something. Now I knew that my school children knew something about this. So I gathered them together and told them that if they were good citizens, they should report to me who did it and God would reward them. So I found out that this was done by some people in the village. When the village people found out their children told me such things, they were very angry. They said that the teachers were teaching their children to disrespect their elders. It is because of things like that that the fathers are taking their children out of school (Grindal: 97–98).

The above implies that the new schools, created for the purposes of aiding and abetting modernization, are quite effective. Without question they do create conflicts between generations and disrupt the transmission of the traditional culture. These effects in themselves are a prelude to change, perhaps a necessary condition. They are not, however, the result of the effectiveness of the schools as educational institutions. Because the curricular content is alien to the existing culture there is little or no reinforcement in the home and family, or in the community as a whole, for what happens in the school. The school is isolated from the cultural system it is intended to serve. As F. Landa Jocano relates concerning the primary school in Malitbog, a barrio in Panay, in the middle Philippines:

> most of what children learn in school is purely verbal imitation and academic memorization, which do not relate with the activities of the children at home. By the time a child reaches the fourth grade he is expected to be competent in reading, writing, arithmetic, and language study. Except for gardening, no other vocational training is taught. The plants that are required to be cultivated, however, are cabbages, lettuce, okra, and other vegetables which are not normally grown and eaten in the barrio. [sentence omitted]
>
> Sanitation is taught in the school, but insofar as my observation went, this is not carried beyond the child's wearing clean clothes. Children may be required to buy toothbrushes, combs, handkerchiefs, and other personal items, and bring these to school for inspection. Because only a few can afford to buy these items, only a few come to school with them. Often these school requirements are the source of troubles at home, a night's crying among the children. . . . [sentence omitted] In the final analysis, such regular school injunctions as "brush your teeth every morning" or "drink milk and eat leafy vegetables" mean nothing to the children. First, none of the families brush their teeth. The toothbrushes the children bring to school are for inspection only. Their parents cannot afford to buy milk. They do not like goats' milk because it is *malangsa* (foul smelling) (Jocano 1969:53).

Nor is it solely a matter of the nonrelatedness of what is taught in the school to what is learned in the home and community. Because the curricular content is alien to the culture as a whole, what is taught tends to become formalized and unrealistic and is taught in a rigid, ritualistic manner. Again, among the Sisala of Northern Ghana, Bruce Grindal describes the classroom environment.

> The classroom environment into which the Sisala child enters is characterized by a mood of rigidity and an almost total absence of spontaneity. A typical school day begins with a fifteen-minute period during which the students talk and play, often running and screaming, while the teacher, who is usually outside talking with his fellow teachers, pays no attention. At 8:30 one of the students rings a bell, and the children immediately take their seats and remove from their desks the materials needed for the first lesson. When the teacher enters the room, everyone falls silent. If the first lesson is English, the teacher begins by reading a passage in the students' readers. He then asks the students to read the section aloud, and if a child makes a mistake, he is told to sit down, after being corrected. Variations of the English lesson consist of having the students write down dictated sentences or spell selected words from a passage on the blackboard. Each lesson lasts exactly forty minutes, at the end of which a bell rings and the students immediately prepare for the next lesson.
>
> Little emphasis is placed upon the content of what is taught; rather, the book

> is strictly adhered to, and the students are drilled by being asked the questions which appear at the end of each assignment. The absence of discussion is due partially to the poor training of the teachers, yet even in the middle schools where the educational standards for teachers are better, an unwillingness exists to discuss or explain the content of the lessons. All subjects except mathematics are lessons in literacy which teach the student to spell, read, and write.
>
> Interaction between the teacher and his students is characterized by an authoritarian rigidity. When the teacher enters the classroom, the students are expected to rise as a sign of respect. If the teacher needs anything done in the classroom, one of the students performs the task. During lessons the student is not expected to ask questions, but instead is supposed to give the "correct" answers to questions posed to him by the teacher. The students are less intent upon what the teacher is saying than they are upon the reading materials before them. When the teacher asks a question, most of the students hurriedly examine their books to find the correct answer and then raise their hands. The teacher calls on one of them, who rises, responds (with his eyes lowered), and then sits down. If the answer is wrong or does not make sense, the teacher corrects him and occasionally derides him for his stupidity. In the latter case the child remains standing with his eyes lowered until the teacher finishes and then sits down without making a response (Grindal 1972:85).

The nonrelatedness of the school to the community in both the content being transmitted and the methods used to transmit it is logically carried into the aspirations of students concerning their own futures. These aspirations are often quite unrealistic. As one of the Sisala school boys said:

> I have in mind this day being a professor so that I will be able to help my country. . . . As a professor I will visit so many countries such as America, Britain, and Holland. In fact, it will be interesting for me and my wife. . . . When I return, my father will be proud seeing his child like this. Just imagine me having a wife and children in my car moving down the street of my village. And when the people are in need of anything, I will help them (Grindal: 89).

Or as another reported in an essay:

> By the time I have attained my graduation certificate from the university, the government will be so happy that they may like to make me president of my beloved country. When I receive my salary, I will divide the money and give part to my father and my wife and children. . . . People say the U.S.A. is a beautiful country. But when they see my village, they will say it is more beautiful. Through my hard studies, my name will rise forever for people to remember (Grindal: 89).

As we have said, the new schools, like the traditional tribal methods of education and schools everywhere, recruit new members of the community into a cultural system and into specific roles and statuses. And they attempt to maintain this system by transmitting the necessary competencies to individuals who are recruited into it via these roles and statuses. The problem with the new schools is that the cultural system they are recruiting for does not exist in its full form. The education the school boys and girls receive is regarded by many as more or less useless, though most people, like the Sisala, agree that at least literacy is necessary if one is to get along in the modern world. However, the experience of the school child goes far beyond training for literacy. The child is removed from the everyday routine of community life and from observation of the work rules of adults. He or she is placed in an artificial, isolated, unrealistic, ritualized environment. Unrealistic aspirations and self-images develop. Harsh reality intrudes abruptly upon graduation. The schoolboy discovers that, except for teaching in the primary schools, few opportunities are open to him. There are some clerical positions in government offices, but they are few. Many graduates migrate in search of jobs concomitant with their expectations, but they usually find that living conditions are more severe than those in the tribal area and end up accepting an occupation and life style similar to that of the illiterate tribesmen who have also migrated to the city. Those who become village teachers are not much better off. One Sisala teacher in his mid-twenties said:

> I am just a small man. I teach and I have a small farm. . . . Maybe someday if I am fortunate, I will buy a tractor and farm for money because there is no future in teaching. When I went to school, I was told that if I got good marks and studied hard, I would be somebody, somebody important. I even thought I would go to America or England. I would still like to go, but I don't think of these things very often because it hurts too much. You see me here drinking and perhaps you think I don't have any sense. I don't know. I don't know why I drink. But I know in two days' time, I must go back and teach school. In X (his home village where he teaches) I am alone; I am nobody (Grindal: 93).

The pessimist will conclude that the new schools, as agents of modernization, are a rank failure. This would be a false conclusion. They are neither failures nor successes. The new schools, like all institutions transforming cultural systems, are not articulated with the other parts of the changing system. The future is not known or knowable. Much of the content taught in the school, as well as the very concept of the school as a place with four walls within which teacher and students are confined for a number of hours each day and regulated by a rigid schedule of "learning" activities, is Western. In many ways the new schools among the Sisala, in Malitbog, and in many other changing cultures are inadequate copies of schools in Europe and in the United States. There is no doubt, however, that formal schooling in all of the developing nations of the world, as disarticulated with the existing cultural context as it is, nevertheless is helping to bring into being a new population of literates, whose aspirations and world view are very different than that of their parents. And of course a whole class of educated elites has been created by colleges and universities in many of the countries. It seems inevitable that eventually the developing cultures will build their own models for schools and education. These new models will not be caricatures of Western schools, although in places, as in the case of the Sisala or the Kanuri of Nigeria described by Alan Peshkin (Peshkin 1972), where the Western influence has been strong for a long time, surely those models will show this influence.

Perhaps one significant part of the problem and the general shape of the solution is implied in the following exchange between two new young teachers in charge of a village school among the Ngoni of Malawi and a senior chief:

> The teachers bent one knee as they gave him the customary greeting, waiting in silence until he spoke.
>
> "How is your school?"
>
> "The classes are full and the children are learning well, Inkosi."
>
> "How do they behave?"
>
> "Like Ngoni children, Inkosi."
>
> "What do they learn?"
>
> "They learn reading, writing, arithmetic, scripture, geography and drill, Inkosi."
>
> "Is that education?"
>
> "It is education, Inkosi."
>
> "No! No! No! Education is *very* broad, *very* deep. It is not only in books, it is learning how to live. I am an old man now. When I was a boy I went with the Ngoni army against the Bemba. Then the mission came and I went to school. I became a teacher. Then I was chief. Then the government came. I have seen our country change, and now there are many schools and many young men go away to work to find money. I tell you that Ngoni children must learn how to live and how to build up our land, not only to work and earn money. Do you hear?"
>
> "Yebo, Inkosi" (Yes, O Chief) (Read 1968:2–3).

The model of education that will eventually emerge in the modernizing nations will be one that puts the school, in its usual formal sense, in perspective, and emphasizes education in its broadest sense, as a part of life and of the dynamic changing community. It must emerge if these cultures are to avoid the tragic errors of miseducation, as the Western nations have experienced them, particularly in the relationships between the schools and minority groups.

Conclusion

In this chapter we started with the question, What are some of the ways culture is transmitted? We answered this question by examining cultural systems where a wide variety of teaching and learning techniques are utilized. One of the most important processes, we found, was the management of discontinuity. Discontinuity occurs at any point in the life cycle when there is an abrupt transition from one mode of being and behaving to another, as for example at weaning and at adolescence. Many cultural systems manage the latter period of discontinuity with dramatic staging and initiation ceremonies, some of which are painful or emotionally disturbing to the initiates. They are public announcements of changes in status. They are also periods of intense cultural compression during which teaching and learning are accelerated. This managed cultural compression and discontinuity functions to enlist new members in the community and maintains the cultural system. Education, whether characterized by sharp discontinuities and culturally compressive periods, or by a relatively smooth progression of accumulating experience and status change, functions in established cultural systems to recruit new members and maintain the existing system. We then turned to a discussion of situations where alien or future-oriented cultural systems are introduced through formal schooling. Schools among the Sisala of Ghana, a modernizing African nation, and a Philippine barrio were used as examples of this relationship and its consequences. The disarticulation of school and community was emphasized. The point was made that children in these situations are intentionally recruited to a cultural system other than the one they originated from, and that the school does not maintain the existing social order, but, in effect, destroys it. This is a kind of discontinuity very different than the one we discussed previously, and produces severe dislocations in life patterns and interpersonal relations as well as potentially positive change.

References and Further Reading

Barnett, Homer G., 1960, *Being a Paluan.* CSCA. New York: Holt, Rinehart and Winston, Inc.

Beals, Alan R., 1962, *Gopalpur: A South Indian Village.* CSCA. New York: Holt, Rinehart and Winston, Inc.

Brown, Judith K., 1963, "A Cross-cultural Study of Female Initiation Rites," *American Anthropologist* 65:837–853.

Chance, Norman A., 1966, *The Eskimo of North Alaska.* CSCA. New York: Holt, Rinehart and Winston, Inc.

Cohen, Yehudi, 1964, *The Transition from Childhood to Adolescence.* Chicago: Aldine Publishing Company.

Deng, Francis Mading, 1972, *The Dinka of the Sudan.* CSCA. New York: Holt, Rinehart and Winston, Inc.

Dozier, Edward P., 1967, *Hano: A Tewa Indian Community in Arizona.* CSCA. New York: Holt, Rinehart and Winston, Inc.

Eggan, Dorothy, 1956, "Instruction and Affect in Hopi Cultural Continuity," *Southwestern Journal of Anthropology* 12:347–370.

Grindal, Bruce T., 1972, *Growing Up in Two Worlds: Education and Transition among the Sisala of Northern Ghana.* CSCA. New York: Holt, Rinehart and Winston, Inc.

Hart, C. W. M., 1963, "Contrasts Between Prepubertal and Postpubertal Education." In G. Spindler, ed., *Education and Culture.* Holt, Rinehart and Winston, Inc.

Henry, Jules, 1960, "A Cross-cultural Outline of Education," *Current Anthropology* 1, 267–305.

———, 1963, *Culture Against Man.* New York: Random House.

Hogbin, Ian, 1964, *A Guadalcanal Society: The Kaoka Speakers.* CSCA. New York: Holt, Rinehart and Winston, Inc.

Jocano, F. Landa, 1969, *Growing Up in a Philippine Barrio.* CSEC. New York: Holt, Rinehart and Winston, Inc.

Lessa, William A., 1966, *Ulithi: A Micronesian Design for Living.* CSCA. New York: Holt, Rinehart and Winston, Inc.

Mead, Margaret, 1949, *Coming of Age in Samoa.* New York: Mentor Books (first published in 1928).

———, 1953, *Growing Up in New Guinea.* New York: Mentor Books (first published in 1930).

———, 1964, *Continuities in Cultural Evolution.* New Haven: Yale University Press.

Peshkin, Alan, 1972, *Kanuri Schoolchildren: Education and Social Mobilization in Nigeria.* CSEC. New York: Holt, Rinehart and Winston, Inc.

Pettit, George A., 1946, *Primitive Education in North America.* Publications in American Archeology and Ethnology, vol. 43.

Pierce, Joe E., 1964, *Life in a Turkish Village.* CSCA. New York: Holt, Rinehart and Winston, Inc.

Read, Margaret, 1968, *Children of Their Fathers: Growing Up Among the Ngoni of Malawi.* CSEC. New York: Holt, Rinehart and Winston, Inc.

Schwartz, Gary, and Don Merten, 1968, "Social Identity and Expressive Symbols: The Meaning of an Initiation Ritual," *American Anthropologist* 70:1117–1131. Reprinted as Chapter 8 in this text.

Spindler, George D., and Louise S. Spindler, 1971, *Dreamers without Power: The Menomini Indians of Wisconsin.* CSCA. New York: Holt, Rinehart and Winston, Inc.

Spiro, Melford, 1958, *Children of the Kibbutz.* Cambridge, Mass.: Harvard University Press.

Van Gennep, Arnold, 1960, *The Rites of Passage.* Chicago: University of Chicago Press.

Whiting, Beatrice B., ed., 1963, *Child Rearing in Six Cultures.* New York: John Wiley & Sons, Inc.

Whiting, John F., R. Kluckhohn, and A. Albert, 1958, "The Function of Male Initiation Ceremonies at Puberty." In E. Maccoby, T. Newcomb, and E. Hartley, eds., *Readings in Social Psychology.* New York: Holt, Rinehart and Winston, Inc.

Williams, Thomas R., 1965, *The Dusun: A North Borneo Society.* CSCA. New York: Holt, Rinehart and Winston, Inc.

Young, Frank, 1965, *Initiation Ceremonies.* Indianapolis: The Bobbs-Merrill Company.

DOROTHY EGGAN

14 Instruction and Affect in Hopi Cultural Continuity*[1]

Education and anthropology have proved in recent years that each has much of interest to say to the other[2] for both are concerned with the transmission of cultural heritage from one generation to another—and with the means by which that transmission is accomplished. And although anthropology has tended to be preoccupied with the processes of cultural *change,* and the conditions under which it takes place, rather than with cultural continuity, it would seem, as Herskovits has said, that cultural change can be best understood when considered in relation to cultural stability (Herskovits 1950:20).

Both education and anthropology are concerned with learned behavior, and the opinion that early learning is of vital significance for the later development of personality, and that emotional factors are important in the learning process, while sometimes implicit rather than explicit, is often found in anthropological literature, particularly in that dealing with "socialization," "ethos" (Redfield 1953), and "values." From Mead's consistent work, for instance, has come a clearer picture of the socialization process in a wide variety of cultures, including our own, and she examines early "identification" as one of the problems central to all of them (Mead 1953). Hallowell, too, speaking of the learning situation in which an individual must acquire a personality pattern, points out that "there are important affective components involved" (Hallowell 1953:610), and elsewhere he emphasizes a "need for further investigation of relations between learning process and affective experience" (Hallowell 1955:251). Kluckholn, writing on values and value-orientation, says that "one of the severest limitations of the classical theory

*Reprinted from *Southwestern Journal of Anthropology* 12(4) 1956, 347–370, with permission.

[1] The substance of this paper was originally presented to the Society for Social Research of the University of Chicago in 1943, and subsequently enlarged in 1954 at the request of Edward Bruner for his class in Anthropology and Education. Discussion with him has greatly clarified my thinking on the problems examined here. Some elimination and revision has been made in order to include references to recently published work and suggestions from Fred Eggan, David Aberle, Clyde Kluckhohn, David Riesman, and Milton Singer. But intimate association with the Hopi over a period of seventeen years has given me this perception of the Hopi world.

[2] See, for example, Mead 1931:669–687; Mead 1943:663–639; Whiting and Child 1953; Spindler (ed.) 1955.

of learning is its neglect of attachments and attitudes in favor of reward and punishment (Kluckhohn 1951:430). And DuBois states explicitly that, "Institutions which may be invested with high emotional value because of patterns in child training are not ones which can be lightly legislated out of existence" (DuBois 1941:281).

In fact, increasing interaction between anthropology and psychiatry (which has long held as established the connection between emotion, learning, and resistance to change in individuals) has in the last decade introduced a theme into anthropology which reminds one of Sapir's statement that "the more fully one tries to understand a culture, the more it takes on the characteristics of a personality organization" (Sapir 1949:594).

Psychologists, while perhaps more cautious in their approach to these problems, since human emotional commitments—particularly as regards permanency—are difficult if not impossible to examine in the laboratory, emphasize their importance in the learning situation, and frequently express dissatisfaction with many existing methods and formulations in the psychology of personality. The shaping factors of emotion—learned as well as innate—are stressed by Asch (1952:29) in his *Social Psychology,* and focus particularly on man's "need to belong." He feels that the "psychology of man needs basic research and a fresh theoretical approach." Allport speaks of past "addiction to machines, rats, or infants" in experimental psychology, and hopes for a "design for personality and social psychology" which will become "better tempered to our subject matter" as we "cease borrowing false notes—whether squeaks, squeals, or squalls . . ." and "read the score of human personality more accurately" (Allport 1951:168–196). And Murphy, starting with the biological foundations of human learning, particularly the individual form this "energy system" immediately assumes, examines man as psychologically structured by early canalizations in which personality is rooted, to which are added an organized symbol system and deeply ingrained habits of perception, and suggests that the structure thus built is highly resistant to change. He says that, "The task of the psychology of personality today is to apply ruthlessly, and to the limit, every promising suggestion of today, but always with the spice of healthy skepticism," while recognizing "the fundamental limitations of the whole present system of conceptions . . ." as a preparation for "rebirth of knowledge" (1947:926–927).

Anthropologists as well as psychologists are aware that any hypotheses in an area so complex must be regarded as tenuous, but since the situations cannot be taken into the laboratory, there is some value in taking the laboratory to the situation. Progress in these amorphous areas can only come about, as Redfield has said, by the mental instrument which he has called a "controlled conversation" (Redfield 1955:148)—this discussion, then, must be considered a conversation between the writer and others who have brought varied interests and techniques to the problem of resistance to cultural change[3] (DuBois 1955). It begins logically with a recent paper on "Cultural Transmission and Cultural Change" in which Bruner discusses two surveys (SSRC, 1954:973–1002; Keesing 1953; Also Spiro 1955:1240–1251) of the literature on acculturation and adds to the hypotheses presented in them another which he finds relevant to the situation among the Mandan-Hidatsa Indians. As stated in his summary paragraph we find the proposition: "That which is learned and internalized in infancy and early childhood is most resistant to contact situations. The hypothesis directs our attention to the age in the individual life career at which each aspect of culture is transmitted, as well as to the full context of the learning situation and the position of the agents of socialization in the larger social system" (Bruner 1956a:197).

This proposition will be further extended by a consideration of the *emotional* commitment involved in the socialization process among the Hopi Indians; here the "conversation" will be directed to emotion in both teaching and learning, and will center around resistance to cultural change which has been remarkably consistent in Hopi society throughout recorded history *until the Second World War brought enforced and drastic changes.*[4] At that time the young men, although legitimately conscientious objectors, were drafted into the army. Leaving the isolation of the reservation where physical violence between adults was rare, they were rapidly introduced to the stark brutality of modern warfare. In army camps alcoholic intoxication, an experience which was the antithesis of the quiet, controlled behavior normally demanded of adult Hopi on their reservation, frequently brought relief from tension and a sense of comradeship with fellow soldiers. Deprived of the young men's work in the fields, many older people and young women were in turn forced to earn a living in railroad and munition centers off the reservation. Thus the gaps in the Hopi "communal walls" were, for the first time, large enough in numbers and long enough in time—and the experiences to which individuals had to adapt were revolutionary enough in character—so that the sturdy structure was damanged. It is emphasized, therefore, that in this discussion *Hopi* refers to those members of the tribe who had reached *adulthood* and were thoroughly committed to their own world view before 1941. Much of it would not apply as forcefully to the children of these people, and would be even less applicable to their grandchildren.

The major hypotheses suggested here, then, are:

1. That the Hopi, as contrasted with ourselves, were experts in the use of *affect* in their educational system, and that this element continued to oper-

[3] Of particular interest in this problem is this paper of DuBois' and the discussion following it. See also Dozier's (1954) analysis of the interaction between the Hopi-Tewa and Hopi; compare Dozier 1955.

[4] An evaluation of these changes has not been reported for the Hopi, although John Connelly is working on the problem; see Adair and Vogt 1949, and Vogt 1951, for discussions of Navajo and Zuñi reactions to the war and postwar situation.

ate throughout the entire life span of each individual as a *reconditioning* factor (Herskovits 1950:325–326, 491, 627); and

2. That this exercise of emotion in teaching and learning was an efficient means of social control which functioned in the absence of other forms of policing and restraint, and also in the maintenance of stability both in the personality structure of the individual and the structure of the society.

These hypotheses may be explored through a consideration of (a) the early and continued conditioning of the individual in the Hopi maternal extended family, which was on every level, an inculcation of *interdependence* as contrasted with our training for *independence;* and (b) an early and continuing emphasis on religious observances and beliefs (also emphasizing interdependence), the most important facet of which—for the purposes of this paper—was the central concept of the Hopi "good heart."[5]

If we examine the educational system by which a Hopi acquired the personal entity which made him so consistently and determinedly Hopi, we find that it was deliberate and systematic (Pettit 1946; Hough 1915:218). Students of Hopi are unanimous on this point but perhaps it can best be illustrated by quoting one of my informants who had spent much time away from the reservation, including many years in a boarding school, and who was considered by herself and other Hopi to be an extremely "acculturated" invididual. In 1938 when she made this statement she was about thirty years old and had brought her children back to the reservation to be "educated." Said she:

> It is very hard to know what to do. In the old days I might have had more babies for I should have married early. Probably some of them would have died. But my comfort would have been both in numbers and in knowing that all women lost babies. Now when I let my little son live on top [a conservative village on top of the mesa] with my mothers, I worry all the time. If he dies with dysentery I will feel like I killed him. Yet he *must* stay on top so the old people can teach him the *important* things. It is his only chance of becoming Hopi, for he would never be a *bahana* (white).

The education which she considered so vital included careful, deliberate instruction in kinship and community obligations, and in Hopi history as it is seen in mythology and as remembered by the old people during their own lifetimes. The Hopi taught youngsters fear as a means of personal and social control and for the purposes of personal and group protection; and they were taught techniques for the displacement of anxiety, as well as procedures which the adults believed would prolong life. Children were instructed in religious lore, in how to work and play, in sexual matters, even in how to deal

[5] The concept of the Hopi "good heart" as contrasted to a "bad heart," which is *Kahopi,* has been documented by every student of Hopi known to the writer, in references too numerous to mention, beginning with Stephen (written in the 1890s but published in 1940) and Hough in 1915. But the clearest understanding of this and other Hopi concepts may be had in Whorf 1941, especially pp. 30–32.

with a *bahana.* Good manners were emphasized, for they were a part of the controlled, orderly conduct necessary to a Hopi good heart.

Constantly one heard during work or play, running through all activity like a connecting thread: "Listen to the old people—they are wise"; or, "Our old uncles taught us that way—it is the *right* way." Around the communal bowl, in the kiva, everywhere this instruction went on; stories, dream adventures, and actual experiences such as journeys away from the reservation were told and retold. And children, in the warmth and security of this intimate extended family and clan group, with no intruding outside experiences to modify the impact until they were forced to go to an alien school, learned what it meant to be a good Hopi from a wide variety of determined teachers who had very definite—and *mutually consistent*—ideas of what a good Hopi is. And they learned all of this in the Hopi language, which, as Whorf has made so clear, has no words with which to express many of our concepts, but which, working together with "a different set of cultural and environmental influences . . . interacted with Hopi linguistic patterns to mould them, to be moulded again by them, and so little by little to shape the world outlook" (Whorf 1941:92).

Eventually these children disappeared into government schools for a time, and in the youth of most of these older Hopi it was a boarding school off the reservation where Indian children from various reservations were sent, often against their own and their parents' wishes.[6] Here white teachers were given the task of "civilizing" and "Christianizing" these wards of the government, but by that time a Hopi child's view of the world and his place in it was very strong. Moreover, trying to transpose our concepts into their language was often very nearly impossible for them, since only Hopi had been spoken at home. Examining Hopi memory of such a method of education we quote a male informant who said:

> I went to school about four years. . . . We worked like slaves for our meals and keep. . . . We didn't learn much. . . . I didn't understand and it was hard to learn. . . . At that time you do what you are told or you get punished. . . . You just wait till you can go home.

And a woman said:

> Policemen gathered us up like sheep. I was scared to death. My mother tried to hide me. I tried to stay away but the police always won. . . . Then we were sent up to Sherman [in California]. . . . It was far away; we were afraid on the train. . . . I didn't like it when I couldn't learn and neither did the teachers. . . . They never punished me, I always got 100 in Deportment. . . . I was there three years. . . . I was so glad to get home that I cried and cried . . . , glad to have Hopi food again, and fun again.

---

[6] See Simmons, 1942, pp. 88–89, for an excellent description of Don Talayesva of the government's use of force in the educational policy of this period; and pp. 134, 178, 199, and 225 for some of the results of this policy. Cf. Aberle 1951 for an analysis of Talayesva's school years and his later reidentification with his people.

As children, the Hopi usually solved this dilemma of enforced education by means of a surface accommodation to the situation until such time as they were able to return to their own meaningful world. For, as Park has said, man can "make his manners a cloak and his face a mask, behind which he is able to preserve . . . inner freedom . . . and independence of thought, even when unable to maintain independence of action."[7] In other words, because the inner core of Hopi identification was already so strong, these children were able to *stay* in a white world, while still *living* in the Hopi world within themselves.[8] And while for some there was a measure of temptation in many of the things learned in white schools so that they "became friendly with whites and accepted their gifts,"[9] the majority of these older Hopi acquired a white education simply as a "necessary accessory";[10] they incorporated parts of our material culture, and learned to deal with Whites astutely, but their values were largely unaffected.

If we now examine more closely the pattern of integration through which the Hopi erected a communcal wall[11] around their children we find in their kinship system the framework of the wall, but interwoven through it and contributing greatly to its strength was a never-ending composition which gave color and form, their religious ceremonies and beliefs.

Let us first contrast briefly the affect implicit in the way a Hopi born into this kinship system experienced relationships and the way in which Western children experience them. In the old days it was rare for a growing primary family to live outside the maternal residence. Normally each lived within it until the birth of several children crowded them out. And in this household each child was eagerly welcomed, for infant mortality was high and the clan was always in need of reinforcement. Thus, in spite of the physical burden on the biological mother, which she sometimes resented, the first strong *clan* sanction which we see in contrast to our own, was the absolute need for and desire for many children. From birth the young of the household were attended, pampered, and disciplined, although very mildly for the first several years, by a wide variety of relatives in addition to the mother. These attentions came both from the household members and from visitors in it. In no way was a baby ever as dependent upon his physical mother as are children in our culture. He was even given the breast of a mother's mother or sister if he cried for food in his mother's absence. True, a Hopi saying states that a

---

[7] Park 1950:361. Cf. Kluckhohn 1951:388–433, who points out that values continue to influence even when they do not function realistically as providers of immediate goal reactions.

[8] Cf. D. Eggan 1955, on the use of the Hopi myth in dreams as a means of "identification."

[9] Simmons 1942:88, and compare pp. 178, 180.

[10] Bruner 1956b:612, indicates that his Mandan-Hidatsa informants were quite conscious of this "lizard-like" quality of protective coloration in white contacts.

[11] Stephen, 1940a:18 says that the Hopi "describe their fundamental organization as a people" by "designating their principal religious ceremonies as the concentric walls of a house." The concept is extended here to include the entire wall of "Hopiness" which they have built around their children.

baby is made "sad" if another baby steals his milk, but it has been my experience that these women may risk making their own babies sad temporarily if another child needs food.

Weaning, of course, when discussed in personality contexts means more than a transition from milk to solid food. It is also a gradual process of achieving independence from the comfort of the mother's body and care, of transferring affection to other persons, and of finding satisfactions within oneself and in the outside world. Most people learn to eat solid food; many of us are never weaned, which has unfortunate consequences in a society where *individual* effort and independence are stressed. The Hopi child, on the other hand, from the day of his birth was being weaned from his biological mother. Many arms gave him comfort, many faces smiled at him, and from a very early age he was given bits of food which were chewed by various members of the family and placed in his mouth. So, for a Hopi, the outside world in which he needed to find satisfaction was never far away. He was not put in a room by himself and told to go to sleep; every room was crowded by sleepers of all ages. He was in no way *forced to find satisfactions within himself;* rather these were provided for him, if possible, by his household and clan group. His weaning, then, was from the breast only, and as he was being weaned from the biological mother, he was at the same time in a situation which *increased* his emotional orientation toward the intimate in-group of the extended family—which was consistent with the interests of Hopi social structure. Thus, considering weaning in its wider implications, a Hopi was never "weaned"; it was not intended that he should be. For these numerous caretakers contributed greatly to a small Hopi's faith in his intimate world—and conversely without question to a feeling of strangeness and *emotional insecurity* as adults in any world outside of this emotional sphere. The Hopi were often successful outside of the reservation, but they have shown a strong tendency to return frequently to the maternal household. Few ever left it permanently.

In addition to his extended family, while a Hopi belonged to one clan only, the clan into which he was born, he was a "child" of his father's clan, and this group took a lively interest in him. There were also numerous ceremonial and adoptive relationships which were close and warm, so that most of the persons in his familiar world had definite reciprocal relations with the child (Eggan 1950:Chap. II; Simmons 1942:Chaps. 3, 4). Since all of these "relatives" lived in his own small village, or in villages nearby, his emotional and physical "boundaries" coincided, were quite definitely delimited, and were explored and perceived at the same time. It cannot be too strongly emphasized that the kinship terms which a Hopi child learned in this intimate atmosphere were not mere verbalizations—as, for instance, where the term "cousin" among ourselves is sometimes applied to someone we have never seen and never will see. On the contrary, each term carried with it definite mutual responsibilities and patterns of behavior, and, through these, definite emotional interaction as well. These affects were taught as proper responses, together with the terms which applied to each individual, as he entered the child's life. This process was deliberately and patiently, but unceasingly, worked at by every older individual in the child's surroundings, so by the time a Hopi was grown kinship reaction patterns were so deeply ingrained in his thinking and feeling, and in his workaday life, that they were as much a part of him as sleeping and eating. He was not merely told that Hopi rules of behavior were right or wise; he lived them as he grew and *in his total environment* (Henry 1955) (as constrasted to our separation of teaching at home, in school, and in Sunday school) until he was simply not conscious that there was any other way to react. Note that I say *conscious!* The unconscious level of feeling, as seen in dreams and life-history materials, and in indirect behavior manifestations (jealousy and gossip), often presents quite a different picture. But while ambivalence toward specific persons among the Hopi—as with mankind everywhere—is a personal burden, the long reinforced conditioned reaction of *interdependence* on both the emotional and overt behavior level was highly uniform and persistent (See Whorf 1941:87, Aberle 1951:93–94, 119–123). Perhaps the strength of kinship conditioning toward interdependence which was conveyed in a large but intimate group, living in close physical contact, can be best illustrated by quoting from an informant:

> My younger sister——was born when I was about four or five, I guess. I used to watch my father's and mother's relatives fuss over her. She didn't look like much to me. I couldn't see why people wanted to go to so much trouble over a wrinkled little thing like that baby. I guess I didn't like babies as well as most girls did. . . . But I had to care for her pretty soon anyway. She got fat and was hard to carry around on my back, for I was pretty little myself. First I had to watch her and joggle the cradle board when she cried. She got too big and wiggled too much and then my mother said to me, "She is *your sister*—take her out in the plaza in your shawl."
>
> She made my back ache. Once I left her and ran off to play with the others for a while. I intended to go right back, but I didn't go so soon, I guess. Someone found her. I got punished for this. My mother's brother said: "You should not have a sister to help you out when you get older. What can a woman do without her sisters?[12] You are not one of us to leave your sister alone to die. If harm had come to her you would never have a clan, no relatives at all. No one would ever help you out or take care of you. Now you have another chance. You owe her more from now on. This is the worst thing that any of my sister's children has ever done. You are going to eat by yourself until you are fit to be one of us." That is what he said. That is the way he talked on and on and on. When meal time came they put a plate of food beside me and said, "Here is your food; eat your food," It was a long time they did this way. It seemed a long time before they looked at me. They were all sad and quiet. They put a pan beside me at meal time and said

[12] In a matrilineal household and clan, cooperation with one's "sisters" is a necessity for the maintenance of both the social structure and the communal unit.

> nothing—nothing at all, not even to scold me. My older sister carried——now, I didn't try to go near her. But I looked at my sisters and thought, "I need you—I will help you if you will help me." I would rather have been beaten or smoked. I was so ashamed all the time. Wherever I went people got sad [i.e., quiet]. After a while [in about ten days as her mother remembered it] they seemed to forget it and I ate with people again. During those awful days Tuvaye [a mother's sister] sometimes touched my head sadly, while I was being punished, I mean. Once or twice she gave me something to eat. But she didn't say much to me. Even she and my grandfather were ashamed and in sorrow over this awful thing I had done.
>
> Sometimes now I dream I leave my children alone in the fields and I wake up in a cold sweat. Sometimes I dream I am alone in a desert place with no water and no one to help me. Then I think of this punishment when I dream this way. It was the worst thing I ever did. It was the worst thing that ever happened to me. No one ever mentioned it to me afterward but——[older male sibling], the mean one. I would hang my head with shame. Finally my father told him sharply that he would be punished if he ever mentioned this to me again. I was about six when this happened, I think.

This informant was about forty when she related this incident, but she cried, even then, as she talked.

Nor was withdrawal of support the only means of punishment. There were bogey Kachinas who "might kidnap" bad children, and who visited the mesas sometimes when children were uncooperative; thus the "stranger" *joined effectively* with the clan in inducing the "ideal" Hopi behavior. But children *shared* this fear, as they also frequently shared other punishments. Dennis has called attention to the fact that a whole group of children often shared the punishment for the wrong-doing of one (Dennis 1941:263). This method may not endear an individual to his age-mates, but it does reinforce the central theme of Hopi belief that each person in the group is responsible for what happens to all, however angry or jealous one may feel toward siblings.

Before we examine the religious composition of the Hopi "communal walls," we might contrast more explicitly the emotional implications of early Hopi conditioning to those experienced in our society. From the day of *our* birth the training toward *independence*—as contrasted to *interdependence*—starts. We sleep alone; we are immediately and increasingly in a world of comparative strangers. A variety of nurses, doctors, relatives, sitters, and teachers march through our lives in a never-ending procession. A few become friends, but *compared with a Hopi child's experiences,* the impersonality and lack of emotional relatedness to so many kinds of people with such widely different backgrounds is startling. Indeed the disparity of the relationships as such is so great that continuity of emotional response is impossible, and so we learn to look for emotional satisfaction in change, which in itself becomes a value (Kluckhohn and Kluckhohn 1947:109). In addition, we grow up aware that there are many ways of life within the American class system; we know that there are many choices which we must make as to profession, behavior, moral code, even religion; and we know that the values of our parents' generation are not necessarily ours. If the permissive intimacy in the primary family in our society—from which both nature and circumstance demand a break in adulthood—is too strong, the individual cannot mature so that he can function efficiently in response to the always changing personalities in his life, and the always changing demands of the society (Riesman 1955; Mead 1948:518). He becomes a dependent neurotic "tentative between extreme polarities (Erikson 1948:198; Murphy 1947:714–733). But precisely because the permissive intimacy, as well as the punishing agencies, in a Hopi child's life were so far and so effectively extended in his formative years, he became *interdependent* with a larger but still definitely delimited group, and tended always to be more comfortable and effective within it. His self-value quickly identified itself with the larger Hopi value (Hallowell 1955:Chap. 4; Erikson 1948: 198n), and to the extent that he could continue throughout his life to identify with his group and function within it, he was secure in his place in the universe.

We have now sketched the situation which surrounded the young Hopi child in his first learning situations, and contrasted these with our own. For descriptive convenience this has been separated from religious instruction, but in the reality experience of the children—with the exception of formal initiation rites—no one facet of learning to be Hopi was separated from others. To understand the meaning his religion had for a Hopi one must first understand the harsh physical environment into which he was born. While it is agreed that it would not be possible to predict the character or the social structure of the Hopi from the circumstances of this physical environment,[13] it is self-evident that their organized social and ritual activities are largely a response to it. And such activities are at once a reflection of man's need to *be,* and his need to justify his existence to himself and others. If those who doubt that the forces of nature are powerful in shaping personality and culture were confined for one year on the Hopi reservation—even though their own economic dependence on "nature" would be negligible—they would still know by personal experience more convincing than scientific experiments the relentless pressure of the environment on their own reaction patterns. They would, for instance, stand, as all Hopis have forever stood, with aching eyes fastened on a blazing sky where thunderheads piled high in promise and were snatched away by "evil winds," and thus return to their homes knowing the tension, the acute bodily need for the "feel" of moisture. When rains do fall, there is the likelihood of a cloudburst which will ruin the fields. And there is a possibility of early frost which will destroy their crops, as well as the absolute certainty of sandstorms, rodents, and worms which will ruin

[13] Redfield 1955:31–32; cf. Titiev 1944:177–178; Whorf 1941:91; D. Eggan 1948 (first published in the *American Anthropologist* 1943, vol. 45); Thompson and Joseph 1944:133.

many plants. These things on a less abstract level than "feeling" resolved themselves into a positive threat of famine and thirst which every Hopi knew had repeatedly ravaged his tribe. It is possible that the effects of this silent battle between man and the elements left no mark on successive generations of individuals? It certainly was the reinforced concrete of Hopi social structure, since strongly conditioned interdependence was the only hope of survival.

Thus, the paramount problem for the Hopi was uncertain rain, and the outward expression of their deep need for divine aid was arranged in a cycle of ceremonies, the most impressive of which, at least among the exoteric rituals, were Kachina (Earle and Kennard 1938) dances. These were, for the observer, colorful pageants in which meticulously trained dancers performed from sunrise until sunset, with short intermissions for food and rest. Their bodies were ceremonially painted; brilliant costumes were worn, along with beautifully carved and painted masks which represented the particular gods who were taking part in the ceremony. The color, the singing and the drums which accompanied the dance, the graceful rhythm and intense concentration of the dancers, all combine into superb artistry which is an hypnotic and impressive form of prayer. Ideally, the Hopi preceded every important act with prayer, and with these older Hopi the ideal was apt to be fact. A bag of sacred cornmeal was part of their daily equipment.

In the religious context also, we must remember the intimate atmosphere which surrounded a Hopi child in the learning situation. Here children were taught that if *all* Hopi behaved properly—that is, if they kept good hearts—the Kachinas would send rain. It was easy for the children to believe this because from earliest babyhood these beautiful creatures had danced before them as they lolled comfortably in convenient laps. There was a happy, holiday atmosphere throughout a village on dance days, but while each dance was being performed, the quiet of profound reverence. Lying in the mother's lap, a baby's hands were often struck together in the rhythm of the dance; as soon as he would walk his feet were likewise directed in such rhythm, and everybody praised a child and laughed affectionately and encouragingly as it tried to dance. As the children grew older, carved likenesses of these gods, as well as other presents, were given to them by the gods themselves. And as he grew in understanding, a child could not fail to realize that these dancers were part of a religious ceremony which was of utmost importance in his world—that the dancers were rain-bringing and thus life-giving gods.

When first initiation revealed that the gods were in reality men who danced in their stead, a *reorganization* of these emotions which had been directed toward them began, and there is much evidence in autobiographical materials of resentment, if not actual trauma, at this point. For some of them the initiation was a physical ordeal, but for those who entered this phase (their education by way of Powamu there was no whipping, although all initiates witnessed the whipping of those who were initiated into the Kachina cult (F. Eggan 1950:47–50; Steward 1931:59ff.).[14] However, the physical ordeal seems to be less fixed in adult memories than disillusion.

In Don Talyesva's account of initiation into Kachina we find:

> I had a great surprise. They were not spirits, but human beings. I recognized nearly every one of them and felt very unhappy because I had been told all my life that the Kachinas were Gods. I was especially shocked and angry when I saw my uncles, fathers, and own clanbrothers dancing as Kachinas. . . . [But] my fathers and uncles showed me ancestral masks and explained that long ago the Kachinas had come regularly to Oraibi and danced in the plaza. They explained that since the people had become so wicked . . . the Kachinas had stopped coming and sent their spirits to enter the masks on dance days. . . . I thought of the flogging and the intitiation as a turning point in my life, and I felt ready at last to listen to my elders and live right (Simmons 1942:84–87).

One of our informants said in part:

> I cried and cried into my sheepskin that night, feeling I had been made a fool of. How could I ever watch the Kachinas dance again? I hated my parents and thought I could never believe the old folks again, wondering if gods had ever danced for the Hopi as they now said and if people really lived after death. I hated to see the other children fooled and felt mad when they said I was a big girl now and should act like one. But I was afraid to tell the others the truth for they might whip me to death. I know now it was best and the *only way to teach* children, but it took me a long time to know that. I hope my children won't feel like that.

This informant was initiated into Powamu and not whipped. She was about thirty when she made this statement to the writer.

Another woman, from a different mesa, speaking of her initiation into the Kachina society, said to me:

> The Kachinas brought us children presents. I was very little when I remember getting my first Kachina doll. I sat in my mother's lap and was "ashamed" [these people often use ashamed for shy or somewhat fearful], but she held out my hand for the doll. I grabbed it and hid in her lap for a long time because the Kachina looked too big to me and I was partly scared. But my mother told me to say "asqualie" [thank you] and I did. The music put me to sleep. I would wake up. The Kachinas would still be there. . . . I dreamed sometimes that the Kachinas were dancing and brought me lots of presents. . . .
>
> When I was initiated into Kachina society I was scared. I heard people whisper about it. . . . Children shook their heads and said it was hard to keep from crying. . . . My mother always put her shawl over my head when the Kachinas left the plaza. When she took it off they would be gone. So I knew they were gods and had

---

[14] The Powamu society is coordinate with the Kachina society and furnishes the "fathers" to the Kachinas on dance occasions. At first initiation parents may choose either of these societies for their children. It is reported that on First Mesa Powamu initiates were whipped, but my Powamu informants from both Second and Third Mesas were not whipped.

> gone back to the San Francisco mountains. . . . My ceremonial mother came for me when it was time to go to the kiva [for initiation] and she looked sad [i.e., serious]. She took most of the whipping on her own legs [a custom widely practiced among the Hopi]. But then I saw my father and my relatives were Kachinas. When they took their masks off this is what I saw. I was all mixed up. I was mad. I began to cry. I wondered how my father became a Kachina and if they [these men, including her father] would all go away when the Kachinas went back to the San Francisco mountains where the dead people live. Then when my father came home I cried again. I was mad at my parents and my ceremonial mother. "These people have made me silly," I said to myself, "and I thought they were supposed to like me so good." I said that to myself. But I was still crying, and the old people told me that only babies cry. They kept saying I would understand better when I got bigger. They said again that the Kachinas had to go away because the Hopi got bad hearts, and they [the Kachinas] couldn't stand quarreling, but they left their heads behind for the Hopis. I said why didn't they rot then like those skulls we found under that house? They said I was being bad and that I should have been whipped more. . . .
>
> When children asked me what happened in the kiva I was afraid to tell them because something would happen to me. Anyway I felt smart because I knew more than those *little* children. It took me a long time to get over this sadness, though. Later I saw that the Kachinas were the most *important thing in life* and that children can't understand these things. . . . It takes a while to see how wise the old people really are. You learn they are always right in the end.

Before we try to find our way with the Hopi to an "understanding of these things" we must examine their concept of the good heart which functions both in their kinship system and religion to maintain the effectiveness of the "wall of Hopiness." Of greatest significance in all activities among these people, and particularly in their religious ceremonies, is the fact that everything of importance is done communally. Thus each individual who has reached maturity is responsible *to* and *for* the whole community. The Hopi speak of this process as "uniting our hearts," which in itself is a form of prayer. A slight mistake in a ceremony can ruin it and thus defeat the community's prayer for rain; so too can a trace of "badness" in one's heart, although it may not be visible to the observer. Thus their religion teaches that *all* distress —from illness to crop failure—is the result of bad hearts, or possibly of witchcraft (here the simple "bad heart" must not be confused with a "Two-heart," *powaka,* witch), an extreme form of personal wickedness in which an individual sacrifices others, particularly his own relatives, to save himself (Titiev 1942; Aberle 1951:94).

This concept of a good heart in *conscious contradistinction* to a bad heart is of greatest importance not only in understanding Hopi philosophy but also in understanding their deep sense of cultural continuity and their resistance to fundamental change. A good heart is a positive thing, something which is never out of a Hopi's mind. It means a heart at peace with itself and one's fellows. There is no worry, unhappiness, envy, malice, nor any other disturbing emotion in a good heart. In this state, cooperation, whether in the extended household or in the fields and ceremonies, was selfless and easy. Unfortunately, such a conception of a good heart is also impossible of attainment. Yet if a Hopi did not keep a good heart he might fall ill and die, or the ceremonies—and thus the vital crops—might fail, for, as has been said, only those with good hearts were effective in prayer. Thus we see that the Hopi concept of a good heart included conformity to all rules of Hopi good conduct, both external and internal. To the extent that it was internalized—and all Hopi biographical material known to the writer suggests strongly that it was effectively internalized—it might reasonably be called a quite universal culturally patterned and culturally consistent Hopi "super-ego."[15]

There was, therefore, a constant probing of one's own heart, well illustrated by the anguished cry of a Hopi friend, "Dorothy, *did* my son die as the old folks said because my heart was not right? Do *you* believe this way, that if parents do not keep good hearts children will die?" And there was a constant examination of one's neighbors' hearts: "Movensie, it is those——— clan people who ruined this ceremony! They have bad hearts and they quarrel too much. That bad wind came up and now we will get no rain." Conversation among the Hopi is rarely censored, and the children heard both of these women's remarks, *feeling,* you may be sure, the *absolute belief* which these "teachers" had in the *danger* which a bad heart carries for everyone in the group.

In such situations, since human beings can bear only a certain amount of guilt,[16] there is a great game of blame-shifting among the Hopi, and this in turn adds a further burden of unconscious guilt, for it is difficult to love properly a neighbor or even a sister who has a bad heart. However, in the absence of political organization, civil and criminal laws, and a formal method of punishment for adults, this consistent "tribal super-ego" has maintained, throughout known history, a record almost devoid of crime and violence within the group,[17] and it has conditioned and ever *reconditioned* a Hopi to feel secure only in being a Hopi.

For through the great strength of the emotional orientation conveyed within the kinship framework and the interwoven religious beliefs, young Hopi learned their world from dedicated teachers whose emotions were involved in teaching what they believed intensely, and this in turn engaged the children's emotions in learning. These experiences early and increasingly

---

[15] See Piers and Singer 1953:6, where Dr. Piers defines "Super-Ego" as stemming from the internalization of the punishing, restrictive aspects of parental images, real or projected.

[16] See Dr. Piers' definition of guilt and shame (Piers and Singer 1953:5, 16). Hopi reactions are not classified here either in terms of guilt or of shame, since, as Singer points out (p. 52), an attempt to do so can confuse rather than clarify. In my opinion, both shame and guilt are operative in the Hopi "good heart," but it is suggested that the reader compare the material discussed here with the hypotheses in *Shame and Guilt,* particularly with Singer's conclusions in Chap. 5.

[17] Cf. Hallowell 1955, Chap. 4, on the positive role anxiety may play in a society.

made explicit in a very personal way the values implicit in the distinction between a good heart and a bad heart. For public opinion, if intensely felt and openly expressed in a closely knit and mutually dependent group—as in the case of the child who left her baby sister alone—can be more effective potential punishment than the electric chair. It is perhaps easier to die quickly than to live in loneliness in a small community in the face of contempt from one's fellows, and particularly from one's clan from whence, as we have seen, comes most of one's physical and emotional security. Small wonder that the children who experience this constant pressure to conform to clan dictates and needs, and at the same time this constant reinforcement of clan solidarity against outsiders, are reluctant as adults to stray too far from the clan's protective familiarity or to defy its wishes.

There was much bickering and tension within the clan and village, of course, and it was a source of constant uneasiness and ambivalence among the Hopi.[18] But tension and bickering, as I have indicated elsewhere, "are not exclusively Hopi"; the Hopi see it constantly among the whites on and off the reservation. What they do *not* find elsewhere is the *emotional satisfaction* of belonging intensely, to which they have been conditioned and reconditioned. For, as Murphy says, "It is not only the 'desire to be accepted' . . . that presses the ego into line. The basic psychology of perception is involved; the individual has learned to see himself as a member of the group, and the self has true 'membership character,' structurally integrated with the perception of group life" (Murphy 1947:855); Asch 1952:334–335, 605). Actually the Hopi clan, even with its in-group tensions and strife, but with all of the advantages emotional and physical it affords the individual, is one of the most successful and meaningful "boarding schools" ever devised for citizenship training.

In this situation, where belonging was so important, and a good heart so vital to the feeling of belonging, gossip is the potential and actual "social cancer" of the Hopi tribe. It is devastating to individual security and is often senselessly false and cruel, but in a country where cooperation was the only hope of survival, it was the *servant* as well as the policeman of the tribe. Not lightly would any Hopi voluntarily acquire the title Kahopi[19] "*not* Hopi," and therefore not good. Throughout the Hopi life span the word *kahopi,* KAHOPI was heard, until it penetrated to the very core of one's mind. It was said softly and gently at first to tiny offenders, through "Kahopi tiyo"

[18] In a short paper it is impossible to discuss both sides of this question adequately, but these tensions, and a Hopi's final acceptance of them, are discussed in D. Eggan 1948, particularly pp. 232–234. Cf. Thompson and Joseph 1944: Chap. 16, where Joseph speaks of fear born of the internally overdisciplined self in Hopi children, and its role both in adult discord and social integration. See also Thompson 1945, for hypotheses regarding the integration of ideal Hopi culture. Aberle (1951) discusses various tensions in Hopi society; see especially p. 94. All authors, however, call attention to the compensations as well as the burdens in Hopi society.

[19] See Brandt 1954. In his study of Hopi ethical concepts, *Kahopi* is discussed on p. 92.

or "Kahopi mana" to older children, still quietly but with stern intent, until the word sometimes assumed a crescendo of feeling as a whole clan or even a whole community might condemn an individual as *Kahopi.*

It it true that we, too, are told we should keep good hearts and love our neighbors as ourselves. But we are not told that, if we do not, our babies will die, *now, this year!* Some children are told that if they do not obey the various "commandments" they learn in different churches they will eventually burn in a lake of hell fire, but they usually know that many of their world doubt this. In contrast, Hopi children constantly *saw* babies die because a parent's heart was not right; they *saw* evil winds come up and crops fail for the same reason; they *saw* adults sicken and die because of bad thoughts or witchcraft (to which bad thoughts rendered a person more vulnerable). Thus they learned to *fear* the results of a bad heart whether it belonged to themselves or to others. There were witches, bogey Kachinas, and in objective reality famine and thirst to fear. Along with these fears were taught mechanisms for the displacement of anxiety, including the services of medicine men, confession and exorcism to get rid of bad thoughts, and cooperative nonaggression with one's fellows, even those who were known to be witches. But the best technique was that which included all the values in the positive process of keeping a good heart, and of "uniting our hearts" in family, clan, and fraternal society—in short, the best protection was to be *Hopi* rather than *Kahopi.*

It is clear throughout the literature on the Hopi, as well as from the quotations given in this discussion, that in finding their way toward the goal of "belonging," Hopi children at first initiation had to deal with religious disenchantment, resentment, and with ever-increasing demands made by their elders for more mature behavior. These factors were undoubtedly important catalyzing agents in Hopi personality formation and should be examined from the standpoint of Benedict's formulations on discontinuity (Benedict 1948:423–424). Here we must remember that shock can operate either to destroy or to mobilize an organism's dormant potentialities. And if a child has been *consistently* conditioned to feel a part of his intimate world, and providing he still lives on in this same world; it seems reasonable to suppose that shock (unless it were so great as to completely disorganize personality, in which case the custom could not have persisted) would reinforce the individual's *need* to belong and thus would tend to reassemble many of his personality resources around this need.

If the world surrounding the Hopi child had changed from warmth to coldness, from all pleasure to all hardship, the discontinuity would have indeed been insupportable. But the new demands made on him, while more insistent, were not unfamiliar in *kind;* all adults, as well as his newly initiated age-mates, faced the same ones. He had shared the shock as he had long since learned to share all else; and he now shared the rewards of "feeling big." He had the satisfaction of increased status along with the burden of increasing responsibility, as the adults continued to teach him "the important things," and conformity gradually became a value in itself—even as we value nonconformity and change. It was both the means *and* the goal. Conformity surrounded the Hopi—child or adult—with everything he could hope to have or to be; outside if there was only the feeling tone of rejection. Since there were no bewildering choices presented (as is the case in our socialization process), the "maturation drive"[20] could only function to produce an ego-ideal in accord with the cultural ideal,[21] however wide the discrepancy between ideal and reality on both levels.

And since the Kachinas played such a vital role in Hopi society throughout, we must consider specifically the way in which the altered faith expressed by informants gradually came about after the first initiation (Aberle 1951: 38–41). First, of course, was the need to find it, since in any environment one must have faith and hope. They also wanted to continue to believe in and to enjoy that which from earliest memory had induced a feeling of pleasure, excitement, and of solidarity within the group. A beginning was undoubtedly made in modifying resentment when the Kachinas whipped each other after first initiation; first, it was again sharing punishment, but this time not only with children but *with adults.* They had long known that suffering came from bad hearts implied by disobedience to the rules of Hopi good conduct and then whipped each other for the same reason; thus there was logic in an initiation which was actually an extension of an already established conception of masked gods who rewarded good behavior with presents but withheld rain if hearts were not right, and who sometimes threatened bad children (Goldfrank 1945:516–539).

Another reorganizing factor explicitly stated in the quotations was "feeling big." They had shared pain with adults, had learned secrets which forever separated them from the world of children, and they were now included in situations from which they had previously been excluded, as their elders continued to teach intensely what they believed intensely: that for them there was only one alternative—Hopi as against Kahopi.

Consistent repetition is a powerful conditioning agent and, as the youngsters watched each initiation, they relived their own, and by again sharing the experience gradually worked out much of the bitter residue from their own memories of it, while also rationalizing and weaving the group emotions ever stronger into their own emotional core—"It takes a while to see how wise the old people really are." An initiated boy, in participating in the Kachina dances, learned to identify again with the Kachinas whom he now impersonated. To put on a mask is to "become a Kachina," and to cooperate actively

[20] See Piers (in Piers and Singer 1953;15) for a discussion of the maturation drive.

[21] Erikson 1948:198, fn.: "The child derives a vitalizing sense of reality from the awareness that his individual way of mastering experience (his ego-synthesis) is a successful variant of a group identity and is in accord with its space-time and life plan."

in bringing about the major goals of Hopi life. And a girl came to know more fully the importance of her clan in its supportive role. These experiences were even more sharply conditioned and directed toward adult life in the tribal initiation ceremonies, of which we have as yet only fragmentary knowledge. Of this one man said to me: "I will not discuss this thing with you only to say that no one can forget it. It is the most wonderful thing any man can have to remember. You know then that you are Hopi. It is one thing whites cannot have, cannot take from us. It is our way of life given to us when the world began."

And since children are, for all mankind, a restatement of one's hopes to be, when these Hopi in turn become teachers (and in a sense they had always been teachers of the younger children in the household from an early age), they continued the process of reliving and rationalizing, or "working out" their experiences with an intensity which is rarely known in our society except, perhaps, on the psychoanalytic couch. But the Hopi had no psychiatrists to guide them—no books which, as Riesman says, "like an invisible monitor, helps liberate the reader from his group and its emotions, and allows the contemplation of alternative responses and the trying on of new emotions" (Riesman 1955:13). They had only the internalized "feeling measure" and "group measure" explicit in the concepts of Hopi versus Kahopi.

On the material level, the obvious advantages of, for instance, wagons versus backs were a temptation. And to the extent to which white influences at first penetrated to these older Hopi it was through this form of temptation. But outside experiences usually included some variation of hostility, scorn, or aggression, as well as a radically different moral code, and these were all viewed and reinterpreted through the Hopi-eye view of the world and in the Hopi language, so that a return to the familiarity of the Hopi world with its solidarity of world view and behavior patterns *was experienced as relief,* and increased the need to feel Hopi, *however, great a burden "being Hopi"* implied.

In summary, the hypothesis here developed, that strong emotional conditioning during the learning process was an instrument in cultural continuity among the Hopi, is suggested as supplementary to that of early learning as being resistant to change. It further suggests that this conditioning was *constantly* as well as *consistently* instilled during the entire lifetime of an individual by a circular pattern of integration. For an individual was surrounded by a series of invisible, but none the less solid, barriers between himself and the outside world. To change him, influences had to breach the concentric walls of social process—as conveyed through the human entities which surrounded him and which were strengthened by his obligation to teach others—and then to recondition his early and ever-increasing emotional involvement in Hopi religion, morals, and mutually dependent lineage and clan groups, as well as those attitudes toward white aggression which he shared with all Indians.

In 1938 one old Hopi, who in his youth had been taken away from his wife and children and kept in a boarding school for several years said to me:

> I am full of curiosity; a great *bahana* [white] education would tell me many things I've wondered about like the stars and how a man's insides work. But I am afraid of it because I've seen what it does to folks. . . . If I raise a family, clothe and feed them well, do my ceremonial duties faithfully, I have succeeded—what do you call success? . . . [And again, while discussing fear in connection with a dream, his comment was] Well, yes, we are afraid of *powakas* [witches] but our medicine men can handle them. Neither your doctors nor your gods can control your governments so you have more to fear. Now you are dragging us into your quarrels. I pity you and I don't envy you. You have more goods than we have, but you don't have peace ever; *it is better to die in famine than in war.*

As the old man anticipated, enforced participation in modern warfare soon replaced instruction for Hopi citizenship, and the concentric walls were finally seriously breached. But for these older Hopi the walls still enclose "our way of life given to us when the world began."

References

Aberle, David F., 1951, *The Psychosocial Analysis of a Hopi Life-History.* Comparative Psychology Monographs 21:1–133. Berkeley and Los Angeles: University of California Press.

Adair, John, and Evon Z. Vogt, 1949, "Navaho and Zuni Veterans: A Study of Contrasting Modes of Culture Change," *American Anthropologist* 51:547–561.

Allport, Gordon W., 1951, "The Personality Trait." In Melvin H. Marx, ed., *Psychological Theory: Contemporary Readings.* New York: The Macmillan Company, pp. 503–507.

Asch, Solomon E., 1952, *Social Psychology.* Englewood Cliffs, N.J.: Prentice-Hall, Inc.

Benedict, Ruth, 1948, "Continuities and Discontinuities in Cultural Conditioning." In Clyde Kluckhohn and Henry A. Murray, eds., *Personality in Nature, Society, and Culture.* New York: Alfred A. Knopf, Inc., pp. 414–423.

Brandt, Richard B., 1954, *Hopi Ethics: A Theoretical Analysis.* Chicago: The University of Chicago Press.

Bruner, Edward M., 1956a, "Cultural Transmission and Cultural Change," *Southwestern Journal of Anthropology* 12:191–199.

———, 1956b, "Primary Group Experience and the Process of Acculturation," *American Anthropologist* 58:605–623.

Dennis, Wayne, 1941, "The Socialization of the Hopi Child." In Leslie Spier, A. Irving Hallowell, and Stanley S. Newman, eds., *Language, Culture, and Personality: Essays in Memory of Edward Sapir.* Menasha, Wis.: Sapir Memorial Publication Fund, pp. 259–271.

Dozier, Edward P., 1954, "The Hopi-Tewa of Arizona, *University of California Publications in American Archaeology and Ethnology* 44:259–376. Berkeley and Los Angeles, Calif.: University of California Press.

———, 1955, "Forced and Permissive Acculturation," *American Anthropologist* 56:973–1002.

DuBois, Cora, 1941, "Attitudes toward Food and Hunger in Alor." In Leslie Spier, A. Irving Hallowell, and Stanley S. Newman, eds., *Language, Culture, and Personality: Essays in Memory of Edward Sapir.* Menasha, Wis.: Sapir Memorial Publication Fund, pp. 272–281.

———, 1955, "Some Notions on Learning Intercultural Understanding." In George D. Spindler, ed., *Education and Anthropology.* Stanford, Calif.: Stanford University Press, pp. 89–126.

Earle, Edwin, and Edward A. Kennard, 1938, *Hopi Kachinas.* New York: J. J. Augustin, Publisher.

Eggan, Dorothy, 1948, "The General Problem of Hopi Adjustment." In Clyde Kluckhohn and Henry A. Murray, eds., *Personality in Nature, Society, and Culture.* New York: Alfred A. Knopf, Inc., pp. 220–235.

———, 1955, "The Personal Use of Myth in Dreams." In "Myth: A Symposium," *Journal of American Folklore* 68:445–453.

Eggan, Fred, 1950, *Social Organization of the Western Pueblos.* Chicago: The University of Chicago Press.

Erikson, Erik Homburger, 1948, "Childhood and Tradition in Two American Indian Tribes, with Some Reflections on the Contemporary American Scene." In Clyde Kluckhohn and Henry A. Murray, eds., *Personality in Nature, Society, and Culture.* New York: Alfred A. Knopf, Inc., pp. 176–203.

Goldfrank, Esther, 1945, "Socialization, Personality, and the Structure of Pueblo Society," *American Anthropologist* 47:516–539.

Hallowell, A. Irving, 1953, "Culture, Personality, and Society." In A. Kroeber, et al., *Anthropology Today: An Encyclopedic Inventory.* Chicago: The University of Chicago Press, pp. 597–620.

———, 1955, *Culture and Experience.* Philadelphia: University of Pennsylvania Press.

Henry, Jules, 1955, "Culture, Education, and Communications Theory." In George D. Spindler, ed., *Education and Anthropology.* Stanford, Calif.: Stanford University Press, pp. 188–215.

Herskovits, Melville J., 1950, *Man and His Works: The Science of Cultural Anthropology.* New York: Alfred A. Knopf, Inc.

Hough, Walter, 1915, *The Hopi Indians.* Cedar Rapids, Iowa: The Torch Press.

Keesing, Felix M., 1953, *Culture Change: An Analysis and Bibliography of Anthropological Sources to 1952,* Stanford, Calif.: Stanford University Press.

Kluckhohn, Clyde, 1951, "Values and Value-Orientations in the Theory of Action: An Exploration in Definition and Classification." In Talcott Parsons and Edward A. Shils, eds., *Toward a General Theory of Action.* Cambridge, Mass.: Harvard University Press, pp. 388–433.

———, and Florence R. Kluckhohn, 1947, "American Culture: Generalized Orientations and Class Patterns." In *Conflicts of Power in Modern Culture,* 1947 Symposium of Conference in Science, Philosophy, and Religion, Chap. 9.

Mead, Margaret, 1931, "The Primitive Child." In *A Handbook of Child Psychology.* Worcester, Mass.: Clark University Press, pp. 669–687.

———, 1943, "Our Education Emphases in Primitive Perspective," *American Journal of Sociology* 48:633–639.

———, 1948, "Social Change and Cultural Surrogates." In Clyde Kluckhohn and Henry A. Murray, eds., *Personality in Nature, Society, and Culture.* New York: Alfred A. Knopf, Inc., pp. 511–522.

———, 1953, *Growing Up in New Guinea.* New York: The New American Library. A Mentor Book (First published in 1930, by William Morrow & Company, Inc.)

Murphy, Gardner, 1947, *Personality: A Biosocial Approach to Origins and Structure.* New York: Harper & Row.

Park, Robert Ezra, 1950, *Race and Culture.* New York: The Free Press.

Pettit, George A., 1946, "Primitive Education in North America," *University of California Publications in American Archaeology and Ethnology* 43:1–182. Berkeley and Los Angeles: University of California Press.

Piers, Gerhart, and Milton B. Singer, 1953, *Shame and Guilt: A Psychoanalytic and a Cultural Study.* Springfield, Ill.: Charles C Thomas, Publishers.

Redfield, Robert, 1953, *The Primitive World and Its Transformations.* Ithaca, N.Y.: Cornell University Press.

———, 1955, *The Little Community: Viewpoints for the Study of a Human Whole.* Chicago: The University of Chicago Press.

Riesman, David, 1955, "The Oral Tradition, The Written Word, and the Screen Image," Founders Day Lecture, no. 1, Antioch College, October 5, 1955.

Riesman, David, in collaboration with Reuel Denney and Nathan Glazer, 1950, *The Lonely Crowd: A Study of the Changing American Character.* New Haven, Conn.: Yale University Press.

Sapir, Edward, 1949, "The Emergence of the Concept of Personality in a Study of Cultures." In David G. Mandelbaum, ed., *Selected Writings of Edward Sapir in Language, Culture, and Personality.* Berkeley and Los Angeles, Calif.: University of California Press, pp. 590–597.

Simmons, Leo W., 1942, *Sun Chief: The Autobiography of a Hopi Indian.* Published for The Institute of Human Relations by Yale University Press, New Haven, Conn.

[SSRC] Social Science Research Council Summer Seminar on Acculturation, 1954, "Acculturation: an Exploratory Formulation," *American Anthropologist* 56:973–1002.

Spindler, George D., ed., 1955, *Education and Anthropology.* Stanford, Calif.: Stanford University Press.

Spiro, Melford E., 1955, "The Acculturation of American Ethnic Groups," *American Anthropologist* 57:1240–1252.

Stephen, Alexander MacGregor, 1940, *Hopi Indians of Arizona.* Southwest Museum Leaflets, no. 14. Highland Park, Los Angeles, Calif.: Southwest Museum.

Steward, Julian H., 1931, "Notes on Hopi Ceremonies in Their Initiatory Form in 1927–1928," *American Anthropologist* 33:56–79.

Thompson, Laura, 1945, "Logico-Aesthetic Integration in Hopi Culture," *American Anthropologist* 47:540–553.

Thompson, Laura, and Alice Joseph, 1944, *The Hopi Way.* Indian Education Research Series, no. 1. Lawrence, Kan.: Haskell Institute.

Titiev, Mischa, 1942, "Notes on Hopi Witchcraft." *Papers of the Michigan Academy of Science, Arts, and Letters* 28:549–557.

———, 1944, *Old Oraibi: A Study of the Hopi Indians of Third Mesa.* Papers of the Peabody Museum of American Archaeology and Ethnology, Harvard University, vol. 22, no. 1.

Vogt, Evon Z., 1951, *Navaho Veterans: A Study of Changing Values.* Papers of the Peabody Museum of American Archaeology and Ethnology, Harvard University, vol. 41, no. 1.

Whiting, John W. M., and Irvin L. Child, 1953, *Child Training and Personality: A Cross-Cultural Study.* New Haven, Conn.: Yale University Press.

Whorf, B. L., 1941, "The Relation of Habitual Thought and Behavior to Language." In Leslie Spier, A. Irving Hallowell, and Stanley S. Newman, eds., *Language, Culture, and Personality: Essays in Memory of Edward Sapir.* Menasha, Wis.: Sapir Memorial Publication Fund, pp. 75–93.

PETER S. SINDELL/*McGill University*

15 *Some Discontinuities in the Enculturation of Mistassini Cree Children**

The establishment of Western schools, especially boarding schools, and curricula in non-Western societies is likely to constitute an extreme type of cultural discontinuity and may do much to force "either-or" choices on their learners (DuBois 1955:102).

Some of the discontinuities which five- or six-year-old Mistassini children experience when they first attend the residential school at La Tuque will be described in this chapter. The world in which these children live before starting school is almost wholly Cree in character. The language spoken at home is Cree, and preschool children have little direct interaction with Euro-Canadians, or "whites." For the small Cree child the most striking figure in the white world is probably the *wabinkiyu,* a form of bogeyman who is thought of as white. When children misbehave parents frequently tell their children that the wabinkiyu is going to take them away.

In the preschool period the children have clear-cut traditional models for identification: parents, grandparents, elder siblings, and other close kin. Most of these kinsmen display behavior and attitudes which conform to traditional Cree values and role expectations.[1] In addition, these kinsmen reward their children, implicitly and explicitly, for conformity to traditional norms.

When the children enter school they must act according to norms which

---

*Printed with permission of the Director of the Canadian Research Center for Anthropology. The author of this paper is a Ph.D. candidate in the Department of Anthropology, Stanford University, Stanford, California, and has been associated with the McGill-Cree Project as a research assistant since July 1966. The research reported on this paper has been supported by the U.S. National Institute of Mental Health grant number MH 13076-01, which is attached to the author's NIMH Pre-Doctoral Fellowship, number 5-F1-MH-24,080-04. This support and the assistance provided by the staff of the McGill-Cree Project are gratefully acknowledged. The author would also like to express his deep appreciation to the Rev. J. E. DeWolf and Mrs. Cynthia Clinton, respectively principal and senior teacher of the LaTuque Indian Residential School.

[1] This is changing now to a certain extent since some of the older children, who have been to school for many years, act in ways which are not traditional. Therefore, they provide their younger siblings with other models for emulation and identification.

contradict a great deal of what they have learned before, master a body of knowledge completely foreign to them, and communicate in an incomprehensible language in a strange environment.

In this chapter I shall discuss self-reliance and dependence, the character of interpersonal relations, cooperation and competition, the expression and inhibition of aggression, and role expectations for children. For each topic the traditional milieu and the first year in the school environment will be compared and contrasted.[2]

As the children attend school, they form ties with their teachers and counselors and learn more about Euro-Canadian culture. Eventually, older students face situations different from those they faced as small children. Upon reaching adolescence, most students experience a conflict in identity which reflects the cultural discontinuities they experience in school, and in alternating between the urban residential school in winter and the trading post during the summer.

The data upon which the following discussion is based were gathered during fieldwork at Mistassini Post and at the La Tuque Indian Residential School from July 1966, to September 1967.[2] The school is operated by the Anglican Church of Canada for the Indian Affairs Branch. It is located in La Tuque, P.Q., which is 180 miles northeast of Montreal and 300 miles south of Mistassini Post by road. Most Mistassini Cree children between the ages of six and sixteen attend the residential school for ten months of each year while their parents go into the bush to hunt and trap. Other children from Mistassini attend the day school at the Post or attend high school in Sault Ste. Marie, Ontario, while living with white families. Only since 1963, when the La Tuque school opened, have the majority of Mistassini children attended school on a regular basis.

In studying the children, interviews were conducted with the children, their parents, teacher, and counselors before, during, and after school. In addition, a series of behavior-rating forms was utilized with the counselors and teacher and hypotheses about the role of imitation and modeling in acculturation were tested in an experiment. Finally, observational protocols were collected on the children's behavior at the Post and in school. The theoretical framework utilized in the study is that of social learning theory as developed by Bandura and Walters (1963). This theory stresses the im-

[2] This chapter was written while the author was in the field, therefore many aspects of the shift from the traditional context to the school environment are not dealt with here. Furthermore, many of the ideas expressed must be considered preliminary until further analysis of the data is completed. The usual biographical apparatus is also attenuated for this reason.

I would like to state that my understanding of Cree culture and enculturation has been greatly enriched by reading the works of A. Irving Hallowell on the Ojibwa, George and Louise Spindler on the Menomini, and Edward and Jean Rogers on the Mistassini. The works of Albert Bandura in the field of social learning theory have also influenced my thinking considerably.

portance of such concepts as modeling, imitation, and social reinforcement in the analysis of behavioral and attitudinal change.

The study of the thirteen children who entered school for the first time in September 1966 is that of the first generation of people who will receive extensive formal education. Many of the cultural conflicts discussed below adumbrate those which the children will face as adolescents and adults when they attempt to adapt changing economic and social conditions in the Waswanipi-Mistassini region.

Self-reliance and Dependence

Before Cree children enter school they experience few limits on their behavior. As infants they are fed on demand. When they grow older they eat when they feel hungry and are free to choose from whatever food is available. Usually something—bannock, dried fish, or dried meat—is readily available. Sleeping too is not rigidly scheduled; and the children simply go to sleep when they are tired.

Further, children are free to explore their natural surroundings, either alone or with siblings or playmates. There are no demarcated territorial boundaries which limit their wanderings at the Post. The number of children in any particular hunting group varies, and therefore, a child may spend much or all of the winter without playmates from his own age group. As a result, children learn to depend upon themselves for amusement. They learn to utilize whatever is available—an old tin stove, a few soft drink bottles, a dead bird, sticks, or stones. Anything the child can reach is a legitimate object for play. If the object is dangerous, parents divert the child's attention or take the object away, but do not reprimand the child. For instance, two- or three-year-old children often handle or play with axes. In general, the only limits placed on a child's behavior relate to specific environmental dangers, for example, children are not allowed go out in boats alone.

Whereas at home the children have experienced few limits on their freedom of action, at school there are many. In order to cope with the large number of children (277 at the time the study was made), the school requires them to conform to many routines. They must eat three times a day at specified hours, must wake up and go to sleep at set times, and must learn to obey many other seemingly arbitrary rules. For example, children are not allowed in the front foyer of the dormitory and are not allowed to use the front stairway. Their environment is circumscribed also by the boundary of the school yard. Occasionally the children leave the school property but only in the company of an adult.

The child is dependent upon others to satisfy almost all of his needs. He must depend on the counselor in his living group ("wing") for clean clothes, soap, toothpaste, and even toilet paper when it runs out. Furthermore, he must line up to receive these supplies at the counselor's convenience. Practically the first English phrase which every child learns is "line up!"

The school, then, reinforces the children into submissive, nonexploratory behavioral patterns. These contravene their previous experiences, which led to self-reliant and exploratory behaviors highly adaptive for life in the bush.

Interpersonal Relations

After a child is weaned he is cared for not only by his mother but increasingly by a wide range of other kin, such as older siblings, young uncles and aunts, and grandparents. Consequently, each child forms close ties with several kinsmen. Fairly frequent shifts in residence and in hunting group composition, early death, and the Cree patterns of adoption, mitigate against the development of extreme dependency on only one or two members of the nuclear family. In fact, it seems likely that some frustration of dependency needs results from the disruption of social relationships noted above. Parents and children interact primarily within networks of close kin. Thus, before they go to school, children gain little experience in interacting with people with whom they do not have close affective ties.

As children enter the school at La Tuque, they interact primarily in the context of large groups: the school class, the wings, and the age groups—Junior Girls (age six to eight) and Junior Boys (age six to ten). The children sleep in rooms with siblings of the same sex, but due to differing schedules on most days they see them only at meals and early in the morning. Since practically all activities are segregated by sex, brothers and sisters have few opportunities to talk to each other. Thus, children's social ties begin to shift from warm affective relations with a small multigenerational kin group comprised of both sexes to shallow contacts with a large peer group of the same sex. Preston notes the implications of this shift for the internalization of social controls (1966:6).

While their peer group expands, the number of adults with whom the children interact shrinks. Each beginning pupil is cared for by only two or three adults: teacher, wing counselor, and Junior counselor. Since each wing counselor is also responsible for an age group, one of the wing counselors is the Junior counselor.

With a large number of children competing for a single adult's attention in any given situation, the children learn to beg for nurturance which they could take for granted at home. Dependent behavior, such as crying and yelling, is reinforced as the children discover its effectiveness in eliciting a response from the adult. At home self-reliance and independence are valued and, therefore, crying is ignored from an early age and children learn not to cry. Children learn in school that the smallest scratch will elicit a great deal of concern because the counselors fear that impetigo will develop. Thus, their early training in silently enduring pain is also contradicted.

In summary, the children openly express far more dependence in school than at home, and this dependence is focused on two or three adults rather than upon a multigenerational kin group. At home the children have supportive relationships but these do not involve a high level of overt expression of dependence (see Spindler 1963:384). Furthermore, the children interact with others far more than they did at home and come to need a high degree of social stimulation.

Cooperation and Competition

Most of the tasks which a child performs at home are done cooperatively and contribute to the welfare of the whole group, usually a nuclear or extended family. Children perform these tasks with siblings, parents or other kin. Cooperation in hunting and in household chores is extremely adaptive since it makes the most efficient use of the group's limited labor resources. Sharing food as well as labor is of major importance in traditional Cree culture. Religious values reinforce this since *"mistapeo,"* the soul spirit, "is pleased with generosity, kindness and help to others" (Speck 1935:44).

Children observe this extensive sharing and cooperation within the kin group and participate directly in it. For example, during the summer, young children often are used to carry gifts of fish, bannock, fowl, and so on, between kin. Observations indicate that the children themselves usually share food and toys readily.

Competition rather than cooperation is the keynote of school life. In class the students are encouraged to compete with each other in answering questions, and those who answer most promptly and correctly gain the teacher's attention and win her approval. Both in school and in the dormitory the children must constantly compete for places in line. Those who are first in line get their food or clothing first or get outside to play soonest. Also, because the dormitory is understaffed, each child must compete with many others to ensure that the counselor attends to his individual needs.

Although the teacher finds it difficult to stimulate many children to respond competitively in class, many older children learn to compete aggressively for food and refuse to share their belongings.

Expression and Inhibition of Aggression

Inhibiting the overt expression of aggression is highly valued in Cree culture and serves to maintain positive affective ties among kinsmen, particularly within the hunting-trapping group. Aggression is defined broadly by the Cree and includes not only fighting but also directly contradicting someone else, refusing a direct request, and raising one's voice inappropriately. (These statements apply particularly to relations between kinsmen.) These forms of behavior are unacceptable except if one is drunk and, thus, considered not responsible for his actions. Fighting when drunk is common and appears to arouse anxiety in children observing this. Laughing at people's mistakes or foibles is not usually defined as aggressive behavior. Gossip, teasing, and the threat of witchcraft are covert means of expressing aggression which are prevalent among the Cree. During enculturation fighting and quarreling are punished.

Punishment seems to be infrequent and usually consists of teasing, ridicule, threats of corporal punishment or reprisals by wabinkiyu, and, occasionally, yelling. But corporal punishment is rare and most often is limited to a light slap with an open hand on top of the head or just above the ear.

In contrast to what they have been taught at home, in school, the children learn to express aggression openly. Counselors and teachers disapprove greatly of the children's constant "tattle taling," which serves to express aggression covertly. On the other hand, overtired and frustrated with the demands of controlling large numbers of children, the adults in the school often yell at the children, speak to them sternly, and, occasionally, swat them. Television and observation of white children are other sources of models for openly aggressive behavior. It is apparent from observing the children that these television models, such as Batman and Tarzan, are very important. Mistassini children also learn to express aggression openly because they are forced to defend themselves against some of the more aggressive children from Dore Lake.

Role Expectations for Children

Cree children learn very early in life the basic components of adult roles through observing their parents and elder siblings. As soon as a child is able to walk he is given small tasks to perform such as carrying a little water or a few pieces of wood. If he does not perform these tasks the child is not punished because Cree parents think he is not old enough to "understand" yet. When the child walks out of the tent for the first time on his own, the "Infants' Rite" is held.

> The essence of the baby's rite is the symbolization of the child's future role as an adult. A boy "kills," brings the kill to camp, and distributes the meat; a girl carries in firewood and boughs. (Rogers and Rogers 1963:20)

All but one of the thirteen children in the sample participated in this rite.

At about five or six years of age children begin to perform chores regularly and are punished if they do not obey. Among their new chores are caring for smaller siblings and washing dishes; in addition, they begin to carry significant quantities of wood, water, and boughs. Children also begin to contribute food to the family at this age. They pick berries, snare rabbits, hunt birds, and sometimes accompany their parents into the bush to check traps or to get wood, water, or boughs. At approximately the same time as the child begins playing a more responsible role in performing tasks, the parents believe that his ability to conceptualize develops.

Parents conceive of their children as developing gradually into responsible adults. Much of the children's play imitates the activities of their parents and, thus, rehearses adult roles. For example, little girls make bannock out of mud, make hammocks and baby sacks for their dolls, and pretend to cook. Little boys hunt birds and butterflies, play with toy boats, and pull cardboard boxes and other objects as if they were pulling toboggans. Little boqs and girls sometimes play together in small "play" tents which their parents make for them.

On the other hand, when they go to school, counselors and teachers expect children to live in a world of play unrelated to their future participation in adult society. There are few chores to do and these are peripheral to satisfaction of the basic needs—food, heat, and water—which concerned them at home. Keeping one's room clean and tidy and making one's bed are the principal chores which smaller children are expected to do. Young children are expected to spend most of their time playing and going to school. In school and in the dormitory most play involves large groups of thirty to forty children and consists mainly of organized games such as "Cat and Mouse," "Simon Says," "London Bridge," and relay races. When play is nondirective children frequently resort to imitative play as they did before coming to school, but sometimes with a new content, for example, playing "Batman," "Spaceghost," or "Counselors."

In discussing the child-rearing practices of some societies like the Cree, Benedict says: "The essential point of such child training is that the child is from infancy continuously conditioned to responsible social participation, while at the same time the tasks that are expected of it are adapted to its capacities" (1954:23–24).

Attending school radically disrupts this development. After only one year of school parents report that their children "only want to play" and are not interested in performing their chores. Thus, children have already begun to reject their parents' definitions of proper behavior. This kind of intergenerational conflict increases dramatically with each year of school experience. It is exacerbated because the children are in school all winter and thus, fail to learn the technical skills related to hunting and trapping as they mature. This has serious implications for identity conflicts in adolescence since the children are unable to fulfill their parents' expectations. Children who do not attend school are able to assume adult economic roles at about the onset of puberty. For example, boys begin to trap seriously and girls can contribute significantly to the cleaning and preparation of pelts.

Conclusions

Traditional Cree encultration takes place primarily in the context of multigenerational kin groups and stresses food sharing and cooperative labor, indirect rather than open expression of aggression, and self-reliance. Interpersonal relations within the kin group are supportive, but verbal expression of dependence is discouraged. Children are viewed as "little adults" and contribute labor and food to the kin group commensurate with their level of maturity. Children's self-reliance is placed in the service of the kin group.

During their first year of residential school the beginners experience radical discontinuities in their enculturation. The values, attitudes, and behavioral expectations which motivate the dormitory counselors and teacher in their interaction with the children differ sharply from those of Mistassini Cree parents. In school, children have few tasks and these rarely relate to the welfare of the whole group. Competition and direct expression of aggression are reinforced rather than punished. The children interact primarily in large groups—school class, age group, and wing—and come to need a high rate of social stimulation. Dependence becomes focused on two or three adults, and overt expression of dependence increases since it is effective in eliciting nurturant behavior.

As the data presented in the body of the chapter make clear, during their first year of formal education Mistassini beginners are exposed to great cultural discontinuity. They learn new ways of behaving and thinking and are rewarded for conformity to norms which contradict those which they learned before coming to school. Consequently, after only one year of school they have already begun to change significantly toward acting in ways which are appropriate in Euro-Canadian culture but inappropriate in their own. As they continue their education this process accelerates. After alternating for five or six years between the traditional milieu in the summer and the urban residential school in the winter severe conflicts in identity arise.

In the six years before starting school the children learn behavioral patterns and values which are highly functional for participating as adults in the traditional hunting-trapping life of their parents. Because they must go to school their development into trappers or wives of trappers is arrested. Prolonged residential school experience makes it difficult if not impossible for children to participate effectively in the hunting-trapping life of their parents. Not only do they fail to learn the requisite technical skills, but they acquire new needs and aspirations which cannot be satisfied on the trapline. Yet most Mistassini parents want their children to return to the bush. It remains to be seen how the students will resolve their dilemma.

References

Bandura, Albert, and Richard H. Walters, 1963, *Social Learning and Personality Development.* New York: Holt, Rinehart and Winston, Inc.

Benedict, Ruth, 1954, "Continuities and Discontinuities in Cultural Conditioning." In Margaret Mead and Martha Wolfenstein, eds., *Childhood in Contemporary Cultures.* Chicago: University of Chicago Press.

DuBois, Cora, 1955, "Some Notions on Learning Intercultural Understanding." In G. D. Spindler, ed., *Education and Anthropology.* Stanford, Calif.: Stanford University Press, p. 89–105.

Preston, Richard J., 1966, "Peer Group versus Trapline; Shifting Directions in Cree Socialization." Paper presented at the Annual Meeting of the Pennsylvania Sociological Society, Haverford, Pa., October 15 (mimeographed).

Rogers, Edward S., and Jean H. Rogers, 1963, "The Individual in Mistassini Society from Birth to Death." In *Contributions to Anthropology,* 1960, Part II, pp. 14–36. (Bulletin 190, National Museum of Canada) Ottawa: Roger Duhamel.

Speck, Frank, 1935, *The Savage Hunters of the Labrador Peninsula.* Norman: University of Oklahoma Press.

Spindler, George D., 1963, "Personality, Sociocultural System, and Education among the Menomini." In G. D. Spindler, ed., *Education and Culture.* New York: Holt, Rinehart and Winston, Inc., pp. 351–399.

C. W. M. HART/*Wichita State University*

16 *Contrasts between Prepubertal and Postpubertal Education**

This chapter represents an attempt to use the body of generally accepted anthropological information as a baseline for considering the educational process. It might be paraphrased as "the educative process, anthropologically considered." I assume that "anthropologically considered" is equivalent to "cross-culturally considered," and I assume that education refers to any process at any stage of life in which new knowledge is acquired or new habits or new attitudes formed. That is, I have taken the question which forms the core problem of this volume and tried to develop a few generalizations about that problem from the general anthropological literature. But it follows that since they are anthropological generalizations their usefulness to education is a matter of opinion. All I claim for them is the old basis upon which anthropology has always justified its preoccupation with the simpler societies, namely that by studying the simpler societies we gain perspective and proportion in really seeing our own society and from that better perspective comes better understanding of common human social processes. I hope that the material contained in this chapter will at least enable the readers interested in education to see our own educative process in better perspective and help them separate what is distinctively American in it from what is general-social and general-human.

My starting point is a distinction that is made by Herskovits. In his chapter on education in the book called *Man and His Works* (1948) he finds it necessary to stress that the training of the young in the simpler societies of the world is carried on through two different vehicles. The child learns a lot of things knocking around underfoot in the home, in the village street, with his brothers and sisters, and in similar environments, and he learns a lot of other things in the rather formidable apparatus of what is usually called in the anthropological literature the initiation ceremonies or the initiation schools.

Herskovits stresses that initiation education takes place outside the home and is worthy to be called schooling, contrasts it with the education the child

---

*Reprinted with minor revision from *Education and Anthropology,* George D. Spindler, Editor, with the permission of the publishers, Stanford University Press; copyright 1955 by the Board of Trustees of the Leland Stanford Junior University.

receives knocking around the household and the village long before the initiation period begins, and decides that the main feature of the latter is that it is within the home, and that it should therefore be called education as contrasted with schooling. There he, and many other writers on the subject, tend to leave the matter.

This tendency, to leave the problem at that point, is rather a pity. Further exploration of these two contrasting vehicles for training of the young will pay rich dividends, and it is to such further exploration that the bulk of this paper is devoted. But before going on, certain unsatisfactory features of Herskovits' treatment must be mentioned. To suggest, as he does, that preinitiation education is "within the home" is misleading to people unacquainted with the character of primitive society. While initiation education is very definitely outside the home and—as we shall see later—this remoteness from home is a very essential feature of it, it does not follow that the other has to be, or even is likely to be, "within the home." The home in most primitive societies is very different indeed from the connotation of "home" in America, and the type of education to which Herskovits is referring takes place in every conceivable type of primary group. The young child in primitive society may be subjected to the learning process in his early years in his household (Eskimo), or in a medley of dozens of households (Samoa); his parents may ignore him and leave him to drag himself up as best he can (Mundugumor); he may be corrected or scolded by any passer-by (Zuñi); his male mentor may not be his father at all but his mother's brother (many Melanesian cultures); and so on.

I do not intend to explore the social-psychological results of this variety of primary-group situations; all I mention them for here is to demonstrate how misleading it is to lump them all together as comprising "education within the home." About the only things they have in common is that they all take place in the earlier years of life and they don't take place within the formal framework of initiation ceremonies. I propose therefore to call all this type of education by the title "preinitiation" or "prepuberty" education (since most initiation ceremonial begins at puberty or later), and the problem I am mainly concerned with is the set of contrasts that exists between what societies do with their children in the preinitiation period and what is done with them in the postinitiation period. In other words, Herskovits' distinction between education and schooling becomes clearer and more useful if they are simply called prepuberty education and postpuberty education.

One further explanatory comment is necessary. Not all primitive societies possess initiation ceremonies of the formal standardized type that anthropology has become familiar with in many parts of the world. How "schooling" or post-puberty education is handled in those primitive societies which lack initiation ceremonies and what the results of such lack are for the adult culture are interesting questions, but they are outside the scope of the present paper. What we are concerned with here is the set of contrasts between prepubertal and postpubertal education in those numerous and widespread societies which include formal initiation ceremonies in their set of official institutions.

Prepubertal and Postpubertal Education—How Do They Differ?

If attention is directed to the ways education is carried on in the prepuberty and postpuberty periods in a large number of simple societies—viz., those "with initiation ceremonies"—some very impressive contrasts begin to appear. They can be dealt with under four heads—(1) Regulation, (2) Personnel, (3) Atmosphere, (4) Curriculum; but the nature of the data will require us to jump back and forth between these four divisions, since they are all interwoven.

1. Regulation

Postpuberty education, in such societies, does not begin until at least the age of twelve or thirteen, and in many cases several years later than that. By that age of course, the child has already acquired a great deal of what we call his culture. How has he acquired the things he knows at the age of twelve or thirteen? The traditional anthropological monographs are said to tell us little or nothing about "early education." I suggest that the reason the older literature tells us so little that is definite about the early prepubertal training of the children is basically for the same reason that we know so little about preschool education in our own culture, or did know so little before Gesell. Until the appearance of *The Child from Five to Ten* (Gesell and Ilg 1946), the information on the preschool "enculturation" of the American child was just as barren as the anthropological literature. Whether Gesell has really answered the question for the American child and whether a Gesell-like job has been done or can be done for a primitive society are questions which need not concern us here except to point up the real question: Why is it so rare to find clear information as to what goes on in the learning process during the preschool years, in any culture?

One possible answer is that preschool education is rarely if ever standardized, rarely if ever regulated around known and visible social norms.[1] It is an area of cultural laissez faire, within very wide limits of tolerance, and society at large does not lay down any firm blueprint which all personnel

[1] *Editor's note:* Nonanthropologist readers should be aware of the fact that Prof. Hart's statements concerning lack of uniformity in prepubertal child training would be contested by many anthropologists, though the same ones might accept his basic position that in comparison to pubertal and postpubertal training the earlier years of experience are *relatively* less structured and less subject to the pressure of public opinion.

engaged in "raising the young" must follow. If, instead of asking for a "pattern" or "norm," we ask the simpler question, "What happens?" it seems to me that the literature is not nearly so barren of information as has been argued. It tends to suggest that anything and everything happens in the same society. For instance Schapera's account of childhood among the Bakgatla is pretty clear: "The Bakgatla say that thrashing makes a child wise. But they also say a growing child is like a little dog and though it may annoy grown-ups, it must be taught proper conduct with patience and forbearance" (Schapera 1940). As Herskovits has pointed out, this mixture of strict and permissive techniques is also reported for Lesu in Melanesia by Powdermaker, for the Apache by Opler, and for the Kwoma by Whiting (Herskovits 1948). This list can readily be added to.

There is no point in counting how many cultures use severe punishment and how many do not. The explicit statements of the fieldworkers just cited are at least implicit in dozens of others. Do the natives beat their children? Yes. Do they fondle and make a fuss over their children? Yes. Do they correct them? Yes. Do they let them get away with murder? Also yes. All this in the same culture. I repeat that it is pretty clear what happens in the prepuberty years in the simpler societies. Anything and everything from extreme punishment to extreme permissiveness may occur and does occur in the same culture.

The fieldworkers do not tell us what the pattern of early education is because there is rarely any one clear-cut pattern. What each individual child learns or is taught or is not taught is determined pretty much by a number of individual variables. A few such variables are: interest or lack of interest of individual parents in teaching their children, size of family and each sibling's position in it, whether the next house or camp is close by or far away, whether the neighbors have children of the same age, the amount of interaction and type of interaction of the particular "peer-groups" of any given child. The number of variables of this type is almost infinite; the child is simply dumped in the midst of them to sink or swim, and as a result no two children in the same culture learn the same things in the same way. One, for example, may learn about sex by spying upon his parents, a second by spying upon a couple of comparative strangers, a third by getting some explicit instruction from his father or his mother (or his elder brother or his mother's brother), a fourth by listening to sniggering gossip in the play group, and a fifth by observing a pair of dogs in the sexual act. Which of these ways of learning is the norm? Obviously none of them is, at least not in the same sense as that in which we say that it is the norm for a person to inherit the property of his mother's brother, or to use an intermediary in courtship, or to learn certain important myths at Stage 6B of the initiation ceremonies.

In asking for a uniform cultural pattern in such a laissez faire, anything-goes area, we are asking for the inherently impossible, or at least the non-existent. There are, of course, some cultural limits set in each society to this near-anarchy: there will, for example, be general outrage and widespread social disapproval if one family shamefully neglects its children or some child goes to what is by general consensus regarded as "too far," but such limits of toleration are very wide indeed in every society. The household is almost sovereign in its rights to do as much or as little as it likes—that is, to do what it likes about its offspring in the *preschool* years. The rest of society is extraordinarily reluctant everywhere to interfere with a household's sovereign right to bring up its preschool children as it wishes. And most primitive parents, being busy with other matters and having numerous children anyway, leave the kids to bring each other up or to just grow like Topsy.

There are other strong lines of evidence supporting this judgment that prepuberty education in the simpler societies is relatively so variable as to be virtually normless. One is the self-evident fact which anybody can verify by reading the monographs, that no fieldworker, not even among those who have specifically investigated the matter of child practices, has ever found a tribe where several reliable informants could give him a rounded and unified account of the preschool educational practices of their tribe comparable to the rounded and generalized picture they can give him, readily and easily, of the local religion, or the folklore, or the moral code for the adults, or the local way of getting married, or the right way to build a canoe or plant a garden. This difference can best be conveyed to an anthropologist audience, perhaps, by contrasting the sort of answer fieldworkers get to such questions as "Tell me some of your myths," or "How do you make silver ornaments?" or "How do you treat your mother-in-law?" with the answer they get to a question like "How do you bring up children?" To the former type of question (not asked as crudely as that, of course) the answers will come (usually) in the form of norms—stereotyped and generalized statements that do not differ a great deal from one informant to the next, or, if they do so differ, will always be referred to a "right" way or a "proper" way: the "right" way to build a canoe, the "proper" way to treat one's mother-in-law, the "correct" form of a myth or a ceremony, and so on. Even in the type of sentence structure the answers come in, they will have this official character—"We do it this way" or "It is our custom here to do thus and so"—and often in case of conflicting versions an argument will develop, not over what the informant himself does but over whether what he says is "right" or socially sanctioned as "the right way."

But given the opportunity to perform a similar generalized descriptive job upon "how children are or should be brought up," informants fail dismally to produce anything of this kind. They either look blank and say little or nothing, or come up with a set of empty platitudes—"All boys should be brought up good boys," "They should all respect their elders," etc.—which clearly have no relation to the facts of life going on all around the speaker; or (most common of all) they fall back onto their own life history and do a Sun Chief or Crashing Thunder sort of job. That is, they give in endless and boring detail an account of how they individually were brought up, or how they bring up their own children, but they clearly have no idea of whether their case is typical or atypical of the tribe at large. And the anthropologist equally has no idea of how representative or unrepresentative this case is. This happens so constantly that we are left with only one conclusion, namely, that if there is a cultural tradition for preschool education (comparable with the cultural tradition for religion or for tabu-observance or for technology), then the average native in a simple society is completely unaware of what it is.

This same conclusion is also supported by another line of evidence, namely, the complete change that comes over the picture when we move from prepuberty education to postpuberty education. Postpuberty education is marked in the simpler societies by the utmost degree of standardization and correctness. At puberty the initiation rituals begin, and perhaps the most universal thing about these is their meticulously patterned character. Every line painted on a boy's body, every movement of a performer, every word or phrase uttered, the right person to make every move, is rigidly prescribed as having to be done in one way only—the right way. A wrongly drawn line, a misplaced phrase, an unsanctioned movement, or the right movement made by the wrong person or at the wrong time, and the whole ritual is ruined. They belong to the same general type of social phenomena as the English Coronation ceremony or the Catholic sacrifice of the Mass; there is only one way of doing them, regardless of the individuals involved, namely the "right" way. By contrast that meticulously patterned feature throws into sharp relief the haphazard, permissive, and unstandardized character of the education that *precedes* the time of puberty.

2. *Personnel*

So far, then, our stress has been on the unregulated character of primitive preschool education. Certain further things become clearer if at this point we switch our attention from the focus of regulation to the focus of personnel —i.e., from the question of whether the education is controlled and standardized to the question of who imparts the education. Anthropologists are coming more and more to realize the importance of the "Who does what?" type of question in fieldwork, and perhaps nowhere is it so important to know who does what than in the area we are discussing. From whom does the child learn in the simpler societies? As far as the preinitiation years are concerned the answer is obvious: He learns from his intimates, whether they be intimates of a senior generation like his parents or intimates of his own generation like his siblings, cousins, playmates, etc. In the preinitiation years he learns nothing or next to nothing from strangers or near-strangers. Strangers and near-strangers are people he rarely sees and even more rarely converses with; and, since learning necessarily involves interaction, it is from the people he interacts with most that he learns most, and from the people he interacts with least that he learns least.

This is so obvious that it needs little comment. But one important point about intimates must be made. In all cultures it appears as if this "learning from intimates" takes two forms. The child learns from his parents or other senior members of his family and he also learns from his play groups. And the interaction processes in these two situations are different in several important respects. The parents are intimates and so are the members of the play group, but there is the important difference that parents, to some extent at least, represent the official culture (are the surrogates of society, in Dollard's phrase), while the play groups do not. All the work upon play groups in Western society has tended to stress what autonomous little subcultures they are, each with its own social organization, its own rules, its own values. The family is a primary group, but one which is tied into the total formal structure of the society and therefore subject to at least some over-all social control. The play group is an autonomous little world of its own, whose rules may be, and often are, directly at variance with the rules of the home or of the wider society.

If, then, as suggested above, it is true that in most societies—simple or modern—each household is allowed a great deal of freedom to bring up its children pretty much as it chooses, and if this wide degree of tolerance leads in turn to a wide variation in the ways in which the culture is presented to different children, then obviously such variation is enormously increased by the role of the play group. Even if we were told of a culture in which all households standardized their child-training practices, it would still fall far short of being convincing evidence of a standardized child-training situation because of the great amount of knowledge which children in all cultures acquire without the household or at least the parents being involved in the transmission process, namely the knowledge which the child "picks up somewhere."

Once we recognize the influence of this second group of intimates on how the child acquires certain aspects of his culture, the case for wide variation in early child training is greatly strengthened. There seems to be no evidence that would suggest that the play group in simple societies functions in any notably different way from the way it functions in modern societies, but unfortunately we have few studies of the "subcultures" of the playworld in other than Western cultures. Among child psychologists dealing with Western cultures, Piaget in particular has some findings that are relevant to the present discussion (Piaget 1929, 1932). These findings tend to show that at least by the age of ten or eleven the child has become empirical and secular in his attitudes toward rules and norms of play behavior, partly because he has learned by that time that each primary group has its own rules, so that there is no "right" way, no over-all norm—at least for children's games such as marbles—for all play groups to conform to. Piaget, of course, is describing European children, but primitive children spend at least as much time in unsupervised play groups as European or American children, and since their preschool period is certainly many years more prolonged, there is no apparent reason why this conclusion of Piaget should not have cross-cultural validity.

However, I am not trying to develop a theory but merely to follow through some of the difficulties that are hidden in the simple statement above that preschool learning is between intimates. There are different sorts of intimacy because of the child's dual relation to his home and to his playmates, and some of his culture is mediated to him by each. We don't know nearly enough about degrees of intimacy, and we may be forced by further research to start making classifications and subdivisions between the different sorts of intimate relationships (different "levels" of primary groups?) to which the child in any culture is exposed in his preschool years. Even if we do, however, the fact still remains that in his preinitiation years the child in primitive society learns nothing from strangers or near-strangers. And this leads to the second comment under the head of Personnel, which is that in his *postpuberty* education in contrast to that of *prepuberty* he *has to* learn from strangers or near-strangers and cannot possibly learn from anybody else. When puberty arrives and the boy is therefore ready for initiation (or the girl for marriage), his family, his siblings, his gangs, his village, all the intimates to whom his training or learning has been left up to now, are roughly pushed aside and a whole new personnel take over his training. Who these new teachers are varies from culture to culture, but a very common feature is that they be nonintimates of the boy, semistrangers drawn from other sections of the tribe (opposite moieties, different districts or villages, hostile or semihostile clans, different age groups, and so on), people with whom he is not at all intimate. Who they are and what they represent is made painfully clear in the ritual. An actual case will help to make clear the nature of the transition.

Among the Tiwi of North Australia, one can see the traumatic nature of the initiation period in very clear form, and part of trauma lies in the sudden switch of personnel with whom the youth has to associate. A boy reaches thirteen or fourteen or so, and the physiological signs of puberty begin to appear. Nothing happens, possibly for many months. Then suddenly one day, toward evening when the people are gathering around their campfires for the main meal of the day after coming in from their day's hunting and food-gathering, a group of three or four heavily armed and taciturn strangers appear in camp. In full war regalia they walk in silence to the camp of the boy and say curtly to the household: "We have come for So-and-So." Immediately pandemonium breaks loose. The mother and the rest of the older women begin to howl and wail. The father rushes for his spears. The boy himself, panic-striken, tries to hide, the younger children begin to cry, and the household dogs begin to bark. It is all terribly similar to the reaction which is provoked by the arrival of the police at an American home to pick up a juvenile delinquent. This similarity extends to the behavior of the neighbors. These carefully abstain from identifying with either the strangers or the stricken household. They watch curiously the goings-on but make no move that can be identified as supporting either side. This is particularly notable in view of the fact that the strangers are strangers to all of them, too, that is, they are men from outside the encampment, or outside the band, who, under any circumstances, would be greeted by a shower of spears. But not under these circumstances (see also Hart and Pilling 1960).

In fact, when we know our way around the culture we realize that the arrival of the strangers is not as unexpected as it appears. The father of the boy and the other adult men of the camp not only knew they were coming but have even agreed with them on a suitable day for them to come. The father's rush for his spears to protect his son and to preserve the sanctity of his household is make-believe. If he puts on too good an act, the older men will intervene and restrain him from interfering with the purposes of the strangers. With the father immobilized the child clings to his mother, but the inexorable strangers soon tear him (literally) from his mother's arms and from the bosom of his bereaved family and, still as grimly as they came, bear him off into the night. No society could symbolize more dramatically that initiation necessitates the forcible taking away of the boy from the bosom of his family, his village, his neighbors, his intimates, his friends. And who are these strangers who forcibly drag the terrified boy off to he knows not what? In Tiwi they are a selected group of his senior male cross-cousins. To people who understand primitive social organization that should convey most of what I want to convey. They are "from the other side of the tribe," men with whom the boy has had little to do and whom he may have never seen before. They belong to the group of men who have married or will marry his sisters, and marriage, it is well to remember, in a primitive society is a semihostile act. As cross-cousins, these men cannot possibly belong to the same clan as the boy, or to the same territorial group, and since only senior and already fully initiated men are eligible for the job they will be men in their thirties or forties, twenty or more years older than he.

By selecting senior cross-cousins to conduct the forcible separation of the boy from the home and thus project him into the postpuberty proceedings, the Tiwi have selected men who are as remote from the boy as possible. The only thing they and he have in common is that they are all members of the same tribe—nothing else. If, then, we have stressed that all training of the child in the prepuberty period is carried on by intimates, we have to stress equally the fact that the postpuberty training has to be in the hands of non-intimates. Anybody who is in any way close to the boy—by blood, by residence, by age, or by any other form of affiliation or association—is *ipso facto* ineligible to have a hand in his postpuberty training.

I selected the Tiwi as my example because the case happens to be rather spectacular in the clarity of its symbolism, but if one examines the literature one finds everywhere or almost everywhere the same emphasis. Those who prefer Freudian symbolism I refer to the initiation ceremonies of the Kiwai Papuans (Landtmann 1927), where during initiation the boy is required to actually step on his mother's stomach; when Landtmann asked the significance of this he was told that it meant the boy was now "finished with the place where he came from" (i.e., his mother's womb). Van Gennep has collected all the older cases in his classic *Rites de passage* (Van Gennep 1909), and no new ones which invalidate his generalizations have been reported since his time.

I therefore suggest two reasonably safe generalizations about initiation rituals: (a) The rituals themselves are designed to emphasize in very clear terms that initiation ceremonies represent a clear break with all home, household, home-town, and friendship-group ties; and (b) as a very basic part of such emphasis the complete handling of all initiation proceedings, and initiation instruction, from their inception at puberty to their final conclusion often more than a decade later, is made the responsibility of men who are comparative strangers to the boy and who are thus as different as possible in their social relationships to him from the teachers, guiders, instructors, and associates he has had up to that time.

3. Atmosphere

It should now be clear what is meant by the third head, Atmosphere. The arrival of the strangers to drag the yelling boy out of his mother's arms is just the spectacular beginning of a long period during which the separation of the boy from everything that has gone before is emphasized in every possible way at every minute of the day and night. So far his life has been easy; now it is hard. Up to now he has never necessarily experienced any great pain, but in the initiation period in many tribes pain, sometimes horrible, intense pain, is an obligatory feature. The boy of twelve or thirteen, used to noisy, boisterous, irresponsible play, is expected and required to sit still for hours and days at a time saying nothing whatever but concentrating upon and endeavoring to understand long intricate instructions and "lectures" given him by his hostile and forbidding preceptors (who are, of course, the men who carried him off to initiation, the "strangers" of the previous section). Life has suddenly become real and earnest, and the initiate is required literally to "put away the things of a child," even the demeanor. The number of tabus and unnatural behaviors enjoined upon the initiate is endless. He mustn't speak unless he is spoken to; he must eat only certain foods, and often only in certain ways, at fixed times, and in certain fixed positions. All contact with females, even speech with them, is rigidly forbidden, and this includes mother and sisters. He cannot even scratch his head with his own hand, but must do it with a special stick and so on, through a long catalogue of special, unnatural, but obligatory behaviors covering practically every daily activity and every hour of the day and night. And during this time he doesn't go home at night or for the week end or on a forty-eight-hour pass, but remains secluded in the bush, almost literally the prisoner of his preceptors, for months and even years at a time. If he is allowed home at rare intervals, he has to carry all his tabus with him, and nothing is more astonishing in Australia than to see some youth who the year before was a noisy, brash, boisterous thirteen-year-old, sitting the following year, after his initiation is begun, in the midst of his family, with downcast head and subdued air, not daring even to smile, still less to speak. He is "home on leave," but he might just as well have stayed in camp for all the freedom from discipline his spell at home is giving him.

The preoccupations of anthropologists with other interests (that of the earlier fieldworkers with the pain-inflicting aspects of the initiations, and the recent preoccupation with early physiological experiences) have directed attention away from what may well be the most important aspect of education in the simpler societies, namely the possibly traumatic aspect of the initiation ceremonies. From whatever aspect we view them their whole tenor is to produce shock, disruption, a sharp break with the past, a violent projection out of the known into the unknown. Perhaps the boys are old enough to take it in their stride and the experience is not really traumatic. If so, it would seem that primitive society goes to an awful lot of trouble and wastes an awful lot of man-hours needlessly. Actually we don't know what the psychological effects of initiation upon the initiates are. All that can be said safely is that judged by the elaboration and the minuteness of detail in the shocking and disruptive features of initiation rituals, they certainly appear to be designed to produce the maximum amount of shock possible for the society to achieve.

This may suggest that our own exaggerated concern with protecting our own adolescents from disturbing experiences is quite unnecessary. If the grueling ordeal of subincision, with all its accompanying disruptive devices, leaves the young Australian psychologically unscathed, we needn't worry that Universal Military Training, for instance, will seriously upset the young American. But perhaps something in the prepuberty training prepares the young Australian and makes him capable of standing the trauma of the initiation period.

4. Curriculum

What is the purpose of all this elaboration of shock ritual? Ask the natives themselves and they will answer vaguely, "to make a child into a man." Occasionally a more specific verb is used and the answer becomes, "to teach a boy to become a man." What is supposed to be learned and what do the preceptors teach in the initiation schools? Perhaps the most surprising thing is what is not taught. It is hard to find in the literature any case where the initiation curriculum contains what might be called "practical subjects," or how to make a basic living. (There appear to be certain exceptions to this generalization, but they are more apparent than real.) The basic food-getting skills of the simpler peoples are never imparted in the initiation schools. Where practical subjects are included (as in Polynesia or in the Poro schools of Liberia and Sierra Leone), they are specialized crafts, not basic food-getting skills. Hunting, gardening, cattle-tending, fishing, are not taught the boy at initiation; he has already learned the rudiments of these at home in his intimate groups before his initiation starts. This is a surprising finding because of the well-known fact that many of these people live pretty close to the starvation point, and none of them manage to extract much more than subsistence from their environment. But despite this, the cultures in question are blissfully oblivious of economic determinism, and blandly leave instruction in basic food production to the laissez-faire, casual, hit-or-miss teaching of parents, friends, play groups, etc. When society itself forcibly takes over the boy in order to make him into a man and teach him the things a man should know, it is not concerned with teaching him to be a better hunter or gardener or tender of cattle or fisherman, even though the economic survival of the tribe clearly depends on all of the adult men being good at one or another of these occupations. The initiation curricula cover instead quite a different series of subjects, which I am tempted to call "cultural subjects"—in either sense of the world "culture."

Of course, there is much variation here from tribe to tribe and region to region, but the imparting of religious knowledge always occupies a prominent place. This (in different cultures) includes such things as the learning of the myths, the tribal accounts of the tribe's own origin and history, and the performance, the meaning, and the sacred connections and connotations of the ceremonials. In brief, novices are taught theology, which in primitive society is inextricably mixed up with astronomy, geology, geography, biology (the mysteries of birth and sex), philosophy, art, and music—in short, the whole cultural heritage of the tribe. As Pettit has pointed out (dealing with North America, but his statement has universal anthropological validity), the instruction in the initiation schools is "a constant challenge to the elders to review, analyze, dramatize, and defend their cultural heritage" (Pettit 1946). That sentence "review, analyze, dramatize, and defend their cultural heritage" is very striking, because you can apply it equally aptly to a group of naked old men in Central Australia sitting talking to a novice in the middle of a treeless desert, and to most lectures in a college of liberal arts in the United States. It serves to draw attention to the fact that, in the simpler societies, the schools run and manned and controlled and financed by the society at large are designed not to make better economic men of the novices, or better food producers, but to produce better citizens, better carriers of the culture through the generations, people better informed about the world they live in and the tribe they belong to. It is here finally, through this sort of curriculum, that each adolescent becomes "enculturated," no matter how haphazard and individualized his learning and his growth may have been up to now. It is through the rigidly disciplined instruction of a common and rigidly prescribed curriculum that he assumes, with all his fellow tribesmen, a common culture. This is where standardization occurs in the educational process of the simpler societies. Everybody who goes through the initiation schools, generation after generation, is presented with the same material, organized and taught in the same way, with no allowances made for individual taste or choice or proclivity, and no substitutions or electives allowed. When we realize how standardized and rigid and uniform this curriculum is, it should help us to realize how variable, how un-uniform, how dictated by chance, accident, and the personal whims of individual parents, individual adult relatives, and the variation in peer and play groups is the "curriculum" on or in which the individual child is trained during the long impressionable period that precedes puberty.

Conclusion

The above discussion has, I hope, provided the basis for some helpful generalizations about education in primitive societies, or at least has opened up some new avenues for further exploration. The main points of this discussion may be summed up as follows:

1. There are typically (though not universally) in primitive societies two sharply contrasting educational vehicles, the preschool process, lasting from birth to puberty, and the initiation procedures, beginning around puberty or a little later and lasting from six months to fifteen years. These two educational vehicles show some highly significant contrasts.

2. From the point of view of regulation, the preschool period is characterized by its loose, vague, unsystematic character. Few primitive societies follow any set standards or rules on how children shall be brought up. It is true that there are frequently, perhaps usually, pretty clear rules (which are actually followed) telling mothers how to hold a baby, correct methods for suckling or weaning, and standardized techniques of toilet training (though I suspect some of these are nothing but copybook maxims), but outside the "physiological areas of child-training" (which therefore have to bear all the weight the Freudians put upon them), it is rare indeed to find in primitive cultures any conformity from family to family or from case to case with regard to anything else in the child's early career. This is not, of course, to deny that there are differences from culture to culture in the degree to which children are loved and fussed over or treated as nuisances or joys. I am not questioning the fact, for example, that the Arapesh love children, whereas the Mundugumor resent them. What I am reiterating is that there is still a wide variation not only possible but inevitable in conditioning and learning between one Mundugumor child and the next.

3. If this view is correct, it raises certain interesting possibilities for theory. Because of the heavy Freudian emphasis in the literature on child training in recent years, there exists a strong and unfortunate tendency to talk of child training as if it were coterminous with swaddling, suckling, weaning and toilet-training practices. But these "physiological" areas or "bodily functions"

areas are only a small part of the preschool education of the primitive child. Even if in primitive cultures the physiological areas of child training are relatively standardized (and this is by no means certain), there is no evidence that the nonphysiological areas are. On the contrary, the evidence points in the other direction. Among adult members of the same society there may be, for example, great variation in apparent strength of the sex drive, or in the overt expression of aggressive or passive personality traits (Hart 1954). Where does such "personality variation" come from? From childhood experiences, say the Freudians. I agree. But in order to demonstrate that personality variation in adult life has its roots in early childhood experiences, it is necessary to show not that childhood experiences are highly standardized in early life and that child training is uniform, but that they are highly variable. How can we account for the self-evident fact of adult personality variation by stressing the uniformity of standardization of childhood training? Surely the more valid hypothesis or the more likely lead is to be found in those aspects of child training which are not uniform and not standardized.

4. So much for the preschool training. But there is also the other vehicle of education and youth training in primitive society, the initiation rituals. The initiation period demonstrates to us what standardization and uniformity of training really mean. When we grasp the meaning of this demonstration we can only conclude that compared with the rigidities of the initiation period, the prepuberty period is a loose, lax period. Social scientists who find it necessary for their theories to stress uniformity and pressures toward conformity in simple societies are badly advised to take the prepuberty period for their examples. The natives themselves know better than this. When they are adults, it is to the happy, unregulated, care-free days of prepuberty that they look back. "Then my initiation began," says the informant, and immediately a grim, guarded "old-man" expression comes over his face, "and I was taken off by the old men." The same old men (and women) who sit around and indulgently watch the vagaries and idiosyncracies of the children without correction become the grim, vigilant, reproving watchers of the initiates, and any departure or attempted departure from tradition is immediately reprimanded.

5. Who are the agents of this discipline? Primitive societies answer in loud and unmistakable tones that discipline cannot be imposed by members of the primary group, that it has to be imposed by "outsiders." The widespread nature of this feature of initiation is, to my mind, very impressive. Making a boy into a man is rarely, anywhere, left to the family, the household, the village, to which he belongs and where he is on intimate terms with people.[2]

[2] In the original draft of this paper I mentioned the Arapesh as one of the few exceptions. At the Stanford conference, however, Dr. Mead pointed out that while it is true that initiation in Arapesh is carried out by intimates, they wear masks. To me this correction of my original remark dramatically emphasizes the main point. The Arapesh social structure is such that there are no "strangers" to use for initiation; therefore they invent them by masking some intimates.

The initiation schools are directed at imparting instruction that cannot be given in the home, under conditions as unlike home conditions as possible, by teachers who are the antithesis of the home teachers the boy has hitherto had. The symbolisms involved in the forcible removal from the home atmosphere; the long list of tabus upon homelike acts, homelike speech, homelike demeanor, homelike habits; the selection of the initiators (i.e., the teachers or preceptors) from the semihostile sections of the tribe—all tell the same story, that the turning of boys into men can only be achieved by making everything about the proceedings as different from the home and the prepuberty situation as possible. Everything that happens to the initiate during initiation has to be as different as it can be made by human ingenuity from the things that happened to him before initiation.

6. This becomes pointed up still more when we remember that what is actually being taught in the initiation schools is the whole value system of the culture, its myths, its religion, its philosophy, its justification of its own entity as a culture. Primitive society clearly values these things, values them so much that it cannot leave them to individual families to pass on to the young. It is willing to trust the haphazard, individually varied teaching methods of families and households and peer groups and gossip to teach children to walk and talk, about sex, how to get along with people, or how to be a good boy; it is even willing to leave to the individual families the teaching of how to hunt or to garden or to fish or to tend cattle; but the tribal philosophy, the religion, the citizenship knowledge, too important to leave to such haphazard methods, must be taught by society at large through its appointed and responsible representatives.

In doing this, society is asserting and underlining its right in the child. The fact that, for example, in Australia it is a group of senior cross-cousins, and elsewhere it is men of the opposite moiety or some other specified group of semihostile relatives, who knock on the door and demand the child from his mourning and wailing family, should not be allowed to disguise the fact that these men are the representatives of society at large, the native equivalents of the truant officer, the policeman, and the draft board, asserting the priority of society's rights over the family's rights in the child. Clearly in every society there is always a family and there is always a state, and equally clearly both have rights in every child born into the society. And no society yet—Western or non-Western—has found any perfect way or equal way of adjudicating or harmonizing public rights and private rights. The state's rights must have priority when matters of citizenship are involved, but the assertion of the state's rights is always greeted with wails of anguish from the family. "I didn't raise my boy to go off and get subincised," wails the Australian mother, but he is carried off and subincised just the same. "I didn't raise my boy for the draft board or the school board," says the American mother, but her protests are of no avail either. It is an inevitable conflict, because it arises from the very structure of society, as long as society is an organization of family units, which it is universally. The only solution is to abolish the family or abolish the state, and no human group has been able to do either.

7. The boy is not ruined for life or a mental cripple as a result of the harrowing initiation experience, but is a social being *in a way he never was before*. He has been made aware of his wider social responsibilities and his wider membership in the total society, but more important in the present context, he has been exposed to a series of social situations in which friendship counts for naught, crying or whining gets one no place, whimsy or charm or boyish attractiveness pays no dividends, and friends, pull, and influence are without effect. The tribal tradition, the culture, treats all individuals alike, and skills and wiles that were so valuable during childhood in gaining preferential treatment or in winning approval or avoiding disapproval are all to no avail. He goes into the initiation period a child, which is a social animal of one sort, but he comes out a responsible enculturated citizen, which is a social animal of a different sort.

8. Primitive societies, then, devote a great deal of time and care to training for citizenship. They make no attempt to even start such training until the boy has reached puberty. But once they start, they do it thoroughly. Citizenship training in these societies means a great deal more than knowing the words of "The Star-Spangled Banner" and memorizing the Bill of Rights. It means exposing the boy under particularly stirring and impressive conditions to the continuity of the cultural tradition, to the awe and majesty of the society itself, emphasizing the subordination of the individual to the group at large and hence the mysteriousness, wonder, and sacredness of the whole individual-society relationship. In Australia, the most sacred part of the whole initiation ritual is when the boys are shown the *churinga,* which are at the same time their own souls and the souls of the tribe which came into existence at the creation of the world. Citizenship, being an awesome and mysterious business in any culture, cannot be imparted or taught or instilled in a secular atmosphere; it must be imparted in an atmosphere replete with symbolism and mystery. Whether it can be taught at all without heavy emphasis on its otherworldliness, without heavy sacred emphasis, whether the teaching of citizenship can ever be a warm, friendly, loving, cozy, and undisturbing process, is a question I leave to the educators. Primitive societies obviously do not believe it can be taught that way, as is proved by the fact that they never try.

9. One last point, implied in much of the above but worth special mention, is the rather surprising fact that technological training, training in "getting a living," is absent from the initiation curricula, despite its obvious vital importance to the survival of the individual, of the household, and of the tribe or society. Mastery of the food-obtaining techniques by the children is left to the hit-or-miss, highly individualistic teaching processes of the home, to the peer groups, and to the whimsies of relatives or friends. The reason for this omission from the socially regulated curricula of the initiation schools is, I

think, pretty clear. In the simpler societies there is nothing particularly mysterious, nothing spiritual or otherwordly about getting a living, or hunting or gardening or cattle-herding. It is true that there is apt to be a lot of magical practice mixed up with these things, but even this heavy magical element is conceived in very secular and individualistic terms. That is, it either works or doesn't work in particular cases, and each man or each household or clan has its own garden magic or cattle magic or hunting magic which differs from the next man's or household's or clan's magic. Dobu, for instance, is a culture riddled with garden magic; so is that of the Trobriands, but each group's magic is individually owned and comparisons of magic are even made between group and group. For this reason, garden skills or hunting skills, even though they include magical elements, can still safely be left by society to the private level of transmission and teaching. Public control, public supervision is minimal.

This leads to two further conclusions, or at least suggestions. (1) On this line of analysis, we can conclude the primitive societies, despite their marginal subsistence and the fact that they are frequently close to the starvation point, devote more care and attention, *as societies,* to the production of good citizens, than to the production of good technicians, and therefore they can be said to value good citizenship more highly than they value the production of good food producers. Can this be said for modern societies, including our own? (2) This relative lack of interest in standardizing subsistence-training, while insisting at the same time on standardizing training in the ideological aspects of culture, may go a long way toward enabling us to explain the old sociological problem called cultural lag. Everybody who has taken an introductory course in social science is acquainted with the fact that change in technology is easier to achieve, and takes place with less resistance than change in nontechnological or ideological fields. I do not suggest that what we have been talking about above offers a complete explanation of the culture lag differential, but it may at least be helpful. I would phrase the relation between culture lag and education like this: that because prepuberty education in the simpler societies is loose, unstructured, and left pretty much to individual household choice, and because such laissez faire prepuberty education typically includes food-getting techniques and the use of food-getting tools (spears, harpoons, hoes, etc.), the attitude toward these techniques and tools that the child develops is a secular one and he carries that secular attitude toward them into his adult life. Hence variations from or alternatives to such tools and techniques are not resisted with anything like the intensity of feeling with which variations from or alternatives to ideological elements will be resisted. From his childhood, the boy believes that in trying to get food anything is a good technique or a good tool, provided only that it works, and he is familiar too with the fact that techniques and tools differ at least slightly from household to household or hunter to hunter. Therefore, as an adult he is, in relation to food-getting techniques and tools, both a secularist and an empiricist, and will adopt the white man's gun or the white man's spade when they are offered without any feeling that he is flouting the tribal gods or the society's conscience. The white man's ideology, or foreign importations in ideology, are treated in quite a different way. They are involved with areas of behavior which have been learned not in the secular, empirical atmosphere of the home and the play groups, but in the awesome, sacred atmosphere of the initiation schools, wherein no individual variation is allowed and the very notion of alternatives is anathema.

To avoid misunderstanding, a brief comment must be made about societies like that of Polynesia and the "schools" of Africa such as the Poro, where specialized technical knowledge is imparted to the adolescent males in special training institutions. The significant point is that in such societies ordinary food-gathering techniques (fishing in Polynesia, gardening in West Africa, cattle-tending in East Africa) are still left to the haphazard teaching methods of the individual household, whereas the craft skills (woodcarving in Polynesia, metalworking in the Poro) are entrusted to vehicles of instruction in which apprenticeship, passing of exams, standardized curricula, unfamiliar or nonintimate teachers, heavy emphasis on ritual and the sacred character of the esoteric knowledge which is being imparted, and the dangers of the slightest variation from the traditional techniques of the craft are all prominent. In such societies, despite the inclusion of some technology in the "schools," basic food-getting techniques remain in the common domain of the culture and are picked up by children haphazardly—only the special craft knowledge is sacredly imparted. (Even as late as Henry VIII's England the crafts were called the "mysteries," the two words being apparently interchangeable.)

To conclude then, we may pull most of the above together into one final summary. In primitive society there are two vehicles of education, the prepuberty process and the postpuberty process. No Western writer has ever succeeded in contrasting them as much as they need to be contrasted, because they are in every possible respect the Alpha and Omega of each other. In time of onset, atmosphere, personnel, techniques of instruction, location, curriculum, the two vehicles represent opposite poles. Everything that is done in or through one vehicle is the antithesis of what is done in the other. Standardization of experience and uniformity of training is markedly present in the postinitiation experience: it is markedly absent in the prepuberty experience of the growing child. If this is accepted as a base line, it has very important implications for the whole field of personality studies, especially for those studies which seem to claim that personality is very homogeneous in the simpler societies and for those allied studies which allege that child training and growing up in primitive society are very different from their equivalents in modern Western cultures. It is suggestive also as a base for attempting to answer a question that nobody has yet attempted to answer: Why do individuals in simple cultures differ from each other so markedly in personality traits, despite their common cultural conditioning? And it furnishes us finally with another link in the complicated chain of phenomena which exists between the problem of personality formation and the problem of culture change.

All these things are brought together, and indeed the whole of this paper is held together by one single thread—namely, that childhood experience is part of the secular world, postpuberty experience part of the sacred world. What is learned in the secular world is learned haphazardly, and varies greatly from individual to individual. Therefore no society can standardize that part of the child's learning which is acquired under secular circumstances. My only claim for this paper is that the use of this starting point for a discussion of primitive education enables us to obtain some insights into educational and cultural processes which are not provided by any alternative starting point.

References

Gesell, Arnold, and Frances L. Ilg, 1946, *The Child from Five to Ten.* New York: Harper & Row.

Hart, C. W. M., 1954, "The Sons of Turimpi," *American Anthropologist* 56:242–261.

———, and Arnold R. Pilling, 1960, *The Tiwi of North Australia.* CSCA. New York: Holt, Rinehart and Winston, Inc.

Herskovits, Melville J., 1948, *Man and His Works.* New York: Alfred A. Knopf, Inc.

Landtmann, Gunnar, 1927, *The Kiwai Papuans of British New Guinea.* London: The Macmillan Company.

Pettit, George A., 1946, "Primitive Education in North America," *University of California Publications in American Archaeology and Ethnology* 43:182.

Piaget, Jean, 1929, *The Child's Conception of the World.* New York: Harcourt, Brace Jovanovich.

———, 1932, *The Moral Judgment of the Child.* London: Routledge & Kegan Paul.

Schapera, I., 1940, *Married Life in an African Tribe.* London: Sheridan House.

Van Gennep, Arnold, 1909, *Les rites de passage.* Paris: E. Nourry. Translated paperback edition, 1960, Chicago: University of Chicago Press.

BRUCE T. GRINDAL/*Florida State University*

17 *Students' Self-Perceptions among the Sisala of Northern Ghana: A Study in Continuity and Change*

The casual Western observer cannot help but be impressed by his first experience of Africa, especially by a certain sense of discontinuity which manifests itself most immediately in the visual imagery he confronts. Walking down the newly paved main street of a medium-sized African town, our observer would see evidences of modern Western civilization—modern office buildings, a hospital, or a newly constructed local branch of a major British overseas bank. All these would constitute manifestations of the familiar which might lead him to conclude that Africa, albeit poorer, is nonetheless well on the road to westernization. This imagery is further confirmed when he looks around at the people. European clothing is the rule; policemen, bank tellers, civil servants, school teachers—all appear to be performing their expected roles. However, were our observer to view this environment more closely, he might see that not far behind the façade of the newly constructed bank, down a winding footpath, there is a traditional African compound constructed of sun-dried adobe brick and roofed with thatch. Within its walls he would see the women, dressed in traditional clothing, preparing the evening meal for their men folk returning from the fields. Such a setting would strike our observer as timeless, unaffected by the "civilizing" world up the road.

The visual imagery of our hypothetical observer is definitely one of disjuncture. He sees, as probably most of us would initially see, two distinct worlds: the timeless world of tradition extending beyond the newly paved road into the vast hinterland of Africa and that small island of European civilization, standing out like a sore thumb in an environment to which it does not seem to belong. To use a visual metaphor, the Western presence may be likened to a transparent overlay map; remove it and everything would go on as it always has.

If the European is inclined to see two Africas, what of the African? What of the schoolboy who spends seven hours in the classroom and who then returns home in the evening to help his illiterate father in the fields? Does he perceive himself as being a part of two worlds? Does he compartmentalize his existence between being European for seven hours and African for the remainder of the day? Perhaps this may sound facetious, and you might be tempted to say, of course he doesn't, he is a human being just like you and me. However, these questions do bring up some very significant issues.

It is easy for us as Western observers and scholars to make an analytical distinction between the traditional and modern sectors of African life. This distinction is useful for many kinds of analyses, but if we are to consider the human factor—the manner in which the African perceives himself and his own existence—the dichotomy of two worlds becomes less significant. To the African growing up in a changing world, the distinction between traditional and modern is not a necessary reality within the existential field of his perception. Obviously, an African schoolboy enacts a different role as student than as son and brother within a traditional household; nonetheless, as a sane individual, he embodies his different roles within a basically integrated personality structure. He simultaneously embodies the continuity and values of the traditional society and the changes brought by colonization and modernization.

In this chapter I shall examine these questions with regard to the Sisala people of northern Ghana. In particular, I am concerned with the manner in which the Sisala schoolboy views himself and his future role as an adult, seeking to understand his imagery as a product of both his experiences and expectations of the modern educational process and his experiences within the traditional educational context of family, village, and tribe.

Background

The Sisala are a tribal society situated in the intensely hot savannah grassland environment of northwest Ghana. As of 1960, approximately 60,000 Sisala resided in Ghana, of which 10,000 live outside of the "native area," primarily in the major urban centers of southern Ghana (Ghana Census Office 1964). In comparison to the more acculturated and urbanized peoples of southern Ghana, the Sisala have encountered a minimal degree of Western influence. The first contact with Europeans did not occur until 1905, when the British established their first colonial outpost in the town of Tumu. Aside from simple maintenance of law and order, the influence of the British was insignificant, and until 1945 there were no serious attempts to educate and prepare the Sisala to assume a meaningful role in the rapidly modernizing larger society.

Today the Sisala people are part of the modern nation state of Ghana. Graded roads cut through the tribal area and motorized vehicles carry people and farm produce to the surrounding trading centers and to the larger cities of southern Ghana. The tribal area, now included within the Tumu Administrative District, boasts of its own local government and representative in the national Parliament.

The modernizing influences of recent times have been felt most significantly in the town of Tumu, capital of the district. On one hand, Tumu is a traditional village consisting of nine lineage settlements which are related through patrilineal descent to form a single clan. The head of the clan is chief, and he, along with the elder men of the other lineage settlements, is responsible for the conduct of traditional village affairs. Superimposed upon this village organization is Tumu, the modern town. Approximately one half of its near 3000 population is made up of "strangers," including traders and artisans from other tribes, government officials and civil servants, and Sisala from other villages. The town has three primary or middle schools and a teacher-training college—a boarding school which houses both Sisala students and those from other major tribes in Ghana. Located at the crossroads of the main transportation routes, Tumu is a kind of cosmopolitan center from which changes spread throughout the tribal area.

However, as one moves away from Tumu along the graded roads and then along the narrow footpaths which wind through the countryside, these modernizing influences become less intense. Small but highly compact villages dot the sparsely populated savannah landscape. Along the road passing through a village, one may occasionally see a mud brick bungalow with a corrugated aluminum roof, built perhaps by one of the wealthier or more acculturated members of the town. However, the far greater percentage of the people live in large mud-walled compounds located upon their traditional ancestral sites. These compounds are more or less circular, made up of rectangular brick dwellings which are linked together so as to present a sturdy wall to the outside world.

Around the compound may be found small gardens in which women grow tomatoes, onions, okra, red peppers, and other minor ingredients used in their cooking. At some distance from the village are located the main farms upon which are grown the dietary staples of the people; these include primarily millet and guinea corn, but also maize, yams, peanuts, rice, and beans. While an occasional farmer might hire a tractor to break the soil, the majority employ the traditional short-handled hoe and digging stick. Large livestock—cattle, sheep, goats—are also kept but are important as subsidiary diet and seldom sold for money; instead they serve as symbols of family prestige and are reserved mainly for customary economic transactions and for sacrifice to family and village shrines.

The Sisala child is born into a large extended family household in which he is viewed as belonging to everyone, not only to his parents. Little value is placed on the child as an individual, and he is seen as a gift of the ancestors, as one who will serve his family and perpetuate its continuity. The infant and small child are seen as inherently dependent and incapable of malice, and the period of early training is characterized by extreme indulgence. When a child reaches the age of six, he is said to have "sense"—the ability to distinguish right from wrong, and he is expected to begin participating in the work tasks of house and farm. However, the "sense" of a child is still "small," and he is considered unable to exert self-control over his behavior. Parents thus discourage innovative behavior and personal autonomy, and the child is expected to comply rigidly with parental teachings and to sublimate individual desires and goals to those of the family. The authority of the father and other male adults in the family is absolute, and the child is expected to demonstrate respect and unquestioning obedience.

The traditional education of children is in no way structured or formalized; rather, the child learns the necessary skills and knowledge through the situational observation of and participation in the daily routine. The educational process is a gradual one wherein the successful performance of a given task is rewarded by being entrusted with further responsibilities and wherein the child is aware, at each stage of his development, of the instrumental importance and social value of his knowledge and skills. When a boy reaches adolescence, he is thought to be capable of controlling and disciplining himself and is no longer subject to parental corporal punishment. His relationship to his father changes gradually from one based upon "fearful respect" to one based upon "respect accruing from generosity, nurturance, and protection." The boy identifies more strongly with his father and with the values his father's role represents, thereby becoming an effective agent in the maintenance of custom and family prestige.

The basic values underlying Sisala society may be ultimately seen as a function of the growth process. After an initially brief period of indulged freedom, the child gradually comes to perceive himself in a negative way as a "small boy"—one who is socially useless, incapable of self-control and judgment, and subject to the domination of those elder to him. This negative self-image generates a strong motivating force whereby the child desires to escape the submissive status of the "small boy" in order to achieve a dominant status similar to that of his elder brother, and eventually that of his father. Thus, to grow older means to grow into and attain the basic rewards and prerogatives of the society: a man successively becomes a father and nurturer of his own children, an owner or co-owner of his family's property, and lastly an elder man, free with leisure time, wealthy with many children, and wise in his years.

Thus, for the majority of the people, the traditional economic and social structure of the society continues to function, and notwithstanding the presence of modern influences, it will probably continue to function. It is in this setting that the average Sisala child grows up, learning the knowledge, values, and skills necessary for successful adjustment to the traditional society. Even the child who attends school seven hours a day is nonetheless inextricably part of this traditional educational environment.

The first primary school was established in the Sisala area in 1945. The response of the people was enthusiastic, and by 1960 there were nineteen primary schools enrolling approximately 12 percent of the school-age population (Ghana Census Office 1962). In addition, two middle or upper primary schools were established in Tumu for students from the seventh through tenth grades. However, prior to these post-World War II developments, a small group of Sisala had been educated in boarding schools outside the tribal area. As fortune would have it, these individuals reached maturity at precisely the time when the British were concerned with developing the Sisala area; as a consequence this small group of literates came to assume relatively important positions within the society. To a large extent, the people's enthusiasm for the establishment of schools stemmed from their perception of this educated elite, and thereby the belief that education was the primary means of achieving success and prestige in a rapidly modernizing world.

The schools in the Sisala area, like those throughout Ghana, are patterned upon the British academic tradition with nationally standardized examinations administered in the sixth and fourth years of the primary and middle schools respectively. The village primary school is constructed of mud and thatch and usually contains two rooms; the six classes meet both in and about the school house. The two middle schools are better constructed, with separate room for each class. Also, in contrast to the primary schools, the teachers are better trained, all having graduated from teaching-training colleges.

Methodology

During the nineteen months I lived among the Sisala, many hours were spent directly observing teachers and students within the classroom setting. In contrast to the traditional educational process, the classroom environment into which the Sisala student enters is characterized by a mood of authoritarian rigidity and an almost total absence of spontaneity. At best, formal education is a process of instilling literacy and memorizing facts, wherein great emphasis is placed upon the student's ability to give "correct" answers to questions posed by the teacher. Moreover, the fact that the curriculum is essential British in both method and content leads one to question whether it is at all relevant to the life experience of the young Sisala student. I was, therefore, very much interested in understanding the impact of the modern educational experience, and discovering how the student views the modern educational process and its relationship to his present position as a schoolboy and his future status as adult.

To accomplish this, I administered a series of projective autobiographical essays entitled "My autobiography from now to the year 2000." This device was used elsewhere by Gillespie and Allport (1955) in a cross-national study of youth's outlook on the future; the essay was administered to over 1800 university students representing ten nations. In my study, the essay was administered to thirty students at the Kanton Teacher Training College in

Tumu and to fifty-three students in the two middle schools of Tumu, and the results were cross-checked by interviews with a sample of the participating students.

The projective essay was extremely easy to administer. After introducing myself, I merely stated that I was very much interested in their writing an essay for me on the above mentioned topic. I stated that even though I would appreciate proper spelling and usage, this essay was not an academic exercise, that it should express the students' own ideas, feelings, and expectations, and that whatever they wrote would be held in confidence. Personal data cards were also collected for each student, and they included information on age, sex, religion, place of birth, place of residence, tribe, level of education, and level of education of mother and father. Fortunately, the teachers in all the classes gave the students as much time as they needed, and the students spent approximately one hour writing. The essays varied in length from 250 to 450 words.

From my experience, I found that students with less than eight years of formal education had difficulty following instructions and were often incapable of expressing themselves in written English. Thus, my sample was chosen from the third and fourth forms of the two middle schools and from the teacher-training college. While the middle schools were predominantly Sisala, the teacher-training college was composed of students representing all major tribes of Ghana, thus furnishing valuable information by which to compare the differential reactions to modern education among the various tribes in Ghana.

The essay results were examined in terms of their dominant themes. Except for making a distinction between Sisala and non-Sisala students, the data were not analyzed with respect to the variables obtained from the personal data cards, nor was any attempt made to quantify the results. Instead, the focus was upon a holistic understanding of these themes within the total cultural context of the student's experience. These essays were particularly valuable since, as I discovered, students were generally reticent when speaking with people in authority while they expressed themselves quite freely in their writings. These materials thus served to uncover questions and provide insights which were subsequently cross-checked by interviews and interpreted within the broader context of my field experience. It is in this perspective then that the following analysis is presented.

Students' Self-Perceptions: An Analysis

One of the dominant characteristics of these essays is the optimistic, and indeed naive perception that an almost one-to-one correspondence exists between formal educational achievement and success in later life. Most essays begin with a methodical outline of the students' educational plans, beginning with graduation from middle school and extending in most cases to university and postgraduate education. At each stage in his life, the student's educational accomplishments are rewarded by the assumption of a prestigious position in the society. These aspirations are usually quite unrealistic and demonstrate little awareness of conditions in the modern world; the essays frequently become heterogeneous mixtures of educational achievements, material acquisitions, and assumed roles. Thus, it is not uncommon for a student to plan to earn three university degrees, buy a radio, automobile, and three-story house, have a zinc roof put on his father's house, marry a white woman, travel and teach in England and America, and then retire to his village with his wife and children.

The following statement demonstrates the staccato style of the essays and the students' perception of a society which is essentially open and in which all things are possible through education.

> In 1967 I will go to form four [middle school]. From there I will take the college exam [i.e., teacher-training college] and I will go to college. After my college I will come to teach in the middle school which I like. About some years to come, I will try again to take an exam to anywhere else. I will go to the university. . . . I will be there till I leave the upper form and then I will be a doctor. I will treat those who are sick and suffering from anything which I can care for. . . . I will be a doctor for a long period. And if I like, I will have my certificate and go and be a lawyer. There I will judge cases, and the guilty ones will always be charged and taken to prison. I will judge my cases honestly and not dishonestly. . . . From there I will go and be the principal of a college or secondary school. There I will not teach but will only work in the office. Also I will see that the school is in a good condition. . . . From there I will go and have a car, and there I will be a big man either an education officer, the district administrator, or the regional administrative officer. There I will have my own car and always carry my wife along with me. From there I will go and be the president of Ghana. There I will be the big man of the country. Whatever I say will be done.

When the essay materials are compared with data derived from interviews, a discrepancy is perceived between the students' aspirations and their actual expectations. It is usually admitted that the essay responses represent ultimate desires; however, students insist that the realization of such desires is possible, and they frequently cite cases of Africans who have risen from humble beginnings to become important men in the society. Thus the student's view of his future is a result of both educational achievement and fate; if he succeeds in life, it is because he has been fortunate enough to pass his leaving and entrance examinations in the various institutions of higher learning; if he does not succeed, it is because fate meant that he should not continue his schooling. As one student aptly stated:

> You see big men. They drive in cars.
> Whether I succeed or not, I don't know.
> Maybe I will become the president of

> Ghana or maybe I will just be a teacher
> in the villages. Nobody knows. It is
> what God wills, and I will be happy with
> whatever I become.

A second characteristic theme in the essays is the relationship between the student's desire to escape his inferior status as a schoolboy and his need to attain a position of power and dominance over others. Students describe their present status as one of wretchedness and poverty. They complain about their dirty appearance, tattered clothes, and insufficient diet; they also recall times when they were bullied or ridiculed by teachers and older students, or publicly humiliated because of their poverty. The expressed desire to achieve success is a reaction to this perceived state of wretchedness. In describing their future occupational roles, students invariably make reference to their interaction with subordinates. Thus to be a magistrate is to pass judgment on evil people, or to be a head teacher is to give orders to classroom teachers. In effect, then, the schoolboy sees himself as escaping his "small boy" status through education, obtaining an occupation or position concommitant with his educational level, and exercising the powers and prerogatives of his status.

The following statements demonstrate the relationship between the student's awareness of his poverty and his desire to achieve.

> When I have finished my schooling, I will sit down and think of the time when I was in middle school. And when I think of how poor I was and how I suffered, I will laugh at myself. For now I will have left the university. I will be a very rich man, and I will be sending some of the money home to my family.
>
> And there were those people who laughed at me when I was poor. But someday they will see me driving in a fine car, and they will be sorry. Maybe too, they will also be poor; and when they see me, they will ask for money. But I was as poor as anything once and God helped, so I will help anyone as poor as I was.

Another aspect to the schoolboy's negative perception of himself involves his familial, village, and ethnic identity. If a boy perceives himself as poor, it is largely because his own father is poor and unable to furnish him with suitable clothing and spending money. Many school children recalled incidents in which they suffered humiliation as a result of their parents' poverty; this is particularly true among students from the villages who feel shame in the presence of the more acculturated Tumu people. Among the older students in the teacher-training college, the self-image of poverty is related to ethnic affiliation as Sisala; in this multitribal setting, the Sisala students often remark that they are referred to as "primitive" or "bush" by the students from the more acculturated tribes of the South.

The strong motivation to achieve thus implies not only a desire to escape the submissive status of the small boy, but also a desire to raise the status of one's family and tribe. This motivational disposition resulting from familial and ethnic status withdrawal is directly related to a third dominant theme in the essays: the desire to serve as an educator and benefactor to one's people.

Whether the schoolboy's aspirations are high or low, he sees his eventual role in life as one of serving his own people. The typical imagery presented by the schoolboy is that of a young man who has become successful, who has traveled around the world and gained prestige, and who returns home to his village as a "big man." He sees himself settling down and building a fine house for his father and his own family. If he is wealthy, he will hire laborers to maintain the farm so that he and his parents will not have to work. He will also be generous both to his village people and to strangers, and with his superior knowledge and financial resources, he will endeavor to improve the conditions of his village.

The following statements illustrate the imagery which students attach to themselves in their future roles as "big men" and benefactors of their communities. The first describes the schoolboy's desire to alleviate the impoverished conditions of his people.

> My village people are dying of thirst. There is no good well there. There is no educated person there yet. I am the only school child. And may God bless me to complete my school, college, and perhaps university with success. During the old regime our fathers were troubled by hunger. Had I been an important person at that time, I would have demanded food from the government.

The second illustrates the schoolboy's impression of himself upon returning to his village as a wealthy and successful man.

> I have in mind this day being a professor so that I will be able to help my country. . . . As a professor I will visit so many countries such as America, Britain, and Holland. In fact it will be interesting for me and my wife. . . . When I return, my father will be proud seeing his child like this. Just imagine me having a wife and children in my car moving down the street of my village. And when the people are in need of anything, I will help them.

The final excerpt involves a student's eventual goal of achieving recognition for the services rendered his people.

> By that time I have attained my graduation certificate from the university, the government will be so happy that they may like to make me president of my beloved country. When I receive my salary, I will divide the money and give part to my father and part to my wife and children. I will take some money to the government to give me some laborers to put up nice buildings so that my village will also be remembered. By that, the people will be proud of what I have done. People say the U.S.A. is a beautiful country. But when they see my village, they will say it is more beautiful. Through my hard studies, my name will rise forever for people to remember.

While the essay responses of Sisala students, as well as those of other northern tribes, show a strong element of discontinuity between the schoolboy's unrealistic aspirations and his strongly dependent relationships to family and kin, the responses of acculturated southern students present a more realistic appraisal of their future living situation. Southerners are very much aware of the limited possibilities of educational and occupational advancement, and their responses reflect a deeper understanding of the actual workings of the modern nation state. Most see themselves as teachers or civil servants, and their eventual life style as that of small, economically independent families. While they recognize the need to maintain customary ties with family and kin, such relationships are not central to their life ambitions. In short, the responses of southern students reflect an accommodation to the acculturative process wherein the customary demands of tribal life are not in conflict with their personal ambitions. Among northerners, on the other hand, greater disparity exists between the realities of the modern plural society and the students' naive perception of their future roles in that society.

This disparity is directly related to a fourth dominant characteristic of the essays: a high incidence of projected and expressed anxiety about the future. In most cases, this consists of a generalized or vague fear of the future and of life outside the tribal area; both are seen as strange and somewhat dangerous. In some of the more imaginative essays, frequent incidents of projected failure in later life occur. Thus one student sees himself working hard for a university degree, but his progress is interrupted by the tragic death of both parents; subsequently, he turns to drink and also dies a tragic death, his great ambitions unrealized. In other essays, anxiety is expressed in terms of an ominous apprehension about the destruction of mankind, but the student sees himself as being able to prevent destruction through the exercise of his powers.

In cross-checking essay responses through interviews, a genuine feeling of insecurity and anxiety was detected in the students' perceptions of the world outside the tribal environment. Many students, especially those in the teacher-training college, remarked that they felt very much alone, lacking real guidance or assistance from their parents. Some admitted that they did not enjoy going home during the holidays because no one in the villages understood what they were studying in school. Yet most of the students stated that they did not wish to leave their tribal areas, except perhaps for a few brief visits to the south. The south, they felt, was more competitive than the north, and they expressed strong doubts whether they could succeed in an environment which they saw as basically inhospitable. Both the essay and oral responses of northern students thus show a genuine ambivalence; on one hand, the students are strongly motivated to attain occupational success; on the other hand, they are held back both by fear of being exposed to the hardships and ethnic prejudice of the modern urban south and by the need to maintain dependent ties with the more understandable world of village and tribe.

Conclusion

The essay responses of Sisala students, therefore, reflect both elements of continuity and discontinuity with respect to the traditional experience. The student's participation in the formal educational process is largely a discontinuous experience, especially when contrasted to the traditional home environment wherein the immediate relevance and social value of the child's knowledge is directly related to his observation of and participation in the daily routine of the adult society. Moreover, education as part of the larger modernizing process has created new awarenesses and new needs. The desire to own an automobile, to travel overseas, and to attain a modern occupation does not have precedent in the traditional society. Also the student's perception of education as the primary means for attaining success and prestige directly bypasses the traditional status system which places emphasis upon age and propertied authority.

However, when seen in the recent historical perspective, these discontinuities are not as profound as they may at first seem. The fact that Sisala students place high expectations upon formal education is due in large part to parental expectations placed upon the school day. Most parents, in one way or another, have experienced and have been involved in the modernizing process. Many have known the experience of living in the urban centers of southern Ghana as temporary migrant workers, and consequently, have been made increasingly aware of alternate modes of life. To a lesser degree, this same increasing awareness holds true for those individuals who have never left the tribal area. As a result, many parents show considerable desire to prepare their children for a world different from that of their early experience. Schooling comes to be viewed as the best means of preparing the child for the future, and many parents, on perceiving the prestigious position of Sisala and other educated elites, have sent their children to school with high expectations for their success. Thus, many of the aspirations contained in the students' essays represent changes in parental attitudes and subsequent modifications in the traditional educational environment.

The most fundamental aspect of continuity in the students' imagery lies in the basic values underlying the notions of achievement and success. The students' perception of achievement as the desire to escape the submissive status of the schoolboy and to attain a position of dominance is directly related to the psychodynamics of growth and attainment of status in the traditional society. Likewise, the idea that one's success is inextricably linked to one's fate or the "will of God" finds precedent in the traditional use of the supernatural explanation to explain success and failure. Also, the theme of expressed anxiety toward the future, while reflecting a basic discontinuity in the students' experience, nonetheless demonstrates a weak development of autonomy which, in turn, may be traced to a traditional educational environment which places strong emphasis upon dependent ties to family and kin. Unlike the Euro-American notion of success which emphasizes self-reliance and personal excellence, the Sisala perceives his own success as inseparable from that of family, village, and tribe. In his future role as a successful adult, the schoolboy aspires to a position similar to that of a prestigious elder man, serving as the nurturant benefactor of his people and gaining personal recognition for his generosity and beneficent power.

As stated in the introduction, it is necessary that we understand the processes of change and modernization in Africa from the perspective of the African experience. Many scholars have made the mistake of reifying the analytical distinction between traditional and modern; as a consequence, the African comes to be viewed as a kind of "schizoid" individual who is continually compartmentalizing and vacillating between the two cultural poles of his existence. By contrast, this paper has attempted to demonstrate that the African perceives and reacts to modernizing influences within the interpretive framework of his total experience. The fact that the African student participates in an essentially European institution of formal education does not mean that his perception of the process and his values with regard to achievement and success are the same as those of his European counterpart.

References

Ghana Census Office, 1962, *1960 Population Census of Ghana: Volume II, Statistics of Localities and Enumeration Areas,* Accra, Ghana: Census Office.

Ghana Census Office, 1964, *1960 Population Census of Ghana: Special Report "E", Tribes in Ghana.* Accra, Ghana: Census Office.

Gillespie, J. M., and G. W. Allport, 1955, *Youth's Outlook on the Future.* New York: Doubleday & Company, Inc.

JOSEPH GLICK/*City University of New York*

18 *Culture and Cognition: Some Theoretical and Methodological Concerns**

Much of our thinking about the relationship between culture and cognition has focused on the role of language in forming cognitive categories. This focus is neither historically nor theoretically inappropriate but may, in fact, obscure other quite important aspects of the relationship.

The choice of language as a cognitive and cultural factor is a powerful one. Language appears to be a unique human capacity, is sufficiently well structured to allow for complex analysis as a cultural "artifact," and appears to play an important role in thought processes. Much of our research on language-cognition relationships has focused on that aspect of language which seems to provide a "conceptual" mapping of the world. An investigation of the terminology and hierarchical structure of language may provide an important clue to the way in which the categories of experience are ordered. Areas of experience in which language in question makes many terminological distinctions may be areas of greater psychological differentiation, whereas those in which few distinctions are made (as in some color names) may be areas of lesser distinctiveness. Some of our own work (Cole, Gay, Glick, and Sharp 1966) has dealt with a case where size comparatives are coded only in an order of increasing size, and we have shown that this has some relationship to the ease with which relative size judgments are made. Other aspects of our work have dealt with ease of communication in areas where few conventionalized terms are available, and again we showed some relationship between codability and communication efficiency (Cole, Gay, and Glick 1969).

I should like to describe some of the research that Michael Cole, John Gay, and I (together with a number of talented and dedicated colleagues) have been conducting over the past few years. Our research started as a cross-cultural investigation focusing on language-cognition and language-learning relationships. It is too early to tell where our work has ended up. It is clear, however, that in order to deal adequately with the culture-cogni-

---

*This chapter was first presented at the American Anthropological Association meetings, New Orleans, November 21, 1969. The research reported here was supported in part by the NSF grant G1221 to M. Cole and NICHD grant 7R01-HD-03947 to the author.

tion relationship, it must be broadened beyond the area of language-cognition relationships. So thorough has been our conversion that we have been led as well to reassess the value of the experimental approach that we had adopted. In fact, one of our greatest learning experiences has been reconceptualizing the meaning of conducting an experiment in a cross-cultural context.

Our investigations originally began with asking the question in terms of whether conceptual categories, as reflected in language, would also be reflected in such basic cognitive operations as class formation and organized memory. Our simplified approach—perhaps overly so—was to isolate class terms in their semantically related instances. A variety of techniques was used for this purpose, ranging from a relatively informal elicitation from informants to more highly structured techniques involving distributional analysis of nouns in different sentence frames. Since all of these operations "converged" to give us similar pictures of the semantic organization of instances into classes, we were confident at the outset that our choice of linguistic classification was appropriate.[1] Using a subset of these linguistically ordered classes, we then attempted to see if nonlinguistic behaviors dealing with classifiable items would show the same conceptual structuring (Cole, Gay, Glick, and Sharp 1971).

Before the story gets ahead of itself I should like to say a few words about the particular population that this general strategy was applied to. Our work has been done mainly among the Kpelle people of north-central Liberia. Until recently the Kpelle have led largely the life of an agricultural people. The main crop is upland rice, which has been grown mainly for subsistence purposes. Cooperative work groups called Kuus are formed to aid in the agricultural process. The main medium of exchange within these groups is the sharing of labor. Only recently, with the advent of a money economy, has money become a means of adjudication of imbalances in the distribution of labor.

Traditional values are strong, although they are increasingly coming under attack from processes of Westernization. Secret tribal initiation societies exist, and serve as a method of cohesion, and as Gibbs (1969) suggests, form a kind of shadow political organization where important matters of law and influence are settled. Status within the society may or may not be correlated with age, but nonetheless the opinions of elders apparently carry greater weight in settling disputes.

---

[1] This confidence applies only to the particular classes used in our sorting and memory experiments. Some of our more grand-scale efforts such as eliciting an hierarchical ordering of the concept of "things" (Seng) have proved quite interesting but more tenuous. For one thing, our elicitation methods enforce a hierarchy that we are not at all positive exists in the heads of the people we are dealing with. Moreover, with any classification system, the elaboration of categories depends upon the initial axis for classification—for example, the chart looks different if the initial ordering is "things" and their types or if the initial ordering is "good and bad." Restricting ourselves to the prosaic (things) and to the more clear-cut "instance class" relationship, we have hoped to avoid some of the very difficult issues involved in more complex semantic mapping.

Medicine, in its physical and spiritual forms, constitutes a large concern for many of the people. In an environment which is, at best, hostile to health and particularly to infant survival, considerable concern for matters of health and fertility is manifest. This concern with medicine penetrates greatly into matters of social relationship. Disputes, which appear to the untutored eye to be frequent, often involve charges of "witching." From the viewpoint of a cognitive psychologist, the medicine relationship seems to involve a great deal of technical skill. It also seems to demand quite a lot in terms of inferences from minimal cues—as to who is witching whom, and so forth. We do not know whether all deviation from the normal and true course of events is attributed to special intervention, but a large portion of experienced discrepancies seem to lead to the "witching" inference.

The educational system in Liberia is presumably universal, but, in fact, it is not. Government schools (often built with U.S. aid funds) exist in many villages, but are often poorly or infrequently attended. For our experimental purposes this presented a nice situation, since the influence of age and of schooling could be separated. In many villages with schools there has developed somewhat of a split between the Westernized or "Kwi" people and the more traditional types. It is not clear to us yet how this split relates to the traditional power relationships which play between the secret society, the organization of wealth and political power within the town, and the degree of Westernization. But it should be noted that several educated people of our acquaintance occupy an important role in the secret society. Still, education is by no means a determiner of importance in itself, nor is it necessarily seen as a natural antagonist to the traditional way.

While the foregoing is merely a glimpse of a society which is richly detailed and well organized, several points should emerge as a context for the rest of the paper. What impressed us most is that much of the life of the Kpelle people is spent in the figuring out and solving of extremely pragmatic problems, from the adjudication of family palavers to the solution of agricultural problems. Neither of these areas has a visible codified set of rules or algorithms for solution—the processes of problem solution seem to be born of the materials of the moment, and settled within that context. Rarely, for example, in law cases is a legal precedent invoked, although there may be one which is implicit at some level of council, or explicit in some form of cultural expression (for example, myth or proverb). It is clear that whatever is codified is sufficiently general to allow for a wide range of solutions in the particular case.

Whether this situation derives from the absence of a shared written language or from some yet to be identified factor of cultural life, the present case seems to be that the Kpelle find themselves in the position of the "bricoleur" (Lévi-Strauss 1966), presented with problems in particular contexts but without context-free algorithms for their solution. The bricoleur is essentially a man with a "bag of tools" which are kept because they may come in handy. His processes of problem solution involve the deployment of this bag of tools in the concrete context, but according to no set formula and no decontextualized codified means of solution. Problems are met and solved in the ongoing process of solution without an overall plan (beyond the simple setting of a goal). A similar contrast has been drawn by Gladwin (1964, 1970) in constrasting Western and Polynesian methods of navigation.

What should be noted at this point is that there is an opposition between these ethnographic ideas and those formally posed by the normal means of conceptualizing the language-cognition relationship. The ethnographic ideas suggest a treatment in terms of the pragmatics of contextualized thinking; the linguistic ideas suggest the presence of categories of formal classification systems which may override particular contexts.

Our research has led us to the posing of this opposition, and we now turn to the data that seemed to demand such an approach.

Our suspicions were raised at the outset of our endeavor when one of our co-workers, a Kpelle college graduate who was entrusted with much of the linguistic elicitation, reported his misgivings about the enterprise to us:

> The idea of a standard or formal grouping of things is so far remote in his [the Kpelle] mind that it cannot be shown by such indirect methods of finding out what is formal—when the informal is what he is used to.
>
> The Kpelle man is able and can usually group things into any group once he can rationalize the reason for such groupings. Such groupings are always inconsistent and informal.

What is suggested here is not the absence of a categorizing ability but the informality of such an ability. Simple categorizations do not exist as principles to be applied to events in vacuo but rather as descriptions of events in context.

Whatever our initial misgivings, we first approached the problem in a direct way. As posed in our first experiment the problem was: If the language categorizes a set of objects in terms of a set of class names, would the linguistic classes dominate the way in which the objects were sorted out by our subjects? Accordingly, we began with a set of twenty objects, which according to both Kpelle and English belong to four classes. These were clothes—head-tie, shirt, singlet, trousers, and hat; tools—knife, hammer, file, cutlass, and hoe; foods—banana, orange, potato, onion, and coconut; and containers—cup, plate, calabash, pan, and pot. These twenty items were at first arranged haphazardly before our subjects, who were told to "put the ones together that belong together." Under these conditions, our Kpelle adult subjects would either isolate the items one by one or, at most, provide matches of two items. The basis for classification offered was in many cases of a functional nature—an orange and a knife would go together because the knife cut the orange. In other cases no explanation of rather exotic co-ocurrences was offered. In an effort to provide greater contextual clues, we decided to constrain the possible response categories. We set out four chairs and instructed our subjects to put all the items that go together on each of the four chairs. Our hope was that as we provided information about the categorical constraints this would clarify an otherwise ambiguous situation. The results of this experiment were disappointing. Our subjects provided no startling evidence of sorting in terms of categories, or, in this instance, of sorting on any other basis. The application of more subtle measure of co-occurrence of items yielded some evidence of categorization, but at very low levels of strength.

Undaunted, we decided to constrain classification even further. In our next experiment only two chairs were provided, and subjects were again asked to put the items that belonged together on one chair. Much to our surprise this manipulation worked. In most of the cases two classes were placed together on a single chair with almost no intrusion of nonsensible items. Moreover, this effect was not due to chance or the enforced greater probability of items from the same category going together only because there were two choices. At first, this particular result seems counterintuitive—shouldn't it be the case that the four-category situation should provide the best clue to the categorical structure of a set of items having, in fact, four categories? Why, when conditions are set up that enforce a mixture of categories, do subjects tend to perform more in categorical terms? Why do their reasons for classifying the way they do shift from functional to categorical reasons as this shift is made?

To form an answer to these questions is probably to understand a lot about the way our subjects think. So, being presumptuous, I should at least like to offer an hypothesis which is testable, but which has not yet been tested. The Kpelle subject, faced with an array of familiar items, functions at first as a pragmatist. His questions are, "How do these things relate to my experiences?" His answers are at first contextual—his experiences are not questioned to the level of linguistic categories, but only to the level of everyday encounters. As we shift the situation for the subject by forcing more and more items into proximity—a proximity that they would not ordinarily manifest—the task shifts from contextual reasoning to conceptual treatment. We are, as it were, shifting the situation from the actual to the hypothetical, from the pragmatic to the "formal."

We are not dealing with a case that represents the presence or absence of a categorical mode, but rather with one that deals with the features of situations that will call forth categorical or other abilities. I believe that throughout the experiments our subjects were performing "reasonably," only in the case of the two-category situation did their criteria of reasonability match ours.

Perhaps an anecdote from some of our early work on this problem is in order here. In the early stages, we were dealing with the unconstrained sorting

---

[2] The type of analysis used is one in which co-occurrence matrices are made up and an hierarchy is forced upon the data. From this sort of analysis the most frequently co-occurring items are bracketed together and are thus bound into a class. By looking at the frequency at which bracketing decisions are made, some index of the strength of association can be garnered (Johnson 1967).

condition and our subjects were producing functional types of categories. When asked to explain what they did, they answered something about the smartness of Kpelle ways—how a wise man would do it only this way. We pressed our subjects to the point of asking how a stupid man would do it—here Western sorting—classificatory behaviors became manifest. The problem was one of reasonableness, not of inability.

Elsewhere (Glick 1968) I have reported a similar instance. In this case we had inadvertently framed a task in a game context, although we imagined it to be a learning-problem-solving task. Subjects, responding to our learning task as if it was a game, seemed unable to learn. However, a minor shift of technique, transforming the "game" to a learning task, produced learning in a manner fully equivalent to that shown by Western graduate students.

More recent work, looking for evidence of the influence of linguistic categorizations on the structure of free recall (recall of memorized items in a subject-determined manner), has demonstrated again the heterogeneity of results that may be obtained (hence the heterogeneity of our characterizations of the cognitive capacities of our subjects), with seemingly minor variations in the contextual variables introduced into our experiments. In some instances the Kpelle will organize free recall in terms of categories (Cole, Gay, Glick, and Sharp 1971).

Masses of data lying behind observations such as these (see Cole et al. 1971) open up real questions about the nature of cross-cultural comparison (for that manner, any comparison where people are judged as being different on the basis of test performances) that are not easily answered. The presence of an ability in one context and not in some other strongly suggests that abstracted statements about "human functioning" are not appropriate. Our interests have shifted more toward questions about the way in which particular contexts bring out particular abilities. We have in this regard made little progress. However, we have begun to toy with some methodological ideas that may in the future allow real progress to be made in the treating of cognitive behaviors both in cross- and intracultural studies.

Methodological Concerns

A good deal of current research in cognitive processes treats these processes as if they were basically context-free, more as a property of the organism (or his head) than as a property of the organism relating to a particular environment.

This basic assumption has allowed us to treat the research enterprise as if it were a sort of psychological test that is applied to the subject. The "test" (or experimental situation) is seen as calling forth certain kinds of abilities. Accordingly, the way in which subjects distribute their scores on the "test" reflects something about their internal processing abilities. Seen in this way the "test" situation can be looked at as a primitive kind of sorting machine—

subjects are thrown into the machine at one end and come out sorted on the other. They are either high x's or low x's, smart or stupid, conceptual sorters or non-conceptual sorters.

As long as the test or experiment is applied to the same population to which the tester or experimenter belongs this model may roughly apply. Not because it is necessarily true, but rather because both tester and subject share certain assumptions about the world which are institutionalized in the testing situation. One need only look beyond this cozy *folie à deux* situation to sense the inadequacies of the model. Many investigators, for example, have argued about the culture bias institutionalized in many I.Q. tests. Our own investigations have helped us to see the arbitrariness of some of the situations that we initially employed. We thought they were the kinds of things that "all rational men" would perform reasonably on. In fact, they were highly specialized cultural patterns of functioning. Our most striking example comes from a case where we wanted to use everyday objects as things to sort. Accordingly, we chose something that was highly familiar to our African subjects—beer bottles of various heights and colors and soda pop bottles of various heights and colors. Our African subjects, though familiar with these objects and their differentiae, refused to subclassify them—all bottles were heaped in a single category. We had made the mistake of using empty bottles, which were clearly "garbage" and nothing else. Preliminary observations with filled bottles shows that these can be classified.

As one reads this example it is striking that there are real differences between Africans and Americans on this kind of task. These differences are not in the ability to classify or not but rather in the constraints of reasonability that allow for the classification operation to be used.

While examples of cultural differences in the way that "test situations" are construed can be multiplied *ad infinitum,* we are left at this juncture with the problem of having to think our way out of the box that we have built for ourselves. Isn't it most reasonable to keep on testing, to keep on refining our tests and trying to make them "culture-free?"

My answer is most certainly no. It appears that the effort to make some test of cognitive functioning "culture-free" is to seriously misunderstand the nature of cognition. Cognition itself is not "culture-free," it is not best conceived of as a set of processing rules independent of the particular circumstances and intentions of the cognizer. In fact, our efforts should be to make our measures of cognitive functioning more culturally sensitive. We should be bending our efforts toward understanding the ways in which particular abilities are brought to bear on particular areas of functioning, to provide a road map of demands and cognitive strategies in the context of those demands.[3]

[3] This, of course, does not deny the possibility of universal forms of cognition. Rather, our point is that these universal forms will be understood only in the context of an organismic analysis of thought forms within cultures. The analyses of Lévi-Strauss bring this point out with particular clarity.

How then can one proceed using experimental methods and all of the other positively valued tools of the experimental psychologist?

A strategy that we have adopted might be termed a fundamental inversion of the testing strategy currently in vogue. In it, any experiment has fixed and variable elements. In the testing-experimental strategy the fixed element is the test-experiment and the variable elements are the subjects and their scores. In our inversion of this procedure we have attempted to make the outcome scores the fixed elements and the subjects and tests the variable elements. What this amounts to is the assertion that some "terminal performance," for example, perfect conceptual sorting, is attainable in all human beings. However, it is attainable under different contextual conditions. Accordingly, when a given test (contextual condition) does not yield the desired terminal performance, the test is varied (we have indicated some of the ways in which this has been done above) until this terminal performance is attained.

A slightly less radical, and perhaps more reasonable, approach is to fix as a terminal point some performance which approaches internal coherence, no matter what its position is with respect to some ideal standard. Both of these variations of approach serve to make more explicit some of the priorities that we have begun to recognize as important in meaningful comparative research.

First the setting of an explicit goal of coherence or particular performance establishes a focus on contextualization—on the understanding of particular behaviors in relationship to the environmental demands for those behaviors. Accordingly, statements coming as the outcome of this type of research will not be "deficit" statements (group X cannot do such and such) but rather positive statements relating behavior to its occasions. This serves to establish a unity of methodological intent between psychologists and other social scientists (anthropologists, for example). In fact, we have termed our own work as experimental anthropology (Cole 1971, 1972).

Second, the posing of our inverted model serves to make explicit one of the major undealt with problems of experimental research—namely, the problem of when to stop an experiment. Look back for a moment on our series of studies dealing with classification. We could have stopped our inquiry at any given time, concluding variously that the Kpelle cannot categorize, or that they can. We had no heuristic to guide us, and hence our decision to continue with the experimental series was a rather chance affair. Premature stopping would, however, have given a highly distorted picture of the Kpelle. By mapping changes in behavior over a variety of environmental situations we have achieved a more differentiated picture of functioning among the members of this African tribal group. This is a picture that poses many puzzles for future research, but one that, at least, does not distort our appreciation of their abilities. By explicitly posing as our goal the achievement of perfect sorting, the series would have been guaranteed to continue. In fact, looking backward we allowed the work to continue because we did pose this goal implicitly.

From the work reviewed above, and other as yet unpublished research, we have gradually come to recognize that the task of the psychologist is broader than that of inventing clever experiments or superior tests. If our goal is to truly understand behavior, then we must see the individual as possessing a variety of modes of functioning, and we must organize our inquiry in such a way as to follow the variations in behavior as environments and contexts vary. Cognition conceived from this point of view is not a "trait" held in greater or lesser degree by people. Rather, it is always an adaptive instrument, suited to the demands of an environment as seen by the subject. We cannot psychologize the subject alone without intimate knowledge of how he construes the environment that he is adapting to.

References

Cole, M., 1972, "Toward an Experimental Anthropology of Thinking." Paper presented at the Joint Meeting of the American Ethnological Society and the Council on Anthropology and Education, Montreal, April 1972.

Cole, M., J. Gay, and J. Glick, 1969, "Communication Skills among the Kpelle of Liberia." Paper presented at the Society for Research in Child Development meetings, Santa Monica, California, March 1969.

Cole, M., J. Gay, J. Glick, and D. Sharpe, 1969, "Linguistic Structure and Transposition," *Science* 164(4):90–91.

———, ———, ———, and ———, 1971, *The Cultural Context of Learning and Thinking: An Exploration in Experimental Anthropology.* New York: Basic Books.

Gibbs, J., 1969, personal communication.

Gladwin, T., 1964, "Culture and Logical Process." In W. Goodenough, ed., *Explorations in Cultural Anthropology.* New York: McGraw-Hill Book Company, pp. 167–177.

———, 1970, *East Is a Big Bird: Navigation and Logic on Puluwat Atoll.* Cambridge, Mass.: Harvard University Press.

Glick, J., 1968 "Cognitive Style among the Kpelle of Liberia." Paper presented at the American Education Research Association meetings, Chicago, February 1968.

———, in press, "Cognitive Development in Cross-Cultural Perspective." In Horowitz et al., eds., *Review of Child Development Research,* vol. 4.

Johnson, S. C., 1967, "Hierarchical Clustering Schemes," *Psychometrika* 32:241–254.

Lévi-Strauss, C., 1966, *The Savage Mind.* Chicago: University of Chicago Press.

PART IV

Approaches to the Study of Schools and Classrooms

PREVIEW

Until quite recently methods of anthropological fieldwork were among the best-kept secrets in the behavioral sciences. As recently as the late fifties and early sixties, graduate students left for the field having read many ethnographies and theoretical papers, but with very little or no idea as to how they should proceed once they arrived in the field. When Louise Spindler and I went out to study the Menomini of Wisconsin in 1948, the most precise advice we received from anyone was from C. W. M. Hart, then at the University of Wisconsin, who suggested to us that we think of ourselves as newspaper reporters—we should talk to people, hang around, and wait for patterns of opinion and behavior to develop. This was, indeed, very sound advice, but from there on we had to devise our own methodology. This resulted in an "experimental design" that allowed some control over our observations, collection of data, and analyses (Spindler and Goldschmidt 1952; Spindler and Spindler 1970).

Anthropology has come a long way since then. In 1962 Gerald Berreman published *Behind Many Masks,* one of the first sophisticated analyses of how an anthropologist takes roles in the social situation he studies. Elenore Smith Bowen's *Return to Laughter* (1964), though presumably fictional, brought us into the delightful but vexing arena in which the anthropologist becomes a human being interacting with other human beings and feeling shame, guilt, sorrow, happiness, rejection, anger, and love—all while striving for objectivity. D. G. Jongmans and Peter Gutkind edited *Anthropologists in the Field* in 1967, a volume particularly notable because it provides contrasts between participant observation and survey research, between the outside and the inside view of a culture. Bronislaw Malinowski's diary, which received very mixed reviews, was published in the same year. It is a very private document and gives us insight into a person quite different from the one we would expect to meet from reading his classic works on the Trobriands. Frances Henry and Satish Saberwal's *Stress and Response in Fieldwork* (1969) demonstrates how anthropologists in four different field situations responded to various forms of personal, social, and political stress. John Middleton, in

Study of the Lugbara: Expectation and Paradox in Anthropological Research (1970), also stresses the paradox of the anthropologist having to live as a human being with other human beings, yet also having to act as an objective observer. In 1970 Peggy Golde brought out *Women in the Field,* showing how twelve female anthropologists adapted to the roles cast for them in the communities they studied and the special advantages and disadvantages relating to these roles. Fieldwork experiences in eleven cultures are discussed in *Being an Anthropologist,* which I edited in 1970. Accounts of these studies appear in the Case Studies in Cultural Anthropology Series, edited by Louise Spindler and myself, and include cases ranging from the hunting and gathering Tiwi of North Australia to the Vice Lords, a black street gang in Chicago. Thus, the situation has changed—there is now a substantial literature for the anthropologist going into the field to draw upon for advice, consolation, warnings, and even specific operational suggestions.

With the exception of a few outstanding pieces, such as Jacquetta Burnett's microethnography of an urban classroom (Burnett 1969), very little of the material published on anthropological fieldwork is related directly to studies of schools and classrooms. Here the sociologist and others—who may or may not have been influenced by anthropological ideas—have taken important first steps. One can find, for example, very useful field research leads in Louis Smith and W. Geoffrey's *Complexities of an Urban Classroom* (1968), as well as in Philip Jackson's *Life in Classrooms* (1968). These studies, however, were not carried out with a participant-observer methodology, which is the keystone of an anthropological approach.

This part of the text, "Approaches to the Study of Schools and Classrooms," focuses on the participant-observer role, although not all of the contributions appropriate to this methodological focus appear in this part. Harry F. Wolcott's chapter on the elementary school principal in Part II could well have been included here. His remarkable study, reported fully in *The Man in the Principal's Office* (1973), contributed significantly to this area of study. Wolcott's paper shows clearly that a sensitive and persistent ethnographic approach to the study of a single role, in this case the principal of an elementary school, can give us an understanding of that role and its context that probably no other means could afford. In my chapter, "Schooling in Schönhausen," also in Part II, I am as much concerned with methodology as with the results of the study. Though it may seem incongruous to think of a middle-aged, 200-pound male anthropologist being a participant-observer in third- and fourth-grade classes, this was actually the case. I sat at a desk in the back of the room and did the same things the children did insofar as my ethnographic recording activities permitted. The children accepted me and my role much more quickly than did the teachers, but both seemed to adapt to the incongruities after a period of several weeks. I can think of no other way that I would have come to an understanding of what the third and fourth grades in the Schönhausen Grundschule were like.

Bud Khleif, in his chapter, anticipates certain themes that appear in various forms in the three papers following. One of them is the problem of *not* having the experience of culture shock, which seems essential to a certain perspective gained in most anthropological fieldwork. The anthropologist in the school is observing and experiencing something that he or she has observed and experienced for years. It is difficult to obtain enough perspective to see it at all, and once having seen it to view it with objectivity.

In his chapter on the teacher as a participant-observer, A. Richard King describes how he operated simultaneously as an anthropological fieldworker and as a fourth-grade teacher in a church-operated residential school for Indian children. It is clear in his essay that the teacher as anthropological participant-observer in the school has certain advantages. For one, he has a role. Novice fieldworkers frequently find that their greatest problem is being seen at first as a person without any legitimate business. Whenever there is such a social vacuum people (i.e., one's potential informants) tend to fill it with stereotypes, mythology, gossip, and very frequently very dark interpretations, such as "secret agent," "government spy," or—in capitalistic countries—Communist. Though the teacher role is fraught with conflicts, ambiguities, and tensions, it is at least a role, and one that puts the fieldworker in direct contact with one's most significant informants, if indeed one is studying the classroom, the school, and their immediate social and cultural context. It is interesting that King develops the concept of "significant friend" as one of the roles that may emerge in the teacher's activity in the community outside the classroom. Most of us have found in our fieldwork that the role of friend is of great importance. In studying the Menomini and the Blood, as well as in the fieldwork in Germany, we found that being friends with people took up more time than any other broad category of activity. This, to be sure, is a potential barrier to productivity. Many a young anthropologist has come back from the field only to find it impossible to write about one's friends with the peculiar distance that at some point the anthropologist must establish in relationship to his informants and the data that he has elicited from or about them. King discusses this problem in the latter part of his chapter.

In "The Teacher as an Enemy," Harry F. Wolcott takes what at first glance appears to be a directly opposed stance to that taken by King. There is an important distinction, however, between roles inside the classroom and outside in the community. My personal impression, knowing both King and Wolcott and the circumstances of their fieldwork quite well, is that indeed the role of friend tended to extend throughout King's relationships to the children as well as to their parents and others in the community, whereas Wolcott's role relationships were quite different. I am not saying that Wolcott was unfriendly to children and that King was friendly. What I am saying is that I believe they went about their teaching and their observation rather differently. The key to the situation that Harry Wolcott faced is contained in his statement, ". . . but I was not assigned to the village to teach villagers their way of life; I was assigned to teach them something about mine." His culture and all the representatives of it had already been defined by the parents, by the children, in fact by the whole community, as enemies. Wolcott's point is that by denying the fact of this perception, he could only mislead himself and the children in his classroom. By acknowledging it, he could move to a useful *rapprochement* in the classroom and with the community. King's position was different in that he came to the school as a person different from anyone the children had experienced before. All of his predecessors had been females who tended to be highly selected for a certain rather limited cultural and emotional role. King also had certain biases about the school situation itself. As most anthropologists, he did not approve of residential schools. He was, therefore, a potential ally of the children and the parents and was more easily cast in the role of enemy by fellow-teachers and educational administrators. I have elaborated upon this in order to call attention to the fact that anthropological field methods do not exist in a vacuum, but are situationally relevant. The transaction in context, plus something we could call personality or personal persuasion, constitutes a complex and rather unpredictable set of vectors that is different in each situation.

The interpretation above is nicely carried forward in Richard L. Warren's chapter on the methodology of his fieldwork in a rural German village, Rebhausen. German post-World War II attitudes toward Americans, the size of the village and its relationship to an urban center, the fact that the village had increased rapidly in size and was adding a new industrial sector, the composition of Warren's family, the strong status orientation of German culture, the housing for Warren's family—these and many other factors interacted to make his situation in his school and community unique. When the reader has finished with Warren's chapter, however, and looks back over the other three chapters contained in this section, he should be able to see how, although each situation is unique, they share common features. The anthropologist is a stranger, he is marginal to the situation, he must find or be assigned some role that permits him to obtain access to sources of information, to people, that will enable him to carry his task of ethnographic field study to a satisfactory conclusion. The anthropologist defends himself as best he can by defining some acceptable kind of role. He and his family, if there is one, must make personal adjustments as well. Friendships are made, some barriers are broken through while others remain, and there is the constant struggle to be objective while being human.

References

Berreman, Gerald, 1962, *Behind Many Masks: Ethnography and Impression Management in a Himalayan Village.* Ithaca, N.Y.: Society for Applied Anthropology, Monograph #4.

Bowen, Elenore Smith, 1964, *Return to Laughter: An Anthropological Novel.* New York: Anchor Books, Doubleday & Company, Inc.

Burnett, Jacquetta, 1969, "Event Description and Analysis in the Microethnography of Urban Classrooms." In Francis Ianni and E. Storey, 1973, *Cultural Relevance and Educational Issues.* Boston: Little, Brown and Company.

Golde, Peggy, ed., 1970, *Women in the Field.* Chicago: Aldine Publishing Company.

Henry, Frances, and Satish Saberwal, eds., 1969, *Stress and Response in Fieldwork.* SAM. New York: Holt, Rinehart and Winston, Inc.

Jackson, P., 1968, *Life in Classrooms.* New York: Holt, Rinehart and Winston, Inc.

Jongmans, D. P., and P. C. W. Gutkind, eds., 1967, *Anthropologists in the Field.* Assen, Holland: Van Gorcum & Company.

Malinowski, Bronislaw, 1967, *A Diary in the Strict Sense of the Word.* Introduction by Raymond Firth. New York: Harcourt Brace Jovanovich.

Middleton, John, 1970, *The Study of the Lugbara: Expectation and Paradox in Anthropological Research.* SAM. New York: Holt, Rinehart and Winston, Inc.

Smith, Louis, and W. Geoffrey, 1968, *Complexities of an Urban Classroom.* New York: Holt, Rinehart and Winston, Inc.

Spindler, G., and L. Spindler, 1970, "Field Work among the Menomini." In G. Spindler, ed., *Eleven Cultures.* New York: Holt, Rinehart and Winston, Inc.

Spindler, George D., and Walter Goldschmidt, 1952, "Experimental Design in the Study of Culture Change," *Southwestern Journal of Anthropology* 8:68–83.

Warren, Richard L., 1967, *Education in Rebhausen: A German Village.* CSEC. New York: Holt, Rinehart and Winston, Inc.

Wolcott, Harry F., 1973, *The Man in the Principal's Office,* CSEC. New York: Holt, Rinehart and Winston, Inc.

BUD B. KHLEIF/*University of New Hampshire*

19 *Issues in Anthropological Fieldwork in the Schools**

It can be said that every profession has three kinds of secrets: open, hidden, and dark. Open secrets are obvious ones, hidden secrets are those that fewer persons outside the profession know, and dark secrets are those the members of the profession would not discuss among themselves nor be inclined to think about. Essentially, open and hidden secrets have to do with occupational ideology, self-justification, and assertion of piety; hidden secrets involve tinkering with clients. Anthropologists, like other members of a profession, have these three kinds of secrets; the general purpose of this chapter is to discuss more openly some of anthropology's hidden (not dark) secrets.

Fieldwork in Exotic Settings versus Fieldwork in Public Schools

One of the hallmarks of anthropology is its insistence on fieldwork as a research method. Fieldwork means the immersion of the anthropologist in the life of the exotic group he studies until he gets to see things much like a native. This requires the use of the self as a research tool, a human filter to screen an unfamiliar reality. However, since the anthropologist as a person had already been culturally programmed by his society, his perception of the approached group tends, to a considerable extent, to be predetermined. The clash between the cultural map as the fieldworker perceives it, and the cultural map that the approached group actually uses is at the root of an intense personal experience for the fieldworker, one akin to a do-it-yourself cultural psychoanalysis. It is this experience of baptism by cross-cultural fire that changes the fieldworker's identity and inducts him into anthropological adulthood. Without it he would not be accepted into anthropological ranks as a full-fledged peer. In short, to be an anthropologist is synonymous with being a fieldworker.

In the fieldwork situation, the completely passive observer is a fallacy (Heisenberg 1959). We read the world around us *on purpose*—vision de-

*This paper was first presented at the American Anthropological Association meeting, New Orleans, November 1969.

pends upon what we put into it. As Goethe said, "We see what we look for, and we look for what we know." In the language of phenomenology we can say: No intentionality, no perception. Intentionality is what we mean when we talk about "selective perception," what the observer sees according to what his culture has taught him to see, and what he brackets out according to what he had been culturally trained to bracket out. It is in this sense that the traditional fieldworker's job as a phenomenologist has been incomplete, for he has written only about the intentionality of the natives and what they take for granted, not about intentionality in his own occupational culture.

What the aforementioned means is that truth—including anthropological truth—is a clash of the conventional wisdoms of the observer and the observed, a tension between opposites, and that in fieldwork, as it is in all human affairs, strict objectivity is a delusion (Polanyi 1958). What the fieldworker has, whether he is studying red-blooded American school natives or non-American natives, is a quest for objectivity, a deliberate attempt to rise above being culture-bound and ethnocentric. Anthropologists, having paid attention to what they call "culture contact" (see Spicer 1961), would do well to study the fieldwork they do as a form of culture contact, and, in addition to discussing the phenomenology of the people studied, to devote some effort to the equally culture-bound phenomenology of anthropology (Du Bois 1967).

The essence of fieldwork in overseas settings is the experience of strangership, a sort of anomie. Collectively, the stages of this experience are known as "culture shock." Culture shock, as the *sine qua non* of fieldwork in exotic settings, is a learning experience; its product is the enlargement of awareness. During culture shock, the fieldworker is culturally debriefed and deprogrammed; his frame of reference is reshuffled; the habitual cultural straitjacket into which he had been imprisoned is loosened. The fieldworker's enlarged awareness tends to dissolve his culturally programmed categories and distinctions, the boundaries between the self and others. He gets to understand the similarity between the perceiver and the perceived, the Bowenesque "return to laughter" (Bowen 1964). Field experience cures him of *a priori* portraits of people and events; his self undergoes a configurational change, and so does his anthropological interpretation. (Obviously, different fieldworkers react to culture shock in a different manner; what we have emphasized is the ideal type.)

There are two important differences between fieldwork in exotic settings and fieldwork in American public schools. First, in the school the fieldworker does not experience culture shock, and second, he is not allowed to be a full-fledged participant. Let me explain these two differences:

1. The fieldworker is familiar with both the language and culture of his society. Therefore he experiences no dramatic change in the self—no culture shock. What he experiences at times may be a sort of revulsion, such as the feeling aroused regarding educators' seeming brutality toward kids. Thus, in some middle-class schools, for example, pupils are allowed only twenty minutes for

lunch because of crowded cafeteria facilities. It is the principal's decree that such pupils are not to talk at all during lunch. Another example is that of some slum schools, where the fieldworker may hear a teacher berating, in a nasty tone of voice, a sixth-grade girl about the noise she is supposedly making when she simply is flipping through her notebook. A third example would be that of a teacher locking up children's sandwiches in a classroom closet and calling them, to their faces, "human mice" (she suspects if the sandwiches are left with their owners, they may be stolen).

2. In the school, and especially in the classroom, the fieldworker cannot be a participant; he neither has the role of teacher or pupil, nor can he take part in classroom interaction (see Hargreaves 1967). Unlike the teacher or pupil, the fieldworker does not participate daily in the school for six or more hours,[1] and most accounts tend to be based on an hour or two of observation per day or week. As Claude Lévi-Strauss maintains, to understand structure in human organization, the fieldworker needs to take the role of the outsider, the observer; to understand process or how a social system is maintained or slowly changed, the fieldworker must go native, that is, be an insider, a participant (Steiner 1966:36). This means that, at best, the fieldworker in public schools can understand only structure, not process, and thus remains more of a stranger than a friend.

Fieldwork in schools lacks both culture shock and avenues for participation. Therefore, the product of such studies tends to be a deliberate application of concepts and notions previously known to the anthropologist about other cultural settings, rather than a generation of new concepts. As Solon Kimball asserts, the fieldworker studying schools allows a dynamic independence to events that schoolmen only passively include in their educational framework, for example, informal networks of pupils and rituals of induction (Kimball 1966). Naming or assigning an independent existence to what is taken for granted in the educational process is essentially an observer's, not a participant's, function.

If lack of culture shock and lack of participation are the two main differences between fieldwork in schools and fieldwork in exotic settings, and if the former is only a special case of the latter, then what are some of the similarities between them? These are interrelated and can be described as follows:

1. Problems of entree: the "spiel" and the "bargain"
2. Image-making and impression management
3. The researcher's roles, reciprocity,, and adaptation
4. Tension between participation and observation in the fieldworker's activity: Being a stranger as well as a friend.

---

[1] *Editor's note:* This is generally true, but the reader should note that the studies by King, Spindler, Warren, and Wolcott reported in this volume are exceptions, and there are others.

Problems of Entree: The "Spiel" and the "Bargain"

In doing fieldwork in schools, one has to "hit" the school system at various levels. Thus, although the social structure of the classroom may be the intended object of study—essentially focusing on pupils and teachers—one has to "get the green light" first from the superintendent and then from all the intervening echelons before reaching the teacher or even the janitor. School systems, being rigid bureaucracies, have a clear chain of command and thus call for the fieldworker's negotiation of his research effort at all levels of the school's hierarchy.

Everett C. Hughes has referred to the problems of entree as the "spiel" and the "research bargain" (personal communication 1965). The spiel is seen as presenting the research activity in a favorable light and as an appeal to cooperation. Since "science" is the central myth of American culture (Du Bois 1967), the fieldworker usually does not have to educate school people on the value of "research"—they already believe in it. The "bargain" is the fieldworker's and educator's answer to the hidden questions during their polite negotiations: "What's in it for me? What's in it for you? What's in it for us?" During the bargain, the fieldworker usually promises to secure the confidentiality of all materials gathered and to present the school personnel with copies of the final summary of his research effort. In addition, he assures educators that his research effort is not to be construed as "evaluation," a word that is anathema—especially to teachers. For school personnel, association with a research project is quite often a source of pride; they like the prestige derived from a partnership with a university or research agency and hope that fieldwork will raise the status of education.

In gaining entree into a school system, as in gaining entree into an exotic community, it is important for the fieldworker to convince those to be observed that he will do them no harm (Cicourel 1964:41).

Image-Making

It is important for the fieldworker to have a plausible explanation of his research, usually phrased in general terms—an interest in studying the "behavior patterns" of children or their "learning experiences."

According to W. J. Hanna (1965), image-making in fieldwork consists of the following components: a convention of equality, imparting to the natives that they have a coequal status; listening with a sympathetic ear and lively interest; avoidance of giving advice; and not passing moral judgments on what is observed. Although these components deal with fieldwork in Africa, they can be said to hold true for image-making in fieldwork done in one's own cultural setting.

The Fieldworker's Roles, Reciprocity, and Adaptation

The quest for a role, whether in nonliterate communities or in literate American schools, is the key to the fieldwork method. Obviously the most important part of the fieldworker's activity is his acceptance as a person. As Florence Kluckhohn observes, "It is reasonable to assume that one learns more from a person if he thinks you want to be like him than if he suspects you are trying to find out why he is different" (Kluckhohn 1940:334). Thus one of the earlier roles of the fieldworker in schools is that of a *learner;* he is there to be educated and enlightened by teachers and pupils.

Throughout fieldwork, the researcher engages in establishing rapport and correcting any misunderstanding of his role, such as that he is in the school to "evaluate" teachers or identify those with a large number of "maladjusted" children. Because his fieldwork data are dependent upon how well he gets along with the people studied and the role definition given him by these people, the researcher tends to gather data that are not of uniform quality. As Robert Janes (1961) maintains, there is a progressive redefinition of the fieldworker's role, ranging from newcomer and learner to oldtimer and immediate migrant. The interrelationship of the quality of data gathered and the progressive redefinition of fieldwork roles is a topic only few researchers have discussed.

Tension Between Participation and Observation

Anthropological accounts are permeated with references to the Janus-like stance that the fieldworker has to take: attraction to the approached group and repulsion from it, involvement and detachment, being a stranger and being a friend at the same time. (For further discussion see Bowen 1964; Gold 1958; Kluckhohn 1940; Malinowski 1961, 1967; Miller 1952; Nash 1963; Powdermaker 1967; Schwartz and Schwartz 1955; and Whyte 1955). Over-rapport with the "natives" of an institution and treatment on a level of personal friendship may result in dropping some penetrating lines of inquiry which are too sensitive to be pursued as well as lead to distortion of data. Thus, in the school situation, by accepting the perspectives of principals or counselors, the fieldworker may become blind to other viewpoints, for example, those of pupils and teachers.

Fieldwork and the Anthropological Mystique

Among those anthropologists who have written about anthropology as a profession and the sociology of knowledge in anthropology are Nash (1963), King (1965), and Braroe and Hicks (1967). Their accounts can be summarized as follows: First, anthropology has always welcomed the stranger, be he informant or colleague. Anthropologists are essentially strangers who can never go home or feel at home. The anthropological community itself is but a haven for strangers (Nash 1963). Second, anthropology tends to attract the marginal and the alienated. As a profession, anthropology is a technique of political disengagement whose hallmark is marginality—being in one's society, yet not being fully committed to its culture. Inasmuch as social science demands a measure of detachment, the anthropologist's alienation is a necessary qualification for research (Braroe and Hicks 1967). Last, the anthropologist keeps away from his own society to reduce his feelings of marginality and alienation. His most intense personal experience—fieldwork—is presumably something that his own society cannot supply (Braroe and Hicks 1967). Thus it is no wonder that the ethos of anthropological fieldwork is "involved detachment" (Nash 1963), an ethos that has both a personal and an occupational basis, an ethos of being *in* society but not *of* it. It is in this sense that we can interpret the anthropological enterprise as basically a search for identity (King 1965). As Margaret Mead has said, fieldwork enables the anthroplogist to come "face to face with himself, without the need to take a special pilgrimage to a Buddhist lamasery" (Mead in Braroe and Hicks 1967:181).

If we accept Braroe and Hicks' view that the anthropological mystique consists of extolling cultural primitivism over civilization, then we can understand why anthropologists, being displeased with their own culture, have become spokesmen for the underdog. If the anthropologist, lacking clear-cut rites of passage in his own society, seeks them outside it and experiences what rites of passage are supposed to make the person experience—a rebirth of identity—then we would expect, as a result of doing fieldwork outside American culture, that the anthropologist would no longer look at his own society in the same manner nor regard it as the only—and thus unquestionable—version of humanity. Inasmuch as fieldwork in non-American settings has enlarged his awareness, and inasmuch as he is an expert in examining intentionality and what people take for granted, then we would expect the anthropologist, when he examines American institutions, to come up with new interpretations about the nature of American society.

Method for What?

From issues of fieldwork as a research method, I now turn to the question of "method for what?" Here I would like to advance a hypothesis: It is only through viewing the familiar as unfamiliar, and the symbolic system of the literate in light of what anthropologists know about the nonliterate, that the American public school can be meaningfully studied as a microcosm of a multiethnic society, that an ethnography of schooling can thus be developed, and that such an ethnography would be illuminative of anthropology itself. Such a hypothesis can be elaborated with a few examples and comments.

1. Very few anthropologists have brought their exotic fieldwork to bear on the problem of American education or have done fieldwork in American public schools. Among those who have maintained a sustained effort in this regard are Margaret Mead, Solon Kimball, George Spindler (1963), Jules Henry (1963), and Murray Wax (1965). To advance such an effort, in my opinion, a deliberate and systematic attempt to use the public school as a lab for examination of American society itself is called for. This means that the anthropologist working in schools must see his work in a larger context and investigate how the larger issues of society—issues "with regard to race, creed, and nationality"—are reflected in the school.

2. If in exotic fieldwork the anthropologist has been given a good accounting of himself and his culture, then we can say that in a very real sense non-American cultures have served as a lab for testing American culture. If that is so, anthropologists can increase their insights further by beginning to apply, to their own literate Americans, concepts and formulations they have clapped on nonliterate peoples.

3. In the same way that the nonliterate community has been used as a lab for testing the taken-for-granted in the fieldworker's culture, the public school could be used as a lab to illuminate general tendencies in American society. If America is a nation of ethnic groups, one may ask—about the school and the society—to what extent the "melting pot" has succeeded in melting and what are the processes that have contributed to its being at times a seething cauldron? To what extent does "cultural pluralism," even in the school, remain an ideal, and what processes have turned it into, and often maintained it as, "cultural particularism"?

It can be asserted that the problem of integrating racial and cultural minorities into American society is no different from integrating tribal peoples into national states (Braroe and Hicks 1967). If science is essentially the conceptualization of hidden similarities, then it would be worthwhile for "urban anthropologists" to study the detribalization of American society as part of the general detribalization going on in literate as well as nonliterate societies. The problem of tribalization and detribalization can be easily examined in public schools. For example, some school systems are basically job monopolies for particular ethnic groups, such as Boston, where schoolmen smilingly ask the fieldworker whether he has met the "only *non-Irish* principal in the system" (author's fieldwork; see also Kozol 1967; Schrag 1967). Italians and others in Boston can become teachers or counselors, but not administrators. In addition, the ethnic vote is an American political reality, and the composition of advisory committees, for the school and in society at large, quite often is based on ethnic and religious representation. It would thus be instructive to examine ethnic, occupational, and other forms of stratification both in the school and outside it.

4. Murray Wax (1965), Ruth Landes (1965), Jules Henry (1963), and George Spindler (1963), among others, have written about what happens in public schools when Indian, Mexican, or Anglo children encounter white teachers, a considerable number of whom are converts to the middle class and thus tend zealously to institutionalize society's prevalent orthodoxy with regard to color, creed, and "cultural deprivation." In addition to focusing on the present, anthropologists may choose to focus on the past and delve into what actually happened to the "whole" child—be he Italian, Indian, or other—under school auspices. Such study would be a heretofore unwritten ethnohistory of American society and its schools.

5. In addition to tribalization and detribalization, two other standard anthropological concepts may be examined in both the school and society: one has to do with mythology, the other with shamanism. First, if science and scientism are the central myth of American society (Du Bois 1967), then the fieldworker may examine the use of I.Q. and achievement tests in schools as a form of magic. How pupils are labeled, graded, and warehoused as ability groups on the basis of standardized test scores and how their future careers are thus determined would be part of the concerns of fieldwork in schools. Second, because of the problems of social dislocation attendant upon a high rate of change in American society, a new secular priesthood has risen to deal especially with emotional crises. This priesthood is composed of psychiatrists, clinical psychologists, social workers, and school counselors. School counselors, for example, love to play "doctor" to pupils, and if need be, to teachers and parents. The "voodoo con games" of Rogerian school counselors, for example, could be studied as one of the varieties of modern clinical magic, something akin to shamanism in nonliterate societies (Khleif 1966). A study of the role of the counselor as a shaman and an analysis of the occupational scriptures of counselors would illuminate, among other things, the nature of American society as a congery of competitive groups, occupational and ethnic.

Conclusion

In this chapter, I have tried to clarify some of the issues of fieldwork in schools as part of the issues of anthropological fieldwork in general. As Poincaré has said, "No one is a privileged observer"; hence, attention has been paid not only to the phenomenology of those studied in fieldwork but to that of fieldworkers themselves.

The public school has been suggested as a lab for the study of American society. As Waller has said in his study of public schools, "It is not necessary for the students of quaint customs to cross the seas to find material" (Waller 1961:103). The American public school can be viewed as exotic and as tribal as any community studied by anthropologists. Among the issues suggested for exploring the linkage between the school and society are such standard anthropological concerns as myth, magic, shamanism, and tribalization and detribalization in the educational "melting pot." In all of this there has been an emphasis on seeing the general in the particular, on conceptualization of hidden similarities, and on the anthropological observer as part of what is observed.

References

Bowen, Elenore S., 1964, *Return to Laughter: An Anthropological Novel.* N.Y.: Doubleday Anchor Books.

Braroe, N. W., and Hicks, G. L., 1967, "Observations on the Mystique of Anthropology," *Sociological Quarterly* 8:173–186; rejoinder by A. S. Wilke, *Sociological Quarterly* 9:400–405, Summer 1968.

Cicourel, A. V., 1964, *Method and Measurement in Sociology,* New York: The Free Press, pp. 39–72.

Du Bois, Cora, 1967, "Is Anthropology Culture Bound?" Paper read at the annual meeting of the American Anthropological Association, Washington, D.C., December 1, 1967.

Gold, R. L., 1958, "Roles in Sociological Field Observations," *Social Forces* 36(3): 217–223.

Gusfield, J. R., 1960, "Field-Work Reciprocities in Studying a Social Movement." In R. N. Adams and J. J. Preiss, eds., *Human Organization Research: Field Relations and Techniques.* Homewood, Ill.: Dorsey Press, pp. 99–108.

Hanna, W. J., 1965, "Image-Making in Field Research: Some Tactical and Ethical Problems of Research in Tropical Africa," *American Behavioral Scientist* 9(1): 15–20.

Hargreaves, D. H., 1967, *Social Relations in a Secondary School.* London: Routledge and Kegan Paul, pp. 193–205.

Heisenberg, Werner, 1959, *Physics and Philosophy.* London: George Allen & Unwin.

Henry, Jules, 1963, *Culture Against Man.* New York: Random House.

Janes, R. W., 1961, "A Note on Phases of the Community Role of the Participant-Observer," *American Sociological Review* 26:446–450.

Khleif, B. B., 1966, "A Socio-Cultural Framework for Studying Guidance in Public Schools." In E. Landy and A. M. Kroll, eds., *Guidance in American Education III: Needs and Influencing Forces.* Cambridge, Mass.: Harvard University Press, pp. 173–196.

Kimball, S. T., 1966. "Educational Development and Anthropology." Paper read at the annual meeting of the American Anthropological Association, Pittsburgh, Pa.

King, A. R., 1965, "The Anthropologist as Man: The Ultimate Paradox." Paper read at the annual meeting of the American Anthropological Association, Denver, Colorado.

Kluckhohn, Florence R., 1940, "The Participant-Observer Technique in Small Communities," *American Journal of Sociology* 56:331–343.

Kozol, Jonathan, 1967, *Death at an Early Age.* Boston: Houghton Mifflin Company.

Landes, Ruth, 1965, *Culture in American Education.* New York: John Wiley & Sons, Inc.

Malinowski, B., 1961, *Argonauts of the Western Pacific: An Account of Native Enterprise and Adventure in the Archipelagoes of Melanesian New Guinea.* New York: E. P. Dutton & Company, pp. 4–17.

———, 1967, *A Diary in the Strict Sense of the Term.* New York: Harcourt Brace Jovanovich.

Miller, S. M., 1952, "The Participant Observer and 'Over-Rapport,'" *American Sociological Review* 17:97–99.

Nash, D., 1963, "The Ethnologist as Stranger: An Essay in the Sociology of Knowledge," *Southwestern Journal of Anthropology* 19(2):149–167.

Polanyi, Michael, 1958. *Personal Knowledge.* London: Routledge & Kegan Paul.

Powdermaker, Hortense, 1967, *Stranger and Friend: The Way of an Anthropologist.* New York: Norton.

Schrag, Peter, 1967, *Village School Downtown.* Boston: Beacon Press.

Schwartz, M. S., and C. G. Schwartz, 1955, "Problems in Participant Observation," *American Journal of Sociology* 60:343–353.

Spicer, E. H., ed., 1961, *Perspectives in American Indian Cultural Change.* Chicago: University of Chicago Press.

Spindler, G. D., ed., 1963, *Education and Culture.* New York: Holt, Rinehart and Winston, Inc.

Steiner, G., 1966, "A Conversation with Claude Lévi-Strauss," *Encounter* 26(4):32–38.

Vaihinger, Hans, 1911, *Philosophie des Als Ob (Philosophy of the "As If").* Germany: Tuebingen.

Waller, Willard, 1961, *The Sociology of Teaching.* New York: Russell and Russell.

Wax, M. L. et al., 1965, *Formal Education in an American Indian Community.* SSSP Monograph, Supplement to Vol. 11, No. 4, of *Social Problems.*

Whyte, W. F., 1955, *Street Corner Society.* Chicago: University of Chicago Press, enlarged edition, pp. 279–358 (Appendix).

Wilson, Colin, 1967, *Introduction to the New Existentialism.* Boston: Houghton-Mifflin Company.

A. RICHARD KING/*University of Victoria, Victoria, B.C.*

20 *The Teacher as a Participant-Observer: A Case Study*

The Teacher Role, Technique and Constraints

The teacher undertaking participant-observation research enters any given situation with an ascribed status integral to the society. Role behavior expectations may vary widely from school to school and among societies, but except in rare situations within a few developing countries, the status of *teacher* exists in one way or another in any community. When a new teacher arrives, he immediately has an opportunity for extensive observation and analysis of a complex domain of behavior indicating overt and covert values as he identifies the role expectations and the boundaries for deviation tolerance in the specific teacher status he occupies.

I found this a useful point of analysis when I, a nonchurch-affiliated male, began working as fourth-grade teacher in a church-operated residential school for Indian children where my predecessors for many years had been females, usually members of the same church, and always members of some church (King 1967). An initial tolerance for my deviant position was undoubtedly included in the fact of my identification as a researcher—although few members of the community really had an understanding of what was meant by that term. My status as male permitted further deviation tolerance. Males in this society are not as avid church members as are females; they are expected to have more active and varied outside interests, to participate more extensively in social affairs, to smoke, drink, and gamble (all preferably in moderation). Nevertheless, despite exhibiting all these and other deviant behaviors, I found my status as *teacher* to be pervasive and overriding. Although I was undoubtedly a threat to some, and certainly a friend to others who had not previously included teachers as friends, I found that wherever I went I was identified first and foremost as "the new teacher" at the residential school. This immediately provided me with an identifiable status in any group. Among those who tended to have a negative reaction to teachers as a class, my deviant behavior was a positive factor leading to more relaxed relationships. Among those who held a more restricted ideal of teacher behavior as a model of traditional Anglo manners, I perhaps shocked occasionally, seldom offended, and was still identifiable as a *teacher* (albeit, perhaps, not the most desirable kind).

The point is that all these varied individual and group adjustments to my idiosyncratic interpretation of teacher role behavior were natural responses, within the cultural framework, to the role variables of an integrated, ascribed status. The persons with whom I interacted were not required to make a basic identification of me as a *stranger* for whom no identification terms existed, or even as an *observer* who would interact briefly and then move on to another observation elsewhere. Although teachers are not necessarily expected to be permanent members of a community (and I was in that community with the specific understanding of spending only one year), the status of teacher is permanently available and the variability of incumbents is an assumed component of the status.

The teacher, then, has the status position ready-made for his entry into any given community and has considerable latitude for variable role behavior as well as a valuable research beginning in identification of the parameters of acceptable behavior as locally defined. Obviously the teacher must be, to borrow Pearsall's terms (1965), either a complete participant or a participant-as-observer. However he determines to operate, he must, as Babchuk points out (1962:226), "perform adequately his role in the capacity for which he is ostensibly in the system." To this I would add that, contrary to Kluckhohn's (1940) prescription that the research intentions cannot be disclosed, the teacher should probably never enter a school system for participant-observation research without the explicit understanding and acceptance of his research intentions by authorities, colleagues, and the general community. It may well be strategic, or even essential, that participant-observation efforts in other situations be kept secret, but this is not the case with teacher research. In the first place, it is not necessary. Perhaps even more important are the ethical implications and the personal considerations of the teacher as an individual who will continue to be a teacher in other schools.

It is not necessary to obscure research intentions because, once they are made explicit (without necessarily elaborating upon them greatly), the primary attention to task performance in the role of teacher will quickly obliterate the observation elements of the teacher's behavior. Observation is a teacher's business (they are continually exhorted to observe more, talk less); recording data is an expected teacher behavior, and interest in the general community as well as individual students and their families is applauded when demonstrated by teachers. It is perfectly possible for any teacher to exhibit these behaviors in an intensified manner, even when people know he is a researcher as well, without establishing an artificial *external observer* set of responses.

The ethical problems of conducting secret research within a school should be obvious, as well as the consequences to the individual. Unlike the anthropologist in the field or the sociologist in the factory who, no matter how fine a rapport they establish with the natives, invariably return to their own kind and their own culture and subculture within which to live the bulk of their lives, the teacher *is* among his own kind as he makes his observations. The ultimate criterion of the effectiveness of his study is that the people among whom he has worked, or at least a sizable segment of them, will agree, "Yes, this is how it is." He cannot write with impunity about the behavior of individuals unless it is relevant to and consistent with culturally patterned behavior that sheds light upon the research problems. Titillating tidbits of personal idiosyncratic behavior are always available to friends of colleagues as one gets to know them well. Such items are frequently injected into ethnographies and often *are* relevant in a peripheral, illustrative manner. It may be necessary for the teacher-researcher to use this class of information also, but only if the observation has been made with full knowledge of the roles of all individuals. To do otherwise would be to label the teacher as a potential spy in any future situation, to say nothing of the irreparable damage to any personal relationships he valued in the studied situation.

In undertaking the study of an Indian residential school while acting the role of teacher, I was initially identified as the new teacher who was from X University and who would be, "doing some research about the school and the community and about some of the dysfunctional elements in the education of Indian children (King 1967)." This introduction was made to the Indian Affairs Branch bureaucracy (I was employed by the Regional Superintendent, who encouraged the research), to the school administration, and to the staff of the school. To the best of my knowledge, no further explicit references were made to my research interests during the year. Occasionally somebody outside the school would make a comment such as, "When you write your book about this place . . . ," but I always diverted this conversational trend away from my potential productivity and toward explication of the information element of the comment. I operated my classes within the prescribed time and curriculum framework, deviating mildly in some situations but always within a reasonable *teacher* behavior interpretation. If there was somewhat more testing and extensive interviews with children and adults than usual, more writing of personal documents by children in class, more involvement of the teacher in nonclassroom activities, none of these were particularly noted as *research* behavior.

At the same time, moving from the domain of *role* to the domain of technique, the teacher has some constraints placed upon him by virtue of his basic task performance requirements. His status as teacher has a determinant effect on what he will see and hear as well as upon his own interpretations of these phenomena. It will open doors of officialdom to files, records, and comments. His queries and observations can range far beyond the school or even the immediate community, yet he must also react to the people in each of the situations from the role of teacher. He will find, as Vidich points out (1955: 354ff), that complete neutrality is impossible; one must *react* to situations and to reactions of respondents. Even silence in such situations is a reaction—a negative reaction in most cases. This aspect of the response set must be taken into account in basic teacher task performance, during observations and interviews, and particularly in the final report. It also shows the importance of timing in the data-gathering process because the response set may alter over time.

An operating school is a complex of social forces and conflict situations. Any participant in this complex will inevitably be drawn into adversary positions—teachers perhaps most of all. Even if one were to assume an ideal student-teacher relationship in the classroom, in which no authoritarian behavior were displayed by the teacher to establish the most immediate adversary relationship (an almost incredible assumption), teachers must evaluate student performance and dispense judgments to the student and to his parents and to others of the school staff. These are value statements, variously but subjectively perceived by others. Inevitably other operating patterns of the school require response by the teacher indicating his value orientation. No ideal behavior is possible for the teacher to prevent variations in the impressions students and others form of the teacher and thus establish differing attitudes which variously and increasingly facilitate or inhibit open communication channels for at least some components of the research task.

A skillful teacher-researcher can delay this process of firm attitude formation perhaps a bit longer than might be expected, but he must face the fact that his channels of information will narrow eventually and his own perceptions will become increasingly selective. Elements of the situation which might be both salient and significant early in the experience will come to be commonplace and apparently insignificant later. People who might easily discuss aspects of the environment early in the teacher's tenure at the school may well become inhibited about such discussion when and if they perceive the teacher's operating procedures. Extensive recording of first impressions is important even when no verification is possible and the impressions later turn out to be inaccurate. Baseline information about attitudes should also be sought early, particularly if these data are essential in the study.

My own experience in the Indian residential school confirmed this importance of timing as well as the almost imperceptible (to me) formation of negative attitudes to inhibit responses. One of my major interests was the attitudes of non-Indian operating personnel toward Indians. Observations of behavior are necessary indicators of these attitudes; but so also are verbal expressions in response to direct questions even if—or perhaps especially if—such expressions are incongruent with observed behavior. As part of the overall design I planned to conduct depth interviews with all of the school operating personnel about their feelings toward Indians and about their identifications and interpretations of Indian behaviors they observed. However, I did not give these interviews a high priority in timing. Higher priorities—after the first priority of classroom teaching tasks—went to achieving a rapport with and establishing an identification of the Indian population. This was, to me, the unknown culture. I felt a compulsion to establish Indian identities, expectations, experiences as the core of my study; then to expand the Indian core by exploring various types of interactions with non-Indians and their perceptions of Indians. Even the weather contributed to my first concentration upon Indians. The school "service community" extends over hundreds of square miles, not all of which could possibly be covered by a working teacher during a school year and much of which is completely inaccessible after the heavy snows of winter set in. So I ranged as far as possible in the early fall.

For these and similar reasons it was well after the end of the first semester before I was ready to make a systematic compilation of non-Indian school staff members' overt attitude statements, and by this time it was too late. Where earlier I could have obtained fairly open expressions—at least expressions unbiased by *my* presence—from nearly all the staff, their observations of my interest in and involvement with Indians during the preceding six months made such expressions impossible for many of them. I had obviously spent much more time among Indians than was customary; my opinions expressed at formal and informal school events demonstrated a bias toward the Indian perspective, not infrequently opposed to non-Indian interpretations of the situations; my probable reaction to any negative value judgments about Indians on the part of the staff members was undoubtedly considered by them to be predictable and unflattering to themselves. Overt hostility was not apparent; we all still greeted each other politely each day and communicated adequately about necessary aspects of school routine; but at least half the non-Indian staff members were unable or unwilling to enter into any sustained conversation with me beyond the necessary business or platitudinous observations about weather or health.

I shifted my approach quickly and prepared a questionnaire for anonymous response by check marks (no writing) to be returned via unmarked envelopes left in my mail box. Approximately half of the questionnaires were returned; fewer than half of those returned contained full responses. Others were partially blank or had such comments as, "Not competent to respond," or "Insufficient knowledge." Since the questions asked only about experiences the respondent had or opinions he held, no special competence or knowledge was required for response. It is clear that my presence had come to be seen as threatening by many of this category of people to the extent of inhibiting responses.

Now, of course, a part of the flexibility of participant-observation research is demonstrated in this case. The very fact that my role behaviors as teacher made me perceived by a substantial portion of one category of personnel as a threatening individual to whom even an anonymous opinion could not be expressed becomes of some significance as data. Further, the significance is not easily apparent by simply relating the incident or by categorizing the nonresponsive staff members with any kind of descriptive terms. It is seen only as a portion of the total matrix of interaction patterns among adults and children, Indians and Whitemen, government and church representatives, and so on. It thus becomes relevant to the major theme of the study but in an unanticipated way. This kind of flexible shift is not uncommon; few preconceived research designs will ever be followed through the participant observation experience without some modification. Yet this was more than modification; it was failure to anticipate the timing needs in relation to the attitudinal dynamics. Had these data been more vital to the outcome of the research, this kind of miscalculation could have led to total failure.

Further constraints in technique are placed upon the teacher as participant-observer by the fact that the school is the focus of his study and the learnings of students during their school experiences are the important variables he seeks to isolate and identify in their broader symbolic context. The entire domain of culture is potentially relevant to the teacher but, from that domain, he must select those elements that operate in the systematic compression process mediated via the school as the child is formed into an adult. The teacher researcher may or may not find kinship patterns, the economy, the language, or other cultural components to be essential understandings to explain his immediate observations, but he will always have to account fully for the school experiences in relation to whatever other cultural factors are determined to be essential for understanding. These determinations, within the concept of *institution,* must be statements of community-shared values and means of acquiring knowledge of those values, not just teacher prescriptions.

The teacher's primary observation arena is the classroom. Each operating classroom constitutes its own system—a subsystem of the school which is, in turn, a subsystem of the total society. Students learn to participate in the classroom system first and regardless of whether or how they master any cognitive skills. Young and Beardsley have demonstrated (1968:175ff) how "The *content* of interaction in schoolrooms is secondary to the *structure* of interaction . . . students must learn to assemble and dissemble the [schoolroom] systems. . . ." The teacher, whether a researcher or not, must recognize this overriding social system component of his classroom and be able to assess it in functional terms. Functional assessment involves at least two levels of abstraction: functionalism in terms of the total school environment of the moment and functionalism in terms of potential for transfer or development of the student role behaviors into appropriate adult behaviors—in terms of the ideal projected outcome of the institutionalized processes of education.

Thus the teacher attempts to provide an adequate explanation of the total culture or subcultures within which the school operates, although in varying depths and emphases. Since culture is identifiable only through analysis of symbols or symbolic behavior, this explanation involves identifying the essence of the symbolic system in some such pattern as Bruyn (1963:227ff) has developed especially for participant-observation methodology. Large segments of the explanation may be subsumed in broad categorizations of ideological, abstract, or emotive symbols. Other elements may require more detailed explanation of specific rules for behavior. Still others may not be susceptible to complete identification and must be left at the level of reported observations.[1]

This kind of prescription is easy to state but it is quite another thing to put it into practice. The teacher is faced daily with about thirty students, all more or less socialized to a classroom and school routine. School procedures, although patterned, are highly variable from school to school and class to class. To say the teacher's first obligation is to his *task performance,* is not enough. This may suffice for doctors who diagnose and prescribe, for nurses who follow rigorous routines in caring for the sick, for factory workers, salespeople, or other roles in which the role behaviors are firmly established and the interactions are usually among peers and dyadic in nature. The teacher-researcher is faced with establishing his thirty individual relationships so they will (1) result in effective daily communication; (2) result in the student achieving adequate personal success for satisfying organizational articulation requirements; (3) be congruent with the expectations of the broader community and bureaucracy; (4) be conducive to furthering his specific research interests; and (5) comply with socialization imperatives without imposing idiosyncratic teacher distortions. (Slight modifications will be introduced in this relationship pattern when the teacher's role does not include direct classroom activities; but essentially the nature of the problem will remain the same for all professional school roles.)

How much of his own personality and personal inclinations should the teacher introduce into the situation? To what extent should he attempt to conform to the modal curriculum and teacher behavior model of the school in efforts to avoid artificial skewing of the total situation? Certainly the teacher-researcher cannot create a totally new pattern to conform either to his philosophical or research inclinations. He must conform to the broad operational framework of the school in which he works. Perhaps ideally he should be as unobtrusive and noninnovative as possible if he hopes to obtain information about the patterns which would operate regardless of which teacher was present. If he experiments, it must be gently, within the acceptable range of school and student definable goal outcomes. Above all, the teacher-researcher needs to differentiate (for himself) between the cognitive

---

[1] I cannot explain, for example, the significance of the fact that girls (and only girls) of my class at the Yukon Indian residential school were able to make quickly and easily the string game pattern, "Osage Diamonds" (*Scientific American* 207(6):154) and frequently did this complicated manipulation as part of their play. No adult women to whom I spoke about this claimed knowledge of the string play. Although I did not investigate intensively, the frequency of the game among children led me to expect it to be something similar to "cat's cradle," and widely known among adults in the society. It was not.

and the affective elements of his mode of classroom behavior. He can work within nearly any curricular pattern with a variety of cognitive skills as the desired result or he can use almost any pedagogical techniques as the means of pursuing such results without distorting the tenor of total school operation, provided he can achieve neutral or positive kinds of affective response patterns among the students.

In addition to the cognitive learnings required by students of schools in order to proceed through the school hierarchy, essential behaviors demonstrating understanding of the cultural values and the culture symbol system are continually exhibited. These must *not* be imposed by the teacher-researcher if he is to achieve his own understanding and provide for others an explanation of the processes in which he is engaged. To the extent that the affective learnings of symbols and values are imposed in the classroom—and they invariably must be to some extent—the teacher-researcher should limit his involvement to that of a channel rather than that of the source. (If chapel attendance is required by the school, the teacher announces time for chapel attendance. If he is not required to escort the students to chapel, he should not simply lead the way but should present the problem of *how* to go to chapel, thus utilizing a specific opportunity to elicit data about interaction patterns, problem attack, authority perceptions, leadership determinations, and similar individual and group behaviors.) In dozens of daily situations the teacher-researcher will find similar opportunities to withdraw himself from the affective learning processes and to observe both these learnings in process and the results of previous learnings of this nature.

The Significant Friend

Our language is inadequate to differentiate among categories to the extent needed for me to elaborate upon the role of *friend* that may well emerge for at least one relationship the teacher develops in the community outside the classroom, whether he is working in his own society or in a cross-cultural context. This role is not dealt with in depth as related to participant-observation methodology—perhaps because it is so utterly nonobjective and objectivity is the great mythology of scientific investigation. Yet I feel the potentiality of the role of *friend* has much to offer to extending the range and reliability of observations and it justifies some careful considerations prior to establishing the relationship. I do not refer to friendly relationships in the common sense, as opposed to hostile or indifferent interactions, but to *friend* in the sense of the unique, intensely personal sharing of perceptions, reactions, preferences, and mutual respect that identifies for all of us a very few select individuals out of the world population.

Casagrande (1960) collected from a group of anthropologists a series of descriptions of a variety of personal informant relationships, some of which included *friends. Informant* is too casual and remote a term to describe the relationship to which I refer, although the person does become in a special way a prime informant. For this reason he should be selected with great care and not too soon in the course of the research. He must be a person with whom a genuine, intimate interaction relationship can be developed, a relationship that all but ignores the primary study objectives of the researcher.

Timing again is important because the researcher must be sure of what he is doing before he permits the relationship to develop. In some cases the newcomer is so eager to effect his entry into the society that he tends to accept uncritically the friendship overtures of atypical persons who eventually may harm the study more than they help. The deviant who is himself barely tolerated in the community, the biased malcontent who, unable to find sources of ego gratification within his own society, grasps any available external audience; these types are likely to be the first to make overtures toward closer relationship with the newcomer. They are interesting cases and create situations worthy of study, provided one is able to marshal facts enough to identify the situations accurately. But if the newcomer's community identity includes the deviant as a basic friend referent, the reliability of his information will be doubtful.

A dual prescription is indicated: initial entry should be with a generalized friendly attitude in all interactions but with definite limits imposed to inhibit close relationships; the close personal friendship should be nurtured actively only when the researcher has determined that the potential friendship will not seal him off from further participation among the broad community. This is not as crass or ruthless as it may sound. Selective friendships are normal human relationships; if a researcher feels that denying himself the close friendship of a complete deviant in a society is rejection of his own basic human values, he probably should not be attempting the research in that society at all. His own biases will never permit arriving at acceptable levels of generalization.

A relationship in which friendship outweighs any other role definition provides opportunities for insights otherwise unobtainable by an outsider. The patterns of salient perceptions and reactions, priorities of time allocation in personal relationships, the flavor of individual life style, the reflections of self-image, and the observations of these perceptions among others as mediated through the friend are all classes of information that emerge only partially, if at all, from more remote formal observations. The long, slow process of getting drunk together, a day spent fishing over several miles of a stream together, hours traveling along a trail to a hunting camp, an afternoon picnic or joint attendance at a funeral or school pageant, all these and dozens of other similar situations provide opportunities in which information obtained more formally and rigorously elsewhere can be evaluated in the operational context of the perceptual patterns of a knowledgeable human (friend) who functions within the cultural framework being studied.

As the relationship develops, the stranger may even assume some degree of privilege—and thus a new dimension of participation—from the host's role in his community and family. Relatives and close friends of the family will develop a special set of behaviors to accommodate the new friend. Often this will include ritual joking behaviors, terminologies relevant to sex taboos (with implications for concurrent sex privileges that would be totally denied to any "stranger" identity), sharing of reminiscences in which the new friend may or may not have participated, special food or residence rights, and generally the establishment of a new set of reciprocal relationships and identity-affirming behaviors within the cultural context. These will be derived from cultural patterns operating in the broader society. The extent to which they are readily available or must be specially created constitutes a powerful insight into the broader cultural processes.

Obviously the genuine friend relationship is the last blow to the myth of objectivity. This, to me, is completely unimportant. The participant-observer may be an objective researcher in another context—and I have used the term *researcher* loosely as his identity in the field situation—but in his field experience he is participating in and observing human experience from the perspective of another human. He should never attempt to do more *research* than to make notes and record data as fully as possible during his participant-observation experience. Analysis and reporting should always await removal of himself and his data from the site of the study.

Analysis

In his analysis of data and the organization of his report, the researcher copes with the problem of objectivity—generalizability. Anyone undertaking participant observation emerges with a wealth of data, much of it intimate, personal, detail. What is relevant and to what is it relevant? What is personal idiosyncracy and what is culturally patterned behavior? What is predictable under what circumstances? What behaviors illustrate the rules? What signs or symbols trigger, modify, or validate such behaviors? What deviations are possible under what circumstances and what constitutes boundaries? And, above all else in schools, to what extent is school behavior relevant as an institutionalized educational process within the total society?

The teacher-researcher is faced with a situation unlike that of the fieldworker in remote primitive societies. The children of a school where the teacher undertakes his study will grow up able to read, to evaluate, perhaps even to make similar studies. Whatever reports are made will be available to the adults of the community within a few years at most. The researcher is faced almost immediately with a population capable of verifying or nullifying on empirical grounds whatever generalizations his analyses lead to. Careful, selective choices of observations are the researcher's only security. The validity and reliability of the data within the total context are of less importance than the accuracy of the observations (Bruyn 1963:232). In some cases completely erroneous interpretations of events may be offered the researcher or totally inappropriate responses may be observed. These *errors* themselves become significant, especially when and as they tend away from isolated specific situations toward patterned role behavior and to the extent that they demonstrate a shared perceptual pattern. When several incidents serve to illustrate a pattern, a parsimonious selection should be made of the minimum required and, to the extent possible, those least likely to identify or to embarrass individuals regardless of the degree of latent interest in the incidents themselves. The desired outcome of the study is not analysis of individual behaviors but a model of an institutionalized social process. Ideally the study culminates with abstractions at a level providing for comparison with similar studies. At the same time it must face the test of projected replication. Even though nobody can completely *replicate* the study by recreating exactly the role interpretations and the situations, the researcher attempts to the best of his ability to answer positively his own question: "If another person had these experiences, would he identify *these* data as significant?"

In the final analysis this becomes a highly personalized and subjective experience, moving into the realm of objectivity only when it meets the ultimate test of those who know, agreeing that it is a useful model. But both teaching and cultural anthropology are, in the final analysis, highly personalized, subjective activities.

Despite this fact, the two domains of interest constitute one of our few hopes for achieving analyses and reformulations of formal educational processes in the world today. Teachers have the social roles but lack the theory and the lexicon; anthropologists have the theory, lexicon, and methodology. A fusion of efforts can permit formulation of a realistic and comparative perspective of the functions of schools. An assertion that schools today are generally dysfunctional needs hardly to be substantiated. Whether one considers minority enclave groups or affluent urban U.S. groups or developing nations struggling to reconstruct and redefine colonially imposed school systems within some culturally valid indigenous context, a universal aspect of modern schools is dysfunctionality.

Every school has a deliberate socialization component, a cultural transmission component including both enculturation and acculturation, and a vocational training component. All of the components are variously overt and covert. Probably all of these components must be retained in schools, but in what mixtures and to what degrees of overtness and covertness?

Little is gained from discrete studies of the components in isolation. The school as a small social structure is interesting but only as the shell in which unidentified learnings take place. Measures of cognitive skill acquisition or vocational aptitudes are useful but obviously only for a fraction of the processes of formal education. Even studies of cultural transmission and culture change as mediated through the formal school organization fall short of providing the whole concept of the school as it relates to the educational process.

This objective will be realized more fully as systematic studies are made of many schools in many societies to develop theory relating to education as a universal social institution, with the formal organization known as *school* functioning as a specialized variable. The common goal of all men in all societies is achievement of optimal adaptation to the environment—an ecological concept of colossal magnitude that demands the magnitude of anthropological theory to encompass it. Education can only be viewed as the process by which the social neophyte achieves this adaptation as he becomes adult. If adults are to continue to function at all on this increasingly overpopulated, overpolluted, and overhostile planet, some new realism must penetrate our social decision-making processes.

References

Bruyn, Severyn, 1963, "The Methodology of Participant Observation," *Human Organization* 22(3)224–235.

Babchuk, Nicholas, 1962, "The Role of the Researcher as Participant Observer and Participant-as-Observer in the Field Situation," *Human Organization* 21(3)225–228.

Casagrande, Joseph B., 1960, *In the Company of Man.* New York: Harper & Row.

King, A. Richard, 1967, *The School at Mopass: A Problem of Identity.* CSEC. New York: Holt, Rinehart and Winston, Inc.

Kluckhohn, F. R., 1940, "The Participant Observer Technique in Small Communities," *American Journal of Sociology* 46:331–343.

Pearsall, Marion, 1965, "Participant Observation as Role and Method in Behavioral Research," *Nursing Research* 14(1):37–42.

Scientific American, 1962, "Osage Diamonds," in "Mathematical Games," edited by Martin Gardner. 207(6):146–154.

Vidich, Arthur J., 1955, "Participant Observation and the Collection and Interpretation of Data" *American Journal of Sociology* 60(4)354–360.

Young, T. R., with P. Beardsley, 1968, "The Sociology of Classroom Teaching: A Microfunctional Analysis," *Journal of Educational Thought* 2(3):175–186. Calgary, Alberta: The University of Calgary.

HARRY F. WOLCOTT/*University of Oregon*

21 *The Teacher as an Enemy*

I don't like Mr. Wolcott
he always make me work
I hate Mr. Wolcott.

A Kwakiutl Indian boy directed these written words to me while he was attending school in his native village on the coast of British Columbia, Canada. At the time I was the teacher at the village school. My purpose in living in the village and teaching at the school was to study the relationship between village life and the formal education of village pupils. An account of my year as teacher and ethnographer at Blackfish Village is contained in *A Kwakiutl Village and School,* which is a case study of the problems of Western education in a contemporary cross-cultural setting (Wolcott 1967).

As the village teacher I had the responsibility for conducting a one-room school for all the resident village children between the ages of six and sixteen. As ethnographer, I wanted to identify and assess the influence of cultural barriers to classroom performance as a way of studying why Indian pupils have so often seemed refractive to the formal educative efforts of the school.

Although I had taught previously in public schools, I was not prepared for the classroom problems which confronted me at the village school. I found there a firmly entrenched pattern of pupil hostility toward the teacher and toward nearly every nonmaterial aspect of the way of life the teacher represented. In the time that has elapsed since the original fieldwork in 1962–1963, I have had the opportunity to reflect upon the experiences of that year and to return for several brief periods of subsequent study. I have been seeking alternative ways of thinking about the role of the teacher in a cross-cultural setting like Blackfish Village.

In a setting in which critical differences between a teacher and his pupils are rooted in antagonisms of cultural rather than classroom origins, I believe that the teacher might succeed in coping more effectively with conflict and in capitalizing on his instructional efforts if he were to recognize and to analyze his ascribed role as "enemy" rather than attempt to ignore or to deny it. To those educators who insist that a teacher must always present a façade of cheery optimism in the classroom, the notion of the teacher as an enemy may seem unacceptable, overly negative, perhaps even dangerous. One might question, however, whether cheery optimism and a determination to accomplish "good" inevitably serve the best interests of culturally different pupils, especially pupils from socially and economically. depressed or deprived sectors of the population. Any teacher who has faced such pupils in the classroom may have recognized that one alternative for him is to try to do less harm rather than more good. Even with so modest a goal, any strategy that may minimize psychological harm either to pupils or to their teachers merits consideration. The strategy of regarding the teacher as an enemy is explored here as it relates to formal education in antagonistic cross-cultural settings.

Antagonistic Acculturation

Anthropologists refer to the modification of one culture through continuous contact with another as acculturation. Often one of the contact cultures is dominant, regardless of whether such dominance is intended. Not infrequently the situation of dominance leads to a relationship which breeds antagonism on the part of the dominated group.

Antagonism rises rather expectedly out of feelings that one's own cherished ways are being eroded and lost or that one's ethnic group belongs to a have-not class. Antagonistic feelings may be aggravated by the attempts of members of the dominant society to hasten the process of assimilation. Frequently antagonisms are aggravated by a contradiction between the ideal of assimilation and the reality of prejudicial treatment accorded to minority groups within the dominant society. This was the case at Blackfish Village, not because of any problem unique to the village but because there had been a concerted, although not very successful, effort by both the Canadian and U.S. governments to hasten and even to complete the assimilation of North American Indian groups. Indian schools run by the federal governments of both countries consciously directed their efforts toward replacing Indian ways with ways more acceptable to and characteristic of the dominant white middle class, although the respective societies have at the same time responded prejudicially to the Indian who attempted to assimilate.

Contemporary social commentary describing the relation of pupils to their schools among the Sioux Indians, along the Mexican-American border, in Harlem and in Puerto Rican East Harlem, in the Deep South, in Boston, in Washington, D.C., or in the inner city everywhere suggests that cultural barriers to classroom performance are not unique to my confrontation with Blackfish pupils. However, I shall relate my discussion to that specific setting. I will describe how the stresses resulting from "antagonistic acculturation" were manifested in microcosm in the behavior of village children in the classroom. First, I shall describe how I perceived the classroom to be organized to thwart my instructional efforts. A rather different picture of the classroom follows as written accounts from some of the older Blackfish pupils suggest how the classroom looked to them.

Classroom Learning Kwakiutl-Style—as Seen by the Teacher

Here are seven important characteristics of the classroom at the Blackfish Indian Day School as I saw it:

1. The pupils set their own pace, not in the ideal sense of an individualized program with each child working independently at an optimum rate, but rather with doing little in lots of time. My inclination, having found them "behind" in their work, was to get them "caught up." Their inclination was, generally, to let the school day slip by without having expended much—or perhaps any—effort in the direction I was so anxious to push them. Their whole orientation to school, I believe, was one of patiently enduring. What my pupils wanted most to get out of school was to get out of school. Since maturity provided the only means to achieve that goal, the amount of school work accomplished in a day had no meaning unless one's peers wanted to engage in a self-imposed competition or unless one really valued the praise of the teacher. But neither the rewards the teacher had to give nor the manner in which he gave them were likely to warrant the effort necessary to attain them or the risk of incurring the displeasure of one's fellow pupils for having done so.

2. Classroom assignments were frequently perceived as a group task. My worksheets and practice papers were treated as though my class was a secretarial pool—older or brighter pupils did papers for younger or slower ones, sometimes because the assignments were difficult, sometimes because they were fun. My pupils, as a class, were organized to cope with me collectively, while I was trying to cope with them individually. The nature of this mutual classroom help among pupils had several concomitant aspects described below.

3. Almost invariably students collaborated as partners in electing to complete or to ignore classroom assignments, in deciding whether to write long diary entries about their day, in making choices when alternative activities were offered, or in preparing answers to my questions. My "divide and conquer" tactic was constantly subverted. I had great difficulty assessing the progress of any given pupil because pupils so frequently teamed up to write daily entries for each other and to work each other's assignments.

One of the most successful classroom activities of the year was the exchange of a series of letters between the older pupils and a sixth-grade class in a California school. As the exchange of letters progressed, some members of the class began receiving more letters than others. Those who received many letters farmed out the excess and had other pupils write the replies. At another time, I gave eight older pupils a sentence-completion test. I later discovered that instead of eight sets of answers I had received four sets of paired answers in return. Before beginning to complete the sentences each pupil chose a partner with whom he worked out a tentative answer, and then both partners wrote a comparable—or identical—response for each sentence.

4. Teasing and bullying were very disruptive elements in class. Often the teasing was related to inter- or intra-family squabbles which had their origin outside of school. Included in the teasing, however, was a process of pupil socialization in which children learned not to outperform their peers. Particularly, I observed change in the behavior of two children, a fourth-grade girl and a first-grade boy, who came to the village after the school year had begun and who seemed to be particularly capable students. Both underwent continual taunting in class, and both learned to display less overt enthusiasm for school and to restrict their academic prowess to tasks on which they could work alone, while they performed only minimally at those tasks on which greater achievement was apparent to their peers. The boy had come from a provincial school where he was one of few Indian pupils; the girl had been attending a day school in another village, one in which school achievement was more acceptable and school success more frequent. Whether the socialization of these children was due to their ability in school, their being outsiders to the village, or a combination of both, I have never been certain. That the quality and quantity of their academic performance diminished, I am sure. The girl traveled to her parents' village for Christmas and never returned to Blackfish Village; the boy survived the year by learning to perform more like other village boys in school, which meant doing very little on group assignments, although he usually worked well alone. He outperformed all the other pupils in the seclusion of two intelligence tests I administered.

5. At the same time that overperformance was restrained through socialization, there was some tendency to help the slower children of one's age or ability group. Such help differs from the help given to younger pupils, because that assistance seemed to be used to get the tasks completed (if the teacher was going to insist on them) while the helping to which I now refer served to keep a pupil from appearing too inadequate in the eyes of the teacher. For the teacher, this "equalizing" behavior among the pupils made the task of finding suitable material or diagnosing individual learning difficulties almost impossible.

The most glaring instance was that of a fifteen-year-old boy who was almost a nonreader. In September I assigned to him a fourth-grade basal reader which was being read by several other boys. It was some time before I realized that he was so used to having difficult words whispered to him by his reading mates that during my limited opportunity to hear the children read aloud he did not necessarily look at the pages to appear to be reading from them. Eventually I realized he could read independently only at grade-one level, and as late as May I recorded in my notes, "He gets so much help from other kids that I still doubt that I know his own capabilities."

As a social phenomenon, the cooperative efforts of my pupils may appear both remarkable and praiseworthy. In each case, however, the extent of their cooperation and organization inevitably thwarted my efforts in both assessing and instructing them, according to the expectations which I held for myself as a teacher. Further, to whatever extent I was able to see the positive aspects of pupil cooperation rather than to feel threatened by it, I was still unable to mobilize the cooperative potential of the pupils to accomplish *my* purposes. I could not make them help each other, be patient toward each other, or socialize each other toward such teacher-approved purposes as keeping the classroom quiet so pupils could read, working quickly enough to allow time for other activities, or letting younger pupils join in the recess play of the older ones.

6. Antagonistic as they were toward so many aspects of school, my pupils nevertheless held very rigid expectations about the activities they considered appropriate for school work. Insistence on attention to the three R's constituted the only legitimate kind of demand which the pupils both expected and accepted on the part of their teacher. Their notion of an ideal classroom was one in which pupils were busily engaged in highly repetitive but relatively easy assignments for long periods of time, uninterrupted by the teacher. Their notion of an ideal teacher, consistent with this, was of a person who meted out assignments but not explanations, a person who had an infinite supply of worksheets and tasks but who never asked a pupil to engage in an exercise he could not already perform. The only favors or rewards expected of a teacher were in the distribution of coveted materials (crayons, water colors, compasses, scissors, puzzles, athletic equipment), the allocation of prestige positions (attendance monitor, bell ringer), and the rationing of school "fun" ("free" time, art periods, extended recesses, classroom parties).

Given their narrow expectations for proper classroom activities, it is not surprising that the pupils responded most favorably to assignments at the specific tasks required in arithmetic and spelling. Occasionally they requested an assignment to repeat a page of arithmetic drill or requested my validation of a self-imposed assignment to write each spelling word three, five, or ten times.

Weeks passed before the older pupils grew accustomed to my daily assignment—making at least a brief entry in a diarylike notebook. Even when they had grown used to this activity as part of our daily program, they were uneasy that I did not "teach" language arts because I did not often use the language arts texts. Although their basal readers and the accompanying workbooks were difficult, dull, and pedantic, the pupils were never satisfied that they were "having reading" unless these readers were before them. They never completely accepted my progressive idea that reading a book of one's own choice was also a legitimate type of classroom reading. Patiently, and sometimes impatiently, they endured my reading aloud to them, because they had been subjected by their teachers to that dubious pleasure for years, but I could seldom induce them to any kind of classroom discussion subsequent to hearing a story. My attempts to relate social studies to their own lives made them uncomfortable both because they perceived this as prying and because I did not depend on textbooks in my approach. They were generally impatient with instruction in concepts that were not included in their texts (for example, notions from the new math). In short, my pupils had very specific expectations for the formal purposes of school, they generally hated school as defined by these expectations, and they refused to have their expectations modified. They disliked school and that is just how they liked it.

7. Let me conclude this description of the classroom as seen by the teacher with one final pattern of pupil behavior, the attempts of the pupils to socialize their teacher. It is misleading to refer to this socialization as "attempts," for my pupils were good teachers, and their techniques were effective. The methods they used to socialize me included giving slow, reluctant responses to my directions, ignoring my comments (by not "hearing" them or occasionally by putting their hands to their ears), mimicking my words or actions, constantly requesting to leave the classroom to go to the toilet, and making me the target of spoken or written expletives. To illustrate, the following note was written to me during the daily writing period by a twelve-year-old boy the day after I took a partially eaten apple away from him and inadvertently forgot to return it:

> We were packing wood yesterday me and Raymond were packing lots of wood. Oh, you little monkey, little asshole you got my apple why don't you mind your own business you think you smart little asshole. Goodbye, that's all I can say now. Goodbye, no more writing because you throw my apple.

The most direct and telling comments were those that identified me as "White man," the outsider, or drew attention to our different cultural origins: "Just like a White man," "That's the trouble with you White guys," or, twice during the year, an angry stare and the comment, "What's the matter; haven't you ever seen an Indian before?" With such a statement as: "We don't have to tell *you* anything," I was at a loss to know whether my distinguishing attribute was that I was white, the teacher, a cranky adult, or all of them.

Classroom Learning Kwakiutl Style—as Seen by the Pupils

Although I have referred frequently to the pupils in the class, the classroom picture presented above is entirely a construct of a teacher's perception. Consequently, it is cast primarily in terms of the teacher's instructional goals and how the subculture of the pupils seemed to be organized to thwart them. Written comments of the older pupils provide some insight into how the class and teacher looked to them.

1. This response was written by a fifteen-year-old girl to an assigned topic, "If I Were the Teacher." Note how she relates her concept of the role of a teacher to perpetuating such middle-class values so revered by teachers as cleanliness, quiet, punctuality, and obedience. Note also the emphasis she

gives to discipline and punishment. The classroom is an orderly, severe, and punishing place.

> If I were the teacher. When I first get here I'd like to meet all the children here. The first day in school I'd tell the pupils what to do. First thing we do is clean the school up then clean the desk and the cupboards. Then straighten the cupboard up for the books. When the school is cleaned up, then I'll give out the books. And ask what grade they're in. Ask how old are they. And give the rules for school. The school starts at 9:00 A.M., recess at 10:30 A.M., dinner at 12:00 P.M., come back in the afternoon at 1:00 P.M., recess at 2:30 P.M. and after school 3:30 P.M. And if anybody's late, they have to write hundred lines.[1] And keep the toilet clean. Their clothes clean and comb hair. First thing they'd do in the morning is Arithmetic, spelling, language, Reading. And the afternoon Science, Social Studies, Health, and free time. And if nobody works they get a strapping. If I had a fourteen year old in my class she or he would take care of grade one and two. And I'd take care of three to eight. If I had a class all in one grade that'll be nice. Then I won't have to bother about other grades except the class I have. And if they get the room dirty they'll sweep the whole classroom. I'd get a monitor for the bath room to be clean and swept. And if anybody talks back. They'd get a strapping. If they get out of their desk they'll have to write lines. If they don't ask permission to sharpen their pencil they'll get strapping. If they wear hats and kerchiefs in class they'll have to stand in the corner for one hour with their hands on their heads. I'd tell the children to draw Indian Design for the room. If they make a noise in class, they all stay in for half an hour. If anybody talks in class they write lines about hundred lines. If anybody's absent they have lots of homework for the next day. And if anybody fights they get a strapping. And I'd have a monitor for the books so nobody touch it except the monitor. Dust the shelves. And on Christmas they'd have to play or sing. And on Halloween they have to dress up for the party.

2. Here is the response of another pupil, a fourteen-year-old girl, to my request for a theme on the same topic, "If I Were the Teacher." Note the contrast she makes between discipline and scholarship. If one of her pupils were to fail to be on time, she would strap him. If he were to fail a comprehensive examination, she would have a talk with him.

> If I were the teacher for Blackfish Village, or someplace else, I'd like my class to be very quiet. If not, they would get a straping from me. They would get a straping if they are late.
>
> They would come to school at nine A.M. No sooner nor later. They would have one recess in the morning and one in the afternoon. In the afternoon they would go home at 3:30 P.M.
>
> The subjects I'd give them in the morning are Math, Spelling, Reading. If they

[1] By "write lines" she refers to the practice of repeatedly writing a sentence like "I will not talk out in class" to the satisfaction of a teacher. In my defense I should add that none of the assortment of disciplinary measures she refers to was used in my classroom, although I did have children put their heads down on their desks as a mild disciplinary measure and sent them out of the classroom for a variety of infractions, including that exquisite pupil weapon, sullenness.

do not get it finished they would have it for homework, same in the afternoon. They would have a story, Language, then Library or drawing.

I'd like my class to be very neat, clothes clean, hair neat. In the morning they could sing "God Save the Queen." In the afternoon they would sing "Oh Canada."

I would choose Monitors for toilets, paints and for blackboards, But of course I would do the Attendance myself. I would given them tests before Christmas, Easter, and the final tests at June. After the tests if anyone fails, I would ask them to tell me why. For example if one of my pupils did fail I'd tell that child to write on a paper to tell me why. If that child has a good excuse, I'd tell that child to "smarten up" and pay attention to his or her work more.

I would go to see their parents to see if they have a normal living, like if they go to sleep before nine o'clock, have good meals every day.

Yes sir! If I were the teacher a lot of changes would be made around here at Blackfish Village. The children would have to listen even if I were a girl teacher.

But I didn't plan the future yet. That's for sure I'm not sticking around here in the future.

3. In most cases where the hostility of the children toward the teacher flared up over a specific incident at school the pupils did not record their perceptions of the event in their classroom writing. Typically at such times they refrained from performing any task that might please the teacher, and writing in their notebooks did win teacher approval. The following excerpt reveals one instance where a pupil did record the anger which she shared with several other pupils. I had refused to admit a group of the older pupils into class when they were late in returning from the morning recess, and at least for this fourteen-year-old, trouble at school had precipitated more trouble at home.

Today is a very horrible day for Norma and me. Of course we would be treaten as babies. When we are late in this dump the teacher would [i.e., *did*] tell us to come back in the afternoon. There was Larry, Joseph, Norma, Tommy, Jack, Herman and me. Norma got in trouble too, of course. My brother would tell on me that brat. This is a strict world for some of us. I thought this was a free world. Norma and me can't even go on Larry's boat and for me I'm not aloud to go to their house! My brother said I was in my aunties house. I guess thats why I ain't aloud in their. All the time I was in Sarah's house. The teacher is so lazy to ring the bell I guess he expects us to hear him when he calls us. That's all!!

4. Two final examples suggest the contrast between the pseudowork and satisfaction of the classroom and the real work and real rewards of adult life. Here is a written comment, in the form of a note to the teacher, from a twelve-year-old boy who recognized that although he was required to attend school, he had a more important contribution to make to his family when he could assist with the work of the men:

I am going to go halibut fishing with my father and Raymond. That's why I asked you is there going to be school tomorrow because I want to go with my father. He

> always has a tough time when he catches halibut [alone]. We got one halibut yesterday.

In a similar vein, the following was written in November by a fifteen-year-old boy. The note mentions only a week's leave, but it was in fact the boy's last classroom assignment forever, because he has never returned to school:

> We are going to Gilford Island tomorrow. I'm going to stay there one week. I'm going to dig clams. There is a big tide this week. I'm not coming to school next week.

The Teacher as an Enemy

In the school at Blackfish Village, or for teachers in any number of comparable settings, I believe there would be real utility in having more than one way of perceiving the reciprocal roles of teacher and pupil. In my own case, experience in both roles prior to my year at Blackfish Village had been within the confines of a middle-class setting of which I am very much part and product. Sometimes, in my twenty years as a student, I had experienced antagonism toward teachers and occasionally I had generated antagonism among my students as a public school and university teacher. Such antagonism, however, was a consequence of immediate psychological or personal incompatibility, never an antagonism rooted in social forces outside the classroom. I had never encountered teachers or pupils with whom I did not share relatively similar expectations regarding behaviors, values, and attitudes.

At Blackfish Village my pupils and I shared few mutual expectations regarding our formal role relationship. Those expectations we did share tended to provide pacts that enabled individual survival in a situation beyond our making rather than opening avenues for trust or understanding. No one, teacher or pupils, ever let his guard down very far. If we were not at any one moment actually engaged in a classroom skirmish, it was only because we were recovering from a prior one or preparing for the next. On the last day of school I reflected that I had not won a battle; instead I felt that all year long I had had a tiger by the tail, and we had merely crossed some kind of symbolic finish line together.

I had anticipated that one of my major problems of the year would be to induce my pupils to come regularly to school. Except for the fact that pupils expected to leave school at about age sixteen, however, my pupils and I did not have to do battle regarding school attendance. Economic sanctions could be taken against families who failed to send their children regularly to school, but in fact attendance (other than a perennial problem in getting pupils from certain families to school on time) was not a major concern. Indeed, parents not only sent their children off to school each day but also ritually endorsed the benefits of formal education with such comments as "Education is the only answer."

I had mistakenly assumed that once the pupils were inside the classroom they could be led to a host of new learnings under the guidance of their dedicated teacher. Ever since my year as a teacher at the Blackfish Indian Day School I have been seeking an alternative teaching perspective, one that would have enabled me to present an instructional program without such personal frustration at my lack of success and without nurturing an atmosphere of hostility where I had intended to create an atmosphere of help.

The direction my quest has taken is *not* to ponder how to "outpsych" or outmaneuver my pupils. Training in anthropology had convinced me of the fact that differences exist among groups of human beings and that the differences may touch every facet of human life from household composition to cognition. But I was not assigned to the village to teach villagers their way of life; I was assigned to teach them something about mine.

I think that I might have been a more effective teacher if I had taken the perspective of regarding the *teacher,* me, *as an enemy.* By effective I mean that I would have remained more objective about my lack of success, and I would have been more sensitive to the high cost for each pupil of accepting me or my instructional program. The "enemy" relationship I use here as my analogy does not refer to entering into combat, although on the worst days we may not have been far from it. More appropriate to antagonistic acculturation as manifested in school might be an analogy to a prisoner-of-war camp. Prisoners of war—inmates and captors alike—are faced with the probability that a long period of time may ensue during which their statuses remain unchanged. While great hostility on the part of either group might be present in the relationship, it is not essential to it, because the enmity is not derived from individual or personal antagonism. Nonetheless, the captors, representing one cultural group, are not expected to convert the prisoners to their way of life, and the prisoners are not expected to acculturate the captors.

So far, a teacher in an instructional role has no place in the analogy. Let us extend the analogy one step further. Suppose that along with the usual cadre of overseers the captors have also provided teachers charged with instructing the prisoners in the ways of, and particularly in the merits of, their culture. The purpose of instruction is to recruit new members into their society by encouraging prisoners to defect, and achieving this by giving them the skills so that they can do so effectively. The teachers are expected to provide information about the captors' way of life and about the skills that this way entails. It has been established that prisoners will attend the classes and that they will not be allowed to disrupt classroom proceedings, but beyond these strictures the teacher is not expected to dwell on the negative aspects that have brought his pupils to him. The teacher is not unaware of the probability, however, that since he is perceived as an enemy, his pupils may not see him playing a very functional role in their lives other than as a representative of the enemy culture.

What purposes might be served in cross-cultural education if a teacher were to draw an analogy between himself and an enemy captor in trying to understand his relationship with his pupils? There are several potential advantages one might anticipate.

First, the teacher who can imagine how pupils might feel toward him as a member of a captor society recognizes a distinction between having pupils physically present in class and having them psychologically receptive to instruction. Cognizance of the pervasive hostile and suspicious influence of the enemy relationship helps the teacher maintain realistic expectations for what he can accomplish in the classroom. Despite his most valiant efforts to make his instruction effective, he is never overcome by feelings of personal inadequacy at a lack of response to his lessons. He realizes that under certain conditions the energy and resources of prisoners are utilized in a desperate struggle to survive and to maintain their own identity in the face of overwhelming odds. The teacher recognizes that the antagonism of his pupils may be addressed to the whole cultural milieu in which they find themselves captive rather than to him as an individual. He understands that any attempt on his part to alter or to ameliorate the basis for antagonism may be met with suspicion. He is not personally disappointed when his pupils show tendencies toward recidivism when they feel themselves being seduced by the constant attention and encouragement of their mentor-enemies. If this is how things seem to the prisoners, the teacher realizes that a modification of a lesson plan or an ingenious new teaching technique is not going to make any important difference to them. Taking the point of view of his pupils, the teacher can ask himself, "Just what is it that a prisoner would ever want to learn from an enemy?"

Second, the teacher who can entertain a perspective that regards himself and his pupils as belonging to enemy cultures acknowledges the possibility that there could be important and systematic differences in life styles and in value-orientation characterizing each group. He is not as inclined to share a perception, common among teachers, that if a pupil does not have the same cultural background as the teacher he does not have any cultural heritage at all. Granted, the teacher can be expected to believe that his own life style is right, but he also recognizes that he is not likely to achieve his purposes by insisting that all other life styles are therefore wrong. Anthropologist Ruth Landes has written cogently in this regard, "The educator, or other authority, can advance his inquiries and explanations by taking the position that he represents one culture talking to another. This minimizes personal and emotional involvements by focusing on the grand designs of each tradition. . . ." (Landes 1965:47).

The teacher's instructional objectives are to try to make his own way of life appear sufficiently manageable to his "enemy" pupils that they may choose to explore it further, and, for those pupils who do make this choice, to provide them with a set of survival skills for living in a different culture and having access to its rewards. Children growing up in Blackfish Village, for example, will have to be able to demonstrate the skill aspects of specific middle-class manners and values such as cleanliness, courtesy, responsibility, punctuality, or how to take orders from a white boss in order to survive in the dominant society. They do not, however, need a teacher who insists that such skills are necessary steps on the road to nirvana. They need a teacher who can identify and instruct them in certain specific behaviors which an individual *must* exhibit if he is going to move successfully in a society that heretofore has been regarded as an alien one.

We would hardly expect the teacher to engage in much "correction" of pupils except for what was essential to the maintenance of an orderly classroom. The language or dialect used by prisoners need not be singled out for ridicule, correction, or extermination. What the teacher might do, however, is to teach a standard dialect of his own language to prisoner-pupils who entertained an intellectual curiosity about it or, especially, to those pupils interested in learning the enemy culture well enough to see if they can survive in it.

Most important, the teacher realizes the meaning that accepting his teaching may have for those prisoners who do accept it. It may mean selling out, defecting, turning traitor, ignoring the succorance and values and pressures of one's peers, one's family, one's own people. It can require terrible and anxious decisions for the prisoner, and it may even require him to sever his most deeply-rooted human ties. The teacher needs constantly to review what these costs mean to any human. As a consequence, the teacher interested in his enemy pupils as humans may find himself less inclined to act as a cultural brainwasher and more inclined to weigh both the difficulties of cultural transition and the ultimate consequences of change. In the latter regard a proverb quoted in Robert Ruark's novel *Something of Value* seems particularly appropriate: "If a man does away with his traditional way of living and throws away his good customs, he had better first make certain he has something of value to replace them" (Basuto proverb).

The teacher may feel a greater need to alert his pupils to the fact that he has *not* been able to provide them with all the prerequisite skills for successfully "passing" in the teacher's own society than to fill them with hopes and promises which few may ever realize. His pupils need to know how much information they actually have, what problems they must anticipate, and which vestiges of their earlier heritage may present almost insurmountable handicaps.

Through the exercise of examining his *own* culture as the alien one, the teacher-enemy may be less aggressive about forcing his lessons on his prisoner-pupils. He may not accept so unhesitatingly the belief that what he is doing is necessarily "good" for them. He may be more inclined to think of teaching as an offer of help to members of the dominated group who seek it rather than as an imposition of help from members of the dominant group who insist on giving it. Pausing to consider the possibility of being regarded by his pupils as a member of an enemy culture offers the teacher a perspective for understanding why pupils might sometimes appear able but unwilling to accept his teaching. This perspective also encourages the teacher to give more help to the potential defectors who seek it, rather than to spend his time bemoaning the lack of defection by the prisoner generation of today.

Conclusion

Cultural systems provide us with practical answers to questions of how we should act and what to think about how we act. But no "culture" ever provides its members with a perfect and complete blueprint of how to act in every situation. If cultures accomplished that, they might never change, and we know that change is inherent in human life and human organization. We do not often pause to examine our own behavior, and it can be with a real sense of surprise that in a new role we suddenly discover that we already know exactly how to act; we may even feel we have "known it all the time." Student teachers, as a case in point, provide themselves and observers with remarkable examples of how well they have internalized the teacher behavior associated with the teacher-pupil role relationship even if they have never formally taken the teacher role before.

When circumstances bring us into contact with others who do not share the same cultural orientation, particularly if our "proper" behavior invites inappropriate responses or no response at all, we become more self-consciously aware of our own patterns of behavior. Initially this may result only in our speaking or gesticulating a bit more emphatically, in a manner characteristic of the American tourist abroad. Under conditions of prolonged contact, one might want to do better than simply wave his hands more or talk louder. Regardless of how much effort he makes at understanding those who are different from him, however, it is from his own repertoire of cultural behaviors that the individual most choose. If he has no perfectly appropriate pattern of behavior, then he has to look for relevant analogous situations. The choice of analogies is crucial.

The teacher working with culturally different pupils exhibits a natural inclination to draw upon a single analogy, that of the idealized teacher-pupil relationship suitable for the monolithic transmission of culture. I do not imagine that teachers will ever escape from drawing upon this analogy. Their very identity as teachers requires that they have specific notions about teacher behavior. Teachers should not be asked perfunctorily to discard their own "good customs."

I have suggested here that the teacher seek out alternative behavior analogs rather than depend solely on the not-always-appropriate model of the ideal teacher in the ideal setting. Like the role relationship between teacher and pupil, the relationship between enemies is also a culturally based one. The enemy relationship may actually draw more heavily upon universal aspects of behavior than does the teacher-pupil role which has tended to become so crystallized in Western civilization. In spite of the negative implications of an enemy role, and barring extremes of physical cruelty, there are certain ways in which pupils equated with captive prisoners might get better treatment than pupils regarded as allies. For example, in thinking of antagonistic pupils as prisoners of war, one comes to recognize that the classroom is neither the underlying source of intercultural antagonism nor the site of its critical campaigns. Such a realization may also help the reform-oriented teacher to recognize that the proper target for his efforts at community reform is the adult community rather than young children in school (Hawthorn et al. 1960:303).

One last dimension of the enemy perspective is that few demands are made of enemy prisoners. Demands are made explicitly; they are not based on assumptions of shared values about fair play, individual rights, ultimate purposes, or the dignity of office. In a sense, the behavior between enemies gives more overt evidence of respecting the other person's cultural ways than does that between friendly groups. Based as it is upon the recognition of vital differences rather than on the recognition of underlying similarities, the perspective of thinking about teachers and their culturally different pupils as enemies invites teachers to examine the kinds of differences cherished by enemies just as they have in the past addressed themselves, at least ritually, to what they and their pupils share in common.

References and Further Reading

Goffman, Erving, 1969, "The Characteristics of Total Institutions," In Amitai Etzioni, ed., *A Sociological Reader on Complex Organizations.* 2d ed. New York: Holt, Rinehart and Winston, Inc. Readers interested in exploring the analogy between pupils and prisoners will find a number of strategies which "inmates" pursue suggested in this essay.

Hawthorn, Harry B., C. S. Belshaw, and S. M. Jamieson, 1960, *The Indians of British Columbia: A Study of Contemporary Social Adjustment.* Berkeley: University of California Press, especially Chap. 23, "Schools and Education."

Henry, Jules, 1955, "Docility, or Giving Teacher What She Wants," *Journal of Social Issues* 11:33–41.

King, A. Richard, 1967, *The School at Mopass: A Problem of Identity.* CSEC. New York: Holt, Rinehart and Winston, Inc.

Landes, Ruth, 1965, *Culture in American Education: Anthropological Approaches to Minority and Dominant Groups in the School.* New York: John Wiley & Sons, Inc.

Rohner, Ronald P., 1965, "Factors Influencing the Academic Performance of Kwakiutl Indian Children in Canada," *Comparative Education Review* 9:331–340.

———, 1967, *The People of Gilford, A Contemporary Kwakiutl Village,* National Museum of Canada, Bulletin 225. Ottawa, Ontario: the Queen's Printer.

———, and Evelyn C. Rohner, 1970, *The Kwakiutl Indians of British Columbia.* CSCA. New York: Holt, Rinehart and Winston, Inc., especially Chap. 4, "Growing Up Kwakiutl."

Ruark, Robert C., 1955, *Something of Value.* New York: Doubleday & Company, Inc.

Smith, Alfred G., 1968, "Communication and Inter-cultural Conflict." In Carl E. Larson and Frank E. X. Dance, eds., *Perspectives on Communication.* Milwaukee: University of Wisconsin Press.

Wax, Murray L., Rosalie H. Wax, and Robert V. Dumont, Jr., 1964, Formal Education in an American Indian Community. *Social Problems, Monograph #1,* Society for the Study of Social Problems.

Wolcott, Harry F., 1967, *A Kwakiutl Village and School.* CSEC. New York: Holt, Rinehart and Winston, Inc.

RICHARD L. WARREN/*University of Kentucky*

22 *The School and Its Community Context: The Methodology of a Field Study*[1]

The educational system of a community constitutes an important vehicle for the transmission of culture. This function may appear to be orderly and stable, if the educational system is viewed primarily as a formal social organization. Goals, curricula, established procedures, hierarchy of authority, formal relationships with community organizations, and other traditional components of the educational process can be identified and described. The result is an assessment of the school as an academically oriented social organization charged with transmitting and mediating the more formal aspects of the culture. The internal organizational requirements of the school, the external expectations of the school's constituency, and the over-all visibility and accessibility of the school's academic program reinforce order and stability in this function.

However, integral to the life of the school are a wide range of activities and functions less subject to organized control and routine. Nuances in disciplinary techniques, teaching styles, faculty and faculty-student interpersonal relationships incorporate and reflect cultural values, norms, and sanctions. They operate often at a less formal, overt level, transmitting aspects of the culture not always clearly defined or articulated but, nevertheless, significantly functional to the life of the school and immediately relevant to assessing the stabilizing and mediating functions the school may perform.

Particular attention was given in this study to the more informal aspects of the educational process and to the role of the teacher in that process. It was assumed that an analysis of these aspects would provide valuable data with regard to the role of the school and the faculty in supporting and maintaining primary cultural directives as well as in effecting a constructive adjustment to change. It was further assumed that the strains and uncertainties created by the process of change would be more manifest in the informal aspects of school life than in the formal, established routine.

---

[1] The study is reported in Richard L. Warren, *Education in Rebhausen: A German Village.* CSEC. New York: Holt, Rinehart and Winston, Inc.

Background for the Selection of a Site

The primary focus of the study was the role of the school in a rural village undergoing rapid cultural changes as a result of industrialization. There were persuasive reasons why a village in West Germany was particularly appropriate.[2] The functional qualities of the educational system have in recent years been the subject of extended debate in West Germany. There exists a growing awareness that the system does not adequately complement the needs of a democratic, industrial society. In the decades since World War II, powerful legacies and developments have tended to converge on German communities, creating different orientations toward the goals and content of the educational system. They include (1) the weight and veneration of historic traditions and loyalties, (2) the reaction to and assessment of the Nazi experience by the younger and older generations, (3) the problem of assimilation involving large numbers of refugees, and (4) the postwar modernization and secularization of German society.

These convergent forces impose on educational institutions problems of cultural maintenance and change. Deeply enmeshed in the relatively isolated, stable folk culture, the schools of the small German community have traditionally operated to maintain and reinforce established cultural patterns—patterns functionally adapted to the local ecology and social system. But the gross and dramatic changes in German society are extending the cultural milieu of the rural community in many directions. Regional differentiations in dialect, religion, and local custom that have traditionally characterized rural Germany are giving way to the leveling influences of an urban way of life. Consequently, the schools are confronted with a perplexing dilemma. The present form and content of education constitute a symbol of cultural stability and continuity, but as a positive force effecting constructive adjustment to change, they are less functional. To sustain a functionally effective role in the community the schools must adjust to the demands of cultural change but at a pace and in a way that will not jeopardize their contribution to cultural maintenance. This kind of adjustment is difficult and fragile. The school which was the object of this study was impressively instrumental in supporting and transmitting the shared community culture, but the response of the school staff to the demands of cultural change was ambivalent.

[2] The more mundane, practical ones included knowledge of the language and the availability of a small grant for research in Germany. In addition, I had spent the years 1947–1949 in Germany as a member of the Education Division of the Office of Military Government for Bavaria. Our policy there sought the democratization of the German educational system—not simply through a "denazification" process but through rather drastic changes in the organization of schools, and to a lesser degree, in the content of the curriculum. This rather pretentious, reformist zeal may have been realistic about the centrality of education to the life of a nation, but it was patently naive about how easily an occupying power could effect changes in so basic an institution. On balance little progress was made during the occupation period. If one examines the changes now being considered and effected in West Germany, there is reason to assess the policy as well-conceived.

Selecting a Site

The size of the community was an important consideration in the selection of a site. The community had to be small enough to make possible a relatively comprehensive analysis of the educational system and of the cultural milieu in which it was situated, and it had to be large enough to maintain an educational system of sufficient size to justify such a study. I had envisioned a population of approximately 2000 as being ideal. As it turned out, Rebhausen,[3] the village selected, had a population of approximately 3000, but for other reasons it appeared to be especially suitable. Although it was located only 15 miles from Waldstadt, a city of some 130,000 people, it was one of a group of villages occupying a hilly and traditionally isolated section of southwest Germany—known for the excellent quality of wine produced and the almost primitive character of life. Rebhausen was, however, significantly different because of a chemical factory, established there in 1958, with a work force which had grown in six years from less than 100 to over 900. The village was originally identified, as one among a number of possibilities, through general information provided in part by Stanford colleagues and German acquaintances who either lived in the region or who had conducted research there, and through several weeks of personal investigation.[4]

The problems of establishing residence may or may not impose constraints on the selection of a site purely on the basis of research interests and design. In my case the problems turned out not to be insurmountable, due in part to fortuitous developments. The problems which had to be resolved were that of introducing the idea of the study to local governmental and school officials and ascertaining their attitude toward it, and then locating housing for myself and family (my wife and two children, a boy, 12, and a girl, 14).

The nature of initial contacts with local officials affects not only entree to the community but also the tenor and productivity of interpersonal relations. Such officials are potentially important informants and able to provide introduction to valuable sources of data. Preparation for a study should therefore include attention to those characteristics of community governance, social structure, and the educational system relevant to introducing the study. In this regard two facets of village life in the region where Rebhausen was located were particularly significant. The village school is an integral part of a state-controlled system of education but is autonomous with respect to research intrusions. Consequently I was beholden only to the principal for permission to conduct the research. Second, the mayor's position in the village is preeminent; his power and influence reaches into all aspects of village life, including the school. Hence his reaction to the research proposal had to be antecedent to a final decision about the selection of a site.

---

[3] The pseudonyms employed in the case study will be used here.

[4] If an exploratory trip to select a site and provide for eventual residence is not possible, time and money have to be expended for such purposes in the initial stage of a study. The more of both one can set aside for preliminary investigation the better, even if it means a financial crisis toward the end of the study—which is probably inevitable anyway.

There may be—in this case there were—important historical considerations which make it especially necessary to ascertain the reaction of local officials. In spite of the generally positive tenor of German-American relations, there was no reason to assume that, in the case of individuals, there would not be a legacy of bitterness as a result of World War II and the subsequent occupation and denazification proceedings. It turned out to be an unnecessary precaution but not, I submit, irrelevant given the ubiquitousness of the American "presence" in today's world. The mayor's response was affirmative; he expressed pleasure that his village was being considered for such research. (His interest and support throughout the study was of inestimable value.)

It was my hope that a village, selected solely on the grounds of research interests, would somehow yield up living accommodations for myself and family. Housing facilities were, however, severely limited—another reason for first soliciting the reaction of the mayor whose manifold duties and powers include housing administration. Nothing was immediately available, the one possibility being the apartment development financed by the factory to insure housing for their employees. The personnel executive informed the mayor I would be considered, conditional on a statement describing my research interests. He especially wanted to know my position on the question of an intermediate school for Rebhausen because educational facilities in the village were an important factor in attracting executive personnel. Formal identification with the factory had potential disadvantages. I submitted the statement and was glad for the serendipitous data the exchange was providing, but was relieved when an apartment outside the factory complex became available in two months.

The housing delay aided the study in quite unanticipated ways. For two months we had to temporize, the first month in Waldstadt (after a week in a hotel we found two rooms in a fraternity house, vacated for the summer, where we had cooking privileges). The second month we rented two rooms from a family in Rebhausen who made it a practice of renting to tourists, the more foreign the better. They had children about the ages of our own and the husband and wife were friendly, open individuals. We saw much of each other as families, and the wife became in time one of my most valuable informants.

Developing the Study of the School

From the very beginning my family's interests and experiences extended the purview of the study. More important, theirs was a more natural participation in the life of the community, and some benefits from this relationship presumably accrued to me. My son became—somewhat reluctantly—the first continuing point of contact with the Rebhausen school.

When we arrived in September, schools were in session. My daughter was too old for the Rebhausen school (grades 1–8). She enrolled in a Waldstadt Gymnasium and thereby shared the experience of those very few Rebhausen children who left the elementary school at the end of the fourth grade to begin the preuniversity training which the gymnasium provided. My son was a seventh-grader. When I had settled on Rebhausen as a site, talked to the mayor and located housing, I had not yet met the principal. He was away for two weeks at a conference. I assumed he would cooperate with the study; the mayor assured me he would and the assistant principal appeared interested in the project. My first formal contact with the school was then through my son, who enrolled in the seventh grade and began attending classes. During the first month I made frequent trips to Rebhausen to bring him to school, to become better acquainted with the faculty, and to observe the community at work.

The principal, when he returned, was favorably disposed toward the research. He invited me to spend as much time as I wanted to in the school, offering to make available whatever statistics and pertinent educational material the school had on file. On the day before the fall vacation (almost the entire month of October, during grape harvest) he arranged a meeting with the faculty to give me an opportunity to describe the study. The teachers appeared receptive to the study, although one faculty member openly expressed some reserve and suspicion. Herr Schenke, the seventh-grade teacher, asked if I had come on assignment from a magazine to write a series of typically American exposés of the "awful" German character. Throughout the study he maintained reservations and was generally of a mood to point out things about American schools he thought I ought to study. For this and other reasons he appeared more sensitive than the other teachers to my presence in the classroom, and because, too, my son was in the seventh grade, I did not spend as much time observing in Herr Schenke's class. So far as I could tell, other faculty members had no such reservations.

As soon as vacation ended I started systematic observations in the school, spending at the outset over a week in each class and moving from the first grade through the eighth. After the completion of three months of concentrated observations, I limited classroom visits to specific grades and teachers relative to certain research questions (a fourth month was spent with a first-grade class, in April when the new school year began). While several class periods and a wide range of special school activities and ceremonies were taped and innumerable photographs taken, most of the data about classroom life were acquired through naturalistic observations.

First encounters with classes did not always result in the unobtrusive presence I naïvely hoped I could be. There was always the formal introduction to the class by the teacher, accompanied in some instances by a stern admonition to behave so that "the professor doesn't take back to America a bad picture of German children." In one instance I was peremptorily given the teacher's desk at the front of the room as an observation post—the better to see the children. After one period of this discomfort I demurred and worked my way to an empty seat in the back.

Extensive observational notes were written. They were infrequent during the first day, until, through informal conversations, I felt I had acquainted the teacher with the study and satisfied whatever initial curiosity she had with respect to my interest in her particular class. There were moments when note-taking was judged to be threatening—and was therefore delayed—when, in particular, the teacher was engaged in a heated disciplinary controversy. In recording anecdotal data attention was focused primarily and almost necessarily on the teacher and on the behavior of those pupils with whom the teacher at any given time was immediately engaged. Random and frequent observations were also made of more inclusive classroom phenomena, such as noise level, pupil attentiveness, generalized responses to teacher behavior, and physical conditions—but these were less systematic.

In preparing to undertake the study, I found myself unable to anticipate clearly how ideally my role as participant-observer ought to evolve, particularly in the school. The literature on participant observation is addressed primarily to the benefits of the participant identity within the broader community context—when the identity is so generalized as to preclude being experienced as a threat except perhaps by single individuals or groups. The boundaries of the participant identity within an institution—when one functions openly as an observer and when, as in a school, the adult roles are themselves the subject of extensive "observation" by the community—are not easily delineated. I had originally anticipated the possibility and value of participating actively in the life of the school as, for example, a teacher of English. In the early months of the study I mentioned this interest in ways I hoped were gentle but persuasive. These attempts failed—a failure which I came to count as a blessing after several experiences of supervising classes in the school.

It was not simply that a teaching responsibility would limit the time available for observation; there was also a question of creating an unnecessary ambivalence, personal and social, with respect to my identity as a researcher and a teacher. Within the school my identity had progressed through different phases. I started out as the father of that American boy in the seventh grade. For some first-graders I was simply the man who was always sitting in the back; for some third-graders I was a county school inspector. For most of the pupils (and adults) I was an American who came to learn about German schools. When, however, classes were turned over to me so that I could administer a questionnaire to the fifth grade (it required three periods over as many different days), I quickly became just another teacher. The behavior of the students structured the kind of authority relationship to which they were accustomed, but not to which I was inclined. When the questionnaire was completed, I was glad to return to the sanctity of the observer role.

The few additional opportunities I had to perform as a teacher I remember now as cases of aborted role-playing. One instance resulted in my having to dry out answers, drenched in beer, to a questionnaire I was giving the eighth grade. It was not easy to find a time and place when I could administer the questionnaire to this class. The pressure of class work made the teacher reluctant to set aside time during school. However, at the end of the year there was a week's lull just before graduation when, for all practical purposes, the class had completed its work. We convened one morning in a local *Gasthaus* (inn)—the most convenient space for the meeting. Herr Kost, the eighth-grade teacher, left me in charge, with the caution that beer and wine were okay but *schnaps* was out. The girls during several breaks stuck to soft drinks; most of the boys had beer to keep them company as they answered questions. The inevitable happened: a bottle was upset. I watched with some consternation as the suds spread slowly over my valuable data.

Questionnaires and essays constituted the two primary sources of systematic data about pupil's perceptions of and attitudes toward various aspects of the life they experienced. The decision about the amount of time and effort to spend eliciting data from pupils was influenced by at least three considerations: (1) Given a study of a school and its sociocultural context, there is a question of achieving an appropriate research balance among three "populations," the community at large, the adults in the school, and the pupils. (2) Given the normal superordinate-subordinate structure of teacher-pupil relationships—emphatically so in this school—there is a question of how extensive an investigation can be made of the subordinate group—with all that implies and requires—without the investigator's appearing to be subverting the relationship to and the research interest in the superordinate group. In this kind of triadic relationship it is difficult for the observer to remain "equidistant" from teachers *and* pupils. (3) Finally, there is a question of how accessible pupils are, that is, what generalized response they exhibit toward, for example, a personal interview, given prevailing norms with respect to adult-child relations.

The considerations are not mutually exclusive. The central question to which the research was addressed was the role of the school in a community experiencing a rural-urban transformation. Conceived, with respect to cultural change, as an agent of stability and potentially of mediation, the instrumental role of the school would appear to be manifest primarily in adult members of the school community. It was the faculty in whom I was most interested; and it was this population and the community at large which I felt required and absorbed most of my research efforts. However, I came to know the students well enough to realize there was an ill-defined but perceptible stirring among the older children—a changing orientation toward urban life to which teachers and parents were beginning to feel they should respond without knowing exactly how. If one is attempting to assess the role of the school in the midst of cultural change, the findings may vary depending on the comparative attention one gives to teachers and students.

In my experience children were not, under any circumstances, very accessible, even for extended informal talks. Their age range and the fact that I was a foreigner may have been factors. Certainly they were not accustomed as pupils to have their attitudes and feelings consulted except generally as part of an academic exercise. Furthermore, it was their nature, teachers insisted, to be reticent to speak up in public, to say what was on their mind.[5] The teachers predicted I would have a difficult time, and I did. Several interviews with small groups of pupils remained stiff and classroomlike; I asked questions and they recited. Interviews with individual pupils, with several exceptions, remained therefore at the level of brief and informal conversations.

Consequently, the most useful sources of data about pupil perceptions of and attitudes toward school, family, and community life were the responses to the questionnaire I administered to the fifth, sixth, and eighth grades and the various essays teachers assigned. The wealth of anecdotal material in the latter had not been anticipated. Beginning with the third grade, pupils are required by the State Ministry of Education to write an essay approximately every three weeks. Over the years, Rebhausen teachers have developed a core of favorite topics for particular grade levels—and, of course, curricular materials from public and private sources are available with limitless suggestions. In most grades there were a wide range of topics covering personal, family, and community life. With certain topics teachers routinely stimulated rather intimate, anecdotal accounts of family life—accounts I would have hesitated to elicit myself. Furthermore, I was at first somewhat surprised that pupils wrote with such apparent ease and openness about personal matters. Admittedly they were in a relatively uncalculating age range, vis-à-vis keeping the teacher at some psychological distance. Nevertheless, the content of the essays violated my expectation as to the inhibitory effect on self-expression and openness which the teacher's authority presumably has. Here it seemed to be simply a question of an assignment that had to be done.

The constraints which teachers imposed on research procedures in which they were involved were minimal but significant. I used a tape recorder quite freely in interviews with most adults in the village, but not with teachers. Assuming the instrument would be intimidating, I waited some months before asking permission to use it. The answer was "No," even by a teacher with whom I felt I had especially good rapport. He had just as soon not, he said; a teacher has to be careful. But I could take notes, and we launched into a series of discussions which totaled more than twenty hours, during which time he spoke freely on what I considered to be for him very controversial and sensitive issues.

It was in this manner that classroom observations of teacher behavior were supplemented. There were formal interviews in which we systematically took up a series of questions to which I wanted all of them to respond. In addition, there were innumerable informal, social occasions involving one teacher or various combinations of teachers and their families, and small

[5] *Schwerfällig* was the word widely used to describe this manner of public behavior, not only of pupils, but as a pervasive characteristic of adults in the region.

groups within the faculty, e.g., the younger teachers. The latter had a weekly coffee klatsch—an excuse to socialize and vent their shared feelings about other members of the faculty and school life in general.

There were sources of data beyond the confines of the school itself. Archives at a nearby institute of history provided material on Rebhausen's educational facilities and personnel going back almost 200 years. Subject-matter workshops sponsored by the county school office, meetings where issues of educational reform were debated, and interviews with the county vocational training officer, the state assistant superintendent in charge of elementary schools, and with others provided data useful in assessing external conditions and forces which impinged on the life of the school.

Developing the Study of the Community

The publication which identifies village residents is not a phone book (less than 5 percent have phones) but an address listing put out by the mayor's office. On the first page is a listing of primary and auxiliary, public and private agencies and institutions. At the head of this listing is the *Gemeindeverwaltung*, a term which is sometimes used very narrowly to designate the mayor's office and staff and sometimes rather broadly to include what are seen as those agencies and institutions basic to and primarily concerned with the general welfare of the village. Hence the *Gemeindeverwaltung* may also include the offices of the county police stationed in the village (strictly speaking there is no local police), the principal of the school, the Evangelical minister, the Catholic priest, the postmaster, the head of the volunteer fire department, and the railroad functionary in charge of the local station operations. In addition, the first page lists addresses of the various Evangelical and Catholic kindergartens, the Evangelical and Catholic emergency first aid stations, the wine cooperative, the savings bank, the local doctor, the dentist, and the nearest veterinarian.

Organizations and industries are listed on the second page. The former include German Red Cross, German Family Association, Evangelical Church Choir, Football Club, Community Library, Business Association, Bee Keepers Association, Catholic Church Choir, Rural Youth Association, Male Chorus, Community Band, Cattlemen's Association, Horsemen's Association, Riding Club, Chess Club, Tennis Club, Gymnastics Club, Union of War Injured, Dispossessed and Welfare Pensioners, and the Adult Education Association.

Organizational participation is important to the life of the community. For individuals it provides opportunities to pursue avocational and recreational interests; it offers a rich, social context in which the individual can reinforce deep, meaningful friendships and maintain acquaintanceships with an impressive number of residents; it makes possible acting in concert with others as an interest group to affect policy at both local and higher levels.

From the standpoint of the community, organizations are functional in several respects. They are a kind of training ground for village leadership; most members of the village council have been or are officers in one or more organizations. They are as well a training ground for the membership, since important decisions affecting the life of the village are considered, debated, and arrived at through a process and within a social context which mirrors the behavior of organizations. Organizational meetings provide opportunities for the mayor, as the preeminent political and governmental official, to reinforce his own role. He attends many of the meetings, if only to pass his blessing on their work. Finally, through organizations and the selection of officers, the village maintains a vital recognition and reward system for those who in their personal, family, and community activities embody the core values of the native culture.

The organizational life of the community was therefore a good place to begin, and in the early days and months provided the widest possible introduction to my research intents. I attended most meetings. The mayor was usually there and invariably introduced me and described my purpose in being in Rebhausen. The format and setting (people sat at tables, wine was always available, extended hours of talk followed the completion of business) made it possible to become acquainted with a number of members, to fix appointments for interviews, and, of course, to participate in informal conversations with both individuals and groups. Furthermore, there was in the organizational life of the village behavioral characteristics similar to that of the school. The latter was also in one sense a network of interlocking collectivities. Students had to learn under the scrutiny of both teachers and classmates how effectively to manage their behavior in at least one of these collectivities. It was instructive to move back and forth between daytime observations of classrooms and nighttime observations of organizations. Since the study and observation of organizations was central to understanding the life of the community, I will examine in more detail one organization, the men's chorus, to illustrate more specifically the kind of data elicited.

The men's chorus is the oldest and most prestigious organization in Rebhausen (in the summer of 1964 it celebrated its 100th anniversary) and in its organization and operation embodies much that is highly valued in the native culture. There are about fifty active singers in the group who, with the exception of one individual, are natives with long-established roots in the village. Farming, however, is no longer the typical occupation among the members as the younger ones move into skilled trades required by or auxiliary to an industrialized economy. Many of the members hold important offices in other organizations.

The chorus rehearses one evening each week. Throughout the year they are invited to and/or are expected to sing at various events and ceremonies: weddings and funerals of members, birthdays of those in the village over eighty, Christmas programs, and dedications. In addition, they are periodically invited to sing in nearby villages. The director is a professional musician who directs several village choruses.

The chorus presents in Rebhausen at least two formal concerts each year —one semipublic, the other public—as a part of the annual meeting. The semipublic concert is "closed" (as the sign reads on the door to the town auditorium) to all but "active" members, namely, those residents who contribute an amount equivalent to at least twenty-five dollars to the chorus each year. Residents who contribute less are classified as "passive" members. The program for the closed meeting included the following:

1. Songs by the chorus were interspersed throughout the evening.
2. Slides of the 100th anniversary celebration were shown. (The celebration had extended over four days, a songfest involving thirty men's choruses from the region.)
3. A movie of Rebhausen, including shots of the celebration, was shown by the operator of the town cinema.
4. The village band provided music for listening and dancing, the latter continuing until after midnight and talking and drinking for another three hours.

The annual meeting was held on a Sunday afternoon, so that the children's chorus could participate. The meeting was open to the public and more than 300 attended. Business transactions were routine and ended with a unanimous voice vote to retain the present slate of officers. Those who had been members for twenty-five years were presented with medallions which had been struck for the 100th anniversary. A bottle of wine and a wine glass were awarded to the individual who had had perfect attendance at chorus rehearsals and performances; large wine glasses went to the four members who missed only once; a small wine glass to those who missed two to four times.

There were certain questions to be resolved. The president served notice that when the chorus was scheduled to sing for an elderly person's birthday, he was going to let that person know the chorus did not want or expect to be served refreshments (contrary to tradition). "The elderly residents are often poor; we should sing and disappear," he observed. The chorus voted on a two-day singing trip, based on the invitations they had received to which the president said they had to respond. The men were not enthusiastic; he had to urge them to vote, and reminded the minority they had to go along with the majority vote. There was much more enthusiasm for the performance of the children's chorus and for ways of encouraging the group.

The men's chorus is meant to be a social and recreational experience. Men join to sing, to enjoy the comradeship of good friends, to be among people they can trust—people who will conduct themselves properly. Extended interviews with the organization's officers and discussions with other members indicated the kind of social behavior considered unacceptable.

1. Drinking too much. (Where the line is drawn is hard to say, except being "drunk" is too much.)
2. Getting in trouble with the law.

3. Having a negative attitude, constantly complaining, and refusing to go along with the majority.
4. Mismanaging one's business affairs, being delinquent in paying bills.
5. Presenting an unkempt, sloppy appearance.
6. Being selfish and greedy. Under no circumstances should private business interests be pushed during meetings.[6]

Data on the men's chorus consisted of observations of rehearsals, formal meetings, concerts, and special celebrations, interviews with members, statistics on membership correlated with family educational and vocational background, even an analysis of their repertoire (they sang with reluctance the few Italian and French numbers the director introduced and preferred instead songs in praise of their native habitat). Such data provided insight into patterns of interpersonal interaction, the distribution and use of authority, social norms and sanctions, and enduring values of the folk culture. Moving constantly back and forth between the life of the school and the life of the community, one could assess the functional relationships between the socialization experience in the school and the social demands of adulthood.

The male chorus was one of a number of institutions whose activities provided data on the community. The operation of the village government was in this regard central. There were few problems in which the power and influence of the mayor's office were not involved. The office is elective, eight years for the first term and twelve thereafter, and the mayor has both executive and judicial responsibilities. The present mayor had been in office for sixteen years and was largely responsible for bringing the chemical factory to Rebhausen. His native background, his aggressive leadership, and his vision of a more prosperous, industrialized village kept him deeply involved in both the traditional and changing facets of community life. Extensive and periodic interviews with him were useful not only for the basic information they provided but also for the opportunity both to reassess accumulated data and identify new lines of investigation. In addition, systematic observations were made of the various operations of the government.

Religious institutions also reflected the tenor of stability and change in the native culture. Along with the mayor and the principal the clergy occupied the apex of the social structure. Both the Catholic priest and the Evangelical minister were in their thirties, vigorous in their administration of parish life, and themselves "students" of village life—in the sense that they saw the native culture as threatened by industrialization and wanted to help their parishioners effect meaningful adjustments while preserving traditional social and moral values. The priest himself was in the midst of change. The Vatican Council was in session and had sanctioned changes in the mass, par-

[6] Two recent cases involved a baker and an auto repair shop owner who berated other members during a meeting for not patronizing them. According to the president, reaction was swift. The men were told openly that that sort of thing was not done and that they therefore were not wanted in the organization. In both cases the men withdrew their memberships.

ticularly with regard to the use by the priest of the native language instead of Latin. The changes the Rebhausen priest chose to make and the reaction of his parishioners were important measures of the rigidity and flexibility of a portion of village life. The Evangelical minister was equally involved in questions of stability and change. He wanted to democratize aspects of church life, including having female representation on the church council, loosening the traditional constraints on age-sex seating arrangements at church services, and persuading members to speak up and participate in church meetings. Every seven years he is expected to make a thorough report to the regional church hierarchy. A report is up to forty pages in length and covers not only church activities but also the social and moral quality of community life. The Rebhausen minister gave me copies dating back to World War I, containing diverse statistics on marriage, divorce, and illegitimate births, as well as descriptions and judgments about political activities and issues and almost every other facet of community life. Both the priest and the minister (supplemented by several of the teachers) conducted religious instruction in the school. Hence in all respects they were important informants.

Questions of Procedure and Data Analysis

Interviews were a basic source of data on the community, as well as the school. They were generally conducted at the respondent's home, in the late afternoon or evening. A rather informal, open-ended interview that had the sense and atmosphere of a social visit proved to be the most efficacious format, primarily because however stiff and formal an interview might be in its inception, the average Rebhausen resident turned it into a social occasion.[7] Consequently, the initiating questions were of a general nature. The talkative propensities of the typical resident made it easy to move informally, through such questions, into the more sensitive areas of community life.

The tape recorder was used extensively with interviews and, depending on the nature of the contact, was introduced at the first or second session. In only two cases was there a preference expressed for its not being used. In the initial interviews the tape recorder was used intermittently with individuals in order to establish a check on its inhibiting influence. An analysis of interview protocols indicated no restrictive influence. The basic procedure followed in the utilization of the material was content analysis. As soon as

[7] If a national image has any effect on the kind of rapport a researcher can establish and sustain with respondents, then the year of this study, 1964–1965, was fortuitous. Among Rebhausen residents there remained great admiration for President Kennedy; during the year the flights of Gemini 3 and 4 added to their sense of appreciation for the accomplishments of U.S. society. Individuals in the village and region with whom I have remained in contact indicate that the violent events of the past few years have cast shadows on this somewhat euphoric view of the United States.

possible after each interview the results were written up, or if the tape recorder was used, transcribed.[8] The primary topics developed were in the areas of education, vocations, economics (with particular attention to the impact of the factory on village life), political and governmental institutions, patterns of childhood training, traditions, norms and sanctions with respect to adolescent behavior, courtship and marriage, and the role of the church. Analysis was directed toward establishing interrelationships among the topics and proceeding in subsequent interviews to examine in more depth the substance of such relationships. Individuals selected for interviews represented different age groups, social and organizational affiliations, vocational pursuits, periods of residence, and relationship to the school.

Another instrument used was modeled after the Instrumental Activities Inventory developed by the Spindlers.[9] The establishment of the factory had created numerous job opportunities for natives, and in the course of five years had noticeably affected vocational patterns. The rhythm and atmosphere of work in the factory was in sharp contrast to the life of the farmer. So it seemed useful to elicit attitudes and value judgments about vocations available to natives in Rebhausen. A list of sixteen vocations was prepared, vocations which generally were traditional in Rebhausen and several of which had been added with the establishment of the factory. At the same time my wife made line drawings of each of the vocations (an individual at work). The drawings were useful in stimulating free-flowing, self-revealing statements and were used in interviews with individuals from two groups, (1) nine factory employees representing practically all levels of job classifications and (2) eleven members of the male chorus representing traditional native vocations. In each instance the drawings were spread out in front of the respondent and he was asked to select three vocations which he liked most and three which he disliked most. These choices were then used in the remainder of the interview to explore the background of the preferences, attitudes toward vocations, and changes in village life.

The process of gathering data naturally required adjustments to the personal qualities and work habits of the populace, an experience that was both socially enjoyable and, at times, professionally frustrating. The people were friendly but busy. They were most talkative in informal situations, amenable

[8] As a general routine I set aside at least two hours each day for studying and typing notes. Transcriptions of taped interviews were done by a secretary I located in a nearby city—one native to the region and able therefore to understand the heavy dialect which the older natives sometimes lapsed into. This item in the budget became before the end of the study a matter of deficit spending. I underestimated the amount of secretarial help I would need because I had no idea what use I could make of a tape recorder. In retrospect no support service was more important to work in the field and processing the data afterwards than that which made it possible to have typescripts of interviews within two weeks after the interview.

[9] George D. Spindler, and Louise Spindler, 1965, "Researching the Perceptions of Cultural Alternatives," in Melford Spiro ed., *Context and Meaning in Cultural Anthropology.* New York: The Free Press.

to and interested in discussing at length life in Rebhausen. But it was not easy to find time. Farming was, most of the year, a typical dawn-to-dusk operation. Regardless of the occupation of their members, most families owned grape holdings, and the working day was long. Consequently, the best time to capitalize on a developing acquaintance was Sunday afternoon, the traditional visiting time in the village. Visits were arranged, and I was usually urged to bring my family along. Whether I did or not, the host's family was there gathered in the living room for after-dinner talk. It was no simple matter to arrange an interview where the respondent could talk freely, unencumbered by the presence of others.

Sensitivity to social protocol was another quality which created problems. At public meetings the mayor always insisted I occupy a place at the speaker's table, not to participate but simply as a special guest. The gesture was appreciated and had practical advantages in the early part of the study when there was good reason to acquaint the populace with my presence and interest. But the speaker's table was not the best vantage point from which to view or experience a meeting, especially one generating controversy between public officials and the populace. Furthermore, the significant transactions at these meetings often took place after the formalities were concluded. Discussions, lubricated by local wine, continued far into the night. People sat at tables throughout the meeting and seldom moved. Groups gathered together regularly and individuals had their traditional associations. I hoped in the course of the meetings to develop productive contacts with these groups, but it was not easy. Even if I entered the hall unobtrusively, so long as the meeting had not begun, the mayor usually located me in the audience and insisted I come to the speaker's table. I finally evolved a countermeasure that had limited success—a matter of making sure the meeting had begun, spotting a likely table or section of the hall, and then sliding in behind some latecomers.

Conclusions

Chronologically speaking, research on Rebhausen proceeded from a study of the primary educational institution, the elementary school, to a consideration of community life in general and of those economic, social, political, and religious organizations and institutions which appeared to be primary in the structuring and guiding of individual and group behavior. While the school was the central focus of the study, no prior assumption was made as to the significance of education compared with other basic institutions in mediating adjustments to cultural change. However, the highly structured content of the educational program, the authoritarian quality of interpersonal relations in the school, and the emphatic enunciation and reinforcement in the school of values and behavioral patterns common to the total community seemed to indicate that the school was the central, pivotal institution in an assessment of cultural stability and change.

In the course of the research it became apparent that new and changing economic institutions, particularly the factory, assumed a significance almost limitless in its possible implications. In a period of only six years the factory had irrevocably changed the tone and tempo of village life. Its beneficent influence on the appearance of the village and on the basic conveniences the village could offer were everywhere noticeable—paved streets where before 1958 there were dirt roads, a sewer system where once there were primitive outhouses, efficient garbage collection where once there was none at all, and, above all, a 7.2 hectare housing and industrial development (with swimming pool, tennis courts, and eventually a seven-story hotel) where once there was farmland.

Certain historical and cultural phenomena have intensified the significance of the factory. The populace remembers village life as having been characterized almost continually by poverty. Nineteenth-century migrations were forced on the village by a series of crop failures, and primitive working conditions in farming required, as late as the 1930s, exhaustive human effort. The moments of relative prosperity have retained a tentative, illusory quality because of the economic collapses which followed—the inflation of the 1920s and the conditions immediately following World War II. The factory has been the immediate agent of prosperity which the village is now enjoying. There is total employment and a wide latitude of reasonably well-paying jobs is available. But the cost of living is high, a constant reminder that the prosperity may be transitory. Consequently, economic developments have led to a kind of hypersensitive, obsessive ambivalence about wealth. The folk of Rebhausen desire what has long been denied them and what is now accessible, but the goal has a refractory quality that blurs the traditional village portrait with which they strongly identify. In this setting, the school is important to study. Its traditional role reaffirms and sustains the values of the folk culture, but its mediating role in the midst of change is tentative and unstructured for parents, pupils, and teachers.

PART V

The Teaching of Anthropology

Preview

23. GEORGE D. SPINDLER *Transcultural Sensitization*
24. TIMOTHY ASCH *Audiovisual Materials in the Teaching of Anthropology from Elementary School through College*
25. PAUL BOHANNAN, MERWYN S. GARBARINO, and EARLE W. CARLSON *An Experimental Ninth-grade Anthropology Course*
26. DIANE A. TROUBETTA REYNOLDS and NORMAN REYNOLDS *The Roots of Prejudice: California Indian History in School Textbooks*

PREVIEW

So far in this book we have encountered models for research, conceptual engagements between anthropology and education, the results of research, and the methods of observation and interpretation stemming from anthropology and applicable to analysis of the educative process. Though much of the discussion has implications for the teaching of anthropology, the implementation of these implications has not been a major theme. This section is devoted to such implementations.

Thanks to several projects, especially the Anthropology Curriculum Study Project, directed by Malcolm Collier (1972), advised by a committee of anthropologists drawn from the American Anthropological Association and supported by the National Science Foundation (Tenenberg and Dethlefsen 1972), and the Social Studies Curriculum Program of the Education Development Center, Inc., of Cambridge, Mass. (Curriculum Development Assoc. 1971), also supported by a grant from the National Science Foundation and directed by Peter Dow with consultants Jerome S. Bruner, Irven DeVore, and Asen Balikci, teachers at both the elementary and secondary school level have available to them useful curricular materials as well as teacher service materials. Thomas Dynneson (1973) provides a study of anthropology in the public schools and makes recommendations for improving project materials from the Anthropology Curriculum Project. There have been a number of other study projects concerned with ways of getting anthropological concepts and data into the social studies curriculum at various points in the public educational system of the United States. It is probably fair to say that although substantial progress has been made in organizing materials and concepts, the influence of anthropology upon the social studies, or any other curriculum, in the majority of public schools in this country is still quite small.

It would be presumptuous to think that in one section of a book we could do justice to the problems of developing relevant curricula for public school programs, though the papers by Bohannan and associates and by Diane and

Norman Reynolds are relevant to these problems. We have emphasized other relationships of anthropology to teaching and to the teaching of anthropology, with the greatest weight upon the latter.

My chapter on transcultural sensitization is concerned with an aspect of the teaching of anthropology at the university or college level, though I believe it is a relevant technique with a relevant purpose for other educational levels. In this chapter I try to describe how students can be shown through their own responses and experience how their observations and interpretations of other cultures are likely to be grievously distorted unless they have some special training. The magnitude of this problem is even larger than the chapter suggests, for indeed it is this kind of transcultural perceptual distortion that is operating in all of the transactions where teachers and students are of different cultures or social classes, as described in the preceding chapters. It would seem important that some such experience be built into teacher-training curricula. I have found it an essential step in preparing Stanford students for fieldwork in German culture at the Stanford University Center in Germany and in the preparation of graduate students in education and anthropology for a relatively objective and sensitized viewing of processes of cultural transmission in other cultural systems in my advanced courses at Stanford in California. The technique could doubtless be improved greatly. What I present here is a beginning.

My chapter and that by Timothy Asch on audiovisual materials in the teaching of anthropology were written at different times and without explicit awareness of what each of us was doing. There is substantial convergence in our points of view and in our techniques, though we have expressed the problems somewhat differently. Asch's chapter makes apparent what would seem to be axiomatic for the teaching of anthropology: that some form of experience, direct or vicarious, with live cultural materials is essential if the basic purposes of anthropological teaching are to be realized. Asch has gone much further than most of us in his experimentation with audiovisual materials in the teaching of anthropology. Many of these materials are drawn from his own films taken in the field in collaboration with other anthropologists, particularly Napoleon Chagnon, the ethnographer of the Yanomamö (Chagnon 1968). In the context of the use of film for both instructional and research purposes, it is relevant here to call attention to the work of John Collier, Jr. (Collier 1967, 1973).

One groans with dismay when one realizes how often anthropology, which should be the most interesting of all subjects, is taught at the university and college level in such a way that the students leave feeling oppressed rather than stimulated and enlightened. This statement applies particularly to the introductory course where beginning students have not yet been, and are unlikely ever to be, motivated by the rewards available to the disciplined professional.

In this introductory course the instructor is very often likely to draw from his professional repertoire the generalizations about culturally variant human behavior that he feels are valid on the basis of his training and experience without much regard for the fact that beginning students do not, and usually will not, go through any of the experiences that he, the instructor, has gone through to arrive at the generalizations or a feeling for their validity. Everything is formulated for the student. The instructor knows and the student does not. The student is presented with abstractions. He is taught *about* anthropology, not about people and their behaviors. Nothing has much relevance to the students' own lives or to their understanding of the world about them. It cannot, for what is taught is relevant to the discipline of anthropology and not to the education of the student.

Audiovisual materials, when used creatively, can be a most important part of the teaching of anthropology. Films or slides, particularly the former, can be used as central points in the unfolding development of a course and its intended communications. As we teach Anthropology I at Stanford, Louise Spindler and I use films as a point of departure for case studies of various ways of life, running the whole gamut of sociopolitical and technological complexity. We move inductively from the case studies to generalizations, most of them tentative and hypothetical rather than finalized. For these purposes, we have also developed case studies in written form in two of our series (Spindler and Spindler) and an inductive text for introductory anthropology (Beals, Spindler, and Spindler 1973). We consider such direct exposures to contrastive ways of life as essential to the teaching of anthropology at every level, but particularly in the introductory course.

This point of view is integral to the experience reported by Paul Bohannan, Merwyn Garbarino, and Earle Carlson in their chapter on an experimental ninth-grade anthropology course. Two of the three came into the teaching experiment without experience in teaching high school students. They discovered that these students could learn a great deal if they were given a variety of case study material rather than finalized abstractions and generalizations. Even the most lively generalized texts in anthropology were not very enthusiastically received by these students. The textbooks were "not about anything," said the students. There were no cultural cases. These three experimenters found that if one uses a considerable amount of good ethnographic fact well presented and organized, ninth-grade students are extremely interested in it and they will make connections between the people they read about and their own lives. The teacher can capitalize upon the inherent comparative aspects of anthropology, as the authors point out, and students are even willing to help create cultural and social theory.

It should be apparent that nowhere in this Preview or in the chapters selected for this section is anyone arguing for a mindless presentation of facts, ethnographic or otherwise. What we are all saying in different ways is that specific cultural materials, case studies, and ethnographies that are about people living in specific settings are basic starting points for a series of inductive steps to broader generalization and abstraction—even to theory. The generalization, the abstraction, or the theoretical statement *cannot* be taught in and of itself, nor do one or two examples abstracted out of cultural context suffice to make a generalization live. Whether we are teaching in the elementary school, high school, or university, and whether we are teaching anthropology as a subject or using anthropological materials in a social studies context, it is my conviction that this is the starting point of effective teaching.

The last chapter in this section, by Diane and Norman Reynolds, is of a different order. It is a hard-hitting analysis of the ways in which public school textbooks have perpetuated and encouraged stereotypic thinking about a minority group, in this case the Indians of California. Their analysis is applicable to the treatment of minority peoples in many other textbooks. Their work shows clearly how deep the transmission of prejudicial beliefs and understandings is in our school system and how much must be overturned and set right if we are to attain anything resembling a fair treatment of all parts of our pluralistic culture in the teaching that occurs in our schools. One of the first steps is to deal with the textbooks and other materials that are used in the classrooms as sources of information and thought organization. This is, of course, just a first step because all of us teachers have been taught by these same kinds of biases in the hands of those who in turn have been taught by them.

We should not delude ourselves into thinking that by introducing anthropological concepts and materials into the public educational system we will correct stereotypic thinking about minority groups or other cultures. Even the best of materials may in the hands of a prejudiced teacher turn sour and misdirect thinking. The retraining and sensitization procedure has to reach deep into the cognitive and attitudinal organization of teachers and deep into the institutional structuring of education at all levels. Nor should we overlook the fact that anthropology as a discipline is far from free of prejudice, bigotry, and blindness. Sometimes in the very act of describing another people anthropologists display latent prejudices. We anthropologists have become more aware of this recently, and through painful self-examination aided by the frank criticisms of some of our erstwhile subjects of inquiry (Indians, blacks, Africans, the urban poor, and so on) are beginning to make some progress toward setting our own house in order.

The complex processes of reeducation, self-education, and other education and the accompanying sensitization cannot be accomplished overnight nor simply. I do believe, however, and I think the people represented in this volume would agree, that anthropology has potential contributions to make to this process that have only been very slightly realized so far.

References

Beals, Alan, George D. Spindler, and Louise Spindler, 1973, *Culture in Process: An Inductive Approach to Anthropology,* 2d edition. New York: Holt, Rinehart and Winston, Inc.

Chagnon, Napoleon, 1968, *Yąnomamö: The Fierce People.* CSCA. New York: Holt, Rinehart and Winston, Inc.

Collier, John Jr., 1967, *Visual Anthropology: Photography as a Research Method.* SAM. New York: Holt, Rinehart and Winston, Inc.

Collier, John, Jr., 1973, *Alaskan Eskimo Education.* CSEC. New York: Holt, Rinehart and Winston, Inc.

Collier, Malcolm, 1972, *Two Way Mirror: Anthropologists and Educators Observe Themselves and Each Other.* Washington, D.C.: American Anthropological Association.

Curriculum Development Associates, Inc., 1971, *Man: a Course of Study.* Cambridge, Mass.: Education Development Center, Inc., Social Studies Curriculum Program.

Dynneson, Thomas, 1973, *Anthropology for the Schools.* Eric/CHESS Service.

Spindler, George D., and Louise Spindler, eds., *Case Studies in Cultural Anthropology; Case Studies in Education and Culture;* and *Studies in Anthropological Method.* Continuing series. New York: Holt, Rinehart and Winston, Inc.

Tenenberg, Morton S., and Edwin S. Dethlefsen, 1972, *Anthropology Curriculum Study Project: Teacher Service Materials.* Washington, D.C.: American Anthropological Association.

GEORGE D. SPINDLER/Stanford University

23 Transcultural Sensitization

This chapter discusses the ways common errors in transcultural observation and interpretation can be anticipated and how sensitivity concerning them can be acquired. The source of data for this discussion is a sensitization technique administered in the winter of 1968, the spring of 1970, the winter of 1971, and in the spring quarters of 1972 and 1973 to Stanford undergraduate students at one of the university's overseas centers, Stanford in Germany. The same technique was used in an advanced education class of ninety-four students during the Stanford University summer session at the home campus in 1970 and in the autumn quarter of 1972, with eighty-six students. I am not concerned in this chapter with the differences between these groups, but rather with the educational purpose of the technique and the kinds of perceptual distortions consistently revealed by it.

There is substantial literature in psychology, and some in anthropology, concerned with cultural variability in perception (see, for example, Segall et al. 1966 and Price-Williams 1969). Very little, however, has been written about the very complex process of perceiving and interpreting culturally relevant material across cultural boundaries in the manner described here. The interpretive principles applied in this chapter are implicit in much of the reported experience of anthropologists in the field (Spindler 1970), but they have not, to my knowledge, been explicitly stated or applied in the specific ways developed here.

At Stanford in Germany there usually are about eighty students, mostly sophomores, in attendance at any given time. For six months they carry on with their regular academic work while learning the language of and becoming exposed to the history, politics, and economics of their host country. The program is designed to enable nearly all interested Stanford students to have an overseas experience irrespective of their major concentrations or future professional plans. The students live together in the various centers (there are also centers in France, Italy, England, and Austria), but do a great deal of traveling and are in constant contact with the population of the areas in which the centers are located.

Whenever I have been in residence, students at Stanford in Germany have done field research in the Remstal, the area near the study center, on the continuity of the folk culture in the small villages and on the urbanization and industrialization overtaking these villages. This field research has, in turn, been related through classroom discussions and lectures to basic generalizations and interpretive principles in cultural anthropology. The purpose of my courses in anthropology as I taught them at Stanford in Germany has been to help develop a cognitive organization for observation and participation in a culture foreign to the student.[1]

German culture cannot be considered, from the anthropological point of view, to be radically divergent from North American culture. Though there are substantial cultural differences between the various European countries and North America, in the larger sense they must all be seen as versions of the same general culture. There are, however, sufficient differences to make the deeper adjustment and accurate perceptions of the European culture problematic for North Americans unless they have systematic help. Contact, even prolonged, does not necessarily result in adjustment on this deeper level. Learning to speak the language is a major step in this direction but does not guarantee accurate perceptions and understandings. Human beings tend to interpret new experience in the light of past experience unless there is decisive intervention in the interpretive process. The anthropology instruction at Stanford in Germany is designed as such an intervention.

The first step in this intervention, as I came to understand and practice it in my instruction, was to alert students to the types of perceptual distortions to which they would be subject and which could be corrected in some degree by transcultural sensitization. The specific way in which we went about this, and some general conclusions concerning the major types of distortions, are the subject of this chapter.

The Technique and Its Results

The technique consists of the administration of ten 35 mm. color slides selected from several hundred I had taken of the Remstal and its internal cultural variations. During the first week overseas the slides are shown and the students are asked to write their responses to each of the pictures and turn them in to me. I use those responses in a simple inductive content analysis, the results of which I utilize in class discussions. A description of the pictures—several of which are included in this text—and their culturally appropriate interpretation, together with the major categories of student reaction to them follows.

Picture No. 1. The first slide is of a small area of vineyards *(Weinberge)* near the Stanford in Germany center. This area is subdivided into many small plots, most of which are not larger than a tenth of an acre. Each plot is terraced and there are poles and wires for the support of the grape vines.

[1] The fieldwork was of such high quality that I was able to utilize it extensively in a Case Study in Cultural Anthropology (G. Spindler and student collaborators 1973).

The picture is very clear and presents no structural or spatial ambiguities. Students are asked to describe what they see in the picture, what it is used for, and what its possible significance might be in the cultural system of the Remstal.

The slide shows very clearly the small, terraced plots of vineyard characteristic of the area. The important point is that the plots are so small and their distribution so fragmented that mechanized cultivation is impossible. Consequently, traditional labor methods are still used for cultivation of the crop and upkeep of the poles and wires. This is a significant support, though one of several, for the entire traditional complex of viniculture and the way of life associated with it.

Students see a very wide range of possibilities in this picture. The majority see it as connected with agriculture, though usually not as vineyard plots but as an irrigation project, feeding troughs for cattle or pigs, a soil conservation project, erosion control, or cribs for grain storage. A sizable minority (about 35 percent) see it as something entirely unrelated to an agricultural operation, such as Roman ruins, rows of chairs for a mass audience, a religious congregation, a guarded border, fields destroyed by war, or gun emplacements.

The problem in accurate perception seems to be that there is no exact counterpart in the culture of the viewers for what is seen on the screen. Though vineyards are known in California, hilly, small, terraced plots of this kind are unknown. Further, there is no functional complex in the culture of the viewers into which this perception fits, even if the perception is accurate. The small size and fragmented distribution of the plots of vineyard have no meaning. Consequently, students seldom see the plots as vineyards, and only a few perceive their functional relevance. In general, the range of interpretations is wide and the level of inaccuracy high. Only about 10 percent of the students grasp the cultural significance of what is observed.

Picture No. 2. This is a picture of a middle-aged woman in dark clothing bending over and tying grapevines onto a wire trellis on a sunny, early spring day (Fig. 23.1). Students are asked to describe what the subject is doing and why her activity might be functionally significant. They are also asked to indicate what they think the subject is thinking and feeling. The type of labor performed here is skilled labor which frequently is obtained, within the traditional economic framework, from the membership of the extended family. This validates these relationships, thus helping to maintain the family and values associated with it. The necessity of such intensive hand labor in the small distributed plots is one factor that has kept traditional folk-oriented adaptation intact up to the present time in this area of Germany.

Most students see that some form of agricultural activity is involved in this picture. Only a small proportion (5–15 percent) expressed an understanding of the significance of the intensive hand labor. Again, as there is no functional counterpart for this kind of work in North American culture, few students can see its cultural or economic significance.

Figure 23.1.

The interpretations of what the subject is thinking and feeling run through a wide gamut, but the modalities that appear have mostly to do with fairly grim states of mind. "Tired," "old," "tedious," "boring," "aching back," "aching bones," "tired muscles," are the responses that predominate. Though the bones and muscles of German women who work in the Weinberge do ache, the interpretation of this sensation is quite different in the traditional subculture of the Remstal than in middle-class America. Labor and its discomforts are regarded as positive and old women complain about no longer being able to work in the Weinberge.[2] Students project from their own culture the meaning of experience appropriate to the activity as perceived.

Picture No. 3. This is a visually ambiguous picture. It shows an older female teacher helping a child of about nine years of age into an old church tower where they are to examine four very large cast bells about which she had lectured in *Heimatkunde* (see Chapter 12) just before the trip to the tower. There are heavy beams in the picture and the surroundings are generally dark and dusty looking. Students are asked to indicate what is "going on" in the picture. Actually, all that is happening is that the teacher is helping the child off the top rung of the ladder into the upper part of the tower where the bells are. Cultural significance is not in question here.

[2] Case endings are not observed in the use of German terms in order to avoid confusing the reader who does not know German.

About one third of the students see the teacher as assisting the child in some way, and about one third see her as punishing the child. The other third of the responses are distributed over a wide range. Those who see the teacher as assisting the child refer to help given in going under a fence, coming out of a mine shaft, a cave, an earthquake-stricken building, or a collapsed basement in a deteriorated slum, or out of a bomb shelter; or, in entirely different directions, as assisting her to go to the toilet or even as preventing suicide. Those who see the teacher as punishing the child usually refer to whipping in a woodshed, spanking because the child had gone some place where she should not have, or being caught because she tried to run away. The interpretations in the third category are too variegated to sample adequately. Most of the interpretations in all categories are irrelevant to the actual situation as it occurred.

It seems clear that the range of possible perceptions and interpretations increases as the situation observed becomes more ambiguous. Ambiguity may be either a product of cultural irrelevance or lack of clarity in spatial or structural relations. Both forms of ambiguity enter into the interpretation of this picture, but the latter are probably most important in this case. Spatial and structural relations are not clear, which is why this picture was selected. The act of climbing into an old church tower to examine bells that have been discussed in class is uncommon in both American and German culture, so the spatial and structural ambiguity is compounded. Perceptions and interpretations, therefore, tend to be fanciful and more or less irrelevant to reality. In actual fieldwork, or in ordinary contact within a foreign culture, situations where ambiguity prevails abound.

Picture No. 4. This slide shows a small bake house *(Backhaus)* in which shifts of several village women bake bread and *Kuchen*[3] together at certain hours each week (Fig. 23.2). The small brick building is technically clear, as is the fire in the furnace inside. A woman is standing by the door with the long ash stirrer in her hand. Students are asked to indicate what it is they are seeing and what its significance could be in the culture of the Remstal. The significance of the Backhaus is not only in the fact that women bake their weekly bread there but in that it is a social-gathering and gossip center for the more conservative women of the village. It thus is a contributing element of social control, as there everyone is talked about and judgments passed on their behavior.

About 30 percent of the students see this as a Backhaus, but virtually none have ever perceived the function of this place as a communication and social-control center. The range of interpretations for the other 70 percent of the students is quite wide, including such perceptions as small-town industry, refinery, one-room house with a coal fireplace, fireplace in an inn, a kiln for making pots, an incinerator, and so forth.

---

[3] Various kinds of baked sweet dough usually served with fruit toppings and whipped cream.

Figure 23.2.

Again, there is no exact cultural counterpart to the Backhaus in U.S. culture, though the general form of the structure and even its purpose may not be unknown. The picture is technically clear. The only ambiguity is the cultural one, which seems to produce a wide range of interpretations as to what is in the picture, and the absence of a cultural counterpart in the culture of the viewer leads to interpretations of significance irrelevant to the local situation.

Picture No. 5. This picture shows a man pumping a liquid of some sort into a trough which empties into a long barrellike container laid lengthwise on a trailer hauled by a small tractor. The man is actually pumping liquid from a pit under the manure pile which is found in front of each *Bauernhaus.*[4] The liquid is then taken in the barrel up to the Weinberge and distributed between the rows of grapevines. This is a substantial contribution to the enrichment of the soil, made possible by the total economic-ecological unit represented by the Bauernhaus. The animals live on the ground floor and the

[4] The traditional structure, quite large, housing humans, cows, pigs, and chickens, hay, and implements used in maintaining agricultural activity.

people above them. There is a functional interdependence between the Bauernhaus and the Weinberge other than that created by the activities of the people themselves.

Only 5 percent of the students in any of the samples have ever seen this as a pump for liquified manure or anything like it. Interpretations range wide: a cement mixer for fixing broken sidewalks or for building houses, crushed grapes being pumped into a container, water for spraying, loading coal, delivery of a pillar, tar for street repairs, pumping insecticide into barrels, filling old barrels with new wine, washing gravel, loading pipe onto a truck, erecting the base for a monument, rinsing off a grinding stone, locating a plumbing fixture, and so forth.

Again, the picture is very clear technically. There is no visual ambiguity because of structural or spatial relationships. The ambiguity is culturally introduced. There is no counterpart for the pump or for the use of liquid manure in agricultural operations in the experience of the majority of American students. They produce, therefore, a wide variety of interpretations.

Figure 23.3.

Picture No. 6. This is a picture of a small boy helping his father pick black currants (Fig. 23.3). It is a pleasant picture filled with sunshine, green leaves, bursting clusters of currants, and a basket heaped with the fruit. Students were asked to indicate what is going on in the picture and how the boy feels and thinks about it. Children in this area of Germany are not required to work until they are ready to do so because their parents want them to enjoy working in the fields and the Weinberge. Most children enjoy helping their parents and older siblings in this way.

About 90 percent of the students see this as an activity connected with the harvesting of grapes or currants. Most, however, see the boy as wishing he could join his comrades in play, hoping that the work will be finished so he can leave, wondering if he is going to grow up to do a tedious and boring job like his father, restive under his father's hand, wishing the sun were not so hot, resigned to the work, feeling hot and scratchy, wishing there were an easier way to do it, feeling restless, resenting the drudgery, and so forth.

Again, students tend to project their own experience or the stereotype of that experience within American culture into the perception and interpretation of events or situations in another culture. Working in the field under the hot sun, perhaps especially with one's father, is perceived as boring, tiresome, and so on, and one "naturally" wants to escape to play with peers, as a projection, it appears, of attitudes common in U.S. culture. Though it is likely that some Remstal children feel this way, it is doubtful that many do, given the particular cultural antecedents to the event and its interpretation in this culture.

It is clear in responses to this and other pictures that when motivations and feelings are identified, the range of perceptions and interpretations

Figure 23.4.

increases and the potential irrelevancy of these perceptions likewise increases, irrespective of the technical clarity of the stimulus.

Picture No. 7. This slide shows a not atypical Bauernhaus with large double doors through which animals and hay pass through to the ground floor where the animals are kept, the manure pile surrounded by its square concrete retaining wall in front with the pump in the center, and two stories and attic under a heavy tiled roof (Fig. 23.4). The Bauernhaus is the traditional structure housing the extended family and livestock and is an especially significant representation of the traditional agricultural "folk" adaptation.

People live in these houses within the villages and farm the many scattered strips of flatland and small plots of Weinberge from it. The Bauernhäuser, small plots, Weinberge, manure pile, and so forth, constitute a whole functioning culture complex. It is a way of life that is disappearing but still very much in evidence.

Students see the Bauernhaus as a warehouse, a gasoline station, a tavern, combined hotel and restaurant, a shop or general store, a feed store, suburban home with a two-stall garage, factory of some kind, store with a loading platform, cheese factory, a garage where cars are fixed, a house of prostitution, a winery, an apartment house, a bakery and family home combined, and an equipment repair shop. Only about 10 percent of the students in the various groups ever saw this structure as a regular domicile, and only about half of those saw it as a structure sheltering both man and beast within the general complex described.

As in the other cases, the responses to this picture contained a wide variety of culturally ready categories imposed from the perceiver's culture upon the situation presented from another culture. Ambiguity is created not because of lack of clarity in spatial or structural relations (the picture is clear and focused), but rather because there is no specific cultural category in the perceiver's culture for the perceived event, object, or situation. Nor is there any functional complex in which the perceived situation would fit even if it were perceived relevantly.

Picture No. 8. This slide shows a male German teacher of about forty years of age standing before a fourth-grade class in the *Grundschule* (see Chapter 12). He is standing in a more or less relaxed posture with his hands behind his back looking at the class. The children are grouped around the tables facing him. The classroom is entirely ordinary. Specific clues to the effect that this is a German classroom are lacking, so students are told that it is. The students are asked to indicate what kind of a classroom atmosphere probably exists here and what kind of a teacher this man is. The teacher, Herr Steinhardt from the Schönhausen School, is not a "permissive" teacher but certainly is not an authoritarian one. I have observed many American classrooms that were much more strictly run than his. The nature of the school and educational philosophy are described in Chapter 12. The children were allowed considerable freedom of movement and expression. Their grouping at tables rather than in traditional, formal rows of stationary seats is symptomatic of this freedom.

The student respondents saw Herr Steinhardt as formal, strict, and orderly, authoritarian, austere, autocratic, dominating, arrogant, stern, meticulous, demanding, stiff, detailed, traditional, old-fashioned, "uptight," and as a "pompous authoritarian" in about 80 percent of all responses to this picture. The classroom was seen consistently in the same framework, that is, one demanding submission from the children, as having an orderly, "didactic," rigid, "alienating," highly disciplined atmosphere.

It is apparent that students responding to this picture have projected a stereotype that is patterned in their own culture about a situation in another culture. American students have stereotypes about how German classrooms are run and what German teachers are like. These stereotypes are projected. The range of perceptions and interpretations is not broad, but the irrelevancy of those offered is marked.

Picture No. 9. This slide shows the same classroom ten seconds after the slide in Picture No. 8 was taken. The teacher is in a more dynamic posture with hand raised and a lively expression on his face, and the children are raising their hands; some are half risen from their seats. Students are asked to indicate whether this slide causes them to change their interpretation of the first picture of this classroom.

About 50 percent of the respondents say that the second picture does not cause them to modify their first perceptions significantly. The other 50 percent describe the classroom as less autocratic than they had thought, less rigid, more free, and more democratic.

It is significant that approximately one half of the students modify their interpretations in the direction of greater freedom in the classroom. This illustrates the importance of time sampling in any particular sequence of behavior, and is also an important element in transcultural sensitization.

Figure 23.5.

Picture No. 10. This slide shows several boys walking into the *Schönhausen* School with Herr Steinhardt standing out in the school yard with one hand raised pointing toward the door (Fig. 23.5). His posture is rather relaxed and his hand and arm are not in a stiff position. Students are asked to indicate what they think the boys are thinking and feeling as they enter the classroom and school.

About one half of the students in the various groups to which these pictures have been shown see the boys as feeling reluctant, fearful, anxious, resigned, and resentful. About one third see the boys as eager to enter excited, anticipatory, wanting to get started, happy, and fascinated. The rest produce a fairly wide range of responses, including "not rushing but o.k," "amenable but not eager," "not thinking or feeling very much," being rewarded for obedience, feeling cheated because the recess break has been cut short, and so forth.

A substantial number of American student respondents appear to draw from their own experience with school. They are probably not only drawing directly from this experience but also from stereotypes about what this experience is like, particularly for boys in U.S. culture. Stereotypes of German classrooms and teachers, and American student responses to these stereotypes, as well as the influence of one's school experience and stereotypes relating to that experience in U.S. culture, are intermingled. This happens frequently in transcultural perception and interpretation.

Conclusions

It should be remembered that the procedures described above are carried out as a part of an instructional program and not primarily for purposes of research on perceptual distortion. With the exception of the two groups at Stanford in California, all of the students were at Stanford in Germany and were about to enter or had already entered into fairly intensive contact with German people and German culture.[5] The cultural sensitization procedure was carried out in order to enrich their overseas experience by making them more sensitive and acute observers, and also to increase the probability of success in fieldwork in the Remstal area.

The pictures were all presented on a large screen with a 35 mm. projector. The responses, as stated, were written by each student and collected at the end of the period. The instructor did a content analysis, resulting in the categories of response described above. These results were presented to each class in two fifty-minute discussion periods during which the pictures were again shown and considerable detail presented by the instructor about the content and significance of each slide. Certain general principles of perceptual distortion in transcultural observation and interpretation were derived inductively in these discussions. I will summarize these general principles

[5] Two of the Stanford in Germany groups had actually been in Germany for one academic quarter at the time the technique was administered. It is interesting that the same types of perceptual errors were displayed by these groups as by the others. The students had no anthropological training during the first quarter.

briefly, as they have already been anticipated in the discussion of the pictures and student responses to them.

It appears that perceptual distortion in transcultural observation increases when:

1. There is no clear counterpart for the perceived object or event in the observer's culture. Responses to the picture of the Bauernhaus, the liquid manure wagon, and the Weinberge all fall into this category. None of these objects, events, or situations occur in North American culture.

2. There is no functional complex into which the object, event, or situation, even if accurately perceived, fits, so the significance is lost or skewed. This applies clearly to the Weinberge and the Backhaus and, to some degree, to most of the rest of the presented pictures. The Weinberge cannot be understood even if seen as Weinberge unless one understands that the size of the plots and their distribution, as well as their terracing, prevents the application of large-scale mechanical power to their maintenance, and that this in turn is related to the necessity for intensive hand labor, in turn related to the extended family as a source of labor and eventually to the utility of the Bauernhaus and the whole traditional complex. Neither can the Backhaus be understood even if perceived as a house where bread and cakes are baked unless it is seen as a communication and gossip center. This same line of reasoning can be applied to a number of the other pictures and responses.

3. There is a stereotype of experience related to the event, object, or situation patterned in the observer's own culture. This seems clear in the interpretation of the boys' feelings as they leave the school yard to go into the school. Boys would rather play, it is said. The school is confining. This is an image of school in American culture, according to the respondents themselves as they retrospected about their reactions to the pictures and their own experience. The same principle applies to the projection of aching backs and bones, the tediousness of labor, and the desire to escape from it in the interpretation of the picture of the women working in the vineyards and the picture of the small boy helping his father pick currants.

4. There is a stereotype of the experience or meaning of the event, object, or situation as it is presumed to exist in another culture. German teachers and classrooms are believed, in American culture, to be authoritarian, strict, and disciplined. This stereotype is applied to the picture of Herr Steinhardt, with the result that the responses are largely irrelevant to the actual situation portrayed in the picture.

5. There is ambiguity due to lack of clarity in the structural or spatial relations surrounding or involved in the event, object, or situation. This applies particularly to the situation where the teacher is helping a child up the last part of the ladder into the loft of the church to see the bells. The range and irrelevancy of responses is great and seems to be a function of the fact that no one understands exactly what is being seen. Potentially meaningful cues are seized upon, such as the heavy structural beams in the tower, the general dinginess of the surroundings, or the white bandage on the child's

hand. There is not only spatial and structural ambiguity involved here but also cultural ambiguity, because the situation is unfamiliar in American culture.

6. There is projection of emotional states ascribed to subjects in another culture. This applies to all situations in which student respondents were asked to indicate what they thought people in the pictures might be thinking or feeling. The emotional states projected are clearly functions of the patterning of experience and beliefs about experience in North American culture. They tend to be quite irrelevant to the specific situations represented in the pictures.

7. There is a single time sample of the action. This applies most directly to the two pictures of the classroom, but it could apply to any of the situations. In order for interpretations to be relevant (i.e., accurate), they must be based upon a sampling of parts of the whole cycle of activity, whatever it is.

Implications

The processes engaged in by students responding to the pictures described above are similar to those experienced by the field anthropologist. They are also similar to those experienced by the teacher faced with a classroom full of children, particularly when they are from different social classes or ethnic groups than his own. Furthermore, the children also represent a youth subculture different from that of the teacher. Teachers make the same types of errors described in this analysis, and for the same reasons the Stanford students made them. Some of these errors are mainly humorous, others suggest why there is constant, serious, often tragic, misinterpretation and noncommunication in classrooms where cultural differences are sharp.

By applying what we know about culture and about the problems of the anthropologist in the field to the analysis of materials that may be brought into the classroom from another culture, such as the slides I used, we may anticipate the kinds of errors that are likely to occur in transcultural perception and interpretation, control them better, and develop some relevant skills in observation. I have called this a transcultural sensitization process. Something similar, I suggest, should be a part of all teacher-training programs. It is one way that an anthropological perspective may help improve teaching.

References

Price-Williams, Douglas, 1969, *Cross-Cultural Studies.* Penguin Modern Psychology Readings Series.

Segall, Marshall H., Donald Campbell, and M. Herskovits, 1966, *The Influence of Culture on Visual Perception.* Indianapolis: The Bobbs-Merrill Company.

Spindler, George, ed., 1970, *Being an Anthropologist: Fieldwork in Eleven Cultures.* New York: Holt, Rinehart and Winston, Inc.

Spindler, George D., and student collaboration, 1973, *Burgbach: Urbanization and Identity in a German Village.* CSCA. New York: Holt, Rinehart and Winston, Inc.

TIMOTHY ASCH/*Brandeis University*

24 *Audiovisual Materials in the Teaching of Anthropology from Elementary School through College*[1]

> The task of teaching a subject to a child at any particular age is one of representing the structure of that subject in terms of the child's way of viewing things. The task can be thought of as one of translation . . . any idea can be represented honestly and usefully in the thought forms of children of school age, and . . . these first representations can later be made more powerful and precise the more easily by virtue of this early learning.
>
> . . . If one respects the ways of thought of the growing child, if one is courteous enough to translate material into his logical forms and challenging enough to tempt him to advance, then it is possible to introduce him at any early age to the ideas and styles that in later life make an educated man (Jerome S. Bruner (1960).

Introduction

This chapter describes ways in which audiovisual material can be used to teach anthropology from elementary school through high school and college. Anthropology is being taught to increasing numbers of students of all ages. It is assumed that a study of man will be of immediate relevance to students and will help them both to understand themselves within a social context and partially to overcome their ethnocentrism. The potential involvement is there, but frequently students complain that these courses are too remote and theoretical, appropriate for the professional anthropologist but irrelevant to the lives of most students.

There is a continuing demand for dynamic classroom materials and greater active participation by students who are challenging the traditional monopoly of lecture and print. Often students who have apparently failed to master traditional academic skills and who seem intellectually lethargic can be reached by the use of different media or classroom techniques.

---

[1] This article was written in 1969, but the bibliography was updated in 1973. Special thanks are due to my colleagues at Brandeis University and to Henry H. Atkins, now District Coordinator of Curriculum for the Newton Public Schools, Newton, Massachusetts, who encouraged me to develop some of these ideas, and to Patsy Asch, Anita Gill, and Barry Levine.

Solomon was such a student in New York City. He appeared ready to quit high school until he encountered a brilliant teacher and sound technician who was teaching special classes. Solomon was told to take home a small Sony tape recorder and record a story. To the boy's question, "How am I going to do that? What am I going to record?" the teacher replied, "There must be something interesting that's happening in your life right now." The boy thought for a moment and then said that his grandfather was dying. The teacher's answer was, "Fine. Write me a story on tape about your grandfather dying." Here, then, was a new medium—there were no old, bad habits to unlearn or fears to overcome. He taped sounds of his grandfather thinking and talking about his life, going back to his early childhood days, and finally dying. Then he taped the sounds of grief in the family, of the relatives that came to visit, and of the funeral. He recorded the things that to him were really important about the death of his grandfather and what this meant to his entire family. Often the tape recorder was put on the table at dinner time, and the whole conversation was recorded. Out of hours and hours and hours of tape, this boy, who could neither read nor write very efficiently, edited one of the most beautiful stories I have ever heard.[2]

By using a new medium free from memories of previous failure, Solomon gained confidence to begin to read and write. He also developed new ways of observing human behavior and gaining insight into a specific social event. For an individual, or even for a class studying anthropology, such an experience could be one of the most significant pieces of ethnographic data to use in contrast with other societies and to relate to theory.

In using audiovisual equipment—films, television, tapes, records, slide tapes, slides, and photographs—the important aspect is not the spectacular things a teacher can do with it, but what the student can do. Often equipment is used as a gimmick. Materials, too, are often designed as entertainment, not as instructional materials that demand student participation. Thus, students are herded into large auditoriums and shown selected footage of disjointed events occurring in another society, held together by a tight narration. When the film is over, there is usually nothing left to say—the images that one has seen have been interpreted in such detail that there is nothing left for the viewer to do. Besides, the footage is selected in a way that does not leave room for any different interpretation.

Those who work in television, movies, and radio are failing to develop this vast potential educational resource. We are aware only in the most superficial sense that there has been a revolution; Marshall McLuhan and others have written much about it, but there is little information to guide us in

---

Editor's note: This, and other field activities of this kind, must be handled with great tact, sensitivity, and respect. What can be a creative, even as in this case, beautiful, experience, can be interpreted as spying, prying, or lack of respect. This was the boy's own grandfather and family and he had full consent and support for doing what he did.

utilizing the media profitably. Expo 67 exhibited what was perhaps the first concerted effort to utilize the potential of the new media to some educational objective. Many teachers came away intrigued by what they saw, but uncertain how it could apply to them and their teaching situations. At this point we do not need more gimmicks or ways to turn students on. What we need are techniques to develop the tools we have, tools which will enable us to teach basic concepts. In recent years there has been a revolution in these techniques. This paper is presented in hope it will provide a few guidelines and examples for those who want to take advantage of this revolution.

Perception

One of the problems encountered in using audiovisual materials is that students of all ages need training to help them see and hear more perceptively in order to make effective use of these materials. I notice in our society that the people who see best are good artists. They have trained eyes, for they are constantly examining and looking at the environment in which they live, whereas most of us take our environment for granted. We get up in the morning, brush our teeth, eat our breakfast, go out of the door, go to work or go to school or whatever without really seeing anything. We have a kind of cognitive map that enables us to trundle about the world we live in without ever giving it so much as a thought, unless something startles our vision, whereupon we stop for a moment, fit it into this cognitive map, and then go on. If there is any learning, the students are going to have to do it themselves, through active participation. The following sequence is one way that I have successfully helped students become visually acute.

First, a very simple photograph is shown. I have used a picture of cows in a field with a farmhouse in the background. The photograph was taken in Nova Scotia, Canada. Although it is an extremely simple photograph, it is amazing how many details become visible as one studies the picture, and how these details can be used to support hypotheses about time of day, season, type of community, kind of people who live there, and the kinds of things they do. By choosing first a simple photograph, yet one rich with detail, the concentrated viewing by students is rewarded.

The second photograph should be much more challenging: I usually use a photograph taken by Laurence Marshall of a Southwest African Bushman family sitting before their fire, with several Bushman huts in the background. The nature of the environment, some of the technology, and several of the social relationships are in evidence in this picture—if one has the eyes to see them. One by one the myriad clues appear, and students begin to piece together the information they need to make an intelligent hypothesis about the phenomena they are viewing.

Other pictures can be used along this same vein, chosen from the students' own society as well as foreign societies. The idea is to show the students the wealth of information contained in a single image and to point out that different people see the same picture differently, in terms of their own experiences, preconceptions, and prejudices. Students gain experience in making inferences, deductions, and conclusions from photographic images.

Another session introduces the students first to the problem of hypothesizing from very little information, and then showing how strongly our hypothesis, once formed, influences our perceptions, even when additional information is contradictory. This activity does not teach students to observe better or to make more useful deductions from information presented to them. What it does is to point out to them that it is often difficult to see things in life for what they are. Using a classical psychological experiment method, I show a slide out of focus; I then ask the viewer to guess what the image is, and gradually bring the image into focus. The first out-of-focus photograph I showed in one fifth-grade classroom was of a road in the snow, with evergreen trees and a blue sky. The children were asked to predict what they would eventually see, and to write down the prediction in their notebooks. They all predicted differently. The slide was brought into focus in five stages, and at each stage they were asked to write down quickly, in one line, what it was they were seeing. Finally in focus it was only shown for two seconds, and then turned off. Many of the students did not see what was in the photograph until it was refocused and left on for many seconds. One student was convinced that she was going to see a church in a large town, and even when the picture was almost completely focused, she was clearly not rethinking her hypothesis on the basis of the clearer image.

In another case I showed a picture of a large acacia tree in Nairobi Game Park which had a leopard sitting on a branch in the middle of the photograph. The students made wild predictions. After the photograph had been clearly in focus for about two seconds, not one child in the class of twenty-six saw the leopard. One child did think he saw a squirrel in a tree. To get the most out of this experiment, one can ask half the class to look at the slide out of focus, and write down what they think it is; and then keep refocusing it for them at intervals, for a whole minute. In the last fifteen seconds the other half of the class, who have had their heads turned in the opposite direction, quickly turn around and look at the slide; they write down what they predict the photograph will look like when it is focused. There is no question, in the end, that those who have seen the slide for only fifteen seconds—but the last and clearest fifteen seconds—have no trouble in making out what the picture shows, but students who have been viewing and predicting for a longer time are not able to change their prediction on the basis of new information.

To demonstrate the difference between people's perceptions, I have often used several photographs from Steichen's *The Family of Man* (1955). In one case, thirty students were shown a picture of a woman who was holding up her hands in front of a child who had a large two-by-four board, that seemed to be raised against her, in his hands (Steichen 1955:46). I asked each student to write down their interpretation of the action. Some students did not realize there was a woman in the picture; others did not realize there was a boy; half the class did not see the stick in the boy's hand; students who did see the stick and thought the woman was threatened were not sure whether the woman was trying to stop the boy from hitting her or whether she was trying to stop him from hitting something else. By comparing and discussing their interpretations, students learned both to study an image more closely before forming an opinion and to recognize that people interpret a given image in many different ways.[3]

I often ask elementary school students to choose from *The Family of Man* slide tape any image that has left an impression on them and write a filmscript about this image—what happened before, what was happening during, and what happened after the picture was taken. This encourages further thought about the relationship between an image and one's interpretation of it.

Having completed these lessons on perception, I usually move to an ethnographic sequence—a series of slides of an event in a foreign society, an event rich with ritual, and one with several primary kin relationships revealed. Viewing such a sequence of activities further improves my students' ability to use visual data, and the class is ready to be led into whatever ethnographic study I wish to pursue with an extensive use of film materials. Some students are quick to perceive details in a photograph, but much practice is needed in drawing conclusions from their observations. The fact that a photograph does not represent the same thing to all students clearly disturbs the students. By the end of the class, students were intrigued with the process of visual perception, and they were learning more about their own process of thinking. Students can become more self-reflecting about perception and thinking not only through these exercises in perception, but by any means that gives them a more objective look at their own society and their relationships with other people.

Elementary School

I shall now describe several kinds of slide tapes that I have used in teaching elementary school social studies. (See Appendix B, p. 483). A slide tape consists of a sequence of slides synchronized with sound on a tape recorder.

[3] It was not until 1936 that the revolutionary new magazine, *Life,* was first published. It was the editors' idea to give the public weekly photographs of the news to read. However, we were not allowed to interpret the images for ourselves: the photographs all had captions and the pictures were very carefully edited. We have often been duped into believing that the picture is in some way a direct imitation of reality: if we see it in a picture, it must be true. Of course this is not so. Pictures can be as much a lie, if not more so, than the written word. The medium itself has no inherent truth in it—it is how the medium is used that determines the representation of reality we finally view.

Ruth MacDonald, a teacher who had spent several years with her husband and children in Aiyetoro, a Yoruba village in western Nigeria, was working on a social studies unit in Nigeria for the Newton, Massachusetts, Public School System. She had taken many photographs while in Aiyetoro and wanted to use these in the curriculum. I helped her make a series of twelve slide tapes. I will describe some of the more important ones we used.

The first slide tape describes the village of Aiyetoro—the occupations, activities, services, churches, and so on,—through intimate images. There are approximately sixty slides in the set, giving one the feeling of walking through a village with the freedom to look closely at people's lives. The image, projected from the rear on a huge screen made of sheets of transparent paper, was approximately life-size (see Appendix D, p. 484, for details). Some students went up and looked at the images more closely. At the end of one showing, I asked if the students would like to see some of the images again; some students said yes, and asked to see particular images. We examined them very carefully, the students asking questions and we answering as best we could. Through examining these sixty images quite carefully, the whole class began to learn about Yoruba society. One child asked to see a close-up photograph of five Yoruba boys—a 10-by-10-foot image completely filled up with five young black faces. The student asked questions about the physical features of the boys. It was obvious to me that in this suburban town the student had probably never been so close to a black child. She said, "He has very strange hair." And I said, "What's strange about it?" She said, "Well—well, I don't know, I mean I—it's not like *our* hair." And I said, "Well, why don't you go back behind the screen and take a look at his hair, see what you think it's really like." "You mean—go back and actually touch it?" And I said, "Yes, go back and feel it, for yourself." Whereupon half the class giggled, and I said, "What's so funny? How does a blind person know the world he lives in, if not by touching things in his environment?" The child went behind the screen, and I noticed immediately that she had turned into a shadow—she was blocking the light, so the screen was filled with the image of the five black faces except where her body was—which was a silhouette of her. (The other students in the class noticed it, too. It meant that later on, if I continued to use rear-screen projection, I could ask students to go behind and walk through the village streets and examine things themselves, without their being inhibited at all, because they had been transformed from their usual selves into a shadow of themselves. This made a great deal of difference in getting them to do role-play later on.) The girl, behind the screen, put her hand over the boy's head to feel his hair. And I said, "What did it feel like?" She said, "Well, it feels very wiry." And I said, "What else?" "Well—it feels kind of greasy." (The photograph obviously was taken on a very hot day, and the children in the photograph were sweating.) And then, for what seemed like a very long moment, she caressed the boy's face, feeling his features, or pretending to. When she was finished, she came back and sat down. I realized for the first time what a powerful instrument the screen, and these photographs, could be for teaching social studies at an elementary school level. The capacity of the ten-year-old to imagine and pretend, when given an opportunity, is a capacity too little appreciated and too little utilized in the classroom. One girl asked to see the procession in the streets of the Aiyetoro picture of the wedding. So we went back to the picture of the wedding, and I said, "And what interests you about the picture of the wedding?" She said, "Well, it's the strange hat—or turban—the woman is wearing. How does one make that?" Luckily I had instructions on how to make such a turban, instructions that should be part of the finished curriculum. With these instructions the children, much more adept at it than I, were able to make Yoruba turbans in no time at all.

I will briefly mention four other slide tapes in this particular curriculum that had great impact on the students.

One tape dealt with the question of death and how the Yoruba reacted to it. It was a slide tape called *Rejoicing,* about a storyteller who died when he was very old, and the people rejoiced at his death. This slide tape had suggestive, nonrepresentational images intercut with the photographs to enable the students to use their own imaginations as freely as possible. Students discussed at length the concept of death in our society and in other societies and the rituals whereby the individual is reincorporated back into his society when he has died. In teaching this particular lesson to ten-year-olds a problem arose; the students were very receptive to many of the basic ideas that might be discussed in an anthropology course at a college level, but their parents were not. I found parents often voiced objections to the fact that social modes of behavior in our own society were being questioned. The assumption seemed to be that questioning would lead to the destruction of these modes and values, not to strengthening them.

A third slide tape was an illustrated Yoruba myth. With the cooperation of two local art dealers—Paul Berneheimer of Cambridge and Boris Mirski of Boston, and the Peabody Museum at Harvard University, I was able to photograph several different pieces of Yoruba sculpture from various angles and distances and in varied lights. I photographed Yoruba twins, gods and goddesses, and animals against a background of old wood and Yoruba cloth until I had 160 images that illustrated the events described in the myth. Students discussed myth as a social charter, and in exploring the role of the storyteller and the function of telling a myth the nature of the socialization process came into question. Yoruba socialization was contrasted to our own educational system.

I kept discovering that it was not the material I presented to students, but what we did with that material that left an impact on them and generated a process of learning. It was at this point that I decided to utilize other talent in the Newton Public School System, and I asked the drama teacher consultant to assist me in preparing a dramatized version, with the students, of another Yoruba myth. I decided to record this dramatization on black and white slides, with sound, to make a sound-synchronous slide tape of the process for teacher-training purposes. I thought I was going to be witnessing a remarkable event. Indeed, it was remarkable, but not for the reasons that I had hoped. And it was going to take me many weeks to figure out just exactly what went wrong that day. The teacher came in and was all set to make a fantastic demonstration: she had the students all organized and lined up and working like beavers from the first minute she walked into the room. Indeed, the play was a fantastic production for her: props were being made, children were rehearsing their lines, it was all going so smoothly. The teacher managed to pull off quite a performance in the end; yet somehow there was something missing. It was a great disappointment to me, but I could not figure out why. At the time I had a great deal else to do, and I had to give up my teaching in that classroom for two weeks. Later the classroom teacher, Beverly Aronson, called me and said that her students had got a play together that they wanted me to see. They had carefully studied the material on Yoruba naming as well as naming in many other societies around the world—how names are chosen, what rituals are involved, and at what point children are considered members of a society (some societies wait a long time before naming a child, fearing he may be only a transient spirit). The students discussed naming, baptism, and social membership in their own society. Finally, after studying the Yoruba naming ceremony carefully, they decided they wanted to do their own play of a Yoruba naming ceremony.

I went to the class quite weary, still wondering what had gone wrong two weeks before with the previous play. The students very simply, and with only a small blanket to represent an infant, went through a naming ceremony that took about fifteen to twenty minutes. They did it very quietly—there were about five of them—and the rest of the class did not speak a word. It was a truly beautiful ceremony. By transforming the material they had studied, the students mastered the data and incorporated it into their own perceptions of the social world.

The last slide tape we made was the most significant of all, because it was made by the students themselves. We were seeking a way to test what the students in one class had learned. Mrs. MacDonald wrote a short story that had many of the social elements that we were trying to examine with the students. The students could read the story, illustrate it, narrate the illustrations, and come back with a version wholly of their own manufacturing, which would either be very close to the original or quite different. We hoped it would be different, but given that, how it would differ would reveal what they had learned.

I read the students a story about a young girl who wanted desperately to go to school, but whose father did not want her to go. It told of a father who had several wives, one of whom bought garden produce from him to sell in a village market. Yoruba women travel great distances to market their wares, and with the money they get, they pay their husbands for the produce. The husbands, in turn, use the money to gain whatever political prestige they can in the village where they live, whereas women, who travel further abroad than men, often want to use the money to educate their children—girls as well as boys. In this case the girl was expected to help her mother in the fields, but had a chance to go to school, too; and she wanted to go to school. I asked each child to illustrate a paragraph that particularly interested him or her by making a drawing. The art teacher, Albert Hurwitz, had briefly shown students a range of things that could be done with "Craypas" to encourage experimentation appropriate to this medium. When they had completed their drawings, I helped each student photograph his illustrations on color film. As some of their pictures were very detailed, I encouraged students to take several pictures, some showing only tiny details, by using a Marcro-Nikkor close-up lens. (Any close-up attachment for a single-lens reflex 35-mm. camera would do.) While I was away for a few days the classroom teacher had each student hold up his picture and narrate it, while she recorded what they said. Later I transferred to regular quarter-inch tape the recordings she had made on the school's cassette portable tape recorder. I then synchronized the children's narrations with their pictures.[4] (A slide-tape synchronizer is not really necessary, as children love programming their own slide shows.) We found that the basic information we had given the children had been assimilated by them and given back to us in different form. It was a pretty good test, as it turned out. The resulting slide tape demonstrated that the children had, on their own terms, understood many of the basic elements that we were interested in having them learn. We do not *teach* this or that objective fact or concept; we express as teachers those facts or concepts as best we can, and they are interpreted by each individual student in his own way, not as objectively or factually as we might assume. That is why teaching can be a creative process. A student may take many years to integrate what he has learned and may appear, at times, to have had a valuable experience, but not to have understood it or generalized from it. One cannot count on receptivity every teaching day, but one can be sure that if the child has partaken creatively in the process of learning he will be able to integrate a great deal of the facts and concepts to which he has been exposed.

Just recently I thought of examining this process of integration further, and asked my eight-year-old son to make a slide tape of a book we had read together. The slide tape was a very interesting explication of what he had got out of the book *Treasure Island* in combination with many other elements of his life drawn from television, skin-diving, other books, and the drawings of his peers.

A final example from my experiences with elementary school students may help to show how the process of integration can be stressed from the

[4] This job took about an hour and a half. A Uher or Norelco slide-tape synchronizer can be used with any monophonic tape recorder; or a Kodak synchronizer can be used with a stereophonic tape recorder.

outset of a course. Three colleagues and I at Education Development Center, Cambridge, Massachusetts, were working on an introduction to a unit on the !Kung Bushmen of southwest Africa.[5] We bought three king-size sheets and strung them on nylon twine around a large space in the gym. From the rear we projected slides onto each sheet with three Carousel slide projectors. The three sheets were arranged so that one was in front of the children and one on either side. The children sat on the floor, watching the images. Sometimes the images were closely related; a single Kalahari scene was spread across three screens with a straight line of horizon; at other times the three screens had quite different images, or only one screen would be used. A lizard, a lion, or a giraffe could fill an entire screen. The sounds of the seasons accompanied the appropriate slides, so that lightning and rain on the screen, for example, could be accompanied by sounds of rain and thunder. The students were markedly impressed by this elaborate show, though sometimes disturbed by those images that were so close and so vivid.

After the showings we asked students to draw, write, or tape record impressions of their experience. It was generally agreed that looking at the Kalahari environment slides had given the children an experience upon which they could build during their entire study of the Bushmen. The question, "What would it be like to live in the Kalahari Desert?" elicited a wide variety of responses, ranging from fear of loneliness to joy and excitement in the openness and the diversity. Most striking about the children's stories was the thematic progression from loneliness, getting lost, being helpless, to taking care of oneself, adapting, and surviving. This encouraged us to believe that this "environment chamber" is more than a *son et lumière.* Rather, it may provide strong psychological groundwork for more conceptual understanding of man's relationship to his environment, his adaptation to it, and his place in the total ecology.

High School

Community Study

The next curriculum that I want to discuss is for a slightly older group of children, thirteen and fifteen years old, whose cognitive skills better enable them to handle more complex material. The following outline is drawn from a proposal I am developing to encourage urban students to study their own communities with the assistance of audiovisual equipment. As I envision it, such a process would involve the students' use of still cameras, 8-mm. films, videotape recordings, painting, sculpture, interviews, journalism, poetry,

[5] All the !Kung Bushman films referred to in this article were made by John K. Marshall. The still photographs and ethnography that I have used for the !Kung Bushman are part of the unique material collected by Laurence and Lorna Marshall.

and music. In the process students would become directly involved, both with the media and with their community, because the use of a new medium often provides the excuse to look and relook at something you think you know. As they examine the underlying structure of their community, students should be able to gain an understanding of their own social relationships within this structure.

Although the United States has always been a pluralistic society, we have often ignored this fact, particularly in education. Education is society's formal mechanism for teaching the young both the skills and the values necessary to be effective adults who will maintain the social system. Obviously our system of public education has often been an important factor in transforming immigrant groups into Americans, but it has also played a role in the development and maintenance of a class system.

In much of America today the curriculum used is a product of past traditions, materials, and social conditions. The gap often is so great between the reality of a child's world outside a school and the history, geography, social studies, and literature presented in school that he frequently discards or rejects his formal training and ends up a "motivation problem." In suburban and rural communities where conditions are closer to the middle-class image of the world, the gap is obviously narrower than in the inner city. Among urban black children whose past is largely ignored, whose people rarely appear in textbooks and fiction, and whose families have difficulty getting good jobs and housing, the gap is enormous.

The wider the gap between a child's own life experience and the story told by his school, the greater the need to select his world and reality as the starting point for regaining both his trust and his belief that what he sees and experiences is real and valuable. It is essential to develop a course with the students themselves, a course which begins wherever they live and closely examines the conditions of this and neighboring communities. Had we begun sooner, such a curriculum might not be necessary, but many children in the last years of elementary school and early grades of high school are no longer willing or able to participate in more traditional courses. A radical break with past educational experience is essential if we want to recapture the attention and interest of these students. An exploration of their environment in detail, in which they are encouraged to express their feelings about this environment in any creative mode they choose, could be such an experience. The context of the course would be the child and his community, why he and his family live there and not somewhere else, why other people do not live there and how "there" compares with other places. In this course we would include anything that would engage a student in his world and in how the people in it do or do not communicate, get along, and understand one another. Things that are stimulating, honest, and that help the student master experience rather than being overwhelmed by it are vital.

At each point, as students work with a given medium, they film, they make taped interviews, they photograph or paint the images, or record or write the music of the streets and buildings (one would discover that some children were sculptors and others poets, on a tape-recorder if not on paper). They can be shown other students' and adults' work from other parts of the country and, from time to time, make field trips to other parts of their city. These trips should not be to traditional places like museums, but to legislative hearings, courtrooms, playgrounds in other communities, stores, banks, clinics—anywhere that would broaden the student's experience in ways he can handle, and help him see his own world clearly. For too long students' formal education has been confined to the walls of a school building. It is important both to stretch beyond the school itself and to bring talent from the community into the school.

By having groups of students periodically make presentations in a variety of media, information and feelings will be integrated into different modes, providing a range of interpretations of the reality of their environment. Processes should be stressed over glossy product, but the content of the product and the struggle to select what belongs in that product will give students needed evidence of their own competence and should help to create respect among them. Herbert Kohl (1967) demonstrates the need of such courses and, of course, of imaginative teachers. The children would become urban anthropologists for their own community. They would discover who really runs the community, who holds it together in time of crisis, the services available in it, the shops, and so on. They would look into questions such as how many services are there? What are the prices for rent? What are food prices? Who owns these services? How much of the community is run by outsiders to the community, like police, fire, schools, merchant stores, and so forth? How much of the community is run by people who live in it?

Language and Social Studies

Audiovisual material can be employed in a multitude of ways, all related to anthropology at the high school level, by students, teachers, and curriculum developers. One final example for high school students contrasts with the previous example of student participation and involves foreign language teaching as well as anthropology. This idea initially came from Harold Beattie, who had proposed a new language program for the Newton Public School System. In order to bring the study of a language, such as French, into a more relevant perspective, we discussed the possibility of finding a community outside of Paris, which was to Paris what Newton is to Boston. It was hoped that a team of people from Newton—teachers, students, and curriculum developers—would go over to this community to discuss the possibilities of forming a joint program where French students would learn English and American students would learn French the following year. During the first summer this team was to make as much of an anthropological study as possible, gathering data and artifacts that could be brought back to American classrooms, all on the subject of youth culture in France. Materials would include novels, relevant movies, songs, narratives of the hopes and desires of young people in that part of France at that time, and their views about all manner of politics and social life. For example, a tape recorder might be placed on the dining table of a French family to record a family dinner conversation. Such tapes could be made throughout the year. The small cassettes could be sent to students in the other country for translation and study. There would be a great problem in translating this tape, but with a good French teacher in the United States, the difficulty could be overcome. Besides, there would be more motivation to learn the language and make a translation, because there would be much more contact between the students in one community and the students in another. Photographs could be exchanged during the year, assignments could be given by members of one country to the members of the other which would help them learn more from a sociological and anthropological point of view about each other's societies. Here the use of the audiovisual media could have great impact.

Students from elementary school through college can learn the same basic concepts if the proper translation into their cognitive mode of thinking is made. Individuals are stimulated in a learning process through varied modes of expression, both in the way things are taught them and ways they are able to express what they have learned, on their own terms. We can observe that growth has occurred in a learning situation, not so much when individuals integrate different bits of information in a particular cognitive mode but when they translate this information from one mode to another. The role of the teacher in the process is not so much to provide an experience for students, but to enable them to reflect on that experience.

College

Field Methods and Techniques

The first course I taught at the college level was designed to introduce undergraduate and some graduate students to good field methods and techniques and in particular, the use of audiovisual techniques in anthropological fieldwork. Students spent the first semester defining a problem that could be researched in the Boston area while they learned to handle the technical aspects of photography and sound. They did some fieldwork and much reading, ending the semester by presenting a scholarly research paper with extensive bibliography of published research on their topic and a bibliography of related materials produced in other forms—films, television, records, newspapers, magazines. The next semester they chose the media they would use to transcribe their field research. In studies such as one on trance states (comparing Bushman dance trances to trances at services in a Baptist church) or on alcoholism in a metropolitan hospital, students used movies, with or without synchronous sound, portable videotape equipment, still photos and slide tapes, with and without synchronous sound. Some students did extremely well in using the new media in a scholarly way, and some students found it impossible to use the media and be anything but subjective about their study.

Some Uses of Audiovisual Materials To Engage College Students in Introductory Anthropology

Traditionally, film has been used in anthropology courses either to demonstrate a technological process or to communicate a general view of a society. For two years we[6] have been experimenting with ways to integrate film with ethnography and ethnology for the teaching of introductory anthropology at Brandeis University. At present this is extremely difficult because so few societies have been filmed in depth by people who understand the social structure and know the filmed individuals well. We have relied heavily on John Marshall's excellent films of the !Kung Bushmen—hunters and gatherers who live in the Kalahari Desert of southwest Africa. And we were fortunate in having Mr. Marshall, Co-Director of our Center for Documentary Anthropology at Brandeis, supervise the use of his thirty-five !Kung films.

In our teaching we have found that a short film of one continuous segment of social interaction, focusing on one or two individuals, is a successful pedagogical device (see Appendix E, pp. 485). Students with a general background in ethnographic and theoretical material may agree on the content of the film but frequently disagree on how to interpret the behavior observed. These differences are discussed and often the same film is shown several times, at both normal and slow speeds. When desired, other sequences can be projected and readings assigned before a film is seen again, so that additional knowledge can be used in analyzing the event.

This use of film, juxtaposed with ethnographic and theoretical readings, is an excellent paradigm for the process by which an anthropologist analyzes observed behavior with the help of other bits and pieces of information and experience. It shows how the anthropologist proceeds from the observed social phenomena to an analysis of what these phenomena mean to the people observed and, occasionally, to a more general understanding of human behavior. Film raises questions about the relationship between models of social behavior—both those constructed by the anthropologist and those expressed by members of the society—and actual behavior. The film process itself can

---

[6] The Center for Documentary Anthropology in the Anthropology Department, Brandeis University. All Bushman and Yąnomamö films in this article are distributed by Documentary Educational Resources, Somerville, Mass. 02143.

be seen as a model because it isolates an event, showing it from one point of view.

Fieldwork assignments have proved to be an important part of our course. Students have gone into a neighboring community to relate the type of social interaction they had previously observed through film to fieldwork in their own society. Such fieldwork helps students see how basic principles of anthropology can be applied to a society which they know. It emphasizes the gap between recorded data and the actual breadth of human experience within any society.

An example of the way we have used film, classroom analysis, and local fieldwork in our course may serve to clarify some essential features of the use of film for teaching anthropology. A film sequence about a !Kung woman preparing to go out gathering is carefully examined in class. The woman tries to persuade her four-year-old son, who is in the midst of a tantrum, to stay at home with his sister. During this loud debate, the woman's husband (the boy's father) remains quietly aloof inside the corner of his hut, lying on his back. The woman finally agrees to take the boy, although she will have to carry him most of the day, along with fifty pounds of roots, berries, and firewood.

Through an analysis of this filmed behavior, students hypothesize that !Kung men play a passive role in disputes between other members of their families and that !Kung parents are permissive, two hypotheses corroborated by the written ethnography.

Students, in male-female pairs, are assigned the task of observing and recording the behavior they see in this film sequence. They are then requested to observe and analyze a comparable situation in the lives of a local family, focusing on a situation in which a mother is trying to manage her children while performing another task, such as cooking dinner. The students prepare field notes containing their observations and later split up in groups to discuss their observations and analysis.

Through the process of recording and discussing their observations, they learn how patterns can be detected in social situations. At the same time they learn why these patterns cannot be generalized without prolonged and intensive ethnographic study and cannot be extrapolated on a comparative basis without the formulation of a verifiable ethnographic interpretation.

Integrated film with readings and field observation is an effective way to introduce the study of anthropology. But extensive experience in analyzing the content of film has an additional advantage. The new communications network that has developed around television has become one of the central institutions in America. Opportunities that enhance a student's ability to understand the ways in which the film medium communicates are valuable educational experiences in themselves. Most television documentaries are tightly scripted films that portray one man's view of a problem by juxtaposing short pieces of footage from a variety of events and personalities. Our films provide a contrast by highlighting the importance of understanding the social context and personalities involved before analyzing either single actions and statements or even short sequences. Our field assignments encourage students to search for the relationship between single examples of social interaction and the range of behavior revealed in similar events throughout the society. These perceptions are important in developing mature responses to the pressures of the television medium.

The Center for Documentary Anthropology has already begun development of a curriculum for teaching introductory anthropology by using available film and other documentary material for three societies: the extensive film material on the !Kung Bushmen of the Kalahari Desert collected by John Marshall in the course of a three-year study; the Ya̧nomamö material collected by Napoleon Chagnon and Timothy Asch; and material about the Dodoth, a pastoral people in northeastern Uganda, also collected by Timothy Asch. The curriculum provides a framework for the comparative analysis of these three societies and makes available to teachers of introductory anthropology a prototype of such a course. However, additional films of the Ya̧nomamö are essential to such an outline to provide rich contrast to the !Kung material and to the students' observations of their own society. Further filming commenced in 1971.

To ensure wide use of the resource materials, we have insisted from the start that they be flexible enough to permit varied combinations. The individual films and articles in the curriculum have independent value and may be adapted separately for instruction in various disciplines.[7]

The prototype course we have been developing at Brandeis deals with the following topics:

ECOLOGY Environmental constraints on !Kung social and economic life and aspects of !Kung social organization that may be adaptive to these constraints are compared with the Ya̧nomamö's relationship to the jungle in which they are able to practice slash-and-burn agriculture. The Ya̧nomamö and !Kung ecological situations are in turn compared to the Dodoth ecology and economy which is based on cattle.

The degree to which a people's social and economic organization constitutes an adjustment to their environment becomes a central question in the study of small, nonindustrial societies. Good film can convey visually a people's place in an ecological system. It can also illustrate efficiently and dramatically a people's technological relationship to the world around them.

SOCIALIZATION A range of examples from the !Kung socialization process, involving individual differences, adult roles, and idealized behaviors, are

[7] At present this film is incomplete and not ready for distribution, but we are considering working with high school teachers to help them adapt it to a lower level, and we shall continue working on the college version.

illustrated in films on child-adult relationships, children's play, and childhood rituals such as the first haircut and the first kill. Similarly, rich film data on the Yąnomamö, which we hope to obtain soon, would be invaluable, since the roles and ideals of the !Kung present marked contrasts to those of the Yąnomamö. In these isolated societies, where children are socialized entirely by close kin, it is much easier to study the relationship between the needed skills and attitudes of adults and the methods used in teaching.

KINSHIP A general study of kinship compares the student's own kinship system, the !Kung kinship system, which supports flexibility in band composition, and the Yąnomamö kinship system, which affects intervillage composition and intravillage alliance. A film such as John Marshall's *An Argument about a Marraige,* based on an incident that threatens traditional social values, illustrates alliance along kin lines and the importance of marriage and bride service to the !Kung. The film shows how people manipulate social relationships in a conflict situation. Film displaying Yąnomamö behavior during conflicts dramatically contrasts patterns of acceptable behavior among these two societies.

The !Kung are also a good example of a society that is organized around extended social ties. Their system of name relationships creates wide social links between people, providing each individual with classificatory kin ties that relate him to !Kung in other bands. Again the Yąnomamö offer an excellent contrast, for although they too are a small society with minimal political organization, physical distance often equates with social danger and the only alliances are close kin ties or active political alliances dependent on frequent exchange of gifts and women, and mutual hostility toward other groups. The conflict between hostility and alliance is readily visible on film (as seen in *The Feast*) and highlights the importance of ritualized behavior during periods of social tension.

ALLIANCE AND RECIPROCITY Two films from the !Kung material used in the course illustrate a system of meat distribution that reinforces solidarity among people living together and provides an economic framework for affinal relationships. One film illustrates a normal distribution in which the meat of a large antelope spreads out through the village in an ever-widening circle. The other film shows what happens when the normal distribution of an antelope is interrupted by a conflict over its ownership. In this instance the ability to preside over the distribution of meat is regarded as a vital part of a man's status.

The exchange of women and gifts and the mounting of joint raiding expeditions are social mechanisms for creating alliances among the Yąnomamö. These alliances are vital to the political future of the village and to the status of its headmen.

Alliance among the Dodoth is shown through the gift of cattle, exchange of women in marriage, and mutual participation in sacrifices and raids.

ROLE AND STATUS In a study of role and status the importance of hunting to male status among the !Kung can be compared with the importance of hunting, raiding, and "fierce behavior" among the Yąnomamö. Among the Dodoth, cattle and women are central to male status. The opportunity we hope to have to make several short films of key Yąnomamö—a headman, a first wife, or a young girl at the point of maturing—will allow us to examine the effect of different roles on an individual's behavior. One Yąnomamö film sequence shows the headman exchanging gifts at a feast where an aggressive stance is appropriate: another shows him relaxing with one of his wives; and in a third he is shown playing with and instructing several of his children.

RELIGION AND RITUAL Film showing ritual events is a valuable aid in teaching anthropology. The intensity of a !Kung Bushman trance or a Yąnomamö hallucinogenic curing ceremony can be conveyed by an exciting visual and acoustic experience difficult to match in words. By combining the film experience with the written models as provided by such authors as Emile Durkheim, Claude Levi-Strauss, Victor Turner, and John Middleton, the student is afforded the opportunity to apply the theoretical analysis to observed behavior.

As demonstrated in the course, the behavior of the members of the three societies forms a spectrum from conspicuously aggressive to relatively peaceful behavior. Yet from a functional standpoint, important elements of social organization are similar among the three groups.

The main goal of our course is to introduce the concepts and the methodology used by anthropologists in their study of man and society. To achieve this we feel that it is important to provide many opportunities for students to observe human beings in action, to question the meaning of specific behavior, and to use the concepts they are learning to sharpen their ability to observe. Film has traditionally been used in courses as entertainment; it is rarely linked to either ethnography or ethnology, and the films are not made with instructional criteria in mind. We intend to show that film can be produced that will have wide educational potential, not just as a pedagogical device attractive to students, but as instructional material and as an additional mode for studying social phenomena.

Following are some interesting and some discouraging answers to a final, ungraded question on an introductory anthropology examination I recently gave my students. They act as an incomplete conclusion to unfinished experiments. The question was: "In terms of the translation of ethnographic material, what, if any, justification do you see for the use of film in teaching Anthropology 1-a?"

The idea of studying anthropology without observing other peoples at least in films if not first hand would be like studying chemistry without ever setting foot in a lab. The written data has no significance unless you have some feeling for the society as a whole. The data can represent the institutions in which we are interested, but social anthropology is generally defined as the study of behavior, that is, the social activities of real people. Furthermore, our field assignments helped me to appreciate first-hand the difficulty of translating field notes into intelligent, meaningful, useful ethnographic material. Finally, I cannot think of a better, more enjoyable way of getting students *interested.* In an introductory course this has to be one of the main objectives. Films, when they are done well, have an uncanny ability to excite people more than any book cover could ever hope to do. Once the interest is aroused, learning is no task at all.

—Cassia Whiteside, Freshman

One picture is worth a thousand words. The footage which our class viewed stands as the most effective argument for the use of film. Watching a tribe in their daily existence allows the viewer to absorb subconsciously more material than he could in any one book. The physical environment, the expressive faces, the voice intonations are all things which the written word simply cannot capture. More importantly, the modern student is quickly bored by extensive reading, and the multi-media film is, in contrast, an immediate learning experience which can so control the viewer's mind that retention often approaches one hundred percent. The written word is, unfortunately perhaps, dying as an educational device. The electronic age, through television (see McLuhan) has brought a generation which cannot wait for something, but must be delivered the article. Film delivers the goods, film explodes in your face, it does not simmer in the cerebrum.

—David Waxler, Sophomore

I started the course, anthropology 1-a, with one question: what is Man? The films glued three pictures in my mind the way no book ever could.

(1) Man is lowlier than Animal. I saw two Ya̧nomamö men squatting on the ground, crosseyed and drooling. They had made themselves sick from drugs. A little dog trotted by, gay, healthy, and untroubled. It didn't have the "sense" to hamper its capacity to achieve its end and enjoy itself.

(2) Man is Human. It was heart-warming to see !Toma kiss his child and women nursing their babies. But I got a spark of insight from a scene in *The Feast.* The Ya̧nomamö society, which notoriously oppresses women, showed me one of women's major contributions. Maybe I saw what is called "a woman's place." A Ya̧nomamö woman was picking lice from her husband's hair and eating them. What struck me was her soothing voice. She was that man's private comfort—his release of anxiety and his relaxation. That voice was beauty, in anyone's language.

(3) Man is close to God. I used to spurn religion because I thought it had nothing to offer that could not be gained by private meditation. In *N/um Tchai,* the curing dance film, I saw the value of community worship. While the Bushmen sang and held each other, I saw men rise above their harsh environment. The group overcame the limits of time and space. I could have read Durkheim to find how society makes religion, but by seeing the film I discovered it for myself. Thus, *the idea was more meaningful to me.*

All this might be wild conjecture. At any rate, the impact was solid.

—Donna Livingstone, Freshman

An experienced anthropologist and competent writer combined can produce an excellent ethnography in the literary form. But one of the most valuable concepts I got from this course is the added advantage and tremendous teaching-learning potential of film. I can remember several specific times when the film really struck me. The first time was the panoramic sweep of the Kalahari Desert (I believe the rain film). It contained the entire atmosphere of the Bushmen's home and it was even more graphic than the narrated shots in "The Hunters." Also, I clearly remember what I was thinking when I saw "The Sacrifice." I had just read the material pertaining to this film, and I remember thinking that I hadn't just been dreaming that they bleed cows [the Dodoth], they really do. For some reason, the fact did not become reality for me till I was watching it on the screen. I have also found that scenes such as these have stuck in my memory. A simple explanation could be that the memory works with images and a book must be translated into imperfect images before the memory will accept them.

Book→words→images(films)→memory. Another valuable impression I have kept from the films is the movement of the bodies. I can remember Di!nai's gentle walk, !Toma's wise facial expressions, and Kaobawa's violent gestures. In my notes I have written, "Anthropologists cannot, should not, must not become a part of the culture, they must not lose objectivity. Films are probably the most objective form of media due to the ease of various interpretations."

—Ann Bergman, Freshman

Appendix A: Some Films That We Have Used

1. Twenty-eight !Kung Bushman films by John Marshall. Of particular importance were:

   Still Birth
   A Curing Ceremony
   !Nai and Debe's Tantrum
   Women under the Baobab
   Playing with Scorpions
   Lion Game
   A Rite of Passage
   Boys Bathing
   The Wasp Nest
   Men Bathing
   N!owa T'ama: The Melon Tossing
   !Nai and Gunda Wake
   A Joking Relationship
   The Meat Fight
   An Argument about a Marriage
   N/um Tchai: The Ceremonial Dance of the !Kung Bushmen
   Bitter Melons

2. Y̨anomamö films by Timothy Asch and Napoleon Chagnon.

   *The Feast**
   Y̨anomamö: An Interdisciplinary Study in Human Genetics
   Magical Death
   Children's Magical Death
   Dedeheiwa Weeds His Garden
   Ocamo Is My Town
   Dedeheiwa Washes His Children

* These films are distributed by Documentary Educational Resources, 24 Dane St., Somerville, Mass. 02143.

Collecting Rasha Fruit
Woman Chops Wood
Arrows
Moawä Weaves a Hammock

3. Netsilik Eskimo films by Asen Balikci and Education Development Center. The most valuable for us were probably:
   Midwinter Camp I, II, III
   Autumn River Camp I, II
   Caribou Hunting I, II
   Fishing at the Stone Weir I, II
4. *Among the Family Herds,* a film of the Dodoth by Timothy Asch
5. Films on the social organization of baboons made by Irven DeVore and Education Development Center, particularly:
   The Young Infant
   Male Dominance in a Baboon Troup
   Evening Activities
   Observing Baboons from a Vehicle
6. *4-Butte-1,* an archeology film by Donald Miller from The University of California Extension Media Center
7. *Invisible Walls,* a film on proximics by Richard Cowan from the University of California Extension Media Center
8. *The River,* by Pare Lorentz
9. Films on birth:
   All My Babies, by George Stoney, a southern midwife training film
   Alexander: Birth of a Boy, Timothy and Patsy Asch—a sterilized, hospital birth
   Curing Ceremony, by John Marshall, a curing ceremony before a Bushman stillbirth

Appendix B: Slide Tapes Used in the Course

Bushman Environment
Politics, Religion and Ritual in an Egalitarian Society, five slide tapes by Timothy Asch of the Dodoth of northeastern Uganda

Appendix C: Slide Tapes

The following is a brief description of how they can be made: The simplest form is merely slides shown with whatever kind of sound one wants from sounds recorded while the slides were being taken, or to music or narration. The slides can be of any subject. Sound and picture are shown simultaneously, with the picture changed at appropriate intervals, either manually in response to the image or to a beep on the sound track or electronically with the use of a Uher or Norelco synchronizer.

Some years ago I went to Uganda to take black and white photographs of the Dodoth for Elizabeth Marshall Thomas. I have since made many slides from negatives by using the following technique:

I converted a bathroom droplight fixture into a small light-table that had a $5 dimmer in it, which would give variable light from a very bright photoflood bulb. A piece of glass was placed on top of the fixture to complete the light-table. A small muffin fan was placed at a cut-away side of the bathroom droplight fixture to blow the hot air from the photoflood lamp away from the glass above where a negative was placed, covered by a second sheet of glass which was hinged with a piece of tape. Above this was a Nikon reflex camera with an inverted 35 mm. lens—any lens would do for this—on a bellows extension. One can then photograph little tiny bits and pieces of each negative, with negative film, thereby producing a positive image. The film used, although a negative film, is called "fine-grain release positive," which is available at most camera stores, and is developed in Dektol Developer. The results are extremely good; the quality is superior to that of a photographic print, because there is much more tonal latitude in negative film than in a print. One could take, then, one negative of a Dodoth sacrifice and photograph eight to nine details, as well as the whole of the picture. With this system one can get so close to the negative that one can photograph easily an area 1/16th of an inch square, and enlarge it to the full frame of a 35-mm. negative.

A quick way to get positive slides from reproductions in a book or regular photographs or paintings in black and white or color is to use Ektachrome color film outside in the shade and have it developed locally.

If one has color slides that are particularly dark, yet would serve to illustrate a point, there is a way of copying them that will make them just as useful as if taken with a normal exposure: project the very dark slide in a very bright Carousel projector onto a Polocote screen held by a tripod clamp on a tripod in front of the projector. The projector will project the image on the Polocote screen, and it is rephotographed from the other side—in other words, you will be looking at, and filming, a rear-screen image. Light, coming through such an image, projected on such a small scale, gives one a very bright, clear image, illuminating detail in the dark areas. For dark color slides, normal copying techniques generally fail to produce a detailed image.

Appendix D: A Huge, Yet Inexpensive Screen

One of the props I experimented with was a very large screen. For elementary school classrooms, I devised a screen made out of tracing paper. One might think this would not be a durable structure, but after four years, the screen is still in good condition. I used a heavy form of tracing paper called Dietzgen #198H, which comes in widths of 40 inches. I laid three 12-foot widths on a clean gym floor and then taped them together on both sides with a very slight overlap, using half-inch Scotch Magic Transparent tape. At the bottom of this big sheet screen I rolled in three folds of paper a piece of quarter-inch by two inch lathing 10 feet long, attaching it with white glue and tape. At the top end I used a rug roller, the type of cardboard roller used as a core for wrapping up rugs by most large rug dealers or rug cleaners, and free for the asking from them. The cardboard is very strong and very light and will not sag over a 10-foot span. I then filled in both ends of the cardboard tube (which was about 3½ inches in diameter) with blocks of round wood, and in the center of these blocks I drilled a small ¾-inch hole and put in a ¾-inch dowel. There are two ways of supporting this large roller once it is upright and the screen has been rolled up. One uses a two-by-three and a Timber Topper can with a spring inside, to put over the top of the two-by-three. If one takes a two-by-three that is cut a few inches shorter than the height of the ceiling of the classroom and puts the can over the top, the spring gives enough pressure on the two-by-three and the ceiling to keep it rigid; indeed, often partitions are made by nailing sheetrock panels to the two-by-three, without putting nails into any existing surface. The top of the Timber-Topper can has a rubber pad on it to protect the ceiling. Now when one has two of these two-by-three uprights, one drills a hole near the top of them (about an inch in diameter); and through that hole one fits the dowel that has been fastened to the end of the wood block in the cardboard tube. We now have a cardboard tube that is 10 feet long, with our screen attached to it, suspended between two two-by-threes.

The next step is to wrap a thin rope around one end of the cardboard tube three times, after having tied the rope in a loop. If one pulls on one side of the loop, the screen will roll up; and if one pulls on the other side, it will roll down. When one has the screen up or down, one can fasten a cleat onto one of the wooden poles, and this will enable you to fasten the rope securely, so the cardboard tube doesn't move. When so desired, the screen can be moved from one end of the classroom to the other.

Another way of making the uprights for the screen is to fasten to a large block of wood (four inches thick and about 12 by 12 inches square) a pipe flange and then screw in a pipe (2½ inches in diameter). Then one fits into the pipe a railing about three feet high (known commonly as bannister railing). This makes an even more mobile structure. The bannister railing then has to be drilled at the top to allow the dowel of the cardboard tube roller to roll freely. At the end of the dowel that slips through either the two-by-three or the bannister railing hole, there should be another hole drilled with a nail that goes through this hole with a rubber band fastened on the sharp end of the nail, to keep it from sliding back out through the hole. When one has a screen, one can use it quite profitably for a whole year, in social studies and other activities, particularly for drama performances and shadow plays. The large screen, when it is down, divides the room quite nicely as a ten-foot wall. If one is going to use a lot of slides or movies in class that year, they can be shown by rear-screen projection—students can sit on the floor in front of the screen without disturbing the huge image. In fact, they can go right up to the image and touch it, and as the image is being projected from the rear, they will not block the light. A 1-inch lens for the projector is required to get a large image in a small room.

Appendix E: Filming

To do a proper job of teaching when using films, good pedagogical films must first be available. We have found so far that the most useful film for teaching anthropology requires a particular kind of shooting: detailed filming of naturally occurring sequences of social interaction. In this sense, sequence is defined as a span of social interaction in which two or more individuals, through the natural course of their social activities, unconsciously reveal patterns of behavior significant in their society.

The filming commences with the initiation of the interaction between individuals, it continues through the period of meaningful exchange, and it dissipates when this phase of interaction ceases: two people see each other from a distance; they meet and discuss the need for a sacrifice, perhaps; they conclude and part. An African market is composed of many sequences, though to varying degrees they are all connected. As people move from one group to another, they move from one sequence to another. Human interaction is composed of these sequences. The number of people involved varies from sequence to sequence; there may be a mob or only two. The film sequence would be a model of such a definable period of behavior.

Because of technical improvements, it is now possible for an individual to go into the field with a small, light camera of professional quality and a Nagra tape recorder (the size of a briefcase) and take film with lip-synchronous sound without wires attached between the recorder and the camera. Each unit remains independent. Previously the cost was prohibitive for ethnographic work, and a truckload of equipment was necessary.

One cannot photograph everything that occurs during a sequence. Inevitably one must be selective. If the photographer knows well the culture that he is filming, his selection can illustrate social relationships important to that culture rather than merely recording the event. He will not be shooting random footage of events in the hope that at some future date he will be able to piece them together to form a coherent whole. Thus the significance of a film is dependent upon the ethnographic knowledge of the photographer when filming and when editing. The photographer himself must be aware of the subtleties of the situation if he hopes to get footage that is of value ethnographically.

Each sequence should be photographed through the behavior and social interaction of a predetermined individual. One cannot hope to film the event insofar as it relates to a specific individual. He provides the necessary theme, or constant element. In a broader sense, an individual could be used to link together a series of sequences, thereby providing insights into his varied relationships and activities within his culture.

One of the biggest technical problems in making a film is photographic field. If one takes a long shot that includes everybody, one has a confusing general picture with individuals and actions too far away to see in detail. But the closer one gets to his subject—to isolated movements—the faster one must cut away from the detail to show the movement or object in its larger context. One must be able to see the external stimuli effecting movement. Close filming becomes a matter of integrating bits of behavior to form a whole, a problem which does not arise with long shots. The use of two cameras eases this problem, but for most fieldwork this is not feasible, as it probably destroys the indigenous social environment.

One of the main goals in filming a sequence is to film in such a way that at any time viewers can agree on the location of the camera and each of the subjects. The essential footage, without cut-aways or narration, must form a coherent pattern. A film sequence must indicate a continuous flow of action throughout, and the audience must be in agreement about the relationship of space and time. To date, few ethnographic or documentary films are constructed this way.

Finally, there are many advantages to developing one's footage while still in the field. This gives one an opportunity to see the quality of the footage and to edit sequences in order to judge their value and to lend insight and direction to future filming. It would be extremely useful to show these films to native informants in order to hear their interpretations of the events and their predictions about what might follow and what to watch for. This also would give added insight into the elements to focus on in future films. In addition, the reaction of members of a culture to their own behavior—whether on tape or on film—may provide further insights for the ethnographer.

It is also important, if money is going to be made available to make this kind of film, to think much more clearly about the film's organization, how it is to be archived, and how it can be best made available to the largest number of people.

Appendix F: The Research Film, the Archive and Retrieval System

An important aspect of our work in curriculum development is a "research film" including all the footage shot (in the order in which it was shot) with two sound tracks: one of the indigenous sound recorded during the shooting and the other containing all the information that the ethnographer can provide about the behavior shown on the unedited footage. Where possible the ethnographer will include a translation (Sorenson 1966). The research film is completed immediately upon returning from the field, by ordering and dating the footage, recording the ethnographer's comments, synchronizing the two tracks with the picture, and by collecting and indexing the available notes, including all relevant publications.

> That new discovery may be made from the retrospective study of ethnographic research films has been the hope which has motivated our developing a method for preparing research film and establishing a research film archive. The problem of utilizing such films for study depends upon the phrasing of questions that can be answered from films and the developing of techniques for this use of film. The phrasing of research questions is a matter for the investigators in each scientific discipline. However, the cinematographer can provide a technology for cataloguing film, for viewing and studying film, for retrieving the images, locating and copying frames, and comparing sequences which may make handling of film data so convenient as to influence workers in various scientific specialties to turn to film documents for original inquiry (Gajdusek and Sorenson 1968:48–49).

In the past two years, many people have wanted to use the ethnographic footage of the Yąnomamö taken by Chagnon and the author for research and curriculum development. However, unless the research film is combined with the ethnographer's comments and the relevant literature, and unless it is stored in an active public archive with the facilities for viewing it, it is extremely difficult for anyone except the film-maker to use the footage. We feel that film supported by public funds should be available to all who could utilize this resource.

At present, we are negotiating with the Smithsonian Institution to provide storage and viewing facilities for existing and future films. The Smithsonian could prove to be an excellent national center for ethnographic research.

A prototype research film archive now exists at NINDS under the direction of Dr. Carleton Gajdusek. Research prints are deposited in the NINDS research film library along with associated copies of field notes, journals, charts, maps, logs, appended typescripts, still pictures, and tape recordings. All these materials are filed by date of collection in the field for cross-reference. Indexed descriptions of the contents of the film are prepared and published, and then the work print goes into a file of material available for special film production.

References and Further Reading

American Anthropologist, Journal of the American Anthropological Association, Washington, D.C. All book and film review issues.

Asch, Timothy, 1971, "Report from the Field: Filming the Yąnomamö Indians of Southern Venezuela," *Program in Ethnographic Film* 3(1). Washington, D.C.: American Anthropological Association.

———, 1972a, "Ethnographic Filming and the Yąnomamö Indians," *Sight Lines* 5(3).

———, 1972b, "Making Ethnographic Film for Teaching and Research," American Anthropological Association Program in Film *Newsletter* 10(2).

———, 1972c, "New Methods for Making and Using Ethnographic Film," Paper presented to the Research Film Committee, African Studies Association, Philadelphia.

———, 1974, "Using Film in Teaching Anthropology: One Pedagogical Approach." Paper presented at the Ninth International Congress of Anthropological and Ethnological Sciences. In Paul Hockings, ed., *Visual Anthropology.* The Hague: Mouton and Company.

———, John Marshall, and Peter Spier, 1973, "Ethnographic Film: Structure and Function," *Annual Review of Anthropology,* Vol. 2. Palo Alto, Calif.: Annual Reviews, Inc.

Balikci, Asen, 1970, *The Netsilik Eskimo.* New York: Natural History Press.

———, and Quentin Brown, 1966, "Ethnographic Filming and the Netsilik Eskimos," Educational Services, Inc., 55 Chapel Street, Newton, Mass. 02158

Benedict, Ruth, 1955, "Continuities and Discontinuities in Cultural Conditioning." In Margaret Mead and Martha Wolfenstein, ed., *Childhood in Contemporary Cultures.* Chicago: University of Chicago Press.

Biocca, Ettore, 1971, *Yanoama* (biography of Helena Valero). New York: E. P. Dutton.

Bruner, Jerome S., 1960, *The Process of Education.* New York: Vantage Books.

———, 1966, *Toward a Theory of Instruction.* New York: W. W. Norton and Company, Inc.

de Brigard, Emily R., 1973, *Anthropological Cinema.* Museum of Modern Art, New York, Department of Film program, May 17–July 3.

———, 1974, *Anthropological Cinema.* New York: Museum of Modern Art, in press.

Carnegie Commission on Higher Education, 1972, *The Fourth Revolution: Instructional Technology in Higher Education.* New York: McGraw-Hill Book Company.

Chagnon, Napoleon A., 1968, "The Culture-Ecology of Shifting (pioneering) Cultivation among the Yąnomamö Indians." In *Ecology in Anthropological and Ethnological Sciences Man-Culture-Habitat Relationship.* Eighth International Congress of Anthropological and Ethnological Sciences, Tokyo.

———, 1968, "Yąnomamö Social Organization and Warfare," in Morton Fried, Marvin Harris, and Robert Murphy, eds., *War: The Anthropology of Armed Conflict and Aggression.* New York: Natural History Press.

———, 1968, *Yąnomamö: The Fierce People.* New York: Holt, Rinehart and Winston, Inc.

———, 1973, *Studying the Yąnomamö.* New York: Holt, Rinehart and Winston, Inc.

Collier, John, Jr., 1967, *Visual Anthropology: Photography as a Research Method.* New York: Holt, Rinehart and Winston, Inc.

Comité International du Film Ethnographique et Sociologique, 1967, *Premier Catalogue Sélectif International de Films Ethnographiques sur l'Afrique Noire,* Paris: UNESCO.

———, 1970, *Premier Catalogue Sélectif International de Films Ethnographique sur la Région du Pacifique.* Paris: UNESCO.

———, 1973, *Premier Catalogue Sélectif International de Films Ethnographique sur l'Asie et le Moyen Orient.* In press.

Documentary Educational Resources, *Film Catalogue,* 24 Dane Street, Somerville, Mass., 02143.

Dow, Peter B., 1972, "If You Were a Baboon, How Would You Tell Your Mother You Were Hungry?" *Natural History* 81(4).

England, Nicholas, in press. *Music Among Bushmen.* Cambridge, Mass.: Harvard University Press.

Gonzalez, Nancie, in press "Anthropology in Grade Schools," *Human Organization.*

Heider, Karl G., 1972, *Films for Anthropological Teaching,* 5th ed. American Anthropological Association, 1703 New Hampshire Ave. N.W., Washington, D.C. 20009

Hockings, Paul, 1972, "Undergraduate Teaching with Film," *Program in Ethnographic Film* 4(1). Washington, D.C.: American Anthropological Association.

Kohl, Herbert, 1967, *36 Children.* New York: New American Library, Inc.

Lee, Richard, 1965, *Subsistence Ecology of !Kung Bushmen.* Doctoral dissertation in anthropology, University of California, Berkeley.

———, and Irven DeVore, in press, *Kalahari Hunters and Gatherers.* Cambridge, Mass.: University Press.

Maranda, Pierre, 1972, *Introduction to Anthropology, A Self-guide.* Englewood Cliffs, N.J.: Prentice-Hall, Inc.

Marshall, John, 1958, "Man as a Hunter," *Natural History* 67(36); and 67(7).

Marshall, Lorna, 1957, "The Kin Terminology System of the !Kung Bushmen, *Africa* 22(1).

———, 1959, "Marriage Among the !Kung Bushmen," *Africa* 29(4).

———, 1960, "!Kung Bushman Bands," *Africa* 30(4).

———, 1961, "Sharing, Talking and Giving: Relief of Social Tension Among !Kung Bushmen," *Africa* 31(3).

———, 1962, "!Kung Bushman Religious Beliefs," *Africa* (32)3.

———, 1965, "The !Kung Bushmen of the Kalahari Desert." In James L. Gibbs, ed., *People of Africa.* New York: Holt, Rinehart and Winston, Inc.

———, 1969, "The Medicine Dance of the !Kung Bushmen," *Africa,* 39(4).

———, in press, *!Kung Bushman Studies.* Cambridge, Mass.: Harvard University Press.

Mauss, Marcel, 1954, *The Gift.* London: Cohen and West (first published in 1925).

Mishler, Anita, 1970, "Protocol Materials To Teach New Perspectives: The Classroom as a Learning Community." Cambridge Mass.: Education Development Center.

Rasmussen, Knud, 1931, *The Netsilik Eskimos.* Report of the Fifth Thule Expedition, 1921–1924, 3 (1 and 2). Copenhagen: Gyldendalske Boghandel, Nordisk Ferlag.

Rossi, Peter H., and Bruce J. Biddle, 1966, *The New Media and Education.* Chicago: Aldine Publishing Company.

Saettler, Paul, 1968, *A History of Instructional Technology.* New York: McGraw-Hill Book Company.

Sorenson, E. R., 1967, "A Research Film Program in the Study of Changing Man," *Current Anthropology* 8(5):443–469.

———, and Carleton Gajdusek, 1963, "Research Films for the Study of Child Growth and Development and Disease Patterns in Primitive Cultures," a catalogue of research films in Ethnopediatrics. Bethesda: N.I.H. Nato Institute of Neurological Diseases and Blindness.

———, and ———, 1966, "The Study of Child Behavior and Development in Primitive Cultures," *Pediatrics* 37(1)2.

Spradley, James P., and David W. McCurdy, 1972, *The Cultural Experience: Ethnography in Complex Society.* Chicago: Science Research Associates, Inc.

Thomas, Elizabeth Marshall, 1959, *The Harmless People.* New York: Alfred A. Knopf.

———, 1963, "Bushmen of the Kalahari," *National Geographic Magazine* 123(6).

PAUL BOHANNAN/*Northwestern University*
MERWYN S. GARBARINO/*University of Illinois at Chicago Circle*
EARLE W. CARLSON/*Northwestern University*

25 *An Experimental Ninth-Grade Anthropology Course*

In 1965–1966 we initiated a full-year course in anthropology for ninth-graders at the North Shore Country Day School in Winnetka, Illinois. The school, a member of the National Association of Independent Schools, has about twenty students in its kindergarten and in each of its first five grades and about forty in each of its sixth through twelfth grades. It is divided, as most independent schools are, into a lower school, middle school (grades six through eight), and an upper school (grades nine through twelve). It is what is commonly called a progressive school because it emphasizes close personal attention to each student, recognizes human capacities beyond the traditional scholarly ones, and tries to train the visual and aural senses as well as the capacities for reading, writing and computing.

Our students met in two sections, each for forty minutes daily with about eighteen students in each section. These students were "selected" in the sense that their capacities ran from average up. We had a few very bright students but none who were not of at least average capacity and achievement. We think it is an important point that the students of the school are not selected primarily for their scholarly capacities—in fact, that is rather far down the list in the requirements. It is, however, assumed that the students are able to absorb and profit from a good high-school education. Therefore, we had no problems with dropouts or with lack of motivation. We had boys with long hair, and, like the rest of the school, we treated it merely as a hair style.

The course was undertaken when, in a discussion with the headmaster of the school, Nathaniel S. French, Bohannan criticized several new curricula that used anthropology and sociology as decorations on a course that was basically economics and history. He felt the right way to handle the material was to treat the principles of sociology and anthropology as the fundamentals, history and ethnology as the primary sources of data on human existence, and economics and political science as the two disciplines most helpful in evaluating today's newspapers.

---

*Reproduced by permission of the American Anthropological Association from the *American Anthropologist* 71(3), 1969.

When an opening occurred in the social studies faculty in the upper school, French suggested that if Bohannan would plan such a course, he (French) would appoint whatever teacher of the course the two of them found satisfactory. Bohannan replied that although he needed a co-worker in this program, he would like to teach part of it himself and would prefer a partnership with a second anthropologist rather than to try directing a program taught by someone else. At that time Garbarino had just finished fieldwork among the Seminole Indians and was writing her dissertation. She agreed to become a partner in this project. Throughout the year the two taught more or less alternate units, one for a few days, then the other for a few days; meanwhile keeping in close touch and exchanging "field notes." We did not find this arrangement difficult, and as far as we know, the students did not find it confusing or objectionable.

From the beginning of the program our goal was to teach students in high school the data, methods, theories, and insights of the behavioral sciences. Although we concentrated on anthropology, we also included a good bit of sociology, no inconsiderable amount of psychoanalytic viewpoint and psychological anthropology, some historical and more prehistorical material, and some theory derived ultimately from economics and political science. Our goal was to provide the best available scaffolding for studying history and comprehending the present-day human situation.

We considered ourselves responsible for the first year. We knew that our students would proceed to at least one more year, and some of them to three more years, of social studies in their high-school careers. We wanted to establish a set of viewpoints that would be useful and expandable in the later years with as little as possible to be relearned, unlearned, or jettisoned. We are aware, of course, that ethnographic details will be forgotten. Nevertheless, we are also aware—and our experience proved overwhelmingly—that only good ethnographic factual material can make such a course interesting.

The year was divided into three quarters. In the first quarter we began with American Indians, proceeded to Africa, and included some theoretical material on cultural theory and the structure of society.

The second quarter dealt with human origins. We taught the principles of evolutionary theory (about three quarters of our students had already studied it in their biology course), the evolution of mankind and the development of man's capacity for culture, and prehistory up to the creation of the ancient civilizations, therefore including the acquisition of agriculture, metalworking and the like.

In the third quarter we made a comparative study of civilization. We began with the ancient Near Eastern civilizations and then discussed the history and culture of the civilizations of China and Japan.

What we accomplished could be called a course in non-Western Civilizations. Although it was anthropologically based, it was not limited to anthropology.

Bohannan and Garbarino came into this teaching experiment without experience in teaching high-school students. (Carlson, who took over in subsequent years, had such experience.) Except for our own children and those of our friends, we had not faced or dealt with teenagers since we ourselves had been teenagers. Our basic fear was, How do you teach social science to people who necessarily, because of their age, have limited social experience? We quickly found the answer: You fill them in. And we soon realized that "filling them in" is as good a definition as any other of a liberal education.

First Quarter: Cultural and Social Anthropology

We began with Theodora Kroeber's *Ishi in Two Worlds* (1963). We found this a very good book for ninth graders because they read it with interest, consider it an adult book, and react emotionally as well as intellectually to its contents. On the first day they were assigned the Prologue to Mrs. Kroeber's book. Ishi, the last surviving member of the Yahi tribe of Central California, was driven by hunger and fear to a slaughterhouse outside of Oroville, California, where he was discovered one morning in a corral. Because no communication was possible and because he was naked and on the verge of exhaustion, he was taken to the Oroville jail. The anthropologists at the University of California in Berkeley were notified, and T. T. Waterman went immediately to Oroville to see him.

In spite of the fact that Mrs. Kroeber goes to some pains to point out that the sheriff's action in putting Ishi into jail was neither stupid nor brutal, our ninth graders had a serious reaction to it. On the basis, then, of no more than the Prologue, they started a discussion in which they blamed their own people, and in a sense themselves, for being inept and guilty of mistreatment of Ishi and the Indians. When this attitude became evident, we asked them what they thought would happen if the last wild Indian were to wander today out of the Skokie lagoons into Winnetka; what would we do with him? After a few minutes discussion one boy raised his hand and said, "We would obviously have to put him in jail." We were encouraged by the first session of the class because we were finding the students willing to get involved in both the material we had assigned to them and the discussion of hypothetical situations set in their own community.

The second chapter of *Ishi* gives background material on California Indians. We had the ninth graders make maps, on the basis of the one Mrs. Kroeber gives, and do a little encyclopedia work on the problem of American Indians. Thereafter, we went through this book a chapter a day. The only part of our teaching techniques that might be difficult for someone who is not a professional anthropologist to emulate is that when students asked questions, we answered them with as precise detail and as much theory as we thought necessary to make the details understood.

By the time they had finished *Ishi,* they were well launched into the study of cultural anthropology. It would, perhaps, be possible to write a teacher's guide for this material. It would be vastly preferable, however, for the teacher to have a few good courses in anthropology and to deal with the questions and the material as it comes up. Our two sections brought up different points; yet we think that they were approximately equal in their achievement at the end of the unit. Certainly we could not have achieved so much if *we* had brought up the points and told them what they were to be interested in.

Next we read Alice Marriott's *Ten Grandmothers* (1945). We found this, like *Ishi,* a superb book for teaching ninth-grade social studies. It is an adult book—a factor that cannot be underestimated. With a series of characters running through the story, Dr. Marriott explains the pressures and responses that led the Kiowa Indians to change and develop as they did in the middle nineteenth century. It is fascinating history and superb anthropology and, like all Dr. Marriott's work, well written. On the basis of this material we discussed Plains Indians at length, and some of the students wrote special reports, taking their materials from such standard books as Spencer and Jennings' *The Native Americans* (1965) and Driver's *Indians of North America* (1961).

When we took up our third Indian group, the Iroquois, we made a serious mistake. We considered, and still do, Hazel Hertzberg's *The Great Tree and the Longhouse* (1966), part of the A.A.A.'s Curriculum Development Project, a very fine book. It is, however, written for the sixth grade, and we did not realize that our ninth graders would not be willing to adjust to what was for them easy reading. The attitude was best summed up by a girl who asked, "When are we going to get through with this kid stuff and back to books written for just people?" This judgment is not a considered judgment on Mrs. Hertzberg's book; it is a statement that ninth graders, in our experience, are not able to utilize material that is easy for them nearly so well as they are able to cope with material that is difficult for them. Although we have not tested this proposition further, it is our hunch that it is probably true in all groups of ninth graders. We found that they could not consider the book as just a book from which they should study and get information and perhaps write things that would bring it up to their level. They didn't see it that way. They felt that we were trying to keep them in a junior role. We think that they understood the intellectual aspects of the problem, but emotionally they nevertheless felt that this book was not for them; we also have a hunch that they would not feel that any book that was written for the schools was for them. They need and want well-written material that can be of interest to an adult.

After discussion of these three books, we gave a few short lectures on introductory aspects of the theories of cultural anthropology. We told students how to take notes on lectures, showed them how lectures should be organized and how to judge a good one, and tried to get them to evaluate critically in the structure of lectures. We graded them on the notes they took on our lectures and found that we had to teach them the outline form.

The lecture material covered the prehistory of the American Indians in a very fast sweep, as well as some statements about the culture areas of North America (we used one created by Garbarino on the basis of all the others available; we think that this makes no difference, and the one in Driver can be utilized with no comparative material at all). For a special project that each student was required to do during the quarter, some of our more advanced students made a study of American Indian origins, basing it primarily on Driver and on Spencer and Jennings. We also led a series of discussions in which the ecology and economic adjustment, the political forms, and the family life of the three peoples we had studied were compared, bringing this into line with other material that the students happened to know, with material they had read for their reports, and with their own experiences in families in the middle and upper middle class in the Middle West.

We then attempted to go over the same general ground, but more briefly and in more depth, for the peoples of Africa. We began with Colin Turnbull's *The Forest People* (1961). This book, about the Pygmies of the Congo, is a superb example of what ought to be written to teach anthropology as a basic subject in the social sciences for high-school students. We might add, parenthetically, that the first twelve chapters are, for this purpose, better than the last three, and would suggest that teachers consider skipping the last three chapters unless they plan to use them for considering how a person from one society reacts to geography and social situations that are strange to him. Since we had already explored this idea in *Ishi,* we did not find the last three chapters as useful as the rest of the book.

But *The Forest People* is a hard act to follow. Therefore, rather than try to use material that we thought less suitable, we went directly to a summary position and used Bohannan's *Africa and Africans* (1964). This book (which has fast become obsolete in all except Chapters 7–14, although a new edition, with Philip Curtin as coauthor, is in the works) was not terribly successful in the ninth grade, because it contains too many generalizations, too much summary, and too few ethnographic examples. What we finally did was take a single point from each one of the chapters around which could be built discussions and outside assignments. Our discussions of slavery, of religion, of witchcraft, and of social organization went very well.

We spent about ten days at the end of the quarter on a summary. We gave lectures on basic ideas and fundamentals of social organization, including the family, political structure, and anthropological ideas of economy and religion. We also assigned Douglas Oliver's *Invitation to Anthropology* (1964). We thought, and still think, that it is a very good, short summary of what anthropology is about. Our students did not concur. The reasons that they gave—and this underscores a point we have made above—was that it was not about anything, by which they meant that there were no ethnographic facts or examples in it.

Our conclusions at the end of the quarter were that if you have a lot of good ethnographic fact, well presented and organized, ninth-grade students are extremely interested in it; they do make an association between the people they read about and their own lives so that the teacher can capitalize on the inherent comparative aspects of anthropology; and they are able to learn and are even willing to help to create cultural and social theory.

Second Quarter: Human Origins and Prehistory

Our course took place before the material created by the Anthropology Curriculum Development Project, directed by Dr. Malcolm Collier, was available, but Carlson used that material in the second and third years. The biggest problem in the first year was the plethora of material—highly repetitious, but with comparatively few outstanding books suitable for ninth graders. The irony, or perhaps one should say it is the cause, is that human origins and prehistory have attracted more nonprofessionals and more writers of "books for young people" than all the rest of anthropology put together. Some of the nonprofessional summaries are good. Others are worse than misleading.

This particular topic presents a problem we do not know how to combat: the primary question that both the writers of the books and our ninth graders ask is "what happened in prehistory?" They want to be given a more or less precise history of the development of man and of his culture and civilization. Obviously, with each new discovery, or at least with each major new theoretical development, it becomes necessary to reconstruct prehistory all over again. This means that each of the books contains a reconstruction and that the reconstructions all too often do not jibe. The reason for this is sometimes to be found simply in the dates of the books, but it is often due to special pleading by the authors. Solving this problem means that the teacher must give a great deal of factual and theoretical material on the evolution of the human animal and culture. We gave this material in lecture form because we did not find books that could do the task for us. The "technician's books" were almost all too detailed for this grade level and for our task. The "writer's books" hurried over the technical problems to get to the romance. Highly technical books on evolution, such as those of Dobzhansky, we did not even try at this grade level. Perhaps we were wrong. We used *Early Man,* by F. Clark Howell and the editors of *Life* (1965). It was extremely useful, but it is difficult to use without supplementary material because there is too much material in it for a casual reading and too little to go into any one aspect of the problem.

Because of limitations both in time and in students' backgrounds in biology, our intention was to teach the concepts rather than the actual mechanisms of evolution. On this level, it was expected that there would be little reason for students who had not had biology to suffer any real disability.

In teaching biological evolution we had to combat the tendency of all the students to take a teleological view of natural selection. We had hoped, by presenting cultural anthropology first, to avoid the problem of purpose in evolution. That is to say, by first showing the present day range of human behavior and then adding the time dimension, we would avoid the bugaboo of tribal peoples seen as contemporary ancestors and would demonstrate that nonliterate peoples have histories, although not written, as long as that of Western man. We think it helped, but we still had to counteract the idea that the aim of evolution was to produce Western man.

We stressed in lecture and discussion that biological and cultural evolution were inseparable in man's development and that through the evolution of culture man was able to move into many new environmental zones without gross biological changes. Culture is thus shown as the extension of man's senses and his nonbiological means of adaptation, including adaptation to the social environment. Man then differs from the other primates primarily because of his culture.

To demonstrate the concept of adaptation we first discussed the exploitative potential of various environments at different stages of cultural evolution, but we hoped to avoid the pitfall of geographic determinism by presenting the environment as permitting a range of forms within its limits. Therefore, even in an extreme environment such as the circumpolar regions, while shelter is an essential, we found many forms shelter could take.

In terms of our stated aims of teaching concepts rather than mechanisms, we believe we were successful in the following ways. The students demonstrated reasonable grasp of natural selection and adaptation, and (within the limits of the facts available to them) they understood the positive feedback relationship between culture and biological evolution. They also learned the generally accepted sequence of fossil forms of the hominid line.

Growing out of our study of adaptation to environment, we progressed to post-Pleistocene times and to culture changes arising from the domestication of plants and animals. Domestication in our presentation was only one of many regional adaptations in response to a slowly changing climate. In this fashion we hoped to avoid the mental image of the neolithic or agricultural revolution as a sudden insight on the part of an individual—a point of view many students have. Indeed, for one of our weekly written assignments we got a lively, imaginative story about *the* woman who invented agriculture. It is quite likely that many students tend toward a similar picture of domestication, and we wanted to correct that view. We think we did.

It was easy to generate interest in the changes in behavior caused by a change from hunting and gathering to food production. In fact, the very concept of domestication as opposed to taming resulted in lively class discussion, and some students became so interested that they did independent study projects, which they reported to the class. Among the topics studied were the attributes selected for domestication and a comparison of productive usefulness of children in hunting and gathering as opposed to agricultural societies. There was some class amusement at the realization that children were usually burdens to hunters whereas they could contribute importantly to an agricultural community. Our students had never before considered children as anything but assets by their mere existence.

Here a note on independent research might be injected. The limitations of the school library presented a real difficulty. This is not to be taken as a criticism of the particular school we taught in, for it is highly unlikely that any high school would have adequate resource material in either cultural or physical anthropology unless some recent attempt had been made to obtain it. The fact is that library materials must be expanded if anthropology is to be taught, and from our experience it would appear that most of the expansion must be in the direction of college-level literature, *not* adaptations written for high school students.

Third Quarter: Comparative Civilizations

By the end of the second quarter we had reached the point of talking about civilization as a subset of culture marked by certain specific terms or traits. The students became interested in the "causes" of civilization, a point we could not have started with. To come up with the necessary and sufficient causes of civilization we turned to the data of the archaic civilizations of the Old and New Worlds—Sumer, Egypt, and Mexico. We went to the various works of V. Gordon Childe, taking his criteria for civilization as a place to start. Then, through discussions with the students, we elicited their ideas of the way these various criteria are to be ranked in importance.

From reading and lectures, discussion ensued, and the students decided that although agriculture was necessary to civilization, it was not sufficient "cause"—that, indeed, no one "cause" was sufficient in itself. That conclusion led to the question of why all agriculturists did not achieve civilization and to a discussion of social and ecological limitations to evolutionary potential.

During the whole unit on early civilization we had the students compare *culture* and the *special form* of culture that is called a civilization. The result was happily more than just a list of traits. It came close to being a statement of cultural process and increasing structural complexity. Without using such professional jargon, the students came up with the recognition that civilization has more components and greater specialization of the components than the noncivilized society. Briefly, we discussed the greater complexities and possibilities of food production with differentiation of primary producers and full-time labor specialists versus food collecting or producing with very little specialization.

The students decided—as anthropologists have known for over a century, but we do not think that we precooked their decision—that the presence of writing was one of the two most important of the several criteria of civilization. The only new thing about this idea is that they discovered it in terms that were not available in the nineteenth century when it was discovered—undoubtedly rediscovered—by anthropologists. They pointed out that the capacity to store culture, created by writing, vastly enlarges the choices open to people. At the same time, it reduces the amount of effort it takes to maintain a cultural level. The result is a proliferation of specialist roles and hence the complexification and cultural achievement that civilization exhibits. We had lively discussions about the fact, which they pointed out with no prodding, that the same thing is happening again today because computers provide new kinds of storage mechanisms for culture and that we are only just beginning to feel the effects of them. In our summary we noted that just as speaking means that the demonstrator is not necessary in all situations of learning, and just as writing means that the actively participating teacher is not necessary in all situations of learning, so in the present situation, the written record has been changed out of recognition so that word symbols too are no longer necessary in all situations of learning. It seemed unlikely to our students—and to us—that computers would replace writing any more than writing replaced speaking or speaking replaced demonstration. (We missed, here, an opportunity to explain a Gutmann scale.)

The other item they thought was of fundamental importance was full-time specialization of arts and industries. However, there were many other characteristics of civilization that we discussed, including oral tradition and common expectations as means of social control in homogeneous societies as opposed to the need for a codification of laws in the heterogeneous society that appeared with early urbanization. Urban culture itself, as a new and different set of relationships, was dwelt upon at some length. Without calling it such, we came close to Redfield's rural-urban continuum as a concept useful in describing development over time as well as change in space.

Largely because the class *demanded* some sort of chronology—we think as a result of prior conditioning—we did a time line of invention from 10,000 BC to AD 1500, comparing Old and New World chronologies. The comparison involved not only the invention of technical improvements, such as the wheel and metallurgy, but also the appearance of major structural change, such as the beginnings of complex village life. The visual stimulus of a time line was important to the students. We think now that throughout the year more visual treatment should have been incorporated, perhaps in the form of films.

We ended the unit on early civilization with a few lectures and some discussion of the European Neolithic, the spread of food production into Europe, the Mediterranean influence in the north, and the steppe pastoralists' introduction of the domesticated horse into central Europe. The emphasis here was on the cultural backwardness of Western man during the formative period of civilization and the importance of diffusion and recombination of many ideas from many sources. Once again we tried to avoid the tendency to think of European as the purposive aim of development and tried to stress the importance of interaction in the spread and elaboration of the few very great simplifying inventions and new combinations of old knowledge.

We spent more time on the ideas of civilization than we had originally planned, so we did not have as much time as we had hoped to deal with non-western civilizations of the nineteenth and twentieth centuries. The class read two books: Etsu Sugimoto's *Daughter of the Samurai* (1934) and Francis Hsu's *Americans and Chinese* (1955).

The *Daughter of the Samurai* is an excellent book, which ninth graders read with great attention. It contains a great deal of ethnographic material, and Mrs. Sugimoto's coming to America, finding the culture strange, and contrasting it with her own makes this good teaching material. Since Bohannan knew some Japanese ethnography and had been in Japan, he was able to fill in the book with materials on Japanese history, the nature of the Meiji Restoration, and how the social structure led to modern economic development in a way that it did not in most other traditional societies. We also went into such things as how properly to sit, stand, walk, and eat. We tried to conduct one class on the floor, sitting Japanese fashion; we lasted about fifteen minutes.

In the case of China, we had Francis Hsu himself come and discuss further some of the ideas in his book. This was an exciting part of the course. At the end, as a summary, we repeated very quickly the criteria for civilization, drawing on Chinese and Japanese examples.

The Following Two Years

Like many another beginner, we tried to put too much into this course, and in the years following it, Carlson (a doctoral candidate at Northwestern), who took the course over from Bohannan and Garbarino, has not proceeded to the third quarter but rather has spread the original material from the first two quarters over the year, finding that in that way, he could get through it without rushing. New materials have also changed the course, and we now use the experimental units of the Anthropology Curriculum Study Project on "Early Man" and "The Great Transformation" of society and culture from hunting and gathering bands to the beginnings of urban civilization.

The basic strategy was, however, left intact: to introduce the students to as much ethnographic material as they could handle in the first half; then to proceed to human origins and culture history, with a strong emphasis on archeological methods and reasoning by inference, in the second half.

This plan, like any other that a teacher of such a course may produce, necessarily demanded some modifications. Students discovered that they needed evolutionary concepts, geographical orientations, and biological insights to deal with ethnographic and, particularly, historical material. These were reinserted.

The plan for the first half was much the same as that outlined above for the first quarter. The materials were the same with the following exceptions. Hazel Hertzberg's book was replaced by Chapter 9, on the Iroquois, from Wendell H. Oswalt's *This Land Was Theirs* (1962). In the Africa section we followed Turnbull's Pygmies with Elizabeth Marshall Thomas's *The Harmless People* (1965), and we inserted there the material from the A.S.C.P. on the Kalahari Bushmen and the materials from *Early Man* in *Life's* Nature Series, edited by F. Clark Howell (1965). This book proved invaluable in this context and later as an introduction to the idea of man's development through the Pleistocene. In the second year talks and discussions on the Tiv were conducted by Laura Bohannan, and her *Return to Laughter* (1965) was read by the class. This book proved stimulating to advanced students, but it can be more safely recommended for the upper grades of high school than for the ninth.

In the third year no appreciable changes in materials or approach were made, but as the terminal assignment of the first half, each student worked through a monograph approved in advance. The student reported to the class, then, the essence of what he had read and commented on its special value for our studies. Invaluable for this assignment were the paperback volumes in the Spindler series,* Kluckhohn and Leighton's *The Navaho* (1962), and Drucker's *Indians of the Northwest Coast* (1963).

Conclusions

We think we have proved that the three of us can teach anthropology to middle-class ninth graders as readily as we can to freshmen and sophomores in college. In many ways, indeed, it is easier to teach ninth graders. There is less resistance on the part of the students, which may, of course, be a characteristic of this particular group of students, although we are not convinced that that is the case. There is a great eagerness to learn the bases and techniques of social life. At this particular time of their lives, students are struggling with becoming adult members of society. Besides being an important educational period and the time when most students go through the experi-

**Editor's note:* The reference here is to the Case Studies in Cultural Anthropology (CSCA) edited by George and Louise Spindler and including nearly 100 studies of cultures around the world. The series is published by Holt, Rinehart and Winston, Inc.

ences of puberty and adolescence, high school (and perhaps this continues for the first two or three years of college) is a rehearsal period for adult life; it is something like watching the prepubertal ten- or eleven-year-old boy rehearsing for adolescence. Social science has a great deal to say directly to these people. It tells them about choices in behavior and allows them to ask questions about behavior in their own society and in comparative contexts. Our students, by and large, were not interested in social sciences merely as subject matter or as the basis on which to make reforms and commitments. They were interested in these things, but they were even more interested in creating their own techniques of social living on an adult plane, and for this reason they gave it an attention that goes beyond the specific data, while at the same time the data allow them to compare and contrast their own situations with it. In short, social science is a good way to learn something about life at this time (and perhaps at any other) of one's own life.

On the other side of the coin, there were some problems we did not expect. Statements in class, in texts, in written themes had to be taken *very* seriously in order to convince students that this was not just another assignment but that their communications carried information about themselves and their culture as well as about the subject matter. This care precipitated some crises for students, who thought they were only to say "nice things" about primitive or prehistoric peoples. We found a stubborn sentimentality for the underdog; we did not allow the sentimentality to go unchallenged, but the process of finding that sentimentality can cover prejudice and that they were not as respectful of other human beings as they had thought, or as they tried to make out, was sometimes painful. There was a tendency to turn the world into good guys and bad guys; Ishi and Turnbull's pygmies were good guys, and White civilization was the bad guy. We did our best to make them examine these ideas and go deeper than a good-guy/bad-guy dichotomy into the religion, world view, technology, and history of the groups, and somehow to gain respect for groups and individuals still closer to themselves in experience without the kind of guilt (which is systematically taught to them somewhere) that ultimately will cripple their attempts to make reforms. At the age of fourteen the biases of mature Americans are not yet entirely internalized; the problems our students faced can be compared with those faced by youth anywhere. We think that the possibility of penetrating cultural biases through anthropological studies appears greater at this age than at eighteen. However, we also think that the problem is that teachers have been brainwashed into saying "What 'they' do is good for 'them.'" A teacher once told Bohannan in a workshop, "Their ways are as good as ours." He asked, "Good for what?" Her immediate reply was, "Good for them," and she could not get beyond that.

This leads to our conviction that the difficulty in applying this sort of program lies largely with the fact that teachers are not adequately trained in anthropology. Bohannan and Garbarino have worked at training teachers in a summer institute and in an extension course for Northwestern (also treated as "in-service training" in some of the local high schools). We found the task overwhelming, and for two reasons. First of all, the better the teacher, the more difficult it is to retrain him. We mean this as a compliment, if a rather left-handed one, to successful and good teachers. What such teachers want, and what they should have, is material to add to their already successful courses. They want material to upgrade and enrich their courses, and they often think of using the social sciences from this point of view. We think that such material should be supplied. We would much rather have good teachers using good materials in ways of which we basically disapprove than to have good teachers using bad materials in ways of which we basically disapprove. We would, in fact, much rather have good teachers teaching things of which we disapprove on professional grounds than to have bad teachers teaching materials we think superb. Therefore, we have come to the conclusion that training social-studies teachers should be done in full-blown M.A. programs for teachers who take a year, or even two years, off to take M.A.s in one of the social sciences, or else that it should be done before a teacher goes out and begins to set up his courses and his style of dealing with them. We hope their superintendents and school boards can be brought to concur. We are of the opinion that good teachers are legion in the schools of this country, at least in the areas with which we are acquainted, and that what they need is more and better teaching materials and a much freer hand in using those materials.

The second reason that we think the teacher-training task is overwhelming and must be done in undergraduate and M.A.T. programs, is that for the scholar or the school administrator to insist upon it is to earn the resentment of people who consider themselves successful and have some pretty good bases for their opinions. Our schools today are burgeoning with new curricula in the social sciences. The "new social studies" has become a jargon term—and a pejorative one. When one looks at the wide variety of the curricula being produced, it is not to be wondered that the very best teachers are skeptical.

It cannot be said after these three years that we have found *the* curriculum or *the* program for the proper study of man in the ninth grade. We *can* say that we are unanimous in our rejection of certain materials for this level and only a little less wholeheartedly unanimous in those we accept; incidentally, our unanimity includes our students.

The greatest challenge is working out curricula that integrate objectives, methods, and materials into a series of units. It is easy enough to make lists of objectives and lesson plans to develop them over time, but the unpredictable nature of ninth graders makes any plan highly tentative. The rationale for *making* such plans is, of course, that it gives the teacher adequate command of his material so that changes of plans will not throw him for a loss. Carlson found in teaching the A.C.S.P. materials that he tended to rely too heavily on following the intricate lesson plans and suggestions uncritically, which means, of course, without reference to the particular students in front of him. Teachers not trained as anthropologists usually find them extremely helpful and rich in material. Carlson often found it profitable to abandon the form while retaining the essence of the A.C.S.P. materials; for all that, we all think these are the best prepared materials we know for teaching anthropology in secondary schools.

Our mode of teaching was based on what today's educators are calling "inductive principles" of "discovery." However, we found that ninth graders also have to be filled in; the teacher must allow himself, his information and opinions, and his character to be used as raw material for the discoveries of his students. "Filling in" is best done, in anthropology courses of this sort, by giving facts. The amount of theory that students need can be determined on a "demand" basis. Theoretical presentations should *follow* the facts if the maximum number of students are to gain some appreciation of theory. Stating a theoretical position and then illustrating it is probably poor pedagogy anywhere (except, perhaps, in graduate seminars that are about theory). Certainly it is bad pedagogy in the ninth grade. By the second semester our students had enough sense of theory to apply it to what they were studying and to demand more when they needed it, although certainly, sometimes we sensed the demand before they did. Obviously, the danger of the "inductive method" is that students may discover things that are either wrong or obsolete. This is an especially great risk in social studies.

Finally, we want to emphasize the vast profit that we ourselves got from teaching this course. We were, in a very real sense, daily driven to the wall. Fourteen-year-olds will not be put off with jargon and expertise. We hope that more of our colleagues will try such courses and that they too will discover that the learning that is part of every teaching experience was never more vivid and more fun than with good high-school students. The anthropological point of view is congenial to young people. Young people test the anthropologist's ingenuity and challenge his professional stereotypes.

References

Anthropology Curriculum Study Project, 1967, *Study of Early Man* and *The Great Transformation.* Chicago, Ill.: 5632 S. Kimbark Avenue.

Bohannan, Paul, 1964, *Africa and Africans.* New York: Natural History Press.

Bowen, Elenore Smith (Laura Bohannan), 1964, *Return to Laughter.* New York: Natural History Press.

Driver, Harold E., 1961, *Indians of North America.* Chicago: University of Chicago Press.

Drucker, Philip, 1963, *Indians of the Northwest Coast.* New York: Natural History Press.

Hertzberg, Hazel W., 1966, *The Great Tree and the Longhouse.* New York: The Macmillan Company.

Hoebel, E. Adamson, 1958, *Man in the Primitive World: An Introduction to Anthropology.* New York: McGraw-Hill Book Company.

Howell, F. Clark, and the Editors of *Life,* 1965, *Early Man.* New York: Time-Life Books.

Hsu, Francis L. K., 1953, *American and Chinese: Two Ways of Life.* New York: Schuman.

Kluckhohn, Clyde, and Dorothea Leighton, 1962, *The Navaho.* New York: Doubleday & Company.

Kroeber, Theodora, 1963, *Ishi in Two Worlds.* Berkeley and Los Angeles: University of California Press.

Marriott, Alice, 1945, *Ten Grandmothers.* Norman: University of Oklahoma Press.

Oliver, Douglas, 1964, *Invitation to Anthropology.* New York: Natural History Press.

Oswalt, Wendell H., 1965, *This Land Was Theirs: A Study of the North American Indian.* New York: John Wiley & Sons.

Spencer, Robert F., and Jesse D. Jennings, 1965, *The Native Americans.* New York: Harper & Row.

Spindler, George, and Louise Spindler, n.d., Case studies in cultural anthropology, continuing series. New York: Holt, Rinehart and Winston, Inc.

Sugimoto, Etsu, 1934, *Daughter of the Samurai.* New York: Doubleday & Company.

Thomas, Elizabeth Marshall, 1965, *The Harmless People.* New York: Random House.

Turnbull, Colin, 1961, *The Forest People.* New York: Simon & Schuster (Reprinted by Natural History Library, N 27).

DIANE A. TROUBETTA REYNOLDS/*Stanford University*
NORMAN T. REYNOLDS/*National Institute of Mental Health*

26 *The Roots of Prejudice: California Indian History in School Textbooks*

For a subject worked and reworked so often in novels, motion pictures, and televisions, American Indians remain probably the least understood and most misunderstood Americans of us all.

American Indians defy any single description. They were and are far too individualistic. They shared no common language and few common customs. But collectively their history is our history and should be part of our shared and remembered heritage. Yet even their heroes are largely unknown to other Americans, particularly in the eastern states, except perhaps for such figures as Chief Joseph and his Nez Perce warriors of the 1870s, Osceola and his magnificent betrayed Seminoles of the 1830s, and possibly Sacagawea, the Shoshoni "bird woman" who guided the lost Lewis and Clark expedition through the mountain passes of Montana.

When we forget great contributions to our American history—when we neglect the heroic past of the American Indians—we thereby weaken our own heritage. We need to remember the contributions our forefathers found here and from which they borrowed liberally.

—John F. Kennedy

This chapter focuses on the ways in which public school textbooks perpetuate and encourage stereotypic thinking about California Indians. We analyze the history of California Indians as it is treated in three textbooks.[1] These books contain the kinds of distortions found in many, perhaps most, public school textbook presentations of American Indians.[2]

We first became aware of the distorted textbook reporting of American Indian history in the fall of 1970 when one of us (D.R.) was teaching social studies at a junior high school, and the other (N.R.) was taking a survey course

[1] J. W. Caughey, *Land of the Free* (1967); M. Williams, *California: A History* (1965); and J. Reith, *California and the West,* (1965). All three were published and approved for use in all California public schools by the California State Department of Education.

[2] American Indians on university campuses and elsewhere frequently refer to themselves as Native Americans. While we in no way denigrate this usage, we use the term "American Indian," since it is more widely used and recognized by the public.

on North American Indians at Stanford University. In the course of these experiences we were struck by the limited knowledge of Indian cultures and by the stereotypes we had acquired through our own educations. We were also struck by the vastness of the literature available on native North American cultures and shocked by the enormous gaps and distortions in the textbooks.

We divide our presentation into four major sections. In the first section, entitled "Content Distortions,"[3] we compare the textbook versions and anthropological and historical sources on the following topics: groups, languages, physical types, political organization, warfare, California Indian history during the Mission Period, and, finally, the fate of the California Indians. We do not attempt to provide complete coverage of all available materials on these subjects. Hopefully, we provide enough information to challenge or refute particular distorted statements and impressions conveyed by the textbooks.

The second section we label "Evaluative Distortions."[4] Here we describe the ways in which the textbooks overtly and covertly encourage ethnocentrism—the feeling that whites are basically superior to Indians and that the cultural traditions brought here by white settlers were and are superior to Indian customs and beliefs. Our examples of content and evaluative distortions sometimes overlap.

The third section of the paper provides discussion of statements and objections that have been put to us by teacher and student groups to whom we have presented the paper. We end the chapter with conclusions and recommendations relevant to teachers, students, textbook authors, publishers, and people generally concerned with the issues of education and prejudice.

Content Distortions

> There is a difference between a book for general readership and one accepted for classroom use. In the first case, the individual has a choice and this choice we must protect. The student has no choice. He is compelled to study from an approved book and in this case, we have the right to insist upon truth, accuracy and objectivity (Statement of the American Indian Historical Society to the California State Board of Education, March 1968).

[3] Content distortions: statements that directly contradict information available in historical and anthropological accounts; also statements that are not factually incorrect in and of themselves but that when left as such or taken with other similar statements leave the reader with a distorted picture of particular customs or cultural institutions.

[4] Evaluative distortions: material presented from an ethnocentric viewpoint, e.g., only as white settlers might have perceived an event; statements that make an overt value judgment without qualifying it as such; statements or methods of presenting material that produce stereotyped thinking about labeled groups.

Ethnic Groups

The textbooks imply that American Indians, or specifically California Indians, were basically of one culture. Each textbook varies in the extent to which cultural uniformity is emphasized and in the particular ways this impression is reinforced. We will concentrate first on one textbook and the ways in which it obscures or distorts the extent of cultural diversity among California Indian groups.

The following is a summary of the material found in *California: A History* which is relevant to California Indians and their cultural diversity. The text points out that different tribal groups lived in pre-Columbian California, and some particular aspects of culture are discussed in some depth. Tribes are mentioned by name and characteristics of some of the tribes are described.[5] Differences and similarities among tribes are also discussed. We will now look more closely at exactly how these areas are covered.

Of the 314 pages of the book, 48 are devoted to a discussion of California's native inhabitants. There are eight chapters within these 48 pages. One chapter is devoted to pointing out that different tribes lived in California. This chapter, entitled "Some of the People Stayed in California," is only one page in length and mentions no Indian groups by name. Thirty-two Indian groups are listed by name on a map on page 30, but in the first 48 pages of the text itself, only seven different tribal names are mentioned. Actual tribal names are used only twenty-four times when referring to California Indian groups. The seven named tribes are discussed in sixty-three sentences, which are just parts of six pages. These six pages, in turn, make up parts of only three chapters out of the total of eight chapters devoted to the natives of California. In the twelve pages of thought questions which follow the chapters on Indians, no tribal names are mentioned.

Despite the fact that this text devotes relatively more space to Indian cultures and does acknowledge in general terms their differences, the small space devoted to discussion of tribal differences and the tendency not to use the names of different Indian groups are part of the way in which the impression of cultural uniformity among Indians is conveyed. Throughout the first eight chapters labels are used to lump different Indian groups together rather than distinguish them from each other. The discussion of spiritual beliefs in Chapter 6, for example, refers to "California Indians" and "the Indians" as all sharing the same beliefs and does not mention the fact that spiritual beliefs differed from one group to another. Again confronted with generalized labels in Chapter 5 on law-making and in Chapter 7 on child-rearing practices, the reader can only come away with the belief that these aspects of culture were uniform throughout all groups in the state.

[5] See our section on political organization of California Indians for an explanation of the term "tribe" and the reasons why this label is technically inappropriate. We use "tribe" occasionally, but prefer the term "ethnic group," which A. Kroeber suggests (1925).

In the discussion of laws there is no mention that there was no single chief for all the California Indians, no tribal council for all California Indians, and no single body of laws for all California Indians. In fact, most ethnic groups were independent and autonomous.

> The extreme of political anarchy is found in the northwest, where there was scarcely a tendency to group villages into higher units, and where even a village was not conceived as an essential unit. . . . The Yurok, Karok, and Hupa, and probably several of the adjacent groups, simply did not recognize any organization which transcended individuals and kin groups (A. Kroeber 1925:830).

Contrast this with the textbook statements:

> There must be rules. . . . The set of rules, or laws, and the way the laws are carried out is called government. People who are to follow the rules like to help decide who is going to see that the rules are carried out. This is true of us. It was true of the Indians. Indians in each village talked over their rules, or laws. . . (Williams 1965:34).

By using general labels instead of mentioning ethnic groups by name, and by failing to point out the extremes of variation among ethnic groups, an impression of cultural uniformity is created. The general impression created is also inaccurate as a description of social and political control and decision-making among California Indians.

When cultural differences among groups are discussed in *California: A History,* they are often of such a general nature that they add nothing to our knowledge of California Indians as opposed to any other people. For example, "Some Indian tribes lived where the weather was often cold or at least cool" (Williams 1965:26); "All the California Indians had special clothes to wear at special times" (1965:27); "Some had tools that others did not have. . . . Some had food that others did not have" (1965:27). Do these statements tell us anything about California Indians that would not be true of peoples of the rest of the world? Note also that in these statements true differences and similarities are alluded to, but without mentioning which tribes these differences and similarities refer to and without giving any concrete examples. When concrete examples are given, as in Chapter 1, where house types are described in some depth, housing structure is related simply to the ecology of an area rather than to named tribes. When an individual ethnic group is described, it is in such a limited manner that one does not derive any real feeling of what the life experience was like for this group. A good example of this is in the description of the Mohave and Yuman groups: "The Mohave and Yuman tribes lived near the Colorado River. They were the only California Indians who learned to plant seeds. They were the only California Indians who learned to plant their own food." Thus, in three sentences are the Mohave and Yumans dispensed with. Nowhere else are they mentioned again. Note that in this space two of the seven tribes mentioned by name are covered. Would one expect a student to have a feeling for the life experience of a Mohave or a Yuman on the basis of such a description? Did their lives consist only of planting food or were there other aspects of their culture? Were Mohave and Yuman life-styles the same, or were there differences between the two groups? Were there differences among individuals within each group?

The text by Williams consistently fails to describe the diversity of life within individual tribal groups. The longest description given of any group is twenty sentences devoted to the Chumash (1965:31). Chumash men are described as boat makers, Chumash women as basket makers, and the Chumash in general as traders. The text does not indicate whether these were the only tasks that they had to perform. Thus the issue of intraethnic variations is avoided. The reader is not encouraged to explore the question or to imagine how the Chumash people as a group accomplished the innumerable tasks necessary for survival.

Languages

The textbooks discount and underemphasize the degrees of linguistic diversity or the variety of Indian cultures. *California and the West* acknowledges linguistic diversity among California Indians with one statement: "Groups of Indians who live in the same way and speak the same language are called tribes" (Reith 1965:50).

Williams' text contains three sentences about languages: "Indians who lived in the same place and spoke the same languages were called a tribe. . . . Each tribe had its own language" (1965:12), and "Tribes that lived near each other sometimes learned to speak each other's language" (1965:29).

This simplistic picture contrasts sharply with anthropological accounts. Dixon and Kroeber state that although exact relationships among the California Indian languages have been difficult to establish, at least twenty-one (mutually unintelligible) linguistic families have been identified (Dixon and Kroeber 1919). Out of a total of ten major language "phyla" for all of Continental North America, Voegelin (1966) locates five in California alone. Theodora Kroeber in writing for school-age children, reports that language variations in California were "even more varied than the large Indo-European stock or family with its Romance and Germanic and Slavic and Hindi divisions" (T. Kroeber 1965:15). Again in her book for school children, she notes that "only parts of the Sudan and the island of New Guinea offer so much language variety within comparable areas" (1965:15–16). Within the Yana language there were even separate dialects for men and women (Sapir 1921).

Textbooks ignore the possible interrelationships between language and culture. For example, psychological differences accompany linguistic differences. Theodora Kroeber hypothesizes that the Yahi dialect may have played a part in determining people's attitudes in facing gradual physical and cultural destruction: "The surviving Yahi seem never to have lost their morale in their long and hopeless struggle to survive." Their language "had equipped its speakers with strong feeling for the importance of speaking and behaving in such a way and no other. . ." (T. Kroeber 1965:21). Whorf has theorized that language is the determinant of one's world view. Reality exists only as it is conceptualized through language (Whorf 1941, 1956). Lee applied Whorf's hypothesis to the California Wintu Indian language in which she looked at Wintu grammar and vocabulary as a means of understanding Wintu world view (Lee 1938, 1943). While some linguists have argued against such linguistic determinism, none would deny that linguistic differences between human beings are likely to be accompanied by pervasive differences in culture. Such a concept could be taught in the context of American Indian history.

Physical Appearance

Descriptions of the Indians' physical appearance in the three textbooks analyzed need qualification. Reith's text (1965:48) states that the people who lived in America before the explorers arrived "had straight black hair, reddish brown skin, and dark eyes." Caughey's text (1967:46) asserts that "experts say the Indians were all basically of the same stock. . . . The Old World people whom the Indians most resemble are those of Asia." Williams' text does not discuss physical appearance at all. Gifford would agree with Reith regarding the physical features mentioned, but adds the qualification that

> Although it is customary to regard the American Indian race as quite homogeneous, as indeed it is when compared with the Caucasian race, we find that in California there are distinctive types in stature, in form of the head, face, and nose, to name only four principal characteristics. . . . California has among its living tribes examples of the shortest and tallest peoples of the American continent. The Yuki Indians of Mendocino County have an average stature for men of 157 cm. The Mohave, of the Colorado River region in Southern California, have an average stature, for men, of 171 cm., making a difference between the averages of more than five inches (Gifford 1926:50).

Therefore, the description in Reith of "Indian" physical appearance is misleading. The statement in Caughey is not only misleading but inaccurate without qualifications.

How closely do Indians resemble Asiatics, and what does "Asiatic" mean? The question of the racial origins of the American Indian is still being discussed in anthropology (Wissler 1950; Heyerdahl 1952). By saying Indians "were all basically of the same stock," Caughey's text avoids dealing with the issue that North American Indians may have originated from, or have been subsequently influenced by, migrations from different parts of Asia or even from other continents at different times and by different routes. For instance, Norsemen (Caucasians) and Pacific Islanders (Polynesian) may have landed at various times in North America and influenced genetic stocks. Furthermore, almost any scholar would balk at the thought that all Asians are basically one racial stock. According to traditional classification, the people of India are Caucasian, the Chinese are Oriental or Mongoloid, and the Japanese Ainu resemble both Mongoloids and Caucasians.

Most textbooks, including the three textbooks we analyzed, fail to point out the ways in which American Indians differ in physical features from Mongoloids. For example, Mongoloids have an epicanthic fold and American Indians do not; there are differences in skin coloring between the two groups; AB and B blood groups are found among American Indians but not among Mongoloids.

There are several reasons why the textbook descriptions of the Indians' physical features are undesirable and detrimental. First, of course, the statements in Caughey's and Reith's textbooks are historically inaccurate. Historical accuracy is especially important in books that purport to describe historical fact. Second, textbook emphasis on the uniform physical appearance of the American Indians reinforces an already common tendency toward stereotyped thinking about racial groups. For example,

> So overpowering is the impact of color upon our perception that we frequently go no further in our judgment of the face. Nor do we perceive the individuality of each face. While we are usually frank in admitting that all Orientals look alike to us, we are scandalized to learn that a common complaint on the part of the Orientals is that "Americans all look alike" (Allport, 1954:134).

Political Organization

The nature and extent of political organization among California Indians is another area that the textbooks either omit or describe in misleading ways. The most conspicuous feature of the chapters on Indians is that they lack all but the most superficial description of the political structures and philosophies represented in these cultures. The only statement in Reith's text referring to political or social organization is:

> The Indians of California lived in small villages. The village leader was called the chief. There was also a group of wise older men, called the council. The chief and the council made the rules for the people of their village (1965:50).

Williams' text devotes only two pages out of forty-seven to a description of Indian government. The text summarizes Indian political structure in the statement: "The California Indians had a simple form of government. Each tribe or village chose a leader. Each leader and his advisors made the laws and saw to it that the laws were obeyed" (1965:276). Caughey's text, after commending the California Indians for their skill in basket making and storytelling, states that "a few other compliments are given the gentle Californians, but not for skill in fighting, government, or turning out goods of much value. Their discoverers were not tempted to stay and have these people work for them" (Caughey 1967:41). Although the text is describing the attitudes of the first explorers, no ethnographic information is provided that would challenge the evaluation of those explorers.

By comparison, ethnographic source material reveals great diversity and complexity of political organization in individual Indian cultures, including those of California. In discussing different Indians of California, the textbook use of the word "tribe" in itself obscures the real nature of political organization among California Indians. A.L. Kroeber clarifies the use of the word "tribe" when he says, "Tribes did not exist in California in the sense in which the word is properly applicable to the greater part of the North American continent. When the term is used, it must therefore be understood as synonymous with 'ethnic group' rather than as denoting political unity" (1925: 830). He again points out the degree of political diversity among native Californians in the following statement:

> The marginal Mohave and the Yuma are the only California groups comparable to what are generally understood as "tribes" in the central and eastern U.S.: namely, a fairly coherent body of 500 to 5,000 souls—usually averaging not far from 2,000; speaking in almost all cases a distinctive dialect or at least subdialect; with a political organization of the loosest, perhaps; but nevertheless possessed of a considerable sentiment of solidarity as against all other bodies, sufficient ordinarily to lead them to act as a unit. . . .
>
> [The opposite extreme in political organization, political anarchy,] is found in the northwest, where there was scarcely a tendency to group villages into higher units, and where even a village was not conceived as an essential unit. . . . [If a northwestern village did act as a body,] it did so either because its inhabitants were kinsmen, or because it contained a man of sufficient wealth to have established personal relations of obligation between himself and individual fellow townsmen not related to him in blood (A. Kroeber 1925:830).

The Yurok, Karok, and Hupa, and probably several nearby groups, did not recognize any organization that transcended individuals and kin groups. Even among these "anarchistic" groups, a set of complex legal principles existed, the establishment and perpetuation of which are difficult for us to understand in a society such as ours, with a legislative, executive, and judicial structure. The complexity of Yurok law and custom are described in detail by A. Kroeber in his *Handbook of the Indians of California* (1925: 22–52).

The complexity of the concept of tribe in relation to political organization is also seen in discussions of political units among the Miwok. Before the disintegrating influence of European contact, "the lineage was anciently . . . a political unit, each lineage dwelling at its ancestral home. . . ." These groups were patrilineal and patrilocal "autonomous, political units" (Gifford 1926; also see a general article by W. Goldschmidt [1948]).

We have found no ethnographic data to support the statement that California Indians elected chiefs to head their governments. To varying extents, wealth and heredity were the primary determinants of chieftainship. According to Kroeber

> Chieftainship is still wrapped in much the same obscurity and vagueness as political bodies. There were no doubt hereditary chiefs in many parts of California. But it is difficult to determine how far inheritance was the formally instituted avenue to office, or was only actually operative in the majority of instances. In general it seems that chieftainship was more definitely hereditary in the southern half or two-thirds of the state than in the north central area. Wealth was a factor of some consequence in relation to chieftainship everywhere, but its influence seems also to have varied according to locality. The northwestern tribes had hereditarily rich men of great influence, but no chiefs. Being without political organization, they could not well have had the latter (A. Kroeber 1925: 832).

Warfare

In the area of warfare also, the textbooks differ from other historical and anthropological accounts. The textbooks stress the peacefulness of the California Indians. Reith's text states: "The Indians did not have to fight each other to get the things they needed. They were peaceful and contented in the pleasant land that was their home" (1965:54).

Ethnographic material supports the idea that California Indian groups were generally not warlike. The Mohave were a striking exception: "The frequent warring expeditions [of the Mohave] were . . . the result of the existence of a distinct class of warriors with whom warfare was an obsession . . . and who were continually eager to join a war party to exercise the military powers conferred upon them by the spirits." The warriors were also set apart by a distinct name, *Kwanamis* (brave men), and "there was no effective control over them" (Steward: 1947). Warfare between the Yuki and Nomlaki is described in another article by Goldschmidt, Foster, and Essene (1939). The same kind of discrepancies can be found in comparing the textbook and ethnographic descriptions of child rearing and socialization, religious beliefs and practices, and literary and artistic traditions among California Indian groups.

Anglo-Indian Relations during the Mission Period

The textbook versions of Anglo-Indian relations during the Mission period are blatantly contradicted by other historical sources. The textbooks emphasize how much the California Indians learned from the Spanish missionaries and how grateful they were for the instruction.

> By 1834 there were 30,000 Indians living at the missions. The mission priests taught the Indians about Christianity. They also taught them how to farm and do other kinds of useful work. . . . The padres were very proud of the Indians,

> and the Indians were very proud of their work. As time went on, many forgot about the way they lived before the coming of the Spanish missionaries (Reith 1965:70–73).

Williams' text states that

> Indian girls were taught by the missionaries to be good homemakers. . . . Indians who had been taught by the missionaries did not often make trouble. . . . Father Serra helped to teach the Indians in the missions of Baja California. . . . He wanted to make their lives easier for them. . . . They trusted him. . . . Before long, the Indians were helping the Spanish men with their work. . . . The Spaniards helped the Indians, too (1965:92–110).

Few Indians ran away from the missions, according to Williams' text; however,

> The Indians in that part of Mexico [Sonora] were not friendly to the Spanish. They would not learn from the priests at the missions. . . . Often the Indians killed white men and carried off women and children. . . . Once in a while a mission Indian had to be punished for something he had done. Sometimes such Indians ran away. . . . The runaway Indians taught the wild [i.e., nonmission] Indians how to steal animals and other things from the missions (1965:115, 126).

The picture that emerges is that the Indians who accepted the teachings of the padres and lived on the missions were happy, grateful, and civilized. The Indians who ran away from the missions or who refused to live on them were "wild" and "made trouble." The incidence of unhappiness or desertion of the missions is said to be slight, and the padres are characterized as uniformly gentle, self-sacrificing, and kind.

Historical accounts of Indian reactions to the Spanish missions and missionaries, and the policies of some of the padres, provide a shocking contrast to the blissful picture painted by the textbooks. First, there is evidence that not only were the nonmission Indians troublesome to the padres, but that the padres played a part, however inadvertent, in decimating the nonmission Indian population. Diseases were spread to the interior tribes by Spanish padres who penetrated beyond mission territory. Venereal and other diseases were also contracted at the missions and further disseminated among the resident population (Cook 1943a:11–12). "Another significant influence in not only reducing and disintegrating the homogeneous nonmission Indian population, but also in wrecking its morale, was the incessant capture and removal of individuals. Here we must reckon captures made for all reasons, including conversions" (1943a:26). Another source of nonmission Indian death and cultural disruption was the policy adopted by the clergy and soldiers of

> using mission neophytes as auxiliaries in warfare with the unconverted heathen. First utilized in a small way . . . the system was later extended on a broad front when elaborate expeditions to the deep interior were carried out. . . . Never in

> California within the knowledge of living man did there occur a profound upheaval or military conquest which threw large numbers of Indians into prolonged and bitter conflict. Precisely this happened after the Spanish occupation (1943a: 29).

The ironic result of assimilation to the Spanish way of life, to the extent of fighting to further the Spanish cause, is illustrated in the following account:

> In 1797 occurred the so-called "Raymundo Affair." This individual, Raymundo el Californio, took some forty neophyte mission Indians on a fugitive hunt in Contra Costa County [looking for runaway mission Indians.] They were set upon by [white] gentiles and virtually destroyed, much to the horror and alarm of the local authorities (Cook 1943a:32–33).

There are also historical documents that contradict the assertion that runaways from the missions were rare. The Indians "generally attempted escape, thus generating the widespread phenomenon of fugitivism. Seldom was the activity positively directed toward active physical resistance or insurrection" (Cook 1943a:31). However, the long-range effect of such resistance by the interior tribes was negative, especially for the Yokuts, Miwok, and Wappo.

> A peaceful, sedentary, highly localized group underwent conversion into a semi-warlike, semi-nomadic group. . . . In the missions in general, the racial fiber of the native decayed morally and culturally. . . . Confinement, labor, punishment, inadequate diet, homesickness, sex anomalies, and other social or cultural forces sapped his collective strength and his will to resistance and survival (Cook 1943b: 31–37).

Historical accounts also do not support the idea that the Spanish missionaries were uniformly kind, filled with affection and regard for the Indians. Indians were not allowed to receive sacramental ordination as secular priests or enter the religious orders during the Colonial era. Mestizos were also barred from the priesthood until 1588 (Madsen 1967). Missionaries used many techniques to force compliance with Christianity, such as forbidding young people in missionary schools to converse in their native languages, "so they would forget their bloody idolatries and excessive sacrifices" (Madsen 1967:373). Much more severe punishments were meted out by Fray Diego de Lánda, who worked primarily among the Maya of Mexico. Lánda organized an Inquisition in 1562 in which some 4549 men and women were tortured by various techniques and an estimated 6330 persons were whipped and shorn. A whipping on the bare flesh included as many as 200 lashes (1967:385). People were punished in other ways for refusing to adopt Christianity. "Indian children spied on their parents and reported idols found at home" (1967:375). Largely as a result of the struggle to convert the Indians, "a chaotic state of civil war emerged. Family fought against family, Christian and gentile against Christian and gentile, purely according to chance. All sense of racial unity was lost" (Cook 1943b).

The effects of the Church on Indian populations were in fact complex and various. We provide only examples of misconduct and cruelty to counterbalance the textbook accounts, which imply that missionary efforts were inspired by only selfless motives, and had only beneficial effects on Indians. By illustrating only the good and failing to point out the abuses Indians suffered directly at the hands of missionaries or indirectly from the missionary presence, the textbooks seriously distort the facts of history.

The Fate of California Indian Groups

Another aspect of Indian-white relations that is completely omitted by the textbooks is the ultimate fate of the Indian population that inhabited California at the time of the first explorations. The textbooks mention warfare between whites and Indians. However, they fail to mention the extent to which warfare led to a decline of the Indian population and the impact of whites on the ecological balance between Indians and their native environment. This disruption of the ecological balance contributed most significantly to a decline in population through disease, malnutrition, psychological demoralization, and cultural erosion.

> From the mission records it is ascertained that approximately 53,000 Indians underwent conversion. At the end of the mission period (1834) there were 14,900 left, a mean annual reduction of 0.9%. The surviving mission Indians together with the remainder of the wild tribes which were subjected to Anglo-American influence from 1848 to 1865 diminished from 72,000 to 23,000, a mean annual depletion of 2.9%. From these figures it is apparent that the impact of the settlement from the U.S. was three times as severe as that of pre-American colonization (Cook 1943c:92).

The three major factors that brought about this decline in population were war, disease, and starvation. The relative effect of warfare on population decline was approximately the same in both the Ibero-American and American periods, estimated at 11.5 and 8.5 percent respectively. The relative effect of disease and dietary maladjustment was much greater than that of warfare. Before and after 1848 an estimated 60 percent of the decline can be attributed to disease. Dietary maladjustment took the form of possible vitamin and mineral deficiencies on the missions, altered birth and death rates among all Indians, and depletion of food resources among unconverted Indians after 1848. "After the gold rush, the universal conversion of fertile valleys into farms, cattle ranching on the hills, and the pollution of the streams all combined to destroy the animal and plant species used for food" (Cook 1943c:92).[6]

---

[6] The specific population numbers mentioned by Cook are estimates and differ from those of other anthropologists. See, for example, Dobyns (1966). However, the relative trends of population decline and the factors which contributed to them are accurate in principle.

[7] We recognize the distortion in the statement. "Life was as it has always been." See Henry's Criteria #5 in Appendix II of this chapter for a general statement describing this kind of distortion.

The statistics on Indian population decline, although impressive, are nevertheless rather dry and impersonal. In the chapters "A Dying People" and "Episodes in Extermination," T. Kroeber in *Ishi in Two Worlds* gives a vivid account of the extinction of the Yana.

> In 1850, ten or more years before Ishi's birth, the Yana occupied some 2,000 to 2,400 square miles of land recognized as their own; they and their Indian neighbors distinguished four linguistic, territorial and cultural groups in the little nation of two or three thousand people—life was as it always had been.[7] By 1872, 22 years later, and when Ishi was perhaps ten years old, there were no southern Yana left; and only some twenty or thirty scattered individuals of the Northern and Central Yana remained alive. As for the fourth group, the Yahi, they were believed to have been entirely exterminated also and so they were except for a handful, Ishi among them. How small, and to the newcomers so unimportant, a fragment of humanity succeeded in involving the U.S. Army as well as citizens and vigilante groups, is a tale soon told, a tale which satisfies the Greek ideal of starkness of tragedy and unity of time. . ." (T. Kroeber 1965:43).

The aggressive and inhuman acts detailed in those two chapters can be labeled nothing less than genocide. Although the Yana and other whole ethnic groups who met similar ends go unmentioned in the textbooks, we are reminded that Anne Hutchinson and her thirteen children were killed by the Indians when she was expelled from her Massachusetts colony (Caughey 1967:63). This history of Indian-white relations between the Colonial period and the present time is also sorely neglected in the textbooks. In a review of the treaties and agreements between whites and Indians from discovery to 1887, McNickle (1957) points out repeated violations by whites. A U.S. Senate report made by the Special Subcommittee on Indian Education notes the following: "A careful review of the historical literature reveals that the dominant policy of the Federal Government toward the American Indians has been one of forced assimilation which has vacillated between two extremes of coercion and persuasion" (1969:9).

Many other aspects of Indian-white relations are either omitted or distorted in the textbooks. The textbooks virtually omit discussion of American Indians as contemporary members of our society. The textbooks ignore the fact that there are significant numbers of Indians living in the United States today, especially in the southwestern states, who continue to struggle to preserve their identities or assimilate to the white establishment in varying degrees. The nature and scope of their cultural identities and the political and cultural conflicts they are engaged in should be discussed in textbooks since their importance must be recognized.

[8] See Forbes (1969) for a discussion of the conflict contemporary Indians face in dealing with the white establishment. Felix Cohen, a professor of law, has written extensively on the conflict between Indian rights and U.S. laws. He gives an overview of the subject and the details of some major contemporary conflicts in his article "The Erosion of Indian Rights, 1950–1953: A Case Study in Bureaucracy" (Cohen 1953). The monthly newspaper *Wassaja* reviews American Indian current events (American Indian Historical Society).

By now the magnitude of the discrepancies between the textbooks and ethnographic accounts of Indian history should be apparent and should make clear the need for a more detailed examination of textbook accuracy.

We wish the reader to note that in the above section we have not specifically covered the varieties of California Indian religious and kinship systems, philosophies of life, healing practices, material culture and technology, and ritual or ceremonial customs. Who would be willing to assume that the textbooks are undistorted in their coverage of these areas? Would you? What reasonable recourse do students have who are required to read this kind of textbook material?

Evaluative Distortions

We now move to an examination of statements in the textbooks that express value judgments rather than factual information and illustrate the degree to which ethnocentrism pervades the textbooks. Ethnocentrism means the attitude that one's own culture is inherently and obviously superior, more desirable, and more natural than any other. The value judgments conveyed in the textbooks are basically that (1) white-European cultures were more desirable than or superior to Indian cultures; (2) Indians were able to see that white-European cultures were more desirable and therefore sought to replace their own culture with that of the white man; (3) by settling in the New World and sharing their culture with the Indians, white-Europeans improved Indian cultures and made life easier and happier for the Indians. In addition, ethnocentrism is revealed in the textbooks' portrayal of the white-European settlers versus the native inhabitants: The settlers are portrayed as full human beings, with a rich variety of abilities and emotions. The common humanity of the Indians is not emphasized. In this section we discuss particular aspects of value distortions under various subsections. The first two subsections are brief and general ones. They reveal the quality and breadth of ethnocentric distortions in the textbooks. Under the third subsection, "We-They Distinctions," we go into the content and implications of this distortion in more detail.

The Superiority of White Culture to Indian Culture

Many textbook statements convey the attitude that white-European culture is more desirable than Indian culture. The statement quoted earlier that the mission Indians were taught to be "good homemakers" by the padres implies that Indian women were formerly poor homemakers. Describing life on the ranches of southern California, Reith's text (1965:77) states that "the rancheros and their families wore much finer clothing than the Indians." Such textbook statements ignore the fact that a preference for one type of material or style of dress over another is relative to one's cultural background and personal preference. Williams' text (1965:17) describes the way in which mountain Indians made houses from logs and then adds, "The house did not look very pretty, but it was a good house." We hope that this kind of ethnocentrism is blatant enough to make further elaboration unnecessary. There is a certain irony, however, in the textbooks' statements which may not be obvious. Despite the alleged superiority of white-European culture, this culture has in fact adopted many Indian elements, to which great pride and admiration are now attached. The *American Home* (1970) magazine recently devoted an entire issue to architecture in the Southwest, which the text and photographs point out is a mixture of Indian, Spanish-Colonial, and European elements. Even more striking are the great number of plants and animals that are now a regular part of the nation's diet thanks to the Indians having discovered and/or cultivated these resources. For example, long before Mendel and modern genetics, some native Americans had hybridized wild corn and propagated many varieties of this plant (Wallace 1956). Crops such as tobacco, potatoes, corn, peanuts, squash, pumpkins, melon, and beans were cultivated by Indians, who later taught whites how to cultivate them. The knowledge of potato cultivation learned from Indians was taken to Europe by whites and played an extremely influential role in the histories of Irish and Russian cultures (Salaman 1949). Today, the potato is one of the major food sources in the world. How many American school children understand the importance to white cultures of what the Indians taught white men about the potato? We will not enumerate here all the various aspects of material cultures, technology, and philosophies that Indians contributed to white cultures and for which they are rarely given credit.[9]

Much evidence exists to dispute the textbooks' assertions that Indians were able to see the superiority of European cultures and that Indian life was much more pleasant after the coming of the white man. Williams' text (1965:123) states that "after the settlers came, the Indians had better food and clothing than they had ever had. They were more comfortable than they had ever been. Life was getting easier with each year that passed." Other statements of this nature can be found in the preceding discussion of the textbook descriptions of the mission Indians. The fact that physical and cultural conditions deteriorated after the white man's arrival (discussed in the section on Indian-white relations) is not mentioned by the textbooks. There is other available evidence that Indians were by no means uniformly eager to adopt all the white man's ways, and in fact are not so inclined even today. There has been no major permanent exodus of Indians from the reservations in the Southwest (Snyder 1968). Indians have not given up or replaced their aboriginal music; the musical forms borrowed have been from fellow Indian groups, not from Anglo and European musical traditions.

[9] See Hallowell (1957, 1959) and the general chapter in Driver (1969) for detailed discussion. Specific contributions of California Indian groups must be culled from these broader discussions.

Denial of the Basic Humanity of Indians

An ethnocentric attitude is conveyed by the textbooks in their treatment of the human qualities of Indians versus Europeans. For example, there are references in each textbook to several of the early settlers and explorers who were killed by Indians. The adventures and eventual death of settlers such as Jedediah Smith, Cabrillo, Rivera, and Drake are mentioned. Statements are made that indicate the settlers were in constant or frequent fear of death at the hands of Indians. "The trip to Oregon Country was difficult and dangerous." There were many hardships on the way. "At times the wagon trains were attacked by Indians who did not want the settlers to cross their land" (Reith 1965:233). In the section entitled "Brave Men Dared to Explore the New World," Williams (1965:92) states that there were many "wild" tribes of Indians in New Spain, and "some of them made trouble when white men tried to move into their lands." In Baja California: "The Indians were not friendly. . . . More than once they stole cattle from the missions. They even killed some of the soldiers and missionaries" (1965:94). None of the textbooks mention Indians by name or mention that Indians also braved many dangers in the New World, suffered hardships, and were often in fear of their lives, especially after the arrival of the Europeans.

Equally ethnocentric is the portrayal of all the early settlers and explorers as brave and good people. Sutter is described by Williams as "generous and brave," yet he had four large cannons installed at each corner of his house to keep troublemakers and unfriendly Indians out. Jedediah Smith is described simply as a trapper in search of new travel routes. In fact, he was one of a group of aliens who entered California surreptitiously or by force and who was hostile to the constituted government (then Mexican).

> The influence of such aliens in accentuating the turmoil among the valley tribes was definitely significant. . . . Their direct effect as homicidal agents, however, is very difficult to assess. Popular tradition and their own accounts give no indication that they were in any way inhibited with respect to killing natives when such action appeared desirable (Cook 1943a:7).

The textbooks do not attribute any admirable qualities to the Indians who fought for the preservation of their lands. Instead they are referred to as "wild" or as troublemakers. No such negative judgment is made of the early white rulers of the New World who were equally determined to keep out competing powers. Before a Spanish settlement was built near San Francisco Bay, the king proclaimed in the face of encroaching Russian trappers: "That land is ours! . . . Keep the strangers out" (Williams 1965: 96). The king is not called wild or a troublemaker for defending what he felt was his.

Similarly, the textbooks do not place the aggressive reactions of the Indians in their proper perspective. The feeling is conveyed that Indian aggression was a result of an inherent wildness or lawlessness in their cultures rather than a typically human response to the threat of physical and cultural destruction. S. F. Cook's description of Indian reactions to kidnappings and the imposition of mission life has been mentioned. These reactions were not always aggressive, and when aggressive they were usually responses to attacks or domination by whites rather than spontaneous manifestations of the aboriginal cultures. One notes an interesting difference in the textbook descriptions of the Indians who resisted white settlement versus those who did not resist. The Indians who were peaceful and friendly are pictured as simple and by implication naive. Those who resisted are termed wild and unprincipled. For example, the Indians near the Colorado were friendly to Jedediah Smith when he first entered California. "Then suddenly they changed!" (Williams 1965:161–162). Smith is ambushed and killed as he stoops, defenseless, to drink at a pool of water. The reader's sympathies are with Mr. Smith. The reader is given no indication that Smith may have committed violence against many Indian people before he was finally killed, or that the Indians had begun to understand the threat to their survival posed by the presence of Smith and other invaders. The textbooks fail to point out that the forceful encroachment of whites on Indian lands resulted in a vicious cycle of violence. Indian raids were not always in direct retaliation to a previous white attack. Instead, Indians and whites were considered by definition enemies and took advantage of many opportunities to do violence to each other. The important point is that this violence was a two-way process and that its origin lay in the forced colonization of the New World by whites.

We-They Distinctions

In both obvious and subtle ways all three textbooks portray the white-Europeans as the "we" or in-group and the Indians as the "they" or out-group. We concentrate here on one of the textbooks, *California and the West,* to detail an example of this process.

In carefully examining Chapters 4–7, we note a startling yet extremely subtle progression of Indians from an ingroup to an outgroup and a constant affirmation of whites as the ingroup. Finally, the whites become the only legitimate ingroup.

Only in the first two pages of Chapter 4, entitled "The First Californians," are Indians acknowledged as the first Californians; nowhere else are Indians again referred to by this label. By the end of the chapter, Indians are referred to simply as Indians, and thus the associations of Indians as the first people of California or even as Californians is dropped. Since the Indians were the first inhabitants of this area, one might have expected that the text would go on to describe Indians as the first discoverers, the first explorers, and the first settlers. Not so. Never are Indians referred to as discoverers, explorers, or settlers, and certainly never as the *first* discoverers, and so on. Instead, when the white Europeans arrive on the scene, they are labeled "the first explorers" of California in the chapter by that same title. Such labeling logically contradicts earlier statements in the text that Indians were the first Californians and by implication questions their right to such a designation.

In subsequent chapters Reith's text refers to whites as "explorers" and "settlers" and to Indians separately as "Indians." Several pages later these "settlers" have become "the Californians." By Chapters 6 and 7, when California becomes a legal part of the United States, these white settlers become "the Americans." Thus the general terms "Californian" and "American" have become so well defined through connotative usage to mean exclusively white that the reader is likely to fail to question the we-they implication of the labeling.

Settlers and Americans are throughout the rest of the book consistently white and distinguished from Indians, as in the following paragraph:

> Soldiers . . . accompanied these settlers. There were also Indians, servants, and large numbers of cattle. For many weeks, the settlers traveled northward through the dusty countryside. Finally on July 1,1769, the last group reached San Diego (Reith 1965:65–66).

It is clear from the paragraph that Indians are grouped with servants and cattle and separated from settlers and soldiers, who were white. If we go to a picture on page 77 of Reith's text, we are specifically told in the caption that "most of the servants on ranchos were Indians." In a description of Jedediah Smith's expedition from Utah to California, Reith states that "no American had ever come to California by land before" (1965:83). Smith's expedition was in 1862, hundreds of years after the first Indians had come to California. On page 81 when Reith asks, "Why were American settlers discontented under Mexican rule?" and, "Why did Americans come to California before 1848?" the meaning of American is again exclusively white and non-Indian. Through the process of repeatedly distinguishing Indians from "Californians" and "Americans," the label "Indian" has come to mean non-Californian, and even worse, non-American. With Indians having been defined as aliens, how can one wonder why many Indians feel alienated from American society?

In Chapters 18 and 19 of Reith, the dichotomy between Americans (whites) and Indians continues. The word "our" is used with the same exclusive connotation of whiteness in terms such as "our country," "our nation," and "our land." Reith's text has completely undone the original definition of Indians as the first Californians.

When in all the earlier chapters "Americans," "Californians," "our people," and "our land" clearly mean European and white, by the end of the book, in Chapter 20, when the word "we" is used, to whom would one logically assume that the word refers? The American identity of the Indians has been completely undermined while that of the European colonizers has been affirmed. The whole question of who had the "right" to the land, Indians or whites, is favorably resolved without any specific reference to the conflict being necessary. Similarly, any potential guilt on the part of the Europeans and their descendants is successfully avoided by considering America unsettled, unexplored, and unclaimed before Columbus. "We" discovered the Indians along with the land, the trees, and the gold, so naturally they all belong to "us."

We are not saying that we-they distinctions did not exist at the time of white-European settlement of America. Distinguishing Indians from whites or Americans and describing Indians as possessions, servants, aliens, or even animals does reflect how many whites viewed the Indians. These sentiments were even reflected in the law. Not until the passage of the Fourteenth Amendment to the U.S. Constitution in 1868 did Indians have the right to become U.S. citizens. Obviously, the passing of a law did not automatically change attitudes of many whites. Since these ethnocentric attitudes existed in reality, we feel that they should be included in the textbooks. We object, however, to the way in which they are currently included. The textbooks never directly and openly identify and discuss the nature and degree of white discrimination against Indians. The textbooks do not discuss the ethics of such prejudice, especially in view of stated American democratic ideals. Instead, the textbooks describe history from a white viewpoint and in doing so, condone it. To the extent that the reader also condones it, he makes a value judgment that the white viewpoint is right or at least acceptable. As a contrast to this approach, we cite the work of Dee Brown (1970), who makes the we-they attitudes of whites an issue in her tragic book *Bury My Heart at Wounded Knee.*

Other Value Distortions

All three textbooks provide examples of value distortions in many other areas. For example, the illustrations are almost exclusively of whites rather than of Indians. There are virtually no pictures of present-day Indians. Europeans are named as individuals much more frequently than are Indians. The hardships of the settlers are described or referred to more often than those of the Indians. The food, climate, and landscape of California are described as bountiful, mild, and hospitable for Indians, while the reader is told that the settlers often braved food shortages, storms, droughts, floods, and forbidding terrain. The Indians are pictured as living passively off of the "gifts of the land" while the white settlers and explorers are portrayed as actively and consciously creating a way of life for themselves. Whites are described as teachers, the Indians as learners. In fact, there was reciprocal cultural exchange.

Because of limited space we do not present in this chapter the detailed results of our analysis of all of the areas of value distortion. We do contend that the distorting processes are similar to the ones we have in part detailed with Reith's use of we-they labels. We wish to emphasize that one statement alone, one distortion of an aspect of culture alone, or even one highly ethnocentric textbook alone, might not suffice to bias a reader's point of view. However, all of these implicit and explicit distortions and value judgments, taken together, in many textbooks, taught over many years of a young child's life, cannot help but produce an ethnocentric bias against Indians and a false image of white superiority. We have analyzed only three textbooks. The Indian Historical Society, using the criteria we quote in Appendix II, analyzed approximately 170 textbooks and found they had none to recommend (Henry 1969).

Discussion

In this section we discuss some of the major effects of ethnocentrically distorted textbooks. We also deal with some of the statements we have frequently encountered when presenting our views to groups of educators and college students. We contend that both the group identities of Indians and non-Indians, as well as the relationship between the two groups, are affected by the kind of history taught in the textbooks we have described. In summary, we maintain the following: (a) The Indian, if he incorporates the image of his cultures presented in the textbooks, will develop a false self-image of inferiority, while the false self-image of the white will be that he is superior to the American Indian. (b) The attitude toward American Indians expressed in the textbooks fosters a paternalistic attitude of whites toward Indians and a reciprocal feeling among Indians of passivity and dependency on whites. The passivity and dependency engendered in some Indians then fulfills the prophecy that Indians are inferior to whites. (c) For both Indians and whites, tolerance and acceptance of cultural diversity is discouraged. Instead, an attitude is fostered that there is one right way of doing things—in this case the white way. (d) The textbooks commit what we term "culturecide," both in the way they gloss over true cultural differences existing between whites and Indians and in the attitude they foster that white cultures are superior and should have predominance over Indian cultures. (e) By failing to admit possible error, bias, or ignorance in their accounts, or even to list the sources of their information, the textbooks discourage, if not prevent, objective evaluation and correction of their descriptions. This is in direct opposition to what should be one of the main goals of public education, to teach students to recognize distortions. In other words, accuracy for accuracy's sake is but a small part of the reason textbooks should strive for accuracy and fairness in their accounts. Our public school system transmits values that become part of our culture as a whole and that affect our behavior in many areas of life outside the classroom.

Self-Image of Indians and Whites

There are several ways in which the textbooks damage the self-image of Indian Americans. The authors deprecate the Indians' native culture while they support and reinforce the attitude that the white-European conquest of the Indians is an indication of the superiority of white-European cultures. The white settlers are pictured as more human, complex, skillful, and wiser than the Indians they conquered. The textbooks are a predominately white yardstick to evaluate everything from architecture to political systems to homemaking. American Indian readers, insofar as they accept the textbooks as true and as representative of popular belief, cannot help but conclude that they are personally and culturally inferior to the average American white. Social, economic, and political discrimination is likely to reinforce this self-image and lead to a variety of possible destructive or self-punitive tendencies (Allport 1954). To persuade a group of people that they are inferior is to inflict immeasurable psychological damage upon them as individuals and to effectively discourage them from productive participation in society.

> A lowly status leaves its mark on persons as truly as the more applauded position does. An old aphorism states that responsibility makes the person. Although this is an important half-truth, the converse is equally true; for occupational subordination and lack of a voice in reciprocities tend to produce either resignation and a feeling of inferiority or a high sensitivity to the implied inequity. Insofar as a culture emphasizes equalitarianism, there is an imputed adverse comparison in all subordinate positions . . . (Hiller 1947:509).

Insofar as white students internalize the textbook versions of American history, their self-image will be unrealistically inflated. The problem of how to evaluate aspects of a culture is left untouched. The possible merits for the future of evaluating the white-European role in American history is lost as well. Instead, the white student is taught that he is better than other people just because he is white. This attitude discourages efforts toward constructive change and hardly prepares students for life in a multicultural world.

We have been told that we are overemphasizing the importance of textbooks in creating these distorted self-images and that we are underestimating children's ability to see through stereotypes and prejudice. We have heard such statements as: "By the time kids are in high school they know they can't take textbooks literally." Substantial evidence exists to the contrary. Hess and Torney, for example, have conducted and reviewed studies that lead them to state that children's political attitudes are shaped significantly by the school (Hess and Torney, 1967). Our personal experience with students who were using the Reith, Caughey, and Williams textbooks did not indicate that students are naturally skeptical about textbook distortions of Indian history. Once presented with supplemental material on Indians, they showed curiosity and interest. Their initial response to the textbooks, however, was passive acceptance. They also did not show signs of having received any less stereotyped a view of whites and Indians in American history in earlier grades, as some teachers have told us should be the case. We also argue that if, in fact, textbooks are not critical and the distortions are not crucial, then efforts to correct the textbooks should not meet with resistance based on strong emotional feelings. From our conversations with several school administrators and directors of multicultural programs, from our observations of some school board meetings, from classroom discussions with college students, and from the documented resistance of authors and publishers (Henry 1969), we have concluded that very strong feelings do exist against altering the textbooks in the ways we suggest.

Teachers have sometimes told us that we are underestimating their own abilities to recognize deficient textbooks and to supplement textbook materials on their own. We offer three arguments for the reader to consider: first, although willing to make a general statement of this nature, very few teachers have been willing to tell us that as individuals they are in fact proficient in the areas of American Indian, Mexican-American, or black history; second, we question the feasibility of stocking public school libraries adequately enough to supplement all the distorted and omitted information in all the textbooks used in all the public schools; third, from our acquaintance with teachers and some familiarity with their average work load, we doubt that the most conscientious, well-meaning, and energetic teacher could find the time necessary to become even minimally familiar with the various histories and cultures that make up the United States today. Placing the full burden on teachers is unfair and might justifiably arouse their resentment. Even cultural anthropologists usually specialize in no more than one culture or culture area because of the amount of time and energy necessary to understand the intricacies of any one culture. Edward Lukes is critical even of the specialized courses on American Indians which have been taught to date. He proposes a course outline for a more balanced presentation of American Indian history. A review of his two-page outline should convince any skeptic of the complexity and quantity of materials which must be mastered by teachers in this field (Lukes 1972).

Another opinion we have encountered is that the textbooks' view of America's European forefathers should be preserved in order to foster a feeling of loyalty to the United States and to make good citizens of its people. The textbooks, in fact, support an idealized view of the development of the present white establishment. We contend that there is a serious risk in basing loyalty on distortions of reality. If these distortions, and whatever part the establishment has played in creating and fostering them, are exposed, the possible risks of such exposure are that loyal citizens may become disillusioned, bitter, and even repudiate the stated ideals of American democracy. Perhaps this process in part explains some of the negative sentiments felt by youth and minority-group members toward the white establishment. We also urge that our readers examine the meaning of the words "citizen" and "loyalty" in the context of the stated ideals of American democracy as put forth in the U.S. Constitution and its amendments.

Several educators and laymen have expressed concern that to admit in textbooks that whites have made mistakes, thus destroying their idealized image, would undermine democracy. The meaning of true democracy, however, is based on the recognition that different viewpoints and opinions do exist among people and that accommodation to these differences need not entail conflict. How can we expect students to understand the democratic process unless we discuss with them how conflicts arise, how they are identified, worked upon, and resolved; and unless we also point out those cases where this process does not occur? A pioneering study of racism in Springfield, Massachusetss, led to several conclusions, including this observation:

> One of the major weaknesses of the previous attempts to inculcate democratic ideas is the fact that the teaching has been too idealized. Youngsters were given to understand that we in this country had already achieved a perfect democracy. . . . They soon became disillusioned because their own observations invalidated the idealizations. Children were taught, for example, that this is a land of equal opportunity and that in this country people are not discriminated against because of race, religion, or creed. . . .
>
> The committee decided, therefore, that issues should be faced squarely; that, while a positive and affirmative position on democratic ideals would be taken, it should be emphasized that we had not yet achieved the perfect democracy which is our goal; that the weaknesses in our democratic processes should be pointed out; and that how these weaknesses could be corrected and how our democratic processes could be strengthened should be discussed realistically.
>
> In order to eradicate blind and intolerant attitudes it is imperative that pupils understand all the constituent elements of our population, the historical backgrounds of these elements, and their contributions to American life.
>
> Finally, it is essential that democratic ideals be presented to students in a dynamic fashion calculated to fire their enthusiasm and to inspire devotion to democracy as the best means of achieving the good life for all our peoples (Halligan 1943:375). Educators themselves may be victims of this idealized education.

Not all educators who seek to force the culturally different student into an Anglo middle-class mold do so . . . because of a conscious desire to implement a superiority complex or because of a compulsive monocultural prejudice. Many have simply never thought of the United States as a culturally heterogeneous nation and, secondly, assume that minority groups must conform in order to compete in an Anglo-dominated society (Forbes 1968:10).

A paternalistic or parental self-image on the part of the white students is encouraged by the textbooks. The settlers are pictured as the strong, superior teachers and the Indians as the weak, inferior pupils. Indians are praised only when they achieve in white terms. The Indian is in almost every case a nonparticipant: He creates neither the standards by which he is judged nor the conditions in which he must perform. The establishment of Indian reservations has been one of the unfortunate consequences of such paternalistic thinking.

The paternalism that characterizes the textbooks undoubtedly encourages Indians to feel childlike and dependent on whites. Indians are taught in school to look to white culture for models and values. The stress on Indian assimilation into white society is often based on the assumption, permeating the textbooks, that Indians should model themselves after whites, rather than on the idea that Indians should share in and contribute to society without obligation to modify their native culture. The possibility of a reciprocal interaction between white and Indian cultures without assimilation of one into the other is disregarded. When, after years of forced isolation and dependency on reservations, Indians do act passively or dependently, many whites take this as proof of Indian inferiority, rather than as evidence of a misguided white policy toward Indians. (See R. K. Merton's discussion of the self-fulfilling prophecy [1948]; see also the 1969 Report of the U.S. Senate Subcommittee on Indian Education for a documentation of the corrosive effects on Indian self-reliance and self-sufficiency resulting from the federal government's Indian policy, see especially the conclusions summarized on page 21 of that report.)

Whatever one's opinions regarding the best relationship between whites and Indians, the point here is that this controversy and its ethical implications are ignored by the textbook authors, who quite casually and consistently adopt a paternalistic attitude in their writings.

For both Indians and whites, the textbooks teach that there is only one way of doing things. The textbooks do not teach tolerance and acceptance of cultural diversity; they do not teach the idea that men share a common humanity which overrides any one culture's judgments about food, clothing, or social customs. To the extent that ethnocentrism makes peaceful relations between groups difficult, it harms both Indians and whites.

Some people have argued that children cannot tolerate the idea that values may be relative and that to expose them to more than one way of doing things would confuse them. Discussion of this argument warrants more space than is available here. Hess and Torney, however, show that children begin learning very abstract and complex concepts such as "justice" and "democracy" in the early school grades. By implication they could learn the concepts of ethnocentrism and cultural relativity. They could be taught that a degree of ambiguity encourages thoughtful inquiry, creative scholarship, and ultimately a better solution to a problem. In fact, such is being tried in the Cupertino school system with some success (Masters 1971). Finally, one could point to Hitler as a man who defined problems concretely, unambiguously, simply, consistently, and thus in a distorted way. The consequences of deluding a whole nation are only too well known.

Culturecide

In effect, the textbooks commit what we term culturecide: the destruction of a culture, either by physical force or through symbolic means. The textbooks contribute to such destruction by distorting and omitting information concerning a cultural tradition. Since culture is primarily symbolic—contained in the minds of men—deprecation of or failure to transmit a cultural tradition is effectively to destroy it. All cultures teach an ethnocentric point of view toward other cultures. Such ethnocentrism becomes dangerous when one culture is more powerful than another. To the extent that one culture can oppress another by practicing ethnocentric distortion without restraint, it denies that oppressed culture's opportunity to perpetuate itself and ultimately to exist. There are many reasons why culturecide should be discouraged. It does harm to the self-image of people who share the cultural tradition being attacked. By destroying knowledge of other cultures we are in effect also preventing ourselves from learning from others' successes and failures. We are eliminating from our consciousness potentially useful alternatives, thus rigidifying our culture and reducing its ultimate chances for survival. Whites as a group are also threatened by the practice of culturecide. Destroying Indian cultures in the United States may not seem particularly dangerous to some whites, since Indians are a politically, militarily, and numerically weak minority. In the context of world demography, however, whites are a minority race. Should the world as a whole have the power to apply this principle of majority ethnocentrism in the future, whites may well experience the oppression of being a minority firsthand.

We have encountered two different kinds of objections to our notion that Indian cultures should be presented in our textbooks. One argument emphasizes practical issues: "It would take 20 volumes to write all the details you talk about. No one could write a textbook if you didn't allow some mistakes and omissions." Another argument is: "Textbooks must be kept general for children." We offer the following references as proof that summaries can be written that are undistorted and easy to understand: The Introduction to Kluckhohn's *The Navajo Door* (1944), the Introduction to *Sun Chief* (Simmons 1942), and Wissler's *Indians of the United States* (1940).[10] Furthermore, throughout his book, Wissler repeatedly points out examples of ethnocentric writing about Indians and also provides an excellent model for teaching the interactional nature of group problems. Theodora Kroeber's book *Ishi in Two Worlds* has been revised especially for school-age children. Although *Ishi* deals with only one Indian group and therefore cannot be used as a summary for all of American history, its widespread popularity among school children and its acceptance by educators indicates that public education can adapt to the principles we espouse in this paper.

The Indian Historian magazine includes a series of book reviews in each of its quarterly issues evaluating new books on the subject of Indians. The book reviewers' evaluations follow the principles quoted in Appendix II of our chapter. *The Weewish Tree* newspaper, using the same principles of evaluation, recommends books for young readers. Virgil Vogel (1968), in evaluating textbook treatment of Indians from a historian's perspective, includes a section of "Recommended Books" at the end of his article. Vogel makes the point well that "Although there is no comprehensive account of the Indian cultural contributions, there are commendable materials available at all [grade] levels" (1968:27).

An excellent multiethnic curriculum for seventh grade by Billie Masters is available and already being used in one school district that we know of.

[10] Wissler himself is not always free of ethnocentrism (1940:34). Because he openly addresses the issue of ethnocentrism as important, however, his ethnocentrism is more apparent, and he would probably be open to criticism leveled against his own ethnocentric biases.

In Appendix I we list the major concepts covered in each of the eight chapters of the curriculum. These chapters emphasize the cultural complexity and sophistication and achievements of Native Americans.

In Lesson I, they introduce the student to the concepts of Anglo-American, majority group, minority group, prejudice, and stereotype in a section under "Vocabulary." In the "Evaluation" section at the end of Lesson I, the student is asked to define those terms and is asked to "write one example of how the Native-American people have been misunderstood," and "In a brief paragraph describe how the Native-American has been wrongly stereotyped by the Anglo majority."

We also wish to emphasize that we are not criticizing the textbooks because of a few errors. What we object to, first of all, is that each textbook is written consistently, page by page, from a biased point of view. Our second objection is that none of the textbooks admit to the possibility of error or teach any self-correcting mechanisms (See Postman 1971); none discuss the problems inherent in writing a multicultural history or even provide a bibliography. Are the textbooks so above possible error that they need not include the sources of their information?

Teachers have reminded us that history is, after all, subjective and that there may be no such thing as truth in history. In that case, why should we teach history from the Indians' point of view when they are such a small minority in this country? We are not advocating the teaching of history from any single point of view, nor do we advocate value-free history books. The one "truth" we say should be taught is that there are different points of view; that is reality. To deny the student access to this truth is to create for him a fundamental misunderstanding of the world and our country as they are.

Jack Forbes, when discussing education and multiculturalism, states:

> Any society which gives a high value to democracy and individual freedom cannot consistently utilize the school as an instrument of enforced culture change. What kind of a democracy would utilize public schools to suppress the heritage of a minority simply because it is a minority (or because it lacks power)? What kind of a free society can use the schools as a means to diminish individual freedom and enforce conformity? (Forbes 1968:24)

Another important truth the textbooks omit is that among whites in America, different values exist, some of which coincide with the beliefs of some Indians. Many whites today, for example, believe that we should maintain the status quo. A history of Indian-white relations could very well be written from this vantage point. Indigenous Indians would then be referred to as the defenders of the status quo, seeking moderation rather than excess. The whites would be the revolutionaries, rabble rousers, invaders, hostile attackers, intruders, exploiters, and mercenaries. Dee Brown (1971) has written a history from such a viewpoint. Conservationists in America are now preaching the same kinds of attitudes and practices toward nature that many Indians have maintained for thousands of years. From the conservationists' point of view, the 1849 gold rush to California could be described as pure economic exploitation for material ends, with a blatant disregard by whites for the ecological balance of nature. The Indians' life-styles, on the other hand, could be used as examples of how to live without destroying natural resources. Perhaps even today whites could learn something about survival by reviewing American Indian philosophies of man's relationship to nature. (For a more complete understanding of the role, deliberate and accidental, that American Indians played in preserving the ecological balance, see Gianella 1972.)

Conclusions and Recommendations

1. We have not pointed out examples of fair reporting and representation in the three textbooks analyzed; instead, we have concentrated on the distortions and ethnocentrism they contain. The textbooks, however, contain few examples of unbiased descriptions of California Indians. Areas of Indian culture and history which are accurately and fairly portrayed are the exception and not the rule. Henry (1969) published very brief reviews of the portrayal of North American Indians in approximately 170 books used in public schools and found none to recommend when using specific criteria. (See Appendix II for Henry's criteria.)

2. In entitling this chapter "The Roots of Prejudice: California Indian History in School Textbooks," we did not intend to imply that textbooks are the only source of prejudice; they are an important vehicle for transmitting values, including those of prejudice. In his article "Teacher Training Designs for Improving Instruction in Interracial Classrooms," M. Chesler (1971) provides a concise description and analysis of other sources of prejudice and interethnic conflict within school systems, including "teachers' own feelings" and "relations with administration." We firmly maintain that textbooks afford a convenient and concrete measure of the degree and nature of prejudice existing in school systems at a particular time. In contrast to textbooks, teachers' attitudes and administrators' policies are more difficult to identify and evaluate objectively; the biases in written material presented year after year on fairly fixed topics are more readily apparent.

Quillen points out the following:

> In the United States, the textbook is the major source of knowledge and understanding in the social studies and other content-subjects. In many schools the textbook is the course of study, and its contents determine, to a very large extent, what children and youth shall learn in school about peoples and places beyond the range of their direct experience. While the influence of the textbook on the building of attitudes has still not been fully determined by educational and psychological research, it must be extensive when considered over the whole range of subjects studied and the whole period of schooling from primary school through high school and college (Quillen 1949:2).

Educators, including textbook authors, are themselves largely educated through textbooks, then pass on textbook-learned biases and misinformation to the next generation of students and into the next set of textbooks and so on. The cycle must be broken at some point. Textbooks are a convenient place to start—to the benefit of both teacher and student. Even if textbooks were the only ethnocentric part of the educational system, we should still look at why and how they have come to be biased, what the effects of their biases are, what forces exist to change textbooks, what forces exist which resist such change, and the dangers which exist in perpetuating the brand and degree of ethnocentric distortion we have identified in this chapter. These are complex processes which deserve careful and detailed study. For example, do textbook authors consciously and deliberately distort information in order to prejudice the reader or are the authors unaware of their own ethnocentric biases? Many of the American Council of Education studies done in the 1940s assume the latter without having studied authors' values, attitudes and motives. Such an assumption is dangerous. The possibility of conscious as well as unintentional ethnocentric attitudes of textbook authors must be carefully considered.

3. The textbook distortions we point out and the changes we recommend in this chapter are similar, and at times identical, to studies and recommendations made in past years. In 1889, the International Peace Conference, after reviewing textbook presentation of wars, urged that, for the sake of international understanding, "textbooks be purged of false ideas about nations and causes of war" (UNESCO 1946). In 1917, James T. Shotwell wrote in the introduction of one of the first analyses of textbook content for international understanding in the United States that "The teaching of history depends largely on the textbooks used in the schools; and upon that teaching rests, to a large degree, our conception as to the character of nations and national policies" (C. Altschul 1917:v). Quillen (1949) reviews the work of organizations which have studied distortions in textbooks up to 1948. He includes discussion of textbook distortions of minority groups, and he specifically recommends publishing the history of minority groups accurately and fairly. An interesting hypothesis that can be derived from Quillen's review is that the impetus for rooting out textbook distortions follows periods of international crises, especially crises of the magnitude of World Wars I and II. We would further speculate that during more peaceful times, incentive decreases and tendencies toward ethnocentric nationalism in textbooks increase.

Also concerned with international relations, but this time concentrating entirely on descriptions of minority groups in textbooks, the American Council of Education analyzed 315 textbooks, 266 of which were being used in the public schools during the years 1944 and 1945. The A.C.E. compares the actual treatment of minority groups in textbooks with stated democratic ideals in the United States. Their findings are discouraging. They found that the overwhelming majority of the textbooks perpetuated notions of white Anglo-Saxon-Protestant superiority over Jews, Catholics and blacks in particular. The principles and recommendations they advocate are an extension of those of Quillen (A.C.E. 1949).

In 1949, the American Council of Education re-examined sixty-one of the textbooks reviewed in 1944–1945. They looked for "a changed point of view or approach to the teaching of intergroup relations." Of those sixty-one books, only twenty-nine had been revised since the American Council on Education study of 1944. Out of those twenty-nine books, only one showed a change and "improved" point of view in its treatment of minorities (American Council on Education 1949:219).

The Anti-Defamation League of B'nai B'rith in 1961 supported a follow-up study using the same methodology as in the two American Council on Education studies mentioned above. Seventeen years after the first report in 1944, the Anti-Defamation League found the same biases existing in textbooks.

> In a study of 48 leading social studies and history textbooks, the ADL found that a majority present largely a white, Protestant, Anglo-Saxon view of history and the current social scene. The complex nature and problems of American minority groups are largely neglected or, in a number of cases, distorted (Marcus 1961:3).

This study updated and again emphasized the criteria which should be used in evaluating textbooks.

In 1968, Virgil Vogel, a historian, published his evaluation of history book, in particular textbook, treatment of American Indians. After examining over 100 books he states, "Historians have used four principal methods to create or perpetuate false impressions of aboriginal Americans, namely: obliteration, defamation, disembodiment, and disparagement" (1968:16). He elaborates on the meaning of these terms and cites examples from textbooks. Although Vogel finds some books to recommend, by his analysis most books are guilty of these techniques of distortion.

In 1969 the U.S. Senate Subcommittee on Indian Education, in examining the education of American Indians, included a review of the presentation of American Indians in public school textbooks. They state: "Textbook studies by a number of states indicate that misconceptions, myths, inaccuracies and stereotypes about Indians are common to the curriculum of most schools." In their Report they cite studies from the states of Alaska, Idaho, Minnesota, and California (1969:23).

The American Indian Historical Society, which provided major testimony at the U.S. Senate Subcommittee hearings mentioned above, in 1969 published its review of more than 170 textbooks currently in use in public schools. Using their criteria, quoted in Appendix II of this chapter, they found no books to recommend.

The Anti-Defamation League in 1970 supported a study of minorities in forty-five social studies textbooks (Kane 1970). Making use of the methodology from previous studies, Kane found in some textbooks a more balanced view of the Indian struggle for survival and for preservation of their cultures. Kane rather generously concludes that textbook Indian history has improved, because eight of the forty-five textbooks he reviewed were "reasonably adequate by the criteria of inclusion, comprehensiveness and balance" (1970: 113). Most of the forty-five textbooks were remarkable for making no reference to Indians whatsoever, or for their brevity and inadequacy when they did mention Indians.

Kane noted that textbooks in general described Indians during periods of warfare and struggle with whites rather than during peacetime. He noted that the portrayal of American Indians in contemporary society was either missing or inaccurate. Although Kane specifically discusses Indians, he devoted only a small amount of space to Indians as one of several minority groups.

We suspect that Indians have been given less space than Jews and blacks in those reviews of minority groups because Indians are more isolated geographically and culturally from the mainstream of American life. This explanation, however, should be no justification for devoting less than thorough effort in exposing the distortions which exist in published descriptions of Indian cultures. Efforts such as ours, Henry's, and Vogel's, should be followed by subsequent studies to determine whether any improvements occur in textbook writing of Indian history in future years.

4. We emphasize that careful study of textbook distortions and stereotypes is not sufficient in and of itself to produce textbook revision. Several authors have already provided exemplary curricula and teaching outlines for the teaching of American Indian history (Forbes 1968 and 1969; Lukes 1972). Henry lists detailed recommendations and criteria specifically for the writing of Indian history (see Appendix II for Henry's criteria).

Resistance to rooting out prejudice in textbooks cannot be attributed simply to lack of awareness of prejudice in textbooks or ignorance about the dynamics of prejudice. Outstanding books such as *The Nature of Prejudice* (Allport 1954) and *Dynamics of Prejudice* (Bettelheim and Janowitz 1952) have been widely circulated since the 1950s. Despite the highly recognized quality of such comprehensive and critical reviews of the phenomenon of prejudice, in general textbook authors have not revised the content of their writings.

5. Several writers have suggested that Indians themselves, as well as trained social scientists, should participate in the writing of Indian history. We share this point of view but with qualification. Many Indians and social scientists themselves may consciously or unconsciously harbor distorted and/or ethnocentric attitudes. Being an Indian or an anthropologist can afford the advantage of a special viewpoint but is not enough in itself to insure objectivity and lack of prejudice. Textbook authors and consultants, of whatever ethnic or educational background, must be actively dedicated to rooting out prejudice in themselves and their writing. This is no easy task.

As we wrote this chapter, we were often struck by our blindness to our own prejudices. For instance, until reading an article by Costo in "The Indian Historian" (Spring 1972), we did not appreciate the degrading aspects of the Indian symbol recently abolished by Stanford University. In contrast, we would have immediately understood opposition to symbols such as the Stanford Jews, Stanford Negroes, or Stanford Caucasians; these groups are visible parts of our everyday lives.

Unfortunately, we did not view Indians in the same way. Instead, we saw the "Stanford Indian" mainly as a symbol representing peoples of the Historic past—relics. What we failed to appreciate was that the "Stanford Indian" is also a symbol of present-day peoples living in our society and already handicapped by many degrading stereotypes. We were similarly struck by our insensitivity to the ramifications of the "Frito Bandito" character recently abolished by the Frito-Lay Company. Initially, the character seemed unimportant and basically neutral to us. When T. Martinez (1969) listed some of the many advertisements which portray Mexicans always as either overweight, lazy, smelly, or dishonest, we began to see that a negative stereotype of Mexicans was being fostered in the mass media.

6. To omit discussion of present-day American Indians, their characteristics, and position in the total society denies them their roles in shaping the present and future of American history; it effectively avoids facing, and diminishes the importance of, current sociocultural conflicts between Indian groups and white society. An accurate historical description of American Indians should be considered only part of the total description of American Indians. American Indians are, in fact, present-day groups of people who differ from each other in their Indian cultural origins and in the degrees to which they are assimilated to various aspects of the majority of white culture. We should be reminded of this in textbooks. (See Forbes 1968 for an excellent discussion of problems present-day Indian groups are facing in the present white establishment.)

7. After extensive reading and after discussing the issues in this chapter with various groups of students and teachers, we conclude that reordering our priorities must be one of the first requirements for solving the problem of prejudice in textbooks. Textbook inaccuracy is presently not a "hot" issue, perhaps because textbooks are read mostly by children who are not attuned to critical reading. In children the effects of biased textbook learning appear gradually and indirectly over the course of years of textbook exposure. The insidious yet powerful nature of this process can too easily be ignored in favor of highly visible spectacular social ills. We firmly believe that identifying and alleviating the negative effects on our society of biased textbooks is critical. For example, what consequences do we suffer as a society when the ideals of human freedom, dignity, equality, and brotherhood are undermined in our basic teaching materials? Should we not insist that textbooks, as well as all teaching resources, "contribute to the development of the understandings, ideals, and competence necessary to both wholesome national citizenship and world citizenship?" (Quillen 1949:73–74). Public education should serve public needs and work for the public benefit. Few would disagree that

American society needs, and would benefit from, greater interethnic communication, understanding, and harmony. Seen in this context, the attitudes learned through textbooks about American majority and minority groups do critically affect the well-being of our whole society.

8. Many detailed and reputable studies have pointed out textbook distortions and have made adequate recommendations for improvements. Why have these studies failed to effect the kinds of changes they recommend? What are the sources of textbook distortions? How much of the failure to revise textbooks is due to lack of awareness and how much to active resistance to revise textbooks?

A study of efforts to introduce multiethnic curricula into public schools might reveal the sources of resistance. To what extent have administrators, school boards, parents, private citizens, teachers, schools of education, and publishers been the sources of resistance? Antisegregation legislation, for example, seems to have ignored the important role of textbooks in perpetuating segregationist values and attitudes. What motivates individuals and groups to resist textbook revision? For example, to what extent are publishers concerned about economic losses if textbooks deviate from traditional models?

At this time more examples of textbook distortions are probably unnecessary and redundant. What is needed is an effective strategy for implementing the recommendations which have already been made. We recommend an examination of the nature and sources of resistance to textbook change as the next necessary step in developing such a strategy.

Appendix I

The following is a portion of the Table of Contents from Billie Masters' multiethnic curriculum entitled *Indian, Native American* (1971) currently in use in the Cupertino Union School District, Cupertino, California.

Lesson 1: Most concepts taught in schools, presented in motion pictures and concerning the Native-American are false.

Lesson 2: The Native-American people share a very complex cultural and ethnic heritage.

Lesson 3: The Native-American has inhabited the continents of North and South America for at least 25,000 years.

Lesson 4: Due to the geographical and related environmental influences, the Native-American people had developed numerous diverse civilizations.

Lesson 5: At the time of the arrival of Columbus in 1492, the Native-American people had developed a systematic way of life based on Indian values which included religion, a form of government and an informal education.

Lesson 6: The Native-American had achieved an ecological balance. He not only had achieved a balance with the earth, but also with his fellow man. The Native-American had maintained this balance for over 20,000 years.

Lesson 7: The world in general and the United States in particular have benefited from the many contributions of the Native-American.

Lesson 8: This is the time of the Great Awakening. (A time of change predicted and anticipated by Native-American religious leaders.)

Appendix II

Henry entitles Chapter III of her book "The General Criteria" and begins:

> In order to judge a particular text, these general Criteria must be adapted to the specific curriculum in which the book is to be used. The general standards of judgment here described are valid for elementary through high school instructional materials, particularly in American history.

Her criteria are as follows:

1. Is the history of the American Indian presented as an integral part of the history of America, at every point of this nation's development?
2. Does the text explain that the first discoverers of America were those Native people whom Columbus described improperly as "Indians?"
3. Is the data contained in the text accurate?
4. Does the textbook faithfully describe the culture and lifeways of the American Indian at that time in history when the Europeans first came in contact with him?
5. Is the culture of the Indian described as dynamic process, so that his social system and lifeways are seen as a developmental process, rather than a static one?
6. Are the contributions of the Indians to the Nation and the world described?
7. Does the textbook accurately describe the special position of the American Indian in the history of the United States of America—socially, economically and politically?
8. Does the textbook describe the religions, philosophies, and contributions to thought, of the American Indian?
9. Does the textbook adequately and accurately describe the life and situation of the American Indian in the world of today?

Acknowledgements

We thank George Spindler for his detailed review of this chapter, especially for his help in improving the clarity of several points we present. E. Fuller Torrey suggested the title and the use of subheadings in the chapter. Frances Hall Smith kindly offered editorial suggestions. We thank Frieda H. Yeaton and the Palo Alto Unified School District for giving us the opportunity to present some of this material for discussion and debate to teachers attending a seminar on multicultural education.

References

Allport, Gordon, 1954, *The Nature of Prejudice.* Reading, Mass.: Addison-Wesley Publishing Company.

Altschul, Charles, 1917, *The American Revolution in Our School Text-Books.* New York: George H. Doran Company, p.v., as quoted in Quillen 1948:3.

American Council on Education, 1949, *Intergroup Relations in Teaching Materials: A Survey and Appraisal.* Washington, D.C.: American Council on Education.

American Indian Historical Society, *Wassaja: A National Newspaper of Indian Americans.* San Francisco: The Indian Historian Press, published monthly since Jan. 1973.

———, *Weewish Tree.* San Francisco: The Indian Historian Press, published monthly during the school year since 1972.

"An American Treasury of Southwest Living," *American Home,* California home edition 73:49–80.

Bettelheim, Bruno, and J. M. Janowitz, 1952, *Dynamics of Prejudice.* New York: Harper & Row.

Brown, Dee, 1970, *Bury My Heart at Wounded Knee.* New York: Bantam Books.

Caughey, C., 1968, *The Land of the Free.* Sacramento: California State Department of Education.

Chesler, M., 1971, "Teacher Training Designs for Improving Instruction in Interracial Classrooms," *Journal of Applied Behavioral Science* 7:612–641.

Cohen, Felix, 1953, "The Erosion of Indian Rights 1950–1953: A Case Study in Bureaucracy," *Yale Law Journal* 62:348–390.

Cook, S. F., 1943a, "The Conflict Between the California Indian and White Civilization: II. The Physical and Demographic Reactions of the Nonmission Indians in Colonial and Provincial California," *Ibero-Americana* 22.

———, 1943b, "The Indian versus the Spanish Mission," *Ibero-Americana* 21.

———, 1943c, "The Conflict Between the California Indian and White Civilization: III. The American Invasion 1848–1870," *Ibero-Americana* 23.

Costo, Rupert, 1972, "Student Petition Gains Support: Stanford Removes Indian Symbol," *The Indian Historian* 5:20–22.

Dixon, R. B., and A. L. Kroeber, 1919, Linguistic Families of California, *UCPAAE* 16:47–118.

Dobyns, H., 1966, "Estimating Aboriginal American Population: An Appraisal of Techniques with a New Hemispheric Estimate," *Current Anthropology,* 7(4): 395–448.

Driver, Harold E., 1969, "Achievements and Contributions." In *Indians of North America.* Chicago: University of Chicago Press, pp. 554–566.

Forbes, Jack D., 1968, *The Education of the Culturally Different: A Multi-Cultural Approach.* Berkeley, Calif.: Far West Laboratory for Educational Research and Development.

———, 1969, *Native Americans of California and Nevada: A Handbook.* Healdsburg, Calif.: Naturegraph Publishers.

Gianella, Bill, 1972, "Misconceptions Shown: Natural and Primitive Areas," *The Indian Historian* 5:11–14.

Gifford, E. W., 1926, "California Indian Types," *Natural History* 26:50–60.

Goldschmidt, W., G. Foster, and F. Essene, 1939, "War Stories for Two Enemy Tribes," *Journal of American Folklore* 52:141–154.

Halligan, A. L., 1943, "A Community's Total War Against Prejudice," *Journal of Educational Sociology* 16:374–380.

Hallowell, Irving, 1957, "The Impact of the American Indian on American Culture," *American Anthropologist* 59:201–217.

———, 1959, "The Backwash of the Frontier: The Impact of the Indian on American Culture," *Annual Report of the Smithsonian Institute for 1958,* pp. 447–472.

Henry, Jeanette, ed., 1969, *Textbooks and The American Indian.* San Francisco: The Indian Historian Press.

Hess, R. D., and J. V. Torney, 1967, *The Development of Political Attitudes in Children.* New York: Doubleday & Company.

Heyerdahl, Thor, 1952, *American Indians in the Pacific.* London: Allen and Unwin.

Hiller, E. T., 1947, *Social Relations and Structures.* New York: Harper & Row.

Kane, M. B., 1970, *Minorities in Textbooks.* Chicago: Quadrangle Books.

Kluckhohn, Clyde, 1944, *The Navajo Door.* Cambridge, Mass.: Harvard University Press.

Kroeber, A. L., 1925, *Handbook of the Indians of California.* Washington, D.C.: Smithsonian Institute, Bureau of American Ethnology, Bulletin 78.

Kroeber, T., 1965, *Ishi in Two Worlds.* Berkeley, Calif.: University of California Press.

Lee, Dorothy, 1938, "Conceptual Implications of an Indian Language," *Philosophy of Science* 5:89–102.

———, 1943, "The Linguistic Aspect of Wintu Acculturation," *American Anthropologist* 45:435–440.

Lukes, Edward A., 1972, "Ethno-History of Indians of the U.S.," *The Indian Historian* 5:23–25.

Madsen, W., 1967, "Religious Syncretism," *Handbook of the Middle American Indians* 6:369–392.

Marcus, Lloyd, 1961, *The Treatment of Minorities in Secondary School Textbooks.* New York: Anti-Defamation League of B'nai B'rith.

Martinez, Thomas, 1969, "How Advertisers Promote Racism," *Civil Rights Digest* 2:5–11.

Masters, Billie, 1971, "Native-American (Grade Seven)," *Inter-Ethnic Curriculum,* Cupertino Union School District, Cupertino, California.

McNickle, D., 1957, "Indian-White Relations from Discovery to 1887," *Annals of the Academy of Political and Social Science* 311:1–11.

Merton, R. K., 1948, "The Self-Fulfilling Prophecy," *Antioch Review* 8:193–210.

Postman, Neil, and Charles Weingartner, 1971, *Teaching as a Subversive Activity.* New York: Dell Publishing Company.

Quillen, James I., 1949, *Textbook Improvement and International Understanding.* Washington, D.C.: American Council on Education.

Reith, J. W., 1965, *California and the West.* Sacramento, Calif.: State Department of Education.

Salaman, R., 1949, *The History and Social Influence of the Potato.* Cambridge University Press.

Sapir, E., 1921, *Language: An Introduction to the Study of Speech.* New York: Harcourt, Brace Jovanovich.

Simmons, Leo W., ed., 1942, *Sun Chief: The Autobiography of a Hopi Indian.* New Haven, Conn.: Yale University Press.

Snyder, P. Z., 1968, "Social Assimilation and Adjustment of Navajo Migrants to Denver, Colorado," *Navajo Urban Relocation Research Report 13.* Denver: University of Colorado Press.

Special Subcommittee on Indian Education (Committee on Labor and Public Welfare, U.S. Senate), 1969, *Indian Education: A National Tragedy—A National Challenge.* Washington, D.C.: Government Printing Office.

Steward, K. M., 1947, "Mohave Warfare," *Southwestern Journal of Anthropology* 3:257–278.

UNESCO, 1946, *Looking at the World through Text-Books.* Paris: UNESCO, p. 2, as quoted in Quillen 1948:2.

Voegelin, C. F., and F. M. Voegelin, 1966, *Map of North American Indian Languages.* Chicago: Rand McNally.

Vogel, Virgil J., 1968, "The Indian in American History Textbooks," *Integrated Education* 6:16–32.

Wallace, H. A., 1956, *Corn and Its Early Fathers.* East Lansing: Michigan State University Press.

Whorf, B. L., 1941, "The Relation of Habitual Thought and Behavior to Language." In L. Spier et. al., ed., *Language, Culture and Personality.* Menasha, Wis.: Supir Memorial Publication Fund, pp. 75–94.

———, 1956, *Language, Thought and Reality.* Cambridge, Mass.: Harvard University Press.

Williams, Mabel Y., 1965, *California: A History.* Sacramento, Calif.: State Department of Education.

Wissler, Clark, 1940, *Indians of the United States.* New York: Doubleday & Company.

———, 1950, *The American Indian.* New York: Peter Smith, pp. 378–388.

GENERAL EDITORS: GEORGE AND LOUISE SPINDLER/*Stanford University*

27 *Case Studies in Education and Culture*

This is a series of descriptive studies of education both in school and out of school in a variety of cultures. Each book examines education in the context of the culture it serves and of which it is an integral part.

John Collier, Jr., 1973, *Alaskan Eskimo Education: A Film Analysis of Cultural Confrontation in the Schools.*
This study is based on analysis of films of classroom activity in schools for Eskimo children taught by white people. The structural reasons for educational failure are clear and are applicable to other situations where politically dominant and minority populations confront each other in the classroom.

John Gay and Michael Cole, 1967, *The New Mathematics and an Old Culture: A Study of Learning among the Kpelle of Liberia.*
The authors demonstrate how a traditional culture affects the learning readiness and the very thinking of children who are being taught concepts for which there are no exact antecedents in their culture.

Bruce T. Grindal, 1972, *Growing Up in Two Worlds: Education and Transition among the Sisala of Northern Ghana.*
This is a study of traditional and modern educational processes at work within a tribal society. These processes are not treated as abstractions. The experience of children with family and kin and with modern schools and migration is discussed in specifics. Wherever traditional systems of culture and the educational processes upholding them are confronted with modernization, the same dilemmas and potential consequences are faced.

John A. Hostetler and Gertrude E. Huntington, 1971, *Children in Amish Society: Socialization and Community Education.*
The community described in this study is one in which families are still stable, people live with a high sense of communal obligation, men and women work with their hands, one hears the clop of horses' hoofs rather than the whine of tires, and the school and community are joined. Given the divergencies between the old order Amish community and its schools and the schools and communities of the outside world, it is inevitable that there should be serious conflict. The struggle to keep control of their schools is one of the dramatic and often heart-rending aspects of contemporary Amish life. The study has many implications for other minorities in conflict with majority society and monolithic educational systems.

F. Landa Jocano, 1969, *Growing Up in a Philippine Barrio.*
This is both an ethnographic account and a case study in education. The author

analyzes the techniques of cultural learning and transmission in the community called Malitbog, a small barrio located in the central region of Panay Island, The Philippines.

A. Richard King, 1967, *The School at Mopass: A Problem of Identity.*
This is a description of the educational process in a residential school for Indian children in the Yukon Territory of northwest Canada where students, because they assimilate the subculture of the school, defeat the intended aims of education. The study makes clear the ways in which children learn to cope with an adult-made social and semantic environment, how they learn a pragmatic gamesmanship to get along in that environment, and how they win the game but lose the battle.

Philip E. Leis, 1972, *Enculturation and Socialization in an Ijaw Village.*
The way Ijaw educate their children to behave and believe in the life-style of Ijaw society and culture is studied here. The Ijaw live in the central part of the Niger Delta where culture change had been relatively slow because of geographical isolation. The author was in a position to study a traditional system of education and changes in recent times. The study engages with a problem of considerable significance to those interested in child development—the early-learning hypothesis.

Nancy Modiano, 1973, *Indian Education in the Chiapas Highlands.*
This study focuses on childhood and the new and formal as well as the relatively informal educational processes in village cultures in the Chiapas Highlands of Mexico. In the final section of the book the author tests the reading capability of children in different schools where Spanish, the national language, is taught in various relationships to the native tongue. This study has implications wherever a standard language is taught to children whose native language is different.

Alan Peshkin, 1972, *Kanuri Schoolchildren: Education and Social Mobilization in Nigeria.*
This case study explores the apparent confrontation between traditional and modern socializing agencies as seen through the lives of four school children. These children, from Muslim families living in northeastern Nigeria, are the first generation in their families to be educated in Western-type schools. A process of social mobilization occurs. Old social, economic, and psychological commitments are eroded or broken and people become available for new patterns of socialization and behavior.

Margaret Read, 1968, *Children of Their Fathers: Growing Up among the Ngoni of Malawi.*
In this study of an African tribal community, the author presents an analysis of an orderly way of life with high standards of conduct and systematic valued ways of transmitting both knowledge and wisdom to each new generation. She shows us how this way of life is transmitted and how these methods have been retained in basic principle despite great change in the technological and economic dimensions of life.

Gerry Rosenfeld, 1971, *"Shut Those Thick Lips!": A Cultural Study of a Slum School.*
The conditions of slum schooling in the United States, as exemplified by the ethnography of a single slum school, are analyzed here. The author demonstrates what going to a slum school and being a black child mean, and discusses the reasons for low achievement by minority children in general.

John Singleton, 1967, *Nichū: A Japanese School.*

This is a study of a Japanese junior high school and the interaction between the school and the local community, the school and the administrative organizations related to it, and the school and various teacher organizations.

Martha C. Ward, 1971, *Them Children: A Study in Language Learning.*

This is a case study of child-rearing practices and family life in a rural black community in southern Louisiana. The emphasis is on the language patterns of mothers and children within the daily routine of community life. Seven families and their activities as relevant to language learning are described. The socialization practices of these families are compared to those of middle-class families.

Richard L. Warren, 1967, *Education in Rebhausen: A German Village.*

This case study examines a rural elementary school in a small German village undergoing rapid cultural change as a result of industrialization. Careful attention is paid to classroom behaviors, teacher management of classes, and faculty relationships. Rebhausen is also in the Schwäbisch-speaking area, as is Schönhausen, described by G. Spindler in Chapter 12 of this volume.

Thomas R. Williams, 1969, *A Borneo Childhood: Enculturation in Dusun Society.*

Notable in this work is the author's attention to reporting the methods of study used; the provision of a summary of information on the general setting of Dusun enculturation; the analysis of changes occurring in Dusun culture and enculturation; and the abstraction of ten patterns of enculturation that he offers as a suggested distillation of the basic processes.

Harry F. Wolcott, 1967, *A Kwakiutl Village and School.*

This study documents the educational process in a one-room school in a tiny Indian village in British Columbia. The author taught at the school for one year and the study was done from the vantage point of a teacher. The conflicts between the purposes of the teacher and the motivations of the students are made clear. The case study is excellent background for Wolcott's paper, "The Teacher as Enemy," in this volume.

Harry F. Wolcott, 1973, *The Man in the Principal's Office.*

This is an ethnography of a comfortable middle-class suburban elementary school, focusing on the day-by-day, hour-by-hour activities of Ed Bell, the principal, as he moves about the school and community. It analyzes the network of relationships occurring between the principal and his staff, parents, officials of the school system, and the children. It is clear that the principal's prime role is that of mediator rather than innovator or commander.

GENERAL EDITORS: GEORGE AND LOUISE SPINDLER/*Stanford University*

28 *Case Studies in Cultural Anthropology Containing Materials on Cultural Transmission*

Francis M. Deng, 1972, *The Dinka of the Sudan.*
Written by the son of a major Dinka Paramount Chief, the book describes the Dinka, a Nilotic people in the Southern Sudan numbering about 2 million. Their lives are presented in terms of the search for values: ideals and everyday preferences, material and spiritual. Their culture is an integrated system with an inner logic. The life cycle is discussed, complete with attention to birth, infancy, childhood, youth, adulthood, aging, and death and related to the cultural system as a whole.

John A. Hostetler and Gertrude E. Huntington, 1967, *The Hutterites in North America.*
The communal Hutterites have been inhabitants of North America since 1874, living in relatively isolated agricultural areas on large collective farms in South Dakota, Montana, and the prairies of Canada. Their educational system is described as one of the major forces for maintenance of the community.

Joe E. Pierce, 1964, *Life in a Turkish Village.*
The first part of the case study sees life in an Anatolian village through the eyes of a small boy who is beginning a long induction into a man's role. The second part shifts from an inside view to a more conventional analysis of Anatolian village life.

George D. Spindler, 1973, *Burgbach: Urbanization and Identity in a German Village.*
A case study of a German village near the industrial city of Stuttgart, this book analyzes the processes of urbanization of a rural wine-growing village as it adjusts to the impact of industrialization and the influx of a new population of workers. A long chapter is devoted to a discussion of schools in Burgbach and Schönhausen, showing how schooling relates to maintenance and change of identities.

George Spindler and Louise Spindler, 1971, *Dreamers without Power: The Menomini Indians.*
This is a study of the adaptive strategies with which the Menomini Indians of Wisconsin have coped with the prolonged confrontation between their culture and that of the whiteman. The thought world of the Menomini is stressed, with much of the text in the Menominis' own words. Educational processes in the traditional group that maintains the Medicine Lodge and the Dream Dance are discussed.

Thomas R. Williams, 1965, *The Dusun: A North Borneo Society.*
The rituals and contests with life and death, health and disease, fortune and misfortune, of the Dusun are examined. Socialization, subsistence, and kinship are explored. This case study makes a useful companion to Dr. Williams' study of Dusun enculturation, annotated above.

INDEXES

Name Index

Subject Index

D

E

F

G

H

T

U

V

W